Disorders of Personality

Disorders of Personality
DSM-III: Axis II

THEODORE MILLON

A Wiley-Interscience Publication

JOHN WILEY & SONS, New York • Chichester • Brisbane • Toronto • Singapore

Quotations from Wilhelm Reich reprinted by permission of Farrar, Straus and Giroux, Inc. From *Character Analysis* by Wilhelm Reich, translated from the German by Vincent R. Carfagno. Copyright © 1972 by Mary Boyd Higgins, as Trustee of The Wilhelm Reich Infant Trust Fund. Quotations from Ernst Kretschmer reprinted by permission of Routledge and Kegan Paul. From *Physique and Character*, English translation. Copyright 1925. Quotations from *Diagnostic and Statistical Manual of Mental Disorders* reprinted by permission of The American Psychiatric Association. Copyright 1980.

Library of Congress Cataloging in Publication Data

Millon, Theodore.
    Disorders of personality.

    "A Wiley-Interscience publication."
    Includes index.
    1. Personality, Disorders of.   2. Personality,
Disorders of—Classification.   I. Title.   [DNLM:
1. Personality disorders.   WM 190 M656d]
RC554.M54   616.85'82   80-28249
ISBN 0-471-06403-3

Printed in the United States of America

10   9   8   7   6   5   4   3

To the Memory of

GARDNER MURPHY, KURT GOLDSTEIN, ERNST KRIS

Gentleman, Teacher, Scholar, each

PREFACE

In many ways this book may be seen as a companion volume to the *Diagnostic and Statistical Manual of Mental Disorders (DSM-III)*, published by the American Psychiatric Association in 1980. Although this most recent edition of the DSM is far more comprehensive descriptively than either of its predecessors, the manual was not designed to provide detailed clinical presentations or the competing theories and etiologies of the syndromes it encompasses. The lack of such materials is especially problematic to those seeking information on the personality disorders. These syndromes have suddenly "come of age," having been transformed from a class of disorders possessing only incidental relevance to the diagnostic enterprise into a class that is central, if not crucial, to the required DSM-III multiaxial format. Although clinicians and researchers will find a substantial literature on most syndromes in current texts and journals, such is not the case, even to a modest degree, for the majority of the personality disorders. Now that these syndromes have been advanced to the status of major clinical entities, the need to develop a literature to fill the void is all the more acute. It is in the sense of filling such a void that this book may be seen as a useful DSM-III companion volume.

This book brings together the sparse, widely scattered, and highly doctrinaire clinical literature on personality disorders, seeking in a single sourcebook to both coordinate and evaluate what has been written on the subject. To maximize scholarly and practical utility, it contains contrasting historical and theoretical viewpoints, serving thereby as a reference guide of alternate conceptions of personality disorder. To enhance its value as a textbook, a full and separate chapter is devoted to each of the disorders. Of particular interest are sections in each chapter that excerpt the writings of the important historical forerunners of contemporary ideas. In addition to providing comprehensive reviews of each of the new personality syndromes—for example, avoidant, narcissistic, borderline, and schizotypal—many of the more common "mixed" personality types are extensively illustrated. Of special utility to clinicians are the detailed discussions of frequent Axis I and Axis II codiagnoses, that is, clinical and personality syndromes that coexist with great regularity. To compensate for the lack of etiologic hypotheses in the DSM-III, significant portions of each chapter are devoted to describing the syndrome's most plausible developmental origins and dynamics.

As one of the initial appointees to the Task Force on Nomenclature and Statistics responsible for developing the DSM-III, I was most fortunate to participate in the group's deliberations from the very start. Especially gratifying were opportunities to persuade colleagues of the utility of an innovative multiaxial format and, more substantively, to provide the initial drafts and diagnostic criteria for each of the personality disorders. Those who are acquainted with my prior writings, especially as formulated in *Modern Psychopathology*, will recognize their influence on the DSM-III and, in turn, their substantial role in this book. I trust that my "followers" will not be dismayed that I have changed my views but minimally; I hope they will be pleased that what they learned previously has not only been retained in great measure, but has now found a significant place in the framework and substance of the DSM-III.

As in the past, it is a pleasure to record the contributions that others have made to improving or expediting my work. First and foremost is my wife Renée, who has never failed me in her editorial talents; as with my previous writings, she has made the text not only more lucid and readable, but also more humane and sensitive.

The five-year stint with my colleagues on the DSM-III Task Force was a joy, a richly rewarding challenge I shall never forget. Among those who made the task intellectually exciting were Don Klein, a brilliant and inventive adversary; Jean Endicott, a conceptualizer and research implementer of the first rank; George Saslow, a gentleman, scholar, and intellectual's intellectual; Henry Pinsker, a compassionate clinician whose feet are planted firmly on the ground; and Bob Spitzer, whose prodigious energy and diplomatic talents as chairman shepherded many a controversial proposition through the thickets of intellectual inertia and resistance. A special word of thanks is due also to Mel Sabshin for having been open to the idea of forming a new, more forward-looking task force in 1974 and for the many thoughtful discussions we shared over the years in Chicago.

Among my current associates, I am especially indebted to Cathy Green for having read drafts of the entire manuscript and for helping refine them through her incisive critiques. Both she and my other primary research colleague, Bob Meagher, have served to keep me honest by insisting that we explore empirically what I might otherwise be disposed only to theorize. Helen Focazio, Sandy Racoobian, and Ruth Srebrenik carried the tasks of typing sequential drafts with intelligence and diligence; Lenny Bard was especially helpful in obtaining reference materials and arranging the indexes.

Acknowledgment is given to several publishers who kindly gave permission to reproduce excerpts of copyrighted materials.

My daughter Adrienne has asked that Chapter 12 be dedicated to her, not for its contents, but to acknowledge her age when she discovered that her dad wrote books that students read.

Little need be said of the three men to whom this text is dedicated; each is well known to the mature reader as among the most innovative thinkers of twentieth century psychology. Without their direct tuition, inspiration, and warm friendship during my student years, the foundations for this work would have never been built.

THEODORE MILLON

Coral Gables, Florida
January 1981

Contents

Disorders of Personality

Part One

The Background of
Personality Disorders

Chapter 1

The Nature of Personality

Personality disorders have historically been in a tangential position among diagnostic syndromes, never having achieved a significant measure of recognition in the literature of either abnormal psychology or clinical psychiatry. Until recently they have been categorized in the official nomenclature with a melange of other, miscellaneous, and essentially secondary syndromes. The advent of the 1980 American Psychiatric Association's *Diagnostic and Statistical Manual of Mental Disorders* (DSM-III) has changed this status radically. Personality disorders now not only hold a place of prominence among syndromal groups but have become central to the diagnostic schema. With the new DSM-III multiaxial format, a significant breakthrough in its own right (Strauss, 1975), personality pathologies comprise, by themselves, one of only two required "mental disorder" axes. Henceforth, diagnoses must assess not only the patient's current symptom picture, via Axis I, but, in addition, those pervasive features which characterize the enduring personality pattern, recorded on Axis II. In effect, the revised multiaxial format requires that symptom states no longer be diagnosed as clinical entities isolated from the broader context of the patient's lifelong style of relating, coping, behaving, thinking, and feeling—that is, his or her personality.

There are substantive grounds for attending to personality influences other than the pragmatics of adhering to DSM-III requirements. These reasons far outweigh the argument that has been recently advanced to the effect that personality disorders fundamentally differ from other forms of psychopathology and, hence, should be excluded from the practice of psychiatry (Schwartz and Schwartz, 1976). This contention represents a failure to recognize that personality disorders reflect pathogenic processes that are identical to those seen in classical "neurotic" and "psychotic" states. More important is the fact that lifelong personality traits serve as a substrate and a context for understanding the more florid and distinct forms of psychopathology.

Since the early 1960s our society has been increasingly committed to the early identification and prevention of mental disorders. This emphasis has led clinicians to attend to both premorbid behavioral signs and the less severe variants of emotional disturbance. Ordinary anxieties, minor personal conflicts, and social inadequacies are now seen as the forerunners of more serious problems. A significant impetus to this movement has been the emergence of community mental health centers whose attentions are directed to the needs of the less seriously disturbed. As a result of these developments the scope of clinical psychopathology has been broadened far beyond its historical province of "State Hospital" psychiatry. It is a field that now encompasses the full spectrum of mild to severe mental disorders. With this as a foundation, diagnosticians will more ably grasp the dynamics and more clearly trace the sequences through which distinct and dramatic clinical symptoms unfold.

ISSUES OF DEFINITION

What is personality?

In the first years of life each child displays a wide variety of behaviors. Although exhibiting a measure of consistency consonant with his or her constitutional disposition, the way in which the child responds to and copes with the environment tends to be largely spontaneous, changeable, and unpredictable. These seemingly random and capricious behaviors serve an important exploratory function. The child is "trying out" a variety of behavioral alternatives for dealing with his/her environment. Over time the child begins to discern which of these actions enable him to achieve his or her desires and avoid discomforts. Endowed with certain capacities, energies, and temperaments, and through experience with parents, sibs, and peers, the child learns to discriminate which activities are both permissible and rewarding, and which are not.

Tracing this sequence over time it can be seen that a shaping process has taken place in which the child's initial range of diverse behaviors gradually becomes narrowed, selective, and, finally, crystallized into preferred ways of relating to others and coping with this world. These learned behaviors not only persist but are accentuated as a result of being repetitively reinforced by a limited social environment. Given continuity in constitutional equipment and a narrow band of experiences for learning behavioral alternatives, the child acquires a pattern of traits that are deeply etched and difficult to modify. These characteristics comprise his/her personality—that is, ingrained and habitual ways of psychological functioning that emerge from the individual's entire developmental history, and which, over time, come to characterize the child's "style."

The traits of which personality is composed are not a potpourri of unrelated perceptions, thoughts, and behaviors but a tightly knit organization of attitudes, habits, and emotions. Although we may start in life with more or less random and diverse feelings and reactions, the repetitive sequences of reinforcing experiences to which we are exposed narrows our repertoire to particular behavioral strategies that become prepotent and characterize our personally distinctive way of coping with others and relating to ourselves.

This conception of personality, now central in the DSM-III, breaks the long-entrenched habit of conceiving syndromes of psychopathology as one or another variant of a disease, that is, some "foreign" entity or lesion that intrudes insidiously within the person to undermine his or her so-called normal functions. The archaic notion that all mental disorders represent external intrusions or internal disease processes is an offshoot of prescientific ideas such as demons or spirits that ostensibly "possess" or cast spells on the person. The role of infectious agents and anatomical lesions in physical medicine has reawakened this archaic view. Of course we no longer see demons, but many still see some alien or malevolent force as invading or unsettling the patient's otherwise healthy status. This view is an appealing simplification to the layman, who can attribute his/her irrationalities to some intrusive or upsetting agent. It also has its appeal to the less sophisticated clinician, for it enables him or her to believe that the insidious intruder can be identified, hunted down, and destroyed.

Such naïve notions carry little weight among modern-day medical and behavioral scientists. Given our increasing awareness of the complex nature of both health and disease, we now recognize, for example, that most physical disorders result from a dynamic and changing interplay between individuals' capacities to cope and the environment within which they live. It is the patients' overall constitutional makeup—their vitality, stamina, and immunological system—that serves as a substrate that inclines them to resist or to succumb to potentially troublesome environmental forces. To illustrate: infectious viruses and bacteria proliferate within the environment; it is the person's interferon defenses that determine whether or not these microbes will take hold, spread, and, ultimately, be experienced as illness. Individuals with robust inteferon activity will counteract the usual range of infectious microbes with ease, whereas those with weakened immunosuppressive capacities will be vulnerable, fail to handle these "intrusions," and quickly succumb. Similarly, structural disorders such as coronary artery disease are not merely a consequence of the food one consumes or the stress of one's life but reflect each individual's metabolic capacity to break down lipoprotein intake; it is the body's ability to process nutritional and adrenergic excess that is the major determinant of whether arterial disease does or does not occur. Those with balanced enzymatic functions will readily transform and dispose of excess lipids, whereas those with less adequate equipment will cumulate arterial plaques that gradually develop into disease. Psychopathology should be conceived as reflecting the same interactive pattern. Here, however, it is not the immunological defenses or enzymatic capacities but the patient's personality pattern—that is, coping skills and adaptive flexibilities—that will determine whether or not the person will master or succumb to his/her psychosocial environment. Just as physical ill health is likely to be less a matter of some alien virus than it is a dysfunction in the body's capacity to deal with infectious agents, so too is psychological ill health likely to be less a product of some intrusive psychic strain than it is a dysfunction in the personality's capacity to cope with life's difficulties. Viewed this way, the structure and characteristics of personality become the foundation for the individual's capacity to function in a mentally healthy or ill way.

This chapter raises a number of empirical and conceptual issues regarding the nature of personality and its disorders. First, however, an attempt is made to clarify alternative terms that have been employed to represent the notion of personality.

Personality, Character, and Temperament

What are the boundaries and principal features of the concept of personality, and how shall it be distinguished from other concepts whose meanings overlap and often are used synonymously with it?

Gordon Allport raised the following concerns in his early text, *Personality: A Psychological Interpretation:*

> The term "personality" is a perilous one for [the psychologist] to use unless he is aware of its many meanings. Since it is remarkably elastic, its use in any context seldom is challenged. Books and periodicals carry it in their titles for no apparent reason other than its cadence, its general attractiveness, and everlasting interest. Both writer and reader lose their way in its ineffectual vagueness, and matters are made much worse by the depreciation of the word in the hands of journalists, beauty doctors and peddlers of gold bricks labeled "self improvement."
>
> "Personality" is one of the most abstract words in our language, and like any abstract word suffering from excessive use, its connotative significance is very broad, its denotative significance negligible. Scarcely any word is more versatile. (1937, pp. 24-25)

Allport sought to clarify the origins of the term and to revitalize this frayed concept. A review of his efforts, along with a similar enterprise by Roback (1927), will prove illuminating to students of the history of personality. The task here, however, is more modest, that of seeking to distinguish among seemingly synonymous concepts and thereby focus the reader more sharply on those features that are most relevant to personality pathology.

Two words, *character* and *temperament,* have often been employed in the literature interchangeably with personality. Each term has a distinguished history, portions of which are elaborated in Chapter 2. Both should be differentiated from the concept of personality, however. In brief, *character* has come to mean those personal qualities that represent the individual's adherence to the values and customs of society; *temperament,* in contrast, has come to signify those biologically based dispositions which underlie the energy level and color the moods of the individual. Let us review their origins briefly.

Derived from the Greek word for "engraving," the term *character* was used initially to signify distinctive features that served as the "mark" of the person. Two distinct meanings of the term evolved over time, and the confusion this raised has rendered its utility for descriptive purposes somewhat less than it would otherwise have been. Most similar to the current meaning of *personality* is the European use of the term *character*, most frequently associated with psychoanalytic writings on *characterology*. In employing the labels "character structure" and "character disorders," analytic theorists refer to those pervasive features of behavior and thinking that are deeply etched and relatively unchanging throughout life. Although this formulation corresponds closely to the concept of personality described earlier, *character* is conceived by analytic writers as somewhat more restricted in scope, as conveyed in this quote from Fenichel:

> Character, as the habitual mode of bringing into harmony the tasks presented by internal demands and by the external world, is necessarily a function of the constant, organized, and integrating part of the personality which is the ego. (1945, p. 467)

As noted above, the analytic concept of character limits its range to only the integrating part of the personality (i.e., the ego), thereby excluding functions carried out by those parts of the personality referred to as *id* and *superego*. It is the second meaning of the term *character*, however, that has proved most problematic. When we speak of a person's character in contemporary language we are likely to be applying a moral standard in judging behavior. In this sense, *character* has taken on (to use psychoanalytic terminology) features associated with the superego, that is, how and to what extent the individual has incorporated the precepts and social customs of his or her cultural group.

In turning to the term *temperament* the focus shifts to the third of the tripartite division of personality formulated by the psychoanalysts, that of the id. The word *temperament* came into the English language in the Middle Ages to represent formulations such as the four humors, and it meant, as it does today, the raw biological materials from which personality emerges. It reflects the constitutional soil, if you will, the biochemistry, endocrinology, and neurological structure that underlie the tendency to respond to stimulation in particular ways. Temperament would be represented in the literature of personality pathology by the individual's prevailing mood, its type, periodicity, and intensity, In the same ways as the term *character* has come to be limited largely to the moral or social valuation dimensions of personality, so too has the term *temperament* come to be restricted to the individual's constitutional disposition to activity and emotionality.

What then is personality?

The word derives from the Greek term *persona* and originally represented the theatrical mask used by dramatic players. Its meaning has changed through history. As a mask assumed by an actor it suggested a pretense of appearance, that is, the possession of traits other than those which actually characterized the individual behind the mask. In time, the term *persona* lost its connotation of pretense and illusion, and began to represent, not the mask, but the real person, his/her apparent, explicit, and manifest features. The third and final meaning that the term *personality* has acquired delves "beneath" the surface impression of the person and turns the spotlight on the inner, less revealed, and hidden psychological qualities of the individual. Thus, through history the term has shifted from meaning external illusion to surface reality, to opaque or veiled inner traits. It is this third meaning that comes closest to contemporary use. Personality is seen today as a complex pattern of deeply embedded psychological characteristics that are largely unconscious, cannot be eradicated easily, and express themselves automatically in almost every facet of functioning. Intrinsic and pervasive, these traits emerge from a complicated matrix of biological dispositions and experiential learnings and now comprise the individual's distinctive pattern of perceiving, feeling, thinking, and coping.

Normality and Pathology of Personality

Numerous attempts have been made to develop definitive criteria for distinguishing psychological normality from abnormality. Some of these criteria focus on features that characterize the so-called normal, or ideal, state of mental health, as illustrated in the writings of Shoben (1957), Jahoda (1958), and Offer and Sabshin (1974); others have sought to specify criteria for concepts such as abnormality or psychopathology, exemplified in the work of Scott (1958) and Buss (1966). The most common criterion employed is a statistical one in which normality is determined by those behaviors that are found most frequently in a social group; and pathology or abnormality, by features that are uncommon in that population. Among diverse criteria used to signify normality are a capacity to function autonomously and competently, a tendency to adjust to one's social environment effectively and efficiently, a subjective sense of contentment and satisfaction, and the ability to self-actualize or to fulfill one's potentials. Psychopathology would be noted by deficits among the preceding.

Central to our understanding of these terms is the recognition that normality and pathology are relative concepts; they represent arbitrary points on a continuum or gradient, since no sharp line divides normal from pathological behavior. Not only is personality so complex that certain areas of psychological functioning operate normally while others do not, but environmental circumstances change such that behaviors and strategies that prove adaptive at one time fail to do so at another. Moreover, features differentiating normal from abnormal functioning must be extracted from a complex of signs that not only wax and wane but often develop in an insidious and unpredictable manner.

Pathology results from the same forces as involved in the development of normal functioning, Important differences in the character, timing, and intensity of these influences will lead some individuals to acquire pathological traits and others to develop adaptive traits. When an individual displays an ability to cope with the environment in a flexible manner, and when his or her typical perceptions and behaviors foster increments in personal satisfaction, then the person may be said to possess a normal or healthy personality. Conversely, when average or everyday responsibilities are responded to inflexibly or defectively, or when the individual's perceptions and behaviors result in increments in personal discomfort or curtail opportunities to learn and to grow, then we may speak of a pathological or maladaptive pattern.

Despite the tenuous and fluctuating nature of the normality-pathology distinction, three features may be abstracted from the flow of behavioral characteristics to serve as differentiating criteria; these are an adaptive inflexibility, a tendency to foster vicious or self-defeating circles, and a tenuous emotional stability under conditions of stress (Millon, 1969). Each is elaborated briefly here.

Adaptive Inflexibility. In this case, the alternative strategies the individual employs for relating to others, for achieving goals, and for coping with stress are not only few in number but appear to be practiced rigidly; that is, they are imposed upon conditions for which they are ill-suited. The individual not only is unable to adapt effectively to the circumstances of his or her life but arranges the environment to avoid objectively neutral events that are perceived as stressful. As a consequence, the individual's opportunities for learning new, more adaptive behaviors are reduced and his/her life experiences become ever more narrowly circumscribed.

Vicious circles. All of us manipulate our environments to suit our needs. What distinguishes pathological from normal patterns is not only their rigidity and inflexibility but their tendency to foster vicious circles. What this means is that the person's habitual perceptions, needs, and behaviors perpetuate and intensify preexisting difficulties. As detailed in Chapter 3, maneuvers such as protective constriction, cognitive distortion, and behavior generalization are processes by which individuals restrict their opportunities for new learning, misconstrue essentially benign events, and provoke reactions from others that reactivate earlier problems. In effect, then, pathological personality patterns are themselves pathogenic; that is, they generate and perpetuate existent dilemmas, provoke new predicaments, and set into motion self-defeating sequences with others, which cause their already established difficulties not only to persist but to be aggravated further.

Tenuous stability. This third feature that distinguishes pathological from normal personalities is a fragility or lack of resilience under conditions of subjective stress. Given the ease with which the already troubled are vulnerable to events that reactivate the past, and given their inflexibility and paucity of effective coping mechanisms, they are now extremely susceptible to new difficulties and disruptions. Faced with recurrent failures, anxious lest old and unresolved conflicts reemerge, and unable to recruit new adaptive strategies, these persons are likely to revert to pathological ways of coping, to less adequate control over their emotions, and, ultimately, to increasingly subjective and distorted perceptions of reality.

Personality Patterns, Symptom Disorders, and Behavior Reactions

A classification system will go awry if its major categories encompass too diverse a range of clinical conditions; there is need to subdivide psychopathology in terms of certain fundamental criteria. In this regard, particular attention must be paid to drawing distinctions among patients who appear overtly similar but differ in ways that have significant prognostic consequences. It is for this reason that an attempt is made here to differentiate among personality *patterns,* symptom *disorders* and behavior *reactions* (Millon, 1969).

The essential criterion for making these distinctions is the extent to which the observed pathology reflects ingrained personal traits versus transient situational difficulties. Thus, personality patterns are defined as clinical syndromes composed of intrinsic, deeply embedded, and pervasive ways of functioning. At the opposite end of a continuum are the behavior reactions, defined as highly specific pathological responses that are precipitated by and largely attributable to circumscribed external events. Between these two extremes lie the symptom disorders, categories of psychopathology that are anchored simultaneously to ingrained personal traits and transient stimulus events. Conceived as intensifications or disruptions in a patient's characteristic style of functioning, symptom disorders are viewed as a reaction to a situation for which the individual's personality is notably vulnerable.

Personality patterns are deeply embedded and pervasive, and are likely to persist, essentially unmodified, over long periods of time. In contrast, behavior reactions are expressed in a narrow range of situations or are weakly anchored to the person's characteristic way of functioning; for these reasons, they can be uprooted readily by proper environmental manipulations. Symptom disorders possess well-delineated clinical features that are less difficult to modify than the ingrained personal traits from which they arise, but are more difficult to extinguish than the situationally manipulable behavior reactions.

Viewed from a different perspective, the traits that comprise personality patterns have an inner momentum and autonomy; they are expressed with or without inducement or external precipitation. In contrast, the responses comprising behavior reactions are stimulus-specific; that is, they are linked to external conditions in that they operate independent of the individual's personality and are elicited by events that are "objectively" troublesome. Symptom disorders are similar to behavior reactions in that they are prompted also by external events, but their close connection to personality results in the intrusion of traits and behaviors that complicate what might otherwise be a simple reaction to the environment.

To further distinguish patterns, disorders, and reactions it might be noted that personality traits "feel right" to the individual who possesses them; the term *ego-syntonic* has been coined to convey this notion of comfort and suitability of one's own characteristics. In contrast, symptom disorders are experienced as *ego-dystonic*, that is, not only uncomfortable but alien, irrational, and strange. This sense of "disorder" and symptom inappropriateness contrasts with the experience of behavior reactions. Not only are reactions straightforward and uncontaminated, but they often seem quite understandable, even justified, given the realistically stressful nature of the external event that precipitated them.

Symptom disorders occur in response to situations that appear rather trivial or innocuous when viewed objectively. Nevertheless, disordered patients feel and respond in a manner similar to that of persons who face realistically distressing situations. As a consequence, symptom disorders fail to "make sense" and often appear irrational and strangely complicated. To the experienced clinician, however, the response signifies the presence of an unusual vulnerability on the part of the patient; in effect, a seemingly neutral stimulus apparently has touched a painful hidden memory or emotion. Viewed in this manner, symptom disorders arise among individuals encumbered with adverse past experiences. They reflect the upsurge of deeply rooted feelings that press to the surface, override present realities, and become the prime stimulus to which the individual responds. It is this flooding into the present of the reactivated past that gives symptom disorders much of their symbolic, bizarre, and hidden meaning.

In contrast to symptom disorders, behavior reactions are simple and straightforward. They do not "pass through" a chain of complicated and circuitous transformations before emerging in manifest form. Uncontaminated by the intrusion of distant memories and intrapsychic processes, behavior reactions tend to be rational and understandable in terms of the precipitating stimulus. Isolated from past emotions and from defensive manipulations, they are expressed in an uncomplicated and consistent fashion—unlike symptom disorders, whose features are highly fluid, wax and wane, and take different forms at different times.

The terminology and categories of the DSM-III are not differentiated in accord with the preceding discussion; the term *disorder* is applied to all clinical syndromes, including those of "personality disorders." Nevertheless, there is reason to reflect further on these distinctions later in the chapter. For the present, this section concludes by noting once more that personality is a concept that represents a network of deeply embedded and broadly exhibited traits that persist over extended periods of time and characterize the individual's distinctive manner of relating to the environment. Pathological personalities are distinguished from their normal counterparts by their adaptive inflexibility, their tendency to foster vicious circles, and their tenuous stability under stressful conditions.

CONCEPTUAL ISSUES

Concepts are not reality. They are not inevitable and "true" representations of the objective world. The conceptual language of a theory is an optional tool utilized to organize observable experience in a logical manner. Theorists engage in intense debates as to which concepts are best, and the poor reader invests much energy in trying to decide who is correct. It is often suggested that what we need are more empirical data to provide "the answer." Unfortunately, pure empiricism overlooks complex philosophical issues. To make sense or give direction to observations it is necessary first to choose the kinds of data that will be conceptualized. Only when we know which data have been selected for this purpose by the various theories will we be able to compare them in terms of their success in giving meaning and coherence to the observations they share in common.

A major source of confusion for students stems from the fact that psychopathologists have traditionally observed different types of data. The complex components of personality lend themselves to being conceived in almost an infinite number of ways. Which observations should be grouped or combined to form conceptual abstractions is a matter of theoretical orientation. Observational units may range from past events to current situations, from specific acts to dimensional traits, from unconscious motives to biological temperaments. No single focus of observation is sufficient to encompass all of the complex and multidimensional components that comprise personality pathology. Psychopathologists have no choice but to approach their subject from different vantage points, selecting only those elements they believe will enable them to best answer the questions they pose.

Two issues related to the data of personality concepts are discussed next. The first pertains to the different levels of data which theorists of psychopathology draw upon for their concepts. The second reflects the fact that the data of personality are organized into trait dimensions by some theorists and into typologies by others.

Alternative Levels of Data

As noted earlier (Millon, 1967), nature does not lend itself to our need to conceptualize a tidy and well-ordered universe. Not only does the complexity of the natural world make it difficult to identify lawful relationships among events, but the relatively simple task of classifying events also proves quite troublesome. In our desire to uncover the essential order of nature we can select only a few of the infinite number of elements that could be chosen. In this selection process we narrow our choices largely in terms of the traditions of our science; it is hoped that this will focus our attention and facilitate our search for answers. Unfortunately, there are diverse traditions in personality pathology, and they suggest competing perspectives as to which data are likely to prove most fruitful. For example, psychopathologists who view patients at a behavioral level are likely to conceive personality as a collection of specific and largely unrelated responses to particular stimulus events. Those who view personality from a phenomenological perspective are inclined to attend to signs of personal discomfort as subjectively experienced and consciously reported. Approached with a biophysical orientation, these same events are likely to be conceived as intricate sequences of neural or chemical activity. Those of a psychoanalytic persuasion will be disposed to organize personality as complex unconscious processes that reflect instinctual drives and the residues of childhood anxieties and conflicts. As a consequence of these diverse perspectives, the raw data of personality may be conceived by some as conditioned habits, by others as cognitive expectancies, or neuro-chemical dysfunctions, or reaction formations, and so on. These alternative levels of data merely are different. However, once a particular level is chosen, it leads to conceptualizations and empirical laws that are potentially different than those likely to be derived following other choices. It is for this reason that theories must be differentiated in terms of the kinds of data they elect to conceptualize. Elaborated in greater detail elsewhere (Millon, 1967, 1973), it will be useful to briefly describe the major levels of data that distinguish contemporary theories.

Biophysical data. Those who follow in the tradition of medical psychia-try are oriented to biophysical data. Most adhere to the medical "disease" model, as illustrated by the search for the origins of disease in infections, obstructions, imbalances, or other disruptions of normal physiological functioning. As regards psychopathology, biophysically oriented theorists are likely to anticipate that structural defects or chemical deficiencies will ultimately be found to account for symptoms such as bizarre behaviors, labile emotions, and disorganized thinking. The major difference they see between psychological and physical disease is that the former, reflecting disruptions in the nervous system, will manifest itself in the realms of behavior, emotions, and thought, whereas the latter, arising from defects in other organ systems, will be manifest in physical symptoms.

Intrapsychic data. Those within the psychodynamic tradition of psychi-atry focus their attention on intrapsychic data. They emphasize the impact of early experience and view adult disorders to be a consequence of the unrelenting and insidious operation of past events. Personality pathology reflects the inappropriate persistence of unconscious defensive maneuvers that were devised initially to protect against the upsurge or recurrence of early difficulties. The obscure and objectively elusive data of the unconscious are uncovered and used for intrapsychic concepts.

Phenomenological data. Theorists whose views reflect humanistic and existential traditions attend primarily to the data of conscious, phenomenological experience. From this perspective, each individual must be studied only on his/her own terms, that is, from the individual's unique perception of the world. No matter how transformed or unconsciously distorted this perception may be, it is the person's idiosyncratic way of seeing and experiencing events which gives meaning to his or her behavior. Concepts must be formulated, therefore, not in terms of objective reality or unconsicous processes, but in accord with how things are directly felt and known by the person.

Behavioral data. Those working in the traditions of academic and experimental psychology direct their observations to overt behavioral data. To them, concepts and propositions are anchored to tangible and measurable properties in the empirical world. Subjective introspection and unconscious dynamics are viewed as unscientific and are replaced by reference to empirically observable events and actions. Environmental influences are given prominence and are conceived as stimulus properties that reinforce and control behavior pathology.

Sociocultural data. Finally, there are theorists whose data derive mainly from sociological and anthropological perspectives. No longer is the focus on the individual, the overt behavior, neurochemical processes, self-concept, or unconscious mechanisms; rather, larger units of sociocultural phenomena such as families, groups, or ethnic and minority status are the primary data. Concepts are devised to represent these social forces and are employed largely to provide a context for understanding pathological behaviors.

Since most researchers and practitioners are oriented to but a small segment of the field as a whole, they often have little sympathy for, or even knowledge of, the concepts employed by those from different traditions. Until such time as a bridge is constructed to coordinate each of these divergent data levels, no one orientation should be viewed as primary; a multiplicity of approaches seems best at this stage of our clinical science.

Categorical Types and Dimensional Traits

A major issue facing theorists concerns the form in which clinical personality data should be organized. Categorization is extremely difficult when, in addition to the specifics of the symptoms themselves, theorists must consider variations in their duration and pervasiveness as well. For example: How does one best cluster symptoms and group patients when it is necessary to weigh the complex and sequential interplay among both recently acquired and long-standing characteristics? It is in response to problems such as these that we find those who favor using trait or dimensional concepts versus those who prefer type or categorical concepts. The issue separating these two approaches may be best stated in the form of a question: Should personality pathology be conceived and organized as a series of dimensional traits that combine to form a unique profile for each individual, or should certain central characteristics be selected to exemplify and categorize personality types found commonly in clinical populations?

The view that personality pathology might best be conceived as dimensional traits has not been widely accepted. Nevertheless, certain trait dimensions have frequently been proposed as relevant to these disorders, notably dominance-submission, extraversion-introversion, and rigidity-flexibility. Some traits have been formulated so that one extreme of a dimension differs significantly from the other in terms of their clinical implications; an example here would be emotional stability versus emotional vulnerability. Other traits are psychologically curvilinear such that both extremes have negative implications; an example of this would be found in an activity dimension such as listlessness versus restlessness.

There are several advantages to dimensional models that should be noted. Most important is that they combine several clinical features or personality traits into a single profile. By their comprehensiveness, little information of potential significance is lost, nor is any single trait given special attention, as when only one distinctive characteristic is brought to the foreground in a typology. Further, a trait profile permits the inclusion of unusual or atypical cases; in typologies, odd, infrequent, or "mixed" conditions often are excluded since they do not fit the prescribed categories. Given the diversity and idiosyncratic character of many clinical personalities, a dimensional system encourages the representation of individuality and uniquesness rather than "forcing" patients into categories for which they are ill-suited. A final advantage of a dimensional format is that the strength of traits is gauged quantitatively, and therefore each characteristic extends into the normal range; as a consequence, normality and abnormality are merely arranged as points on a continuum rather than as distinct and separable phenomena.

Despite their seeming advantages, dimension systems have not fared well in the diagnosis of personality pathology. Numerous complications and limitations have been noted in the literature, and these should be recorded also.

First is the fact there there is little agreement among dimensional theorists concerning the number of traits necessary to represent personality. For example, Menninger (1963) contends that a single dimension will suffice; Eysenck (1960) asserts that three are needed, whereas Cattell (1965) claims to have identified as many as 33 and believes there to be many more. It appears, in fact, that theorists invent dimensions in accord with their expectations rather than "discovering" them as if they were intrinsic to nature, merely awaiting scientific detection. The number of traits required to assess personality is not determined by the ability of our research to disclose some inherent truth but rather by our predilections for conceiving and organizing our observations.

Second, describing personality with more than a few trait dimensions produces such complex and intricate schemas as to require geometric or algebraic representation. There is nothing intrinsically wrong with such quantitative formats, but they do pose considerable difficulty both in comprehension and in communication among professionals. Most mental health workers are hesitant about working with complex multivariate statistics, and the consequent feeling that one is lost in one's own professional discipline is not likely to make such schemas attractive, no less practical for everyday use. Apart from matters of convenience and comfort, algebraic representations must be grouped into categories before the information they contain can be communicated. In effect, once a population has been identified as possessing a similar profile or dimensional pattern, it comprises a category. Thus, although the original format may have been dimensional, those who are grouped within it invariably are spoken of as a "type."

Typological models are the preferred schema for representing clinical syndromes. There are several reasons for this preference. First, most contemporary typologies neither imply nor are constructed to be all-or-none categories. Although singling out and giving prominence to certain features of behavior, they do not overlook the others but merely assign them lesser significance. It is the process of assigning centrality or relative dominance to particular characteristics that distinguishes a schema of categories from one composed of trait dimensions. A comparison of the concepts of response, habit, trait, and type may help clarify this distinction. In effect, these four concepts may be arranged in a hierarchy such that each higher-order concept abstracts and subsumes several features represented in the next, lower-order concept; in this manner the higher-order concept is more comprehensive and includes only those features of lower-order concepts which are judged clinically most significant.

More concretely stated, at the level of direct observation all we perceive at any single moment is that a patient *responds* to a specific situation in a particular way. If, over time, we observe the patient to make that response in a variety of different situations, we may decide that these responses represent a general *habit*. Taking our observations one step further, we may note that the patient exhibits a group of response habits that co-occur and form a repetitive way of psychological functioning or relating to the environment; at this point we may begin to speak of these related habits as a *trait*. Last, if we note that several of these traits display important psychological connections that can be understood in terms of a particular central or overarching characteristic, we may decide to speak of this distinguishing or coordinating characteristic as a *type* of personality functioning. Conceived in this manner, a type simply becomes a superordinate category that subsumes and integrates psychologically covariant traits that, in turn, represent a set of correlated habits that, in their turn, stand for a response displayed in a variety of situations.When this superordinate type is found with some frequency in clinical populations, we have reason to conclude that it may be useful as a concept that gives coherence to seemingly diverse symptoms. Exemplified and labeled in accord with its prominent and unifying feature, the type may, in time, become established as a formal clinical syndrome.

Among the advantages of typologies is their ease of use by clinicians who must make relatively rapid diagnoses with large numbers of patients whom they see briefly. Although clinical attention in these cases is drawn to only the most salient features of the patient, a broad range of traits that have not been directly observed are strongly suggested. It is this capacity to suggest characteristics beyond the immediately observed that adds special value to an established system of types. For example, let us assume that an individual is diagnosed as a histrionic personality following the observation that his behaviors were seductive and dramatic; although the data base was limited there is reason to believe that the person is likely to be characterized also as stimulus seeking, needful of attention, interpersonally capricious, emotionally labile, and so on. In effect, assignment to a particular type or category often proves useful by alerting the clinician to a range of unobserved but frequently correlated behaviors. This process of extending the scope of associated characteristics contrasts wtih the tendency of dimensional schemas to fractionate personality into separate and uncoordinated traits. Typologies restore and recompose the unity of personality by integrating seemingly diverse elements into a single coordinated syndrome. Moreover, the availability of well-established syndromes will provide standard references for clinicians who would otherwise be faced with repeated analyses and de novo personality constructions.

There are, of course, objections to the use of typologies in personality. They contribute to the fallacious belief that psychopathological syndromes are discrete entities, even medical "diseases," when, in fact, they are merely concepts that help focus and coordinate observations. Further, typologies often fail to identify and include important aspects of behavior since they reflect a decision to narrow the list of characteristics that are considered primary. Of course, the discarding of information is not limited to typologies; dimensional schemas also choose certain traits to the exclusion of others. The problem, however, is that types give primacy to only a single characteristic. Another criticism is that the number and diversity of types are far less than the individual differences observed in clinical work. Not only are there problems in assigning many patients to the limited categories available, but clinicians often claim that the more they know a patient, the greater the difficulty they have in fitting him or her in a single category. A final criticism reflects the diversity of competing systems available; as is detailed in Chapter 2, numerous typologies have been formulated in the past century and one may question whether any system is worth utilizing if there is so little consensus among typologists themselves.

What solution is there to the question of how the data of personality pathology might best be organized? Is it possible to conclude from this review that typological or dimensional schemas are potentially more useful? A surprising and illuminating answer may have been provided by Cattell, who wrote:

> The description by attributes [traits] and the description by types must ... be considered face and obverse of the same descriptive system. Any object whatever can be defined either by listing measurements for it on a set of [trait] attributes or by sequestering it to a particular named [type] category. (1970, p. 40)

In effect, Cattell has concluded that the issue of choosing between dimensional traits and categorical types is both naive and specious since they are two sides of the same coin. The essential distinction to be made between these models is that of comprehensiveness. Types are higher-order syntheses of lower-order dimensional traits; they encompass a wider scope of generality. For certain purposes it may be useful to narrow attention to specific traits; in other circumstances a more inclusive level of integration may be appropriate. Since the concept of personality itself is so comprehensive in scope, it was inevitable that both clinicians and researchers would show a clear preference in choosing typologies for organizing the data of personality pathology.

EMPIRICAL ISSUES

The previous section dealt with conceptual issues concerning the organization of personality data. Questions raised by these issues are resolved largely by logic, utility, and preference. In contrast, the two issues addressed in this section, and the questions they raise, are approached empirically; that is, answers must be sought through objective and quantitative research. The first of these issues, touched upon only in passing previously, pertains to whether clinical syndromes are or are not discrete entities; that is, is each syndrome a separate unit composed of distinct constituent symptoms or do syndromes overlap and interrelate by virtue of important shared symptoms? Referred to as *syndromal continuity* versus *discontinuity*, the problem is similar in certain respects to the conceptual issue of types versus dimensions. The second empirical issue is whether personality characteristics do, in fact, display consistency from one time and situation to another, or whether they are transient and situationally specific. We would have great difficulty in justifying the concept of personality if little or no behavioral stability was observed over time and circumstance.

Syndromal Continuity versus Discontinuity

The notion of syndromal discontinuity is an outgrowth of the belief that all psychopathologies are qualitatively distinct disease entities. Syndromal continuity reflects the view that all psychological abnormalities are quantitative deviations from the average on a distribution of traits. Discontinuity implies that some unusual process has intruded upon the individual's functioning, which now sets this person apart from others who vary normally from each other in accord with natural individual differences. The discontinuity thesis is strongly supported if it can be demonstrated empirically that a clear boundary exists between the features of one syndrome and those of others. Kendell has stated this issue as follows:

> If the putative boundary lies between one syndrome and another this means demonstrating, on an unselected population, that patients with features of both conditions are less common than those with symptoms appropriate only to one or the other. And in the related case where the presumed boundary lies between a syndrome and normality, it means demonstrating that patients with partial or half-fledged symptoms are less common than those who have all or none. Either way the mixed forms, the greys, must be shown to be less common than the pure forms, the blacks and the whites. The mere existence of patients with mixed symptoms is not evidence that the boundary is not a genuine one, any more than the existence of a few hermaphrodites invalidates the distinction between male and female, but such interforms must be relatively infrequent. In graphical terms, this means that the distribution curve of the total population must be bimodal rather than unimodal. (1975, p. 65)

Empirical research does little to support the view that syndromes can be clearly separated, nor is there evidence that distribution curves tend to be bimodal. For example, the work of Beck (1967) and Kendell (1968, 1975) indicates the presence of numerous borderline cases between supposedly discrete categories. Some investigators have uncovered an occasional bimodality, but these findings appear to reflect methodological artifacts. Strauss (1973), for example, has noted several complications with studies that report bimodal findings, including sampling problems, procedural distortions, poor interjudge reliabilities, rater preconceptions, and so on.

Both factor and cluster analytic techniques have been employed to demonstrate the existence of discrete syndromes. Findings obtained with factorial techniques have been seriously questioned, however. For example, factors may be mere artifacts of redundant variables or preselected patient populations. Others have questioned whether the characteristics included in most factor studies represent meaningful clinical features found in patients (Armstrong and Solberg, 1968; Maxwell, 1971). Although cluster analysis is the most advanced technique for identifying patient similarities, the groupings it derives do not represent commonalities inherent in patients; rather, they reflect statistical maneuvers that impose group clusters on data even when there is little to support them as discrete clinical syndromes (Fleiss and Zubin, 1969; Bartko, Strauss, and Carpenter, 1971). Particularly disturbing is the fact that different cluster computer programs frequently produce dissimilar patient groupings, a finding that strongly suggests that the statistical method, rather than the raw data themselves, plays the major role in producing what patterns or categories emerge.

Where then do we stand on the issue of syndromal continuity or discontinuity?

It would appear that the view that mental disorders are composed of distinct entities reflects our level of scientific development more than the intrinsic characteristics of psychopathological phenomena. For example, Hempel (1961) has noted that all sciences, in their early stages, tend to order their variables into separate or discrete classes. As progress occurs, advanced methods of analysis become available to enable scientists to deal with the interplay of elements comprising their field and, thereby, specify how formerly unconnected characteristics overlap and interrelate. It would appear, then, that as our science progresses, syndromes should be conceived less as discrete and independent, and more as converging and reciprocal, exhibiting both interconnected and distinct features—that is, displaying greater continuity.

A first step toward the goal of simultaneous differentiation and coordination has been taken in the DSM-III, where the two major axes are separate yet interrelated. Axis I consists of clinical symptom disorders, those syndromes that wax and wane in their severity over time, and that display themselves as the acute and more dramatic forms of psychopathology. On Axis II are found the personality syndromes representing those enduring and pervasive characteristics that often underlie and provide a context and foundation for understanding the more florid and transient symptomatology recorded on Axis I. Each axis is recorded separately, yet they are conceived as representing interrelated clinical features. In its multiaxial construction, therefore, the DSM-III has sought to encourage clinicians to explore relationships among diagnostic categories. It was hoped that clinical syndromes would no longer be seen as standing on their own as discrete entities; rather, they would be viewed either as precursors, extensions, or substrates for one another. More specifically, the symptom disorders of Axis I would be understood to be disruptions of functioning among the personality types listed on Axis II, springing forth, so to speak, to dominate the clinical picture under stressful or otherwise vulnerable circumstances. Envisioned in this fashion, a symptom disorder is no longer a distinct diagnostic entity but a single element or expression of a complex of personality characteristics that is exhibited under special conditions.

Personality Consistency versus Situational Specificity

The assumption that the way an individual behaves typically at one time or in one situation will be closely related to the way he or she behaves at others has been seriously questioned in recent years. That traits endure or persist over time has been spoken of as *stability;* that behaviors displayed in one situation will be exhibited in others has been referred to as *consistency.*

Temporal stability and cross-situational consistency are fundamental to the concept of personality. If individuals fail to exhibit reasonably stable and consistent behaviors, then the very notion of personality itself may be in jeopardy. Although it is intuitively self-evident that people exhibit both stability and consistency, there are those who have vigorously argued that research fails to support both assumptions. Mischel, a former proponent of this critical view, raised the following question in an early paper on the topic:

> How does one reconcile our shared perceptions of continuity with the equally impressive evidence that on virtually all of our dispositional measures of personality substantial changes occur in the characteristics of the individual longitudinally over time and, even more dramatically across seemingly similar settings cross-sectionally? (1969, p. 1012)

To Mischel, as well as to other critics in the early 1970s, behavioral consistency had not been empirically demonstrated, and, hence, the concept of personality traits itself was considered untenable. Needless to say, attacks such as these provoked a rather lively debate in the literature. Among the more illuminating papers on the topic were the following: Alker, 1972; Bem, 1972; Ekehammer, 1974; Endler and Magnusson, 1976; Epstein, 1977, 1979; Magnusson and Endler, 1977; Mischel, 1968, 1969, 1973a, 1973b, 1979; and Wachtel, 1973. This is not the place for a detailed review of the "situationist versus personologist" positions; it will suffice for present purposes to note a few of the major pro and con arguments.

Mischel, in an early critique favoring the situationist position, presented a wide array of evidence indicating that behaviors over time and situation rarely achieve correlations beyond the .30 level (1969). In contrast, he referred to a substantial body of data that show that behaviors are affected significantly by situational variations. Mischel also pointed out that the data of studies finding purported consistency were, in fact, spurious, a consequence of anticipated and rater-imposed regularities.

Several personologists, in rebuttal to Mischel, presented counterarguments in support of both stability and consistency assumptions. Few have taken a rigid position on these matters, fully recognizing the role of situational influences on behavior. However, they claimed that the fact that behaviors vary across situations did not preclude the existence of a certain measure of consistency and, more importantly, a high degree of what was termed *coherence.* Coherence, to the personologist, means that stability and consistency are to be found in logical patterns or regularities rather than in sameness. Wachtel described this notion with an illustration of contradictory behaviors:

> Even where seemingly inconsistent behaviors appear, the viewpoint of most psychodynamic thinkers points toward a search for underlying organizational principles....
>
> Such a characterization of psychodynamic approaches as seeking coherence in people's behavior may at first glance seem inconsistent with the strong emphasis of psychodynamicists on conflict. But an examination of the explanatory role of conflict in most psychodynamic theories reveals that often *conflict itself* is the organizing principle providing coherence in the seeming diversity of everyday

behavior. For example, excessive timidity in one context and extreme aggressiveness in another may both be seen as manifestations of a strong conflict over aggression.... Such divergent extremes are viewed from a psychodynamic perspective, especially one that emphasizes the analysis of character, with an eye toward finding underlying unities, though these unities lie in the organizing role of conflict or apparent *dis*unity. (1973, p. 324)

In addition to noting that behavioral diversity often reflects an underlying coherence, personologists have taken the offensive, so to speak, in pointing to the methodological weaknesses of studies ostensibly demonstrating that behavioral stability and consistency are invalid (Block, 1977; Epstein, 1979). In addition, they have reported on numerous well-designed investigations that support the position that behavior is stable and consistent (Block, 1971, 1977; Olweus, 1977; Epstein, 1979). These longitudinal and cross-sectional studies impressively demonstrate that, in contrast to situational variables, a significant portion of behavioral variance is attributable to personality.

The issue of consistency versus specificity has become a pseudoissue in recent years. Mischel (1979), for example, has asserted that the controversy never existed since it has always been known that people behave in a stable manner in certain situations and variably in others. In his first rethinking of this matter, he phrased his position as follows: "No one suggests that the organism approaches every new situation with an empty head, nor is it questioned by anyone that different individuals differ markedly in how they deal with most stimulus conditions" (1973a, p. 255). What Mischel has come around to is referred to in the literature as the *interactionist position*. Ekehammer (1974), in a review of interactionism, has concluded that the situationist-personologist issue should be reformulated as follows: Which personality and situational factors interact to produce consistent behaviors and which to produce variable behaviors? Behavior, from this viewpoint, results from reciprocal transactions between personality and situational characteristics.

It is unfortunate that the personologist, situationist, and interactionist perspectives are formulated as three contrasting positions, as if only one could be right. If we step back from the debate we may recognize that all three are logical in that each focuses on a different point on a continuum of influences. It may be useful to elaborate this "eclectic" view with reference to personality pathology.

Interactionism would be supported by those cases in which a known personality vulnerability is precipitated into a florid disorder only by situational events that expose the vulnerability. The personological position would be strengthened by evidence that a particular form of behavior is exhibited by a patient repetitively, despite environmental changes. Finally, situationism would be reinforced when certain circumstances produce essentially identical reactions in individuals who are known to possess diverse personality traits. Each of these perspectives will find clinical events and conditions to support their views.

To tie a prior discussion into the present topic, the three positions on the consistency-specificity issue correspond closely to earlier distinctions made in differentiating personality patterns, behavioral reactions, and symptom disorders. Personality patterns were conceived as enduring (stable) and pervasive (consistent) characteristics of behavior, that is, pathological traits that persist over time and are displayed across situations. At the other end of the continuum are the behavior reactions, described as situationally specific pathological responses induced by the conditions of the environment. Symptom disorders lie between these two and were formulated as pathological phenomena that reflect the interaction of personality vulnerabilities and situational stimuli. In essence, symptom disorders represent the interactionist view concerning the origin of pathological symptoms; behavior reactions reflect the situationist position; and personality patterns, the prime topic of this text, correspond to the personological perspective. By differentiating the major categories of pathology in accord with the threefold schema of patterns, reactions, and disorders, a small step will be taken toward distinguishing syndromes in a manner that parallels the three primary sources of pathogenesis, the individual (personological), the environment (situational), and their interaction.

As a final paragraph to the chapter reference should be made to recent empirical research that shows that individuals differ in the degree to which their behaviors exhibit consistency (Endler and Magnusson, 1976; Epstein, 1979). Moreover, each individual displays consistency only in certain characteristics; that is, each of us possesses particular traits that are resistant to situational influence and others that can be readily modified. Stated differently, the several characteristics comprised in our personality do not display equal degrees of consistency and stability. Furthermore, the traits that exhibit consistency in one person may not exhibit consistency in others. In general, consistency is found only in traits that are central to the individual's style of functioning. For some, what is of significance is being compliant and agreeable, never differing or having conflict; for another, it may be crucial to keep one's distance from people so as to avoid rejection or the feeling of being humiliated; and for a third, the influential characteristic may be that of asserting one's will and dominating others. Thus, each individual possesses a small and distinct group of primary traits that persist and endure, and exhibit a high degree of consistency across situations. These enduring (stable) and pervasive (consistent) characteristics are what we mean when we speak of personality. Going one step further, personality pathology comprises those stable and consistent traits that persist inflexibly, are exhibited inappropriately, and foster vicious circles that perpetuate and intensify already present difficulties.

Chapter 2

Systems of Personality Classification

Current classifications of personality are the result of a long and continuing history. Despite the desultory nature of our path to knowledge, there appear to be certain themes and concepts to which clinicians and theorists return time and again; these are noted as the discussion proceeds in this chapter. Commonalities notwithstanding, the classification schemas to be summarized here represent different notions concerning which data are important to observe and how they should be organized to best represent personality. Thus, to Kretschmer (1925), body morphology was a significant variable in conceptualizing pathological types; for Cattell (1957, 1965), statistically derived trait dimensions were given preeminence; for Horney (1950), it was the interpersonal orientation developed to resolve unconscious conflicts that received emphasis.

What should be especially heartening is that theorists and classifiers have been convinced that the complexities and intricacies of personality can, in fact, be studied systematically and will, it is hoped, yield to our efforts at scientific comprehension. Each classification schema is not only a model for arranging thinking about personality but poses significant questions and provides interesting, if not necessarily valid, answers to them. Moreover, these abstract formulations furnish frameworks to organize clinical concepts and to appraise the everyday utility of observations.

It is not the intent of this chapter to enable the reader to master the details of personality classification. The purpose is simply that of outlining the diverse theories into which personality pathology has been cast through history. Much is to be gained by reading original or primary sources, but the aim of this synopsis is to distill the essentials of what theorists have written and to present them as an orientation to the personality syndromes described in later chapters.

HISTORICAL APPROACHES

The history of formal personality characterization can be traced to the early Greeks. A survey of these notions can be found in the detailed reviews published by Roback (1927) and Allport (1937). Given these fine secondary sources, there is no reason to record here any but the most central concepts of these early characterologists. Also worthy of brief mention are those who may be considered the forerunners of contemporary systems of classification.

Literary Characterology

Allport has referred to "character writing" as a minor literary style originating in Athens, probably invented by Aristotle and brought to its finest and most brilliant form through the pen of Theophrastus. Presented as "verbal" portraits, these depictions of character are brief sketches that capture certain common types so aptly as to be identified and appreciated by readers in all walks of life. In these crisp delineations, a dominant trait is brought to the forefront and accentuated and embellished to highlight the major flaws or foibles of the individual. In essence, they are stylized simplifications that often border on the precious or burlesque. Among literature's most incisive and brilliant portrayals are the character depictions found in the works of Butler, Carlyle, Chaucer, Donne, Eliot, La Bruyère, La Rochefoucault, Montesquieu, Pascal, Proust, Stendhal, and Tolstoy.

Whether the work is penetrating or poignant, novelists are free to write about their subjects without the constraints of psychologic or scientific caution. Lively and spirited characterizations most assuredly capture one's interest, but many mislead us regarding the true nature of causes and correlates. Allport noted the facile word play of literary characterology and its frequent insubstantial nature in the following:

> One of his characters may have "menial blood in his veins," another "a weak chin." A hand may possess "a wonderfully cruel greed" and a blond head "radiate fickleness." Such undisciplined metaphors give cadence and inspire a kind of bland credulity, but for science they are mere idle phrases. (1937, p. 62)

For all its graphic and compelling qualities, literary characterology is a limited and often misleading form of personality description. In the hands of an astute observer, sensitive to the subtleties and contradictions of behavior, such portrayals provide a pithy analysis of both the humor and anguish of personal functioning. However, the very unique and picturesque quality of the presentations draws attention to the fascinating, and away from the mundane behaviors that typify everyday human conduct. Artistic accentuations may serve the purpose of dramatic rendition but falsify the true nature of psychic operations. Intriguing though such portrayals may be, they often depict types that are either unidimensional or rarely seen in clinical observation, and are, hence, of minimal diagnostic utility. Perhaps less delightful and amusing, the characteristics required for purposes of clinical classification must be both more systematic and more commonplace.

Humoral Doctrines

The first explanatory system to specify personality dimensions is likely to have been the doctrine of bodily humors posited by early Greeks some 25 centuries ago. Interestingly, history appears to have come full circle. The humoral doctrine sought to explain personality with reference to alleged body fluids, whereas much of contemporary psychiatry seeks answers with bio-chemical and endocrinological hypotheses.

In the fourth century B.C. Hippocrates concluded that all disease stemmed from an excess of or imbalance among four bodily humors: yellow bile, black bile, blood, and phlegm. Humors were the embodiment of earth, water, fire, and air—the declared basic components of the universe according to the philosopher Empedocles. Hippocrates identified four basic temperaments, the choleric, melancholic, sanguine, and phlegmatic; these corresponded, respectively, to excesses in yellow bile, black bile, blood, and phelgm. Modified by Galen centuries later, the choleric temperament was associated with a tendency toward irascibility, the sanguine temperament prompted the individual toward optimism, the melancholic temperament was characterized by an inclination toward sadness, and the phlegmatic temperament was conceived as an apathetic disposition. Although the doctrine of humors has been abandoned, giving way to scientific studies on topics such as neuro-hormone chemistry, its terminology and connotations still persist in such contemporary expressions as being sanguine or *good humored.*

Physiognomy and Phrenology

The ancients speculated also that body structure was associated with the character of personality. Whereas the humoral doctrine may be seen as the forerunner of contemporary psychiatric endocrinology, phrenology and physiognomy may be conceived as forerunners of modern psychiatric morphology.

Physiognomy, first recorded in the writings of Aristotle, seeks to identify personality characteristics by outward appearances, particularly facial con-figurations and expressions. People have sought to appraise others through-out history by observing their countenance, the play in their face, and the cast of their eyes, as well as their postural attitudes and the style of their movements. It was not until the late eighteenth century, however, that the first systematic effort was made to analyze external morphology and its relation to psychological functions.

Despite its discredited side, phrenology, as practiced by Franz Josef Gall, was an honest and serious attempt to construct a science of personology. Although Gall referred to his studies of "brain physiology" as "organology" and "crainoscopy," the term *phrenology*, coined by a younger associate, came to be its popular designation. The rationale that Gall presented for measuring contour variations of the skull was not at all illogical given the limited knowledge of eighteenth-century anatomy. In fact, his work signified an important advance over the naïve and subjective studies of physiognomy of his time in that he sought to employ objective and quantitative methods to deduce the inner structure of the brain. Seeking to decipher personality characteristics by their ostensible correlations with the nervous system, he was among the first to claim that a direct relationship existed between mind and body. Contending that the brain was the central organ of thought and emotion, Gall concluded, quite reasonably, that both the intensity and character of thoughts and emotions would correlate with variations in the size and shape of the brain or its encasement, the cranium. Thus, Gall asserted that just as it is logical to assume that persons with large bicep muscles are stronger than those with thin or small ones, so too would it be logical to assume that persons possessing large cranial projections would display corresponding psychological characteristics to a greater extent than those who evidence smaller protuberances. That these assertions proved invalid should not be surprising when we recognize, as we do today, the exceedingly complex structure of neuroanatomy and its tangential status as a substrate for personality functions. Despite the now transparent weaknesses of Gall's system, he was the first to attempt a reasoned thesis for the view that personality characteristics may correlate with body structure.

EARLY TWENTIETH-CENTURY THEORISTS

Attempts to classify nosological systems are doubly problematic; not only must we identify the essential quality that each classifier intends as the core of the schema, but we must also find a framework by which these diverse systems themselves can be grouped. Unfortunately, no principle exists to unify or organize the various classifications that have been proposed throughout history. One useful distinction that may be made differentiates those that focus on normal as opposed to abnormal personalities. In accord with this distinction, this discussion separates theorists of character and temperament, who concern themselves with nonpathological traits and types, from psychiatric theorists, who are likely to attend to pathological symptoms and syndromes.

The majority of theorists presented in this section are of European origin, as were most scientific contributors in the early decades of this century. As psychological interest and talent crossed the Atlantic, and as psychoanalysis gained its preeminent status in the 1940s and 1950s, acquaintance with the theorists discussed here faded rapidly. The loss of their contributions is most unfortunate in that many of them proposed concepts that had to be "rediscovered" in contemporary work. Present thinking might have progressed more rapidly had their ideas been in more common use.

Character Propositions

Ribot. A late nineteenth-century French psychologist, T. Ribot (1890) attempted to formulate character types in a manner analogous to botanical classifications. By varying the intensity level of two traits, those of sensitivity and activity, Ribot sought to construct several major types. Among the personalities proposed were: (1) the "humble character," noted by excess sensibility and limited energy; (2) the "contemplative character," marked by keen sensibility and passive behavior; and (3) the "emotional type," combining extreme impressionability and an active disposition. Among other major categories were the "apathetic" and the "calculative" characters.

Queyrat. A similar method of permutation was applied by another French theorist, F. Queyrat (1896), in his formulation of nine normal character types; this was achieved by intensity combinations of three dispositions: emotionality, activity, and meditation. Where only one disposition was preeminent, the character took the form of a pure emotional, active, or meditative type. A second group of normal characters were noted by the simultaneous predominance of two dispositions, yielding an active-emotional, or "passionate," type; an active-meditative, or "voluntary," character; and a meditative-emotional, or "sentimental," personality. In the third set of characters Queyrat identified those in which the three dispositions were balanced: Here were noted the "equilibrated," the "amorphous," and the "apathetic" characters. When one or more of the three tendencies functioned irregularly or erratically, Queyrat designated them as semimorbid characters, specifically the "unstable," the "irresolute," and the "contradictory" types.

Heymans and Wiersma. Writing a decade or so later were a number of theorists from other European nations. Most notable among them were the Dutch psychologists G. Heymans and E. Wiersma (1906-1909). On the basis of a series of highly sophisticated empirical studies, they identified three "fundamental criteria" for evaluating character: activity level, emotionality, and susceptibility to external versus internal stimulation. These criteria anticipated identical threefold schemas (each based, however, on highly dissimilar theoretical models) developed by McDougall (1908), Meumann (1910), Freud (1915a), and Millon (1969). By combining these criteria, Heymans and Wiersma deduced the presence of eight character types, namely: (1) the "amorphous" character, reflecting the interplay of passive, nonemotional, and external susceptibility; (2) the "apathetic" character, developing from a passive, nonemotional, and internal orientation; (3) the "nervous" character, a product of a passive, emotional, and external responsiveness; (4) the "sentimental" character, who is passive, emotional, and internally impressed; (5) the "sanguine" character, noted as active, nonemotional, and externally receptive; (6) the "phlegmatic" character, typified by active, nonemotional, and internal tendencies; (7) the "choleric" character, reflecting an active, emotional, and external susceptibility; and (8) the "impassioned" character, representing an active, emotional, and internal sensitivity. As noted, the criteria developed by Heymans and Wiersma correspond extremely well with clinical dimensions derived by later theorists, specifically the polarities of activity-passivity, pleasure-pain emotionality, and an internal, or self, responsivity versus an external, or other, responsivity.

Lazursky. Finally, brief note should be made of the work of the Russian psychologist A. Lazursky, whose book *An Outline of a Science of Characters* was first published in 1906. Lazursky had been greatly influenced by the experimental approach of Pavlov and his colleagues. Foreshadowing personality dimensions that were given special significance in later decades, Lazursky concluded, following a series of "systematic" studies, that the seeming diversity among characters can be grouped into three higher-order types: (1) those who relate to society negatively, appear detached from everyday affairs, and are only minimally adapted to the demands of their environment; (2) those who are molded by their environment and dependent upon external circumstances to guide their behavior and actions; and (3) those who are masters of their fate, controlling their environment and capable of functioning independently of the will of others.

Temperament Hypotheses

Attempts were made in the early twentieth century to identify the constituents of temperament and determine the ways in which they blend into distinctive patterns. The ideas proposed by three theorists are briefly described to illustrate this trend of thinking.

McDougall. Best known in the United States was William McDougall, who proposed the "consolidation of sentiments" in his *Introduction to Social Psychology*, first published in 1908. In a manner not dissimilar from Heymans and Wiersma, McDougall derived eight "tempers" based on different combinations of three fundamental dimensions: the intensity (strength and urgency), the persistency (inward versus outward expression), and the affectivity (emotional susceptibility) of behavioral impulses. Those of high intensity were viewed as active individuals, whereas those disposed to low intensity were seen as passive. High persistency directed the person to the external world, whereas those with low persistency were oriented toward internal matters. By affectivity McDougall meant susceptibility to pleasure and pain such that those characterized by high affectivity were particularly susceptible to these influences, whereas those of low affectivity were not. Combining these three dimensions led McDougall to form the following eight tempers: (1) the "steadfast" temper, noted by high intensity, high persistency, and low affectivity; (2) the "fickle" temper, characterized by low intensity, high persistency, and high affectivity; (3) the "unstable" temper, defined by high intensity, low persistency, and high affectivity; (4) the "despondent" temper, distinguished by high intensity, low persistency, and low affectivity; (5) the "anxious" temper, designated by low intensity, high persistency, and high affectivity; (6) the "hopeful" temper, identified by high intensity, high persistency, and high affectivity; (7) the "placid" temper, depicted by low intensity, high persistency, and low affectivity; and (8) the "sluggish" temper, specified by low intensity, low persistency, and low affectivity.

Of interest is the similarity between McDougall's temperament typology and the characterology of Heymans and Wiersma, especially with regard to parallels between their basic dimensions of intensity and those of activity-passivity, between persistency and the internal versus external orientation, and between affectivity and the emotions of pain and pleasure. As noted earlier, frameworks based on essentially the same three dimensions were formulated by other theorists, such as the two discussed next.

Meumann.   A major effort to construct a theory of temperament was proposed by the distinguished German psychologist E. Meumann in his 1910 text *Intelligenz und Wille*. Meumann specified eight fundamental qualities of feeling. Central among them were the polarity of pleasure versus displeasure and the two excitative modes of expression, the active and the passive. A number of other features were considered by Meumann to be of lesser significance, such as the ease of excitability and the intensity of affect. By combining the pleasure-displeasure and active-passive dimensions Meumann sought to account for the four classical humors. For example, the active mode and the pleasurable quality blended to produce the sanguine temperament, an active mode merged with displeasurable feelings to form the choleric temperament, the combination of a passive mode with a pleasurable feeling accounted for the phlegmatic temperament, and the passive and displeasure amalgam created the melancholic temperament.

Kollarits.   Another schema was formulated by the Hungarian psychiatrist J. Kollarits in his *Charakter und Nervositat*, published in 1912. Here again the dimensions of pleasantness versus unpleasantness and of excited (active) versus calm (passive) were brought to the foreground as a basis for deriving major character types. For example, Kollarits spoke of the pleasantly toned "calm euphoric," whom he contrasted with both the "calm depressive," who is unpleasantly toned, and the "indifferent," who lacks the capacity to experience both pleasant and unpleasant affects. In a manner similar to

Meumann, Kollarits related these dimensions to the four humors. In his schema, the sanguine temperament reflected an interaction of the calm and unpleasant modes, the choleric was an excited and unpleasant blending, and the phlegmatic corresponded essentially to the indifferent type.

Psychiatric Conceptions

Just prior to the turn of the century the professions of psychology and psychiatry began one of their first, albeit tentative, mergers. Psychologists and psychiatrists undertook to study in each other's laboratories, to read each other's treatises, and to explore the overlap between normal and abnormal characteristics of behavior. The following paragraphs note a number of contributions made by psychiatrists who broadened their primary focus on psychopathological "diseases" so as to include the "morbid" personalities, that is, the "deviant" character types described by psychologists.

Hirt. Among the first of these psychiatrists was E. Hirt, director of a German asylum and author of *Die Temperamente*, published in 1902. Extrapolating from work with institutionalized cases, Hirt divided temperament in accord with the classical four humors, but, in addition, he attempted to find their parallels among psychiatric populations. To Hirt, those who possessed an accentuated phlegmatic temperament were inclined to exhibit a morbid apathy such as seen in cases of dementia praecox; these patients were not only inactive but lacked insight, seemed detached from the world, and were too indifferent to complain about their plight. Patients endowed with a sanguine temperament to an extreme degree were characterized by superficial excitability, enthusiasm, and unreliability, and were therefore typically diagnosed as hysterical types; to Hirt, vanity, a craving for attention, and the seeking of enjoyment served as their primary stimuli for action. The choleric temperament was found among several subcategories of patients, including suspicious characters who were forever anticipating treachery and ill-will, and grumbling types who were invariably critical of others, claiming their personal superiority to all "if only they were given a chance." Those of a melancholic disposition were divided into two categories: Those of an active inclination were filled with an irritable pessimism and bitterness, and those more passively inclined were found among speculative and brooding types.

Kraepelin. The prime psychiatric nosologist at the turn of the century, Emil Kraepelin, did not systematize his thinking on personality disorders until the eighth edition of his major text, in 1913. Until then, Kraepelin paid but scant attention to personality disturbances, concentrating his organizing efforts on the two major syndromes of dementia praecox and maniacal-depressive insanity. In his efforts to trace the early course of these syndromes, Kraepelin "uncovered" two premorbid types: the "cyclothymic disposition," exhibited in four variants, each inclined to maniacal-depressive insanity; and the "autistic temperament," notably disposed to dementia praecox. In addition, Kraepelin wrote on a number of so-called morbid personalities, those whom he judged as tending toward criminality and other dissolute activites.

The four varieties of the cyclothymic disposition were labeled the "hypo-manic," the "depressive," the "irascible," and the "emotionally unstable." Kraepelin stated the following with regard to the hypomanic type:

> They acquire, as a rule, but scant education, with gaps and unevenness, as they show no perseverance in their studies, are disinclined to make an effort, and seek all sorts of ways to escape from the constraints of a systematic mental culture. The emotional tone of these patients is persistently elated, carefree, self-confident. Toward others they are overbearing, arbitrary, impatient, insolent, defiant. They mix into everything, overstep their prerogatives, make un-authorized arrangements, as they prove themselves everywhere useless. (p. 221)

Turning to the depressive personality, Kraepelin noted the following:

> There exists in these patients from youth a special sensitiveness to the cares, troubles, and disappointments of life. They take all things hard and feel the little unpleasantnesses in every occurrence. They lack self-confidence, decision, and seek the advice of others on the slightest occasions. Owing to the timidity these patients never come to a quick decision. (p. 221)

Those categorized as displaying the irascible makeup are ostensibly endowed simultaneously with both hypomanic and depressive inclinations. To Kraepelin:

> They are easily offended, hot-headed, and on trivial occasions become enraged and give way to boundless outbursts of energy. Ordinarily the patients are, perhaps, serene, self-assertive, ill-controlled; periods, however, intervene in which they are cross and sullen. (p. 222)

The emotionally unstable variant presumably also possesses both hypo-manic and depressive dispositions but manifests them in an alternating or, as Kraepelin viewed it, true cyclothymic pattern. He described these patients as follows:

> It is seen in those persons who constantly swing back and forth between the 2 opposite poles of emotion, now shouting with joy to heaven, now grieved to death. Today lively, sparkling, radiant, full of the joy of life, enterprise, they meet us after a while depressed, listless, dejected, only to show again several months later the former liveliness and elasticity. (p. 222)

Kraepelin's *autistic* temperament serves as the constitutional soil for the development of dementia praecox. The most fundamental trait of this type is a narrowing or reduction of external interests and an increasing preoccupation with inner ruminations. Of particular note was Kraepelin's observation (1919) that children of this temperament frequently "exhibited a quiet, shy, retiring disposition, made no friendships, and lived only for themselves" (p. 109). They were disinclined to be open and become involved with others, were seclusive, and had difficulty adapting to new situations. They showed little interest in what went on about them, often refrained from participating in games and other pleasures, seemed resistant to influence (but in a passive rather than active way), and were inclined to withdraw increasingly in a world of their own fantasies.

Among the "morbid personalities," Kraepelin included a wide range of types disposed to criminal activities; he described in considerable detail the so-called shiftless, impulsive types, liars and swindlers, troublemakers, and other disreputable characters.

Psychiatric typologies prior to the First World War were also formulated by other clinical theorists, notably Bleuler and Weygandt. Their lists are bypassed since they overlap substantially with the conceptions of Hirt and Kraepelin. Attention is turned next to those personality systems that gained recognition after the First World War and have retained to the present some following in either Europe or the United States.

MODERN FORMULATIONS

As noted earlier, there is no simple principle or intrinsic logic to suggest the order in which various personality classifications might best be presented. They could be separated into those which focus on "normal" versus "abnormal" subjects, as sketchily done in the previous section. This format breaks down too readily among modern classifiers, who frequently include both normal and abnormal types within their purview. Instead, and by no means resolving all complications, the sequence followed here presents, in rough order, theorists who draw upon biological dispositions as the basis for their personality classification, followed by theorists who give primacy to experiential learning.

Constitutional Models

Perhaps the most perceptive observer of human character, Shakespeare, wrote the following in *Julius Caesar* (Act I, Scene 2):

> Let me have men about me that are fat;
> Sleek-headed men and such as sleep o'nights;
> Yon Cassius has a lean and hungry look;
> He thinks too much; such men are dangerous.

Since times of antiquity observant persons have noted that bodily form was in some way related to characteristics of behavior. This section briefly discusses the views of a few theorists who have furnished a rationale for this relationship.

Kretschmer. Ernst Kretschmer is the prime modern constitutionalist, suggesting a series of inventive propositions that he sought to support empirically (1925). In his early research, Kretschmer categorized individuals in accord with their physical build and attempted to relate morphological differences to schizophrenia and manic-depressive psychosis. As his work progressed he extended the presumed relationship of physique, not only to severe pathology but also to premorbid personality and to "normal" temperament. Kretschmer proposed that people could be grouped into four basic physical types: the "pyknic," viewed as compactly built, with a large thorax and abdomen, soft and poorly muscled limbs, and a tendency toward obesity; the "athletic," noted for extensive muscular development and a broad skeletal endowment; the "asthenic," seen as fragile, possessing thin muscularity and a frail bone structure; and the "dysplastic," a mixture of the other three variants that formed an awkwardly constructed bodily structure. Kretschmer's early findings led him to claim a clear-cut relationship between manic-depressive disease and the pyknic build, and a similarly strong correlation between schizophrenia and the asthenic type.

Kretschmer considered psychotic disorders to be accentuations of essentially normal personality types, a position not commonly held by the majority of his psychiatric colleagues. Thus, the schizophrenic, the schizoid, and the schizothymic possessed different quantities of the same disposition or temperament; a distinctly pathological level existed among schizophrenics, a moderate degree among schizoids, and a minimal amount among relatively well-adjusted schizothymics. Similarly, cycloids were viewed as moderately affected variants of those with manic-depressive psychosis, and cyclothymic personalities were normal types possessing minor portions of the disposition. As far as the relationship between bodily structure and temperament are concerned, Kretschmer contended that normal asthenic individuals were inclined toward introversion, timidity, and a lack of personal warmth—that is, lesser intensities of the more withdrawn and unresponsive schizophrenics to whom they were akin. Normal pyknics were conceived as gregarious, friendly, and interpersonally dependent—that is, less extreme variants of the moody and socially excitable manic-depressive.

To complicate matters somewhat, Kretschmer expanded his notions into what he termed the four fundamental reaction types. The first of these, the "asthenic" reaction, was noted by depressive lethargy, a tendency toward sadness and weariness, and an inability to gather sufficient energy to be anxious about life's events. The second, the "primitive" reaction, was to be found in individuals who discharged the impact of their experiences immediately, who lacked a capacity to retain and integrate experience—a pattern Kretschmer found most clearly among those he termed the "explosive," "shiftless," "delinquent," "instinct-driven," and "immature" personality types. The third set, the "expansive" reactions, included patients who were highly vulnerable to distressing events, overly sensitive to the thoughts of others, and unable to deal with social frustrations; their supersensitivity and irritability disposed them toward suspicious and aggressively paranoid behaviors. The fourth reaction pattern was labeled the "sensitive type," and was distinguished by inclinations to "dam up" emotions, a high level of intrapsychic activity, and poor powers of expression—all of which resulted in a brooding, anxious, restricted, and unconfident behavioral style. In addition, Kretschmer identified a number of intermediary types, notably the "placating," the "submissive," and the "histrionic."

Sheldon. William H. Sheldon is the best-known American constitutional theorist (1940, 1954; Sheldon and Stevens, 1942). A disciple of Kretschmer, Sheldon also formulated a series of hypotheses concerning the relationship between body physique, temperament, and psychopathology. He identified three basic dimensions in his morphological schema: first is "endomorphy," noted by a predominance of body roundness and softness; second is "mesomorphy," characterized by muscular and connective tissue dominance; and third is "ectomorphy," identified by a linearity and fragility of structure. In his temperament typology Sheldon specified three clusters: "viscerotonia," "somatotonia," and "cerebrotonia." The viscerotonic component, which parallels endomorphy, is characterized by gregariousness, an easy expression of feeling and emotion, a love of comfort and relaxation, an avoidance of pain, and a dependence on social approval. Somatotonia, the counterpart to mesomorphy, is noted by assertiveness, physical energy, low anxiety, indifference to pain, courage, social callousness, and a need for action and power when troubled. Cerebrotonia, corresponding to ectomorphy, is defined by a tendency toward restraint, self-consciousness, introversion, social awkwardness, and a desire for solitude when troubled.

Correlating measures of morphology and temperament to psychiatric syndromes led Sheldon to construct what he termed the three primary components of psychopathology. The first was labeled the "affective" found in its extreme from among manic-depressive patients; Sheldon proposed that a high relationship exists between this component, the endomorphic physique, and the viscerotonic temperament. The affective component is characterized by a low threshold for behavioral reaction and emotional expression, and results from a weakened or feeble inhibitory capacity; with minimal prompting these individuals display either marked elation or intense dejection, depending on the nature of events in their immediate environment. The "paranoid" component corresponds in its most intense form to the traditional diagnostic category of the same name and to both mesomorphy and somatotonia. It reflects a "fighting against something," a driving antagonism and resentment that is projected against the environment; the power delusions of persecution that characterize paranoids are seen as extremes of this dimension. If physically capable, the patient will be overtly aggressive and arrogant; if weak or otherwise deterred from manifesting hostility, the patient will use circuitous methods of attack or become preoccupied ideationally with feelings of persecution. The third component, labeled by Sheldon as "heboid," is typified by marked withdrawal and regression, features characteristic of the traditional diagnosis of hebephrenic schizophrenia. It is found in ectomorphic individuals since these individuals lack both energy and viscerotonic affect. These patients learn to withdraw from social participation and actively avoid the disastrous consequences of attempting, with their feeble energies, to cope and compete with others.

Temperament Dimensions

Theorists included under this rubric are similar to those grouped as constitutionalists; they differ in that their focus is not on explicit structural or morphological features but on implicit endocrinological or neuroanatomical variations. It should be noted that temperament is a psychological, and not a physiological, concept; it attempts to represent psychologically relevant physiological processes inferred from observed differences in behavioral activity, persistence, intensity, variability, and, especially, susceptibility to emotional stimulation.

Sjöbring. The major Scandinavian theorist of personality is J. Sjöbring (1914, 1973). Influenced primarily by Dutch psychologist Heymans and, to a lesser extent, Janet and Kraepelin, Sjöbring formulated his first ideas about temperament in 1913. Writing over a 45-year span, he termed the various temperaments as basic "physiological constructs" that underlie interindividual or personality variations. The four main constructs were labeled: "capacity," denoting the genetic substrate for intellectual development; "validity," indicating the degree of energy available for nervous system functioning; "stability," meaning the maximum potential achievable given the person's nervous substrate; and "solidity," signifying the extent to which this potential must be replenished by experience to maintain its maximum level. Sjöbring conceived each of these four factors as independent of the others and distributed in accord with the normal curve. Although personality combinations of these constructs were recognized, clinical interest centered on features that characterized those who were high (super) and those who were low (sub) on each of the four factors. Among the eight "pure" types are the "subcapable," referring to those who are seen as inadaptable, crude, coarse, and blunt. They contrast with the "supercapable," who are appraised as sensitive, subtle, talented, and adaptable. "Subvalid" personalities are conceived as cautious, reserved, precise, industrious, and scrupulous; "supervalid" types are characterized as venturesome, active, perservering, alert, and confident. Those judged to be primarily "substable" types are identified as warm, hearty, clumsy, naïve and sociable; whereas "superstables" are described as cool, clever, abstract, sophisticated, and elegant. The "subsolid" person is assessed as quick, agile, histrionic, unpredictable, subjective, and impulsive; finally, the "supersolid" individual is noted as slow, steady, earnest, dependable, circumspect, and dependable.

Kahn. An early classification of temperaments for personality pathology was also constructed by E. Kahn, in 1928. Interweaving the concepts of impulse, temperament, and character, Kahn constructed several innovative types. In line with earlier theorists, Kahn identified a number of basic dimensions, notably the polarities of activity versus passivity, self-orientation versus non-self-orientation, negative versus positive outlook, and so on. On the bases of their interaction, Kahn deduced the presence of four basic temperaments: the "hyperthymic," noted by excitability, rapidity, and explosiveness; the "athymic," characterized by dull or weak affect; the "dysphoric," identified by an anxious timidity and peevishness; and the "poikilothymic," distinguished by a high degree of emotional lability. Unusual among temperament theorists was Kahn's proposal that biological bases may exist to orient the person either toward the self and individual needs or toward others and the extenal environment.

Tramer. Another early system of temperament classification was constructed by M. Tramer in 1931. Twelve types were derived from his schema. The "hyperthyme" was noted by a ready emotionality and a sanguine disposition; in its extreme form, Tramer categorized the troublemakers, the shiftless, and the unreliable. The "depressive" personality was characterized by a phlegmatic and sluggishly reacting temperament; among them were found the morose and ill-tempered depressives. The "labile" types and the "impulsive" characters were distinguished by their inflammable moods, which died down quickly after discharge; among them were the cyclothymics and those disposed to immature acting out. Tramer also identified a "hypothymic" personality, those who exhibited little or no affect, often found among the more withdrawn and schizoid types. "Explosive" personalities gave evidence of a passionate temperament that tended to short-circuit reactions; these individuals were disposed, according to Tramer, to conversion reactions and alcoholism. The seventh type, the "suspicious," or hypersensitive, temperament was seen clinically among paranoids. The "suggestible," or weak-willed, types encompassed addicts, the thin-skinned, and the "morally inferior." Following the lead of Kahn, Tramer included types that represent two aspects governing the self; the sense of self may be either strong or weak, and the relation to the environment may be active or passive. Among the passive types with a weak sense of self were found those who give evidence of "martyrdom" and masochistic tendencies; among the active types could be found the "reformers" and adventurers. The eleventh subtype, the "attention seekers," were noted by their exhibitionism and boastfulness, and were often inclined toward hysterical disorders. Finally, Tramer noted the "poorly integrated," insecure types who lacked confidence, had difficulty in discharging tensions, and were disposed to obsessive-compulsive conditions.

New York Medical School-Menninger Foundation. Although they have not derived clinical personality types from their work, mention should be made of the studies conducted by two groups of collaborators, one associated with New York Medical School (Thomas et al., 1963, 1968, 1977) and the other with the Menninger Foundation (Escalona and Leitch, 1953; Escalona and Heider, 1959; Murphy et al., 1962; Escalona, 1968; Murphy and Moriarty, 1976). Their research has been especially useful in identifying temperament characteristics in the young child. Several hundred infants were observed from birth through the early years of adolescence. Several rating scales were employed to quantify behavior dimensions such as activity level, rhythmicity, inclinations toward approach or withdrawal, adaptability, intensity of reaction, quality of mood, and so on. It was found that the majority of children displayed a recognizable and distinctive way of behaving from the first few months of life. Some were predictably regular in their schedule, while others followed chaotic sequences. Some reached out for everything presented; others avoided anything new. Although children could be differentiated on any of a number of different dimensions, two subsumed several characteristics considered significant, if not crucial, to later development. The first of these was labeled the child's "activity pattern." Active children displayed a decisiveness and vigor in their behavior; they related continuously to their environment and insisted that events take place in accord with their desires. In contrast, passive children displayed a receptive orientation; they seemed to be content to wait and see what would be done to meet their needs, accepting matters until their wishes were ultimately fulfilled. The second set of central temperament constellations was organized around what the researchers termed "adaptability." One group of children was characterized by a regularity, a positive approach to new stimuli, and a high degree of flexibility in response to changing conditions. Another group displayed irregularity in their biological functions, exhibited withdrawal reactions to new stimuli, showed minimal flexibility in response to change, and expressed intense and often negative moods.

Maddi et al. A recent temperament theory that gives primacy to the activity-passivity dimension has been proposed by Salvadore Maddi and his colleagues (Fiske and Maddi, 1961; Maddi, 1968; Maddi and Propst, 1971). High-activation people are seen as spending the major portion of their time pursuing stimuli so as to keep their behavior level from falling too low; in addition, those who possess what Maddi terms the "active trait" take the initiative in influencing their environment. Low-activation people spend their time avoiding the impact of stimulation in order to maintain low levels of behavior; although only certain low-activation persons display the "passive trait," those with this characteristic tend to be indolent and permit themselves to be influenced by events over which they assert little control. Although Maddi indicates that 24 different temperaments may be derived from his schema, he details only four primary variants, high- and low-activation types, each divided into two subcategories depending on the presence of "internal" or "external" traits; this latter distinction signifies a distinction between introversive, or self-oriented, behaviors versus extraversive, or other-oriented, behaviors. High-activation persons with external traits are seen as "go-getters," people who seek out challenges, are disposed to be energetic pursuers of causes, and are inclined to curiosity and adventure. High-activation persons with internal traits are disposed to pursue stimulation through thinking, seeking challenges of a subtle, intellectual kind, and inclined toward originality or creativity. Those with low activation and external traits tend to be conservative, disposed to negotiate, conform, and control; they oversimplify problems, avoid ambiguity, find routines, and prefer the familiar to the new. The fourth category, the low-activation person with internal traits, is also conservative, carefully avoiding excesses and indulgences of any kind, and disposed to function in a stable manner, devoid of inconsistencies and flamboyance.

Buss and Plomin. Grounded firmly on an empirical research base is the temperament theory of personality development recently proposed by Arnold Buss and Robert Plomin (1975). They have suggested four fundamental temperaments; activity, emotionality, sociability, and impulsivity. "Activity" refers to total energy output such that active persons are typically busy, in a hurry, constantly moving and seemingly tireless, whereas passive or lethargic persons display opposite inclinations. "Emotionality" is conceived as equivalent to intensity of reaction; thus, the emotional person is easily aroused, has an excess of affect, and displays strong tempers, violent mood swings, and a high degree of expressiveness. The third temperament, that of "sociability," consists of a need to be with others. Those at the "gregarious" extreme of the sociability dimension find that interaction with others is very gratifying, far more rewarding than nonsocial experiences; they contrast with those at the opposite extreme of the dimension, which Buss and Plomin refer to as "detached". "Impulsivity" involves a tendency to respond quickly, rather than inhibiting one's responsiveness; its opposite extreme is noted as "deliberateness." Although all possible permutations of two, three, or four temperaments might be expected theoretically, Buss and Plomin stated that this is not supported in either the research or clinical literature. Among clinically relevant combinations is the pairing of high activity and high impulsivity, seen most clearly in manic disorders. Low activity or passivity combined with high emotionality appears to underlie agitated depressions. A blend of high emotionality and high impulsivity would lead to impetuous and seductive tendencies such as found in histrionic personality types. Those high in emotionality and sociability would be inclined to seek the company of others but would perhaps be inhibited by strong anxieties over potential rejection and ridicule. The combination of high sociability and high impulsivity is seen as relating to the classical extrovert pattern, whereas those low in both temperaments are conceived as similar to the introvert.

Factorial Categories

Factor analysis is a statistical method that calculates intercorrelations among a large group of variables such as traits, behaviors, symptoms, and so on. Patterns or clusters among these correlations are referred to as first-order, or primary, factors; the elements making up these factors are interpreted to provide them with relevant psychological meaning. Second- or higher-order, factors may be derived from the original factors by clustering them into larger units; it is usually these second-order factors that possess the scope necessary to correspond to the breadth of a concept such as personality. This section summarizes the research of a few factor analysts, making particular reference to the dimensions or typologies they have derived from their work.

Cattell.   The most productive of those utilizing a factorial approach to the construction of personality dimensions is Raymond Cattell (1957, 1965). His research has led him to identify 16 primary factors, or source traits, which he then arranged in sets of biopolar dimensions. They include: "schizothymia" (reserved, detached, aloof) versus "cyclothymia" (outgoing, warm, sociable); "dull" (low intelligence, concrete thinking) versus "bright" (intelligent, abstract thinking); "low ego strength" (easily upset, emotionally unstable) versus "high ego strength" (mature, calm, stable); "submissiveness" (obedient, conforming) versus "dominance" (assertive, independent); "desurgency" (serious, glum, sober) versus "surgency" (enthusiastic, happy-go-lucky); "low superego strength" (expedient, casual, undependable) versus "high superego strength" (conscientious, rule-bound, persistent); "threctia" (timid, restrained, fearful) versus "parmia" (adventurous, thick-skinned, uninhibited); "harria" (tough, self-reliant, realistic) versus "prensia" (sensitive, overprotected, tender minded); "alaxia" (trusting, easy to get on with) versus "protension" (suspicious, jealous, opinionated); "praxernia" (practical, careful, conventional) versus "autia" (imaginative, unconcerned, unconventional); "naïvete" (forthright, guileless, natural) versus "shrewdness" (calculating, sophisticated, polished);. "confident" (self-assured, placid, unshakeable) versus "guilt prone" (apprehensive, troubled, insecure); "conservatism" (traditional, uncritical) versus "radicalism" (experimental, liberal); "group adherence" (joiner, follower, imitator) versus "self-sufficiency" (resourceful, independent minded); "weak willed" (aimless, careless, impulsive) versus "self-disciplined" (controlled, compulsive, socially precise); and "low ergic tension" (relaxed, tranquil, phlegmatic) versus "high ergic tension" (tense, overwrought, driven).

Cattell's second-order factor dimensions may be described as follows: creativity versus conventionality, independence versus dependence, tough versus sensitive, neurotic versus stable, leadership versus followership, high anxiety versus low anxiety, and introversion versus extroversion, Cattell gives primacy to the latter two second-order factors in constructing four personality types. The first type, "high anxiety–introversion," is noted as being tense, excitable, suspicious, insecure, jealous, unstable, silent, timid, and shy. The second type, "low anxiety–introversion," tends to be phlegmatic, unshakeable, trustful, adaptable, mature, calm, self-sufficient, cold, timid, unconcerned, and resourceful. In the third personality type, the "high anxiety-extroversion" group, is found someone who is tense, excitable, insecure, suspicious, jealous, and unstable but, at the same time, sociable, enthusiastic, talkative, practical, and dependent. The last of the types, "low anxiety-extraversion," is identified by being phlegmatic, confident, unshakeable, adaptable, mature, calm, warm, sociable, enthusiastic, practical, and conventional. As noted in the first chapter, problems arise when efforts are made to synthesize trait dimensions into a diverse set of coherent clinical types. This problem is clearly evident in Cattell's typology since the traits that cluster factorially in his work neither consolidate into clinically relevant syndromes nor generate enough variety to comprise a comprehensive classification.

Several other factor analysts at work today are worthy of note.

Eysenck. Hans Eysenck (1952, 1960; Eysenck and Eysenck, 1969) has contributed to many areas of learning and behavioral research. On the basis of his studies he has selected three dimensions of personality that are fundamental to psychopathology: "neuroticism," "introversion–extroversion," and "psychoticism." Stimulated by the ideas of Jung, Kretschmer, and Pavlov, Eysenck has built an explanatory schema in terms of autonomic nervous system reactivity and ease of conditionability. Those who are highly reactive autonomically are prone to neurotic disorders, whereas those who readily form conditioned responses are inclined to introverted behavior. People at the high end of both conditionability and autonomic reactivity are disposed to develop fears and compulsions, whereas those who are subject to minimal conditioning are likely to become extroverted and potentially antisocial. As in the case of Cattell, Eysenck's formulations provide us with a rather skimpy range of clinically diverse personality types.

Lorr and Phillips. Both Maurice Lorr (Lorr, 1975; Lorr and Manning, 1978) and Leslie Phillips (1968) have contributed interesting factor analytic models of personality. Lorr is best known for having developed a typology of psychotics; more recently, however, he has begun to explore less severe disorders. In developing second-order factors with psychotics, Lorr suggested that there are three broad categories of patients: (1) those who express self-directed hostility and guilt behaviors, often associated with both dependency and depression; (2) those evidencing seclusiveness and social withdrawal, often accompanied in severe form by thought disorders and personality decompensation; and (3) those inclined to hostile, belligerent, and irritable combativeness, often coexisting with delusional thinking. Studies with "normal" populations have not produced a clear typology but have suggested the following personality dimensions: socialized-unsocialized, extroverted-introverted, independent-dependent, structure seeking–structure avoiding, stable-anxious, and "tempo."

Projects carried out by Phillips support proposals that clinical symptoms may be grouped into three interpersonal styles. The first style is described as a "turning against the self," expressed either directly, in action, or in thought. The second group reflects a "turning against others," as in temper outbursts and socially disapproved behaviors. The third interpersonal style is characterized as an "avoidance of others," either through withdrawal behaviors, fantasy preoccupations, or other indices of social detachment. The similarity between Phillips's styles, Lorr's second-order categories, and the classical trichotomy of affective, paranoid, and schizoid pathologies is worth noting.

Psychiatric Syndromes

The typologists included in this section have contributed atheoretical lists of personality disorders derived from experience as practicing psychiatrists. Though exhibiting certain similarities, the proposals formulated for the most part overlap minimally. Nevertheless, each list provides a glimpse into the many and diverse types seen in clinical work.

Schneider. The best-known European classification has been proposed by Kurt Schneider, first published in 1923 and revised through several editions (1950). Schneider differed from many of his contemporaries, most notably Kretschmer, in that he did not view personality pathology to be a precursor to other mental disorders but conceived it as a separate entity that covaried with them. In the last edition of his text on "psychopathologic personalities," Schneider described the following 10 variants seen often in psychiatric work.

"Hyperthymic" personalities reflect a mix of high activity, optimism, and shallowness; they tend to be uncritical, cocksure, impulsive, and undependable. Many seem unable to concentrate, and those who achieve occasional insights fail to retain them as lasting impressions. Those in the second category, the "depressive" personalities, have a skeptical view of life, tend to take things seriously, and display little capacity for enjoyment. They are often excessively critical and deprecatory of others; at the same time, they are full of self-reproach and exhibit hypochondriacal anxieties. "Insecure" personalities are grouped by Schneider into two subvarieties, the "sensitives" and the "anankasts" (compulsives). These individuals ruminate excessively over everyday experience but have little capacity for expressing or discharging the feelings these thoughts stir up. Chronically unsure of themselves, they are apt to see life as a series of unfortunate events. They tend to behave in a strict and disciplined manner, holding closely to what is judged as socially correct. "Fanatic" personalities are expansive individuals inclined to be uninhibited, combative, and aggressive in promoting their views; they are often querulous and litigious. Among the "attention-seeking" personalities are those with heightened emotional responses, who delight in novelty and give evidence of excess enthusiasms, vivid imaginations, and a striving to be in the limelight; showy and capricious, many are boastful and inclined to lie and distort. "Labile" personalities do not evidence a simple chronic emotionality but are characterized by abrupt and volatile mood changes, impulsive urges, sudden dislikes, and a "shiftless" immaturity. The "explosive" personality is characterized by being impulsively violent, disposed to be fractious, and likely to become combative without warning and without provocation. "Affectionless" personalities lack compassion and are often considered callous and cold; they appear distant or indifferent to friends and strangers alike. Historically, these patients correspond to those identified in the literature as exhibiting "moral insanity." The so-called weak-willed personalities are not only docile and unassuming but are easily subjected to seduction by others and readily exploited "to no good end"; they are inevitably fated to trouble and disillusionment. The last of Schneider's types, the "asthenic" personality, subjects him/herself to intense hypochondriacal scrutiny and is so preoccupied with bodily functions that external events fade into the background and appear strange or unreal.

Sullivan. Although central to the development of the interpersonal orientation in psychiatry, the personality typology presented by Harry Stack Sullivan (1947) may best be grouped with that of Schneider's in that both are atheoretical, comprise 10 varieties, and attempt to identify syndromes seen in everyday clinical practice. The first type, labeled "nonintegrative" personalities, is characterized by fleeting involvements with people, a failure to profit from experience, and a disregard for the consequences of one's behavior; these individuals constantly disappoint others by their superficiality and wandering inclinations, but this does not dispose them to experience discontent or to wonder why others react as they do. The second of Sullivan's syndromes, termed the "self-absorbed," or fantastic, personality, is characterized by autistic and wish-fulfilling thinking. Conflicted as to whether the world is essentially "good or bad," these persons see relationships as either marvelous or despicable; they engage in a series of intimacies that inevitably terminate in profound disillusionment, only to be sought after and repeated again. The "incorrigible" personality is identified by hostility toward others and a pattern of unfriendly, morose, and forbidding behaviors. Authority is viewed as especially hostile and there is a tendency to complain bitterly about those in superior positions. The fourth syndrome is termed the "negativistic" personality, individuals who cope with their considerable insecurity by refusing to subscribe to the views of others, by passively or subtlely resisting social norms, or by a cynical form of conciliation. The fifth type, what Sullivan conceives as a super-negativisitic variety, is termed the "stammerer"; stammering is perceived as a symptom disorder by most theorists, and Sullivan offers little reason for conceiving them as a personality type. "Ambition-ridden" personalities are noted by their exploitation of others, their competitiveness and unscrupulous manipulations. Those with the seventh syndrome, "asocial" personalities, are typically detached and lonely, unable to establish and maintain warm and gratifying personal relationships. They seem unable to appreciate the possibility that others may value them; though some asocials are sensitive, others seem obtuse and drift through life without intimate relationships. The "inadequate" personality is distinguished by a need for guidance from a strong person who will take responsibility for everyday decisions; these persons appear to have learned that a clinging helplessness is an adequate adaptation to life. The ninth syndrome is labeled by Sullivan the "homosexual" personality; its distinguishing feature is that love appears to extend only to persons of the same sex. Here, again, Sullivan has identified a specific symptom with the totality of personality. The final syndrome is labeled the "chronically adolescent" personality. These individuals are perennially seeking to achieve ideals but rarely are able to fulfill their aspirations in either love-objects or mature vocations; some will ultimately resolve their frustrations, whereas some will become cynical, others will turn lustful, or celibate, and so on.

Walton et al.   Finally, mention should be made of the recent work of the Scottish psychiatrist H. J. Walton and his associates (Walton et al., 1970; Walton and Presley, 1973 a, b). Although Walton has employed clustering procedures in his studies, this research has led him to conclude that a dimensional format is likely to be a more accurate means of representing personality than categorical schemas. Walton differentiates personality disorders into three levels of severity: mild, moderate, and gross. Mild personalities are individuals who are dissatisfied with the quality of their lives or relationships; they characteristically seek assistance on their own initiative rather than being brought to the attention of clinicians because of difficulties with others. Mild personality pathologies are termed "character disorders" and Walton specifies three varieties: the "withdrawn" type, noted by being socially isolated and emotionally inhibited; the "dependent" type, characterized by compliance, helplessness, and a seeking of support; and the "overassertive" type, identified by an overbearing or officious style, often associated with feelings of guilt. Moderately severe personalities are those whose maladjustments are associated with other mental disturbances, such as psychosomatic ailments or neurotic symptoms; in addition, their behaviors are sufficiently unusual or eccentric to be evident to others. Among moderately severe types, referred to by Walton as "personality disorders," may be found five varieties: the "schizoid" type, noted by being reserved, aloof, and lonely, often appearing queer and incapable of intimacy; the "hysterical" type, characterized by histrionic dress and behavior, sociability and vivaciousness, and a tendency toward the theatrical, shallow, and insincere; the "paranoid" type, seen as basically mistrustful, hypersensitive, upset by imagined criticism, and envious and suspicious of others; the "cyclothymic" type, giving evidence of mood phases, with spells of spontaneous, outgoing activity turning into dejection and loss of drive; the "obsessional" type, noted by being orderly, neat, punctual, and pedantic, and by tightly controlled emotions. The third level of severity, the gross personality disorders, refers to persons whose deviance is so marked that they are unable to fit into their social group and often come into conflict with its laws and customs. Among these are two major types: the "aggressive sociopath," those unable to inhibit aggressive impulses, affectionless, harmful to society, and cannot form close relationships or loyalty to others; and the "passive sociopath," noted as inept, inclined to poor judgment, lacking in drive and stamina, aimless, and having poor work records and few ties to others.

Psychoanalytic Theorists

The best-known and perhaps most fully conceptualized of personality disorders are those formulated by psychoanalytic theorists.

Freud and Abraham.   It was Sigmund Freud (1908, 1932), Karl Abraham (1921, 1925), and Wilhelm Reich (1933) who laid the foundation of the psychoanalytic character typology. These categories were conceived initially as a product of frustrations or indulgences of instinctual or libidinous drives, especially in conjunction with specific psychosexual stages of maturation. Since the essentials of this typology may be traced to Freud, it may be of value to note alternative formulations he proposed at different times as potential schemas for personality, that is, schemas based on conceptions other than psychosexual theory.

Freud wrote in 1915 what many consider to be his most seminal papers, those on metapsychology and, in particular, the section entitled "Instincts and Their Vicissitudes." Speculations that foreshadowed several concepts developed more fully later were presented in this paper. Particularly notable is a framework that Freud proposed as central to the understanding of personality functioning; unfortunately, this framework was never fully developed as a system for personality dynamics, as Freud appears to have intended. His conception was formulated as follows:

> . . . Our mental life as a whole is governed by three polarities, namely, the following antitheses:
>
> Subject (ego)—Object (external world),
> Pleasure—Pain,
> Active—Passive.

> The three polarities within the mind are connected with one another in various highly significant ways. (1915a, pp. 76-77)
> We may sum up by saying that the essential feature in the vicissitudes undergone by instincts is *their subjection to the influences of the three great polarities that govern mental life.* Of these three polarities we might describe

that of activity-passivity as the *biological,* that of the ego-external world as the *real,* and finally that of pleasure-pain as the *economic* respectively. (1915a, p. 83).

These same three dimensions were well known prior to Freud's writings in 1915; recall earlier references to the ideas of Heymans and Wiersma, McDougall, Meumann, and Kollarits, each of whom identified the pain-pleasure, active-passive, and subject-object distinction as central. Despite the prominence Freud gave these three polarities by identifying them as the elements that govern all of mental life, he failed to capitalize on them as a framework for formulating character types. Some 50 years later Millon (1969) utilized these same polarities in constructing a series of eight basic personality patterns.

At another time in his exploration of personality dimensions, Freud speculated that character classification might best be based on his threefold structural distinction of id, ego, and superego. Thus, in 1932 he sought to devise character types in accord with which intrapsychic structure was dominant. First, he proposed an "erotic" type whose life is governed by the instinctual demands of the id; second, in what he termed the "narcissistic" type, are found persons so dominated by the ego that neither other persons nor the demands of id or superego can affect them; third, he suggested a "compulsive" type whose life is regulated by the strictness of the superego such that all other functions are dominated; and last, Freud identified a series of mixed types in which combinations of two of the three intrapsychic structures outweigh the third. Freud's compulsive character type has been well represented in the literature, but only in the past 10 years have his proposals for a narcissistic personality disorder gained attention.

Freud's 1908 paper set the seeds for psychoanalytic character types. Freud's primary interest at that time was not in tracing the formation of character structure but rather in discovering the derivatives of instincts as they evolve during particular psychosexual stages. Although Freud noted that developmental conflicts give rise to broadly generalized defensive tendencies, these were noted only incidentally, written largely as minor digressions from the main point of his early papers; unlike Karl Abraham, he did not focus on character structure derivatives but attempted to identify the psychosexual roots of specific and narrowly circumscribed symptoms, such as compulsions or conversions.

Reich.   It was not until the writings of Wilhelm Reich in 1933 that the concept of character appeared in its current psychoanalytic formulation. Reich asserted that the neurotic solution of psychosexual conflicts was accomplished by a pervasive restructuring of the individual's defensive style, a set of changes that ultimately crystallizes into what he spoke of as a "total formation" of character. In contrast to his forerunners, Reich claimed that the emergence of specific pathological symptoms was of secondary importance when compared to the total character structuring that evolved as a consequence of these experiences. As Reich put it: "Our problem is not the content or the nature of this or that character trait" (1949, p. 46). To him, the particular defensive modes acquired in dealing with early experience become stable, even ossified, or as he put it, "a character armor." As the consolidation process hardens, the response to earlier conflicts becomes "transformed into chronic attitudes, into chronic automatic modes of reaction" (p. 46).

Reich's contribution broadened the impact of early instinctual vicissitudes from that of specific symptom formations to that of character or personality types. However, it remained a limited notion in that it failed to specify nondefensive ways in which character traits or structures might develop. Character formations, according to Reich, had an exclusively defensive function, comprising an inflexible armor against threats from the external and internal world. While the habits of character were employed in dealing with current realities and were no longer limited to early conflicts, these functions remained exclusively defensive and protective; thus, Reich did not recognize that character traits may emerge from sources other than early conflicts. It is in this last regard that contemporary modifications to psychoanalytic characterology have been proposed, notably in Otto Fenichel's text (1945) and, more recently, in the writings of ego theorists such as Heinz Hartmann (1958) and Erik Erikson (1950).

Fenichel, Hartmann, and Erikson. Fenichel classified character traits into "sublimation" and "reactive" types, depending on whether normally maturing instinctual energies were compatible with the ego, and thereby fashioned into conflict-free or neutral patterns (sublimation), or whether they were "dammed up" by the aims of the ego and "countermanded" by conflict-resolving defensive measures (reactive). In making this distinction Fenichel was the first to recognize that instinctual energy can develop into character forms free of conflict resolution. Although Fenichel considered the sublimation character traits to be as deeply ingrained as the reactive types, he viewed them to be nonpathological and, hence, paid little attention to the diverse forms into which they might take shape. In this regard, he failed to recognize the possibility that pathological personality traits could arise from conflict-free sources, that is, simply result from deficient or other inappropriate experiences that set the seeds for maladaptive behaviors. Fenichel limited his attention to reactive characters and differentiated them into the "avoidance" and "oppositional" types, each representing a major form of defensive control. Fenichel died without being fully satisfied with the classification schema he had just begun to sort out; his well-delineated, yet somewhat disjointed, format is not detailed here, but the reader might benefit by studying his original text (1945).

Both Hartmann and Erikson also recognized that the origins of character may be found in instinctual energies that are independent of conflicts and their resolutions. To Hartmann, both ego and id instincts derive from a common matrix of biological potentials, differentiating into separable energies for adaptive functioning. Termed "autonomous apparatuses," these ego potentials were seen as "preadapted to handle average expectable environments." Erikson extended this notion by stating that character development emerges out of three interwoven roots: instinctual energies, the maturational capacities of the ego, and the external standards that society provides at each developmental stage. It would appear logical for Hartmann and Erikson to have taken the next step and propose character types that develop from conflict-free ego energies—that is, nonreactive traits that prove to be pathological because they are inadequate or ill-suited to the expectancies of the social environment. Since neither attempted such a characterology, the schema of psychoanalytic character types remains largely that formulated by Freud, Abraham, and Reich some 50 years ago.

Psychoanalytic Character Types

It may be useful at this point to briefly summarize the major character types. Organizing the various formulations that have been proposed in psycho-analytic literature is no simple task. The most common practice, and the one followed here, differentiates types into the psychosexual stage associated with their development.

Oral Characters. The oral period is usually differentiated into two phases: the oral-sucking phase, in which food is accepted indiscriminately, followed by the oral-biting phase, in which food is accepted selectively, occasionally rejected, and aggressively chewed. An overly indulgent sucking stage leads to what is frequently referred to as the *oral-dependent* type. Characteristic of these individuals is an imperturbable optimism and naïve self-assurance; such persons are inclined to be happy-go-lucky and emotion-aly immature in that serious matters do not seem to affect them. An ungratified sucking period is associated with excessive dependency and gullibility—for example, deprived children may learn to "swallow" anything in order to ensure that they get something; here, external supplies are all important, but the children yearn for them passively.

Frustrations experienced at the oral-biting stage typically lead to the development of aggressive oral tendencies such as sarcasm and verbal hostility in adulthood. Sometimes referred to as the *oral-sadistic* character, this person is in many ways characterologically the opposite of the oral-sucking or dependent character. The basic pattern is one of pessimistic distrust, an inclination to blame the world for unpleasant matters, and a tendency to be cantankerous and petulant.

Anal Characters. Difficulties associated with the anal period likewise lead to distinctive modes of adult personality. During this time children can both control their sphincter muscles and comprehend the expectancies of their parents; for the first time in their lives, children have the power to actively and knowingly thwart their parents' demands, and they now have the option of either pleasing or spoiling their desires. Depending on the outcome, children will adopt attitudes toward authority that will have far-reaching effects. So-called anal characters are quite different from each other depending on whether their conflict resolutions are during the anal-expulsive or the anal-retentive period. Characteristics emerging from the *anal-expulsive* period are primarily those of suspiciousness and megalomania, a tendency toward extreme conceit and ambitiousness, and a pattern of self-assertion, disorderliness, and negativism. Difficulties that emerge in the late anal, or *anal-retentive*, phase are usually associated with frugality, obstinacy, and orderliness. There is a predominance of parsimony and pedantry, a hair-splitting meticulousness, and a rigid devotion to societal rules and regulations. As Fenichel (1945) put it, these individuals are in constant conflict between "I want to be naughty" and "I must be good."

Although writers such as Fenichel (1945) have proposed what may be called a *urethral* character, there is little consensus that a distinct pattern exists. The most outstanding personality features attributed here are those of ambition and competitiveness, both of which are presumed to be reactions against feelings of shame and inadequacy.

Phallic Characters. The next major psychosexual phase in which a distinct set of character types are associated is the so-called phallic stage. This period of psychosexual development is one that Reich (1933) conceived as troubled by narcissistic sexuality. Although libidinal impulses normally are directed toward the opposite sex, they may become excessively self-oriented. Either intense frustration or overindulgence during this period of need for genital contact may produce conflict and defensive armoring. As a result, according to Reich, there will be a striving for leadership, a need to stand out in a group, and poor reactions to even minor "defeats." The traits of this *phallic narcissistic* character were depicted by Reich as vain, brash, arrogant, self-confident, vigorous, cold, reserved, and defensively aggressive. If these persons succeed in gaining the attentions of others, they often become delightful and spontaneous high achievers; conversely, if they are not greatly appreciated or sought after, they are inclined to downgrade themselves or to become exhibitionistic and provocative.

In early analytic theory the genital stage was viewed as the pinnacle of maturity, the attainment of a fully socialized and adjusted adult. However, Reich, in disagreement with other analysts, saw two pathological complications associated with this final period: the *hysterical* and the *masochistic* characters. Among the hysterical characters are people fixated at the genital level, who have little inclination to sublimate their impulses and are preoccupied with sexual excitations and discharge. They are noted by a characteristic fearfulness and skittishness, a pseudoseductiveness, interpersonal superficiality and flightiness, and an inability to sustain endeavors. In what he refers to as the masochistic character, Reich describes a pattern that results from the repression of exhibitionistic tendencies during the genital stage. The masochist is characterized by self-criticism, a querulous disposition, and a habit of tormenting both self and others. The masochist is in a terrible bind, however. Love and affection are sought but result in pain; by making themselves unlovable, masochists avoid pain but, as a consequence, prevent themselves from achieving the love they desire.

Kernberg. Although numerous analytic theorists have contributed in recent years to the study of character, the work of Otto Kernberg deserves special note (1967, 1975, 1980). Offering little in terms of a new characterology, Kernberg nevertheless has constructed a useful framework for organizing types in terms of their level of severity. Breaking away from a rigid adherence to the psychosexual model, Kernberg proposes another dimension as primary, that of structural organization. Coordinating character types in accord with severity and structural organization leads Kernberg to speak of "higher, intermediate and lower levels" of character pathology; both intermediate and lower levels are referrred to as "borderline" personality organizations. To illustrate his ordering of types, Kernberg assigns most hysterical, obsessive-compulsive, and depressive personalities to the higher level. At the intermediate level of organization Kernberg locates the "infantile" and most narcissistic personalities. Last, clear-cut antisocial personalities are classified as distinctly of a lower borderline organization. Despite having been strongly influenced by the major ego theorists, and despite the innovative nature of his proposals, Kernberg has remained anchored to the view that all pathological character types are inevitably "reactive" in their formation rather than potentially conflict-free in their origins.

Life-style Types

This section turns to the proposals of Carl Gustav Jung and Alfred Alder, early disciples of Freud known best as the first dissidents. Both present essentially "normal" character typologies free of clinical symptomatology. Parallels do exist between their types and various personality syndromes, but their intent was to provide a theoretical foundation for normal life-styles.

Jung. Jung is among the more seminal thinkers in psychopathology. Most practitioners and laymen are acquainted with his distinction between extraversion and introversion; few, however, are aware of their subdivisions and characteristics. To refresh the reader's memory, *extraversion* represents the flowing of energy toward the outer world, whereas *introversion* is a flow inward (Jung, 1921). Extraverts explain events from the viewpoint of the environment, seeing things as coming from without. The introvert's approach is essentially subjective, drawing from the environment whatever is perceived as necessary to satisfy inner inclinations. Interacting with introversion and extraversion are four psychological modes of adaptation or functioning:

thinking, feeling, sensation, and intuition. "Thinking" refers to logical and directed thought such that situations are approached in a cool, detached, and rational fashion. "Feeling" is a subjective and value-laden process to be distinguished from emotion in that the former is a more rational and less impulsive activity. "Sensation" refers to perceptions geared to the present moment that are experienced immediately by the senses and by bodily excitations. "Intuition," in contrast, relates to a future orientation that anticipates situational possibilities. Thinking and feeling are conceived as rational functions, whereas sensation and intuition are viewed as irrational. Jung created a four-by-two matrix of eight basic types by combining his extraverion-introversion dimension with each of the four psychological functions.

The "extraverted thinking" type is inclined to base actions only on intellectual appraisals and to reconstruct events in line with these appraisals. Intellectual formulas serve as ruling life principles to which people are expected to subordinate themselves. As a consequence, such persons are often considered martinets or quibblers who force their views on others. In the "extraverted feeling" type is found a predominance of traditional standards, a willingness to adjust to external expectations, and an avoidance of criticism and reflection. Personal judgments are suppressed and efforts are made to be consistent and loyal, and to adhere to the standards of others. The "extraverted sensation" type pursues enjoyment as the true reality. There is little inclination to reflect on matters and no desire to examine either the past or the future. What is not experienced spontaneously is seen as suspect. Thoughts and feelings are reduced to their immediate, so-called objective qualities. Such individuals are inclined to become crude pleasure seekers, "degenerates," or "unscrupulous effetes." In the "extraverted intuitive" type there are expectations concerning the potential of things, a search for the new and for the possibilities in people. Stability is experienced as monotonous and suffocating; new situations are seized upon with intensity, only to be abandoned as soon as their potentials are anticipated.

Turning to the introverted types, there is a shift from the environment toward inner processes, a centering in the self as opposed to external objects or persons. The "introverted thinking" type does not draw from objective data, as does the extraverted thinker, but from subjective reflections. Such thinkers often are inarticulate because they construct images that have little correspondence to objective events. Often taciturn, this type only rarely makes the effort to gain the approval of others. The "introverted feeling" type also tends to be silent and inaccessible, and frequently hides behind a mask of childishness and melancholy. Although appearing reserved at times, these persons feel intensely but tend to express it in a personal manner such as in art or poetry. The "introverted sensation" type is characterized by peculiarities that stem from highly subjective reactions to objective events. There is often no logical relationship between reality and subjective response; as a consequence, these persons tend to be seen as unpredictable and arbitrary in their behaviors. Persons of this type often become involved in the spiritual interests that are not accessible to objective understanding. Finally the "introverted intuitive" type draws from the deepest layer of the unconscious and is inclined to mystical dreaming and artistic forms of expression. Often an enigma to others, these persons may appear aloof and unrelated to conventional reality.

Jung's typology has but limited utility to the understanding of patients since it reflects his theoretical speculations about the essence of personality structure and not the problems of everyday clinical practice. Difficulties in extrapolating Jung's types to clinical reality are found also in the classification formulated by Freud's other early disciple, and later dissident, Alfred Adler.

Adler. As the reader may recall, the cardinal concept in Adler's (1964) theoretical system is that of *overcompensation*, an inborn tendency to counteract deficiencies or inadequacies through reparative striving. Compensation for feelings of inferiority takes the form of what Adler referred to as fictive goals, that is, unrealistic aspirations by which the individual could redress shortcomings. Compensating strategies, which Adler termed "neurotic safeguards," help the individual keep fictive goals intact by various protective maneuvers. The individual's "style of life" represents distinctive patterns of striving that derive from shortcomings and the adaptive compensations employed to cope with them. Adler formulated his life-style typology on the basis of two polarities, active-passive and constructive-destructive. The "active-passive" dimension reflects whether the individual has learned to be a giver and initiator as opposed to being a receiver or getter. The "constructive-destructive" polarity refers essentially to levels of social interest. High levels of social interest reflect the constructive orientation, and low levels signify a destructive orientation. Combining the two polar extremes led Adler to propose four basic life-styles: active-constructive, passive-constructive, active-destructive, and passive-destructive (Ansbacher and Ansbacher, 1956; Adler, 1964).

It is the "active-constructive" life-style that Adler considers the healthy or ideal individual. He described these persons as feeling at home in life and sensing their existence to be worthwhile; such individuals are disposed to face advantages and disadvantages with equal firmness, to be concerned with serving humanity, and to overcome difficulties with creative efforts. The "passive-destructive" style is characterized by oppositional tendencies. These individuals are seen as accusatory; they are inclined to fix blame, expect to get things from others, lean on them, and act in a passive-aggressive and despairing fashion—or what Adler described as a neurotic style of life. The "passive-constructive" life-style is noted by attention seeking, behaving in a charming manner, and seeking to gain recognition simply by being oneself rather than for what one has achieved. The final group, the "active-destructive" style, is one in which attention getting takes the form of becoming a nuisance, of behaving in a rebellious, vicious, tyrannical, and often delinquent manner with others.

Interpersonal Orientations

Both Jung and Adler reoriented characterology toward the social aspects of personal functioning. What ultimately became the interpersonal orientation took its clearest form in the personality descriptions of Karen Horney, Erich Fromm, and Timothy Leary. Although Harry Stack Sullivan contributed significantly to this interpersonal school, his personality typology reflected this interest only minimally.

Horney. Karen Horney's descriptive eloquence is perhaps without peer; nevertheless, difficulties arise in attempting to summarize what she refers to as the major "solutions" to life's basic conflicts. Although her primary publications were written over a short period, she utilized different terms to represent similar conceptions (1937, 1939, 1942, 1945, 1950). An attempt is made here to synthesize these diverse formulations, albeit briefly. Faced with the insecurities and inevitable frustrations of life, Horney identified three broad modes of relating that will emerge: "moving toward" people, "moving against" people, or "moving away" from them. In her 1945 book Horney formulated three character types to reflect each of these three solutions: Moving toward is found in a "compliant" type; moving against, in an "aggressive" type; and moving away, in a "detached" type. In 1950 Horney reconceptualized her typology in line with the manner in which individuals solve intrapsychic conflicts. Corresponding roughly to the prior trichotomies, they were termed the "self-effacement" solution, the "expansive" solution, and the solution of "neurotic resignation." Although these sets of three do not match perfectly, they do correspond to the essential themes of Horney's characterology, which are briefly summarized next.

In the moving-toward, compliant, and self-effacing orientation are individuals with a marked need for affection and approval, a willingness to deny personal aspirations and self-assertion, and an assumption that love solves all problems. Self-esteem is determined by what others think, personal desires are subordinated, and there are tendencies toward self-accusation, helplessness, passivity, and self-belittlement. In the extreme form, a morbid dependency emerges; at a more advanced and complicated level, there is a masochistic wallowing in guilt and self-degradation.

In the moving-against, aggressive type with expansive solutions, individuals glorify themselves, and there is a rigid denial of weakness and inadequacy. Life is seen as a struggle for survival; there is a need to control or exploit others, to excel, to outsmart and to belittle those who have power. Three subdivisions of this solution were described by Horney. The first, the "narcissistic" solution, suggests that individuals believe that they are, in fact, their idealized selves; and, to the extent that others reinforce this belief, they are able to maintain their sense of eliteness and superiority. The second subdivision is referred to as "perfectionism"; persons in this type believe that they are, in fact, what social standards expect them to be, and they are heavily invested in repressing all indications that they may fail to live up to these standards. The third subdivision, most similar to the aggressive type that Horney described in her earlier work, is referred to as "vindictive sadism," in which individuals arrogate to themselves all powers and rights, and seek to deny them to others. In the extreme form there is an effort to be omnipotent, invulnerable, and inviolable. Satisfaction is gained by subjecting others to pain or indignity, and there is a perverse joy in sadistically deprecating them; through these actions vindictive types feel that they restore their pride and glory.

The third of the triad is the moving-away, detached type. Employing the solution of neurotic resignation, these persons have as their primary goal the active avoidance of others, fearing that relationships will evoke feelings and desires that will lead ultimately only to conflict and frustration. They restrict their life, become detached onlookers, and achieve peace by curtailing needs and wishes. In extreme form this type becomes severely alienated, moves to the periphery of life, and becomes an automaton who drifts in a dream, unconnected to others.

Fromm.   Erich Fromm (1947) was one of the early theorists to reinterpret Freud's psychopathological theories along social lines. Although constructing his model in accord with themes first formulated by Freud, Fromm questioned the relevance of libidinous forces as the prime elements in character development. Primary emphasis was given to the interpersonal transactions at each stage between parent and child. For example, the compulsive pattern was seen to result not from frustrations experienced at the anal stage but from the behavioral models exhibited by a rigid and meticulous parent who imposed cleanliness and orderliness as standards for the child during toilet training. Fromm distinguished five character orientations that develop from such interpersonal learning experiences; four are identified as nonproductive orientations and are of primary interest. The first is termed the "receptive orientation" and is characterized by a deep need for external support from parents, friends, and authorities. All things that are good or necessary are found outside one's self. A search takes place for a "magic helper," and anxiety is experienced when external sources of support and nurturance are threatened. Similar to the classical analytic oral-sucking character, these individuals find consolation in eating and drinking, and in dependency on others; they behave in an optimistic, receptive, and friendly manner, except when anticipating loss or rebuff. The second orientation is entitled the "exploitative" character; these persons seek to extract what they wish from others by either force or cunning. Pessimistic, suspicious, and angry, these individuals feel they are not capable of producing on their own and, hence, must usurp or steal what they can, claiming that what they take from others is of greater value than what they can produce themselves. This type is similar to the analytic oral-biting character and to Horney's aggressive style. The third orientation, labeled the "hoarding" character by Fromm, is closest to the psychoanalytic anal-retentive type. Security for these personalities is achieved by saving and keeping, by surrounding oneself with a protective wall and drawing in as much as possible, while letting out virtually nothing. There is a rigid and compulsive orderliness, a miserliness in the sharing of both possessions and thoughts, and an inability to express love, as well as an unreceptiveness to both feelings and new ideas. In the "marketing orientation" Fromm has made an original contribution to characterology, that is, one not developed by earlier writers. Such individuals mold themselves to fit whatever others expect or require of them; they have little that is stable and genuine in their makeup since they are ever-ready to adapt and "sell" themselves to fulfill the desires that others wish of them. There is a superficiality, a lack of depth and genuineness in one's relationships, a manipulation of oneself to appeal to the fashions of the moment. The fifth of Fromm's orientations, the "productive" character, is seen as the healthy and creative personality, one who fully develops his/her powers, is capable of thinking independently while respecting the views of others, and is responsive to the experience of love and the sensuous pleasures, without being either indulgent or self-centered.

Leary. Drawing inspiration from the work of Horney, Fromm, and Sullivan, Timothy Leary (1957), along with associates at the Kaiser Permanente Foundation, constructed an interpersonal typology based on two dimensions: dominance-submission and hate-love. Utilizing gradations and permutations, Leary separated 16 behavioral segments, which he then grouped into eight distinct interpersonal types. Each is identified by two variants, a mild and an extreme form; two labels are used here to designate each of the eight types, the first to signify the mild or more adaptive variant; the second, the more extreme or pathological variant. The "rebellious-distrustful" personality, the first of Leary's types, is characterized by an attitude of resentment and by feelings of deprivation. These persons handle anxiety and frustration by actively distancing themselves from others and by displays of bitterness, cynicism, and passively resistant behaviors. Although not wishing to be distant, desiring both closeness and tenderness as alternatives, experience has taught them that it is best not to trust others, to be skeptical of the so-called goodwill of others, and to be alert to and rebel against signs of phoniness and deceit on their part. In the "self-effacing-masochistic" personality there is a modesty and an unpretentious reserve, a tendency to avoid appearing capable and confident; in extreme form, efforts are made to evoke deprecation and humiliation from others, with consequent feelings of depression and uncertainty. The behavior of the "docile-dependent" personality is primarily submissive and is characterized by overt displays of both friendliness and affiliation. Its central feature is that of soliciting help by behaving weak and incompetent, and by voicing unusual trust and admiration of others; in the extreme form we might observe an ingratiating and clinging dependency, and a constant beseeching for help, advice, and direction. The fourth pattern, the "cooperative-overconventional" personality, identifies those who strive to be liked and accepted by others, and who display an extraverted friendliness and sociability. There is a willingness to compromise to maintain harmony; in more extreme form this personality displays an effusiveness, a shallow optimism, an immature naïvete, a histrionic or dramatic expressiveness, and a hyperdistractibility. The "responsible-hypernormal" personality is noted by efforts to maintain the appearance of personal integrity, self-sacrifice, and concern for others. Variants of this type strive excessively to achieve an inner ideal of proper and conventional behavior, and to avoid appearances of emotionality and weakness; they are orderly and perfectionistic, and are intolerant of impulsive feelings such as anger in either themselves or others. In extreme form, this personality may experience life as a "hollow man," isolated by pretentions of propriety and correctness from both the external realities of life and from one's own inner feelings. The "managerial-autocratic" personality is characterized by an air of strength and confidence, and by communicating an attitude of leadership that often evokes obedience and respect from others. In the maladaptive form we might observe domineering and dictatorial attempts to control others, power-ridden manipulations of their lives, an inability to relax, and an insistence that others behave efficiently and competently. In the "competitive-narcissistic" personality is seen a proud, independent, self-enhancing style in which others are either exploited, put down, or benignly invited to be submissive. These personalities are most secure when they are in control, independent of others, feel triumphant, or are assured of a competitive advantage or superior status. In pathological form there is a blind selfishness, a frantic effort to impress, and a boastfulness and exhibitionism that becomes flagrant and irrational. The eighth and final of Leary's types is the "aggressive-sadistic" personality, individuals noted by their cold sternness and punitiveness, who gain security and pleasure in mocking others, acting hardboiled, and in provoking fear through intimidating displays of power; although intentionally provocative, these persons may feel a measure of guilt over the consequences of their behaviors.

Learned Coping Patterns

Nearly 70 years ago Karl Jaspers (1913, 1948) wrote the following:

> While the work of the psychiatrist is entirely with individual cases, he nevertheless requires to be also a psychopathologist, to look for general concepts and rules, in order to solve the problems presented by the individual case.... He wishes to know and understand, characterize and analyze, not the individual person but the general case.... He requires ideas which can be conceptualized, which can be communicated, which can be fitted into an orderly scheme and which can be systematized. (1948, p. 87)

What Jaspers recommended then is equally true today, that an effort be made to construct a consistent framework that will create order and give coherence to the broad spectrum of mental disorders. A review of the theorists described earlier in this chapter indicates that many have pursued this goal, but few, if any, have succeeded in formulating as comprehensive and integrated a framework as is necessary to encompass even the personality disorders. Given the intrinsic difficulty of the task, one must ask whether there are good reasons to continue the pursuit of systematizing our knowledge of psychopathology in a theoretically anchored fashion? This question is briefly answered before describing the classification model for this section.

There are several benefits that derive from systematizing knowledge in a theoretically anchored fashion. For example, given the countless ways in which the complex of clinical behaviors can be observed and analyzed, a system of explanatory propositions becomes an extremely useful guide and focus. Thus, rather than shifting from one aspect of behavior to another, according to momentary impressions of importance, the clinician is led to pursue only those aspects that are likely to prove fruitful and clinically relevant. Another major value of a theoretical system is that it enables researchers to generate hypotheses about relationships that have not been observed before. Thus, in the same manner as in nuclear physics (where theory may predict the presence of particles that have yet to be experimentally observed), psychopathology theory may accurately deduce the presence of clinical entities even though they may never have been previously conceived as syndromal types. In this way, theoretical frameworks may enlarge the scope of knowledge by directing observers to potentially significant clinical relationships and constellations. More commonplace, yet significant, is that a theory may enable the clinician to tie new and old observations into an orderly and coherent pattern.

Although general psychopathology theories can prove extremely useful, it is important that the personality pathologies they subsume be as diverse in scope as possible. One of the problems noted in the review of earlier formulations is the limited number of syndromes subsumed within most classifications. For example, though extremely rich in its clinical details, the analytic psychosexual theory generates no more than five or six personality characters; factor analytic theorist Eysenck specifies only three types; Sheldon also notes only three basic categories, as does Horney in her three "solutions," and so on. None provide distinctions sufficient in number to correspond to the diversity seen in clinical work. Of equal importance, they do not match in reasonable detail the list of personality disorders described in the DSM classification schema. Thus, in evaluating the utility and accuracy of a theory of personality pathology, the clinician must ask whether it generates a typology that both encompasses and corresponds to all of the established and formally recognized personality syndromes. Only in this manner can the prime goal of a clinical science be achieved, that of establishing agreement between theory and empirical observation.

Millon.   This section now turns to a recent formulation that employs a set of theoretical concepts for deducing and coordinating personality syndromes. The full scope of this schema has been published by the author in an earlier text (Millon, 1969) and summarized in later writings (Millon and Millon, 1974; Millon, 1977). Identified as a *biosocial-learning theory*, it attempts to generate the established and recognized personality categories through formal deduction and to show their covariation with other mental disorders.

In reviewing the many theories that are presented in this chapter, the reader cannot help but be impressed by both the number and diversity of concepts and types. In fact, one might well be inclined to ask, first, where the catalog of possibilities will end and, second, whether these different frameworks overlap sufficiently to enable the identification of common trends or themes. In response to this second question, we find that theorists, going back to the turn of the century, began to propose a threefold group of dimensions that were used time and again as the raw materials for personality construction. Thus, Freud's "three polarities that govern all of mental life" were "discovered" by theorists both earlier and later than he—in France, Germany, Russia, and other European nations, as well as in the United States. The dimensions of active-passive, subject-object, and pleasure-pain were identified either in part or in all their components by Heymans and Wiersma (1906), McDougall (1908), Meumann (1910), Kollarits (1912), Kahn (1928), Fiske and Maddi (1961), and others. For example, the subject-object distinction parallels Jung's introversive-extroversive dichotomy; active-passive is the same polarity utilized by Adler and is traceable directly to a major distinction drawn by Aristotle. Clearly, then, a review of the basic ingredients selected for building personality typologies since the turn of the century uncovers an unusual consensus. It is these very concepts that were "discovered" once more by Millon (1969).

When theorists speak of the *active-passive* dimension they usually mean that the vast range of behaviors engaged in by a person may be fundamentally grouped in terms of whether the individual takes the initiative in shaping surrounding events or whether behavior is largely reactive to those events. The distinction of *pleasure-pain* recognizes that motivations are ultimately aimed in one of two directions, toward events which are attractive or positively reinforcing versus away from those which are aversive or negatively reinforcing. Similarly, the distinction of subject-object, or *self-other*, recognizes that among all objects and things in our environment there are two that stand out above all others in their power to affect us: our own selves and others. Using this threefold framework as a foundation, Millon (1969) derived personality "coping patterns" that correspond in close detail to each of the "official" personality disorders in the DSM-III.

Learned coping patterns may be viewed as complex forms of instrumental behavior, that is, ways of achieving positive reinforcements and avoiding negative reinforcements. These strategies reflect what kinds of reinforcements individuals have learned to seek or avoid (pleasure-pain), where individuals look to obtain them (self-others), and how individuals have learned to behave in order to elicit or escape them (active-passive). Eight basic coping patterns and three severe variants were derived by combining the *nature* (positive or pleasure versus negative or pain), the *source* (self versus others), and the *instrumental behaviors* (active versus passive) engaged in to achieve various reinforcements. Describing pathological strategies of behavior in reinforcement terms merely casts them in a somewhat different language than that utilized in the past.

A major distinction derived from the theoretical model is that people may be differentiated in terms of whether their primary source of reinforcement is within themselves or within others. This distinction corresponds to the dependent and independent patterns. *Dependent* personalities have learned that feeling good, secure, confident, and so on—that is, those feelings associated with pleasure or the avoidance of pain—are best provided by others. Behaviorally, these personalities display a strong need for external support and attention; should they be deprived of affection and nurturance they will experience marked discomfort, if not sadness and anxiety. *Independent* personality patterns, in contrast, are characterized by a reliance on the self. These individuals have learned that they obtain maximum pleasure and minimum pain if they depend on themselves rather than others. In both dependent and independent patterns, individuals demonstrate a distinct preference as to whether to turn to others or to themselves to gain security and comfort. Such clear-cut commitments are not made by all personalities. Some, those whom Millon speaks of as *ambivalent*, remain unsure as to which way to turn; that is, they are in conflict regarding whether to depend on themselves for reinforcement or on others. Some of these patients vacillate between turning to others in an agreeable conformity one time, and turning to themselves in efforts at independence, the next. Other ambivalent personalities display overt dependence and compliance; beneath these outwardly conforming behaviors, however, are strong desires to assert independent and often hostile feelings and impulses. Finally, certain patients are characterized by their diminished ability to experience both pain and pleasure; they have neither a normal need for pleasure nor a normal need to avoid punishment. Another group of patients are also distinguished by a diminished ability to feel pleasurable reinforcers, but they are notably sensitive to pain; life is experienced as possessing few gratifications but much anguish. Both groups share a deficit capacity to sense pleasurable reinforcers, although one is hyperreactive to pain. Millon describes both of these as *detached* patterns; unable to experience rewards from themselves or from others, they drift increasingly into socially isolated and self-alienated behaviors.

Another theory-derived distinction reflects the fact that we instrumentally elicit the reinforcements we seek in essentially one of two ways: actively or passively. Descriptively, those who are typically *active* tend to be characterized by their alertness, vigilance, persistence, decisiveness, and ambitiousness in a goal-directed behavior. They plan strategies, scan alternatives, manipulate events, and circumvent obstacles, all to the end of eliciting pleasures and rewards, or avoiding the distress of punishment, rejection, and anxiety. Although their goals may differ from time to time, they initiate events and are enterprising and energetically intent on controlling the circumstances of their environment. By contrast, *passive* personalities engage in few overtly manipulative strategies to gain their ends. They often display a seeming inertness, a lack of ambition and persistence, an acquiescence, and a resigned attitude in which they initiate little to shape events and wait for the circumstances of their environment to take their course.

Using these classical polarities as a basis, Millon (1969) derived a classification that combined in a four-by-two matrix the dependent, independent, ambivalent, and detached styles with the activity-passivity dimension. This produced eight basic types, to which three severe disorders were added, for a total of 11 theory-derived personality patterns. Despite their close correspondence to the official DSM-III personality disorders, these coping patterns should be conceived as provisional and heuristic, and not as reified diagnostic entities. In the following paragraphs the eight well-compensated or mildly pathological patterns are described first, followed by three more severe or borderline variants.

1. The *passive-dependent* pattern (Millon Submissive personality; DSM-III Dependent disorder) is characterized by a search for relationships in which one can lean upon others for affection, security, and leadership. This personality's lack of both initiative and autonomy is often a consequence of parental overprotection. As a function of these early experiences, these individuals have simply learned the comforts of assuming a passive role in interpersonal relations, accepting whatever kindness and support they may find, and willingly submitting to the wishes of others in order to maintain their affection.

2. The *active-dependent* pattern (Millon Gregarious personality; DSM-III Histrionic disorder) shows an insatiable and indiscriminate search for stimulation and affection. This personality's sociable and capricious behaviors give the appearance of considerable independence of others, but beneath this guise lies a fear of autonomy and an intense need for signs of social approval and attention. Affection must be replenished constantly and must be obtained from every source of interpersonal contact.

3. The *passive-independent* pattern (Millon Narcissistic personality; DSM-III Narcissistic disorder) is noted by an egotistic self-involvement. As a function of early experience these persons have learned to overvalue their self-worth; their confidence in their superiority may, however, be based on false

premises. Nevertheless, they assume that others will recognize their special-ness, maintain an air of arrogant self-assurance, and, without much thought or even conscious intent, benignly exploit others to their own advantage.

4. The *active-independent* pattern (Millon Aggressive personality; DSM-III Antisocial disorder) reflects a learned mistrust of others and a desire for autonomy and retribution for what are felt as past injustices. There is an indiscriminate striving for power and a disposition to be rejecting of others; these actions are seen as justified because people are unreliable and du-plicitous. Autonomy and hostility are claimed to be the only means to head off deceit and betrayal.

5. The *passive-ambivalent* pattern (Millon Conforming personality; DSM-III Compulsive disorder) is based on a conflict between hostility toward others and a fear of social disapproval. These persons resolve their ambival-ence not only by supressing resentment but by overconforming and over-complying, at least on the surface. Lurking behind this front of propriety and restraint, however, are anger and intense oppositional feelings that, on occasion, break through their controls.

6. The *active-ambivalent* pattern (Millon Negativistic personality; DSM-III Passive-aggressive disorder) represents an inabiity to resolve conflicts similar to those of the passive-ambivalent; however, this ambivalence remains close to consciousness and intrudes into everyday life. These individuals get themselves into endless wrangles and disappointments as they vacillate between deference and conformity, at one time, and aggressive negativism, the next. Their behavior displays an erratic pattern of explosive anger or stubborness intermingled with moments of guilt and shame.

7. The *passive-detached* pattern (Millon Asocial personality; DSM-III Schizoid disorder) is characterized by social impassivity. Affectionate needs and emotional feelings are minimal, and the individual functions as a passive observer detached from the rewards and affections, as well as from the demands, of human relationships.

8. The *active-detached* pattern (Millon Avoidant personality; DSM-III Avoidant disorder) represents a fear and mistrust of others. These individuals maintain a constant vigil lest their impulses and longing for affection result in a repetition of the pain and anguish they have experienced with others previously. Only by active withdrawal can they protect themselves. Despite desires to relate, they have learned that it is best to deny these feelings and keep an interpersonal distance.

Three additional personality patterns are identified at the moderately severe or borderline level of pathology. These are differentiated from the first eight by several criteria, notably deficits in social competence and periodic (but reversible) psychotic episodes. Less integrated and effective in coping than their milder personality counterparts, they appear especially vulnerable to the strains of everyday life. Their major features and similarities to DSM-III personality disorders are briefly summarized.

9. The *cycloid personality* corresponds to the DSM-III "borderline

personality disorder" and represents a moderately dysfunctional dependent or ambivalent orientation. These personalities experience intense endogeneous moods, with recurring periods of dejection and apathy interspersed with spells of anger, anxiety, or euphoria. Many reveal recurring self-mutilating and suicidal thoughts, appear preoccupied with securing affection, and display a cognitive-affective ambivalence evident in simultaneous feelings of rage, love, and guilt toward others.

10.   The *paranoid* personality is described in a similar fashion in both Millon and the DSM-III. Here are seen a vigilant mistrust of others and an edgy defensiveness against anticipated criticism and deception. There is an abrasive irritability and a tendency to precipitate exasperation and anger in others. Expressed often is a fear of losing independence, leading this personality to vigorously resist external influence and control.

11.   The DSM-III schizotypal disorder and Millon's *schizoid* personality both display a constellation of behaviors that reflect a poorly integrated or dysfunctional detached personality pattern. These persons prefer isolation with minimal personal attachments and obligations. Behavioral eccentricities are notable, and the individual is often perceived by others as strange or different. Depending on whether the pattern is passive or active, there will be either an anxious wariness and hypersensitivity, or an emotional flattening and deficiency of affect.

The DSM-III Personality Disorders

The Task Force assigned to develop the DSM-III acknowledged that the personality disorders represented syndromes that were "fuzzy at the edges" (Task Force, 1976). On the one hand, these disorders shade imperceptibly into "normal problems of everyday life"; and, on the other, they have few clear and distinguishing symptoms to serve as identifying markers. Nevertheless, the Task Force recognized that personality disorders possess features that are not shared with other syndromes, qualities noted more by the pervasiveness and duration of their expression rather than by their symptomatological distinctiveness. It was recognized, further, that personality "traits" had to be differentiated from personality "disorders." Although the behaviors that signify traits often underlie and may be difficult to discriminate from those comprising disorders, they can be distinguished on two grounds: Disorders are associated with subjective feelings of distress and/or significantly impaired social functioning.

This text is arranged in accord with DSM-III categories for several reasons other than the fact that it is the standard and official schema. Despite the many compromises its products represent, the end result is a reasonable reflection of the "state of the art" as judged by a well-respected and highly competent committee of practicing clinicians and academic researchers. Moreover, the syndromes included in the final draft had been extensively pretested in two studies with large and representative samples of mental health professionals.

Earlier drafts were revised in light of these studies, and several categories were proposed anew while others were dropped.

A major goal of the committee was to include as many clinically useful personality syndromes as justified. Despite objections from certain quarters, a decision was made to incorporate categories that had not been "fully validated" by systematic research but nevertheless had much to commend them in terms of their everyday clinical applicability. Failure to include these "tentative," but clinically useful, categories would have deprived the profession of an opportunity to encourage the systematic research necessary to determine whether these syndromes hold up under careful clinical and research scrutiny.

An early aspiration of the committee was the differentiation of personality types along the dimension of severity; unfortunately, criteria for such distinctions were never developed. Rather than drawing severity discriminations, as proposed by both Kernberg (1967, 1970) and Millon (1969), associates of the Task Force grouped the personality syndromes into three symptomatological clusters. The first includes the paranoid, schizoid, and schizotypal disorders, unified as a group in that their behaviors appear odd and eccentric. The second cluster subsumes the histrionic, narcissistic, antisocial, and borderline disorders, grouped together on the basis of their tendency to behave dramatically, emotionally, or erratically. The third cluster groups the avoidant, dependent, compulsive, and passive-aggressive personalities on the grounds that these types often appear anxious or fearful. A memo distributed by the author for discussion at the Task Force meeting of June 1978 addressed these recommended clusters as follows:

> I never quite understood the importance of those dimensions that led us to cluster personality disorders in the manner described. Any number of different dimensions could have been selected to group the eleven personality disorders in any of an almost infinite arrangement of sets or combinations. Why the specific one suggested in the text was selected out of these is not clear to me. Does it have some prognostic significance, some etiological import, logic in terms of a deductive theoretical model? If I were to develop a cluster or factorial framework for the personality disorders I am sure I would come up with a different schema than the one suggested. The characteristics specified are clear enough, but of what value is it to know that three are "eccentric," that four are "emotional," and that four appear "anxious"?
>
> My own preference would be either to drop the grouping entirely and list them alphabetically or to group them in terms of their known prevalence or potential severity. The likely severity of pathology, such as the probability to which these syndromes succumb to severe versus mild disorders, strikes me as a useful distinction if we are to make any one at all among these disorders. If we look through our list we might note that disorders such as paranoid, schizotypal and borderline, and possibly schizoid and avoidant, are likely to exhibit a greater propensity to severe pathology than the others. Conversely, types such as the histrionic, narcissistic, antisocial, dependent and compulsive, and perhaps passive-aggressive, tend to stabilize at the mild-to-moderate level of severity.

If we follow the above suggestion we would have a logical distinction of some clinical import among the categories. It would be at least in line with earlier plans to note the dimension of severity with each personality disorder.

In presenting the syndromes of personality disorder in the following chapters, this text sequences them in terms of their usual level of severity. However, before doing so, a question must be asked: How shall severity levels be gauged; that is, what criteria should be employed to determine whether one personality disorder is typically more severe than another?

Two classification systems in current use pay special attention to criteria differentiating personality disorders along the dimension of severity, those of Kernberg (1967, 1970) and of Millon (1969). Direct comparison is not feasible since the character types presented by Kernberg do not correspond to the DSM-III personality disorders. Nevertheless, it will be useful to put aside DSM-III comparability and consider the conceptual distinctions that differentiate Kernberg's views from those of Millon.

As noted earlier, Kernberg groups personality disorders into higher, intermediate, and lower levels of character pathology. Millon also categorizes his types into three subsets, including eight mild, three moderate, and three of marked severity; the markedly severe, or psychotic level, is bypassed for current purposes, leaving 11 personality syndromes. The major distinction between Kernberg and Millon is not found in the clinical signs they include to gauge severity but rather in the ones they choose to emphasize. For Kernberg, primary attention is given to the *internal* structural characteristics of the personality, whereas for Millon the *external* social system and interpersonal dynamics are given a status equal that of internal organization.

Kernberg focuses on "nonspecific manifestations of ego weakness," as illustrated in shifts toward primary process thinking, defensive operations characterized as "splitting," increasingly primitive idealizations, and early forms of projection and omnipotence. Though differences do exist, Millon and Kernberg identify the following similar features: loss of impulse control, disturbed psychological cohesion, rigid versus diffused ego functions, adaptive inflexibility, ambivalent or conflict-ridden defenses, blurrings of self and nonself, and so on. Millon goes beyond these, however, by stressing a systems perspective that interprets the internal structure as being functional or dysfunctional depending on its efficacy and stability within the context of interpersonal, familial, and other social dynamics. Thus, he speaks additionally of such severity criteria as deficits in social competence, checkered personal relationships, digressions from early aspirations, and repetitive interpersonal quandries and disappointments. From this view, severity is conceived as a person-field interaction that includes not only intrapsychic dynamics but interpersonal dynamics as well. Although Kernberg recognizes the importance of internalized object relations (1975), Millon assigns them a major role by stressing both "internalized" past and contemporary "real" social relationships. In this way, the boundaries of both structure and dynamics are expanded such that internal structural features are placed within a context or system of external social dynamics.

A positive consequence of broadening the criteria of severity is that personality pathology need no longer be traced exclusively to intrapsychic origins in conflict and defense. By enlarging our vista so as to include interpersonal efficacy within a social context, our reference base for conceptualizing disordered personality has been expanded. A shift from the view that all pathogenic sources derive from internal conflicts is consistent with Fenichel's notion of "sublimation" character types and reinforces the ego analysts' assertion of conflict-free spheres of development and learning. No longer restricted by the limiting intrapsychic outlook, personality disorders can now be conceived best as any behavior pattern that is consistently inappropriate, maladaptive, or deficient in the social and familial system within which the individual operates. And, in accord with this broader systems perspective, several personality syndromes described in Millon (1969) and formulated for the DSM-III are recognized as having developed "conflict-free"—that is, they are products of inadequate or misguided learning; others, of course, are conceived more traditionally as primarily "reactive"—that is, they are consequences of conflict resolutions. For example, some dependent personalities unfold in large measure as a result of simple parental overprotection and insufficiently learned autonomous behaviors, and not from instinctual conflicts and regressive adaptations.

The logic for broadening the criteria of severity to include the interplay of both individual and social systems seems especially appropriate when considering personality syndromes. Not only do personality traits express themselves primarily within group and familial environments, but the patient's style of communication, interpersonal competency, and social skill will, in great measure, elicit reactions that feed back to shape the future course of whatever impairments the person may already have. Thus, the behavior and attitudes that individuals exhibit with others will evoke reciprocal reactions that influence whether their problems will improve, stabilize or intensify. Internal organization or structure is significant, of course, but the character or style of relating interpersonally may have as much to do with whether the sequence of social dynamics will prove rewarding or destructive. It is not only the structural ego capacity, therefore, but also the particular features of social and familial behavior that will dispose the patient to relate to others in a manner that will prove increasingly adaptive or maladaptive.

Utilizing a systems perspective that includes the interplay of both internal and external dynamics groups the 11 personality disorders of the DSM-III into three broad categories.

The *first* includes the dependent, histrionic, narcissistic, and antisocial personality disorders. These four personality patterns are *either* dependent or independent in their style of interpersonal functioning. Their intrapsychic structures enable them to conceive of themselves and to deal with others in a relatively coherent, "nonsplit," or nonconflictual manner—that is, in a reasonably consistent and focused rather than a diffused or divided way. Moreover, because the needs and traits that underlie their coping style dispose them to seek out others and to relate socially, they are able either to adapt to or to control their interpersonal environment so as to be sustained and nourished emotionally, and thereby maintain their psychic cohesion.

The *second* group, that viewed at a mid-level of personality severity, includes the compulsive, passive-aggressive, schizoid, and avoidant personality disorders. These represent a lower level of functioning than the first group for several reasons. In the two ambivalent types, the compulsive and passive-aggressive personalities, there is a split within both their interpersonal and their intrapsychic orientations; they are unable to find a coherent or consistent direction to focus either their personal relationships or their defensive operations. They are in conflict, split between assuming an independent or dependent stance; hence, they often undo or reverse their social behaviors and frequently feel internally divided. The second pair of this foursome, the two detached types, labeled the schizoid and avoidant personalities in the DSM-III, are judged at a mid-level of severity because they are characteristically isolated or estranged from external support systems. As a consequence, they are likely to have few subliminatory channels and fewer still interpersonal sources of nurturance and stability, the lack of which will dispose them to increasingly autistic preoccupations and regressions.

The *third* set, reflecting still lower levels of personality functioning, includes the DSM-III borderline, paranoid, and schizotypal disorders. All three are socially "incompetent," difficult to relate to, and often isolated, hostile, or confused; hence, they are not likely to elicit the interpersonal support that could bolster their flagging defenses and orient them to a more effective and satisfying life-style. Moreover, a clear breakdown in the cohesion of personality organization is seen in both schizotypal and borderline disorders. The converse is evident in the paranoid, where there is an overly rigid and narrow focus to the personality structure. In the former pair there has been a dissolution or diffusion of ego capacities; in the latter, the paranoid pattern, there is an inelasticity and constriction of personality, giving rise to a fragility and inadaptability of functions.

The sequential order just outlined is used in the presentation of DSM-III personality disorders in following chapters. Before describing these types in greater detail, Chapter 3 will present some of the major influences that serve as precursors of personality pathology.

Chapter 3

Personality Development

Interaction and continuity are the major themes of this chapter. The discussion stresses the fact that numerous biogenic and psychogenic determinants covary to shape personality, the relative weights of each varying as a function of time and circumstance. Further, this interaction of influences persists over time such that the course of later characteristics is related intrinsically to earlier events. Personality development must be viewed, therefore, as a process in which organismic and environmental forces display not only a mutuality and circularity of influence but an orderly and sequential continuity throughout the life of the individual.

For pedagogical purposes, it is often necessary to separate biogenic from psychogenic factors as influences in personality development; this bifurcation does not exist in reality. Biological and experiential determinants combine in an inextricable interplay throughout life. Thus, constitutional dispositions not only shape the character of experience but are themselves modified in a constant interchange with the environment. This sequence of biogenic-psychogenic interaction creates a never-ending spiral; each step in the interplay builds upon prior interactions and creates, in turn, new potentials for future reactivity and experience.

The circular feedback and the serially unfolding character of the developmental process defy simplification, and must constantly be kept in mind when analyzing the background of personality. There are no unidirectional effects in development; it is a multideterminant transaction in which unique biogenic potentials and distinctive psychogenic influences mold each other in reciprocal and successively more intricate ways.

BIOLOGICAL INFLUENCES

It is inconceivable that characteristics of anatomic morphology, endocrine physiology, and brain chemistry would not be instrumental in shaping development and behavior. Biological scientists know that the central nervous system cannot be viewed as a simple and faithful follower of what is fed into it from the environment; not only does it maintain a rhythmic activity of its own, but it plays an active role in regulating sensitivity and controlling the amplitude of what is picked up by peripheral organs. Unlike a machine, which passively responds to external stimulation, the brain has a directing function that determines substantially what, when, and how events will be experienced. Each individual's nervous system selects, transforms, and registers objective events in accord with its distinctive biological character- istics. Unusual sensitivities in this delicate orienting system can lead to marked distortions in perception and behavior. Any disturbance which produces a breakdown in the smooth integration of functions, or a failure to retrieve previously stored information, is likely to create chaos and pathology. Normal psychological functioning depends on the integrity of certain key areas of biological structure, and any impairment of this substrate will result in disturbed thought, emotion, and behavior. It must be carefully noted, however, that although biogenic dysfunctions or defects may produce the basic break from normality, psychological and social determinants almost invariably shape the form of its expression. It should be understood, therefore, that acceptance of the role of biogenic influences does not negate the role of social experience and learning.

Although the exact mechanisms by which biological functions undergird personality and behavior will remain obscure for some time, the belief that biogenic factors are intimately involved is not new. Scientists have been gathering data for decades, applying a wide variety of research methods across a broad spectrum of biophysical functions. The number of techniques used and the variety of variables studied are legion. These variables often are different avenues for exploring the same basic hypotheses. For example, researchers focusing on biochemical dysfunctions often assume that these dysfunctions result from genetic error. However, the methods they employ and the data they produce are quite different from those of researchers who approach the role of heredity through research comparing monozygotic with dizygotic twins. With this in mind, this chapter proceeds to subdivide the subject of development into several arbitrary (but traditional) compartments, beginning first with heredity.

Heredity

The role of heredity is usually inferred from evidence based on correlations among traits in members of the same family. Most psychopathologists admit that heredity must play a role in personality development, but they insist that genetic dispositions are modified substantially by the operation of environ- mental factors. This view states that heredity operates not as a fixed constant but as a disposition that takes different forms depending on the circumstances of an individual's upbringing. Hereditary theorists may take a more inflexible position, referring to a body of data that implicate genetic factors in a wide range of psychopathologies. Although they are likely to agree that variations in these disorders may be produced by environmental conditions, they are equally likely to assert that these are merely superficial influences that cannot prevent the individual from succumbing to his or her hereditary inclination. The overall evidence seems to suggest that genetic factors serve as predispositions to certain traits, but, with few exceptions, similarly affected individuals display important differences in their symptoms and developmental histories. Moreover, genetically disposed disorders can be aided by psychological therapies, and similar symptomatologies often arise without such genetic dispositions.

Unfortunately, most genetic research has been limited to hospitalized patients and their families, since they have been readily available as study populations and because theorists assume that severe levels of psychopathology represent the clearest form of expression of a genetic disease. Despite the paucity of work with less severe disorders, a number of theorists have suggested that the milder pathologies represent undeveloped or minimally expressed defective genes; for example, the schizoid personality possesses the schizophrenic genotype, but the defective gene is weakened by the operation of beneficial modifying genes or favorable environmental experiences. An alternate explanation might be formulated in terms of polygenic action; polygenes have minute, quantitatively similar, and cumulative effects. Thus, a continuum of increasing pathological severity can be accounted for by the cumulative effects of a large number of minor genes acting upon the same trait. No systematic research in psychiatry has utilized a polygenic model of inheritance despite its appropriateness as an explanatory vehicle for such less severe and less sharply delineated pathologies as personality disorders. This reflects the preoccupation of researchers with easily diagnosed, severe patients and the dominant, if erroneous, belief that all forms of psychopathology are best conceived in a dichotomous model of health versus disease, with no intermediary steps.

The idea that psychopathological syndromes comprise well-circumscribed disease entities is an attractive assumption for those who sought a Mendelian or single-gene model of inheritance. Recent thinking forces us to question the validity of this approach to nosology and to the relevance of Mendelian genetic action. Defects in the infinitely complex central nervous system can arise from innumerable genetic anomalies. Moreover, even convinced geneticists make reference to the notion of phenocopies, a concept signifying that characteristics that usually are traceable to genetic action can be simulated by environmental factors; thus, overtly identical forms of pathology may arise from either genetic or environmental sources. As a consequence, the clinical picture of a disorder may give no clue to its origins since similar appearances do not necessarily signify similar etiologies. To complicate matters further, different genes vary in their responsiveness to environmental influences; some produce uniform effects under all environmental conditions, whereas others can be entirely suppressed in certain environments. Moreover, it appears that genes have their effects at particular times of maturation and that their interaction with environmental conditions is minimal both before and after these periods.

Despite these ambiguities and complications, there can be little question that genetic factors do play some dispositional role in shaping the morphological and biochemical substrate of certain traits. However, these factors are by no means necessary to the development of personality pathology, nor are they likely to be sufficient in themselves to elicit pathological behaviors. They may serve, however, as a physiological base which makes the person susceptible to dysfunction under stress or inclined to learn behaviors which prove socially troublesome.

Temperament Dispositions of Childhood

Each child enters the world with a distinctive pattern of dispositions and sensitivities. Nurses know that infants differ from the moment they are born, and every perceptive mother notices distinct differences in her successive offspring. Some infants suck vigorously; others seem indifferent and hold the nipple feebly. Some infants have a regular cycle of hunger, elimination, and sleep, whereas others vary unpredictably. Some twist fitfully in their sleep, while others lie peacefully awake in hectic surroundings. Some are robust and energetic; others seem tense and cranky.

Proving that children are temperamentally different may seem to be laboring the obvious, but important implications of the obvious may too readily be overlooked. The question that must be posed is not whether children differ but whether a particular sequence of subsequent life experiences will result as a consequence of these differences; childhood temperament would be of little significance if it did not persist and establish lifelong patterns of functioning. In this regard the clinician must ask whether the child's characteristics evoke distinctive reactions from his/her parents and whether these reactions have a beneficial or a detrimental effect upon the child's development. Rather than limit attention to the traditional question of what effect the environment has upon the child, the focus might be changed to ask what effect the child has on the environment and what the consequences of these are upon the child's development.

It would appear that patterns of behavior observed in the first few months of life are of biogenic rather than psychogenic origin. Some researchers speak of these patterns as "primary" because they are displayed before postnatal experience can account for them. Investigators have found that infants show a consistent pattern of autonomic system reactivity; others have reported stable differences on such biological measures as sensory threshold, quality and intensity of emotional tone, and electroencephalographic waves. Because the pertinence of psychophysiological differences to later personality is unknown, investigators have turned attention to the relationship between observable behavior and later development.

The studies of two research groups mentioned briefly in Chapter 2 (Thomas et al., 1963, 1968; Thomas and Chess, 1977; Escalona and Leitch, 1953; Escalona and Heider, 1959; Escalona, 1968; Murphy et al., 1962; Murphy and Moriarty, 1976) have been especially fruitful in this regard. Their work has contributed not only to an understanding of personality development in general but to the development of psychopathology in particular. Several behavioral dimensions were found to differentiate the temperament patterns of infants. Children differ in the regularity of their biological functions; they differ in their autonomic reactivity, gauged by initial responses to new situations; they differ in sensory alertness to stimuli and in adaptability to change; they display characteristic moods that are clearly negative or positive; they show differing levels and intensities of response and differ in distractibility and persistence. Although early patterns were modified only slightly from infancy to childhood, this continuity could not be attributed entirely to the persistence of innate endowments. Subsequent experiences served to reinforce the characteristics that were displayed in early life. This occurred in great measure because the infant's initial behaviors transformed the environment in ways that intensified and accentuated initial behaviors.

Since so little attention has been paid to children's own contribution to their development, theorists have viewed disorders to be the result of experiences that individuals had no part in producing themselves. This is a simplification of a complex interaction. Each infant possesses a biologically based pattern of sensitivities and dispositions that shape the nature of his or her experiences. The interaction of biological dispositions and environmental experience is not a readily disentangled web but an intricate feedback system of crisscrossing influences. Two components of this process—adaptive learning and reciprocal reinforcement—are elaborated because of their pertinence to development.

Adaptive learning. The biological dispositions of the maturing child are important because they strengthen the probability that certain kinds of behavior will be learned. For example, highly active and responsive children relate to and learn rapidly about events and persons in their environment. Their zest and energy may lead them to experience personal gratification quickly or, conversely, their lively and exploratory behavior may result in painful frustrations if they run repetitively into insuperable barriers. Unable to fulfill their activity needs, they may strike out in erratic and maladaptive ways.

Adaptive learning in constitutionally passive children is shaped also by their biological constitution. Ill-disposed to deal with their environment assertively and disinclined to discharge their tensions physically, they may learn to avoid conflicts and step aside when difficulties arise. They may be less likely to develop guilt feelings about misbehavior than active youngsters, who more frequently get into trouble and receive punishment, and who are therefore inclined to develop aggressive feelings toward others. Passive youngsters may also deprive themselves of rewarding experiences, feel "left out of things," and depend on others to protect them from events they feel ill-equipped to handle on their own.

Reciprocal reinforcement. Childhood temperament evokes counterreactions from others that accentuate the initial disposition. Biological moods and activity levels shape not only the child's own behaviors but those of the parents as well. If the infant's disposition is cheerful and adaptable, and has made care easy, the mother will quickly display a positive reciprocal attitude. Conversely, if the child is tense, or if his/her care is difficult and time consuming, the mother may react with dismay, fatigue, or hostility. Through this distinctive behavioral disposition, then, the child elicits parental reactions that reinforce the initial pattern. Innate dispositions can be reversed, of course, by strong environmental pressures. A cheerful outlook can be crushed by parental contempt and ridicule. Conversely, shy and reticent children may become more self-confident in a thoroughly encouraging family atmosphere. Unfortunately, the reciprocal interplay of temperamental patterns and parental reactions has not been sufficiently explored. It may prove to be a fruitful sphere of research exploring the origins of personality pathology.

An obstacle to the assumption that early temperamental patterns persist throughout life is the recognition that maturation rates differ from child to child. Not all features of an individual's constitution are activated at the moment of birth. Potentials may unfold only gradually as maturation progresses. Thus, biologically rooted temperament patterns may not emerge until the youngster is well into adolescence, and it is not inconceivable that late-blooming patterns may supplant those displayed earlier.

A crucial determinant of whether a particular temperament will lead to personality pathology appears to be parental acceptance of the child's individuality. Parents who accept their child's temperament, and then modify their practices accordingly, can deter what might otherwise become pathological. On the other hand, if parents experience daily feelings of failure, frustration, anger, and guilt, regardless of the child's disposition, they are likely to contribute to a progressive worsening of the child's adjustment. These comments point once more to the fact that biogenic and psychogenic factors interact in complex ways. In the following section, which deals primarily with biogenic factors in adulthood, the operation of this interplay is seen again.

Biophysical Individuality

The general role that neurological lesions and physiochemical imbalances play in producing pathology can be grasped with only a minimal understanding of the structural organization and functional character of the brain. However, it is important that readers possessing limited knowledge in this sphere avoid the naïve, but often held, belief that psychological functions can be localized in neurohormonal depots or precise regions of the brain. Psychological processes such as thought, behavior, and emotion derive from complex and circular feedback properties of brain activity. Unless we recognize that awesomely intricate connections within the brain subserve these psychological functions, we will be inclined to simplistic propositions that clinical or personality traits can arise as a consequence of specific chemical imbalances or focal lesions. Psychological concepts such as emotion, behavior, and thought represent diverse and complex processes that are grouped together by theorists and researchers as a means of simplifying their observations. These conceptual labels must not be confused with tangible events and properties within the brain. Certain regions are more involved in particular psychological functions than others, but it is clear that higher processes are a product of brain area interactions. For example, the frontal lobes of the cortex orchestrate a dynamic pattern of impulses by selectively enhancing the sensitivity of receptors, comparing impulses arising in other brain spheres and guiding them along myriad arrangements and sequences. In this regnant function it facilitates or inhibits a wide range of psychological functions.

The point to be emphasized is that clinical signs and symptoms cannot be conceived as localized or fixed to one or another sphere of the brain. Rather, they arise from a network of complex interactions and feedbacks. All stimuli, whether generated externally or internally, follow long chains of reverberating circuits that modulate a wide range of activities. Psychological traits and processes must be conceived, therefore, as the product of a widespread and self-regulating pattern of interneuronal stimulation. If we keep in mind the intricate neural interdependencies underlying these functions, we should avoid falling prey to the error of interpretive simplification.

With the exception of a few well-circumscribed lesions that are directly associated with specific organic syndromes, the data relating neurological damage to psychopathology are equivocal. We are only beginning to cross the threshold of knowledge about normal brain functions. When we have a firm grasp of these normal processes, we may have an adequate base for specifying how disruptions impair psychological processes. At present, theoretical speculations are extrapolated from surgical, brain scan, chemotherapeutic, and electric stimulation studies; as such, they must be approached with a healthy degree of skepticism. Ingenious though they may be, these deductions are imaginary suppositions based on minimal empirical data.

The problem of correlating psychopathology with neurological structures is complicated immensely by individual differences in the organization of the brain. There is more variability in internal morphology than there is in external morphology. The location of and interconnections among brain regions differ markedly from person to person. These naturally occurring individual differences are important in another regard. Variations among individuals in the constitutional density, range, and branching of comparable brain regions will have a direct bearing on emerging psychological functions.

Possessing more or less of the neurological substrate for a particular function, such as pleasure or pain, can markedly influence the character of experience and the course of learning and development. Quite evidently, the role of neuroanatomical structures in psychopathology is not limited to problems of tissue defect or damage. Natural interindividual differences in structural anatomy and organization can result in a wide continuum of relevant psychological effects.

If we recognize the network of neural structures that are upset by a specific lesion, and add the tremendous natural variability in brain morphology, we may begin to see the difficulties involved in tracing the role of a neurological disturbance. If the technical skills required to assess the psychological consequences of a specific brain lesion are difficult, one can only begin to imagine the staggering task of determining the psychological correlates of natural anatomic differences.

Anatomic differences are only part of the story. The highly popular current search for biochemical dysfunctions in psychopathology is equally handicapped by the high degree of natural variability in physiochemical processes among humans. Roger Williams (1973), the eminent biochemist, has made us aware that each individual possesses a distinctive physiochemical pattern that is wholly unlike others and bears no relationship to a hypothetical norm. Such patterns of biological individuality comprise crucial factors that must be built into the equation before we can properly appraise the role of biogenic influences in the development of personality pathology. Certainly the checkered history of ill-conceived theories and the tendency of biogenic researchers to report evidence favoring their hypotheses prematurely have given ample justification for caution, if not cynicism. Nevertheless, new insights and bold ideas should not be discarded. Cynicism at this point will only deter us from seeking suggestive trends that may lead to important discoveries.

In summary, the search for biogenic determinants will be handicapped unless researchers recognize the high degree of biophysical individuality among humans. These patterns of individuality should be viewed not as a methodological complication but as an opportunity. The notion of a continuum of natural constitutional variations in neurological structure and physiochemical functioning may, in the long run, prove to be more productive to the study of biogenic factors than the current search for diseases, defects, and dysfunctions.

EARLY DEVELOPMENT

The previous section stressed the view that biological functions play an active role in regulating what, when, and how events will be experienced; the nervous and endocrine systems do not passively accept what is fed into them. Moreover, although behavior pathology may be activated by biogenic abnormalities, the mere specification of a biogenic cause is not sufficient for etiologic analysis. Even where clear-cut biogenic factors can be identified, it is necessary to trace the sequence of experiences that transform them into manifest forms of pathology. The need for this more extensive analysis is made evident by the fact that some persons with biological defects function effectively, whereas other, similarly afflicted individuals succumb to maladaptation. The biological defect, in itself, cannot account for such divergences. Pathological behaviors that are precipitated initially by biological abnormalities are not simple products of these defects; rather, they emerge through a complex sequence of interactions that include environmental experience and social learning.

A major theme of this book is that personality pathology develops as a result of an intimate interplay of intraorganismic and environmental forces; such interactions begin at conception and continue throughout life. Individuals with similar biological potentials emerge with different personality patterns depending on their environmental experiences. These patterns unfold as new maturations interweave with new environmental encounters. In time, learned attitudes and behaviors stabilize into a distinctive hierarchy of traits that remain relatively consistent through the ever-changing stream of experience.

A number of ways in which biological factors can shape, facilitate, or limit the nature of experience and learning were noted previously. For example, the same objective events will be perceived as different by individuals possessing different biological sensibilities; people register the same stimuli at varying intensities in accord with their unique patterns of alertness and acuity. Not only is experience itself shaped by the biological equipment of the person, but these built-in dispositions will influence the probability that certain forms of behavior will be learned. Thus, body morphology, strength, energy, and autonomic ractivity will not only influence how stimuli are perceived and felt but will determine, in large measure, which behaviors the person is likely to find are successful in dealing with these experiences.

It should be noted further that the interaction between biological and psychological factors is not unidirectional such that biological determinants always precede and influence the course of learning; the order of effects may be reversed, especially in early development. Biological maturation is dependent on favorable environmental experience, and the development of the biological substrate itself can be disrupted, even totally arrested, by depriving the maturing organism of stimulation at sensitive periods of neurological growth. Nevertheless, there is an intrinsic continuity throughout life. The author contends that childhood events are more significant to personality formation than later events, and that later behaviors are related in a determinant way to early experience. Despite an occasional disjunctiveness in development, there is an orderly and sequential continuity, fostered by mechanisms of self-perpetuation and social reinforcement, which links the past to the present. The characteristics of early development that create the foundations of lifelong continuity are discussed next.

Maturational Plasticity

Deeply embedded behavior patterns may arise as a consequence of psychological experiences that affect developing biological structures so profoundly as to transform them into something substantially different from what they might otherwise have been. Circumstances that exert so profound an effect are usually those experienced during infancy and early childhood, a view that can be traced to the seminal writings of Freud at the turn of the century. The observations of ethologists on the consequences of early stimulation upon adult animal behaviors add substantial evidence for this position. Experimental work on early developmental periods also has shown that environmental stimulation is crucial to the maturation of psychological functions. In essence, psychological capacities fail to develop fully if their biological substrates are subjected to impoverished stimulation; conversely, these capacities may develop to an excessive degree as a consequence of enriched stimulation.

Maturation refers to the intricate sequence of ontogenetic development in which initially inchoate bodily structures progressively unfold into specific functional units. Early stages of differentiation precede and overlap with more advanced states such that simpler and more diffuse structures interweave and connect into a complex and integrated network of functions displayed ultimately in the adult organism. It was once believed that the course of maturation—from diffusion to differentiation to integration—arose exclusively from inexorable forces within the genes. Maturation was thought to evolve according to a preset timetable that unfolded independently of environmental conditions. This view is no longer tenable. Maturation follows an orderly progression, but the developmental sequence and level of ultimate biological function are substantially dependent on environmental stimuli and nutritional supplies. Thus, maturation does not progress in a fixed course leading to a predetermined level but is subject to numerous variations that reflect the character of environmental experience.

The answer to why early experiences are more central to development than later experiences derives in part from the fact that peak periods of structural maturation occur from prenatal stages through the first years of postnatal life. An example may illustrate this point well. In the nervous system, prenatal deficiencies in nutrition will retard the differentiation of gross tissue into separable neural cells; early postnatal deficiencies will deter the proliferation of neural collaterals and their integration. However, deficiences arising later in life will have but little effect on the development of these neural structures.

Stimulus Nutriment

Nutrition should be viewed more broadly than is commonly done in order to understand biological maturation. Nutrition includes not only obvious components, such as food, but additionally what Rapaport has termed "stimulus nutriment" (1958). This concept suggests that the impingement of environmental stimuli upon the maturing organism has a direct bearing on the chemical composition, ultimate size, and patterns of neural branching within the brain.

The belief that the maturing organism requires periodic stimulus nutriments for proper development has led some to suggest that the organism actively seeks an optimum level of stimulation. Thus, just as the infant cries out in search of food when deprived or wails in response to pain, so too may it engage in behaviors that provide it with sensory stimulation requisite to maturation. Although infants are restricted largely to stimulation supplied by others, they often engage in what appear to be random exercises that, in effect, furnish them with the stimulation they require. In the first months of life, infants can be seen to track auditory and visual stimuli; as they mature further, they grasp incidental objects and then mouth and fondle them. Furthermore, the young of all species display more exploratory and frolicsome behavior than adults. These seemingly "functionless" play activities are not functionless at all; they may be essential to growth, a means of self-stimulation indispensable to the maturation and maintenance of biological capacities.

It may be deduced from the foregoing that unless certain chemicals and structures are activated by environmental stimulation, the biological substrate for a variety of psychological functions may be impaired irrevocably. Furthermore, deficiencies in functions that normally mature in early life may set the stage for a progressive retardation of later functions.

What evidence is there that serious consequences may result from an inadequate supply of early stimulation?

Numerous investigators have shown that impoverished early environment results in permanent adaptational difficulties. For example, primates reared in isolation tend to be deficient in traits such as emotionality, activity level, social behavior, curiosity, and learning ability. As adult organisms they possess a reduced capacity to cope with their environments, to discriminate essentials, to devise strategies and manage stress. Comparable results are found among humans. Children reared under unusually severe restrictions, such as in orphanages, evidence deficits in social awareness and reactivity, are impulsive and susceptible to sensorimotor dysfunctions, and display a generally low resistance to stress and disease. These early difficulties have double-barreled effects. Not only is the child hampered by specific deficiencies, but each of them yields to progressive and long-range consequences in that they retard the development of more complex capacities.

Intense levels of early stimulation also appear to have effects. Several investigators have demonstrated that enriched environments in early life resulted in measurable changes in brain chemistry and brain weight. Others have found that early stimulation accelerated the maturation of the pituitary-adrenal system, whereas equivalent later stimulation was ineffective. On the behavioral level, enriched environments in animals enhance problem-solving abilities and the capacity to withstand stress; comparable data among humans, however, are equivocal.

There has been little research on the potential detrimental effects of environmental enrichment, since clinicians are inclined to assume that impoverishment, not enrichment, is more conducive to pathological consequences. This assumption is probably correct, but the possibility should not be overlooked that excess stimulation may result in overdevelopments in biological substrates that are disruptive to effective psychological functioning. For example, just as excess food leads to obesity and physical ill health, so too may stimulus enrichment of certain neural substrates, such as those subserving emotional reactivity, dispose the organism to overreact to social situations. The predominance of certain biological response tendencies may throw off what might otherwise be a more balanced pattern of functioning. Whether enhanced psychological processes prove advantageous or disadvantageous depends on which capacities have been enriched, and whether the resultant overall pattern of functions is balanced or unbalanced.

NEUROPSYCHOLOGICAL STAGES

The previous discussion was limited to the effects of the magnitude of early stimulation. Attention here turns from the issue of "how much" to that of "when." This section explores the question of whether the specific maturational period of stimulation has any bearing on its effect. The concept of sensitive periods of development states that there are limited time periods during which particular stimuli are necessary for the full maturation of an organism, and that if these stimuli are experienced either before or after those periods, they will have minimal or no effects. Without proper stimulus nourishment at these periods, the organism will suffer various maldevelopments which are irremediable and cannot be compensated for by the presentation of stimuli at a later date.

Embryological research suggests that the effects of environmental stimuli upon morphological structure are most pronounced when tissue growth is rapid. It is unclear at present as to the mechanisms that account for the special interaction between stimulation and periods of rapid neural growth. Stimulation itself promotes a proliferation of neural collaterals, and this effect is most pronounced when growth potential is greatest. Also, early stimulation creates selective growth so that certain collaterals establish particular interneuronal connections to the exclusion of others. Once these connections are biologically embedded, the first set of stimuli that traverse them appear to preempt the circuit and thereby decrease the chance that subsequent stimuli will have comparable effects. Whatever the mechanisms may be, research supports the view that stimulation effects are maximal at periods of rapid tissue growth.

Numerous developmental theorists have proposed, either by intention or inadvertently, schemas based on a concept of sensitive periods. Among these are Heinz Werner (1940), Jean Piaget (1952, 1956), and, of course, both Sigmund Freud and Erik Erikson. Despite the brilliance of their formulations, none has presented their notions in terms of *neurological growth* stages.

As noted earlier, the logic for a concept of sensitive periods rests on evidence that environmental stimuli have their most pronounced effects at times of rapid neural growth. It would seem reasonable, therefore, to construct a developmental model in line with periods of neurological maturation rather than psychosexual stages or cognitive functions. Cast in this fashion, it will have a firm basis as a theory of sensitive developmental phases and will be formulated in terms that are consonant with our growing knowledge of the neurological substrate of psychological maturation. A model of this nature (Millon, 1969) is briefly summarized in the following paragraphs.

A number of qualifications should be noted before describing the features of the model. First, it would be erroneous to assume that children of the same chronological age are comparable in the level and character of their biological capacities. Second, not only does each infant start life with distinctive neurological, physiochemical, and sensory equipment, but the child progresses at his or her own maturational rate toward some ultimate but unknown level of potential. Thus, beyond initial differences and their not insignificant consequences are differences in the rate with which maturation unfolds. Different systems within a single child may mature at different rates. Third, the potential level of development of each of these neurological substrates will vary widely, not only among children but within each child. Thus, a youngster may be constitutionally disposed to mature a sparse substrate for sensory functions and a dense and well-balanced one for integrative functions.

A brief rationale of the neuropsychological-stage model and its relation to personality development may be useful before describing its separate periods and their consequences.

The capacities of each organism are established by genetic factors. The sequence in which these capacities unfold follows a general species-specific order. However, the rate and level to which these capacities mature are determined in large measure by the amount of stimulation experienced at certain peak periods of neural growth. During growth, the organism utilizes its established capacities to provide itself with the stimulus nutriment required for further development. Failure in stimulus nourishment leads to an undermaturation or retarded progression in development; overstimulation may lead to an overmaturing or unbalanced development. When the optimal sensitive period of neural growth has passed, further development is slow and difficult to accomplish. For all essential purposes, the organism's neuropsychological capacity has begun to reach its likely upper limits.

The characteristics and consequences of the three stages of neuropsychological development are discussed next.

Stage 1: Sensory-Attachment

The first year of life is dominated by *sensory* processes, functions basic to subsequent development in that they enable the infant to construct some order out of the initial diffusion experienced in the stimulus world. This period has also been termed that of *attachment* because infants cannot survive on their own and must "fasten" themselves to others who will protect, nurture, and stimulate them.

Sensory capacities.   The early neonatal period is characterized as one of undifferentiation in which the organism behaves in a diffuse and unintegrated way, and perceptions are unfocused and gross. Although Freud recognized that the mouth region is a richly endowed receptor system through which neonates establish their first significant relationship to the stimulus world, it is clear that this oral unit is merely the focal point of a more diverse system of sensory capacities. Through oral and other tactile contacts the infant establishes a sense, or "feel," of the environment.

According to neuropsychological theory, it would be expected that the amount and quality of tactile stimulation to which the neonate is exposed will contribute significantly to the infant's development. Not only may different levels of stimulation result in sensory precocities or retardations, but the quality and pattern of this stimulation may lead the infant to experience diffuse feelings that are as diverse as isolation, tension, or pleasure.

Attachment behaviors.   The neonate cannot differentiate between objects and persons; both are experienced simply as stimuli. How does this initial indiscriminateness become progressively refined into specific attachments? For all essential purposes, the infant is helpless and dependent on others to supply its needs. Separated from the womb, the neonate has lost its physical attachment to the mother's body and the nurturance it provided. It must turn toward other regions or sources of attachment if it is to survive and obtain nourishment and stimulation for further development. Attachment behaviors may be viewed, albeit figuratively, as an attempt to reestablish the intimate unity lost at birth. Since it will be years before the child can furnish its own needs, it must learn to identify which objects in its environment provide nourishment and stimulation.

Impoverishment.   A wealth of clinical evidence is available showing that humans deprived of adequate maternal care in infancy display a variety of pathological behaviors. We cannot, of course, design studies to disentangle precisely which of the complex of variables that compromise maternal care account for these irreparable consequences; the lives of babies cannot be manipulated to meet our scientific needs. It is here that the value of animal research is clear since we can arrange conditions for a reasonably precise analysis of the problem.

Extensive reviews of the consequences in animals of early stimulus impoverishment show that sensory neural fibers atrophy and cannot be regenerated by subsequent stimulation. Almost any means of stimulation (e.g., stroking, tossing, shaking, or shocking) provides the requisite activation for neural development. Inadequate stimulation in any major receptor function usually results in decrements in the capacity to utilize these sensory processes in later life. The profound effects of social isolation have been studied thoroughly and show that deprived monkeys are incapable at maturity of relating to peers, of participating effectively in sexual activity, and of assuming adequate roles as mothers.

Little has been researched concerning the potential effects of moderate levels of early sensory impoverishment. It should be noted that degree of sensory impoverishment is a gradient or continuum, not an all-or-none effect. There is every reason to believe that children who receive less than an optimum degree of sensory stimulation will be likely to grow up less "sensory oriented" and less "socially attached" than those who have experienced more. Such variations are especially relevant to the study of personality disorders where symptoms are matters of degree.

Enrichment. Data on the consequences of too much, or enriched, early sensory stimulation are few and far between; researchers have concerned themselves with the effects of deficit rather than excess stimulation.

It would not be unreasonable to hypothesize, however, that excess stimulation during the stage of sensory-attachment would result in over-developments among associated neural structures; these may lead to receptor oversensitivities that, in turn, may result in a potentially maladaptive dominance of sensory functions. It was along this line that Freud hypothesized that excess indulgence at the oral stage was conducive to fixations at that period. Eschewing both oral and fixation notions, the author proposes that excess sensory development in childhood would require a high level of stimulus maintenance in adulthood, as seen in persistent sensory-seeking behaviors. These individuals might be characterized by their repetitive search for excitement and stimulation, their boredom with routine, and their capricious involvement in incidental and momentary adventures. Exactly what neural or chemical mechanisms undergird this stimulus-seeking pattern is a matter for speculation. Whatever the mechanisms may be, it appears plausible both neurologically and clinically that overenriched early stimulation can result in pathological stimulus-seeking behavior.

Turning to attachment behavior, it seems reasonable to assume that excess stimulation, especially if anchored exclusively to the mother, would result in an overattachment to her. This consequence is demonstrated most clearly in the symbiotic child, where there is an abnormal clinging to the mother and a persistent resistance to stimulation from other sources. Feelings of isolation and panic often overtake these children, such as when they are sent to nursery school or "replaced" by a newborn sibling.

Stage 2: Sensorimotor-Autonomy

It is not until the end of the first year that infants have sufficiently matured to engage in actions independent of parental support. Holding the drinking cup, the first few steps, or a word or two, all signify a growing capacity to act autonomously. As the child develops the functions that characterize this stage, he or she begins to comprehend the attitudes and feelings communicated by stimulative sources. No longer is rough parental handling merely excess stimulation, undistinguished from the playful tossing of an affectionate father; the child now discerns the difference between harshness and good-natured roughhousing.

Sensorimotor capacities. The unorganized movements of the neonate progressively give way to focused muscular activity. As the neural substrate for muscular control unfolds, the aimless motor behavior of the infant is supplanted by focused movements. These newly emergent functions co-ordinate with sensory capacities to enable the child to explore, manipulate, play, sit, crawl, babble, throw, walk, catch, and talk. The maturing fusion between the substrates of sensory and motor functions is strengthened by the child's exploratory behavior. Manipulative play and the formation of babbling sounds are methods of self-stimulation that facilitate the growth of interneuronal connections; the child is building a neural foundation for more complicated and refined skills such as running, handling utensils, con-trolling sphincter muscles, and articulating precise speech. Children's intrinsic tendency to "entertain" themselves is a necessary step in establishing capacities that are more substantial than maturation alone would have furnished. Stimulative experiences, either self-provided or through the actions of others, are requisites for the development of normal sensorimotor skills. Unless retarded by environmental restrictions or biological handicaps, toddlers' growing sensorimotor capacities prepare them to cope with the environment with increasing competence and autonomy.

Autonomous behaviors. Perhaps the most significant aspect of sensori-motor development is that it enables children to begin to do things for themselves, to influence their environment, to free themselves from domina-tion, and to outgrow the dependencies of their first years. Children become aware of their increasing competence and seek new ventures. Needless to say, conflicts and restrictions arise as they assert themselves. These are seen clearly during toilet training, when youngsters often resist submitting to the demands of their parents. A delicate exchange of power and cunning often ensues. Opportunities arise for the child to extract promises or deny wishes; in response, parents may mete out punishments, submit meekly, or shift inconsistently. Important precedents for attitudes toward authority, power and autonomy are generated during this period of parent-child interaction.

Impoverishment. A lack of stimulation of sensorimotor capacities can lead to retardations in functions necessary to the development of autonomy and initiative. This is seen most clearly in children of overprotective parents. Spoon-fed, excused from "chores," restrained from exploration, curtailed in friendships, and protected from "danger"—all illustrate controls that restrict growing children's opportunities to exercise their sensorimotor skills and develop the means for autonomous behavior. A self-perpetuating cycle often unfolds. These children may fear abandoning their overlearned dependency upon their parents since they are ill-equipped to meet other children on the latter's terms. They may become timid and submissive when forced to venture out into the world, likely to avoid the give and take of competition with their peers, and they may seek out older children who will protect them and upon whom they can lean.

Enrichment. The consequences of excessive enrichment during the sensorimotor-autonomy stage are found most often in children of lax, permissive, or overindulgent parents. Given free rein with minimal restraint and stimulated to explore and manipulate things to their suiting without guidance or control, these children will soon become irresponsibly undisciplined in their behaviors. Carried into the wider environment, however, these behaviors run up against the desires of other children and the restrictions of less permissive adults. Unless the youngsters are extremely adept, they will find that their self-centered and free-wheeling tactics fail miserably. For the few who succeed, however, a pattern of egocentrism, unbridled self-expression, and social arrogance may become dominant. The majority of these youngsters fail to gain acceptance by peers and never quite acquire the give-and-take skills of normal social relationships.

Stage 3: Intracortical-Initiative

The peak period of neurological maturation for certain psychological functions generally occurs between the ages of 4 and 18, and the total amount of environmental stimulation at these times of rapid growth will have a strong bearing on the degree to which these functions mature. What are the capacities which unfold during this stage, and what consequences can be attributed to differences in the magnitude of relevant stimulus experience?

Intracortical capacities. Progressively more complex arrangements of neural cells become possible as children advance in maturation. Although these higher-order connections begin in early infancy, they do not form into structures capable of rational foresight and planning until the youngsters have fully developed their more basic sensorimotor skills. With these capacities as a base, they are able to differentiate and arrange the objects of the physical world. As verbal skills unfold, they learn to symbolize concrete objects; soon they are able to manipulate and coordinate these symbols as well as, if not better than, the tangible events themselves. Free of the need to make direct reference to the concrete world, they are able to recall past events and anticipate future ones. As increasingly complex cortical connections are established, higher conceptual abstractions are formulated, enabling the children to transfer, associate, and coordinate these symbols into ideas of finer differentiation, greater intricacy, and broader integration. It is their own internal representations of reality, their own symbolic thought, and their own construction of events—past, present, and future—that take over as the primary elements of the stimulus world.

Somewhere between the eleventh and fifteenth years a rather sweeping series of hormonal changes unsettle the level of intracortical integration so carefully constructed in preceding years. These changes reflect the onset of puberty—the emergence of strong sexual impulses and adultlike features of anatomy, voice, and bearing. Erratic moods, changing self-images, new urges, hopeful expectancies, and a growing physical and social awkwardness, all upset the relative equanimity of an earlier age. Disruptive as it may be, this turbulent stage of growth activates and ties together the remaining elements of the youngster's biological potential; it is a preparatory phase for the forthcoming independence from parental direction.

Initiative behaviors. When the inner world of symbols is mastered, giving objective reality an order and integration, youngsters are able to create some consistency and continuity in their lives. No longer are they buffeted from one mood or action to another by the swirl of changing events; they now have an internal anchor, a nucleus of cognitions that serves as a base and imposes a sameness upon an otherwise fluid environment. As they grow in their capacity to organize and integrate their world, one configuration predominates. Accrued from experiences with others and their reactions to the child, an image of self-as-object takes shape. This highest order of abstraction, the sense of individual identity, becomes the dominant source of stimuli that guides the child's style of behavior. External events no longer have the power they once exerted; the youngster now has an ever-present and stable sphere of internal stimuli that governs his/her course of action and from which events are initiated.

Impoverishment. The task of integration is not an easy one in a world of changing events and values. From what source can a consistent sense of self be consolidated?

The fabric of society is designed to inculcate the young. Family, school, and church set implicit values and explicit rules by which the child is guided in behaving and thinking in a manner consonant with those of others. The youngster not only is subject to cultural pressures but requires them to give direction to his/her proliferating capacities and impulses. Without them, potentials may become overly diffuse and scattered; conversely, too much guidance may narrow the child's potentials and restrict their flexibility and adaptiveness. Once basic patterns of thought are shaped during this period, it is difficult to orient them along new pathways.

What are the effects of inadequate or erratic stimulation during the peak years of intracortical integration? Without direct tuition from elders, youngsters are left to their own devices to master the complexities of a varied world, to control intense urges, to channel fantasies, and to pursue the goals to which they aspire. They may become victims of their own growth, unable to orient their impulses or fashion acceptable means for expressing their desires. Scattered and unguided, they may be unable to construct a sense of personal identity, a consistent direction and purpose to their existence. They may vacillate at every turn, overly responsive to fleeting stimuli, shifting from one erratic course to another. Without an inner core or anchor to guide their future, they may flounder or stagnate.

Evidently, the impoverishment of integrative stimuli will have a profound effect. Fortunately, there is an abundance of untapped cortical cells in the adult brain; thus, the "immaturity and irresponsibility" of many adolescents may be salvaged in later years. But for others, the inability to settle down into a consolidated path may become a problem of increasingly severe proportions.

Enrichment.   The negative consequences of overenrichment at the third stage usually occur when parents have been excessively controlling and perfectionistic. Overly trained, overly disciplined, and overly integrated youngsters are given little opportunity to create their own destiny. Whether by coercion or enticement, children who are led too early to control their feelings, to focus their thoughts along defined paths, and to follow the prescriptions of parental demands, have been subverted into adopting the identities of others. Whatever individuality they may have acquired is drowned in adult orderliness, propriety, and virtue. Such oversocialized youngsters lack the spontaneity, flexibility, and creativeness we expect of the young; they have been trained to be too narrow in perspective to respond to the excitement, variety, and challenge of new events. Overenrichment at this stage has set them on a restrictive course and has deprived them of the opportunity to become themselves.

It would be an error to leave this discussion of neuropsychological development with the impression that personality growth is merely a function of stimulation at sensitive maturational periods. Impoverishment and enrichment have their profound effects, but the quality or kind of stimulation the youngster experiences is often of greater importance. The impact of parental harshness or inconsistency, of sibling rivalry or social failure, is more than a matter of stimulus volume and timing. Different dimensions of experience take precedence as the meaning conveyed by the source of stimulation becomes clear to the growing child. This facet of psychogenesis is considered next.

SIGNIFICANT LEARNINGS

Normal psychological processes depend on a substrate of orderly neuronal connections. The development of this intricate neural substrate unfolds within the organism in accord with genetically determined mechanisms, but there remain substantial numbers of fibers whose direction of growth is modifiable. To summarize the previous section, it might be said that the basic architecture of the nervous system is laid down in a relatively fixed manner, but refinements in this linkage system do not develop without the aid of stimulative experiences. Environmental experience not only activates neural collaterals but alters these structures so as to preempt them for similar subsequent experiences. Thus, early experiences not only construct new neural pathways but, in addition, selectively prepare them to be receptive to later stimuli that are qualitatively similar.

This second consequence of stimulus experience, representing the selective lowering of thresholds for the transmission of similar subsequent stimuli, is described in the conceptual language of psychology as *learning*. It reflects the observation that behaviors that have been subject to prior experience are reactivated with increasing ease. With this second consequence of stimulation, we begin to conceive the nervous system as more than a network of abstract pathways; it is now viewed as possessing the residues of specific classes of environmental stimuli. These environmentally anchored neural connections interweave to form patterns of perception and behavior that relate to discriminable events in the external world. By including qualitatively discriminable features of the stimulus world within our purview, we shift our attention to observational units that transcend neural mechanisms located strictly within the anatomical limits of the body. It is necessary to represent these complex external-internal relationships in a conceptual language that is broader in scope than that of neurology. Since learning concepts are formulated in terms of behavior-environment interactions, it would appear reasonable, when including the properties of qualitatively discriminable stimulus events, to utilize the conceptual language of learning.

Learning Concepts

Principles derived from learning research describe features of psychological behavior that cannot begin to be handled in neurological terms. It should be noted, however, that learning concepts and neurological concepts do not represent intrinsically different processes; the former are used here because they have been more finely and relevantly differentiated as tools for formulating qualitatively different stimulus-behavior interactions.

Contiguity learning.   The simplest method of acquiring new perceptions and behaviors is known as contiguity learning. It represents the observation that any set of stimuli and behaviors that occurs either simultaneously or in close temporal order are likely to become associated with each other. If one element in the set recurs in the future, other elements with which it had been associated are likely to be anticipated or elicited.

Instrumental learning.   People learn to discriminate between stimuli that portend pain and those that promise pleasure. In time, they learn to engage intentionally in acts that are reinforcing, that is, avoid pain or produce pleasure. They anticipate and actively manipulate the environment once they have learned that reinforcements are contingent on performing certain prior acts. The process of acquiring these manipulative behaviors is known as instrumental learning or, as Skinner (1953) has termed it, "operant conditioning." Either through direct tuition or chance events individuals learn which acts ultimately lead to the desired result of obtaining a positive reinforcement or escaping a noxious one. When these instrumental acts prove consistently effective in a wide variety of situations they begin to take the form of an ingrained and broadly generalized behavior pattern. These learned patterns of instrumental behavior gradually develop into what are termed "strategies"—that is, complex series of manipulative acts employed in relation to events or people that enable the individual to avoid difficulties and provide gratification.

Vicarious learning. Patterns of behavior are extraordinarily complex. For each child to learn the intricacies of civilized behavior by trial-and-error reinforcement methods alone would be no more possible than it would be for a primitive culture to advance, in one generation, to a full-fledged industrial society. Rather than struggling to acquire each of the many components of human behavior piece by piece, children adopt whole sequences of behaviors and attitudes provided through the incidental actions and formal precepts espoused by members of their social group. These complex patterns are acquired in toto merely by observing, vicariously learning, and then imitating what others do and think; it is an efficient and necessary means by which children become "civilized" in an amazingly short period of time. Vicarious learning may be acquired quite incidentally by simple contiguity (e.g., being exposed to social belief systems or observing exemplary forms of behavior) or by complex instrumental strategies (e.g., adopting patterns of behavior manifested by parents as a means of obtaining their approval).

Implicit learning. Much of what is learned occurs implicitly, that is, without being manifest in overt responses or being a direct consequence of external environmental effects. "Thinking" organisms are capable of arranging the memories of learned experience into new patterns of association. Furthermore, ideational processes enable individuals to engage in the self-reinforcements of imaginative fantasy. As children develop a symbolic repertoire of words and images, they are no longer dependent on fortuitous or laboriously attained reinforcements of "real" experience to form new learnings. By manipulating their storehouse of symbols and images, they can create new associations among objectively unconnected events; they can reinforce themselves by fantasy; they can make future plans by anticipating novel sequences and can concoct new strategies for dealing with their environment. By modeling their internal symbolic world, then, they supplement objective events with thoughts that lead them to new learnings and to self-administered reinforcements.

Learning Interpersonal and Self-Attitudes

Experience is likely to have a more profound effect at certain stages in the developmental sequence than at others. This statement reiterates a conviction stated earlier that pronounced environmental influences occur at periods of rapid neurological growth. A further reason for the stage-specific significance of experience is the observation that children are exposed to a succession of social tasks that they are expected to fulfill at different points in the developmental sequence. These stage-specific tasks are timed to coincide with periods of rapid neurological growth (e.g., the training of bladder control is begun when the child possesses the requisite neural equipment for such control; similarly, children are taught to read when intracortical development has advanced sufficiently to enable a measure of consistent success). In short, a reciprocity appears between periods of rapid neurological growth and exposure to related experiences and tasks. To use Erikson's (1950) terms, the child's newly emerging neurological potentials are challenged by a series of "crises" with the environment. Children are especially vulnerable at these critical stages since experience both shapes their neurological patterns and results in learning a series of fundamental attitudes about themselves and others.

What experiences typically arise at the three neuropsychological stages described earlier, and what are the central attitudes learned during these periods?

In seeking answers to these questions, this discussion turns to the fertile ideas of Freud and Erikson. Briefly, during the sensory-attachment stage, the critical attitude learned deals with one's "trust of others," the sensorimotor-autonomy stage is noted by learning attitudes concerning "self-competence," and the intracortical-initiative stage is characterized by the acquisition of a "personal identity." A brief elaboration of these is in order.

Stage 1: Learning trust of others.   Trust may be described as a feeling that one can rely on the affections and support of others. There are few periods of life when an individual is so wholly dependent on the goodwill and care of others than during the helpless state of infancy. Nothing is more crucial to the infant's well-being than the nurture and protection afforded by his/her caretakers. It is through the quality and consistency of this support that deeply ingrained feelings of trust are etched within the child.

Needless to say, the young infant makes only the grossest of discriminations at this period. In part, it is a result of this perceptual indiscriminateness that what is learned is so very significant. Thus, feelings and expectancies arising from specific experiences become highly generalized and come to characterize the child's image of the entire environment. It is because children are unable to make fine discriminations that early learning become pervasive and widespread. Nurtured well and given comfort and affection, they will acquire a far-reaching trust of others; they learn that discomfort will be moderated and that others will assist them and provide for their needs. Deprived of warmth and security or handled severely and painfully, they will learn to mistrust their environment, to anticipate further stress, and view others as harsh and undependable. Rather than developing an optimistic and confident attitude toward the future, they will be disposed to withdraw and avoid people for fear that these persons will recreate the discomfort and anguish that were experienced in the past.

Stage 2: Learning self-competence. Children become progressively less dependent on their caretakers during the sensorimotor-autonomy stage. By the second and third years they are ambulatory and possess the power of speech and control over many elements in their environment. They have acquired the manipulative skills to venture forth and test their competence to handle events on their own.

Subtle, as well as obvious, parental attitudes shape children's confidence in their competencies. These attitudes markedly influence behavior since it is not only what the children can do that determines their actions but how they feel about what they can do. The rewards and punishments to which they are exposed and the degree of encouragement and affection surrounding their first performances will contribute to their confidence in themselves. Severe discipline for transgressions, humiliating comments in response to efforts at self-achievement, embarrassment over social awkwardness, deprecations associated with poor school performance, and shame among one's peers as a result of physical inadequacies, all weigh heavily to diminish self-esteem. Faced with rebuffs and ridicule, children learn to doubt their competence and adequacy. Whether they actually possess the skills to handle events is no longer the issue; they simply lack the confidence to try, to venture out or to compete.

Stage 3: Learning personal-identity. The emergence of the intracortical-initiative stage—with its capacities for thinking, evaluating, and planning—leads children to formulate a distinct image of themselves as a certain "kind of person," an identity discernible from others, one capable of having independent judgments and of fashioning their own course of action. Healthy children must acquire a coherent system of internalized values that will guide them through a changing and varied environment. They must find their own anchor and compass by which to keep to a steady and independent course through life. Equipped by successful efforts toward autonomy, they will have confidence that they possess a direction in life that is valued by others and one that can safely withstand the buffeting of changing events. Deprived of rewarded achievements and unable to construct a picture of a valued identity, they will lack the means to meet life's tasks and challenges and be unable to handle discouraging and divisive forces that may arise. Without an integrated and coherent sense of self, of "who I am" and "where I am going," the growing adolescent or adult will flounder from one tentative course to another and be beset with amorphous and vague feelings of discontent and uselessness.

Learning Coping Strategies

Children learn complicated attitudes, reactions, and expectancies in response to life experiences. Initially, these responses tend to be specific to the events that prompted them. However, over the course of time, children form a pattern of stable instrumental strategies for coping with everyday events. These coping strategies come to characterize the individual child's way of relating to others and comprise a major facet of his/her personality pattern. Usually arrived at after years of groping through trial and error learning, these resources are not routine or mechanical reactions to the environment. Rather, healthy children display a flexibility in their coping maneuvers, deploying only those behaviors suited to the particulars of each situation. When feasible, a direct, task-oriented solution to problems will be attempted. Once having made a conscious appraisal of reality, children will initiate actions that they have learned previously are successful in comparable situations. Should these learned strategies prove inadequate, a child may innovate, devising novel approaches until one seems adequate to the task. Along with more rational and task-oriented behaviors, the child may come to employ any of a number of intrapsychic processes. These essentially unconscious mechanisms ameliorate the discomforts experienced when children are unable to resolve their problems directly. Any of the classical defense mechanisms—repression, sublimation, rationalization—will serve to relieve the anguish; they are useful also in that they enable the person to maintain equilibrium until a better solution can be mustered. Healthy coping may be characterized, then, both by retreat and self-deception if the objective conditions of the environment prevent a direct solution to a problem. Only when the person persistently distorts and denies the objective world do these unconscious mechanisms interfere with effective functioning.

When routine conscious and unconscious strategies fail repeatedly in dealing with life events, children will resort to more circuitous devices and to more distorting and denying mechanisms. If these secondary maneuvers restore balance, the children will have a respite, an opportunity to reequip themselves with behaviors that may be more adequate than those employed in the past. But if the threat faced is too severe, or too persistent and unremitting, the children dare not divert their attentions and let down their guard. Exposed to repeated threats and frustrations, they may learn to expect that problems never subside and that they must always be prepared to avoid problems or react to them before they recur. Even when no objective discomfort exists, these children must be ready to forestall what they expect. As they begin to "cope" with nonexistent (but anticipated) events, their behavior becomes inflexible. Their acquired coping strategy is no longer adaptive; it has become an indiscriminate and autonomously acting behavior pattern. Designed initially to protect against recurrences of the painful past, it now distracts and misguides the children. The importance of self-perpetuation as an element in psychogenesis is elaborated in a later section.

In Chapter 2, as well as in previous publications (Millon, 1969; Millon and Millon, 1974), a scheme is proposed in which these persistent, yet defective, strategies are derived in terms of the types of reinforcements (positive/pleasure versus negative/pain) an individual has learned to seek, the sources (self versus others) the person has learned provide these reinforcements, and the instrumental behaviors (passive versus active) the person has learned to employ to achieve them. Describing pathological coping strategies in these terms casts them in a language that may help point more clearly to their basic features. By constructing a theoretical model in terms of *what* reinforcements the individual is seeking, *where* the individual is looking to find them, and *how* the individual performs in order to obtain them, we may see more simply and sharply the essential strategies that guide coping behaviors. As noted in Chapter 2, these three polarities correspond closely to those formulated by early twentieth-century theorists who sought the "raw materials" from which personality classifications might best be composed.

Using the elements of this threefold polarity results in a four-by-two arrangement that combines dependent, independent, ambivalent, and detached reinforcement styles with the activity-passivity dimension, and leads to eight basic personality types characterized by their learned coping strategies. They are briefly described in the following paragraphs.

1. *Passive-dependent strategy (submissive personality)*: These individuals have learned not only to depend on others for reinforcements but to await the other's leadership in providing them. They tend to be unambitious, helpless, and clinging; display little autonomy or initiative; and seem content to sit by compliantly and put their fate in the hands of others.

2. *Active-dependent strategy (gregarious personality)*: These individuals use others as their primary source of reinforcement but engage busily in manipulative maneuvers to secure the attention and approval they seek. They are typically sociable, charming, demonstrative, affectionate, and clever, ever-ready to change their tune to attract praise or avoid hostility.

3. *Passive-independent strategy (narcissistic personality)*: These individuals experience their primary rewards simply by being themselves. They exhibit an egocentric self-assurance, an air of snobbish and pretentious superiority that they believe requires little confirmation through genuine accomplishments. Their confidence that things will work out well leaves them with little incentive to engage in the reciprocal give-and-take of social life.

4. *Active-independent strategy (aggressive personality)*: These persons counter the expectation of negative reinforcements by vigorous, assertive, and aggressive actions. Their resentment and envy of others leads them to become

self-reliant, domineering, and cunning—strategies designed to exploit and control others for their personal gain.

5. *Passive-ambivalent strategy (conforming personality)*: These individuals have been intimidated and coerced into accepting the values and desires of others. By a disciplined self-restraint they inhibit their own desires and deny their feelings; they learn to remain passive and to conform to the expectations of their environment in a prudent, controlled, and perfectionistic way.

6. *Active-ambivalent strategy (negativistic personality)*: These individuals struggle between following the demands and expectations of others as opposed to those desired by themselves. They get into endless wrangles because of their moodiness and erratic behaviors, tend to be restless and discontent, and to feel misunderstood and unappreciated.

7. *Passive-detached strategy (asocial personality)*: These persons lack the drive or capacity to experience either positive or negative reinforcements. They are typically apathetic, listless, unresponsive, distant, withdrawn, and asocial.

8. *Active-detached strategy (avoidant personality)*: These individuals are apprehensive, suspicious, and mistrustful. They experience few positive reinforcements or pleasures in life; they are vigilant, perennially on guard, and ever-ready to avoid actively their anxious anticipation of negatively reinforcing experiences.

As noted earlier, care must be taken to avoid being carried away by the oversimplifications of a classification scheme. What has been proposed in the Millon system is merely a tool, a way of thinking about the complicated and diverse patterns of coping behavior manifested by patients. The labels attached to patient behaviors are abstractions designed to facilitate clinicians' thinking and understanding; they should not lead to seeing more than the patient conveys or to oversimplification of what is. Labels are conceptual tools of limited utility and do not represent tangible or circumscribed "illnesses."

PATHOGENIC SOURCES OF LEARNING

Behavior and attitudes may be learned from explicit indoctrination, but most of what is learned stems from haphazard and casual events to which the child is incidentally exposed. Not only are rewards and punishments meted out most often in a spontaneous and erratic fashion, but the everyday and ordinary activities of parents provide the child with unintended models to imitate.

Without awareness or intention, parents suggest through incidental behaviors how "people" think, talk, fear, love, solve problems and relate to others. Aversons, irritabilities, anxieties, and styles of relating and communicating are adopted by children as they observe the everyday actions of parents and older siblings. Children mirror complex behaviors without understanding their significance and without parental intentions to transmit them. Since many pathological patterns have their beginnings in offhand behaviors and attitudes to which children are incidentally exposed, it is important to recognize that such learnings accrue less from intentional training than from adventitious experience.

Pathogenic learnings arise essentially from three sources. *First,* there are events that create intense anxieties because they undermine feelings of security. When these events persist they elicit adaptive and self-protective reactions that (though successful in diminishing discomfort in the short run) may establish long-term coping styles and anticipations that ultimately intrude upon and undermine healthy functioning. *Second* are emotionally neutral conditions or models of behavior that *do not* activate protective or defensive behaviors, as do emotionally disruptive events. However, they do suggest and do reinforce styles of behavior that prove deleterious when exhibited or generalized to settings other than those for which they are suitable. The roots of these difficulties do not lie in anxious events or unconscious defense mechanisms but in the simple conditioning or imitation of maladaptive behaviors. The *third* source of pathogenicity reflects an insufficiency of experiences requisite to learning adaptive behaviors. Thus, stimulus impoverishment or minimal social experience may produce deficits in learned coping behaviors. The lack of skills and competencies for mastering the environment is a form of pathological *under*learning that may prove as severe as those generated by stress or defective models of behavior.

Feelings and Attitudes

Since the ebb and flow of life consists of many interwoven elements, we must keep in mind that the features we may separate for analysis represent only single facets of an ongoing and inextricable constellation of events.

An atmosphere, a way of handling the routine of life, a tone to ways of relating and communicating day in and day out, all come to characterize the family setting within which the child develops. In contrast to the occasional and scattered events of the outside environment, the circumstances of daily family life have cumulative effects upon the entire fabric of children's learning. Within this setting children establish feelings of security, imitate the way people relate interpersonally, acquire impressions of how others feel about them, develop a sense of self-worth, and learn to cope with the stresses of life.

The most pervasive and perhaps most important aspect of learned experience is the extent to which children develop a feeling of acceptance or rejection by parents. To be exposed throughout one's early life to parents who view one as unwanted or troublesome can establish only a deep and overriding feeling of isolation and worthlessness. Deprived of security at home, the child may be disinclined to venture forth to face struggles in the outer world. Rejected by parents, the child is likely to anticipate equal devaluation by others. As a defense against further pain, the child may learn to avoid others and utilize indifference as a protective cloak to minimize what is now expected from others. Different strategies may evolve, of course. Thus, some rejected children may imitate parental scorn and ridicule, and learn to handle their disturbed feelings by acting in a hostile and vindictive fashion.

Rejection is not the only parental attitude that can produce insidious damage. Attitudes such as seduction, exploitation, and deception contribute their share of damage as well. However, it is usually the sense of being unwanted and unloved that proves to have the most pervasive and destructive of effects. Children can usually tolerate considerable buffeting from their environment if they sense a basic feeling of love and support from their parents.

Behavior Control

Parents disposed to intimidate their offspring, using punitive or repressive measures of control, may set the stage for a variety of maladaptive patterns. If children submit and fulfill parental expectations, they are apt to become overly obedient and circumspect. These children not only learn to keep their impulses and contrary thoughts in check but, by observations and imitation, often adopt the parental model and become punitive themselves in response to the deviant behaviors of others. Should their youngsters fail to satisfy parental demands and be subject to continued harassment, they may develop a pervasive anxiety about personal relationships, leading to feeling discouraged and resulting in social avoidance and withdrawal. Others, faced with similar punitive experiences, may incorporate the pattern of parental harshness and develop hostile and aggressively rebellious behaviors. Which learned strategy evolves depends on the larger configuration of factors involved.

Some parents rarely are punitive but expect that certain behaviors will be performed *prior* to giving encouragement or reward. Positive reinforcement is contingent, therefore, upon approved performance. Youngsters reared under these conditions tend to be socially pleasant and affable but, quite often, seem to have an insatiable and indiscriminate need for social acceptance. Contingent reward methods appear to condition children to develop an excessive need for approval.

Other parental methods of control may be characteristically inconsistent, contradictory, and capricious. Some degree of variability is inevitable in every child's life, but there are parents who display an extreme inconsistency in their standards and expectations, and an extreme unpredictability in their application of rewards and punishments. Youngsters exposed to such chaotic or capricious treatment cannot learn consistently and cannot devise a nonconflictive style of adaptive behavior. To avoid the anxiety of unpredictable reactions, the child may become protectively noncommittal. Others, imitating what they have been exposed to, may come to be characterized by their own ambivalent tendency to vacillate from one action or feeling to another.

Some parents protectively narrow the experiences to which their children are exposed such that the youngsters fail to learn the rudiments of autonomous behaviors. Overprotective parents not only succeed in forestalling the growth of normal competencies but, indirectly, give children a feeling that they are inferior and frail. And, observing their actual inadequacies, the children have verification that they are, in fact, weak, inept, and dependent.

Overly indulgent, lax or undisciplined parents may allow children full rein to explore and assert their every whim. Moreover, by their own lack of discipline these parents provide a model to be imitated, which only further strengthens the child's tendency to be irresponsible. Unconstrained by parental control, these youngsters display inconsiderate and tyrannical characteristics, and are often exploitive, uncooperative, and antisocially aggressive. Unless rebuffed by external discipline, they frequently become difficult members of society.

Styles of Communication

The styles of interpersonal communication to which children are exposed serve as models for attending, organizing, and reacting to the expressions, thoughts, and feelings of others. Unless this framework of communication is rational and reciprocal, they will be ill-equipped to relate in an effective way with others. Thus, the very capacity which enables humans to symbolize their environment so successfully may lend itself to serious misdirections and confusions. Illogical ideas, irrational reactions, and irrelevant and bizarre verbalizations most often arise as a consequence of emotional stress, but the roots can also be traced to an early exposure to peculiar or disjointed styles of interpersonal communication.

The effects of amorphous, fragmented, or confusing communications have been explored by numerous investigators. Not only are messages attended to in certain families in a vague or erratic fashion, with a consequent disjunctiveness and loss of focus, but when they are attended to, they frequently convey equivocal or contradictory meanings. Exposed to such communications, the child's conception of reality may become deviant, if not precarious. To avoid these confusions, some children may learn to distort or deny conflicting signals, but in this defensive maneuver they may succumb even further to irrational thinking. Unable to interpret intentions and feelings correctly, they may fall prey to an increasing estrangement from others.

Content of Learnings

Parents transmit values and attitudes through either direct tuition or unintentional commentary. Through these explicit and implicit teachings the child learns to think about and react to events and people in particular ways. What teachings lend themselves to learning potentially pathological attitudes and behaviors?

The most insidious of these teachings is training in anxiety. Parents who fret over health, investigate every potential ailment, or are preoccupied with failures and the dismal turn of events, teach and furnish models for anxiety proneness in their children. Few attitudes transcend the pernicious effects of a chronically anxious and apprehensive household.

Guilt and shame are generated in the teachings of many homes. Failure to live up to parental expectations, a feeling that one has caused undue sacrifices, or that one has transgressed rules and embarrassed the family, illustrate events that undermine the individual's self-worth and produce marked feelings of shame and guilt. The sacrificing and guilt-laden atmosphere of such parental homes often provides a model for behavioral imitation. Admonished and reproached repeatedly for minor digressions, such children develop a deep and pervasive self-image of failure. To protect against feelings of self-condemnation, these youngsters may restrict their activities, deny themselves the normal joys and indulgences of life, and learn to control their impulses far beyond that required to eschew shame and guilt.

Other destructive attitudes can be taught directly through narrow parental outlooks. Particularly damaging are those associated with anger, affection, and sexual urges. Unrealistic standards which condemn these common behaviors and feelings create unnecessary fears and strong guilt feelings.

Family Structure

The formal composition of the childhood family unit often sets the stage for learning pathogenic attitudes and relationships. The lack of significant adult figures within the family often deprives children of the opportunity to acquire, through observation, many of the complex patterns of behavior required in adult life. The most serious deficit usually is the unavailability of the same-sex parental model. For example, the frequent absence of fathers in underprivileged homes, or the vocational preoccupations of fathers in well-to-do homes, may give rise to a lack among sons of a mature sense of masculine identity.

Children subject to persistent parental bickering are not only exposed to destructive models but are faced with a repeated upsetting influence. The stability of life necessary for acquiring a consistent pattern of behaving and thinking is shattered when strife and controversy prevail. Children frequently become scapegoats, subject to displaced parental hostilities, constantly dragged into the arena of parental strife or involved in competitions and coalitions that determine who receives affection and who receives antagonism.

Sibling relationships often are overlooked as a major element in shaping the pattern of peer and other intimate "competitions." When disproportionate affections are allocated to one child, seeds of discontent and rivalry flourish. Since hostility fails to eliminate the competitor and gains, not the sought-for attention, but parental disapproval, the aggrieved child often reverts to maneuvers such as pouting, illness, or depression. If these methods succeed in gaining parental love, the youngster will have been reinforced to continue these ultimately troublesome techniques. More often than not, however, efforts to alter parental preferences succeed only partially, and the child continues both to display these partially successful maneuvers and still experience deep resentment and insecurity. Such persons often acquire a distrust of affections, fearing that those who express them will prove to be as fickle as their parents.

Traumatic Experiences

Popular psychology has it that most forms of psychopathology can be traced to a single, very severe experience, the residues of which account for the manifest disorder. Freud's early writings gave impetus to this notion, but he reversed himself when he was made aware that patient reports of trauma often were imaginative fabrications. Current thinking indicates that most pathological behaviors accrue gradually through repetitive learning experiences.

There are occasions, however, when a particularly painful event can shatter equanimity and leave deeply embedded attitudes that cannot be readily extinguished. The impact of these events may be especially severe with young children since they are usually ill-prepared for them and lack a perspective that might serve as a context for moderating their effects. If a traumatic event is the first exposure to a particular class of experiences, the feelings it evokes may intrude and color all subsequent events of that kind.

The consequences of traumatic events are likely to persevere for essentially two reasons. First, a high level of neural activation occurs in response to situations of marked distress. This suggests that many and diverse neural associations become connected to the event; the greater the level of neural involvement, the more ingrained and pervasive will be the learned reaction. Second, during heightened stress there is often a decrement in the ability to make clear distinctions among the elements of the environment. As a consequence, the traumatized individual is likely to generalize the emotional reaction to a variety of objects and persons only incidentally associated with the traumatic source. More is said in the next section about the difficulty in extinguishing such learned attitudes and feelings.

PERSISTENCE AND CONTINUITY OF EARLY LEARNINGS

This section concentrates on the notion of continuity in behavior since the author believes that the significance of early experience lies not only in the intensity of its impact but in its durability and persistence. Early experiences are not only ingrained more pervasively and forcefully, but their effects tend to persist and are more difficult to modify than the effects of later experiences.

Although part of this continuity may be ascribed in the stability of constitutional and temperamental factors, there are numerous psychological processes that contribute to it as well. Because these processes—resistance to extinction, social reinforcement, and self-perpetuation—enable us to see more clearly how pathology develops and persists, we cannot take them for granted or merely enumerate them without elaboration.

Resistance to Extinction

Acquired behaviors and attitudes usually are not permanent. What has been learned can be modified under appropriate conditions, a process referred to as extinction. Extinction entails exposure to experiences that are similar to the conditions of original learning but provide opportunities for new learning to occur.

What occurs when the conditions of original learning cannot be duplicated? Essentially, failure to provide opportunities for interfering with and replacing old habits means that they are likely to remain unmodified and persist over time.

The question to be asked next is whether the events of early life are experienced in such a manner as to make them difficult to reproduce and, therefore, make what was learned earlier difficult to unlearn later. Several factors lead the author to conclude that the answer is yes; the discussion turns next to processes that contribute to the resistance of early learning to extinction.

Presymbolic learning. The nervous system of young children is primitive and incomplete; they perceive the world from momentary and changing vantage points and are unable to discriminate many of the elements of their experience. What they learn about the environment through their infantile perceptual and cognitive systems will never again be experienced in the same manner in later life.

This presymbolic world of fleeting impressions recedes gradually as children acquire the ability to identify and symbolize experience. By the time they are 4 or 5 years old, they group and symbolize objects and events in a stable way, a way quite different from that of infancy. Once the children's perceptions have taken on symbolic forms, they can no longer duplicate the perceptually amorphous and diffusely inchoate experiences of their earlier years. Unable to reproduce these early experiences, they will not be able to extinguish what they learned in response; no longer perceiving events as initially sensed, they cannot replace their early reactions with new ones. These early learnings will persist beneath the level of symbolic awareness in the form of feelings, attitudes, and expectancies that crop up in a vague and diffuse way.

Random learning. Young children lack not only the ability to form precise images of the environment but the means to discern logical relationships among its elements. Their world of objects and people is connected in an unclear and often random fashion. Clusters of concurrent, but only incidentally related, events are fused erroneously. Experiencing fear in response to a father's harsh voice, a child may learn to fear not only that voice but the setting, the atmosphere, the pictures, the furniture, and a variety of incidental objects that by chance were present at that time. Unable to discriminate the precise source that "caused" the fear, the child connects his or her discomfort to all, and now each becomes a precipitant for these feelings.

Random associations arising in early life cannot be duplicated as children develop the capacity for logical thinking and perception. To advise them that they are reacting to a picture, a setting, or a piece of furniture simply will be rejected; they cannot identify the true elements that continue to evoke their feelings, since these sources are so foreign to the children's new, more rational mode of thought. Not only is it difficult for them to reexperience the world as it once may have been, but they will be misled in their search for causes if they apply their mature reasoning powers.

Generalized learning. As children begin to differentiate the elements comprised in their world, they group and label them into broad and unrefined categories. Thus, all men become "daddy," and all four-legged animals are called "doggie." When children learn to fear a particular dog they will learn to fear not only that dog but all strange, mobile, four-legged creatures. At this level of discrimination, all of these animals are one of a kind. As the undifferentiated mass of early experiences become more finely differentiated, learning gets more focused, specific, and precise; a ten-year-old may learn to fear bulldogs but will not necessarily generalize this fear to collies or poodles, since the child can discern differences among them.

Generalized learning is difficult to extinguish in young children because their learned reactions are attached to a broader class of objects than called for by their specific experiences. To extinguish broadly generalized reactions in later life, when discriminative capacities are much more precise, requires that an individual be exposed to many and diverse experiences. An illustration may be useful to clarify this notion.

Assume that a 2-year-old had been frightened by a cocker spaniel. Given the child's discriminative capacity, this experience conditioned him to fear dogs, cats, and other small animals. In later life the child was exposed repeatedly to a friendly cocker spaniel. As a consequence of this experience, the child's fear was extinguished, but only the fear of cocker spaniels, not of dogs in general, cats, or other small animals. The child's later experience, seen through the discriminative capacities of an older child, was that spaniels are friendly, not dogs in general. The extinction experience applied to only one part of the original, generalized complex of fears acquired. The child's original learning incorporated a broader range of stimuli than his later experience, even though the objective stimulus was essentially the same. The child now must have his fear extinguished with a variety of animals to compensate for the single, but widely generalized, early experience.

Social Reinforcement

As noted earlier, personality patterns develop as a consequence of enduring experiences generated in everyday, incidental relationships with members of one's immediate family. Here attention is on those aspects of relationships that strengthen what has been learned and lead to perpetuation of these learnings.

Repetitive experiences. The typical life of daily activities in which young children participate is restricted and repetitive. Day after day they play with the same toys, remain in the same physical environment, and relate to the same people. Repeated exposure to a narrow range of family attitudes and training methods not only builds deeply etched habits and expectations but prevents children from new experiences that are essential to change. The dependency of children keeps them restricted to a tight little world with few alternatives for learning new attitudes and responses. Early behaviors may fail to change, therefore, not because they have jelled permanently but because the same slender band of experiences that formed them initially continue and persist for many years.

Reciprocal reinforcement. The notion that children's early behaviors may be accentuated by their parents' response to them was raised earlier. For example, unusually sensitive or cranky infants frequently elicit feelings on the part of their mothers that perpetuate the infants' original tendencies.

This model of circular, or reciprocal, influences applies not only to the perpetuation of biological dispositions but also to behaviors that are acquired by learning. Many distinctive and potentially troublesome behaviors provoke or "pull" from others certain reactions that result in their repetition. For example, a chip-on-the-shoulder, defiant child eventually will force others to counter with exasperation and anger. An ever-widening gulf of irritation and defiance may develop as parents of such children withdraw, become punitive, or 'throw up their hands in disgust." Each participant, in feedback fashion, contributes fuel to the fire, and the original level of hostile behavior is further aggravated. The process has gotten out of hand, and it may continue its inexorable course until some benign influence interferes or until it deteriorates further.

Social stereotypes. The child's early behaviors form a distinct impression upon others. Once established, people expect the child to behave in this manner, and, in time, they develop a fixed image of "what kind of person the child is." The term *stereotype* represents this tendency to simplify and categorize the attributes of others.

People no longer view a child passively and objectively once they have formed a stereotype of the child. They are sensitized to those distinctive features they have learned to expect, and the stereotype begins to operate as a screen through which the child's behaviors are selectively perceived so as to fit the attributed characteristics. Cast in such molds, children begin to experience a consistency in the way in which others react to them, ways that fail to take cognizance of the varieties and complexities of their behaviors. No matter what efforts they make to alter them, children find that their behaviors are interpreted in the same fixed and rigid manner. Unable to break the stereotypes into which they have been cast, children may give up and continue to behave as they did originally, and as others expect.

Self-Perpetuation

The residues of past experience are never fully lost, persisting as influences into the present. Moreover, they shape and distort the present, as described in the following (Millon, 1969):

> Significant experiences of early life may never recur again, but their effects remain and leave their mark. Physiologically, we may say they have etched a neurochemical change; psychologically, they are registered as memories, a permanent trace and an embedded internal stimulus. In contrast to the fleeting stimuli of the external world, these memory traces become part and parcel of every stimulus complex which activates behavior. Once registered, the effects of the past are indelible, incessant and inescapable. They now are intrinsic elements of the individual's make-up; they latch on and intrude into the current events of life, coloring, transforming and distorting the passing scene. Although the residuals of subsequent experiences may override them, becoming more dominant internal stimuli, the presence of earlier memory traces remains in one form or another. In every thought and action, the individual cannot help but carry these remnants into the present. Every current behavior is a perpetuation, then, of the past, a continuation and intrusion of these inner stimulus traces.
>
> The residuals of the past do more than passively contribute their share to the present. By temporal precedence, if nothing else, they guide, shape or distort the character of current events. Not only are they ever present, then, but they operate insidiously to transform new stimulus experiences in line with past. (p. 200)

A number of these self-perpetuating processes are elaborated here.

Protective constriction. Painful memories are kept out of consciousness, a process referred to as *repression*. Similarly, experiences which reactivate repressed memories are judiciously avoided. The individual develops a network of protective maneuvers to decrease the likelihood that distressing memories or experiences will recur. As a consequence of these efforts, however, the person's world is constricted. Repression thwarts the individual from "unlearning" disturbed feelings or learning new, potentially more constructive ways of coping with them. Likewise, by reducing activities to situations that will not activate painful memories, the individual precludes the possibility of learning to be less anxious than in the past.

As a result of their own protective actions, these persons preserve unaltered their memories of the past. In addition, these defensive maneuvers force them along paths that prevent resolution. Moreover, the more vigilant the protective steps and the more constrictive the boundaries, the more limited will be the competencies for effective functioning.

Perceptual and cognitive distortion.

Certain actions not only preserve the past but transform the present in line with the past. Once individuals acquire a system of expectancies, they respond with increasing alertness to similar elements in their life situation. For example, persons who develop bodily anxieties often become hyperalert to physiological signs that most people experience but ignore.

People acquire anticipatory attitudes as a consequence of all forms of past experience. These cognitions guide, screen, code, and evaluate new experiences in line with expectancies. The role of habits of language as factors in shaping perceptions is of particular interest. The words we use transform our experiences in line with the meaning of these words. For example, children whose parents responded to every minor mishap as "a shattering experience" will tend to use these terms themselves and conceive every setback they experience as "shattering" because they have labeled it as such.

The importance of expectancies, sensitivities, and language habits lies in the fact that they lead to the distortion of objective realities. These distortions channel attention, magnify awareness of insignificant features of the environment, and intrude constantly to obscure and warp an accurate perception of reality. The following quote from Beck (1963) illustrates this process well:

> A depressed patient reported the following sequence of events which occurred within a period of half an hour before he left the house: His wife was upset because the children were slow in getting dressed. He thought, "I'm a poor father because the children are not better disciplined." He then noticed a faucet was leaky and thought this showed he was also a poor husband. While driving to work, he thought, "I must be a poor driver or other cars would not be passing me." As he arrived at work he noticed some other personnel had already arrived. He thought, "I can't be very dedicated or I would have come earlier." When he noticed folders and papers piled up on his desk, he concluded, "I'm a poor organizer because I have so much work to do." (p. 329)

Such distortions have an insidiously cumulative and spiraling effect. By misconstruing reality to make it corroborate expectancies, individuals intensify their misery. These persons subjectively experience neutral events as if they were threatening; in this process, they create painful experiences for themselves where none, in fact, exists. Once a pathological process of distortion has begun, these patients may become caught in a downward spiral in which everything, no matter how objectively "good" it might be, is perceived as distressing. Distortion has built up its own momentum, resulting not only in its perpetuation but in its intensification.

Behavior generalization. From the viewpoint of efficiency, behavioral generalization enables us to apply what we have learned, that is, to react in the same way to situations that are comparable. A problem arises when we transfer responses incorrectly because we have failed to discriminate between dissimilar situations—for example, reacting to novel circumstances in the present as if they were duplicates of the past. The tendency to generalize inappropriate behaviors has far-reaching consequences since it elicits reactions from others that not only perpetuate these behaviors but often aggravate the conditions that gave rise to them.

In what way does the generalization of behavior tend to perpetuate the conditions that originally gave rise to these behaviors? An example may help illustrate the point. Youngsters who anticipate punitive reactions from their parents may become hyperalert to signs of rejection from others. They may distort innocuous comments, seeing them as indications of hostility. In preparing themselves to counter the hostility they expect, they freeze their posture, stare coldly and rigidly, and pass a few aggressive comments. These actions communicate a message quickly sensed by others as antagonistic. Before long, others begin to withdraw and display real, rather than imagined, hostility.The youngsters' generalized suspicious behavior has evoked the punitive responses they expected. They now have experienced an objective form of rejection similar to that received at the hands of their parents, which leads them to be even more suspicious and arrogant, beginning the vicious circle over again.

Almost all forms of generalized behavior set up reciprocal reactions that intensify these behaviors; docile or fearful actions, for example, draw domineering and manipulative responses, and confidence and self-assurance elicit admiration and submissiveness. What is especially notable is that generalization is not only a form of perpetuation itself but one that creates conditions that promote further perpetuation.

FINAL COMMENT

The author has taken the liberty in this chapter of bringing together many notions that theorists have used to identify the principal psychogenic sources of personality pathology. Only rarely has the discussion commented on the adequacy of these notions or the data employed in deriving them. The presentation would be amiss if it failed to comment, albeit briefly, on the soundness of the evidence.

That early experience plays a decisive part in determining personality is assumed by psychiatrists and psychologists of all theoretical persuasions. The "hard data," the unequivocal evidence derived from well-designed and well-executed research, are sorely lacking, however. There are findings that show no substantial difference in deleterious childhood experiences between normal persons and psychiatric patients. It is known also that adults who have been reared in devastating childhood environments not only survive but thrive, whereas others, raised under ideal conditions, often deteriorate into severe pathological patterns. Clearly, the events and sequences involved in producing pathology are awesomely complex and difficult to unravel. Only minimal reference to specific research has been made in this chapter lest the reader be led to believe that there are supportive data from well-designed studies. The author believes that the notions presented here are fundamentally sound and justified. Nevertheless, the reader should approach them as propositions to be sustained in future research.

Part Two

Basic Personality Disorders

Chapter 4

Dependent Personality: The Submissive Pattern

Dependent personalities are distinguished from other pathological patterns by their marked need for social approval and affection, and by their willingness to live in accord with the desires of others. Dependent persons' "centers of gravity" lie in others, not in themselves. They adapt their behavior to please those upon whom they depend, and their search for love leads them to deny thoughts and feelings that may arouse the displeasure of others. They avoid asserting themselves lest their actions be seen as aggressive. Dependents may feel paralyzed when alone and need repeated assurances that they will not be abandoned. Exceedingly sensitive to disapproval, they may experience criticism as devastating.

Dependent personalities tend to denigrate themselves and their accomplishments. What self-esteem they possess is determined largely by the support and encouragement of others. Unable to draw upon themselves as a major source of comfort and gratification, they must arrange their lives to ensure a constant supply of nurturance and reinforcement from their environment. However, by turning exclusively to external sources for sustenance, dependents leave themselves open to the whims and moods of others. Losing the affection and protection of those upon whom they depend leads them to feel exposed to the void of self-determination. To protect themselves, dependents quickly submit and comply with what others wish, or make themselves so pleasing that no one could possibly want to abandon them.

Dependents are notably self-effacing, obsequious, ever-agreeable, docile, and ingratiating. A clinging helplessness and a search for support and reassurance characterize them. They tend to be self-depreciating, feel inferior to others, and avoid displaying initiative and self-determination. Except for needing signs of belonging and acceptance, they refrain from making demands on others. They deny their individuality, subordinate their desires, and hide what vestiges they possess as identities apart from others. They often submit to abuse and intimidation in the hope of avoiding isolation, loneliness, and the dread of abandonment. Paralyzed and empty if left on their own, they feel the need for guidance in fulfilling even simple tasks or making routine decisions.

Many dependent individuals search for a single, all-powerful "magic helper," a partner in whom they can place their trust and depend on to protect them from having to assume responsibilities or face the competitive struggles of life alone. Supplied with a nurturant partner, they may function with ease, be sociable, and display warmth, affection, and generosity. Deprived of this support, they withdraw into themselves and become tense, despondent, and forlorn.

Despite the well-known prevalence of this personality pattern, there was only passing reference to it in the DSM-I and no provision at all in the DSM-II. The closest approximation in the DSM-II, though far from sufficient in either scope or clarity, was the "inadequate personality." Fortunately, the DSM-III has taken cognizance of this important syndrome and has given it the status of a separate and major personality disorder. The following quote is taken from this official manual, and it highlights the essential features and diagnostic criteria selected to represent the syndrome:

> The individual passively allows others to assume responsibility for major areas of his or her life because of a lack of self-confidence and an inability to function independently; the individual subordinates his or her own needs to those of others on whom he or she is dependent in order to avoid any possibility of having to be self-reliant.
>
> Such individuals leave major decisions to others. For example, an adult with this disorder will typically assume a passive role and allow his or her spouse to decide where they should live, what kind of job he or she should have, and with which neighbors they shoud be friendly.
>
> Generally individuals with this disorder are unwilling to make demands on supporting people for fear of jeopardizing these relationships and being forced to rely on themselves.
>
> Individuals with this disorder invariably lack self-confidence. They tend to belittle their abilities and assets. (p. 324)

HISTORICAL AND THEORETICAL ANTECEDENTS

Before elaborating the clinical picture of the DSM-III dependent personality it will be useful and illuminating to briefly review formulations of a parallel nature that have been published by early as well as contemporary clinical theorists.

The features of passively allowing others to assume responsibility and the characteristic receptivity to external influence were first described under the labels of the "shiftless" type by Kraepelin (1913) and the "weak-willed" personality by Schneider (1923). Both theorists made little reference to the need for and the seeking of external support that typify dependent patients, stressing instead "their irresoluteness of will" and the ease with which they can be "seduced" by others. Schneider noted, "as far as their pliable natures will allow they are responsive to good influences, show regret for their lapses and display good intentions" (p. 133). Kraepelin considered these types to be a product of delayed maturation. Viewing them as readily "exploited to no good end," both Kraepelin and Schneider conceived these personalities as not merely minimally competent to handle their affairs and susceptible to influence, but as easy prey to "bad notions" and ready targets for social forms of misconduct such as addiction and thievery.

A distinct shift from the notion that these personalities were potentially immoral characters was taken by psychoanalytic theorists who were also writing in the first two decades of this century. Evolving their formulations in line with libidinal or psychosexual stage theory, both Freud and Abraham gradually constructed the "oral character" type and, more specifically, what has been termed either the "oral-sucking" or "oral-receptive" character. Most clearly presented by Karl Abraham in 1924, he writes of this major precursor of the DSM-III dependent personality as follows:

> According to my experience we are here concerned with persons in whom the sucking was undisturbed and highly pleasurable. They have brought with them from this happy period a deeply rooted conviction that everything will always be well with them. They face life with an imperturbable optimism which often does in fact help them to achieve their aims. But we also meet with less favourable types of development. Some people are dominated by the belief that there will always be some kind person—a representative of the mother, of course—to care for them and to give them everything they need. This optimistic belief condemns them to inactivity . . . they make no kind of effort, and in some cases they even disdain to undertake a bread-winning occupation. (1924a, pp. 399–400)

Elaborating on this early statement, Fenichel highlighted other prime traits of the oral character, particularly those individuals who have experienced deprivation at this stage:

> If a person remains fixated to the world of oral wishes, he will, in his general behavior, present a disinclination to take care of himself, and require others to look after him. . . . The behavior of persons with oral characters frequently shows signs of identification with the object by whom they want to be fed. Certain persons act as nursing mothers in all their object relationships. They are always generous and shower everybody with presents and help. (1945, p. 489)

Sullivan, although drawing from a different theoretical framework than libidinal theory, described in his "inadequate" personality a series of characteristics that correspond in many respects to the current DSM-III criteria:

> Some of these people have been obedient children of a dominating parent. They go through life needing a strong person to make decisions for them. Some

of them learned their helplessness and clinging vine adaptation from parental example. (1947, p. 84)

Perhaps the closest parallel to the DSM-III dependent personality is found in the descriptive features of the "compliant" type as formulated by Karen Horney:

> He shows a marked need for affection and approval and an especial need for a "partner"—that is, a friend, lover, husband or wife who is to fulfill all expectations of life and take responsibility for good and evil....
> This type has certain characteristic attitudes toward himself. One is the pervasive feeling that he is weak and helpless—a "poor little me" feeling.... A second characteristic grows out of his tendency to subordinate himself. He takes for granted that everyone is superior to him.... The third feature ... is his unconscious tendency to rate himself by what others think of him. His self-esteem rises and falls with their approval or disapproval, their affection or lack of it. (1945, pp. 49-54)

A similar set of traits was provided by Erich Fromm in his characterization of the "receptive orientation."

> In the receptive orientation a person feels "the source of all good" to be outside, and he believes that the only way to get what he wants—be it something material, be it affection, love, knowledge, pleasure—is to receive it from that outside source....
> They are dependent not only on authorities for knowledge and help but on people in general for any kind of support. They feel lost when alone because they feel that they cannot do anything without help. This helplessness is especially important with regard to those acts by which their very nature can only be done alone—making decisions and taking responsibility. (1947, pp. 67-63)

As noted earlier—and quite surprisingly given its extensive reference in the literature—the dependent personality syndrome was accorded only brief mention in the DSM-I, noted as a subvariant of the passive-aggressive disorder, and it was totally overlooked in the DSM-II. Features of dependency were most closely represented in the *inadequate* personality disorder, but these failed to provide either a comprehensive or coherent picture of the clinical type. For reference purposes, the salient aspects of the inadequate personality were noted as follows:

> This behavior pattern is characterized by ineffectual responses to emotional, social, intellectual and physical demands. While the patient seems neither physically nor mentally deficient, he does manifest inadaptability, ineptness, poor judgment, social instability and lack of physical and emotional stamina. (p. 44)

Of potential interest are factor analytic studies of "oral character" traits. For example, in a series of cross-validated projects designed to assess the factorial unity of certain presumed psychoanalytic types, Lazare, Klerman, and Armor (1966, 1970) identified the following characteristics as covarying to a high degree in what they termed the "oral factor": dependence, pessimism, passivity, self-doubt, fear of sexuality, and suggestibility. Along similar lines, Walton and Presley (1973a, 1973b) rated a population of patients on an inventory of personality traits and extracted a major component that they labeled "submissiveness"; it was composed of the following items: timidity, meekness, submissiveness, intropunitiveness, indecisiveness, and avoidance of competition. In noting possible parallels to this component in the clinical literature, Walton and Presley referred to the "obviously related" dependent personality, a classification well known to practicing professionals but one that did not appear in either the DSM-II or the ICD system.

Millon drew upon his theoretically derived passive-dependent pesonality pattern (1969), and in 1975 he provided the following descriptive features and criteria as the initial working draft for the personality subcommittee of the DSM-III Task Force.

> This pattern is typified by a passive-dependency, general social naivete and a friendly and obliging temperament. There is a striking lack of initiative and competitiveness, self-effacement of aptitudes and a general avoidance of autonomy. Appeasing and conciliatory submission to others is notable, as is a conspicuous seeking and clinging to supporting persons. Except where dependency is at stake, social difficulties are cognitively denied or neutralized by an uncritical and charitable outlook.
>
> Since adolescence or early adulthood at least 3 of the following have been present to a notably greater degree than in most people and were not limited to discrete periods nor necessarily prompted by stressful life events.

1. Pacific temperament (e.g., is characteristically docile and noncompetitive; avoids social tension and interpersonal conflicts).
2. Interpersonal submissiveness (e.g., needs a stronger, nurturing figure, and without one feels anxiously helpless; is often conciliatory, placating, and self-sacrificing).
3. Inadequate self-image (e.g., perceives self as weak, fragile and ineffectual; exhibits lack of confidence by belittling own aptitudes and competencies).
4. Pollyana cognitive style (e.g., reveals a naive or benign attitude toward interpersonal difficulties; smooths over troubling events).
5. Initiative deficit (e.g., prefers a subdued, uneventful and passive life style; avoids self-assertion and refuses autonomous responsibilities).

In a second draft revision of the criteria, the following list was written by the author in 1977 for review by his DSM-III Task Force associates.

A. Excessive dependency (e.g., displays a chronic and conspicuous need for supporting or nurturant persons).
B. Isolation anxiety (e.g., cannot tolerate being alone for more than brief periods).

    C. Lack of confidence and initiative (e.g., perceives self as weak, belittles aptitudes and is non-competitive).

    D. Submissive and socially conciliatory (e.g., avoids self-assertion, is self-sacrificing and pollyanna-like).

    E. Abdication of responsibilities (e.g., seeks others to assume leadership and direction for one's affairs).

CLINICAL PICTURE

With the foregoing as a précis, there is a reasonable foundation for detailing the major clinical characteristics of the dependent personality. Although the analysis is separated into four sections, the traits described should be seen as forming a coherent picture. Congruity among the four descriptive realms of behavior, self-report, intrapsychic processes, and interpersonal coping style should be expected since a distinguishing characteristic of a personality trait is its pervasiveness—that is, its tendency to operate in all spheres of psychological functioning. It should not be surprising, therefore, that each section provides a clinical impression similar to the others.

Behavioral Features

Among the most notable features of dependents is their lack of self-confidence, a characteristic apparent in their posture, voice, and mannerisms. They tend to be overly cooperative and acquiescent, preferring to yield and placate rather than be assertive. Large social groups and noisy events are abhorrent, and they go to great pains to avoid attention by underplaying both their attractiveness and their achievements. They are often viewed by friends as generous and thoughtful, and at times as unduly apologetic and obsequious. Neighbors may be impressed by their humility, cordiality, and graciousness, and by the "softness" and gentility of their behavior.

    Beneath their warmth and affability may lie a plaintive and solemn quality, a searching for assurances of acceptance and approval. These needs may be especially manifest under conditions of stress. At these times, dependents are likely to exhibit overt signs of helplessness and clinging behaviors. They may actively solicit and plead for attention and encouragement. A depressive tone will often color their mood, and they may become overtly wistful or mournful. Maudlin and sentimental by disposition, they may also become excessively conciliatory and self-sacrificing in their relationships.

Self-Descriptions and Complaints

It is characteristic of dependents to limit awareness of self and others to a narrow sphere, well within comfortable boundaries. They constrict their world and are minimally introspective and pollyannalike with regard to difficulties that surround them. From an introspective view dependent personalities tend to be naïve, unperceptive, and uncritical. They are inclined to see only the "good" in things, the pleasant side of troubling events.

Underneath their pollyanna veneer, dependent personalities often feel little of the joy of living. Once their "hair is let down" they may report feeling pessimistic, discouraged, and dejected. Their "suffering" is done in silence, however, away from those for whom they must appear pleased and content with life.

Dependents see themselves, at least superficially, as considerate, thoughtful, and cooperative, disinclined to be ambitious and modest in their aspirations. Closer probing, however, is likely to evoke marked feelings of personal inadequacy and insecurity. Dependents tend to downgrade themselves, claiming to lack abilities, virtues, and attractiveness. They are disposed to magnify their failures and defects. When comparing themselves to others they minimize their attainments, underplay their attributes, note their inferiorities, and assume personal blame for problems they feel they have brought upon others. Of course, much of this self-belittling has little basis in reality. Clinically, this pattern of self-deprecation may best be conceived as a strategy by which dependents elicit assurances that they are not unworthy and unloved. Hence, it serves as an instrument for evoking praise and commendation.

Inferred Intrapsychic Dynamics

By claiming weakness and inferiority, dependents effectively absolve themselves of the responsibilities they know they should assume but would rather not. In a similar manner, self-depreciation evokes sympathy and attention from others, for which dependents are bound to feel guilt. Maneuvers and conflicts such as these are difficult for dependents to tolerate consciously. To experience comfort with themselves, dependents are likely to deny the feelings they experience and the deceptive strategies they employ. Likewise, they may cover up their obvious need to be dependent by rationalizing their inadequacies—that is, by attributing them to some physical illness, unfortunate circumstance, and the like. And to prevent social condemnation, they are careful to restrain assertive impulses and to deny feelings that might provoke criticism and rejection.

Dependents' social affability and good-naturedness not only forestall social deprecation but reflect a gentility toward the self, a tender indulgence that protects them from being overly harsh with their own shortcomings. To maintain equilibrium, they must take care not to overplay their expressions of guilt, shame, and self-condemnation. They are able to maintain a balance between moderate and severe self-deprecation by a pollyanna tolerance of the self, "sweetening" their own failures with the same saccharine attitude that they use to dilute the shortcomings of others.

The inadequacies that dependents see within themselves may provoke feelings of emptiness and the dread of being alone. These terrifying thoughts are often controlled by identification, a process by which they imagine themselves to be an integral part of a more powerful and supporting figure. By allying themselves with the competencies of their partners, they can avoid the anxieties evoked by the thought of their own impotence. Not only are they uplifted by illusions of shared competence, but through identification they may find solace in the belief that the bonds they have constructed are firm and inseparable.

Denial mechanisms also characterize the dependent's defensive style. This is seen most clearly in the pollyanna quality of dependents' thoughts. Dependents are ever-alert to soften the edges of interpersonal strain and discomfort. A syrupy sweetness may typify their speech, and they may persistently cover up or smooth over troublesome events. Especially threatening are their own hostile impulses; any inner feeling or thought that might endanger their security and acceptance is quickly staved off. A torrent of contrition and self-debasement may burst forth to expiate momentary transgressions.

Interpersonal Coping Style

What interpersonal behaviors do dependents use to manipulate their environment, and how do they arrange their relationships to achieve their aims?

A major problem for dependent individuals is that they not only find little reinforcement within themselves but feel that they are inept and stumbling, and thus lacking in the skills necessary to secure their needs elsewhere. As they see it, only others possess the requisite talents and experience to attain the rewards of life. Given these attitudes, they conclude that it is best to abdicate self-responsibility, to leave matters to others, and to place their fate in others' hands. Others are so much better equipped to shoulder responsibilities, to navigate the intricacies of a complex world, and to discover and achieve the pleasures to be found in the competitions of life.

To achieve their goals, dependent personalities learn to attach themselves to others, to submerge their individuality, to deny points of difference, to avoid expressions of power, and to ask for little other than acceptance and support— in other words, to assume an attitude of helplessness, submission, and compliance. Moreover, by acting weak, expressing self-doubt, communicating a need for assurance, and displaying a willingness to comply and submit, dependents are likely to elicit the nurture and protection they seek.

Dependents must be more than meek and docile if they are to secure and retain their "hold" on others. They must be admiring, loving, and willing to give their "all." Only by total submission and loyalty can they be assured of consistent care and affection. Fortunately, most dependents have learned through parental models how to behave affectionately and admiringly. Most possess an ingrained capacity for expressing tenderness and consideration, essential elements in holding their protectors. Also important is that most have learned the "inferior" role well. They are able, thereby, to provide their "superior" partners with the feeling of being useful, sympathetic, stronger, and competent—precisely those behaviors that dependents seek in their mates.

From many sources, then, dependent personalities have learned interpersonal strategies that succeed well in achieving the goals they seek.

ASSOCIATED DISORDERS

Before detailing the disorders that frequently accompany the dependent personality, it may be useful to reiterate an earlier discussion in Chapter 1 concerning distinctions between personality and symptom disorders.

Essentially, the behaviors that typify personality persist as permanent features of the individual's way of life and seem to have an inner autonomy; that is, they exhibit themselves with or without external precipitants. In contrast, the behaviors that characterize Axis I symptom disorders arise as a reaction to stressful situations and tend to be transient; that is, they are of brief duration, subsiding or disappearing shortly after these conditions are removed. The clinical features of personality are highly complex and widely generalized, with many attitudes and habits exhibited only in subtle and indirect ways. In contrast, symptom disorders tend to be characterized by isolated and dramatic behaviors that often simplify, accentuate, and carica-ture the more prosaic features of the patient's personality. That is, they stand out in sharp relief against the background of more enduring and typical modes of functioning. Furthermore, personality traits feel "right" to the patients. They seem to be part and parcel of their makeup. In contrast, symptom disorders often are experienced as discrepant, irrational, and uncomfortable. The behaviors, thoughts, and feelings of disorders seem strange and alien not only to others but to the patients themselves. They often feel as if they were driven by forces beyond their control.

It is the contention of this book that a full understanding of Axis I symptom disorders requires the study of Axis II personalities. Symptom disorders are but an outgrowth of deeply rooted sensitivities and coping strategies. What events a person perceives as threatening or rewarding, and what behaviors and mechanisms he or she employs in response to them reflects a long history of interwoven biogenic and psychogenic factors that have formed the person's basic personality pattern.

Several qualifications should be noted lest the discussion imply an overly simplified relation between Axis I and Axis II syndromes. First, symptom disorders do not arise in one personality pattern only. Second, in many cases several Axis I symptom disorders may be simultaneously present since they reflect the operation of similar coping processes. Third, symptoms are likely to be transient since their underlying functions wax and wane as the need for them changes. And last, Axis I symptoms should, in large measure, be interchangeable, with one symptom appearing dominant at one time and a different one at another.

Despite the fact that Axis I symptom disorders often covary and are frequently interchangeable, we would expect some measure of symptom dominance and durability among different Axis II personalities. No one-to-one correspondence should be expected, of course, but differences in lifelong coping habits should lead us to anticipate that certain personalities would be more inclined to exhibit certain symptoms than others. In the compulsive personality, for example, where ingrained mechanisms such as reaction formation and undoing have been present for years, we would expect the patient to display symptoms that reflect these mechanisms. Similarly, histrionic personalities should exhibit the more dramatic and attention-getting symptoms since exhibitionistic histrionics have characterized their coping behaviors.

There are other reasons not to overstate the correspondence between personality and symptom disorders. Thus, symptoms that are often indistin-guishable from those exhibited by pathological personalities arise also in normal persons. More importantly, there are endless variations in the particular experiences to which different members of the same personality syndrome have been exposed. To illustrate, compare two individuals who have been "trained" to become dependent personalities. One was exposed to a mother who was chronically ill, a pattern of behavior that brought her considerable sympathy and freedom from many daily burdens. With this as the background, the patient in question followed the model observed in the mother when faced with undue anxiety and threat, and thereby displayed hypochondriacal symptoms. A second dependent personality learned to imitate a mother who expressed endless fears about every kind of event and situation. In this case, phobic symptoms arose in response to stressful and anxiety-laden circumstances. In short, the specific symptom "choice" is not a function solely of the patient's personality but may reflect particular and entirely incidental events of prior experience and learning.

Concomitant Axis I Symptoms

This section (also provided in each of the following chapters) briefly discusses the prime Axis I disorders that often covary with the personality syndrome under review. In addition to identifying the most frequent of these accom-panying difficulties, there is also a description of the more common sensitivities and vulnerabilities that dispose this personality to react in a "disordered" fashion. Further, note is made of several of the hypothesized dynamics and secondary gains that characteristically occur among these personalities when they exhibit the Axis I disorder under discussion.

As noted earlier, objective precipitants in symptom disorders play a secondary role to those which exist internally. It is the patients' anticipatory sensitivities that dispose them to transform innocuous elements of reality so that they are duplicates of the past. As in a vicious circle, this distorted perception stirs up a wide range of associated past reactions. To specify the source of an Axis I disorder, then, we must look not so much to the objective conditions of reality, though these may in fact exist, as to the deeply rooted personality vulnerabilities of the patient.

Identifying these sensitivities is a highly speculative task since no one can specify exactly what goes on intrapsychically. The best we can do is to make theoretically and clinically informed guesses as to which attitudes in each of the major personality types are likely to give rise to the vulnerability. There is, of course, no single "cause" for Axis I symptom disorders, even in patients with similar personalities. Moreover, not only do triggering precipitants differ from patient to patient, but different sensitivities may take precedence from one time to another within a single patient. The discussion proceeds with these cautions in mind.

Anxiety disorders. Dependent personalities are extremely vulnerable to anxiety disorders, especially those referred to as separation anxieties. Having placed their welfare entirely in the hands of others, they expose themselves to conditions that are ripe for generalized anxieties. There may be an ever-present worry of being abandoned by their sole benefactor and left alone to struggle with their meager competencies. Another factor that may give rise to *panic anxiety* attacks is the anticipation and dread of new responsibilities. Their sense of personal inadequacy and the fear that new burdens may tax their limited competencies (thereby bringing disapproval from others) may precipitate a dramatic change from calmness to marked anxiety. It should be noted, of course, that anxious displays often serve to evoke nurtural and supporting responses from others. Thus, an anxiety disorder may come to be used as a tool that enables the dependent to avoid the discomforting responsibilities of autonomy and independence.

Phobic disorders. Dependent personalities develop phobic disorders when their security is threatened or when demands are made which exceed their feelings of competence. They avoid responsibility, especially actions which require self-assertion and independence. To ensure the safety of their dependency, they will quickly displace or transform any thought or impulse that may provoke rebuke. *Social phobias* are not uncommon among these personalities. Not only do phobic symptoms externalize anxiety and avoid threats to security, but by anchoring inner tensions to tangible outside sources dependents prompt others to come to their assistance. For these reasons, dependents are especially vulnerable to *agoraphobic attacks.* These anticipatory fears of leaving familiar and secure settings, most frequently one's home, serve well as a means of soliciting care and protection. Thus, the phobic maneuver achieves secondary gains that are fully consonant with the patient's basic dependent orientation.

Obsessive-compulsive disorders. Often preoccupied with self-doubts, dependent personalities may be subject to a variety of obsessive-compulsive disorders. These symptoms usually stem from reactivated feelings of inadequacy and are precipitated by situations calling for independence and responsibility. At these times, they are likely to weigh interminably the pros and cons of the situation and thereby endlessly postpone any change in their dependent status. Obsessional thoughts and compulsive acts may also arise in response to feelings of separation anxiety or repressed anger. Here, coping is an aid (through reaction formation or undoing) in countering tensions that stem from the isolation or discharge of security-jeopardizing impulses. These symptoms often take the form of "sweet" thoughts and approval-gaining acts.

Somatoform disorders. Dependent personalities may develop somatoform disorders as a means of controlling the upsurge of forbidden impulses. More commonly, these symptoms promote the avoidance of onerous responsibilities and help recruit secondary gains such as sympathy and nurture. By displaying physical helplessness, dependents often succeed in eliciting the attention and care they need. *Conversion* symptoms may be a form of self-punishment for feelings of guilt and worthlessness. Dependents tend, however, not to be too harsh with themselves. Their conversion symptoms are likely to take the form of relatively mild sensory anesthesias such as a generalized numbness in the hands and feet. It is notable that their symptoms often are located in their limbs, a way perhaps of demonstrating to others that they are "disabled" and, therefore, incapable of performing even routine chores.

Among the principal goals of *hypochondriacal* and *somatization* disorders are dependents' desires to solicit attention and nurture from others and to evoke assurances that they will be loved and cared for, despite weaknesses and inadequacy. By their "illness," dependents divert attention from the true source of their dismay, the feeling that others are showing little interest and paying little attention to them. Without complaining directly about their disappointment and resentment, dependents still manage through their physical ailments to attract and rekindle the flagging devotions of others. Not to be overlooked also is that illness complaints may be employed to control others, make them feel guilty, and thereby retaliate for the disinterest and mistreatment dependents may feel they have suffered. In some cases, pain and nagging symptoms represent a form of self-punishment, an attack upon oneself that is disguised in bodily ailments and physical exhaustion.

Factitious disorders. Since dependent personalities have been well trained to view themselves as weak and inadequate, it would not be unlike them to readily assume the role of "the patient" and, hence, be disposed to factitious disorders. Overdependency and excessive parental solicitousness may have taught them as children to protect themselves, not to exert their frail capacities or assume responsibilities that may strain their delicate bodies. Any source of tension, be it externally precipitated or based on the control of forbidden impulses, may lead to an anxious conservation of energy. Having learned that frailty and weakness elicit protective and nurtural reactions from others, dependents may "allow" themselves to succumb to physical exhaustion or illness as a device to ensure these desired responses. It is not unlikely that genuinely felt guilt may be stirred up when dependents recognize how thoughtless and ineffectual they have been in carrying out their responsibilities. But here again, physical weariness and bodily illness come to the rescue as a rationalization to exempt them from assuming their share of chores.

Dissociative disorders. Although infrequent, dependent personalities may develop dissociative disorders. These dreamlike trance states may occur when they are faced with responsibilities that surpass their feelings of competence. Through this process the dependent effectively fades out of contact with threatening realities. Amnesic episodes, however, are likely to be rare since they would prompt to intensify existent separation anxieties. Repetitive somnabulistic states may not be as uncommon. Here dependents may vent minor forbidden impulses or seek to secure affect and nurture. Brief, frenzied actions may arise if the patient is in a decompensated state. Here dependents may feel an upsurge of intense hostile impulses that can threaten their dependency security. By these means, contrary feelings are discharged without the patient knowing it and therefore without having to assume blame. Irrational acts such as these are so uncharacteristic of this personality that these behaviors are seen by others as a sure sign of "sickness," thereby eliciting support (rather than rejecting) responses.

Affective disorders. Since dependent personalities are especially susceptible to separation anxiety, feelings of helplessness readily come to the fore when they anticipate abandonment. The actual loss of a significant person is very likely to prompt any number of affective disorders, including a *major depression.* Actual abandonment may prompt the dependent to plead for reassurance and support. Expressions of guilt and self-condemnation are not uncommon since these verbalizations often deflect criticisms and transform threats into sympathy. Guilt may be employed as a defense against outbursts of resentment and hostility. Dependents usually contain their anger since they dread provoking retribution. To prevent this, dependents typically turn their aggressive impulses inward, discharging them through self-derisive comments, guilt, and contrition. These statements not only temper the exasperation of others but often prompt them to respond in ways which make the patient feel redeemed and loved.

On occasion, dependent personalities exhibit a marked, although usually temporary, reversal of their more subdued and acquiescent style. In these cases of *bipolar disorder,* with their unusual *manic* episodes, the happy-go-lucky air, boundless energy, and buoyant optimism are merely a front, an act in which they try to convince themselves as well as others that "all will be well." What we see at these times is a desperate effort to counter the beginning signs of hopelessness and depression, a last-ditch attempt to deny what they really feel and to recapture the attention and security they fear they have lost.

Schizoaffective and catatonic disorders.   Dependent personalities succumb on rare occasion to schizoaffective disorders. Here we often see a coloring of sadness that draws others to, rather than away, from the patient. The tone of inner softness reflects an inclination to acquiesce to the wishes of others in the hope of maintaining some measure of affection and support from them. It is in dependent patients that we often see the cataleptic waxy flexibility of the catatonic disorder. This willingness to be molded according to the desires of others signifies the personality's complete abandonment of self-initiative and its total dependence and submission to external directives. At the heart of these patients' passive acquiescence is the deep need that dependents have to counter their separation anxieties and to avoid actions that might result in disapproval and rejection.

Concurrent Axis II Personalities

Although all combinations are possible theoretically, experience and research show that only certain personality types tend to overlap or coexist (Millon, 1977). This discussion draws upon the evidence of several statistical cluster studies employing the Millon Clinical Multiaxial Inventory (MCMI) to supplement what theoretical deduction and observation suggests as the most prevalent personality mixtures. To furnish a picture of the more prominent characteristics of these clusters, sections are included from clinical reports generated by an MCMI computer program devised and written specifically to provide assessments of personality profile combinations.

Dependent-avoidant mixed personality.   Perhaps the most common personality disorder found concurrently with the dependent is the new DSM-III avoidant personality, which is described in detail in Chapter 11. This combination has been identified as highly prevalent in centers such as V.A. outpatient clinics and other settings that minister to ambulatory chronic patients who are sustained in a dependent and largely parasitic state by virtue of institutional rewards and requirements. The MCMI computer report of a 57-year-old married and unemployed World War II veteran follows. He has remained in outpatient treatment at a mental hygiene clinic for varying periods since the early 1950s and has continued to receive a 75 percent psychiatric disability. The report was "blind" concerning background data and history.

The patient's behavior may be characterized as submissively dependent, self-effacing, and noncompetitive. Others are leaned upon for guidance and security, and a passive role is assumed in relationships. There is a striking lack of initiative and a general avoidance of autonomy. The patient is exceedingly dependent, not only in needing attention and support from others to maintain equanimity but in being especially vulnerable to separation from those who provide support. However, intense resentment is felt toward those upon whom there is dependence since he has been subjected to frequent rebuff and disapproval. Outbursts of anger have been directed toward others for having failed to appreciate the patient's needs for affection and nurturance. The very security that he needs is threatened, however, when such resentments are expressed.

The patient has become apprehensive and has acquired a pattern of withdrawing from social encounters. Further, he has built a tight armor to damp-down and deaden excessive sensitivity to rejection. Loneliness and isolation are commonly experienced. Although efforts are made to be pleasant and agreeable, there is an underlying tension and emotional dysphoria, expressed in disturbing mixtures of anxious, sad, and guilt-ridden feelings. Insecurity and fears of abandonment underlie what may appear on the surface to be a quiet, submissive, and benign attitude toward difficulties. Despite past rebuff and fears of isolation, he continues to evidence a clinging helplessness and a persistent search for support and reassurance.

Complaints of weakness and easy fatiguability may reflect an underlying mood of depression. Having experienced continuing rebuff from others, the patient may succumb to physical exhaustion and illness. Under these circumstances, simple responsibilities demand more energy than the patient can muster. He expresses the feeling that life is empty but heavy, experiencing a pervasive sense of fatigue and apathy.

Dependent-histrionic mixed personality.　Another frequent combination is found between the dependent and histrionic personalities. Cluster research suggests that this mixture is particularly prevalent among women as they approach mid-life, and it appears to be commonly diagnosed in private practice settings as well as at marital and family agencies. The following MCMI report was computer generated on the basis of replies given by a 37-year-old woman with three adolescent children who was facing the imminent possibility of an undesired divorce.

The patient's behavior is best characterized by a submissive dependency and a leaning upon others for affection, nurturance, and security. The fear of being abandoned leads the patient to be overly compliant and obliging. At times, she handles this fear by being socially gregarious and superficially charming, often evident in the seeking of attention and in self-dramatizing behaviors. The patient typically reveals a naïve attitude toward interpersonal problems. Critical thinking rarely is evident and most cognitive knowledge appears to be unreflected and scattered. In an effort to maintain an air of buoyancy, she tends to deny all disturbing emotions, covering inner disharmonies by short-lived enthusiasms. In part, this may stem from a tendency to be genuinely docile, soft-hearted, and sensitive to the desires of others. The patient is more than merely accommodating and docile in efforts to secure dependency needs. She is admiring and loving, giving all to those upon whom there is dependence. The patient has also learned to play the inferior role well, providing partners with the rewards of feeling useful, sympathetic, stronger, and more competent. There is often an active solicitousness of praise, a marketing of appeal, and a tendency to be seductive and entertaining.

The patient persistently seeks harmony with others, if necessary at the expense of internal values and beliefs, and is likely to actively avoid all situations that may involve personal conflict. To minimize distressing relationships, she avoids self-assertion and abdicates autonomous responsibilities, preferring to leave matters in the hands of others. The preoccupation with external rewards and approval has left her bereft of an identity apart from others. The patient values herself not in terms of intrinsic traits but in terms of relationships. By submerging or allying herself with the competencies and virtues of others, the patient not only is bolstered by the illusion of shared competence but finds solace in the belief that bonds so constructed are firm and inseparable.

The patient feels helpless when faced with responsibilities that demand autonomy or initiative. The loss of a significant source of support or identification often prompts severe dejection. Under such conditions of potential rejection or loss, she will openly solicit signs of reassurance and approval. Guilt, illness, anxiety, and depression are frankly displayed since these tend to deflect criticism and transform threats of disapproval into those of support and sympathy. When dependency security is genuinely threatened, the patient will manifest an anxious depressiveness covarying with other, more extreme reactions such as brief manic periods of either euphoria or disorganized hostility.

The picture portrayed clearly reflects both dependent and histrionic personality features. Not included in the report are sections that dealt with her current symptom state, notably a moderate level of separation anxiety and considerable situational depression.

Differential Diagnostic Signs

Since multiple diagnoses among mental disorders are not only possible but encouraged by the DSM-III multiaxial schema, the importance of differential diagnosis, so central to conventional medical assessment, has clearly diminished. Despite its lessened role, there are justifications for insisting on clear differentiations among disorders. The main reason is to reduce diagnostic confusion, not to separate syndromes that naturally overlap. Diagnostic clarity is important because it bears on the nature and goals of treatment. For example, if a dependent personality style accounts for a particular set of symptoms more accurately than a transient or situationally specific agoraphobia, the therapist will likely decide that cognitive or intrapsychic, rather than behavioral, methods are most suitable to the case.

Turning to diagnostic discriminations involving the dependent personality, we find that confusions are made most often with the two personality patterns with which they frequently overlap—the histrionic and the avoidant. The key features differentiating the dependent from the *histrionic* are the passivity, submissiveness, self-effacement, and docility of the former—in contrast to the actively manipulative, gregarious, charming, and frequently seductive attention-getting behaviors of the latter. As far as differentiating *avoidant* from dependent personalities, the primary distinction relates to matters of trust; both have strong needs for affection and nurturance, but the avoidant fears and strongly doubts the good faith of others, anticipating instead both rejection and humiliation, whereas the dependent is not only receptive to others and willing to rely on their goodwill but has learned to anticipate gratifying consequences when turning to them.

Occasional difficulties may arise in drawing the line between decompensated dependent personalities and personalities diagnosed in accord with DSM-III criteria as *borderline* types. The degree of overlap may be substantial, and further, if viewed longitudinally, borderline patients may be understood best as progressively impaired or deteriorated variants of other personality types, such as the dependent. Not only do the severe features of the borderline overlap and shade into personality types that are characteristically less impaired, but these features often reflect the insidious and progressive disintegration of formerly adaptive functions. For purposes of differential diagnosis it would appear most apt, where the collapse of coping and self-control has advanced significantly, to apply the label of borderline. However, it is the author's view that a double entry, including both borderline and dependent diagnoses, would be more suitable and informative in that it would convey simultaneously the long-term and characteristic dependent style, and the more recent and decompensated level to which this style has regressed.

Few problems should be encountered when separating personality syndromes from disorders listed under Axis I. Given the fact that multiaxial diagnosis requires a listing of impairments from both Axis I and Axis II, the task should not be primarily that of differentiating between these two spheres but of finding which categories in the first axis covary with which categories in the second. Nevertheless, if the behaviors under scrutiny give evidence of having been lifelong, then they should be identified as representing a personality, rather than a symptom, disorder. Similarly, if the clinical features manifest themselves across a wide variety of settings and circumstances, rather than being limited to specific situations, then a personality diagnosis is again the likely correct one.

There are two Axis I syndromes that present more than the usual level of differential diagnostic difficulty with the dependent personaltiy. The first of these potentially confusing classifications is "chronic depressive disorder"; the second is "agoraphobia." In the first of these syndromes, the problem centers on the so-called stability, or long-standing nature, of the Axis I category; *chronic* means enduring, that is, for an extended period of time. However, the descriptive criteria for this diagnosis focuses almost exclusively on the patient's depressed mood and fails to include the diverse clinical traits that comprise the dependent personality complex. Of course, the Axis I chronic depression disorder may be diagnosed as concurrent with the Axis II dependent personality.

As far as agoraphobia is concerned, the issue is essentially one of duration and pervasiveness of symptomatology. Quite typically, the symptoms of agoraphobics are situationally specific and arise episodically. Moreover, the dependent's hesitations in assuming responsibility and autonomy take a passive form, whereas agoraphobics are insistent and demanding of the support of others. Additionally, the dependents' interpersonal submissiveness and feelings of inadequacy are characteristics that are not found in most patients who have an agoraphobic fear of being alone or in "unprotected" situations. Again, where appropriate, the simultaneous diagnosis of an agoraphobic Axis I disorder and a dependent Axis II personality is available to the clinician.

PREDISPOSING BACKGROUND

The discussion now turns to hypotheses concerning the developmental background of dependent traits. Before listing a number of influences that ostensibly shape the dependent pattern, three points should be reiterated. First, most hypotheses in psychopathology are conjectural. Second, a role ascribed to constitutional or biological determinants in no way precludes comparable effects of learning and experience. Third, biogenic and psychogenic factors interact; they are separated only for pedagogic purposes.

Hypothesized Biogenic Factors

The thesis that dispositions to behavior may be rooted in genetic factors is no less plausible in dependent patterns than in any other personality; convincing research evidence is lacking, however. Similarities within a family group may suggest the operation of hereditary determinants, but these findings can reflect environmental influences as well. "Common sense" tells us that individuals' inherited machinery inclines them to perceive and react to experiences in certain ways. Dependency per se is never inherited, of course, but certain types of genetic endowments are likely to have reasonably high probabilities of evolving, under "normal" life experiences, into a dependent style of functioning.

If one's constitutional makeup is moderately consistent throughout life, it would seem reasonable to hypothesize that many adult dependents would have displayed a tendency to a soft, gentle, peaceful, and, perhaps, somewhat sad quality in early childhood. Similarly, they may have shown hesitance about asserting themselves, a restraint in new situations, and a fear of venturing into the world to test their growing capacities.

Early temperamental dispositions elicit distinctive reactions from parents. A gentle but fearful infant is likely to evoke warmth and overprotectiveness from a concerned mother. Such children invite excessive care from others, which may result in their learning to be overly dependent and comfortable with caretakers. Rather than overcoming their initial dispositions, the reactions they evoke from others may lead them to be even less assertive and venturesome than they would otherwise have been.

A somewhat intricate pattern of neural organization may be hypothesized to account for the development of dependent personality traits. Reticular arousal mechanisms may be sluggish in these individuals, giving rise to deficit coping under conditions of stress. At the same time, they may be overly endowed in limbic regions associated with fear, pain, and sadness. Given these neural characteristics, such persons may learn to turn to others for assistance. Their "limbic" attributes dispose them to feel difficulties intensely, and their "reticular" attributes prevent them from mustering the reactive powers needed to cope with these difficulties. Fortunate in having thoughtful and protective caretakers, such persons will quickly learn to depend on others to execute the defensive actions they cannot manage on their own. Turning more and more to their caretakers to aid them in coping only "binds" them further to others and the protection they provide. As a consequence, they may progress into increasingly greater dependencies.

The speculation proposed regarding neurological imbalances may be applied to physiochemical impairments as well. It may be conjectured that adrenal reactivity to stress is sufficient for short periods but is rapidly depleted before restitutive mechanisms can be mustered. Such individuals may experience intense emotional turmoil but lack the sustained adrenal reaction necessary for effective coping responses. Experiencing threat, but unable to "follow through," they may learn to lean on others either to protect them from distress or to resolve it for them when it occurs.

Characteristic Experiential History

It would not be difficult to enumerate a score of influences that might contribute to the development of the dependent personality. The determinants described in this section have been chosen because they appear often in the history of these individuals and seem to carry weight in initiating, as well in shaping, their personality style. They are relevant because they contribute both to the development of attachment learnings and to the avoidance of independent behaviors.

Every infant is helplessly dependent on caretakers for both protection and nurturance. During the first months of life, the child acquires a notion of which objects are associated with increments in comfort and gratification; as a consequence, the child becomes "attached" to these objects. Difficulties arise if these attachments are too narrowly restricted or so rooted as to deter the growth of the child's competencies for self-direction and autonomy. It may be of interest to follow the course of these pathological attachments through the three stages of neuropsychological development outlined in Chapter 3.

1. The first stage of neuropsychological development, that of sensory-attachment, serves as a foundation for future growth. Supplied with beneficial stimulation, the child is likely to develop interpersonal sensitivity and trust. However, infants who receive excessive stimulation and nur-

turance, and experience these almost exclusively from one source, usually the mother, will be disposed to develop dependent traits. As a consequence of a narrow sphere of object relations, the infant will form a singular attachment, a fixation if you will, to one object source to the exclusion of others. A variety of events may give rise to this exclusive attachment. Unusual illnesses or prolonged physical complications in the child's health may prompt a normal mother to tend excessively to her infant. On the other hand, an overly worrisome and anxious mother may be hyperalert to real and fantasied needs she sees in her normal child, resulting in undue attention and cuddling. Occasionally, special circumstances such as a father leaving for an overseas war assignment may throw the infant and mother together into a "symbiotic" dependency.

2. Infants who retain their exclusive attachment to the mother during the second neuropsychological stage, that of sensorimotor-autonomy, will have their earlier training in dependency behaviors strengthened and perpetuated. There are many youngsters, however, who were not especially attached to their mothers in the first stage who also develop the dependent pattern. The sensorimotor-autonomy stage is distinguished by the opportunity to learn skills associated with competence and independent behaviors. Circumstances that undermine the acquistion of these competencies can foster pathological dependency. What conditions during this period result in learning these inadequacy behaviors?

A not uncommon factor is the child's own deficits and temperament dispositions, such as physical inadequacies, fear of new challenges, anguish when left alone, and so on. Whether by virtue of constitutional temperament or earlier learning, some children elicit protective behaviors from others. Unwittingly, their parents may have acceded to overprotective habits because the child "forced" them to do so. In a similar manner, children who have suffered prolonged illnesses may have been prevented from exercising their maturing capacities because of a realistic physical limitation or the judgments of justifiably concerned parents.

Barring constitutional or physical deficits, average youngsters assert their growing capacities and strive to do more things by themselves. This progression toward self-competence and environmental mastery may be interfered with by excessive parental anxieties. Thus, some parents discourage independence for fear of losing "their baby"; they place barriers and diversions to keep their children from gaining autonomy. These parents restrict ventures outside the home, worry lest the children strain themselves, make no demands for self-responsibility, and provide them with every comfort and reward so long as they keep close to mother. Rather than let children stumble and fumble with their new skills, the parents do things for them and make things unnecessarily easy. Time and again they will be discouraged from the impulse to "try it on their own." Because of the ease with which they can obtain gratification by leaning on their parents, these children will give up their feeble efforts at independence. Hence, they may never learn the wherewithal to act on their own to secure the rewards of life. There is no need to acquire self-initiated instrumental behaviors; all they must do is sit back passively and "leave it to mother."

3. Parental overprotection that is continued into the third neuropsychological stage, referred to as intracortical-initiative, may have a devastating effect upon the child's self-image. These children may fail to develop a distinct picture of themselves apart from their caretakers since their dependence on others has denied them the opportunity to do things for themselves, to form an impression of what they are good at and who they are. Failure to break dependency deprives them of experiences necessary to the development of attributes that distinguish them as individuals. Moreover, parental overprotection implies that these children cannot take care of themselves. Thus, pampered children are likely to view themselves, as their parents do, as persons who need special care and supervision because they are incompetent, prone to illness, oversensitive, and so on. Their self-image will, therefore, mirror the parental image of them as weak and inferior. Additionally, when they begin to venture into the outside world, they are likely to find that their "inferiority" is confirmed, that they objectively are less competent and mature than others of their age. Viewing themselves to be inadequate, they have little recourse but to revert to their learned pattern of turning to others to arrange their life and to provide for them.

Some nonparental factors alluded to in the last paragraph may also dispose children to develop a dependent pattern. The major factor here concerns events or relationships that lead children either to believe that they cannot compete with others or to learn that a submissive rather than assertive role will assure less discomfort and more reward. For example, a family situation in which the growing youngster is exposed to a more aggressive, competent, or troublesome sibling may set the stage for a dependent personality style. A more assertive and effective sibling may lead to unfavorable self-comparisons. Similarly, a difficult-to-manage sibling may invite the child to adopt the "good boy" image, one who acquiesces to mother's every mood and wish so as to gain comparative favor. In a third family, a child who is repeatedly subjected to the lashing of an angry or jealous sib may run so often for parental cover that the child learns to cling to them whenever a difficult world must be confronted.

Similar difficulties may be generated in experiences with one's peer group. Feelings of unattractiveness and inadequacy, especially during adolescence, often result in social humiliation and self-doubt. These youngsters are fortunate in the sense that they can usually retreat to their parents, where they find both love and acceptance. Although the immediate refuge of home is not to be demeaned, it may, in the long run, prove a disservice to these children since they must ultimately learn to stand on their own.

Note should be made of the fact that more women than men develop the dependent pattern. Some researchers attribute this fact to an inherent, temperamental dependency on the part of the female sex. Equally plausible is the view that the cultural roles sanctioned and encouraged in most societies reinforce the learning of passive and dependent behaviors among women.

PROGNOSTIC CONSIDERATIONS

It may appear strange, even paradoxical, that the genuine affection and acceptance experienced in childhood by dependent personalities should dispose them to pathology. For most of these individuals, childhood was a time of warmth and security, a period marked by few anxieties that were not quickly dispelled by parental attention and care. Too much of a "good" thing, however, can turn bad. Excessive parental shielding may establish habits and expectancies that are detrimental in the long run since they ill prepare the children to cope on their own with life. Accustomed to support from others and ill-equipped without them, dependents stand implanted, rooted to the deep attachments of their childhood. Unable to free themselves from their dependence, they face the constant danger of loss, dread desertion, and fear the abyss into which they will fall if left on their own. Beneath their pleasant and affable exterior, then, lies an extreme vulnerability, a sense of helplessness, and a fear of abandonment. Dependents' lack of resources and their self-doubts compel them to seek safe partners, trustworthy figures "like mother" who can be depended on to assure them that they are loved and will not be deserted.

What does the future usually hold for dependents, how and why do they remain fixed in their ways, and what approaches are best when intervening therapeutically? It is questions such as these that are addressed, albeit briefly, in this final section of the chapter.

Perpetuation of the Dependent Pattern

Dependent personalities, despite claims to ineptness and inadequacy, employ an interpersonal coping strategy that recruits the nurture and support they need. Moreover, it is a style that forestalls their sinking into deeper levels of psychopathology. By soliciting attention and affection, dependents remain in close touch with the "real" world and are exposed constantly to social relationships that keep them from straying too far into the abyss of subjective distortion. Despite the fact that dependency behaviors protect against the pernicious and decompensating effects of social withdrawal and autistic distortion, the problem remains that the coping strategy persists far beyond its origins and ultimate utility. More importantly, it leads the person into self-defeating vicious circles. A brief review follows of some of the features that result in the aggravation of the dependent's characteristic inadequacies.

Self-deprecation. Dependents not only observe real deficits in their competence, but they deprecate what virtues and talents they may possess. This is done to prevent others from expecting them to assume responsibilities they would rather avoid. Successful as a shield against discomfort and in protecting their dependency needs, these actions are carried out at the cost of demeaning one's own self-respect. Their rationalizations of inadequacy, offered for the benefit of others, have an impact on their own person. Each time dependents announce their defects, they convince themselves as well as others and thereby deepen their self-image of incompetence. Trapped by their own persuasiveness, they further reinforce their belief in the futility of standing on their own, and they are, hence, likely to try less and less to overcome their inadequacies. Their strategy has fostered a vicious circle of increased helplessness and dependency.

Avoidance of adult activities. Dependents' sense of inadequacy, fear of failure, and hesitation about antagonizing others cause them to refrain from activities that may facilitate a more mature and independent life-style. For example, despite ample opportunities to learn skills and to assume more "manly" roles, some dependent men shy away from these "threats," fear they could never succeed, and prefer instead to remain inept but good-natured and easy to get along with. Self-imposed restrictions will diminish short-term embarrassments and anxieties associated with failure, but they also diminish the probability that the dependents will acquire competence and confidence that will enable them to function more maturely. By making themselves less accessible to growth opportunities, they effectively preclude further maturation, and, hence, become evermore needful of others.

Clinging social behaviors. Although dependents appease others and apologize for their incompetence, their need for affection and assurance that they will not be abandoned may become so persistent as to exasperate and alienate those upon whom they lean most heavily. Of course, exasperation and alienation on the part of others only serve to increase the dependents' neediness. As the vicious circle persists, they may become more desperate, more ingratiating, and more urgently pleading and clinging, until they become "millstones around their partner's necks." Wearying of demands to prove fealty and love, the stronger partner may come to openly express annoyance, dissapproval, and, finally, rejection. Seriously rebuffed, a cycle of decompensation may begin or take on an increased pace. Overt expressions of self-blame, self-criticism, and self-condemnation may come to the fore. Fearful of expressing hostility, lest this result in further loss, dependents are likely to turn these feelings inward—first, to reproach themselves for their shortcomings and, second, to promise to be "different" and redeem themselves for their past mistakes. The "new leaf" they plan to "turn" takes the form of promises of greater competence and less dependence—aspirations that run counter to their lifelong personality style. These goals rarely are achieved, and it is at this point that we often see the emergence of a serious symptom disorder such as a major depression.

Remedial Intervention

Despite the possibilities of decompensation just noted, the prognosis for the dependent pattern is relatively good. Dependents are likely to have had a supporting relationship with at least one parent and this provided them with a reservoir of security and of feeling loved and wanted. Each of these positive emotions will sustain a dependent through difficult periods. Additionally, affectionate parents serve as models for imitative learning, equipping dependents with reciprocal habits of affection and generosity. Moreover, as noted earlier, dependency needs assure interpersonal contact, thereby forestalling the potentially decompensating effects of self-preoccupation and subjective distortion.

As far as therapy is concerned, dependents are not only receptive to being involved in treatment but are disposed to seek assistance wherever they can. The strength and authority of the therapist comforts them and gives them a feeling of assurance that an all-powerful person will not only come to their rescue but provide them with the kindness and helpfulness they crave. Moreover, the task of unburdening their woes to a therapist calls for little effort on their part. Although they may lack accurate insight into their difficulties, dependents will provide ample data to lead the therapist to uncover the origins of their problem. Furthermore, dependents are disposed to trust others, especially therapists, in whom they are likely to invest great powers and the highest of virtues.

The dependent's receptiveness and the auspicious beginning of therapy may create a misleading impression that future progress will be rapid. Quite naturally, these patients will seek a dependent relationship with their therapists. Despite "promises" to the contrary, they will resist efforts to guide them into assuming independence and autonomy. Assisting them in relinquishing their dependency habits will prove a slow and arduous process. Building an image of competence and self-esteem must proceed one step at a time through a program of strengthening attributes and dislodging the habit of leaning on others.

Environmental changes may be introduced to maximize growth and to minimize continued dependency. Psychopharmacologic treatment, notably certain antidepressants and antianxiety agents, may prove useful toward the end of promoting increased alertness and vigor since dependents often are plagued by fatigue, lethargy, and diffuse anxieties—states that incline them to postpone efforts at independence. It is important also that the relationship between therapist and patient not reestablish the dominance-submission pattern that has characterized the history of these patients. Nondirective and humanistic approaches are more likely to foster the growth of autonomy and self-confidence than more directive cognitive reorientation methods. It may be necessary to utilize psychodynamic approaches in order to rework deeper object attachments and to construct a base for competency strivings. Group therapy may be pursued fruitfully as a means of learning autonomous skills and as an aid to the dependent's growth of social confidence.

Chapter 5

Histrionic Personality:
The Gregarious Pattern

Dependent and histrionic personalities share important traits. Both turn to others for protection and the rewards of life. Beneath the social affability that characterizes them lies an intense need for attention and affection. They require constant affirmation of approval and acceptance, are vulnerable to the moods and attitudes of those upon whom they depend, and often experience a sense of helplessness when anticipating disinterest from others or when threatened with desertion.

The previous chapter described the dependent personality who not only finds security through the support of others, but who turns passively to them in the hope that they will be kind enough to bestow approval and affection. This passivity in securing acceptance contrasts markedly with the more active and manipulative style of the histrionic personality. Histrionics are no less dependent upon others for attention and affection but, in contrast to dependents, take the initiative in assuring these reinforcements. Rather than placing their fate in the hands of others, and thereby having their security in constant jeopardy, histrionic personalities actively solicit the interest of others through a series of seductive ploys that are likely to assure receipt of the admiration and esteem they need. Toward these ends histrionics develop an exquisite sensitivity to the moods and thoughts of those they wish to please. This hyperalertness enables them to quickly assess what maneuvers will succeed in attaining the ends they desire. This extreme "other-directedness," devised in the service of achieving approval, results, however, in a life-style characterized by a shifting and fickle pattern of behaviors and emotions. Unlike dependent personalities, who anchor themselves usually to only one object of attachment, the histrionic tends to be lacking in fidelity and loyalty. The dissatisfaction with single attachments, combined with a need for constant stimulation and attention, results in a seductive, dramatic, and capricious pattern of personal relationships.

This well-known syndrome, missing entirely in the official 1952 nosology, was reinstated in the DSM-II, though under the archaic label of the "hysterical personality." A less controversial and more appropriate appellation, that of "histrionic personality disorder," has been officially introduced as its designation in the DSM-III. The following excerpt is quoted from this latest manual.

> Individuals with this disorder are lively and dramatic, and are prone to exaggeration in order to dramatize their view of a particular situation ...
>
> Behavior is overly reactive and intensely expressed. Minor stimuli give rise to emotional excitability, such as irrational, angry outbursts or tantrums. Individuals with this disorder crave novelty, stimulation and excitement, and quickly become bored with normal routines.
>
> There are characteristic disturbances in interpersonal relations. Initially people with this disorder are apt to be perceived by others as shallow and lacking genuineness, even if superficially charming and appealing. Although frequently quick to form friendships, once a relationship is established, they often become either demanding, egocentric, and inconsiderate, which may result in manipulative suicidal threats, gestures or attempts, or dependent and helpless, constantly seeking reassurance. In some cases both patterns are present in the same relationship. Their actions are frequently inconsistent and are often misinterpreted by others.
>
> Such individuals are typically attractive and seductive and attempt to control the opposite sex or enter into a dependent relationship. Flights into romantic fantasy are common, and in both sexes overt behavior often is a caricature of femininity. The actual quality of their sexual relationships is variable. Some individuals are promiscuous, others naïve and sexually unresponsive, while others have an apparently normal sexual adjustment.
>
> Individuals with this disorder often experience periods of intense dissatisfaction and a variety of dysphoric moods, usually related to obvious changes in external circumstances.
>
> Usually these individuals show little interest in intellectual achievement and careful, analytic thinking, although they often are creative and imaginative.
>
> Individuals with this disorder are often impressionable and easily influenced by others or by fads. They tend to be overly trusting of others, suggestible, and show an intially positive response to any strong figure of authority who they think can provide a magical solution for their problems. Though they adopt convictions strongly and readily, their judgment is not firmly rooted, and they often play hunches. (p. 313)

HISTORICAL AND THEORETICAL ANTECEDENTS

Although recommended as a diagnostic label by several theorists over the last two decades, the designation "histrionic personality" achieved recognition as an official classification for the first time in the formal listings of the DSM-III, published in 1980. The term has replaced that of "hysterical personality," a syndrome whose origins in the word hysteria can be traced to the early days of both the Egyptians and the Greeks (Chodoff, 1974). The first descriptions of what we now refer to as histrionic personality traits were written in the mid-nineteenth century; since then the attributes of the syndrome have been well recognized and richly portrayed in the literature.

Ernst von Feuchtersleben (1847) depicted women disposed to hysterical symptoms as being sexually heightened, selfish, and "overprivileged with satiety and boredom." Attributing these traits to the unfortunate nature of female education, he wrote: "It combines everything that can heighten sensibility, weaken spontaneity, give a preponderance to the sexual sphere, and sanction the feelings and impulse that relate to it." Less oriented to matters of sexuality, Wilhem Griesinger (1845), the major psychiatric nosologist of mid-nineteenth-century Germany, wrote that hysterical women displayed an "immoderate sensitiveness, especially to the slightest reproach [in which there is a] tendency to refer everything to themselves, great irritability, great change of disposition on the least, or even from no, external motive." Among other distinguishing characteristics, according to Griesinger, were their volatile humor, their senseless caprices, and their inclination to deception, prevarication, jealousy, and malice.

Classificatory theorists of personality at the turn of the century were not concerned with clinical entities per se. However, their speculative models enabled them to derive character types that corresponded closely to the prime features of the "histrionic." As noted briefly in Chapter 2, Ribot (1890) formulated an "emotional" type characterized by an active disposition and extreme impressionability; along similar lines is Queyrat's active-emotional "passionate" type (1896). Heymans and Wiersma's (1906–1909) "choleric" character is noted by active, emotional, and external susceptibility; the same descriptive features are to be found in McDougall's "fickle" temper (1908). Hirt (1902), seeking to connect the classical four humors to psychiatric populations, assigned extremes in the sanguine temperament to the hysterical type, depicting them as superficially excitable, enthusiastic, unreliable, attention craving, and vain.

Two major strands of thinking concerning personality types emerged in the early twentieth century. On the one hand were the classical descriptive psychiatrists such as Kraepelin, Bleuler, Kretschmer, and Schneider; on the other were those of a psychoanalytic persuasion, notably Freud, Abraham, and Reich. Despite their chronologic overlap they are separated here for purposes of considering their views of the so-called hysterical personality.

Kraepelin provided a variety of different portraits of the hysterical type, noting as characteristic their delight in novelty, enthusiasm, vivid imagination, great excitability, mood lability, romantic preoccupation, capriciousness, and impulsiveness. In his classic lectures on psychiatry, published first in 1904, he provided the following delineation of a seriously disturbed hysterical patient.

> The emotional sympathies of the patient are more and more confined to the
> selfish furthering of her own wishes. She tries ruthlessly to extort the most

careful attention from those around her...is extremely sensitive to any supposed neglect, is jealous...and tries to make [others] give in to her by complaints, accusations, and outbursts of temper. The sacrifices made by others...only serve to pave the way for new demands. To secure the sympathy of those around her, she has recourse to...histrionic exaggeration. (1904, p. 253)

A similar description was formulated in 1901 by Pierre Janet in his list of the "stigmata" of hysteria; included here were the characteristic exhibitionistic, flamboyant, and demanding behaviors. Bleuler also articulated these classic features in his standard 1924 textbook. According to Karl Jaspers (1925), the essential feature of this personality was the "attempt to seem more than one is." Tracing the evolution of the disorder, Jaspers noted that the more self-deception and histrionics crept in, the more there was a loss of contact with genuine feelings; ultimately, nothing was left but "counterfeit demonstrativeness." Schneider (1923) assigned the label "attention-seeking" (*Geltungsbeduerftig*) as a substitute for "hysterical," claiming that the latter term implied a moral judgment and had acquired too broad and vague a meaning; a central feature in Schneider's account of these personalities was their proclivity to exaggeration and pathological lying, employed in the service of making themselves appear more interesting or attractive to others.

An especially apt and colorful summary of the features of the "hysterical character" was written by Kretschmer. In many of its details it could be substituted for the descriptive text written for the DSM-III:

> An overlively and overidealistic psychic sexuality with prudish rejection of its physical correlate, a rapidly vanishing elan of feelings, enthusiasm for impressive persons, a preference for what is loud and lively, a theatrical pathos, an inclination for brilliant roles, to dream themselves into big purposes in life, the playing with suicide, the contrast between enthusiastic self-sacrificial abandonment and a naïve, sulky, childish egotism, and especially a mixture of the droll and tragic in their way of living. (1926, p. 26)

Before moving to the evolving formulations of psychoanalytic theorists this discussion takes a brief excursion to characterizations by Jung and Adler that conform in several respects to the histrionic style. Specifically, in his "extraverted-intuitive" type, Jung conceived a set of features that correspond closely to the hysterical personality as described in his day. Jung wrote as follows:

> There is a marked dependence on external situations...he has a keen nose for anything new in the making. Because he is always seeking out new possibilities, stable conditions suffocate him. He seizes on new objects or situations with great intensity...only to abandon them cold-bloodedly, without any compunction...as soon as their range is known. (1921, p. 368)

Adler's (1964) "passive-constructive" life-style also depicts traits characteristic of the histrionic, notably attention seeking, behaving in a charming manner, and wishing to be recognized as special even if one has few achievements to deserve it.

As evident from the preceding paragraphs, psychiatrists and psychologists began to write about the traits of so-called hysterical characters as early as the mid-1800s. Although psychoanalytic theory had its origins in Freud's explication of the hysterical symptom, it was not until 1932 that he elucidated his views on the hysterical character. Similarly, and despite Abraham's signal role in formulating the concepts of oral and anal characters in early 1920s, Freud's interest focused on the relationship between libidinal development and hysterical symptoms, not on hysterical character traits. Fritz Wittels was the first analyst to provide a systematic description of the hysterical structure (1930); he asserted that despite important relationships connecting the hysterical symptom and the hysterical character, a significant segment of character operates independent of the symptom. Further—and in contrast to Abraham, who anchored the hysteric symptom to phallic-stage failures— Wittels ascribed the formation of character to fixations at the infantile or pregenital level. He wrote as follows:

> The hysterical character never frees itself from its fixation at the infantile level. Hence it cannot attain its actuality as a grown-up human being; it plays the part of a child, and also of the woman. The hysteric person has no actuality, she confuses fantasy and reality. (1930, p. 187)

In Freud's 1932 paper on "libidinal types," he spoke of those cases in which the id has become predominant as the "erotic" character. In his discussion of parallels between libidinal and character structures, he stated: "It seems easy to infer that when persons of the erotic type fall ill they will develop hysteria" (p. 250). To Freud, the distinguishing motive that governs the behavior of hysterics is the "dread of loss of love," which results in becoming "particularly dependent on those who may withhold their love from them" (p. 250).

As noted in Chapter 2, it was Reich who, in 1933, provided the first solid underpinnings to the psychoanalytic theory of character formation. In portraying what he termed the "outstanding characteristics" of the hysterical types, he wrote as follows:

> Disguised or undisguised coquetry in gait, look, or speech betrays, especially in women, the hysterical character type. In the case of men, besides softness and excessive politeness, a feminine facial expression and a feminine bearing also appear.
>
> We find fickleness of reactions, i.e., a tendency to change one's attitudes unexpectedly and unintentionally; a strong suggestibility, which never appears alone but is coupled with a strong tendency to reactions of disappointment.
>
> An attitude of compliance is usually followed by its opposite, swift deprecation and groundless disparagement. (1949, pp. 204–205)

Otto Fenichel has reinforced and added to these formulations in describing the hysterical characters as

> Persons who are inclined to sexualize all nonsexual relations, toward suggestibility, irrational emotional outbreaks, chaotic behavior, dramatization and histrionic behavior, even toward mendacity and in its extreme form, pseudologic phantastica...
>
> The histrionic quality...is a turning from reality to fantasy and probably also an attempt to master anxiety by "acting" actively what otherwise might happen passively...hysterical "acting" is...directed toward an audience. It is an attempt to induce others to participate in the daydreaming. (1945, pp. 527–528)

Within psychoanalytic circles, views concerning the development and varieties of hysterical character remain controversial. A seminal paper by Marmor (1953) has raised questions concerning whether the psychosexual origin of its formation is primarily oral rather than phallic; Easser and Lesser (1965), Kernberg (1967), and Zetzel (1968), although adhering to the classical themes of earlier writers, suggest several differentiations within the hysterical character spectrum. However, it is in quarters that have deviated significantly from psychoanalysis that we find some new and perceptive formulations; a number of them are discussed in the following paragraphs.

Although both Sullivan (1947) and Horney (1950) described personality types akin to the classical hysterical character, it was Fromm among the neo-Freudian social theorists who captured its modern variant most acutely in his delineation of the "marketing orientation."

> Success depends largely on how well a person sells himself on the market, how well he gets his personality across, how nice a "package" he is; whether he is "cheerful," "sound," "aggressive," "reliable," "ambitious."...
>
> Since success depends largely on how one sells one's personality, one experiences oneself as a commodity...A person is not concerned with his life and happiness, but with becoming salable.
>
> In the marketing orientation man encounters his own powers as commodities alienated from him. He is not one with them but they are masked from him because what matters is not his self-realization...but his success in the process of selling them. Both his powers and what they create become estranged...something for others to judge and to use; thus, his feeling of identity becomes as shaky as his self-esteem; it is constituted by the sum total of roles one can play: "I am as you desire me."
>
> The premise of the marketing orientation is emptiness, the lack of any specific quality which could not be subject to change...The marketing personality must be free, free of all individuality. (1947, pp. 69–78)

At an entirely different level, Donald Klein, a psychopharmacologically oriented theorist (1967, 1971, 1972, 1975), has suggested that the hysterical personality as formulated in the DSM-II was an amalgam of three subgroups that respond differently to psychotropic drugs: the histrionic, the emotionally unstable, and what he termed the "hysteroid dysphoric." Noting that cross-sectional distinctions are difficult to draw, and that diagnosis often requires prolonged longitudinal study, Klein nevertheless identified several key factors to delineate their respective characters. All three variants give evidence of the classical signs of lability, vanity, and dependency; but the "histrionic" is noted especially by "role-playing and symptom imitation"—that is, "symptoms may not be the direct external manifestations of intolerable affective states but rather may be environmentally oriented, learned manipulative devices" (1972, p. 355). Klein contrasted them to the "emotionally unstable" type who are predominantly

> female adolescents whose mood disorder consists of short periods of tense, empty unhappiness, accompanied by inactivity, withdrawal, depression, irritability and sulking, alternating suddenly with impulsiveness, giddiness, low frustration tolerance, rejection of rules and shortsighted hedonism. (1972, p. 356)

Last, in portraying the "hysteroid dysphoric," Klein wrote:

> They are fickle, emotionally labile, irresponsible, shallow, love-intoxicated, giddy and shortsighted...Seductive, manipulative, exploitative and sexually provocative, they think emotionally and illogically. Easy prey to flattery and compliments...they are possessive, grasping, demanding, romantic...when frustrated or disappointed, they become reproachful, tearful, abusive and vindictive... Rejection sensitivity is perhaps their outstanding common clinical feature. (1972, p. 237)

Whether Klein's distinctions merely represent different expressions of the same basic syndrome or are types deserving clear differentiation on the basis of their response to psychopharmacologic agents, as Klein contends, cannot be gauged at this time. Regardless, they are illuminating and effective portrayals of classical hysterical characters.

Brief note should be made of the factor analytic studies by Lazare, Klerman, and Armor (1966, 1970) and by Walton and Presley (1973a, b). The latter study uncovered a small group of traits that paralleled those assigned to the traditional hysterical personality category, notably ingratiation, need for attention, excessive emotional display, unlikability, and insincerity, In a cross-validation investigation to confirm and elaborate earlier findings, Lazare et al. noted that only four of seven traits that are classically associated with the hysterical character clustered together as anticipated. Traits that held up as strongly as predicted were emotionality, exhibitionism, egocentricity, and sexual provocativeness; those clearly failing to do so were suggestibility and fear of sexuality; the trait of dependency fell into an intermediary position. Among the unanticipated characteristics uncovered in the hysterical cluster were aggression, oral expression, obstinacy, and rejection of others. On the basis of these latter findings, Lazare et al. concluded that their "hysterical" population may have corresponded to the "infantile" personality described by Kernberg (1967), a type characterized as a primitive or regressed hysterical variant.

A fine early paper by Chodoff and Lyons (1958), which summarized the history and contrasted the hysterical symptom with the hysterical character, furnished a brief description that has been referred to time and again in the literature. Following a listing of cardinal qualities, they summarized:

> The hysterical personality is a term applicable to persons who are vain and egocentric, who display labile and excitable but shallow affectivity, whose dramatic, attention-seeking and histrionic behavior may go to the extremes of lying and even pseudologic phantastica, who are very conscious of sex, sexually provocative yet frigid, and who are dependently demanding in interpersonal situations. (1958, p. 736)

Moving to more recent work, Millon, using his theoretically derived active-dependent personality pattern as a basis (1969), summarized the distinguishing features of the "histrionic-gregarious" type in the following descriptions and diagnostic criteria; these were written in 1975 as the initial working draft for the DSM-III Task Force personality subcommittee.

> This pattern is typified by a gregarious, facile and superficially charming social lifestyle. There is a persistent seeking of attention, stimulation and excitement, usually expressed in seductive, immaturely exhibitionistic and self-dramatizing behaviors. Interpersonal relationships are characteristically shallow, frivolous and fleeting. A general intolerance of delay and inactivity often results in impulsive and over-reactive behaviors. Thought processes are typically insubstantial, unreflected and scattered. Highly labile emotions are notable by their easy and short-lived enthusiasms followed by rapid boredom.
>
> Since adolescence or early adulthood at least 3 of the following have been present to a notably greater degree than in most people and were not limited to discrete periods nor necessarily prompted by stressful life events.
>
> 1. Fickle affectivity (e.g., displays short-lived, dramatic and superficial affects; reports tendency to be easily excited and as easily bored.)
> 2. Sociable self-image (e.g., perceives self as gregarious, stimulating and charming; attracts fleeting acquaintances and enjoys rapidly-paced social life).
> 3. Interpersonal seductiveness (e.g., actively solicits praise and manipulates others to gain attention and approval; exhibits self-dramatizing and childishly exhibitionistic behaviors).
> 4. Cognitive dissociation (e.g., integrates experiences poorly which results in scattered learning and unexamined thought; reveals undependable, erratic and flighty judgment).
> 5. Immature stimulus-seeking behavior (e.g., is intolerant of inactivity, leading to unreflected and impulsive responsiveness; describes penchant for momentary excitements, fleeting adventures and short-sighted hedonism).

A revision of the preceding emerged following committee discussion; the focus shifted somewhat and resulted in these recommended criteria:

A. Persistent attention-seeking (e.g., socially seductive and childishly exhibitionistic as a means of soliciting praise and approval).

B. Interpersonally demanding (e.g., insistent on getting own way by manipulating others to achieve ends).

C. Overly reactive and intensely expressed affect (e.g., displays short-lived, dramatic and superficial emotion; is easily excited and quickly bored).

D. Socially gregarious (e.g., pursues active social life and is successful in attracting fleeting acquaintances).

E. Immature stimulus-seeking (e.g., penchant for momentary excitements, impulsively adventurous, and short-sighted hedonism).

The final criteria reflect further modifications, but the classic distinguishing features remain close to what has been written for well over 100 years.

CLINICAL PICTURE

Histrionic personalities often demonstrate, albeit in caricature and mild pathological form, what our society tends to foster and admire in its members—to be well liked, successful, popular, extraverted, attractive, and sociable. Beneath this surface portrayal we often see a driven quality, a consuming need for approval, a desperate striving to be conspicuous and to evoke affection or attract attention at all costs. Despite the frequent rewards these behaviors produce, they stem from needs that are pathologically inflexible, repetitious, and persistent.

In this section the histrionic picture is detailed in line with the four spheres of clinical observation and analysis employed in Chapter 4 for description of the dependent personality.

Behavioral Features

Histrionic personalities often impress one at first meeting by the ease with which they express their thoughts and feelings, by their flair for the dramatic, and by their capacity to draw attention to themselves. These exhibitionistic and expressive talents are manifested, however, in a series of rapidly changing, short-lived, and superficial affects. Histrionic personalities tend to be capricious, easily excited, and intolerant of frustration, delay, and disappointment. Moreover, the words and feelings they express appear shallow and simulated rather than deep or real.

Histrionics are more than merely friendly and helpful in their relationships: They are actively solicitous of praise, "market" their appeal, and are often entertaining and sexually provocative. Since affection and attention are primary goals, histrionics engage in a variety of maneuvers to elicit a favorable response. Women may behave in a charming or coquettish manner;

men are typically generous in praise and, on occasion, overtly seductive. Both men and women often display an interesting mixture of being carefree and sophisticated, on the one hand, and inhibited and naïve, on the other. In the sphere of sexuality, for example, many histrionics are quite at ease while "playing the game" but become confused, immature, or apprehensive once matters get serious.

Characteristically, histrionics are unable to follow through and sustain the initial impression of goodwill and sophistication they convey. Social life is one in which there are "many acquaintances but few friends." In most areas of personal activity they put up a good show at the start but often falter and withdraw when depth and durability in relationships are required.

Self-Descriptions and Complaints

Histrionic personalities view themselves as sociable, friendly, and agreeable people. Many lack insight, however, failing to recognize, or admit recognizing, signs of inner turmoil, weakness, depression, or hostility.

The preoccupation of histrionic personalities with external rewards and approvals often leaves them bereft of an identity apart from others. They describe themselves not in terms of their own traits but in terms of their relationships and their effects upon others. Histrionics behave like "empty organisms" who react more to external stimuli than to promptings from within. They show an extraordinary sensitivity to the thoughts and moods of those from whom they desire approval and affection. This well-developed "radar" system serves them well, for it not only alerts them to signs of impending rejection but enables them to manipulate the object of their designs with consummate skill.

This orientation toward external stimuli leads histrionics to pay fleeting, impressionistic, and scattered attention to details, and accounts in part for their characteristic distractible and flighty behaviors. The susceptibility of histrionics to transient events parallels their superficial cognitive style, their lack of genuine curiosity, and their inability to think in a concentrated and logical fashion. Habits of superficiality and dilettantism may represent an intellectual evasiveness and a desire to eschew troublesome thoughts or emotionally charged feelings. Part of the flightiness of histrionic personalities derives from an avoidance of potentially disruptive ideas and urges, especially those which might bring to awareness their deeply hidden dependency needs. For these and other reasons they "steer clear" of self-knowledge and depth in personal relationships. In effect, histrionics dissociate themselves from thoughts, from people, and from activities that might upset their strategy of superficiality.

Inferred Intrapsychic Dynamics

As already noted, histrionics actively seek to avoid introspection and responsible thinking. Not only are they characteristically attuned to external rather than internal events, but their lifelong orientation toward what others think and feel has prevented them from learning to deal with their own inner thoughts and feelings. As a consequence, they lack intrapsychic skills and must resort to gross mechanisms to handle unconscious emotions. What they have learned best is to simply seal off, repress, or dissociate entire segments of memory and feeling that may prompt discomfort. As a result, much of their past is a blank, devoid of the complex reservoir of attitudes and emotions they should have acquired through experiences.

Having deprived themselves of past learnings, histrionics are less able to function on their own and thereby perpetuate their dependency on others. Moreover, to compensate for the void of their past, and for the guidance these learnings could provide, they remain locked into the present. In short, the intrapsychic world of the histrionic personality is skimpy and insubstantial. Their preoccupation with external immediacies has led to an impoverishment of inner richness and depth.

To the degree that histrionics possesses an inner world of thought, memory, and emotion, they try to repress it and to keep it from intruding into their conscious life. This they do for several reasons. First, their own sense of worth depends on the judgment of others; there is no reason to explore the inner self, for they alone cannot appraise their personal value or provide acceptance or approval. Second, by turning attentions inward histrionics distract themselves from attending to the outer world. This divided attention can prove troublesome since they feel they must be ever-alert to the desires and moods of others. To preserve their exteroceptive vigilance, they must reduce "inner" distractions, especially those that may be potentially disturbing. Third, histrionics seek actively to blot out any awareness of the barrenness of their intrapsychic world. This inner emptiness is especially intolerable since it points to the fraudulence that exists between the impressions they seek to convey to others and their true cognitive sterility and emotional poverty. The contrast between their pretensions and objective reality leads histrionics to repress not only one or two deficiencies within themselves but all of their inner self; it is the triviality of their entire being, its pervasive emptiness and paucity of substance, that must be kept from awareness. Repression is therefore applied across the board; it is massive and absolute.

Interpersonal Coping Style

Most persons seek stimulation, attention, and approval, but it is only the histrionic personality who possesses an insatiable striving for these experiences, who feels devoid of an inner self and seeks constant nourishment to fill that void. Lacking a core identity apart from others, histrionics must draw nurture from those around them. It is others who supply the sustenance of life without which the histrionic will feel an emptiness, a fear of collapse, and a falling apart in disarray. How do histrionics manipulate their interpersonal world to assure the stimulation and approval they require?

It may be useful before proceeding to note again that the interpersonal behaviors of most pathological personalities do not usually appear strikingly different from that seen among "normal" individuals. Their distinction lies not so much in their uniqueness or bizarreness but in their inflexibility and persistence.

Histrionics are often successful in accomplishing their aims of eliciting stimulation and captivating the attentions of others. Their strategies are considered pathological because they fail to limit their manipulations to situations in which they are appropriate. Rather, theyaare applied indiscriminantly and persistently, seeking to attract the attentions of insignificant persons in unsuitable circumstances. Histrionics' need for recognition and approval appear insatiable. As soon as they receive attention from one source, they turn their unquenchable thirst for approval to others. The histrionic is a bottomless pit into which esteem and tribute may be poured. Equally important is the observation that a failure to evoke attention and approval often results in dejection and anxiety. Signs of indifference or neutrality on the part of others often are interpreted as rejections and result in feelings of emptiness and unworthiness.

It is toward the end of achieving these goals and avoiding these fears that histrionics have learned to manipulate others to their suiting. More than merely agreeable and friendly, they "sell" themselves by employing their talents and charm to elicit recognition and esteem. This is done by presenting an attractive front, by seductive pretensions, by a dilettante sophistication, and by a show of postures and acts to impress and amuse others. Displays and exhibitions, dramatic gestures, attractive coiffures, frivolous comments, clever stories, and shocking clothes, all are designed not to "express themselves" but to draw interest, stimulation, and attention. In short, histrionics use themselves as a commodity with a bag of tricks, a conspicuous "personality" that corners all of the attention of those with whom they come into contact.

Histrionic personalities not only acquire skill in sensing what is salable or will "get across" to others, but they learn to be alert to signs of potential hostility and rejection. This hypervigilance enables them to quickly adapt their behaviors to minimize indifference and disapproval. Their interpersonal facility extends, therefore, not only to evoking praise but to avoiding rejection. By paying close attention to the signals that people transmit, histrionics can fashion their reactions to conform with the desires of others. Then they need not fear indifference or desertion since they are always ready to maneuver themselves to do things that correspond to the wishes and expectations of others.

Despite the charm and talent for "pleasing" others, the histrionic fails to provide them with genuinely sustained affection. All that histrionic personalities offer in return for the approval they seek are fleeting and often superficial displays of affection. Having failed throughout life to develop the richness of inner feelings and lacking resources from which they can draw, histrionics have difficulty in maintaining a full, meaningful, and stable relationship with another. At some level they also sense the disparity that exists between the favorable but superficial impression they give to others and their real lack of inner substance. As a result, they are likely to shy from prolonged contact with others for fear that their fraudulence will be uncovered. In sum, the facile emotions of histrionics are shallow, fleeting, and illusory; not only are they unable to sustain close relationships, but they quickly abandon what few they may have had before the "truth" be known.

ASSOCIATED DISORDERS

As in the previous chapter (and as in each of the subsequent ones), a brief discussion ensues concerning the major varieties of both Axis I and II syndromes that frequently coexist with the personality type under review. Equally important, in the author's judgment, is the opportunity these presentations provide for elaborating the distinctive manner and form in which each personality pattern expresses the symptom disorders they share in common. For example, experienced clinicians know (and Chodoff and Lyons [1958] have shown) that hysterical conversion symptoms are found as frequently among nonhysterical as among hysterical personalities. Symptom disorders signify different vulnerabilities and coping responses in different personality styles; there is value, therefore, in elaborating their interface. Reference should be made to the discussion of the coping functions associated with these disorders in Chapter 4. This section now turns, however, to those Axis I disorders to which the histrionic personality is most susceptible, identifying not only the manner in which the various symptoms are manifested but also the probable dynamics and secondary gains with which they are typically associated.

Concomitant Axis I Symptoms

Anxiety disorders. Histrionics are vulnerable to *separation anxieties* to only a slightly lesser extent than are dependent personalities. The conditions that give rise to these feelings, however, are quite different. Histrionics promote their own anxieties by their tendency to seek diverse sources of support and stimulation. Moreover, they quickly get bored with old attachments and excitements. As a consequence, they frequently set themselves up to be isolated and alone, stranded for extended periods with no one to lean on and nothing to be occupied with. During these empty times they feel at loose ends and experience a marked restlessness and generalized anxiety until some new romance or excitement attracts their interst. Histrionic patients experience genuine discomforts during these vacant periods, but they tend to overdramatize their distress as a means of soliciting attention and support. The use of exhibitionistic displays of anxiety as an attention-getting tool is notable.

Phobic disorders.   Histrionics exhibit phobic symptoms somewhat less frequently than dependent personalities. Feelings of emptiness and aloneness may be symbolized and transformed into brief *agoraphobias*. Similarly, an upsurge of socially unacceptable aggressive impulses may serve to prompt the formation of a protective or neutralizing phobic symptom. Symptoms such as these are also displayed exhibitionistically, that is, utilized as dramatic vehicles to gain attention and support from others. Histrionics are likely to be quite open about their symptom, in contrast to most other personalities with phobic problems. In essence, they will often try to get as much attention-gaining mileage out of their discomforts as they can.

Obsessive compulsive disorders.   Obsessional symptoms occur infrequently among histrionics. However, as a consequence of their lack of a cohesive personality organization, their thoughts and emotions may become scattered and disconnected. These unconnected or free-floating obsessional thoughts illustrate a variant of the dissociative thesis first posited by Janet (1901). Contributing further to these symptoms is the tendency of these patients to exhibit dramatic emotion in response to matters of minimal significance; similarly, but conversely, they are inclined to discuss serious problems with an air of cool detachment. The ease with which intense affects and ideas can be isolated from one another contributes to the emergence of seemingly unconnected and unanchored obsessive symptoms. The poor psychic integration of histrionics means that with little strain or tension they can disconnect an emotion from its associated content. Not unfrequently, histrionics report experiencing a "free-floating" erotic emotion or sexual impulse, without an external precipitant or focus. In parallel fashion, they often speak of hostile thoughts that obsessively preoccupy them but lack normally associated feelings of anger. Which behavior or emotion will be expressed and which will be repressed is usually determined by their goal of seeking social approval and minimizing social rebuke; for example, histrionics rarely vent hostility but often manifest unfeeling seductive behaviors.

Somatoform disorders.   Histrionic personalities openly and dramatically exhibit *conversion symptoms*. This is consistent with their desire to attract attention to themselves. Among the more common conversions in this personality are mutism and persistent laryngitis; this usually serves to protect against an unconscious impulse to verbalize hostile thoughts that may provoke social reproval. Moreover, these symptoms are quite eye-catching and enable the patients both to dramatize their plight and to draw the total attention of others to their only means of communication, those of gesticulation and pantomime.

Histrionics also utilize *hypochondriacal* and *somatization* symptoms as instruments for attracting attention and nurture. To be fussed over with care and concern is rewarding for most individuals. In histrionics, it is "like a drug" that is needed to sustain them. When histrionics feel a sense of emptiness and isolation, they desperately seek a diet of constant concern and approval. To be ill is a simple solution since it requires little effort yet produces guaranteed attention. Thus, if nothing else "works," *factitiously* created symptoms may be depended upon as a means of achieving these ends. Moreover, if life becomes humdrum and boring, physical ailments not only evoke attention from others but provide a new preoccupation and source of stimulation. *Psychogenic pain* and aches are another form of preoccupation and stimulation to fill the empty moments. Only rarely, however, do histrionics display somatic fatigue since this symptom runs counter to their active stimulus-seeking style. They prefer to use obvious and dramatic complaints to draw attention to themselves, for these behaviors enable them to continue to participate actively in social affairs.

Dissociative disorders.   The lack of an integrated personality organization among histrionics makes it difficult for them, even in normal times, to unify the disparate elements of their lives. During periods of strain and discord, this integrative deficiency may result in the development of a dissociative disorder. *Psychogenic fugue* states may not be uncommon; they usually take form in a search for attention and stimulation when the person feels unwanted or otherwise deprived. Daytime *depersonalization* episodes are unusual, however, since histrionic patients seek to be alert to their environment. Also rare are *psychogenic amnesia* and *multiple personality* states. When they do occur, these symptoms usually signify the histrionic's attempt to break away from a confining and stultifying environment. Faced with internal psychic poverty and external boredom or constraint, histrionics may seek the gains of a more exciting and dramatic life in which they can achieve the attention and approval they crave.

Affective disorders.   Histrionic personalities characteristically overplay their feelings of *dysthymic* disorder, expressing them through dramatic and eye-catching gestures. This contrasts to the flat and somber picture typically seen in the dependent, and to the tense and guilt-ridden quality seen, for example, among compulsive and passive-aggressive personalities. The exhibitionistic display of mood is a natural outgrowth of their basic style of actively soliciting attention and approval. Episodes of milder depression in histrionics are usually prompted less by a fear of abandonment than by a sense of emptiness and inactivity. It arises most often when they feel stranded between one fleeting attachment and another or between one transitory excitement and the next. At these times of noninvolvement, histrionics sense a lack of direction and begin to experience a fearful void and aloneness. Depressive complaints tend to be expressed in popular jargon. Histrionics philosophize about their "existential anxiety" or the alienation that we all share in this "age of mass society." This use of fashionable language provides them with a bridge to others. It gives them a feeling of belonging during times when they are most isolated from the social life they so desperately seek.

Moreover, their pseudosophistication about up-to-date matters not only enables them to rationalize their personal emptiness and confusion but also allows them to maintain their appeal in the eyes of "interesting" people. By adopting currently popular modes of disenchantment, they reinstate themselves as participants of an "in" subgroup and thereby manage to draw attention to themselves. Expressions of dissent also provide an outlet for venting resentments and tensions. However, should feelings of hostility be discharged without sanction, they may be quickly withdrawn and replaced with dramatic declarations of guilt and contrition.

Histrionics are likely to evidence agitated rather than retarded *major depressions*. The primary precipitant tends to be anticipated losses in dependency security. Histrionics may wail aloud and make well known their feelings of helplessness and abandonment, all in the hope of soliciting support and nurture. Their agitation does not reflect an internal struggle, as in more ambivalent personality types, but is a direct and simple expression of the worrisome apprehension they seek to resolve.

Among other Axis I symptoms to which histrionics are particularly susceptible are *biopolar disorders* and *cyclothymic disorders*; these syndromes are consistent with their characteristic socially gregarious and exuberant style. Confronted with severe separation anxieties or anticipating a loss of social approval, histrionic personalities may intensify their habitual behavior pattern until it reaches the forced and frantic congeniality we term *manic* or *hypomanic*. Here we may observe a frenetic search for attention, a release of tension through hyperactivity, and an effort to stave off the growing feeling of depressive hopelessness.

Concurrent Axis II Personalities

As noted in the previous chapter, this book draws upon research carried out with the Millon Clinical Multiaxial Inventory (MCMI) to provide an empirical base for determining frequently coexisting personality disorders. Sections of MCMI computer-generated reports are included to illustrate clinical syntheses of profiles composed of these personality pairings.

Histrionic-narcissistic mixed personality. A common association has been found between the histrionic and the narcissistic personalities. Prevalence data indicate that this covariation occurs with considerable frequency in settings such as drug treatment programs, marital counseling clinics, and centers for handling youth offenders. Those who score high on MCMI histrionic and narcissistic personality scales tend to be clever, charming, flippant, and capable of weaving fanciful images that intrigue and seduce the naïve. Driven by a need for excitement and stimulation, this amalgam acts impulsively, is unable to delay gratification, and evidences a penchant for momentary excitements and fleeting adventures, with minimal regard for later consequences. These individuals are notably thrill seeking, easily infatuated, and overly, but transiently, attached to one thing or person following another. There is often a lack of social dependability, and a disdain for the effects of one's behaviors, as the individual pursues the restless chase of satisfying one whim after another. There may be a capricious disregard for agreements hastily assumed, and a trail may be left of broken promises and contracts, squandered funds, distraught employers, and so on. Lacking inner substance and self-discipline, tempted by new and exciting stimuli, and skilled in attracting and seducing others, such narcissistic-histrionic personalities may travel an erratic course of flagrant irresponsibility and leave in their wake the scattered debris of once promising but now abandoned hopes.

Histrionic-antisocial mixed personality. Another major composite is found in the fusion of histrionic and antisocial personalities. These combinations are prevalent also in drug treatment programs but are found most commonly in prison populations and other criminal-related detention centers. The following material from a MCMI "blind" computer printout is based on the responses of a 27-year-old male involved in the early stages of a drug rehabilitation program; his record of both minor and major crimes (consisting of burglaries, mugging, and check forgeries) was traced back to the age of 16.

This patient's behavior is typified by a veneer of friendliness and sociability. Although making a superficially good impression upon acquaintances, his more characteristic unreliability, impulsive tendencies, and deep resentments and moodiness are seen frequently among family members and other close associates. The socially facile life-style may be noted in a persistent seeking of attention and excitement, often expressed in seductive and self-dramatizing behaviors. Relationships are shallow and fleeting, frequently disrupted by caustic comments and hostile outbursts. Impulses are acted upon with insufficient deliberation and poor judgment.

The patient is frequently seen as irresponsible and undependable, exhibiting short-lived enthusiasms and immature stimulus-seeking behaviors. Not likely to admit responsibility for personal or family difficulties, he manifests a testy defensiveness and vigorous denial of psychological tensions or conflicts. Interpersonal difficulties are rationalized and blame is projected upon others. Although egocentrically self-indulgent and insistent on attention, he provides others with minimal loyalty and reciprocal affection.

The patient is fearful lest others see him as indecisive or soft-hearted, and antagonism is often expressed toward those upon whom there is dependence. Tendencies to act out antisocially may be present. When mildly crossed, subject to minor pressures, or faced with potential embarrassment, this patient may be quickly provoked to anger, often expressed in a revengeful or vindictive way. A characteristic undercurrent of defensive vigilance and hostility rarely subsides. The air of superficial affability is extremely precarious and he is ready to depreciate anyone whose attitudes touch a sensitive theme. Temper outbursts may reach intense proportions and sudden, unanticipated violence may be expressed. Although infrequent, when the thin veneer of sociability is eroded there may be momentary upsurges of abuse and uncontrollable rage.

Histrionic-borderline mixed personality. A compound of histrionic and borderline personality features is not uncommon. Kernberg (1967) refers to a mix akin to this union as the "infantile personality," noted by labile and diffuse emotions, childlike pouting, and demanding-clinging behaviors, as well as a crude and direct sexual provocativeness; in many respects this type might be best conceived as a decompensated or a primitively developed and poorly organized histrionic. The following "blind" MCMI computer report illustrates a mixture of histrionic, compulsive, and borderline personality features; it was obtained from response data given by a 34-year-old divorcee with a history since adolescence of both manic and depressive episodes.

> This patient's behavior is typified by a veneer of sociability, maturity, and independence. Beneath this veneer is a fear of genuine autonomy, a need to present a good public front, and a deeply conflictful submission to the expectancies of others. Her front of social propriety and self-assurance cloaks deep and increasingly intense but suppressed antagonisms. To control these oppositional tendencies, she struggles to maintain a disciplined self-restraint and a socially agreeable affability, perhaps with moments of dramatic conviviality. This patient engages in a wide variety of interpersonal maneuvers designed to elicit favorable attention and social approval. There is a long-standing pattern of being deferential and ingratiating with superiors, going out of the way to impress them with efficiency and seriousmindedness.
>
> Recent failures to evoke authority approval have led to depressive periods and chronic anxiety. She is now high-strung and moody, straining to express attitudes contrary to her inner feelings of tension, anger, and dejection. To avoid these discomforts, she has become increasingly sensitive to the moods and expectations of others. Although she views herself as prudent and disciplined, the extreme other-directedness utilized in the service of achieving approval has resulted in a life-style characterized by its high adaptability. She has also learned to be alert to signs of potential hostility and rejection. By paying close attention to the signals that others transmit, the patient usually avoids disapproval, adapting all behaviors to conform with their desires. This pattern has been central to her life-style, that is, doing that which corresponds to the wishes of others. Moreover, by identifying with the views of authorities and adhering to the rules of bureaucracies, she has acquired a feeling of importance and significance. This preoccupation with external approval, however, has resulted in a growing sense of personal impotence and social dependency.
>
> This patient denies awareness of her inner deficiencies since it would point up the fraudulence that exists between the overt impressions she seeks to create and her personally felt sterility and emotional poverty. This tendency to seal off and deny the elements of inner life further intensifies her dependence on others. Increasingly, deep resentments toward those to whom she conforms and depends on have begun to emerge. These antagonisms have periodically broken through surface constraints, erupting in outbursts of guilt and contrition. These vacillations in behavior between periods of submissive compliance and testy negativism compound her discomforts. Such public displays of inconsistency and impulse expression contrast markedly with her self-image. There are bitter complaints about being treated unfairly, of expecting to be disappointed and

disapproved by others, and of no longer being appreciated for her diligence, sociability, and respectability. With the persistence of these ambivalent feelings, she has begun to suffer somatic discomforts, voicing growing distress about a wide range of physical symptoms.

Differential Diagnostic Signs

In Chapter 4 several reasons were presented for a decreased concern over matters of differential diagnosis. Essentially, the multiaxial format of DSM-III encourages the recording of overlapping diagnoses within each axis, and, more importantly, it *requires* the listing of impairments from both Axis I and Axis II. Multiple diagnoses notwithstanding, there are areas in which diagnostic confusions can occur—that is, where the issue is *not* overlap but a matter of distinguishing among fundamentally different processes that appear similar on the surface. Two such syndromes should be discussed: cyclothymic disorder and narcissistic personality disorder.

Overlap with the *cyclothymic disorder* is possible, of course. However, hypomanic periods, as observed in these disorders, are found among numerous personality types other than the histrionic and it is for this reason that distinctions may be needed. The symptoms of elevated, expansive, and irritable mood are notable in both syndromes, but there is an urgency, restlessness, and intensity about the hypomanic phase of cylothymia that does not typify the everyday behaviors of the histrionic. Similarly, as a personality pattern, the histrionic has learned to behave in a reasonably skillful social manner, gregariously maneuvering and manipulating others in a way that is usually seen as "attractive" rather than "infantile" and desperate. Although occasionally inappropriate, the usual pattern of the histrionic's life-style is adaptive in that it does not interfere with routine social and occupational functioning, as does the behavior and mood of the cyclothymic disorder.

Superficial similarities between histrionics and *narcissists* in their desire to be the center of attention, in behaving exhibitionistically, and in their characteristic bouyant (if fickle) moods lead frequently to initial differential diagnostic difficulties; of course, these two personality patterns may, and frequently do, coexist. A clear distinction, rather than a multiple diagnosis, should be made when warranted, however. The essential difference is found in the relative dominance or centrality of seeking dependence upon versus independence from others. Histrionics seek close, if not necessarily enduring, relationships and are willing to subscribe to popular fads and conventions if they give promise of attention and favor. Narcissists disdain acts of dependency, turning away from group fashions and regulations, acting as if they were above the responsibilities of shared social life. Rather than being on the "in" or seeking to "outdo" others in identifying with social styles, as do histrionics, narcissists avoid and depreciate such "demeaning" behaviors. Their style interpersonally is exploitive rather than seductive, as in the histrionic. Furthermore, narcissists struggle to convey a consistently cool and nonchalant air rather than displaying the histrionic's short-lived and dramatic moods.

PREDISPOSING BACKGROUND

As noted in the introduction to a parallel section in Chapter 4, the influences posited here as significant in forming the histrionic personality must be understood to be conjectural. Further, the distinction made in grouping these influences into biogenic and experiential sections is merely pedagogic; the pattern of determinants is not only interactive but is reciprocal and sequentially interconnected. With these caveats, discussion of the topic proceeds.

Hypothetical Biogenic Factors

The biological underpinnings of the histrionic personality are difficult to infer. Conceived in temperamental terms, histrionic behavior suggests both a high level of energy and activation, and a low threshold for autonomic reactivity. Histrionics tend, in general, to be quick and responsive, especially with regard to the expression of emotions. Feelings of both a positive and negative variety come forth with extreme ease, suggesting either an unusually high degree of sensory irritability, excessive sympathetic activity, or a lack of cortical inhibition. No single temperament label readily captures the intense, erratic, and wide range of emotions to which they are disposed.

The role of heredity cannot be overlooked in searching for the origins of the histrionic pattern. The neural and chemical substrate for sensory alertness and emotional reactivity may logically be traced to genetic influences. Evidence demonstrating a high degree of family correspondence in these traits is suggestive, of course, but can be explained also by common experience and learning.

It would seem reasonable that histrionic adults would have displayed a high degree of emotional responsiveness in infancy and early childhood. This inference derives from the facts that constitutional traits are essentially stable throughout life and that active and responsive children are likely to foster and intensify their initial responsiveness by evoking stimulating reactions from others.

Among the possible sites that may be posited for the emotional responsivity of the histrionic are the limbic and reticular systems. A neurally dense or abundantly branched limbic region may account for both the intensity and ease with which emotions are expressed. Low thresholds for reticular activation, stemming from idiosyncratic features of that region, may underlie their excitability and diffuse reactivity. Similarly, ease of sympathetic arousal, adrenal hyperreactivity, and neurochemical imbalances may facilitate a rapid transmission of impulses across synaptic junctions, resulting in the tendency of histrionics to be labile, distractible, and excitable.

The hypotheses just noted must be viewed as highly conjectural. Even if the evidence can be adduced in their support, the question remains as to why some persons who possess these constitutional characteristics become histrionics, whereas others develop different pathological patterns and most remain normal.

Characteristic Experiential History

Biogenic influences are likely to be minimally relevant in the development of the histrionic pattern. It would be logical, therefore, to focus our attention on psychological experience and learning as primary etiological variables.

Constitutionally alert and responsive infants are likely to experience greater and more diverse stimulation in their first months of life than dull and phlegmatic infants. As a consequence, their tendency is reinforced to look "outward" to the external world for rewards rather than "inward" to themselves. Similarly, normally alert infants may develop this exteroceptive attitude if their caretakers, by virtue of indulgence and playfulness, expose them to excessive stimulation during their first, or what we have termed their "sensory-attachment," stage (Millon, 1969). Future histrionic personalities may have been exposed to a number of different sources that provided brief, highly charged, and irregular stimulus reinforcements. For example, they may have had many different caretakers in infancy (parents, siblings, grandparents, and foster parents) who supplied them with intense, short-lived stimulus gratifications that came at irregular or haphazard intervals. Such experiences may not only have built in a high level of sensory capacity, requiring constant "feeding" to be sustained, but may also have conditioned the child to expect stimulus reinforcements in short, concentrated spurts from a melange of different sources. Viewed in this way, the persistent yet erratic dependency behaviors of the histrionic personality may reflect a pathological form of intense stimulus seeking that is traceable to highly charged, varied, and irregular stimulus reinforcements associated with early attachment learning. Shifting from one source of gratification to another, the histrionic's search for new stimulus adventures, penchant for creating excitement, and inability to tolerate boredom and routine, all may represent the consequences of these unusual early experiences.

In addition to differences in the variety, regularity, and intensity of stimulus enrichments in the sensory-attachment stage, the childhood experiences of the future histrionic may be distinguished, for example, from those of the future dependent personality. It appears that dependents received attention and affection from their caretakers, regardless of their behavior; they did not need to "perform" to elicit parental nurturance and protection. As a consequence of passively waiting for their parents to tend to their needs, dependents failed to develop adequate competencies and autonomy. The future histrionics, in contrast, learned that they had to engage in certain sanctioned behaviors and had to satisfy certain parental desires and expectations in order to receive attention and affection. In other words, future histrionics learned that parental approval was contingent on performance, such as "looking pretty," or showing their latest "artistic masterpiece," or the "fancy ballet steps" they just learned in dancing school.

The conditions for learning histrionic behaviors seem to be characterized by the following three features: minimal negative reinforcement (e.g., parents rarely criticize or punish the child), positive reinforcement contingent upon performance of parentally approved behaviors (e.g., favorable comments are conveyed only if one "is pretty" or "did well"), and irregularity in positive reinforcement (e.g., parents periodically fail to take cognizance of the child's efforts even when the child attempts to attract their attention). Stated in conventional language, the parents of the future histrionic rarely punish their children, they distribute rewards only for what they approve and admire, but they often fail to bestow these rewards even when the child behaves acceptably.

These experiences have several consequences in terms of personality. They appear to create behaviors that are designed primarily to evoke rewards, create a feeling of competence and acceptance *only* if others acknowledge and commend one's performances, and build a habit of seeking approval for its own sake. All three of these traits are characteristic of the histrionic personality. The following paragraphs consider their development in some detail.

Children who receive few punishments and many rewards will develop strong and unambivalent inclinations to relate to others. If a child such as this learns that the achievement of rewards is dependent on fulfilling the expectations and desires of others, he or she will develop a set of instrumental behaviors designed to please others and thereby elicit these rewards. However, if these behaviors succeed sometimes but not always, the child will persist in using them well beyond all reason—until they do succeed, which they eventually will. In other words, these reward- and attention-seeking behaviors will not be easily extinguished, even if they fail much of the time. As a consequence, these children become actively, rather than passively, oriented toward others. Furthermore, they will learn to look to others rather than to themselves for rewards, since their actions are only a preliminary and not a sufficient condition for achieving reinforcement. Despite the fact that the child always behaves in a manner to please and perform well for others, it is always *they* who determine whether or not the child will be rewarded. Future histrionics learn to look to others for the judgment of whether their efforts justify approval; it is others who define the adequacy of the child's behavior. Appeal and achievement are gauged by the attentions of others, not by the intrinsic merit or lack of merit of their actual behaviors. Moreover, since favorable recognition of acceptance occurs only irregularly—that is, not every time the child performs—future histrionics are never sure of their appeal and attractiveness, and therefore continue to look to others, even after repeated failures, to express a favorable response. Because of the irregularity with which attention is bestowed, the search takes on a "life of its own," a habit of soliciting signs of approval that becomes so firmly established that it eventually is pursued for its own sake.

Two additional features of family life often contribute to the development of the histrionic pattern—parental models who themselves are histrionic and certain patterns of sibling rivalry.

As discussed in Chapter 3, children learn, quite unconsciously and unintentionally, to mimic what they are exposed to. The prevailing attitudes, feelings, and incidental behaviors displayed every day by family members serve as models which children imitate and take as their own long before they can recognize what they are doing or why. Vicarious learning of this sort is made especially easy if parental behaviors and feelings are unusually pronounced or dramatic. When parents bring attention to themselves and create strong emotional reactions in their child, the child cannot help but see and learn clearly how people behave and feel. Specifically, the daily input of a histrionic parent who exhibits feelings and attitudes rather dramatically provides a sharply defined model for vicarious and imitative learning.

Another family condition conducive to histrionic learning arises among children who struggle long and hard to capture the attention and affection of their parents under conditions of sibling rivalry. These children often continue to utilize the devices that led to their periodic successes long after the rivalry ceased in reality. Thus, if the child learned to employ cuteness, charm, attractiveness, and seduction as a strategy to secure parental attention, these interpersonal behaviors may persist and take the form of a lifelong histrionic pattern.

Not to be overlooked, despite its apparent "simple-minded" nature, is the fact that aesthetically appealing girls and likable or athletic boys need expend little effort to draw attention and approval to themselves. Merely being themselves is sufficient to attract others. Rewarding as these experiences may be in building self-esteem, they do have negative consequences. Such youngsters come to be excessively dependent on the approval of others since they are accustomed to special recognition and have learned to expect attention at all times. Many will experience considerable discomfort when attention fails to materialize. In order to assure the continuation of these rewards, many may learn to "play up" their attractiveness. For example, the formerly attractive young girl, in order to elicit the attention that came so readily in youth, goes to great pains as she matures to remain a pretty woman; similarly, a formerly successful young athlete struggles to keep his trim figure as he progresses into mid-life. Both of these individuals may have failed to acquire more substantial talents in their youth since they needed none to elicit social rewards. What we may observe in later life is a childish exhibitionism and an adolescent and flirtatious style of relating, both of which characterize the histrionic personality.

Finally, there are parents who fail to provide their children with a consistent or stabilizing set of values. Some are intellectually committed to a "laissez-faire" policy; others are vacillating themselves; a third group is so preoccupied that they have little time to guide their child's development. Whatever the reason, many children are left to fend for themselves, to discover their own direction in the complex and changing world which surrounds them. Given the character of an evolving society, these children find little clarity or consistency; one set of values is espoused here, and another, entirely contradictory set is presented there. No firm footing is to be found anywhere. As a consequence, such children often learn that the best course of action is to size up each situation as they face it and to guide themselves in accord with the particulars of that situation, and no other. Rather than establishing an internal set of consistent standards, they acquire a hyperflexibility, a facile and quick adaptiveness to changing circumstances. To believe in anything wholeheartedly is foolish since events change and one must be ready to adjust to them. Such youngsters are devoid of any internal and stable belief system to which they are committed. Their identities are multiple and diffuse. Life progresses, not with an internal gyroscope, but with a radar system that is sensitive to changing values and expectations. Unsure of who they are, these youngsters must remain hyperalert and hyperadaptive to their environment. Restlessly shifting from one belief and fleeting course of action to another is a trait that often comes to characterize the future histrionic.

PROGNOSTIC CONSIDERATIONS

We all engage in automatic and persistent behaviors that are "senseless" if viewed in terms of their objective utility. The difference between the persistent behaviors we consider normal and those that are pathological lies in the fact that "normal" senseless and repetitive acts do not create problems or intensify existent ones. Pathological behaviors, no matter what their immediate utility, ultimately foster new difficulties and perpetuate old ones. This section considers aspects of histrionic behaviors that foster these consequences.

Perpetuation of the Histrionic Pattern

Three characteristics of the histrionic pattern are discussed in this section since each tends to set up vicious circles that promote new problems.

External preoccupations.   This chapter has already recorded the observations that histrionics orient their attention to the external world and that their perceptions and cognitions tend to be fleeting, impressionistic, and undeveloped. This preoccupation with incidental and passing details prevents experiences from being digested and embedded within the individual's inner world. In effect, histrionics show little integration and few well-examined reflective processes that intervene between perception and action; behaviors are emitted before they have been connected and organized by the operation of memory and thought. The disadvantages of this hyperalertness to external stimuli may outweigh its advantages. Unless life events are digested and integrated, the individual gains little from them. Interpersonal transactions and learnings pass through the person as if he or she were a sieve. There is little opportunity to develop inner skills and few memory traces against which future experience can be evaluated. Indiscriminate and scattered responsiveness leaves the person devoid of an inner reservoir of articulated memories and a storehouse of examined ideas and thoughts. In short, an excessive preoccupation with external events perpetuates the histrionic's "empty shell" and further fosters dependence on others as the only source of guidance.

Massive repression. The tendency of histrionics to seal off, repress, and make inaccessible substantial portions of their meager inner life further aggravates their dependence on others. By insulating their emotions and cognitions from the stream of everyday life, histrionics deny themselves opportunities to learn new alternatives for their behavior, to modify their self-image, or to become more genuinely skillful and knowledgeable persons. As long as they block the merger that should occur between new and old experiences they are likely to remain stagnant, unaltered, and impoverished. Deprived of opportunities to learn and grow, they will further perpetuate the vicious circle of dependency on others. As a consequence, the histrionic progresses little beyond childhood and retains the values and modes of behavior of an adolescent.

Superficial social relationships. The histrionic personality requires a retinue of changing events and people to replenish the need for stimulation and approval. Thus, as life progresses, histrionics move capriciously from one source to another. One consequence of these fleeting and erratic relationships is that histrionics can never be sure of securing the affection and support they crave. By moving constantly and by devouring the affections of one person and then another, they place themselves in jeopardy of having nothing to tide them over the times between. They may be left high and dry, alone and abandoned with nothing to do and no excitement with which to be preoccupied. Cut off from external supplies, histrionics are likely either to engage in a frantic search for stimulation and approval or to become dejected and forlorn. They may proceed through cyclical swings, alternating moments of simulated euphoria and excitement intermingled with longer periods of hopelessness, futility, and self-condemnation. Should deprivation be frequent or prolonged, the probability is high that these personalities will display the signs of a clear and serious affective disorder.

Despite their lack of well-developed inner resources, histrionics have a reasonably good prognosis because they possess motivation and skills for maintaining satisfactory interpersonal relationships. Given their desire to relate to others and their facility for eliciting attention and approval, the probability is slight that they will succumb to prolonged pathology.

Remedial Intervention

Histrionics rarely seek therapy. When they do, it usually follows a period of social disapproval or deprivation. Their complaints take the form initially of rather vague feelings such as boredom, restlessness, discontent, and loneliness. The histrionic personality often reports a growing disaffection with his or her mate, a feeling that the vitality that supposedly characterized their earlier years together have now palled. Sexual interest may have faded and the frequency of relations may have dropped due to impotence or frigidity. As disaffection intensifies, conflicts and tension may rise, prompting the patient to feel not only a sense of loss but of rejection and hostility from his or her mate. Life feels as if it has taken on a purposeless and meaningless quality. The patient may begin to dramatize his or her plight, feeling that every recourse is hopeless and futile.

A first therapeutic step might be to curtail the patient's tendency to overemotionalize and thereby aggravate his or her distraught feelings. Once calmed and more objectively oriented it would be wise to strengthen the patient's previously successful, but currently flagging, life-style. The therapist must be prepared to be viewed by the patient initially as an object possessing magical powers. This is transient. Nevertheless, the illusion should not be immediately counteracted since it may be used to reestablish the patient's equilibrium.

Few histrionic personalities retain motivation for long-term therapy unless life experiences persist as discouraging. Most quickly regain the feeling of being able to secure affection and approval. Not untypically, this decision to "go it alone" occurs when they begin to experience anxiety following serious therapeutic probing. Should treatment be extended beyond brief intervention, the therapist's efforts are best directed toward the goal of building self-reliance and the capacity to develop sustained emotional attachments.

The technique of environmental management, psychopharmacologic treatment, and behavior modification appear to be of minimal value with these personalities. Supportive therapy is indicated to tide them over their "rough periods." If the patient is so inclined, the procedures of cognitive reorientation may prove useful in developing insight and a rich inner life. Psychoanalytic psychotherapy may be a worthy approach if there is time and motivation to undertake a reconstruction of the basic personality style. Of frequent value, also, are group and family methods, which may aid the person in developing more genuine and sustaining ways of relating to others.

Chapter 6

Narcissistic Personality: The Egotistic Pattern

In contrast to dependent and histrionic personalities, who look to others to provide the reinforcements of life, both the narcissistic and antisocial patterns (described in this and the next chapter) are independent in their orientation. That is, they turn inward for gratification, having learned to rely on themselves rather than others for safety and self-esteem. Weakness and dependency are threatening. Since both personalities are preoccupied with matters of adequacy, power, and prestige, status and superiority must always be in their favor. They fear the loss of self-determination, proudly display their achievements, and strive to enhance themselves and to be ascendant, stronger, more beautiful, wealthier, and more important than others. In sum, it is what they think of themselves, not what others say or can provide for them, that serves as the touchstone for their security and contentment.

The "independent" personality style has been divided into two subtypes in earlier writings (Millon, 1969): the passive-independent, or *narcissistic, personalities,* who are confident of their self-worth and who feel they need be merely themselves to justify being content and secure; and the active-independent, or *aggressive, personalities* (DSM-III, antisocial personality), who struggle to "prove" themselves, who insist on their rights and will be harsh and ruthless when necessary to retaliate or gain power over others. For the narcissistic type, self-esteem is based on a blind and naïve assumption of personal worth and superiority. For the aggressive or antisocial type, it stems from distrust, as assumption that others will be humiliating and exploitive. To these personalities, whose independence from others takes on an active and angry character, self-determination is a protective maneuver; it is a means of countering, with their own power and prestige, the hostility, deception, and victimization they anticipate from others. Although both passive- (narcissists) and active-independents (antisocials) devalue the standards and opinions of others, finding gratification primarily within themselves, their life histories and the strategies they employ for achieving their needs are substantially different.

This chapter focuses on the narcissistic personality, a character pattern that has gained considerable recognition in the past decade. Rather sadly, it has grown into a diagnostic "fad" among certain groups of mental health professionals, notably those of a psychoanalytic persuasion. This shift in status from a largely unknown clinical entity to *the* paramount and most prevalent personality syndrome diagnosed in several analytic centers is less a commentary on our times (Lasch, 1978) than on the fervor characterizing insular schools of thought that may be undergoing popular decline or serious external appraisal (Millon, 1967). In the opening paragraphs of an earlier work describing the narcissistic personality, the author wrote as follows:

> This rather fascinating pattern, though well known in contemporary life, and depicted so well in literary writings, has been given but scant theoretical and clinical attention. For example, the recent DSM-II has no diagnostic category that approximates the clinical features of this personality type. (1969, p. 261)

Drafted initially in 1966, and updated just prior to publication, this statement could not be written today, except facetiously. Analytic theorists Otto Kernberg and Heinz Kohut have carried many of their colleagues along a path that has promised a renewed vitality for psychoanalytic theory and therapy; it is narcissism that serves as the cornerstone of this enthusiastic revival. Fortunately, the concept of a narcissistic personality syndrome does not stand or fall on the vagaries of the future of psychoanalysis. As formulated in this chapter, the syndrome is well ensconced in the DSM-III and reflects the thinking, not only of Kernberg and Kohut but of biosocial and learning theories such as utilized by the author; its viability is more solidly rooted than its current faddistic character might suggest.

The label "narcissistic" connotes more than mere egocentricity, a characteristic found in all individuals who are driven primarily by their needs and anxieties. More particularly, narcissism signifies that these individuals overvalue their personal worth, direct their affections toward themselves rather than others, and expect that others will not only recognize but cater to the high esteem in which narcissists hold themselves. This form of self-confidence and self-assurance is conducive to success and the evocation of admiration in our "other-directed" society. It falters as a life-style, however, if the person's illusion of specialness is poorly founded in fact or if the supercilious air is so exaggerated as to grate on and alienate significant others.

In contrast to the antisocial personality, the self-centeredness of the narcissist is not anchored to feelings of deep hostility and animosity. Narcissistic individuals are benignly arrogant. They exhibit a disdainful indifference to the standards of shared social behavior and feel themselves "above" the conventions of the cultural group, exempt from the responsibilities that govern and give order and reciprocity to societal living. It is assumed that others will submerge their desires in favor of the narcissists' comfort and welfare; they operate on the fantastic assumption that their mere desire is justification for possessing whatever they seek. Thus, their disdainfulness is matched by their exploitiveness, their assumption that they are entitled to be served and to have their own wishes take precedence over others, without expending any effort to merit such favor. In short, narcissists possess illusions of an inherent superior self-worth and move through life with the belief that it is their inalienable right to receive special considerations.

It will be useful before proceeding further to present appropriate excerpts from the brief DSM-III text describing the narcissistic personality:

> There are a grandiose sense of self-importance or uniqueness; preoccupation with fantasies of unlimited success; an exhibitionistic need for constant attention and admiration; characteristic responses to threats to self-esteem; and characteristic disturbances in interpersonal relationships, such as entitlement, interpersonal exploitiveness, relationships that alternate between the extremes of overidealization and devaluation, and lack of empathy.
>
> The exaggerated sense of self-importance may be manifested as extreme self-centeredness and self-absorption. Abilities and achievements tend to be unrealistically overestimated. Frequently the sense of self-importance will alternate with feelings of special unworthiness.
>
> Although ... fantasies frequently substitute for realistic activity, when these goals are actually pursued, there is often a "driven" pleasureless quality, and an ambition that cannot be satisfied.
>
> Self-esteem is invaribly fragile and the individual is preoccuppied with concerns as to how well he or she is doing and how well regarded by others. In response to criticism, defeat or disappointment, there is either a cool indifference or marked feelings of rage, inferiority, shame, humiliation, or emptiness.
>
> Interpersonal relationships are invariably disturbed. There is commonly a lack of empathy and inability to recognize and experience how others feel.
>
> Entitlement, the expectation of special favors without assuming reciprocal responsibilities, is usually present.
>
> Interpersonal exploitiveness, in which others are taken advantage of in order to indulge one's own desires or for self-aggrandizement, is common, and the personal integrity and rights of others are disregarded.
>
> Relations with others lack sustained positive regard. Close relationships tend to alternate between idealization and devaluation. (1980, pp. 315–316)

HISTORICAL AND THEORETICAL ANTECEDENTS

It was Havelock Ellis (1898) who first gave psychological significance to the term *narcissism* by conceptualizing it as *autoeroticism*, that is, sexual gratification without stimulation or evocation by another person. Paul Näcke (1899) used the term in a similar manner, applying it to the perversion of being preoccuppied with the sight and pleasures of one's own body in a manner usually reserved for those of the opposite sex. In 1908 J. Sadger extended the concept to other so-called perversions, notably that of homosexuality.

Freud's first formulation of narcissism (1910, 1911) conceived it as a normal phase of development standing midway between autoeroticism and object love. During this transitory period, initially diverse and unconnected auto-erotic sensations were fused into what was experienced as one's body, which then become a single, unified love-object. In 1914 Freud aligned narcissism with libido theory and proposed that it ultimately matured and diffused into object relationships. Shortly thereafter he reformulated his thinking on the developmental sequence and spoke of the autoerotic phase as the "primary narcissistic condition." This first phase became the initial repository of libido, from which emerged not only the love of self but love in general. In time, narcissism was conceived by Freud as a universal developmental process that continued through life but unfolded through sequential stages. He recognized that difficulties may arise in this normal, sequential progression. First, there may be failures to advance from libidinal self-love to object-love, and, second, "peculiarities" may occur in the way the person expresses narcissistic love. Freud described this latter difficulty as follows:

> We have found, especially in persons whose libidinal development has suffered some disturbance, as in perverts and homosexuals, that in their choice of love-object they have taken as their model not the mother but their own selves. They are plainly seeking themselves as love-object and their type of object-choice may be termed narcissistic. (1914, p. 45)

In this only major paper devoted exclusively to narcissism (1914), Freud suggested that in certain cases—notably among "perverts and homosexuals"—libidinal self-centeredness stems from the child's feeling that caretakers cannot be depended upon to provide love reliably. Either rebuffed by their parents or subjected to fickle and erratic attention—seductive one moment and deprecating the next—these children "give up" as far as trusting and investing in others as love-objects. Rather than rely on the capriciousness of others or risk their rejection, future narcissistics avoid the lasting attachment they achingly desire and decide instead that it is only themselves they can trust and therefore love.

It is important to note in light of current debates within psychoanalytic circles that the developmental origin of the term *narcissism* described here was only one of several concepts that Freud posited as the source of libidinal self-cathexis. Moreover, the paper was *not* written for the purpose of formulating either a narcissistic personality type or a narcissistic character structure. Rather, Freud's interest lay in exploring and elaborating variations in both the development and the nature of libidinal cathexis. As far as clinical syndromes were concerned, Freud referred in this paper to characteristics observed among paraphrenics (paranoid schizophrenics), megalomaniacs, and hypochon-driacs. When he wrote, for the first time in 1932, of a narcissistic libidinal type, he described this individual as follows:

> The main interest is focused on self-perservation; the type is independent and not easily overawed . . . People of this type impress others as being 'personalities';

it is on them that their fellow men are specially likely to lean; they readily assume the role of leader, give a fresh stimulus to cultural development or break down existing conditions. (1932, p. 249)

What is striking in this quote is Freud's characterization of the narcissist's strength and confidence, especially since it contrasts so markedly with the low self-esteem, feelings of emptiness, pain, and depression that certain of his recent disciples (Kohut, 1971; Forman, 1975) attribute to this personality. Disparities in characterizations such as these often arise as a consequence of shifts in Freud's formulations from one period to another over his productive and long career. In this case, it can be traced to the fact that Freud identified several origins of narcissistic self-cathexis, only one of which is the type of parental caprice and rejection that may lead to feelings of emptiness and low self-esteem. As evident from earlier excerpts, and as later elaborated further, Freud's description of the narcissistic libidinal type, brief though it is, corresponds much more closely to the DSM-III portrayal of the narcissistic personality than do several contemporary characterizations that trace its antecedents to either parental rebuff or unreliability. Relevant to this issue is a quote of Freud's reproduced later in the chapter that suggests that narcissistic self-investment is more likely to be a product of parental overvaluation than of parental devaluation.

Moving back somewhat in historical sequence, it was Wilhelm Reich who claimed to have first formulated what he termed the "phallic-narcissistic" character at a Vienna Psychoanalytic Society meeting in 1926. Published in Germany as a comprehensive exposition of his general theory in 1933, Reich characterized this type as follows in a subsequent English translation:

The typical phallic-narcissistic character, on the other hand, is self-assured, sometimes arrogant, elastic, energetic, often impressive in his bearing.

The most pronounced types tend to achieve leading positions in life and are ill suited to subordinate positions among the rank and file.

If their vanity is offended, they react with cold disdain, marked ill-humor, or downright aggression. Their narcissism, as opposed to that of other character types, is expressed not in an infantile but in a blatantly self-confident way, with a flagrant display of superiority and dignity. (1949, pp. 217–218)

Notable is the close correspondence between Reich's depiction and Freud's 1932 formulation of the narcissistic libidinal type; both provide clear descriptions that anticipate the text of the DSM-III. In contrast to both Freud and more contemporary analytic theorists, Reich attributed the origins of narcissism to fixations at the libidinal phallic stage and conceived it as a compensation and wish-fulfilling reaction to conflicts associated with the castration complex.

Significant shifts in emphasis among psychoanalytic thinkers began in the mid-1930s and resulted in the emergence of a series of new orientations. Spawned at that time were neo-Freudian schools of ego, self, object relations, and social theory.

Karen Horney, a prime "social" theorist, addressed the concept of narcissism in an important early book, formulating the central features of the personality type as follows:

> If narcissism is considered not genetically but with reference to its actual meaning it should, in my judgment, be described as essentially self-inflation. Psychic inflation, like economic inflation, means presenting greater values than really exist. It means that the person loves and admires himself for values for which there is no adequate foundation. Similarly, it means that he expects love and admiration from others for qualities that he does not possess, or does not possess to as large an extent as he supposes. (1939, pp. 89–90)

Leary, a disciple of Horney and others of the social and interpersonal school of analysis, extended their notions as follows:

> In its maladaptive extreme it becomes a smug, cold, selfish, exploitive social role. In this case the adaptive self-confidence and independence become exaggerated into a self-oriented rejection of others...
> These individuals feel most secure when they are independent of other people... The narcissist puts... distance between himself and others—wants to be independent of and superior to the "other one". Dependence is terrifying.
> He is driven to compete, to exhibit, to exploit. (1957, pp. 332–334)

Relevant to the recent growth of interest in narcissism among more orthodox analytic groups were the suggestive notions presented in the early 1960s by A. Reich (1960), E. Jacobson (1964), H. Nagera (1964), and H. Rosenfeld (1964). For example, in describing the narcissistic patient, Rosenfeld wrote:

> [This] patient... feels that he is loved by everyone, or demands to be loved by everyone, because he is so lovable. All these patients seem to have in common the feeling that they contain all the goodness which would otherwise be experienced in a relationship to an object. We usually encounter simultaneously a highly idealized self-image... and anything interfering with this picture is rigorously defended against and omnipotently denied. (1964, p. 333)

Recent and insightful characterizations of various narcissistic types have been presented by Bursten (1973), but the most enthusiastically received revisions in psychoanalytic thought by far are those formulated by Otto Kernberg (1967, 1970) and Heinz Kohut (1966, 1968, 1971). The author has neither the space nor the inclination here to trace the circuitous labyrinths through which their metapsychological assertions wind their way. Nor is the clinical utility of their views confirmed by debates that have filled recent analytic journals. Nonetheless, a reasonably detailed synopsis of their major themes is in order.

Kernberg, in his restructuring of a diagnostic framework for characterology, de-emphasized the psychoanalytic classification schema that has traditionally been based on libidinal development. Stage sequences are referred to as a means of identifying levels of instinctual maturation (e.g., pregenital, genital). The vicissitudes of maturation give rise to the clinical features, defensive operations, level of severity, prognosis, and, most centrally, the structural integration or organization that is likely to characterize the individual's personality. Employing his framework of levels of structural organization as a model for constructing "a psychoanalytic classification of character pathology," Kernberg described the features of the narcissist as follows:

> These patients present an unusual degree of self-reference in their interactions with other people, a great need to be loved and admired by others, and a curious apparent contradiction between a very inflated concept of themselves and an inordinate need for tribute from others. Their emotional life is shallow. They experience little empathy for the feelings of others, they obtain very little enjoyment from life other than from the tributes they receive from others or from their own grandiose fantasies, and they feel restless and bored when external glitter wears off and no new sources feed their self-regard. They envy others, tend to idealize some people from whom they expect narcissistic supplies, and to depreciate and treat with contempt those from whom they do not expect anything (often their former idols). In general, their relationships with other people are clearly exploitative and sometimes parasitic. It is as if they feel they have the right to control and possess others and to exploit them without guilt feelings—and behind a surface which very often is charming and engaging, one senses coldness and ruthlessness. Very often such patients are considered to be "dependent" because they need so much tribute and adoration from others, but on a deeper level they are completely unable really to depend on anybody because of their deep distrust and depreciation of others. (1967, p. 655)

Kernberg asserted that the haughty and grandiose constellation of behaviors that characterize the narcissist is a defense against the projection of "oral" rage that, in turn, stems from the narcissist's incapacity to depend on "internalized good objects." In this etiologic formulation, Kernberg claimed that the experiential background of most narcissists includes chronically cold parental figures who exhibit either indifference or covert, but spitefully aggressive, attitudes toward their children. At the same time, the young, future narcissist is often found to possess some special talent or status within the family, such as playing the role of "genius" or being the "only child." This quality of specialness serves as a refuge, at first only temporarily but ultimately an often-returned-to haven that reliably offsets the underlying feeling of having been unloved by the vengefully rejecting parent.

Kohut's views are more difficult to summarize than those of Kernberg, perhaps as a consequence of their greater originality. Despite having been written in esoteric, if not obscure, psychoanalytic jargon and having been formulated in an ingenious, if at times ponderous and tautalogical fashion, Kohut's work has attracted numerous disciples. Fortunately, a score of "interpreters" have sought to elucidate his metapsychological assertions, which many consider among the more imaginative advances in recent analytic theory (Gedo and Goldberg, 1973; Forman, 1975; Wolf, 1976; Palombo, 1976).

Kohut rejects the traditional Freudian and Kernbergian thesis that narcissistic self-investment results from a defensive withdrawal of object-love attachments following a pattern of chronic parental coldness or vengeful spite. This classical view contends that narcissism is a result of developmental arrests or regressions to earlier points of fixation. Thus, the future narcissist, according to standard analytic metapsychology, regresses to or fails to progress through the usual developmental sequence of initial undifferentiated libido, followed by autoeroticism, narcissism, and, finally, object love. It is not the content as such but the sequence of libidinal maturation that Kohut challenges. His clinical observations have led him to assert that the primitive narcissistic libido has its own developmental line and sequence of continuity into adulthood. That is, it does not "fade away" by becoming transformed into object-libido, as contended by classical theorists, but unfolds into its own set of mature narcissistic processes and structures. In healthy form, for example, these processes might include behaviors such as humor and creativity; similarly, and most significantly, it is through this narcissistic developmental sequence that the cohesive psychic structure of "self" ultimately emerges.

Pathology in narcissistic development, according to Kohut, occurs as a consequence of failures to integrate one of two major spheres of self-maturation, the "grandiose self" and the "idealized parental imago." Confronted by realistic shortcomings that undermine early feelings of grandiose omnipotence, or subsequently recognizing the equally illusory nature of the idealized powers they have attributed to their parents, these children must find a way to overcome their "disappointments" so as not to "fragment." If disillusioned, rejected, or experiencing cold and unempathic care at the earliest stages of self-development, serious pathology, such as psychotic or borderline states, will occur. Trauma or disappointment at a later phase will have somewhat different repercussions depending on whether the difficulty centered on the development of the grandiose self or on the parental imago. In the former, the child will fail to develop the sense of fulfillment and self-confidence that comes from feeling worthwhile and valued; as a consequence, these needs will "split off" and result in the persistent seeking of "narcissistic" recognition through adulthood. Along the second line of self-development, children who are unable to "idealize" their parents because of the latter's indifference or rejection will feel devastated, depressed, and empty. Through adulthood they will seek idealized parental surrogates who, inevitably, will fail to live up to the omnipotent powers the narcissists hoped to find within them. Since they desperately seek an ideal that is "greater" than themselves, they are often led to behave in a weak and self-effacing manner, a style that will enable others to overshadow them.

What is notable is that Kohut's is a developmental theory of self and not a personality characterization. Nevertheless, it leads to a clinical picture that is at variance with those of Freud, Kernberg, and the DSM-III. The features that emerge from Kohut's descriptions have been summarized by Forman (1975). Listed among the more prominent are: (1) low self-esteem, (2) tendencies toward periodic hypochondriasis, and (3) feelings of emptiness or deadness. To illustrate their contrasting views, for example, the episodic depression that Kohut finds so characteristic of narcissistically injured persons is not seen by Kernberg to be a true depression at all. Rather, Kernberg contends that when "narcissists" feel seriously disappointed or abandoned they may appear depressed on superficial examination, but they are, in fact, smoldering with constrained anger and revengeful resentment.

It is not only in psychoanalytic circles that narcissism has acquired its faddistic status and intellectual fascination. We appear to be witnessing the "me" generation, a subculture immersed in what has been popularly described as "our narcissistic society." Fortunately, the validity of the narcissistic personality as a conceptual entity does not rest solely on the speculations of analytic theory nor the passing character of contemporary lifestyles. Social learning theory (Millon, 1969), also provides a foundation for deriving the behavioral constellation that typifies the narcissistic clinical pattern. Conceived neither in terms of libidinal regressions nor "disappointments" with formerly omnipotent parents, this social learning formulation is relatively straightforward, tracing the origin of the narcissistic style to the unrealistic overvaluation by parents of the child's worth, that is, creating an enhanced self-image that cannot be sustained in the "outer" world. Unable to live up to their now internalized parental illusions of self-worth, narcissists will display a wide range of behaviors that typify this personality syndrome. This formulation of the narcissist is elaborated throughout the current chapter. The following excerpts present some of the features and diagnostic criteria as drafted by the author in 1975 to serve as the initial working draft for the DSM-III personality subcommittee:

> This pattern is typified by an inflated sense of self-worth, an air of supercilious imperturbability and a benign indifference to shared responsibilities and the welfare of others. A special status for self is taken for granted and there is little awareness that exploitive behavior is inconsiderate and presumptuous. Achievement deficits and social irresponsibilites are justified and sustained by a boastful arrogance, expansive fantasies, facile rationalizations and frank prevarications. Marked rebuffs to self-esteem may provoke serious disruptions in the characteristic unruffled composure.
>
> Since adolescence or early adulthood at least 3 of the following have been present to a notably greater degree than in most people and were not limited to discrete periods nor necessarily prompted by stressful life events.
>
> 1. Inflated self-image (e.g., displays pretentious self-assurance and exaggerates achievements and talents; often seen by others as egotistic, haughty, and arrogant).
> 2. Interpersonal exploitiveness (e.g., divulges taking others for granted and

using them to enhance self and indulge desires; expects special favors and status without assuming reciprocal responsibilities).

3. Cognitive expansiveness (e.g., exhibits immature fantasies and an undisciplined imagination; is minimally constrained by objective reality, takes liberties with facts and often prevaricates to redeem self-illusion).

4. Insouciant temperament (e.g., manifests a general air of nonchalance and imperturbability; except when narcissistic confidence is shaken, appears coolly unimpressionable or buoyantly optimistic).

5. Deficient social conscience (e.g., reports flouting conventional rules of shared social living, viewing them as naive or inapplicable to self; reveals a careless disregard for personal integrity and an indifference to the rights of others).

Minor revisions of this draft were introduced in 1977, resulting in the following recommended criteria:

A. Inflated self-esteem (e.g., exaggerates achievements and talents; displays pretentious self-assurance).

B. Interpersonal exploitiveness (e.g., uses others to indulge desires; expects favors without assuming reciprocal responsibilities).

C. Expansive imagination (e.g., exhibits immature and undisciplined fantasies; often prevaricates to redeem self-illusions).

D. Supercilious imperturbability (e.g., except when narcissistic confidence is shaken appears nonchalant and coolly unimpressionable).

E. Deficient social conscience (e.g., flouts conventions of shared social living; reveals disregard for personal integrity and the rights of others).

Modified in certain details, notably in specifying symptoms manifested when confidence in self is shaken (e.g., rage, humiliation, unworthiness, and emptiness), the central features of these criteria served to guide the final version.

CLINICAL PICTURE

The discussion turns next to the typical characteristics of the narcissistic personality using the four-way analysis format.

Behavioral Features

Narcissists convey a calm and self-assured quality in their social behavior. Their seemingly untroubled and self-satisfied air is viewed, by some, as a sign of confident equanimity. Others respond to it much less favorably. To them, these behaviors reflect immodesty, presumptuousness, pretentiousness, and a haughty, snobbish, cocksure, and arrogant way of relating to people.

Narcissists appear to lack humility and are overly self-centered and ungenerous. They characteristically, but usually unwittingly, exploit others, take them for granted, and expect others to serve them, without giving much in return. Their self-conceit is viewed by most as unwarranted; it smacks of being "uppish" and superior, without the requisite substance to justify it.

Self-Descriptions and Complaints

Narcissists feel justified in their claim for special status, and they have little conception that their behaviors may be objectionable, even irrational. Their self-image is that they are superior persons, "extra-special" individuals who are entitled to unusual rights and privileges. This view of their self-worth is fixed so firmly in their minds that they rarely question whether it is valid. Moreover, anyone who fails to respect them is viewed with contempt and scorn.

Narcissists are cognitively expansive. They place few limits on either their fantasies or rationalizations, and their imagination is left to run free of the constraints of reality or the views of others. They are inclined to exaggerate their powers, to freely transform failures into successes, to construct lengthy and intricate rationalizations that inflate their self-worth or justify what they feel is their due, quickly depreciating those who refuse to accept or enhance their self-image.

Roused by the facile workings of their imagination, narcissists experience a pervasive sense of well-being in their everyday life, a buoyance of mood and an optimism of outlook. Affect, though based often on their semigrandiose distortions of reality, is generally relaxed, if not cheerful and carefree. Should the balloon be burst, however, there is a rapid turn to either an edgy irritability and annoyance with others or to repeated bouts of dejection that are characterized by feeling humiliated and empty.

Inferred Intrapsychic Dynamics

Narcissists suffer few conflicts; their past has supplied them, perhaps too well, with high expectations and encouragement. As a result, they are inclined to trust others and to feel confident that matters will work out well for them. As detailed in a later section, this sanguine outlook on life is founded on an unusual set of early experiences that only rarely are duplicated in later life. Essentially, narcissists were led by their parents to believe that they were almost invariably lovable and perfect, regardless of whether what they did and how they thought amounted to much objectively. Such an idyllic existence cannot long endure; the world beyond home will not be so benign and accepting.

Reality bears down heavily at times. Even the routine demands of everyday life may be viewed as annoying incursions by narcissists. Such responsibilities are experienced as demeaning, for they intrude upon the narcissist's cherished illusion of self as almost godlike. Alibis to avoid "pedestrian" tasks are easily mustered since narcissistics are convinced that what they believe must be true and what they wish must be right. Not only do they display considerable talent in rationalizing their social inconsiderateness, but they utilize a variety of other intrapsychic mechanisms with equal facility. However, since they reflect minimally on what others think, their defensive maneuvers are transparent, a poor camouflage to a discerning eye. This failure to bother dissembling more thoroughly also contributes to their being seen as cocksure and arrogant.

What happens if narcissistics are not succesful, if they face personal failures and social humiliations? What if realistic events topple them from their illusory world of eminence and superiority? What behaviors do they show and what mechanisms do they employ to salve their wounds?

Initially dejected, shamed, and feeling a sense of emptiness, narcissists have no recourse but to turn for solace to their fantasies. In contrast to the antisocial personality (described in the next chapter), narcissists have not learned to be ruthless, to be competitively assertive and aggressive when frustrated. Neither have they acquired the seductive strategies of the histrionic to solicit rewards and protections. Failing to achieve their aims and at a loss as to what they can do next, they are likely to revert to themselves to provide comfort and consolation. It is at these times that their lifelong talent for imagination takes over. These facile processes enable them to create a fanciful world in which they can redeem themselves and reassert their pride and status. Since narcissists are unaccustomed to self-control and objective reality testing, their powers of imagination have free rein to weave intricate resolutions to their difficulties.

What the narcissist is unable to work out through fantasy is simply repressed, put out of mind and kept from awareness. Beyond these, narcissists invent alibis, excuses, and "proofs" that seem plausible and consistent, and convince them of their continued stature and perfection. These flimsily substantiated rationalizations are offered with an air of confidence and authority. As noted earlier, however, narcissists may never have learned to be skillful at public deception; they usually said and did what they liked without a care for what others thought. Their poorly conceived rationalizations may, therefore, fail to bring relief and, more seriously, may evoke scrutiny and deprecating comments from others. At these times narcissists may be pushed to the point of employing projection as a defense. Unable to disentangle themselves from lies and inconsistencies, and driven by their need to maintain their illusion of superiority, they may begin to turn against others, accusing the latter of their own deceptions, their own selfishness, and their own irrationalities. It is at these, not very typical, times that the fragility and pathology of the narcissist becomes clearly evident. "Breakdowns" in the defensive structure of this personality, however, are not too common. More typically, the exploitive behaviors and intrapsychic maneuvers of narcissists prove highly adaptive and provide them with the means of thwarting serious or prolonged periods of dejection or decompensation.

Interpersonal Coping Style

It is not difficult to see why the behaviors of narcissists are so gratifying to them. By treating themselves kindly; by imagining their own prowess, beauty, and intelligence; and by reveling in their "obvious" superiorities and talents, they gain, through self-reinforcement, the rewards that most people must struggle to achieve through genuine attainments. Narcissists need depend on no one else to provide gratification; there is always themselves to "keep them warm."

Unfortunately for them, narcissists must come to terms with the fact that they live in a world composed of others. No matter how preferred their fantasies may be, they must relate and deal with all the complications and frustrations that real relationships entail. Furthermore, and no matter how satisfying it may be to reinforce oneself, it is all the more gratifying if one can arrange one's environment so that others will contribute their applause as well. Of course, true to their fashion, narcissists will seek to accomplish this with minimal effort and reciprocity on their part. In contrast to the dependent personality, who must submit and acquiesce to evoke favorable rewards; or the histrionic, who must perform and be attractive to win praise from others—narcissists are likely to contribute little or nothing in return for the gratifications they seek. In fact, some narcissists assume that others feel "honored" in having a relationship with them, and that others receive as much pleasure in providing them with favors and attention as the narcissist experiences in accepting these tributes.

It should not be surprising that the sheer presumptuousness and confidence exuded by the narcissist often elicits admiration and obedience from others. Furthermore, narcissists typically size up those around them and quickly train those who are so disposed to honor them; for example, narcissists frequently select a dependent mate who will be obeisant, solicitous, and subservient, without expecting anything in return except strength and assurances of fidelity. It is central to narcissists' interpersonal style that good fortune will come to them without reciprocity. Since they feel entitled to get what they wish and have been successful in having others provide them with comforts they have not deserved, narcissists have little reason to discontinue their habitual presumptuous and exploitive behaviors.

ASSOCIATED DISORDERS

Following the sequence established in the prior two chapters, attention turns next to the major Axis I and Axis II syndromes that covary with the personality under review. Note again that where personalities share a vulnerability to the same disorder, each manifests the characteristic symptoms in a somewhat distinctive way.

Concomitant Axis I Symptoms

Affective disorders. *Dysthymic* disorder is perhaps the most common symptom disorder seen among narcissists. Faced with repeated failures and social humiliations, and unable to find some way of living up to their inflated self-image, narcissists may succumb to uncertainty and dissatisfaction, losing self-confidence and convincing themselves that they are, and perhaps have always been, fraudulent and phony. Kernberg has described this process of self-disillusionment well:

> For them, to accept the breakdown of the illusion of grandiosity means to accept the dangerous, lingering awareness of the depreciated self—the hungry, empty, lonely primitive self surrounded by a world of dangerous, sadistically frustrating and revengeful objects. (1975, p. 311)

Recounting the psychic consequences of the loss of stature in a national political figure, Kernberg described the steps of decompensation into a *major depression* as follows:

> He became depressed and developed deep feelings of defeat and humiliation accompanied by fantasies in which his political opponents were gloating with satisfaction over his defeat. His depression diminished. He went into retirement, but gradually devaluated the areas of political science in which he had been an expert. This was a narcissistic depreciation of that in which he was no longer triumphant, which brought about a general loss of interest in professional, cultural and intellectual matters. His primary areas of professional and intellectual interests no longer seemed exciting and reminded him again of his failure...
>
> He experienced an increasing sense of estrangement which finally evolved into the recurrence of a now severe, chronic depression, with a predominance of impotent rage over mourning processes. (1975, pp. 311-312)

Since depression is not experienced as consonant with the narcissist's self-image, it rarely endures for extended periods unless the psychic blow is irreparable, as in the case just described. Most typically, we observe rapid shifts in the character of the depressive symptomatology as narcissists succumb at first to their feelings of apathy and worthlessness, and then abruptly seek to retrieve their grandiose self-confidence and reassert themselves. At one time, they may express their depressive mood dramatically; at other times, in a cranky and irritable manner; and at yet another, in a dreamy, vague, and philosophically abstract way. Not untypically, narcissists will utilize their mood as a rationalization for their increasing indecisiveness and failures. Here, their complaints are likely to be colored with subtle accusations and claims that others have not supported or cared for them, thus fostering their growing sense of futility and ineffectuality. As is characteristic of the passive-aggressive personality, narcissists may vacillate for a brief period between anxious futility and self-depreciation at one time and a bitter discontent and demanding attitude the next. A struggle ensues between venting and curtailing the rage felt toward others simply for being witness to their shame and humiliation. Moody and pessimistic complaints are not only genuinely expressed but are a useful outlet for mounting resentments. Moreover, depressively toned hostility often serves to intimidate others, and it thereby functions as a form of retribution or vengeance for their failure to rescue the narcissist from his or her own deficiencies.

Anxiety disorders. Narcissistic personalities do not characteristically exhibit anxiety disorders. However, anxiety may be manifest for brief periods until the patient cloaks or restrains the overt expression of these embarrassing feelings. The image of being weak conveyed by a public display of anxiety is anathema to narcissists. Rarely is it overt, tending instead to be neutralized or camouflaged by other symptoms such as touchy irritability and sudden resentments. Anxiety precipitants in narcissists usually relate to shame and failure such as might arise in a public disparity between their illusion of superiority and the facts of reality.

Somatoform disorders. There is a reasonable likelihood that narcissists will exhibit *hypochondriacal* symptoms following the shame of a humiliating defeat or embarrassment. Unable to solicit the tribute they expect from others, narcissists become their own source of solicitude by nurturing their wounds symbolically. Their hypochondriacal concerns are a form of self-ministering, an act of providing the affection and attention they can no longer obtain from others. As Fenichel (1945) has stated regarding hypochondriasis: "Narcissistic withdrawal means a transfer of libido from object representations to organ representations" (p. 261). Not to be overlooked also among the secondary gains of these symptoms is their use as a rationalization for failures and shortcomings. Discomforting though it may be to admit to any frailty, it impugns narcissists' competence somewhat less if they can ascribe their "defeats" to a physical illness rather than to a self-implicating psychological shortcoming. Additionally, physical complaints are often a useful disguise for discharging anger and resentment. Discontent over their own inadequacies and too ashamed to express anger directly, narcissists may cloak their resentments by using their physical impairments as an excuse. Thus, they may become "household tyrants," not only by creating guilt in others for the latter's failure to attend to the needs of a "sick person" but by demanding that their claims for special status be instituted once again.

Paranoid disorders. Under conditions of unrelieved adversity and failure narcissists may decompensate into paranoid disorders. Owing to their excessive use of fantasy mechanisms, they are disposed to misinterpret events and to construct delusional beliefs. Unwilling to accept constraints on their independence and unable to accept the viewpoints of others, narcissists may isolate themselves from the corrective effects of shared thinking. Alone, they may ruminate and weave their beliefs into a network of fanciful and totally invalid suspicions. Among narcissists, delusions often take form after a serious challenge or setback in which their image of superiority and omnipotence has been upset. They tend to exhibit compensatory grandiosity and jealousy delusions in which they reconstruct reality to match the image they are unable or unwilling to give up. Delusional systems may also develop as a result of having felt betrayed and humiliated. Here we may see the rapid unfolding of persecutory delusions and an arrogant grandiosity characterized by verbal attacks and bombast. Rarely physically abusive, anger among narcissists usually takes the form of oral vituperation and argumentativeness. This may be seen in a flow of irrational and caustic comments in which others are upbraided and denounced as stupid and beneath contempt. These onslaughts usually have little objective justification, are often colored by delusions, and may be directed in a wild, hit-or-miss fashion in which the narcissist lashes out at those who have failed to acknowledge the exalted status in which he/she demands to be seen.

Concurrent Axis II Personalities

Clinical experience and research employing the Millon Clinical Multiaxial Inventory (Millon, 1977) suggest several personality blends that incorporate distinct narcissistic features. The preceding chapter includes a description of the association frequently found between histrionic and narcissistic personality syndromes; readers may wish to refer back to these pages to refresh their memory of the clinical features these patterns display in combination.

Narcissistic-antisocial (aggressive) mixed personality. The second most prevalent concurrence of types that includes the narcissist is found in conjunction with the DSM-III antisocial personality. This amalgam is seen with substantial frequency in drug rehabilitation programs, centers for youth offenders, juvenile courts, and in jails and prisons; it is somewhat less common in marital and family clinics and divorce courts.

The distinctive feature of this personality mix is an indifferent conscience, an aloofness to truth and social responsibility that, if brought to the individual's attention, elicits an attitude of nonchalant innocence. Though totally self-oriented, these individuals are facile in the ways of social influence, often feign an air of dignity and confidence, and are rather skilled in deceiving others with their clever glibness.

Not infrequently, they leave behind them a trail of outrageous acts such as swindling, sexual excesses, pathological lying, and fraud. This disregard for truth and the talent for exploitation and deception are often neither hostile nor malicious in intent. These personality elements appear to derive from an attitude of omnipotence and self-assurance, a feeling that the rules of society do not apply to them and that they are above the responsibilities of shared living. As with the pure antisocial pattern, individuals with this mixture are cooly indifferent to the welfare and rights of others, whom they use as a means of enhancing and indulging their whims and desires. Flagrant antisocial acts may emerge when persons of this type realize that they must become productive and contributing members of society. Caring little to shoulder genuine responsibilities and unwilling to change their ways, the narcissist-antisocial mix refuses to "buckle down" like everyone else and expend effort to prove their worth. Never having learned to control their fantasies or be concerned with matters of social integrity, they will maintain their attitude of superiority if need be by deception, fraud, lying, and by charming others through craft and wit. Rather than apply their talents toward the goal of tangible achievements, they will devote their energies to construct intricate lies, to cleverly exploit others, and to slyly contrive ways to extract from others what they unjustly believe is their due. Untroubled by conscience and needing nourishment for their overinflated self-image, they will fabricate stories that enhance their worth and succeed in seducing others into supporting their excesses. Criticism and punishment are likely to prove of no avail since this personality quickly dismisses them as the product of jealous inferiors.

The following "blind" MCMI computer report was based on the responses of a 20-year-old male who was apprehended following involvement in a series of schemes to swindle elderly widows seeking companionship in a fraudulent "social club."

> The patient's behavior is characterized by an arrogant sense of self-worth, an indifference to the welfare of others, and a mixed seductive and intimidating social manner. There is a tendency to exploit others, expecting special recognition and consideration without assuming reciprocal responsibilities. A deficient social conscience is evident in his tendency to flout conventions, engage in actions that raise questions of personal integrity, and to disregard the rights of others. Achievement deficits and social irresponsibilities are justified by expansive fantasies and frank pervarications.
>
> There is pride in self-reliance, unsentimentality, and hard-boiled competitive values. He evidences a rash willingness to risk harm and is notably fearless in the face of threats and punitive action. Malicious tendencies are projected outward, precipitating frequent personal and family difficulties, as well as occasional legal entanglements. Vindictive gratification is often obtained by humiliating and dominating others. When matters are well under control, the patient is successful in attracting attention and enjoying a rapid-paced social life with short-lived periods of dramatic acting out. More characteristically, he evidences a jealously of others, being wary and suspicious of their motives, feeling unfairly treated, and easily provoked to irritability and authority; and he appears to feel secure only when possessing control and power over others. The thin facade of sociability gives way readily to quick antagonisms and caustic comments. Antisocial tendencies, alcoholism, or drug problems may be prominent.
>
> The patient displays an indifference to truth that, if brought to his attention,

is likely to elicit an attitude of nonchalant indifference. He is skillful in the ways of social influence, is capable of feigning an air of justified innocence, and is adept in deceiving others with charm and glibness. Lacking any deep feelings of loyalty, he may successfully scheme beneath a veneer of politeness and civility. His principal orientation is that of outwitting others, getting power and exploiting them "before they do it to you." He often carries a chip-on-the-shoulder attitude, a readiness to attack those who are distrusted or who can be used as scapegoats.

This patient attempts to maintain an image of cool strength, acting tough, arrogant, and fearless. To prove his courage, he may invite danger and punishment. But punishment only verifies his expectation of unjust treatment. Rather than having a deterrent effect, it only reinforces his suspiciousness and rebelliousness. If unsuccessful in channeling these ever-present aggressive impulses, resentments may mount into overt acts of hostility.

Differential Diagnostic Signs

The major sphere of confusion that may have some clinical import lies in differentiating narcissistic from *histrionic* personalities; as noted earlier, these patterns do frequently merge into a single diagnostic blend. The major points of differentiation were drawn in Chapter 5 and need but minimal repetition here. Essentially, the distinguishing feature of narcissists is their desire to avoid dependence on others and to view themselves as "cool" and "above" the responsibilities of shared living. By contrast, histrionic personalities, though equally needy of recognition and tribute, can be warmly expressive, often seek close (if fleeting) relationships, and willingly subscribe to the conventions and fashions of social life if these give promise of bringing the approval and attentions they desire.

Much has been written in the recent literature seeking to clarify similarities and differences between narcissistic and *borderline* personalities. This preoccupation reflects confusions that exist in the field concerning what these new syndromes constitute in the first place. As presented in contemporary psychoanalytic literature, both syndromes are formulated often as obscure matrices of intangible metapsychological concepts that lack clear clinical referents, often leading the less experienced clinician to conclude that they are quite similar and difficult to disentangle. No difficulty of this sort will exist among readers who review each set of diagnostic criteria spelled out in the DSM-III. In brief, the similarities between these syndromes are miniscule, and each is clearly delineated and comprehensible, even to the clinical novice.

Differential problems may be faced in distinguishing narcissistic from *paranoid* personalities. In many cases overlap may be considerable. According to Millon (1969) and Meissner (1979), paranoid personalities are frequently, though not invariably, advanced or more severe variants of the narcissistic personality, reflecting the progressive deterioration of formerly adaptive functions. More is said concerning this process of decompensation in later chapters. To this author it appears that recording both diagnoses, when appropriate, will convey both the long-term narcissistic personality structure and the more recently evolved paranoid pattern to which the individual has deteriorated.

Difficulties in distinguishing narcissistic syndromes from Axis I symptoms should not occur. Short-lived hypomanic episodes often convey the confident ebullience frequently seen among narcissistic personalities, but narcissists lack the frenetic and driven quality of the manic disorder. Where they coexist, of course, both may properly be diagnosed.

PREDISPOSING BACKGROUND

An attempt is made in this section to trace some of the influences that are likely to have shaped the development of narcissistic traits. Primary consideration is given to propositions derived from social learning theory; analytic formulations have been extensively reviewed in the literature, and they are summarized earlier in the chapter.

Hypothesized Biogenic Factors

The role of biological influences in narcissistic personality development is unclear. Although evidence adduced in support of such determinants among other personality patterns was largely speculative, there was at least some (albeit tenuous) justification for these speculations. In the case of the narcissist, where even the existence of distinctive temperaments seems lacking, conjectures have an usually weak grounding; hence none is proposed.

Characteristic Experiential Histories

Since no evidence for the development of narcissistic traits can be provided from biological hypotheses, the roots of the pattern are traced to psychogenic influences.

Whatever the reasons may be, some parents come to view their child as "God's gift to mankind." These parents pamper and indulge their youngsters in ways that teach them that their every wish is a command, that they can receive without giving in return, and that they deserve prominence without even minimal effort. It may be instructive to reproduce an excerpt from Freud's seminal paper "On Narcissism" to point up a central contributor to the development of narcissism. It signifies Freud's awareness that narcissism need not stem from rejection or disillusion, as Kernberg and Kohut contend, but may be a direct consequence of parental overvaluation. In describing these parents, Freud wrote:

> They are impelled to ascribe to the child all manner of perfections which sober observation would not confirm, to gloss over and forget all his shortcomings . . . Moreover, they are inclined to suspend in the child's favour the operation of all

those cultural requirements which their own narcissism has been forced to respect, and to renew in his person the claims for privileges which were long ago given up by themselves. The child shall have things better than his parents; he shall not be subject to the necessities which they have recognized as dominating life... restrictions on his own will are not to touch him; the laws of nature, like those of society, are to be abrogated in his favour; he is really to be the center and heart of creation. (1914, p. 48)

Horney presented a similar developmental history in the following quote:

Parents who transfer their own ambitions to the child and regard the boy as an embryonic genius or the girl as a princess, thereby develop in the child the feeling that he is loved for imaginary qualities rather than for his true self. (1939, p. 91)

In short order, children with such experiences will learn to view themselves as special beings, and learn to expect subservience from others; they begin to recognize that their mere existence is sufficient to provide pleasure to others and that their every action evokes commendation and praise. Unfortunately, they fail to learn how to cooperate and share or to think of the desires and interests of others. They acquire little sense of interpersonal responsibility and few skills for the give-and-take of social life. The family world revolves about them. They are egotistic in their attentions and narcissistic in the expression of their love and affect.

Children that have been exposed repeatedly to acquiescent and indulgent parents will expect comparable treatment from others, and they learn to employ the presumptuous and demanding strategies that quickly elicited favored reactions when these were not immediately forthcoming from their parents. Thus, when their desires are frustrated, they need act only in one way—feel entitled and assume that their wishes will automatically be met.

Such youngsters learn not only to take others for granted and to exploit them for personal benefit, but they also learn to see others as weak and subservient. By their fawning and self-demeaning behaviors, the parents of future narcissists have provided them with an image of others as manipulable, docile, and yielding. This view not only enhances narcissists' image of their own specialness but serves to strengthen their inclination to exploit others. Seeing others as weak and submissive allows them to ride roughshod over their interests with impunity.

It may be useful to trace the effects of parental overvaluation through the stages of neuropsychological development (Millon, 1969).

Feelings of omnipotence begin shortly after birth but do not take hold in a meaningful fashion until the sensorimotor-autonomy stage. Every minor achievement of future narcissists is responded to with such favor as to give them a deluded sense of their own extraordinary self-worth. Extreme confidence in one's child need not be a disservice, if it is well earned. In the case of the future narcissist, however, a marked disparity will exist between the child's actual competence and the impression he/she has of it.

Failures in parental guidance and control will play an important role during the intracortical-initiative stage. The child is encouraged to imagine, explore, and act without discipline and regulation. Unrestrained by the imposition of parental limits, the child's thoughts and behaviors may stray far beyond accepted boundaries of social reality. Untutored by parental discipline regarding the constraints of fear, guilt, and shame, the child may fail to develop those internal regulating mechanisms that result in self-control and social responsibility.

Mention should be made of the high frequency with which the conditions noted here arise among only children. Such youngsters often are cherished by their parents as possessions of extraordinary value. Not only are these children fawned over, but they frequently experience few of the restrictions and learn few of the responsibilities of sharing acquired by youngsters with siblings.

PROGNOSTIC CONSIDERATIONS

A major factor in the perniciousness of personality pathology is that its characterological behaviors are themselves pathogenic. Pathological personality patterns perpetuate themselves by setting into motion new and frequently more troublesome experiences than existed in the past. This section turns to a number of these self-perpetuating features.

Perpetuation of the Narcissistic Pattern

As with all personalities, narcissists exhibit their style with persistence and inflexibility. They cannot alter their strategy since these patterns are deeply ingrained. Rather than modifying their behavior when faced with failure, they may revert more intractably to their characteristic style; this is likely to intensify and foster new difficulties. In their attempts to cope with shame and defeat, they set up vicious circles that only perpetuate their problems. Three of these are elaborated next.

Illusion of competence. Narcissists assume that the presumption of superiority will suffice as its proof. Conditioned to think of themselves as able and admirable, they see little reason to waste the effort needed to acquire these virtues. Why bother engaging in such demeaning labors as systematic and disciplined study if one already possesses talent and aptitude? Moreover, it is beneath one's dignity to struggle as others do. Since they believe that they are well endowed from the start, there is no need to exert their energies to achieve what they already have. They simply assume that what they wish will come to them with little or no effort on their part.

Many narcissists begin to recognize in time that they cannot "live up" to their self-made publicity and fear trying themselves out in the real world. Rather than face genuine challenges, they may temporize and boast, but they never venture to test their adequacy. By acting in this way they can retain their illusion of superiority without fear of disproof. As a consequence, however, narcissists paralyze themselves. Their unfounded sense of confidence and their omnipotent belief in their perfection inhibit them from developing whatever aptitudes they may in fact possess. Unwilling or fearful of expending the effort, they may slip increasingly behind others in actual attainments. Their deficits may become pronounced over time, making them, as well as others, increasingly aware of their shortcomings. Since the belief in their superiority is the bedrock of their existence, the disparity between their genuine and their illusory competence becomes extraordinarily painful. The strain of maintaining their false self-image may cause them to feel fraudulent, empty, and disconsolate. They may succumb to periodic depressions or may slip slowly into paranoid irritabilities and delusions.

Lack of self-controls. The narcissist's illusion of superiority and entitlement is but one facet of a more generalized disdain for reality. Narcissists are neither diposed to stick to objective facts nor to restrict their actions within the boundaries of social custom or cooperative living. Unrestrained by childhood discipline and confident of their worth and prowess, they may take liberties with rules and reality, and prevaricate and fantasize at will. Free to wander in their private world of fiction, narcissists may lose touch with reality, lose their sense of proportion, and begin to think along peculiar and deviant lines. Their facile imagination may ultimately evoke comments from others concerning their arrogance and conceit. Ill-disposed to accept critical comments about their "creativity" and needing to retain their admirable self-image, narcissists are likely to turn further to their habit of self-glorification. Lacking social or self-controls, however, their fantasies may take flight and recede increasingly from objective reality.

Social alienation. Were narcissists able to respect others, allow themselves to value others' opinions, or see the world through others' eyes, their tendencies toward illusion and unreality might be checked or curtailed. Unfortunately, narcissists have learned to devalue others, not to trust their judgments, and to think of them as naïve and simpleminded. Thus, rather than question the correctness of their own beliefs, they assume that it is the views of others that are at fault. Hence, the more disagreement they have with others, the more convinced they are of their own superiority and the more isolated and alienated they are likely to become. These ideational difficulties are magnified further by their inability to participate skillfully in the give-and-take of shared social life. Their characteristic selfishness and ungenerosity often evoke condemnation and disparagement from others. These reactions drive narcissists further into their world of fantasy and only strengthen their alienation. And this isolation further prevents them from understanding the intentions and actions of others. They are increasingly unable to assess situations objectively, thereby failing further to grasp why they have been rebuffed and misunderstood. Distressed by these repeated and perplexing social failures, they are likely, at first, to become depressed and morose. However, true to their fashion, they will begin to elaborate new and fantastic rationales to account for their fate. But the more they conjecture and ruminate, the more they will lose touch, distort, and perceive things that are not there. They may begin to be suspicious of others, to question the latter's intentions, and to criticize them for ostensive deceptions. In time, narcissists' actions will drive away potential well-wishers, a reaction that will only serve to "prove" their suspicions.

Deficient in social controls and self-discipline, the narcissist's tendency to fantasize and distort may speed up. The air of grandiosity may become more flagrant. They may find hidden and deprecatory meanings in the incidental behavior of others, becoming convinced of others' malicious motives, claims upon them, and attempts to undo them. As their behaviors and thoughts transgress the line of reality, their alienation will mount, and they may seek to protect their phantom image of superiority more vigorously and vigilantly than ever. Trapped by the consequences of their own actions, they may become bewildered and frightened as the downward spiral progresses through its inexorable course. No longer in touch with reality, they begin to accuse others and hold them responsible for their own shame and failures. They may build a "logic" based on irrelevant and entirely circumstantial "evidence" and ultimately construct a delusional system to protect themselves from unbearable reality.

Remedial Interventions

Despite the potential for serious decompensation, as described above, most narcissists function successfully in society if they possess even a modicum of substance and talent to back their confidence. Difficulties arise only when a marked disparity exists between their presumptions and their actual competence. The inexhaustible reservoir of self-faith of narcissists can withstand considerable draining before it runs dry.

Narcissists are not inclined to seek therapy. Their pride disposes them to reject the "weak" role of patient. Most are convinced they can get along quite well on their own. How demeaning it is to admit shortcomings. Why should one consider changing if one is already perfect. And adding insult to injury, why should one be guided by a less talented being, namely the therapist. In sum, narcissists will not accede to therapy willingly. Moreover, once involved, they will maintain a well-measured distance from the therapist, resist the searching probes of personal exploration, become indignant over implications of deficiencies on their part, and seek to shift responsibility for these lacks to others. This evasiveness and unwillingness may seriously interfere with progress. The treatment setting may give witness to struggles in which narcissists seek to outwit the therapist and assert their dominance. Great patience and equanimity are required to establish a spirit of genuine confidence and respect.

Only after a particularly painful blow to their pride will narcissists be precipitated into therapy. A severe occupational failure, an embarrassing loss of public esteem, or a sudden change of attitude on the part of a previously idolizing marital partner illustrate the kinds of events that may prompt the voluntary acceptance of treatment. Once involved in treatment, the therapist can hold narcissists' initial interest by allowing them to focus attention upon themselves. Further, by encouraging discussions of their past achievements, the therapist may enable narcissists to rebuild their recently depleted self-esteem. Not infrequently, self-confidence in narcissists is restored merely by talking about themselves, by recalling and elaborating their attributes and competencies in front of a knowing and accepting person. If comfort and regained confidence are the goals, these can often be achieved in a few sessions.

Therapeutic aims are usually more substantial than merely reestablishing former levels of functioning, especially since rebuilding narcissists' superiority illusions may prove, in the long run, to be a disservice to them. Thus, the therapist might assist patients in acquiring greater self-control, becoming more sensitive and aware of reality, and learning to accept the constraints and responsibilities of shared social living. However, the therapist must first strengthen narcissists' capacity to confront their weaknesses and deficiencies. Until they can deal with themselves on a more realistic basis than before, it is not likely that narcissists will be motivated to develop socially cooperative attitudes and behaviors.

Turning to specific methods of intervention, the procedures of environmental management, psychopharmacologic treatment, and behavior modification appear of limited value. Changing attitudes toward self and others may best be begun through procedures of cognitive reorientation. Once a baseline of rapport has been established with such techniques, narcissists may be able to withstand more directive methods designed to probe and modify their self-attitudes and social habits. Psychoanalytic techniques have been recommended recently as applicable to these cases, although the narcissist's illusions often are reinforced too strongly by the imaginative freedom this method fosters. Group and family therapy may prove profitable in assisting patients to view themselves in a more realistic social light and to learn the skills of interpersonal sharing and cooperation.

Chapter 7

Antisocial Personality: The Aggressive Pattern

Independent personalities are identified by their inclination to turn to themselves as the primary source for fulfilling needs (Millon, 1969). A major distinction has been drawn, however, between those who are passively versus those who are actively independent. Passive-independents, or what the author and the DSM-III have termed narcissistic personalities, are characterized by their sublime, if unjustified, self-confidence and their deeply rooted faith in themselves as superior human beings. In contrast, active-independents—what the author has designated as aggressive personalities and are labeled in the DSM-III as antisocial personalities—are driven by a need to prove their superiority; strivings for independence stem not so much from a belief in self-worth as from a mistrust of others. Aggressive personalities, both nonantisocial and antisocial types, have faith only in themselves and are secure only when they are independent of those who they fear may undo, harm, or humiliate them.

The DSM-III label of "antisocial" as the designation for this personality syndrome places, the author believes, too great an emphasis on the delinquent, criminal, and other undersirable social consequences often found among these patients. Of course, some active-independent or aggressive personalities are openly and flagrantly illegal in their social behavior and, therefore, may properly be spoken of as antisocial. Other individuals with essentially similar "basic" personalities, however, fit into the mainstream of society, displaying their characteristic traits through socially acceptable avenues. The author considers it a major regressive step that the DSM has returned to an accusatory judgment rather than a dispassionate clinical formulation; what we have before us is but a minor variation of earlier, ill-considered, and deplorable notions such as "moral insanity" and "constitutional psychopathic inferiority."

Only a minor subset of the aggressive personality pattern comes into conflict with the law. Many find themselves commended and reinforced in our competitive society, where tough, hard-headed "realism" is admired as an attribute necessary for survival. Most find a socially valued niche for themselves in the rugged side of the business, military, or political world. Their behaviors are seen, for example, in the arrogant patriotism of nationalists whose truculence is "justified" by the hostility of "alien" groups. Such behavior is evident also in the machinations of politicans whose facade of good intentions cloaks a lust for power that leads to repressive legislation. Less dramatically, and more frequently, these individuals participate in the ordinary affairs of everyday life: the harshly punitive father; the puritanical, fear-inducing minister; the vengeful dean; and the irritable, guilt-producing mother.

The aggressive actions of these personalities appear to spring from their anticipation that others will be hostile. Their anger and vengeful behaviors are a preemptive counterattack, a fending off of the malice and humiliation they have learned to expect; in effect, they want to "beat the other fellow to the punch." To accomplish this, they seek to grab as much power as they can to prevent others from having and using it to exploit and harm them. Once seizing power, however, they become even more ruthless and vindictive than others may have been to them. They now use their strength for retribution, striking back at those who they feel mistreated and betrayed them in the past.

Although the author takes strong exception to the narrow view promulgated in the DSM-III, relevant excerpts are reproduced here for reference purposes. Before doing so, a quote is given from a comment prepared by the author in 1978 in criticism of the draft version that served as the basis for the final text of the DSM-III antisocial personality.

> I have never felt comfortable with the write-up for the antisocial personality disorder. I very much agree with those who contend that the focus given is oriented too much toward the "criminal personality" and not sufficiently toward those with similar propensities who have avoided criminal involvements. More importantly, the write-up fails to deal with personality characteristics at all, but rather lists a series of antisocial behaviors that stem from such characteristics. In that sense we have shifted the level of our focus in this disorder from that employed in describing all of the other personality disorders. The list comprising the antisocial diagnostic criteria is merely a sequence of picayunish specifics (e.g., thefts, three or more traffic arrests, etc.). These details make us delude ourselves that we are a mature empirical science when, in actuality, they derive from the data of one, highly biased research study. I would very much like to see a shift back from these narrow "empirical" details toward our "standard format." The semi-abstract criterion concepts of our standard format capture the underlying tone of the relevant trait or symptom we are addressing; we can record particular acts as illustrative examples....
>
> Traits that I consider to be prominent diagnostic criterion features that capture the essence of these antisocial individuals are the following. A major characteristic is what I would term "hostile affectivity;" this is illustrated by the fact that many of these personalities have an irascible temper that flares quickly into argument and attack, as evidenced in frequent verbally abusive and physically cruel behaviors. Another characteristic that I think coheres the scattered details of our description is the theme of "social rebelliousness" as

evidenced by the fact that these patients are contemptuous toward authority, tradition, sentimentality and humanistic concerns. Moreover, they exhibit a social "vindictiveness," a tendency, if you will, to enjoy and gain a peculiar satisfaction when derogating and humiliating others. Another notable feature is their frequent fearless attitude in which many of them seem to be not merely undaunted by danger and punishment, but seem to seek, provoke and be attracted to it.

It is these more general traits that I would like to see us list as diagnostic criteria. If there is some value in specifying particular illustrations to exemplify them, then, and only then, should we list such details (e.g., persistent lying, early aggressive sexual behavior, vandalism).

With these comments as a précis, the discussion turns to the descriptive text as printed in the DSM-III. It reflects a compromise following criticisms such as just noted. However, the diagnostic criteria, which are not reproduced here, remain narrow in focus.

The essential feature is a Personality Disorder in which there are a history of continuous and chronic antisocial behavior in which the rights of others are violated, persistence into adult life of a pattern of antisocial behavior that began before the age of 15, and failure to sustain good job performance over a period of several years (although this may not be evident in individuals who are self-employed or who have not been in a position to demonstrate this feature, e.g., student or housewife).

Lying, stealing, fighting, truancy, and resisting authority are typical early childhood signs. In adolescence, unusually early or aggressive sexual behavior, excessive drinking and use of illicit drugs are frequent. In adulthood, these kinds of behaviors continue, with the addition of inability to sustain consistent work performance, lack of ability to function as a responsible parent, and failure to accept social norms with respect to lawful behavior. After age 30 the more flagrant aspects may diminish, particularly sexual promiscuity, fighting, criminality, and vagrancy.

Despite the stereotype of a normal mental status in this disorder, frequently there are signs of personal distress, including complaints of tension, inability to tolerate boredom, depression, and the conviction (often correct) that others are hostile towards them. The interpersonal difficulties and dysphoria tend to persist into late adult life even when the more flagrant antisocial behavior has diminished. Almost invariably there is markedly impaired capacity to sustain lasting, close, warm, and responsible relationships with family, friends, or sexual partners. (p. 317–318)

HISTORICAL AND THEORETICAL ANTECEDENTS

Because of its extensive and divergent literature, the following review of the antecedent concepts and theories of this personality pattern is more detailed than usual. Its origins and clinical characteristics have been formulated and reformulated innumerable times over the past two centuries. Throughout this checkered history, the notion of an antisocial character has served to designate a rather varied collection of behaviors that have little in common other than being viewed as repugnant to the social mores of the time. Despite disagreements concerning its nature and origins, few clinicians today will fail to "get the picture" when they hear the designations "sociopath" or "antisocial personality." However, in a recent review of the last 50 years of research and theory on the "elusive category" of the psychopathic personality, the well-known British psychiatrist Sir Aubrey Lewis commented as follows:

> These reveal a preoccupation with the nosological status of the concept . . . its forensic implications, its subdivisions, limits [and] the propriety of identifying psychopathic personality with antisocial behavior. The effect of reading solid blocks of literature is disheartening; there is so much fine-spun theorizing, repetitive argument, and therapeutic gloom. (1974, pp. 137–138)

Fifty years ago the same issues were in the forefront, notably whether the psychopathic personality was or was not synonymous with overt antisocial behavior. Partridge's detailed review of the conceptions of the psychopath then prevalent began as follows:

> Ideas relating to psychopathic personality are scattered widely throughout psychiatric and criminological works. Much that has been written is somewhat incidental to the study of delinquency as a whole; some relate to the various types of mental disorders in which deviations of personality are involved. (1930, p. 53)

In addressing the issue of whether psychopathy and antisocial behavior are one and the same, Partridge wrote:

> There is comparatively little attention paid to [psychopathological] personality deviations which, though distinct, are not expressed in antisocial behavior.
> . . .
> There is an assumption that at least some types of chronic misbehavior are the visible extensions, so to speak, of deep [personality] ledges. (1930, p. 75)

In reporting on covariations found between diagnosed psychopathy and recorded histories of criminal or delinquent behavior, he noted:

> The proportionate importance of the psychopath in the production of the total of delinquency has been given some attention. Some, we have seen, find a very large proportion of psychopathic personality in criminal groups or delinquents in general, some seem to find only a small one. (1930, p. 93)

In the conclusion of his analysis, Partridge wondered whether the tendency of nosologists to focus on antisocial behaviors, at the expense of the deeper personality structure and its nonsociopathic variants, simply reflects the fact that these behaviors are "obvious." He wrote:

One reason why there has arisen confusion about the so-called psychopaths is that, in these cases, the personality deviations become *apparent* at an early age in a distinct form.... The main difference ... being that the sociopathic forms are more objective, merely in their manifestations or adjustment patterns—at least more fully revealed. (1930, pp. 98–99)

The issue of whether the antisocial form is but only one of several manifestations of a more complex personality substrate continues as controversial in the literature. The DSM-III committee voted to retain the decision promulgated for the first time in the DSM-II that the "antisocial" label serve to represent a distinct personality type rather than a form of behavior observed in several personality types. This decision signified a shift from the DSM-I, which considered "sociopathic reactions" to be a syndrome symptomatic of any of several underlying personality disorders. As contended earlier, undue prominence is given the delinquent or criminal expression of the personality by designating it as "antisocial." This formulation fails to recognize that the same fundamental personality structure, with its characteristic pattern of ruthless and vindictive behavior, is often displayed in ways that are not socially disreputable, irresponsible, or illegal. Using personal repugnance and conventional morals as a basis for diagnostic syndromes runs contrary to contemporary efforts to expunge social judgments as clinical entities (e.g., the reevaluation of the concept of homosexuality as a syndrome). The label "antisocial" reflects a return toward earlier value-laden concepts; attention turns to this history next.

The first clear presentation of the clinical features of this personality arose when psychiatrists at the end of the eighteenth century were drawn into age-old arguments concerning free will and whether certain moral transgressors were capable of "understanding" the consequences of their acts. It was Philippe Pinel (1801, 1806), referring to a form of madness known at the time as *la folie raisonnante,* who noted that certain patients engage in impulsive and self-damaging acts, despite the fact that their reasoning abilities were unimpaired and they fully grasped the irrationality of what they were doing. Describing these cases under the name *manie sans délire* ("insanity without delirium"), his description was among the first to recognize that madness need not signify the presence of a deficit in reasoning powers. As Pinel described it:

I was not a little surprised to find many maniacs who at no period gave evidence of any lesion of understanding, but who were under the dominion of instinctive and abstract fury, as if the faculties of affect alone had sustained injury. (1801)

Until Pinel forcefully argued the legitimacy of this psychopathological entity, it was universally held that all mental disorders were disorders of the mind; since mind was equated with reason, only a disintegration in the faculties of reason and intellect would be judged as insanity. However, beginning with Pinel there arose the belief that one could be insane *(manie)* without a confusion of mind *(sans délire)*.

Benjamin Rush, the well-known American physician, wrote in the early 1800s of similar perplexing cases characterized by lucidity of thought combined with socially deranged behaviors. He spoke of these individuals as possessing an "innate, preternatural moral depravity" in which "there is probably an original defective organization in those parts of the body which are preoccupied by the moral faculties of the mind" (1812, p. 112). Rush appears to have been the first theorist to have taken Pinel's morally neutral clinical observation of defects in "passion and affect" and turned it into a social condemnation. He claimed that a lifelong pattern of irresponsibility was displayed by these individuals without a corresponding feeling of shame or hesitation over the personally destructive consequences of their actions. Describing the features characterizing this type, Rush wrote:

> The will might be deranged even in many instances of persons of sound understandings... the will becoming the involuntary vehicle of vicious actions through the instrumentality of the passions. Persons thus diseased cannot speak the truth upon any subject.... Their falsehoods are seldom calculated to injure anybody but themselves. (1812, p. 124)

As evident from the dates mentioned in the preceding paragraphs, the British alienist J. C. Prichard (1835)—credited by many as having been the first to formulate the concept of "moral insanity"—was, in fact, preceded in this realization by several theorists; nevertheless, he was the first to label it as such and to give it wide readership in English-speaking nations. Although he accepted Pinel's notion of *manie sans délire,* he dissented from Pinel's morally neutral attitude toward these disorders and became the major exponent of the view that these behaviors signified a reprehensible defect in character that deserved social condemnation. He also broadened the scope of the original syndrome by including under the label "moral insanity" a wide range of previously diverse mental and emotional conditions. All of these patients ostensibly shared a common defect in the power to guide themselves in accord with "natural feelings"—that is, a spontaneous and intrinsic sense of rightness, goodness, and responsibility. Those afflicted by this disease were swayed, despite their ability to intellectually understand the choices before them, by overpowering "affections" that compelled them to engage in socially repugnant behaviors. As Prichard described it:

> There is a form of mental derangement in which the intellectual functions appear to have sustained little or no injury, while the disorder is manifested principally or alone in the state of the feelings, temper or habits. In cases of this nature the moral or active principles of the mind are strangely perverted or depraved; the power of self-government is lost or greatly impaired and the individual is found to be incapable, not of talking or reasoning upon any subject proposed to him, but of conducting himself with decency and propriety in the business of life. (1835, p. 85)

The separation between insanity due to defects in reasoning versus those owing to defects in "natural affections" espoused by Prichard led to a major and long-standing controversy among British legal scholars and alienists. The discussion returns to this controversy after a few comments on the terminology of the day.

1. The word *moral* was imposed upon Pinel's concept by both Rush and Prichard. Pinel's syndrome signified the inability to restrain the affections (emotions) without a corresponding loss of reasoning; it was entirely neutral with regard to conventional notions of morality. Immersed in the British philosophical doctrine of "natural rights," which stressed both the state's and the individual's responsibility for social action, Rush and Prichard took Pinel's neutral clinical observation and transformed it into an entity consisting of moral censure and social depravity. In seeking to counter this intrusion of irrelevant philosophical and moralistic values upon clinical judgments, the distinguished British psychiatrist of the mid-nineteenth century, Daniel Hack Tuke, proposed (1892) that Prichard's label be dropped and the syndrome renamed "inhibitory insanity," thereby recapturing the essence and moral neutrality of Pinel's original formulations.

2. Prichard's entity of "moral insanity" has little in common as a clinical syndrome with contemporary notions of psychopathy or antisocial personality. So diverse a group of disorders were subsumed in Prichard's category that almost all mental conditions, other than mental retardation and schizophrenia, would be so diagnosed today. If we sorted the "morally insane" into contemporary categories, the syndrome would be depleted so severely as to leave but a minor fraction that could be characterized by current notions of antisocial behavior.

Prichard did make one important positive contribution in that he was the first theorist to have differentiated the prognosis of long-standing clinical traits from those that arise in response to transient stresses. He stated this original idea as follows:

> When the disorder is connected with a strong natural predisposition, it can scarcely be expected to terminate in recovery. Such we must conclude to be the case in those instances in which the phenomena bear the appearance of an increase or exaltation of peculiarities natural to the individual, and noted as remarkable traits in his previous habits. If, however, this morbid state of mind has been the effect of any external and accidental cause, which admits of removal, or if the individual can be extracted from its influence or helped defend against it, there is reason to hope that the disorder will gradually subside. (1835, p. 122)

The concept of moral insanity continued as a major source of contention and preoccupation in England for more than 70 years. In contrast to Daniel Hack Tuke, Henry Maudsley, another leading British psychiatrist of the period, not only sided unequivocally with Prichard but contended that there existed a specific cerebral center underlying "natural moral feelings." His views concerning the morally insane were stated thus:

> As there are persons who cannot distinguish certain colours, having what is
> called colour blindness, so there are some who are congenitally deprived of
> moral sense. (1874, p. 11)

To the notion that there were cerebral deficits among the morally depraved
were added several anthropological "stigmata," as proposed by Lombroso
(1872–1885) and Gouster (1878). Dismissing the primitive physical anthrop-
ology, what is striking about Lombroso's exposition is how closely it
corresponds to the thinking of current DSM criteria. Lombroso was explicit in
proposing the idea of a "born delinquent," whereas the DSM-III only implies
a similar notion. According to Lombroso, constitutionally disposed criminal
types display a notably large and projective lower jaw, outstretched ears,
retreating forehead, left-handedness, robust physique, precocious sexual
development, tactile insensibility, muscular agility, and so on. Behaviorally,
they are emotionally hyperactive, temperamentally irascible, impetuous in
action, and deficient in altruistic feelings. Gouster's list of stigmata parallels
other aspects of the DSM-III antisocial personality criteria. Most similar is the
symptom cluster characterized by moral perversion from early life, as
evidenced in headstrong, malicious, disobedient, irascible, lying, neglectful,
and frequently violent and brutal behaviors; also noted are a delight in
intrigue and mischief, and a tendency toward excesses in seeking excitement
and passion.

Toward the end of the nineteenth century, German psychiatrists turned
their attentions away from the value-laden theories of the English alienists
and toward what they judged to be observational research. Prominent among
this group was J. L. Koch (1891), who proposed that the label *moral insanity*
be replaced by the term *psychopathic inferiority*, under which he included:

> all mental irregularities whether congenital or acquired which influence a
> man in his personal life and cause him, even in the most favorable cases, to seem
> not fully in possession of normal mental capacity. (1891, p. 67)

The term *psychopathic*, a generic label for all personality disorders until
recent decades, was selected by Koch to signify his belief that a physical basis
existed for these impairments. Thus, he stated:

> They always remain psychopathic in that they are caused by organic states and
> changes which are beyond the limits of physiological normality. They stem
> from a congenital or acquired inferiority of brain constitution. (1891, p. 54)

As with Prichard, Koch included a wide group of conditions in his category of
psychopathic inferiorities, only a small portion of which would be considered
within our current rendering of an antisocial or sociopathic syndrome. His
subgroups of "psychopathic disposition" *(Zartheit)*, noted by tension and
high sensitivity; "psychopathic taint" *(Belastung)*, seen clinically in those
with pecularities, egocentricities, and impulsive fury; and "psychopathic

degeneration," manifested predominantly in borderline mental states, all rested on presumptive physical defects, none of which Koch admitted could be structurally or physiologically verified.

The concept of a "constitutionally inferior" type was introduced into American literature at the turn of the century by Adolf Meyer, shortly after his arrival from Germany. Although following Koch's ideas in the main, Meyer sought to separate psychopathic cases from psychoneurotic disorders, both of which were grouped together in Koch's "psychopathic inferiorities" classification. Meyer was convinced that the etiology of the neuroses was primarily psychogenic, that is, colored less by inherent physical defects or by "constitutional inferiorities." The line of distinction he drew between these groups remained clear and sharp for many years in American nosology. The label "inferiority," however, did not fare as well since its deprecatory connotation was anathema to both the verbalized social values and medical practices of the day. "Constitutional psychopathic state" and "psychopathic personality" evolved as the two popular American designations through the first half of the twentieth century.

It is necessary to step back again in this review to bring into sharper focus the fact that for the first three decades of this century the label *psychopathic* conveyed nothing more than Koch's contention that the individual's personality was physically rooted or constitutional. Further, the term *inferiority* implied nothing more, insofar as specific clinical characteristics were concerned, than the observation that these personalities deviated unfavorably from the norm. In time, the term took on a more specific cast, assuming the features connoted by the designation "moral insanity," the historical precursor that Koch sought to escape. Recall that the meaning of the category *manie sans délire*, as originally formulated by Pinel, had nothing whatsoever to do with the value judgments ascribed to it by Prichard in his construction of "moral insanity." Similarly, Koch's effort to obviate the moral pejoratives in Prichard's conception was slowly undermined as his designation gradually evolved to mean quite the opposite of what he intended. This fascinating transmutation of the meaning of a diagnostic label is not unique in the history of clinical science. Moreover, to add further insult to the injury of having *psychopathy* so misconstrued, Koch's intent that a physical etiology for these syndromes be clearly affirmed was undone in later years when the designation was changed to *sociopathy*, a means of signifying its now ostensive social origins. The shifting sands of our terminologies and theories in this field should give us good reason to question current formulations that appear to be throwbacks to earlier, discarded notions. Although the label "antisocial personality" may seem less pejorative than "constitutional psychopathic inferior," it does hark back to its ancestral forerunner, "moral insanity."

The threads of this historical review are now picked up with the descriptions provided by Emil Kraepelin; the successive editions of his important text reflect the changing emphases given the psychopathic syndrome. In the second edition of this major work (1887), Kraepelin identified the "morally insane" as suffering congenital defects in their ability to restrain the "reckless gratification of... immediate egotistical desires" (p. 281). The fifth edition, in 1896, referred to these conditions as "psychopathic states" for the first time, asserting that these constitutional disorders display themselves as lifelong morbid personalities. The next edition, published in 1899, referred to psychopathic states as one of several forms of degeneration, along with syndromes such as obsessions, impulsive insanity, and sexual perversions. Retaining the theme of degeneration in his seventh edition of 1903-1904, Kraepelin now referred to these states as "psychopathic personalities," by which he meant:

> Those peculiar morbid forms of personality development which we have grounds for regarding as degenerative. The characteristic of degeneration is a lasting morbid reaction to the stresses of life. (p. 547)

By the eighth edition of his work (1909-1915), Kraepelin described psychopaths as deficient in either affect or volition. He separated them into two varieties, those of morbid disposition, consisting of obsessives, impulsives, and sexual deviants; and those exhibiting personality peculiarities. The latter group was differentiated into seven classes: the excitable *(Erregbaren)*, the unstable *(Haltlosen)*, the impulsive *(Triebmenschen)*, the eccentric *(Verschobenen)*, the liars and swindlers *(Luegner und Schwindler)*, the antisocial *(Gessellschaftsfeinde)*, and the quarrelsome *(Streitsuechtige)*. Only the latter three possess features akin to current notions of the antisocial. Liars and swindlers are "naturally cheats and occasionally thieves"; sexual offenses are common to them, and they are "uncertain and capricious in everything." The quarrelsome personality is "in constant trouble"; they think others are always against them and their judgment is "warped and unreliable." Last, antisocial personalities, the explicit and prime forerunners of our contemporary nomenclature, are:

> the enemies of society... characterized by a blunting of the moral elements. They are often destructive and threatening... [and] there is a lack of deep emotional reaction; and of sympathy and affection they have little. They are apt to have been troublesome in school, given to truancy and running away. Early thievery is common among them and they commit crimes of various kinds. (Partridge, 1930, pp. 88-89)

The details characterized by Kraepelin in the final edition of his monumental text are almost identical to the diagnostic criteria spelled out for the younger antisocial in the DSM-III. Were Kraepelin's views the final word? Apparently many of his contemporaries thought not.

K. Birnbaum (1914), writing in Germany at the time of Kraepelin's final edition, was the first to suggest that the term *sociopathic* might be the most apt designation for the majority of these cases. To him, not all delinquents of the degenerative psychopathic type were either morally defective or constitutionally inclined to criminality. Birnbaum asserted that antisocial behavior only rarely stems from inherent immoral traits of character; rather, it reflects most often the operation of societal forces that make the more acceptable forms of behavior and adaptation difficult to acquire. This social-conditioning thesis did not become a prominent alternative in psychiatric circles until the later 1920s, largely gaining serious consideration through the writings of Healy and Bronner (1926) and Partridge (1930) in the United States. In the interim decades, psychopathy was conceived internationally in the manner most explicitly stated in the British Mental Deficiency Act of 1913; still wedded to Prichard's conception of moral insanity developed some 80 years earlier, it was judged a constitutional defect that manifested "strong vicious or criminal propensities on which punishment has had little or no deterrent effect."

Both K. Schneider (1923) and E. Kahn (1931) presented detailed and thoughtful personality typologies to which they gave the label "psychopathic." Their concept of psychopathy, however, was that of constitutional disposition, not of antisocial predilection. Although some of their types correspond with current notions of the antisocial personality, they are largely more detailed descriptions of what Kraepelin presented in the final edition of his text a decade or so earlier.

Before turning to the writings of the psychoanalysts during the third and fourth decades of this century, the views of several other pre-World War II contributors should be noted briefly. G. E. Partridge (1927, 1928, 1930), a leading American clinician of the period, systematically studied several populations of diagnosed psychopathic personalities and concluded that the label was "meaningless" and should be dropped in favor of Birnbaum's concept of sociopathy. Efforts to divide these personalities into subtypes would be only a futile endeavor, according to Partridge; to him, the only justification for membership among the "essential sociopaths" was that the individual's behavior consistently deviated from the norms of his or her social group.

The leading British theorist of the thirties, D. K. Henderson (1939), allied himself with Partridge's basic conclusions but felt that a useful distinction could be drawn between three subtypes: (1) the predominantly aggressive, (2) the predominantly passive or inadequate, and (3) the predominantly creative. Original at the time was Henderson's suggestion that these individuals feel themselves to be outcasts, rarely understood by others, and stigmatized and scapegoated unjustly. Because of his prominence in British circles, certain of Henderson's views gained quick attention and stirred much debate. Notable among the issues he raised was his inclusion of a passive-inadequate type, considered by most of his psychiatric colleagues to be more properly diagnosed as neurotic; even more controversial was his proposal of a "creative psychopath," a brilliant, aggressively active, though erratic and moody person, exemplified by individuals such as Lawrence of Arabia. As elsewhere, controversy raged, not over matters of empirical substance or theoretic logic but as a consequence of terminological confusion and issues of syndromal scope.

An incisive and thorough clinical description was provided by H. Cleckley in his book *The Mask of Sanity*, first published in 1941. Attempting to clarify problem terminologies and seeking to counter the trend of including evermore diverse disorders under the rubric of "psychopathy," Cleckley proposed replacing the term with the label "semantic dementia" to signify what he viewed to be the syndrome's prime feature, the tendency to say one thing and to do another. More important than his proposal of a new nomenclature, which attracted little following, was the clarity of Cleckley's description of the psychopath's primary traits—guiltlessness, incapacity for object love, impulsivity, emotional shallowness, superficial social charm, and an inability to profit from experience. No less significant was Cleckley's assertion that these personalities are found not only in prisons but in society's most respected roles and settings. Cleckley illustrated this thesis with several examples of "successful" businessmen, scientists, physicians, and psychiatrists. He wrote as follows:

> In these personalities...a very deep seated disorder often exists. The true difference between them and the psychopaths who continually go to jails or to psychiatric hospitals is that they keep up a far better and more consistent outward appearance of being normal.
>
> The chief difference...lies perhaps in whether the mask or facade of psychobiologic health is extended into superficial material success. (1941, pp. 198-199)

As the novel concepts and theories of psychoanalysis took root in the 1920s, preliminary and scattered notions concerning the "character" of psychopaths began to be published by clinicians oriented by this school of thought. Thus, in commenting on papers presented by more traditional psychiatrists, Coriat suggested in 1927 that the "constitutional psychopathic" was an antisocial character who fixated at infantile levels, had unresolved oedipal conflicts, and never learned to replace the ego ideals of childhood with the ego ideals of society. Partridge (1927), employing psychoanalytic concepts, perceived the demands of the psychopath as stemming from unfulfilled oral needs.

It was not until the work of Franz Alexander (1923, 1930, 1935), however, that the first assessment of psychopathy and criminal behavior was undertaken from a thoroughgoing psychoanalytic perspective. Alexander was prompted to this task by an intriguing paper of Freud's (1915b) entitled "Some Character Types Met with in Psychoanalytic Work"; here Freud described "peculiar acts" that appear out of character for the individual. In exposing the dynamics of a subgroup of these cases, referred to as "criminality from a sense of guilt," Freud wrote:

> Analytic work then afforded the surprising conclusion that such deeds are done precisely *because* they are forbidden, and because by carrying them out the

doer enjoys a sense of mental relief. He suffered an oppressive feeling of guilt, of which he did not know the origin, and after he had committed a misdeed the oppression was mitigated. (1915b, p. 342)

This paper served as the impetus for a number of subsequent clinical reports by other analysts. Among those written in the early mid-1920s was Aichorn's "Wayward Youth," Reich's study the "Impulse Ridden Character," and Abraham's analysis of the life and development of an imposter.

In Alexander's 1923 text *Psychoanalysis of the Total Personality,* he distinguished several levels of personality psychopathology; a similar thesis was presented in a 1930 paper, "The Neurotic Character." Four levels of pathology were proposed: neuroses, neurotic character, psychosis, and true criminality. They were arranged in this sequence to reflect diminishing levels of the ego's ability to restrain unconscious impulses, the neurotic displaying the greatest capacity and the criminal the least. The neurotic character was conceived by Alexander to be the underlying personality of psychopaths. To Alexander, neurotic characters act out their conflicts rather than transforming them intrapsychically. Alexander wrote:

They live out their impulses, many of their tendencies are asocial and foreign to the ego, and yet they cannot be considered true criminals. It is precisely because one part of such an individual's personality continues to sit in judgment upon the other . . . that his total personality is easily differentiated from the more homogeneous, unified and antisocial personality of the criminal. The singular and only apparently irrational drive to self-destruction met with in such people indicates rather definitely the existence of inner self-condemnation.

Their conduct arises from unconscious motives which are not directly accessible to their conscious personality. . . . Admonition, encouragement or punishment coming from the environment is as useless as his own resolution, "I am beginning a new life tomorrow."

A large proportion of such individuals, neurotically driven by unconscious motives, now to commit a transgression, then to seek punishment, sooner or later fall foul of the law. . . .

[Their] lives are full of dramatic action . . . something is always happening, as if they were literally driven by the demonic compulsion. . . . Here is where the adventurers belong whose manifold activities give expression to an underlying revolt against public authority. They always manage to be punished unjustifiably from their highly subjective point of view. (1930, pp. 11-15)

A similar formulation was made that year by another analyst, L. Bartemeier:

The neurotic character is more bold and daring than the neurotic personality. He does not allow society to intimidate him into mere phantasy but dramatizes his primitive impulses in real action. . . . He maintains a social spite against civilization and its restrictions. The life of such a person. . . . is made up of socially ruthless indulgences and subsequent insistences upon punishment. These people only commit crime with emotional conflict while true criminals experience no such stress. (1930, p. 516)

Lest the analytic model of the psychopath be viewed as näive, it may be helpful to record a few quotations from Alexander's study the *Roots of Crime* (1935), quotations that indicate his thorough awareness that antisocial behaviors reflect an inextricable interplay among intrapsychic processes, social forces, and constitutional dispositions.

> The chief difference between neurosis and criminal behavior is that in the neurosis the emotional conflict results in symbolic gratifications of unsatisfied urges, whereas in criminal behavior it leads to overt misdeeds. Those needs which are frustrated by economic conditions... cannot be satisfied as easily by the symbolic gratifications of phantasy as can the emotional tensions of love and hate. The emotional conflicts and deprivations of childhood, the resentments of parents and siblings, find a powerful ally in resentment against the social situation, and this combined emotional tension seeks a realistic expression in criminal acts and cannot be relieved by mere phantasy products that are exhibited in neurotic symptoms.
>
> We found that criminality in some cases is a direct expression of a protest against certain deprivations, a reaction of spite against certain members of the family, the expression of jealousy, envy, hostile competition, all of which are strengthened by early sufferings or the lack of love and support on the part of adults. But, we must add, intense hostilities in such cases frequently create strong guilt feelings, which in turn lead to an unconscious need for punishment....
>
> Certain unacquired bases of the instinctive life (constitution), apart from the environmental influences, must be partly responsible for the fact that similar emotional conflicts may, depending on the make-up of the individual, result either in criminality or in neurosis. The introverted nature of the neurotic, his readiness to content himself with gratifications in phantasy and to renounce real satisfaction, seems to be founded on some constitutional factor. And, on the other hand, certain individuals are characterized by a more robust, expansive instinctual life which contents itself only with outgoing behavior. (1935, pp. 278–279)

The last paragraph is of special interest in that it presages, in almost exact detail, the views of later, vigorously antianalytic critics such as Eysenck, whose work is discussed shortly. Alexander was the first prominent psychoanalyst to invest a significant portion of his attention to antisocial behavior. Subsequent, similarly inclined writers (Wittels, 1937; Karpman, 1941; Fenichel, 1945; Freidlander, 1945; Greenacre, 1945; Allen, 1950; Levy, 1951) also sought a rationale for the development of these behaviors with reference to intrapsychic processes and early parent-child relations. For example, Wittels differentiated neurotic psychopaths from simple psychopaths; the former, fixated ostensibly at the phallic stage, fear their bisexual impulses, whereas the latter directly indulge their bisexuality. Karpman distinguished two variants of psychopathy also, the "idiopathic" and the "symptomatic." The former were judged to be the true psychopaths in that they were constitutionally guiltless, insensitive to the feelings of others, and disposed to acquisitiveness and aggression; moreover, no psychogenic history could be observed that would account for their antisocial inclination. Karpman's symptomatic group was composed of neurotics who "paraded" as psychopaths; they were akin to Alexander's neurotic characters and could not be considered true psychopaths because their actions stemmed from unresolved unconscious difficulties. Levy proposed another subdivision to represent what he saw as clearly different forms of early experience. Termed by Levy the "deprived psychopath" and the "indulged psychopath," they are similar in conception to Millon's (1969) distinction between "aggressive" and "narcissistic" sociopaths, the former being a product of a harsh upbringing; and the latter, of parental overvaluation.

Although Horney's contributions were seen by her orthodox psychoanalytic colleagues as deviating from the mainstream, the distinctions she drew were deeply rooted in analytic theory. Attentive to conditions encountered in conventional clinical practice, as opposed to juvenile courts and prisons, Horney was fully aware that "antisocial" types were prevalent in all walks of life. Describing such a personality pattern, which she characterized as displaying "sadistic trends," Horney wrote:

> In degrading others he not only allays his intolerable self-contempt but at the same time gives himself a feeling of superiority.... When he exploits others emotionally he provides a vicarious emotional life for himself that lessens his own sense of barrenness. When he defeats others he wins a triumphant elation which obscures his own hopeless defeat. This craving for vindictive triumph is perhaps his most intense motivating force.
>
> All his pursuits serve as well to gratify his hunger for thrills and excitement.
>
> Last but not least, his sadistic dealings with others provide him with a feeling of strength and pride which reinforce his unconscious feeling of omnipotence. (1945, pp. 206–207)

A recent psychoanalytic theorist, B. Bursten (1972), has proposed that the essential features of classical sociopaths are their need to bolster their self-esteem by being contemptuous of others and "needing to put something over them." Referring to this pattern as "the manipulative personality," Bursten wrote:

> This conceptualization begins to throw some light on why the sociopath seems not to learn from experience; we are looking at the wrong experience. Frequently these people are quite bright and do learn. They are quite adept at assessing social situations. Indeed it is their very sharpness and their ability to size up a situation which inspires simultaneously our admiration and our anger. They have well learned from experience what to expect in certain social situations. Nevertheless, the sociopath's behavior has baffled us because we have misunderstood the main purpose of his behavior. (1972, p. 319).

Of particular note also is Bursten's effort to counter the moral and judgmental implications of the "antisocial" label by substituting what he viewed to be a value-free designation. He phrased his proposal as follows:

By describing such people as manipulative personalities, we get further away from the mixture of psychiatric concepts and concepts involving offenses against society. The manipulation is an interpersonal event resting in great measure on the internal dynamics of the manipulative personality; whether he comes into conflict with society is now immaterial as far as the diagnostic category is concerned.

What the shift from antisocial personality to manipulative personality can add is the further separation of the personality configuration from the social conflict. For indeed, there are many people who are internally driven to manipulate and who do not get into serious conflict with society. People with similar character structures may manifest their dynamic processes in a variety of ways [depending on] the options for expression which society offers them.

The category... includes some successful businessmen, politicans, administrators... as well as those who come into open conflict with society. (1972, p. 320)

Bursten's specific proposals for the manipulative personality are highly debatable, but his desire to protect personality diagnoses from value judgments and his assertion that these personalities are to be found in all sectors of social life are both relevant and appropriate.

The discussion now turns from the frequently overlooked psychoanalytic contribution to the antisocial personality to the even less recognized work of research psychologists. For example, Eysenck (1957, 1967) offers evidence for the thesis that psychopaths possess an inherited temperamental disposition to extraversion that inclines them to acquire antisocial behaviors. According to the learning theory espoused by Eysenck, extraverts condition slowly and therefore, in contrast to normals, are able to acquire the values and inhibitions of their social group to only a minimal degree. Eysenck's thesis leaves many details of psychopathic development unclear, and laboratory evidence for its central assumptions is scanty at best. Whereas Eysenck's theory rests on the assumption of innate constitutional dispositions, other learning theorists who have studied aggressive sociopathic behavior base their interpretations solely in terms such as vicarious learning and reinforcement. Thus, Bandura and Walters (1959), following a social learning model that is not dissimilar in content from the views of many analysts, gave primary attention to the role of parent-child interactions. For example, hostile parents are viewed as models that the child imitates and uses as a guide to establish antisocial relationships with others. In other cases, parents may mete out rewards and punishments in a manner that produces a style of superficial affability cloaking fundamentally devious attitudes. A series of extensive studies by Quay and his associates (1964, 1979) focused on delinquent populations and used multivariate statistical techniques to identify distinct clusters or types. Four characteristic patterns have been obtained repeatedly across a variety of population samples: conduct disorder, anxiety-withdrawal, immaturity, and socialized-aggressive disorder.

An empirical approach of special note is the work of Robins (1966) and her colleagues, which has attempted to unravel the juvenile antecedents of adult psychopathy and antisocial behavior. What is noteworthy in her findings is the close correspondence they show to the behaviors specified as characteristic of psychopathic personalities some half-century earlier by Kraepelin. What makes these data so important is that they comprise, in almost every detail, the diagnostic criteria for the DSM-III antisocial personality; despite the history of alternative models and theories available for consideration, the DSM-III Task Force voted to base its diagnostic guidelines in accord with this single, albeit well-designed, follow-up study of delinquency cases referred to one child guidance clinic in a large midwestern city.

A quote concerning the evolving history of "psychopathy," written by Cameron and Magaret in the early 1950s, is as apt today as it was then:

> The residue of this tortuous and perplexing historical development is unfortunately still with us. For example, the popular labels for social deviation now . . . seem merely to be a restatement of the outmoded category of "constitutional psychopathic inferiority." They do not refer to new concepts. Moreover, the accounts of psychopathic behavior given by present-day behavior pathologists are still likely to be accusations rather than descriptions. The evaluative attitudes of nineteenth-century psychiatry continue to tinge our modern classifications; and the psychopath stands accused of crime, of exploitation and of inability to profit from corrective procedures.
>
> The background of "psychopathic personality" in nineteenth-century psychiatry, although relevant as past history, need not dictate the present and future development of the concept. Nor can we afford to perpetuate the implication that social deviation is morally bad. We cannot ignore the effects of parental emphasis, of others' reactions and of self-reactions in training a growing child to socially deviant behavior. (1951, pp. 190–191)

This plea that we progress beyond the perspective of moral and social judgments as a basis for clinical concepts is as relevant today as it was when written.

The final model for this review anchors "psychopathic" behaviors to developmental learning and psychological dynamics. Proposed by Millon (1969) in his formulation of the active-independent personality, the following descriptions and criteria served as the initial working draft for what was ultimately labeled by the DSM-III Task Force as the "antisocial personality." A synthesis of the more concretistic and research-oriented criteria in the final DSM-III draft and the more abstract and clinically oriented criteria that follow may prove useful to the reader. The draft proposals stated:

> This pattern is typified by a self-assertive, temperamentally hostile and socially forceful and intimidating manner. There is pride in self-reliance, unsentimentality and hard-boiled competitive values. Malicious personal tendencies are projected outward, precipitating frequent outbursts of explosive anger. Vindictive gratification is obtained by humiliating and dominating others. A rash willingness to risk harm is notable as is a fearlessness in the face of threats and punitive action. Frank antisocial behaviors (e.g., truancy, non-traffic

arrests, frequent fighting) are common among adolescent and post-adolescent aggressive personalities, as well as in certain socioeconomic sub-populations. However, the majority of these personalities do not exhibit flagrant antisocial behaviors, finding a sanctioned niche in conventional roles.

Since adolescence or early adulthood at least 3 of the following have been present to a notably greater degree than in most people and were not limited to discrete periods nor necessarily prompted by stressful life events.

1. Hostile affectivity (e.g., pugnacious and irascible temper flares readily into argument and attack; exhibits frequent verbally abusive and physically cruel behaviors).
2. Assertive self-image (e.g., proudly characterizes self as self-reliant, vigorously energetic and hard-headed; values tough, competitive and power-oriented life style).
3. Interpersonal vindictiveness (e.g., reveals satisfaction in derogating and humiliating others; contemptuous of sentimentality, social compassion and humanistic values).
4. Hyperthymic fearlessness (e.g., high activation level evident in impulsive, accelerated and forceful responding; attracted to and undaunted by danger and punishment).
5. Malevolent projection (e.g., claims that most persons are devious, controlling and punitive; justifies own mistrustful, hostile and vengeful attitudes by ascribing them to others).

These criteria are drawn upon for the next section's more comprehensive presentation of those clinical features that exemplify this personality.

CLINICAL PICTURE

The major features of this personality pattern are approached in line with the four levels of data used in previous chapters. Identifying characteristics that are relatively specific to the antisocial variant of the aggressive personality syndrome are used to distinguish them from what the author calls, for lack of a simple term, the "nonantisocial aggressive" type. Unless the specification is noted, the features described should be assumed applicable to both antisocial and nonantisocial forms.

Behavioral Features

Many people shy away from these personalities, feeling intimidated by their brusque and belligerent manner. They sense them to be cold and callous, insensitive to the feelings of others, gaining what pleasure they can competing with and humiliating everyone and anyone. These aggressively oriented personalities tend to be argumentative and contentious. Not infrequently, they are abrusive, cruel, and malicious. They often insist on being seen as faultless, invariably are dogmatic in their opinions, and rarely concede on any issue despite clear evidence negating the validity of their argument. Most behave as if the "softer" emotions were tinged with poison. They avoid expressions of warmth and intimacy and are suspicious of gentility, compassion, and kindness, often seeming to doubt the genuineness of these feelings.

Many of these personalities evidence a low tolerance for frustration, seem to act impetuously, and cannot delay, let alone forego, prospects for immediate pleasure. Antisocial types appear easily bored and restless, unable to endure the tedium of routine or to persist at the day-to-day responsibilities of marriage or a job. Others of this variant are characteristically prone to taking chances and seeking thrills, acting as if they were immune from danger. There is a tendency to jump from one exciting and momentarily gratifying escapade to another, with little or no care for potentially detrimental consequences. When matters go their way, these antisocial variants often act in a gracious, cheerful, saucy, and clever manner. More characteristically, their behavior is brash, arrogant, and resentful. They have a low tolerance for frustration. When pushed on personal matters or faced with embarrassment, they are likely to respond quickly and to become furious and vindictive; easily provoked to attack, their first inclination is to demean and to dominate.

Self-Descriptions and Complaints

Most of these personalities exhibit both clarity and logic in their cognitive capacities, an observation traceable to Pinel's earliest writings. Yet they show a marked deficit in self-insight and rarely exhibit the foresight that one would expect, given their capacity to understand (at least intellectually) the implications of their behavior. Thus, despite the fact that they have a clear grasp of why they should alter their less attractive behaviors, they fail repeatedly to make such modifications.

Despite their seemingly crude and callous actions, many are finely attuned to the subtle elements of human interaction. A minor segment within this group may be constitutionally gross and insensitive, but the great majority, though appearing to be coarse and imperceptive, are in fact quite keenly aware of the moods and feelings of others. Their ostensive insensitivity stems from their tendency to use what weaknesses they see in others for purposes of upsetting the latter's equilibrium. In short, they take advantage of their perception of the foibles and sensitivities of others to manipulate and be intentionally callous.

It should be evident that many of these personalities are unable to change because they possess deeply rooted habits that are highly resistant to conscious reasoning. To make their more repugnant behaviors more palatable to others, antisocial types are likely to concoct plausible explanations and excuses, usually those of "poor upbringing" and past "misfortunes." By feigning innocent victimization, they seek to absolve themselves of blame, remain guiltless and justified in continuing their irresponsible behaviors. Should their rationalizations fail to convince others, as when they are caught in obvious and repeated lies and dishonesties, many will affect an air of total innocence, claiming without a trace of shame that they have been unfairly accused.

The nonantisocial aggressive variants are likely to view themselves as assertive, energetic, self-reliant, and perhaps hardboiled, but honest, strong, and realistic. If we accept their premise that ours is a dog-eat-dog world, we can understand why they value being tough, forthright, and unsentimental. In their jungle philosophy of life, where "might makes right," the only course open is to be bold, critical, assertive, even ruthless. The harsh and anti-humanistic feelings of the aggressive personality are seen in a variety of ways. They are adept at pointing out the hypocrisy and ineffectuality of so-called do-gooders. They rail against the devastating consequences of international appeasement. They justify their toughness and cunning by pointing to the hostile and exploitive behavior of others. Contemptuous of the weak and the underprivileged, they do not care one iota if they are looked upon with disfavor. They claim that "good guys come in last," and so on. To them, the only way to survive in this world is to dominate and control it.

The basic aggressive type dreads the thought of being weak, of being deceived, and of being humiliated. These persons assume they will receive no greater kindness from others than the latter should expect from them. Others are seen as potentially threatening, and they claim they must be aggressive to defend themselves. Their principal task is to outsmart others, to gain power over them before the others outfox and dominate them. People are ruthless. It is this "fact" that makes them act as they do. They must outmaneuver others at their own game. Personal feelings are a sign of weakness and of maudlin and sloppy sentimentality. No one can make it in this life if he/she lets feelings get in the way.

Beyond their callous disdain for the rights of others, these personalities seem deficient in the capacity to share tender feelings, to experience genuine affection and love for another or to empathize with their needs. Among the more antisocial types, pleasure is gained in both the thought and process of hurting others and in seeing them downtrodden and suffering pain. Thus, antisocial personalities not only are devoid of guilt or remorse for their malicious acts, but they obtain a perverse and cruel satisfaction thereby. To achieve these malevolent ends, antisocial variants go out of their way to intimidate and harm others, enjoying not only the tangible fruits of their abuse and deceit but the distress and misery they leave in their wake.

Inferred Intrapsychic Dynamics

Most of these personalities act out their impulses, rather than reworking them through intrapsychic mechanisms. Although showing restraint under certain conditions, there is a tendency to blurt out feelings and vent urges directly. Rather than inhibit or reshape thoughts, this personality is inclined to express them precipitously and forcibly. This directness may be viewed by some as commendable, an indication of a frankness and forthrightness. Such an appraisal may be valid at times, but this personality manifests these behaviors, not as an expression of "honesty and integrity," but from a desire to shock and intimidate others.

Despite the relative openness with which nonantisocial aggressives voice their thoughts and feelings, they have learned that there are times when it is best to restrain and transmute them. One cannot function effectively in society if one constantly bursts forth with hostility. To soften and redirect these urges, these individuals depend primarily on three mechanisms: rationalization, sublimation, and projection.

The simplest means of justifying one's aggressive urges is to find a plausible and socially acceptable excuse for them. Thus, the blunt directness that characterizes the aggressive's social behavior is rationalized as signifying frankness and honesty, a lack of hypocrisy, and a willingness to face issues head-on—as being realistic and not mealymouthed and softheaded. More long-range and socially sanctioned resolutions of hostile urges are seen in the occupations to which these aggressive personalities gravitate. Many sublimate their impulses in highly competitive business enterprises, in military careers, the legal profession, and so on. Disposed to ward off threat by aggressive counteraction, this type accentuates the disapproval they anticipate from others by projecting their own hostility onto them. This act enables these personalities to justify their aggressive actions since they perceive themselves to be the object of unjust persecution.

Projection is the prime mechanism employed by antisocial aggressives. Accustomed throughout life to anticipate hostility from others and exquisitely attuned to the subtlest signs of contempt and derision, they are ever-ready to interpret the incidental behaviors and remarks of others as fresh attacks upon them. Given their perception of the environment, they need not rationalize their outbursts. These are fully "justified" as a response to the malevolence of others. The antisocial aggressive is the victim, an indignant bystander subjected to unjust persecution and hostility. Through this projection maneuver, then, they not only disown their malicious impulses but attribute the evil to others. As persecuted victims, they feel free to counter-attack and gain restitution and vindication.

Interpersonal Coping Style

If we look at the world through the eyes of both antisocial and nonantisocial variants of this aggressive personality—a place fraught with frustration and danger, a place where they must be on guard against the malevolence and cruelty of others—we can better understand why they behave as they do. They have no choice. You cannot trust what others will do. They will abuse, exploit, and dispossess you, strip you of all gratifications, and dominate and brutalize you, if they can. To avoid a fate such as this, one must arrogate all the power one can to oneself; one must block others from possessing the means to be belittling, exploitive, and harmful. Only by an alert vigilance and vigorous counteraction can one withstand and obstruct their malice. Displaying weakness or being willing to appease and compromise are fatal concessions to be avoided at all costs. Only by acquiring power can one be assured of gaining the rewards of life. Further, only by usurping the powers that others command can one thwart them from misusing it. Given these fears and attitudes, we can readily see why these personalities have taken the course they have. It is only through self-sufficiency and decisive action that they can forestall the dangers in the environment and maximize the bounties of life.

Aggressive acts serve more than the function of counteracting hostility for these personalities. They are driven by a desire to dominate and humiliate others, to wreak vengeance upon those whom they see as having mistreated them. Not only do they covet both power and possessions, but they gain special pleasure in usurping and taking from others. For some, what can be plagiarized, swindled, and extorted are fruits far sweeter than those earned through honest labor. Once having drained all one can from one source, others are sought to exploit, bleed, and then cast aside. Pleasure in the misfortunes of others is particularly notable among antisocial types.

Having learned to place their trust only in themselves, these personalities have few feelings of loyalty and may be treacherous and scheming beneath a veneer of politeness and civility. People are used as a means to an end, often subordinated and demeaned so that they can vindicate themselves for the grievances, misery, and humiliations they experienced in the past. By provoking fear and intimidating others, they seek to undo the lowly caste into which they feel they were thrust in childhood. Their search for power, therefore, is not benign; it springs from a deep well of hate and the desire for retribution and vindication.

Not only does the strategy of assertion and domination gain release from past injustices, but, as with most coping maneuvers, it often proves successful in achieving current material rewards; this is especially true among the basic nonantisocial type. Since most persons are intimidated by hostility, sarcasm, criticism, and threats of physical violence, the aggressive demeanor of these personalities is a powerful instrumentality for coercing others and for frightening them into fearful respect and submission. Thus, aggressive personalities frequently find a successful niche for themselves in roles where their hostile and belligerent behaviors are not only sanctioned but admired. The ruthless and cleverly conniving businessman, the intimidating and brutalizing sergeant, the self-righteous and punitive headmistress, the demanding and dominating surgical chief, all illustrate roles that provide outlets for vengeful hostility cloaked in the guise of a socially responsible and admirable function.

The most distinctive characteristic of antisocial variants is their tendency to flout conventional authority and rules. They act as if established social customs and guidelines for self-discipline and cooperative behavior do not apply to them. In some, this disdain is evidenced in petty adolescent disobedience or in the adoption of unconventional values, dress, and demeanor. Many express their arrogance and social rebelliousness in illegal acts and deceits, coming into frequent difficulty with educational and law enforcement authorities. Still others are flagrantly hostile, exhibiting malicious physical brutalities and gaining a sadistic pleasure in seeing others intimidated and pained.

Despite the disrespect they show for the rights of others, many antisocial types present a social mask, not only of civility but of sincerity and maturity. Untroubled by guilt and loyalty, they develop a talent for pathological lying. Unconstrained by honesty and truth, they weave impressive tales of competency and reliability. Many are disarmingly charming in initial encounters and become skillful swindlers and imposters. Alert to weaknesses in others, they play their games of deception with considerable skill. However, the pleasure they gain from their ruse often flags once the rewards of deceit have been achieved. Before long their true unreliability may be revealed as they stop "working at" their deception or as their "need" grows to let others know how cleverly cunning they have been.

ASSOCIATED DISORDERS

As in other chapters before, this section is designed to aid the clinician in fulfilling the tasks of identifying overlapping or mixed syndromes, and in discriminating among similar, but fundamentally different, syndromes.

Concomitant Axis I Symptoms

Despite the misconception that most of these aggressive personalities are devoid of emotional sensitivity, there is ample clinical evidence that both antisocial and nonantisocial variants often experience inner tensions and dysphoric moods. What appears to differentiate them from other personality types is their *un*willingness to tolerate extended periods of psychic discomfort and frustration. It is the quick warding off of anxiety and the immediate discharge of tensions that is characteristic, not their failure or inability to experience either anxiety or tension. Their defense is geared toward rapid relief and impulsive acting out, rather than internal and intrapsychic resolutions. It is for this reason that classical Axis I symptom disorders occur infrequently among these personalities. In forming "neurotic" symptoms patients refashion their tensions through intrapsychic transformations; this occurs in patients who wish to camouflage the source and content of their emotions so as to make them personally more tolerable, socially more acceptable, and, they hope, capable of eliciting support and nurture from others. This contrasts with the behaviors of both aggressive personalities, who not only care little whether their actions are socially approved but often gain gratification in flouting convention and in upsetting others; hence, there are few Axis I symptoms.

Anxiety disorders. Despite their general infrequency, these aggressive personalities do experience brief periods of anxiety prior to discharge and acting out. The major precipitant for these feelings is the dread of being controlled by others. Events that reactivate memories of similar and painful experiences in the past will evoke strong mixtures of anxiety and hostility. A severe panic attack may occur if the patient senses being particularly helpless or at the mercy of an obviously more powerful and hostile force. In contrast to the "free-floating" anxiety that persists in most other personality patterns, these patients quickly find an external source to which they ascribe their inner discomfort. Chronic anxiety, therefore, is rarely seen. For many, especially the nonantisocial variant, the surplus energy generated by anxiety is transformed and utilized to spur vigorous self-assertive action. Much of the aggressive drive that characterizes these persons reflects the exploitation of anxious energy in the service of manipulating and dominating others.

Paranoid disorders. Acute paranoid episodes characterized by hostile excitement may be displayed by these personalities. Particularly prone to this disorder as a result of their hypersensitivity to betrayal, they have learned to cope with threat by acting out aggressively and, at times, explosively. Faced with repeated failures and frustrations, their fragile controls may be overwhelmed by undischarged and deeply felt angers and resentments. These hostile feelings, spurred by the memories and emotions of the past, may surge unrestrained to the surface, spilling into wild and delusional rages.

Concurrent Axis II Personalities

Psychopaths, sociopaths, and antisocial personalities have been described in the past by a parade of seemingly contradictory characteristics. Some clinicians have described them as impulsive, immature, naïve, aimless, and flighty. No less frequently it has been said that they are sly, cunning, and well-educated sorts who are capable of making clever long-range plans to deceive and exploit others. To complicate the clinical picture further, they have been noted for their cruel aggressiveness and for the keen pleasures they derive in disrupting and intimidating others. At still other times, they are pictured as lacking true hostility and are believed to feel considerable discomfort when their actions prove harmful to others. This confusion stems in part from a failure to recognize that antisocial behaviors may spring from appreciably different personality combinations or mixtures.

Two of these combinations have been described in the preceding chapters: the *histrionic*-antisocial and the *narcissistic*-antisocial. The third most common mixture may be found in combination with the *paranoid* personality. Together, these three profile combinations appear to comprise the great majority of so-called antisocial personality types. Although the focus in this section is on those features that distinguish the antisocial-paranoid amalgam, it should be noted that all three combinations exhibit certain commonalities, most notably their marked self-centeredness and disdain for others. Security and gratification are achieved primarily by attending to oneself; the interests and needs of others are given incidental consideration, if attended to at all. Each of these personality mixtures views the world-at-large as composed of opportunities for exploitation and self-gratification.

Antisocial (aggressive)-paranoid mixed personality. The antisocial-paranoid combination epitomizes the least attractive of the antisocial variants since these individuals are especially vindictive and hostile. Their impulse toward retribution is discharged in a hateful and destructive defiance of conventional social life. Distrustful of others and anticipating betrayal and punishment, they have acquired a cold-blooded ruthlessness, an intense desire to gain revenge for the real or imagined mistreatment they were subjected to in childhood. Here we see a sweeping rejection of tender emotions and a deep suspicion that the goodwill efforts expressed by others are merely ploys to deceive and undo them. They assume a chip-on-the-shoulder attitude, a readiness to lash out at those whom they distrust or those whom they can use as scapegoats for their seething impulse to destroy. Dreading the thought that others may view them as weak, or that others may manipulate them into submission, they rigidly maintain an image of hard-boiled strength, carrying themselves truculently and acting tough, callous, and fearless. To "prove" their courage, they court danger and punishment. But punishment only verifies their anticipation of unjust treatment. Rather than being a deterrent, it only reinforces their rebelliousness and desire for retribution. In positions of power, they often brutalize others to confirm their self-image of strength. If faced with persistent failure, beaten down in efforts to dominate and control others, or finding aspirations far outdistancing their luck, feelings of frustration, resentment, and anger may mount until controls give way to a raw brutality and vengeful hostility. Spurred by repeated rejection and driven by an increasing need for power and retribution, their aggressive impulses surge into the open. At these times, their behaviors may become outrageously irresponsible and flagrantly antisocial. Not only will they be devoid of guilt or remorse for what they may have done, but they are likely to display an arrogant contempt for the rights of the others they so churlishly cast aside.

Differential Diagnostic Signs

As noted in an earlier chapter, differential diagnostic considerations have diminished in importance because of the DSM-III multiaxial format. Nevertheless, there are assessment pitfalls that one should be alert to and avoid. For example, the persuasiveness and facile emotions of some antisocial aggressive personalities, particularly those with either histrionic or narcissistic features, may be so masterful as to "con" even experienced diagnosticians into believing that these patients are "depressed," "normal," "schizophrenic," or what have you. It is imperative when dealing with such glib and charming, but duplicitous, patients to inquire into their past history and to investigate inconsistencies. The discussion now turns from matters of deception to specific syndrome differentiations.

Although they often coexist, a clear distinction between aggressive and *paranoid personalities* may be justified. In general, the paranoid patient exhibits fewer emotional controls and is more inclined to irrational behaviors. The prime distinction, of course, is the hypervigilance and suspiciousness of paranoids. They are extremely guarded and secretive, hypersensitive and readily slighted. Paranoids have difficulty relaxing and invariably expect to be tricked by others. This tense, edgy, and suspicious quality is usually lacking in aggressives, who typically act in a forward, brash, and self-confident manner despite their vigilance and mistrust. Paranoids may also be readily differentiated from the antisocial variant in that few paranoids ever engage in explicit illegal acts.

An important distinction to be drawn here is that between the antisocial variant of the aggressive personality and the condition labeled in the DSM-III as *adult antisocial behavior.* This latter designation is essentially what previously was termed "dyssocial reaction"; it is now grouped among "conditions not attributable to a mental disorder that are a focus of attention or treatment." Both antisocial conditions are characterized by a disdain for social conventions. They differ in terms of the extent to which the behaviors they manifest reflect the operation of deeply ingrained and pervasive personality characteristics. As conceived in the DSM-III, the behavior of antisocial personalities stems from internal psychological dynamics and broadly generalized environmental sensitivities. The actions of those evidencing the "adult antisocial behavior" condition are stimulus specific, usually provide material gain, and are acquired and sustained by the operation of vicarious or imitative group learning. Although the actions of the adult behavior group develop as a result of a less than ideal past, these experiences and associations did not destroy the acquisition of loyalty, trust, and the capacity for personal affection. Nor are these antisocial behaviors driven by unconscious and irrational needs; rather, they appear to be both discriminating and understandable in terms of material advantages and practical realities. Adult antisocial behaviors often grow as a consequence of group loyalties in which the individual joins others in shared criminal acts or plans collaborative illegal operations to achieve a tangible and profitable reward. By contrast, antisocial aggressive personalities tend to be "loners" with little or no loyalty to anyone or anything. Driven primarily by the need to discharge unconscious tensions stirred up from the past, their goals often appear indiscriminate and impulsively pursued. For example, an antisocial aggressive personality, following a disagreement with an employer, may impulsively pilfer essentially worthless office items or decide to forge a series of small checks, despite the fact that he/she has no financial need, may end up losing a decent job, and create a personal and family scandal. Compelled by the dictates of the unconscious, this behavior is objectively foolish and seemingly purposeless, enacted without apparent rhyme or reason.

PREDISPOSING BACKGROUND

For pedagogic purposes biogenic factors are again differentiated from experiential influences. The usual caveat concerning the conjectural nature of the hypotheses that follow is also applicable. There is a marked paucity of established empirical findings, even in this group of disorders where more research has been undertaken than in any other personality syndrome. Although some of the conjectures proposed in the following paragraphs derive from findings that are reasonably consistent, it would still be wise to view them with a skeptical eye.

Hypothesized Biogenic Factors

A number of constitutional features have been reported to occur with disproportionately high frequency among these personalities. In the realm of activation, for example, they have been judged to be energetic, to react with high intensity to stimuli, and to have a low threshold for responding physically but a high threshold for responding emotionally. Unbounded in energy, they appear assertive and intrude upon others like the proverbial "bull in a china shop." Others display an irritability upon stimulation, respond before thinking, act impulsively, and are unable to delay or inhibit their first reaction, and therefore behave in an unreflective and uncontrolled manner. With regard to affect and temperament, there are indications that many of these personalities are constitutionally fearless, unblanched by events that most people experience as dangerous and frightening. Some evidence a foolhardy courageousness, a venturesomeness seemingly blind to the potential of serious consequences. Others appear easily provoked to anger; they appear so constituted as to respond with hostility "at the drop of a hat." Thus, in contrast to their high threshold for experiencing fear or anxiety, their threshold for anger is so low that the mildest of provocations can elicit intensely hostile reactions.

The high frequency of correspondence in antisocial aggressive behaviors observed among family members suggests that genetic dispositions may play a developmental role. Of course, observed similarities in family behavior patterns can be accounted for quite readily by shared experiences. Despite the questionable linkage that had been posited between XYY chromosomes and antisocial tendencies, it seems reasonable to hold to the view that if there are biophysical substrates for such tendencies, they may in part be transmitted by heredity.

Worthy of note is the fact that parents who bring their acting-out children to clinics often report that their youngsters "always were that way." A common complaint is that the child displayed temper tantrums from infancy and would get furious when frustrated, either when awaiting the bottle or feeling uncomfortable in a wet diaper. As these children mature they are often described as having had a "hot temper" and a bullying attitude toward sibs and other children. Quite commonly, parents remark that these children were undaunted by punishment and generally quite unmanageable. Moreover, many evidenced a daring boldness, an audacious and foolhardy willingness to chance physical harm. Many seemed thick-skinned and unaffected by pain. Temperamental dispositions such as these in early life are significant not only in themselves but for the experiences they produce and the reactions they evoke from others. More venturesome, such children explore, challenge, and compete in their environment assertively. Moreover, they intrude and upset the peaceful existence that others seek. Not only are they likely to precipitate more trouble than most, but their seeming recalcitrance results in their receiving more punishment than that required to control most children. Thus, given a "nasty" and "incorrigible" disposition from the start, these children provoke an excess of exasperation and counterhostility from others. Their temperament initiates a vicious circle in which they not only prompt frequent aggression but learn to expect it.

As suggested earlier, a disposition to hostile and irritable behaviors may be based in part on low thresholds for activation. Similarly, the insensitivity to pain and anxiety often attributed to these personalities may derive from high thresholds for autonomic reactivity. Moreover, should reticular pathways for arousal be unusually dense or laid out to short circuit the inhibitory effects of cortical intervention, the individual may exhibit the characteristic intense and impulsive behaviors. An unusual anatomical distribution in the limbic system also may contribute to the distinctive pattern of affectivity and to the bold and seemingly fearless outlook. We may speculate, finally, that the biophysical substrate for "rage and anger" may be copious or extensively branched, resulting in the rapid and frequently activated hostile behaviors.

Characteristic Experiential Histories

Although the characteristics of this personality may be traced, albeit quite speculatively, to biogenic dispositions, psychogenic factors will undoubtedly shape the content and direction of these inclinations. Moreover, experience and learning often are sufficient in themselves to prompt these behaviors. Keep in mind, however, that as far as personality patterns are concerned, biogenic and psychogenic factors inevitably weave a complex sequence of influences that cannot be readily disentangled.

The primary experiential agent for this pattern is likely to be parental rejection, discontent, or hostility. This reaction may be prompted in part when the newborn infant, for constitutional reasons, proves to be "cold," sullen, testy, or otherwise difficult to manage. It does not take too long for a child with a disposition such as this to be stereotyped as a "miserable, ill-tempered, and disagreeable little beast." Once categorized in this manner, reciprocal negative feelings build up into a lifelong cycle of parent-child feuding.

Parental hostility may stem from any number of sources other than the child's initial disposition. Many children are convenient scapegoats for displaced anger that has been generated elsewhere, such as in a parent's occupational, marital, or social frustrations. Whatever its initial source, a major cause for the development of this personality pattern is exposure to parental cruelty and domination. The reason that these experiences have so pronounced an impact is fairly straightforward. Hostility breeds hostility, not only in generating intense feelings of anger and resentment on the part of the recipient but, even more importantly, by establishing a model for vicarious learning. It makes little difference as to whether the child desires consciously to imitate parental hostility; mere exposure to these behaviors—especially in childhood, when there are few alternatives to be observed—serves as a template or model as to how people feel and relate to one another. Thus, mean, irresponsible, and abusive parents arouse and release strong counter feelings of hostility in their children. Moreover, they demonstrate in their roughshod and inconsiderate behaviors both a model for imitation and an implicit sanction for similar abusive behaviors whenever the children themselves feel a rush of anger or frustration.

Tracing the effects of parental thoughtlessness and abuse in line with the three stages of neuropsychological development will provide additional insights into the complex pattern of habits and attitudes displayed by both major variants of this personality.

1. The distinguishing feature of the sensory-attachment stage is not likely to have been the amount of stimulation to which the infant was exposed, but rather its quality. Rough or harsh treatment conveys a tone, a "feeling" in the neonate that the world is an unkind, painful, and dangerous place, that discomfort and frustration are to be expected and to be prepared for. Early parental abuse and hostility cue the infant to mistrust the environment and to view it with suspicion.

2. Having learned to expect a world that will treat them harshly, these children enter the sensorimotor-autonomy stage with a feeling that they cannot depend on others, that they must turn to themselves to provide pleasure and to avoid pain. Having no alternatives, the youngsters rapidly acquire the skills of autonomy and self-reliance. By the end of the second neuropsychological stage, then, they are both deeply mistrustful and substantially independent of their parents.

3. Being both suspicious of others and increasingly confident in their powers of self-sufficiency, these youngsters begin the intracortical-initiative stage with a determination to reject the guidance and domination of others. Why should they accept the restrictions and demands that others seek to impose upon them when they have nothing to gain and, in addition, are convinced that they can manage better on their own? Subjected to parental abuse and disinterest throughout these growing years, the children learn not

only to reject their parents but to oppose the values and standards of the adult world they represent. Thus, they set out to shape their own identity, one that is contrary to those espoused by their elders; in so doing, they embark on a course of self-sufficiency and mistrust.

One consequence of rejecting "authorities" is to lose the guidance society provides for handling and directing impulses. By rejecting traditional values and customs, these youngsters are left on their own. They must devise, either on their own or by imitating peer models, ways and means to handle their emotions. During this period, when adolescent children are driven strongly by both erotic and hostile impulses, we find that few acquire self-developed controls adequate to their emotions. Most have difficulty in deferring gratifications, in resisting temptations, and in inhibiting angry reactions to even the slightest of frustrations. Such youngsters pursue their desires with little concern for the dangers or complications they invite.

In summary, children who are exposed to parental abuse acquire enduring resentments toward others, and they incorporate the parental model of hostility as a guide for venting these feelings. This background is one of the most common found among the antisocial variants of the aggressive personality, but by no means is it the only pathogenic source for this pattern.

Another important contributor, particularly in shaping antisocial types, is the lack of parental models. If parents provide little or no guidance for their children, they are left to fend for themselves, to observe and to emulate whatever models they can for guidance. Broken families, especially those in which the father has abandoned both wife and children, often characterize this state of affairs. With the model and authority of the breadwinner out of sight, and the mother frequently harassed by overwork and financial insecurity, the youngster is often left to roam the streets, unguided and unrestrained by the affection and controls of an attending parent. Moreover, the disappearance of the father and the preoccupations of a distracted mother are felt as rejections. To find a model or belief by which their identity can be mobilized and given meaning, these children must often turn to their peers, to those other barren and lost souls who are also bereft of parental attention, and who likewise wander aimlessly in an indifferent, if not hostile, world.

Together with their fellow outcasts, these nascent antisocial personalities quickly learn that they are viewed by others as society's misfits, and that their misfortunes will only be further compounded by the deprecatory and closed-minded attitudes of the larger community. They soon learn that it is only by toughness and cunning that they will find a means of survival. Unfortunately, this adaptive strategy sets into play a vicious circle. As they venture into the deviant remains left behind for them and their fellow scavengers by the larger society, that very same society points a finger of disapproval and castigates and condemns them. As their resentments mount over the injustice and entrapment they feel, the circle of hostility and counter hostility feeds back and gains momentum. With little hope of changing their fate and little promise of advancement—and struggling mightily, if cunningly and brutally, to keep a foothold in the dog-eat-dog world into which they have been cast—they are driven further and further into an antisocial and vindictive life-style.

PROGNOSTIC CONSIDERATIONS

Turning to the future prospects of these patterns, this discussion notes both the factors that contribute to their persistence and the steps that may be taken to head them off.

Perpetuation of the Aggressive Pattern

Despite the fact that behavioral strategies have been learned to optimize positive experiences, they produce, as do all pathological strategies, certain self-defeating actions. They are not only adaptively inflexible and thereby ineffective in dealing with novel challenges, but they rest upon a rather tenuous and easily upset psychic balance. Perhaps their most destructive consequence is that they foster rather than resolve problems.

Perceptual and cognitive distortions. Most of what is communicated and experienced in life is fragmentary in nature—a few words, an intonation, a gesture. On the basis of these suggestive, but incomplete, messages we come to some conclusion or inference as to what others seek to convey. We constantly "read between the lines" on the basis of past experiences, enabling us thereby to give these incidental cues their coherence and meaning. Among the determinants of what we "fill in" are our moods and anticipations. If we expect someone to be cruel and abusive we are likely to piece together the hazy elements of the communication in line with this expectancy. If we feel down-hearted some days, it appears that the whole world is downcast and gloomy with us. Since the outlook and moods of most of us are episodic and temporary, these intrusions tend to be counterbalanced. That is, we may be suspicious of certain persons but overly naïve with others; we may feel "blue" some days but cheerful and optimistic on others. This pattern of variability and balancing of mood and attitude is less typical of pathological than "normal" personalities. In the aggressively antisocial individual, for example, there is an ever-present undertone of anger and resentment, a persistent expectation that others will be devious and hostile. Because these moods and expectancies endure, these personalities are likely to repeatedly distort the incidental remarks and actions of others so that they appear to deprecate and vilify them. They persist in misinterpreting what they see and hear, and magnify minor slights into major insults and slanders.

Despite the fact that this personality's aggressive reaction to external threat is understandable, given past experience, it promotes repetitive self-defeating consequences. For example, by perceiving rejection where none exists these individuals prevent themselves from recognizing and appreciating the objective goodwill of others when it is there. Their reality is what they perceive, not what objectively exists. Thus, their vulnerability to rejection blocks them from recognizing the presence of experiences that might prove gratifying and thereby change the course of their outlook and attitudes. Moreover, their distortion aggravates their misfortunes by creating, through anticipation, fictitious dangers that duplicate those of the past. Rather than avoiding further pain and abuse, the antisocial's hypersensitivity uncovers them where they do not exist. In essence, their moods and defenses have fabricated dangers from which antisocials cannot escape since they derive from within themselves.

Demeaning of affection and cooperative behavior. This personality is not only suspicious of, but tends to depreciate, sentimentality, intimate feelings, tenderness, and social cooperativeness. These individuals lack sympathy for the weak and oppressed, and are often contemptuous of those who express compassion and concern for the "underdog." Given their past, there is little reason to expect that the aggressive personality would be empathic and sentimental. What affection and consideration did they enjoy in childhood? They learned too well that it is best to trust no one. Why be sympathetic and kindly? Should they chance again the rebuffs they believe they suffered at the hands of their parents and later, in the case of the antisocial subtype, from society as a whole? Will not others undo them and infringe upon the freedom and autonomy that they have sought, and that are so vital to them?

By denying tender feelings, they protect themselves against the memory of painful parental rejections. Furthermore, feelings of sympathy would be antithetical to the credo they have carved for themselves as a philosophy of life. To express the "softer" emotions would only undermine the foundations of their coping strategy and reactivate feelings that they have rigidly denied for years. Why upset things and be abused and exploited again? Sympathy and tender feelings only "get in the way," distract and divert one from being the hardheaded realist one must be. Of course, this very attitude creates a vicious circle. By restraining positive feelings and repudiating intimacy and co-operative behaviors, these personalities provoke others to withdraw from them. Their cold and abusive manner intimidates others and blocks them from expressing warmth and affection. Once again, by their own action, they create experiences that only perpetuate the frosty, condemning, and rejecting environment of their childhood.

Creating realistic antagonisms. Both the basic aggressive and overtly antisocial variants of this personality evoke hostility, not only as an incidental consequence of their behaviors and attitudes but because they intentionally provoke others into conflict. They carry a "chip on their shoulder," often seem to be spoiling for a fight, and appear to enjoy tangling with others to prove their strength and test their competencies and powers. Having been periodically successful in past aggressive ventures, they feel confident of their prowess. They may seek out dangers and challenges. Not only are they unconcerned and reckless, but they appear poised and bristling, ready to vent resentments, demonstrate their invulnerability, and restore their pride.

Unfortunately, as with their perceptions and attitudes, these aggressive, conflict-seeking behaviors only perpetuate their fears and misery. More than merely fostering distance and rejection, they have now provoked others into justified counterhostility. By spoiling for a fight and by precipitous and irrational arrogance, they create not only a distant reserve on the part of others but intense and well-justified animosity. Now they must face real aggression, and now they have a real basis for anticipating retaliation. Objective threats and resentments do exist in the environment now, and the vicious circle is perpetuated anew. Their vigilant state cannot be relaxed; they must ready themselves, no longer for suspected threat and imagined hostility, but for the real thing.

Remedial Interventions

The prognostic picture for this personality cannot be viewed as promising, unless the person has found a socially sanctioned sphere in which to channel his or her energies and hostilities. Because differences in style and environment have significant implications for treatment, the basic aggressive type is discussed separately from the antisocial variant.

The nonantisocial aggressive pattern will not be readily altered since mistrust is both chronic and deep. Moreover, these individuals will resist exploring their motives, and their defenses are resolute. It is an understatement to say that these personalities are not willing participants in therapy. The submissive and help-seeking role of patient is anathema to these power-oriented people. When they "submit" to therapy it is usually under the press of severe marital discord or work conflicts. For example, they may be in a jam as a consequence of aggressive or abusive behavior on their job, or as a result of incessant quarrels and brutality toward their spouse or children. Rarely do they experience guilt or accept blame for the turmoil they cause. To them, the problem can always be traced to the other person's stupidity, laziness, or hostility. Even when they accept a measure of responsibility for their difficulties, one senses an underlying resentment of their "do-gooder" therapist, who tricked them into admitting it.

Not uncommonly, these personalities will challenge therapists and seek to outwit them. These patients will set up situations to test the therapist's skills, to catch inconsistencies, to arouse ire, and, if possible, to belittle and humiliate the therapist. It is no easy task for the therapist to restrain the impulse to "do battle" or to express a condemning attitude; great effort must be expended at times to check these counterhostile feelings. Therapists may have to remind themselves that these patients' plight was not of their own doing, that they were the unfortunate recipients of a harsh upbringing, and that only by a respectful and sympathetic approach can they be helped to get on the right track.

To accomplish this goal therapists must be ready not only to see things from the patient's point of view but to convey a sense of trust and create a feeling of sharing an alliance. It is important, however, that the building of rapport not be interpreted by the patient as a sign of the therapist's capitulation, of the latter having been intimidated by bluff and arrogance. A balance of professional firmness and authority, mixed with tolerance for the patient's less attractive traits, must be maintained. By building an image of being a fair-minded and strong authority figure, the therapist may encourage these patients to change their expectancies. Through quiet and thoughtful comments, the therapist may provide a model for learning the mix of power, reason, and fairness. By this process, patients may develop more wholesome attitudes toward others and be led to direct their energies more constructively than in the past.

Among specific therapeutic techniques are drugs that modulate both the threshold and intensity of reactivity. Changes such as these may minimize the frequency and depth of hostile feelings and thereby decrease some of the self-perpetuating consequences of aggressive behavior. The less confrontive cognitive approaches may provide patients with opportunities to "vent their spleen"; once drained of venom, they may be led to explore their habitual feelings and attitudes, and be guided into less destructive perceptions and outlets than before. Psychoanalytic procedures are not likely to prove beneficial unless a more thorough reworking of the patient's defensive strategies seems mandatory. As far as group methods are concerned, these patients often intrude and disrupt therapeutic functions. On the other hand, many aggressive patients become useful catalysts for group interaction and appear to gain useful insights and constructive social skills.

Approaches to be employed with the more antisocial of the aggressive pattern are considered next.

In general, antisocial behaviors appear in pronounced form for the first time during the middle teens and recede in frequency in later years. Most clinicians are pessimistic about the prospects of modifying "delinquent" types, even in later years. Nevertheless, there is a decline in incidence in middle age, a decline that probably reflects two factors entirely incidental to the intrinsic character of the disorder. First, those whose antisocial behaviors persist, are ultimately imprisoned for prolonged periods; they are, in effect, "out of commission" by 25 or 30 years of age. Second, those who survive in the mainstrain of society are likely to have learned to channel their abusive and impulsive tendencies more skillfully or into more socially acceptable endeavors. It is not probable that their basic personality has been altered, only that it expresses itself in a less obviously flagrant and public way.

As with their nonantisocial counterparts, antisocial aggressive types are highly resistant to therapeutic efforts. Rarely are they convinced that they need treatment. Many are remanded to therapy by court action. Once in treatment, they tend to be either openly defiant or extremely congenial but cleverly evasive. Militating against the success of therapy is the fact that these patients often achieve both material and emotional rewards in conjunction with their antisocial behaviors. This contrasts with the byproducts of other personality types who experience considerable discomfort in association with their symptoms and, hence, are usually motivated to seek the relief that therapy promises.

Directive and punitive methods have proved of little value in controlling the actions of antisocial aggressive personalities. Nevertheless, efforts should be made to eliminate the pernicious effects of environmental influences that sustain and reinforce their destructive behaviors. Psychopharmacologic methods also make few, if any, inroads. Intrapsychic techniques seem equally fruitless. Supportive procedures may be of value in establishing rapport, whereas cognitive methods of reorientation may be useful in exploring misconceptions and channelling more constructive behaviors. Behavioral modification procedures may help extinguish certain repugnant forms of acting out, although their effectiveness in cases such as these has not been sufficiently documented. Of promise are group self-help procedures in which antisocial patients share and freely discuss their attitudes. This can be done without feeling the implicit derogation these patients often experience when facing so conventional an authority as a professional therapist. As they explore their feelings and behaviors, they may learn a measure of loyalty and group responsibility that, it is hoped, will generalize to nontherapeutic social settings.

Chapter 8

Compulsive Personality: The Conforming Pattern

This chapter begins the discussion of personality patterns judged to be of moderate rather than mild severity. The four preceding personalities—the dependent, histrionic, narcissistic, and aggressive (antisocial)—possess traits that have the potential of being intrinsically satisfying and reasonably adaptive. This stems from the fact that the interpersonal and intrapsychic orientations of these four personalities are relatively focused and coherent. Being *either* dependent or independent in outlook enables them to think of themselves and deal with others in a nonconflictful manner. These four types contrast with the two ambivalent personalities, which are discussed here and in Chapter 9, in that their feelings about themselves are not "split," nor are their attitudes toward others divided and divergent. The milder personality pathologies are able to relate to others in a manner that is often personally satisfying. This state of personal satisfaction is not as possible in the four moderately severe types. Even if their environments are both benign and accepting, these individuals will either undo their chances for satisfaction or simply find themselves unable to experience contentment. The two ambivalent types—the compulsive and the passive-aggressive—are beset by severe internal conflicts that they can neither escape, since they are an intrinsic part of themselves, nor resolve through external manipulation. This chapter elaborates the "entrapment" of compulsive personalities who strive to find a niche in society that others will judge responsible and productive. However, they face an internal struggle in which the more they adapt, the more they feel anger and resentment.

Feeling ambivalent and experiencing conflict are inevitable parts of living. Each of us faces these "no win" struggles periodically, but some individuals are constantly plagued in that ambivalence is an ongoing part of their makeup. Most of the conflicts we experience are fairly obvious and conscious to us, but some, usually the more troubling ones, tend to be kept from awareness, that is, are unconscious. Certain conflicts may be considered as especially troublesome in the sense that they disrupt significant segments of life or lead to resolutions that have broad and enduring effects. One of these more troublesome conflicts is relevant to the two "ambivalent" personality patterns. It relates to whether individuals turn primarily to themselves *or* to others to find the security and rewards they desire. Stated in the form of the conflict it represents, it is a struggle between obedience and defiance, to use terms suggested by Rado (1959). What distinguishes the ambivalent personalities from other pathological types is their failure to adequately resolve this conflict. This section elaborates the nature of ambivalence in these personalities.

Most individuals learn to feel comfortable with themselves *and* with others; they are able to seek rewards and satisfactions from both sources. The pathological personalities discussed in previous chapters may have faced a conflict between turning to others for comfort versus turning to themselves; each has opted, albeit unconsciously, to choose one course rather than the other. Dependent and histrionic personalities have "decided" to obtain their rewards from the outer world; as a consequence, they will look only rarely for pleasure or comfort to themselves. The situation is reversed among narcissistic and aggressive (antisocial) personalities; experience has taught them that the bounties and securities of life are to be found within oneself. Despite the fact that each of the four milder personality types will occasionally reconsider their choice, the decision as to where to turn for reward and protection is essentially settled. With minor exceptions, they feel comfort with their choice and have little doubt that it is best for them.

This resoluteness does not characterize all pathological personalities; in fact, it is the failure to come to terms with the choice of self versus others that is the central difficulty among ambivalent patterns (Millon, 1969). Two types have been identified: those whose ambivalence is seen clearly in their overt vacillation and inconsistencies (active-ambivalent), and those who, on surface impression, appear to have resolved their conflict through "obedience" but are struggling at a deeper level to restrain their "defiance" (passive-ambivalent). Both of these personalities have intense, conflictual feelings toward both themselves and others.

The active-ambivalent pattern, referred to in the DSM-III as the passive-aggressive personality, experiences the turmoil of indecision daily. These persons get into endless wrangles and disappointments as they vacillate between submissive obedience and conformity, at one time, and stubborn defiance and resolute autonomy, the next. The passive-ambivalent pattern, referred to in the DSM-III as the compulsive personality, appears entirely different. These individuals manifest extraordinary consistency, a rigid and unvarying uniformity in all significant settings. They accomplish this by repressing urges toward autonomy and independence. They comply to the strictures and conform to the rules set down by others. Their restraint, however, is merely a cloak with which they deceive both themselves and others; it serves also as a straitjacket to control intense resentment and anger.

The conflict within the compulsive personality may be understood best as comprising the diametrically opposite qualities of two, milder pathological patterns, the dependent and the aggressive (antisocial) personalities. These personalities are like the aggressive in that they possess a strong, albeit unconscious, desire to assert themselves, act independent, and even defy the regulations imposed by others. At the same time, their conscious attitudes and overt behaviors are akin to the dependent; they are not only overly obedient but fully incorporate the strictures of others and submerge all vestiges of individuality. Inwardly, they churn with defiance like the aggressive personality; consciously and behaviorally, they submit and comply like the dependent. To bind their rebellious and oppositional urges, and to ensure that these do not break through their controls, compulsives become overly conforming and overly submissive. Not only do they adhere to societal rules and customs, but they vigorously espouse and defend them. As a consequence, they are often seen as moralistic, legalistic, and self-righteous. Their insistence that events and relationships be systematized and regulated becomes a caricature of the virtues of order and propriety. Proceeding meticulously through their daily routines, they are likely to get lost in the minutiae, in the form and not the substance of everyday life. These rigid behaviors are necessary if compulsives are to succeed in controlling their seething, if repressed, antagonisms. Moreover, they cling grimly to the rules of society since these help restrain and protect them against their own impulses. They dare not take the chance of deviating from an absolute adherence to these injunctions lest their anger burst out of control, and lest they expose to others and themselves the resentment they "really" feel.

The DSM-III employs the label "compulsive personality" to characterize this syndrome. The author considers this designation to be inappropriate since the great majority of these patients exhibit neither compulsions nor obsessions. Moreover, there is an "obsessive-compulsive" anxiety syndrome with which the personality diagnosis may readily be confused. For reference purposes, the descriptive text for the DSM-III compulsive personality states the following:

> The essential feature is a Personality Disorder in which there generally are restricted ability to express warm and tender emotions; perfectionism that interferes with the ability to grasp "the big picture;" insistence that others submit to his or her way of doing things; excessive devotion to work and productivity to the exclusion of pleasure; and indecisiveness.
>
> Individuals with this disorder are stingy with their emotions and material possessions.... Everyday relationships have a conventional, formal, and serious quality. Others often perceive these individuals as stilted and "stiff."
>
> Preoccupation with matters of rules, efficiency, trivial details, procedures, or form interferes with the ability to take a broad view of things.... Time is poorly allocated, the most important tasks being left to the last moment. Although efficiency and perfection are idealized, they are not attained.
>
> Individuals with this disorder are always mindful of their relative status in dominant-submissive relationships. Although they resist the authority of others, they stubbornly insist that people conform to their way of doing things.

Work and productivity are prized to the exclusion of pleasure and the value of interpersonal relationships. When pleasure is considered, it is something to be planned and worked for.

Decision-making is either avoided, postponed, or protracted, perhaps because of an inordinate fear of making a mistake.

Individuals with this disorder may complain of difficulty expressing tender feelings. Considerable distress is often associated with their indecisiveness and general ineffectiveness. . . . Individuals with this disorder tend to be excessively conscientious, moralistic, scrupulous or judgmental of self or others. . . . Frequently there is extreme sensitivity to social criticism, especially if it comes from someone with considerable status or authority. (p. 326–327).

HISTORICAL AND THEORETICAL ANTECEDENTS

The first portrayals of what we now refer to as compulsive states were rendered by German and French clinicians at the beginning of the nineteenth century. The German term for compulsion (*Zwang*) was first used by Krafft-Ebing in 1867; however, he did not utilize the label in the same sense as we do today, applying it to represent the constricted thinking of depressives. A posthumous paper of Griesinger's, published in 1868, employed the term *Zwang* in a manner more consistent with contemporary usage; in describing several of his cases he identified the properties of compulsive questioning, compulsive curiosity, and compulsive doubting. In the last quarter of the nineteenth century a debate arose as to whether compulsions necessarily signified the operation of hidden emotions; Westphal (1877) was the prime naysayer, whereas Kraepelin (1887) was among those convinced that emotions were centrally involved. To represent this latter view, Donath (1897) proposed that the label *Zwang*, which by now had acquired differing meanings and translations (e.g., obsession in London, compulsion in New York), be replaced by the designation *anankast*, a term that has gained some favor on the Continent, but none in the United States.

It was not until the second or third decades of this century that the literature turned from an exclusive interest in obsessive and compulsive symptoms to that of the personality or character type of the same name. This change evolved as a consequence of the writings of Freud and Abraham, particularly their formulations concerning the "anal character." Before detailing the contributions made by psychoanalytic thinkers, this discussion steps ahead in time to record briefly the views of K. Schneider and E. Kretschmer, two nonanalytic theorists of note who wrote important treatises on personality disorders in the first third of this century.

In his description of the "insecure" personality type, Schneider (1923) brought together several earlier proposals made by clinical observers that he felt could be grouped under the designation *anankast*. Among his prime features were the following:

[This personality] is always trying to hide a nagging inner uncertainty under various forms of compensatory or overcompensatory activity, especially where the inferiority feelings are of a physical or social character. Outer correctness covers an imprisoning inner insecurity....

To the onlooker anankasts appear as carefully dressed people, pedantic, correct, scrupulous and yet with it all somehow exceedingly insecure. The compensations they reach often seem unnatural and constrained....

Severe anankasts with their compulsion to control... are extremely constricted people and indeed at times become reduced to almost complete immobility. (1950, pp. 87, 92, 93).

Kretschmer described what we would consider to be the essential features of the compulsive personality under the designation of "sensitive types" (1918). By this term Kretschmer meant persons who are burdened by affect-laden complexes that they must deal with intrapsychically because of their inability to externalize or discharge them. Highly impressionable but deficient in powers of active expression, they engage in a "pent-up working over" of even minor and irrelevant daily experiences. Beset by their inability to take decisive action, they become uncertain over both large and small matters. In order to compensate for their indecisiveness and lack of self-confidence they hold fast to standards set with conviction by others, often becoming "men of conscience." Ethical and moral issues are prominent matters in their thinking, as are conflicts over sexuality. Experienced as especially humiliating and shameful are their sexual phantasies, which appear to lodge in their thoughts and resist all efforts at suppression. The contrast between their internalized standards and these persistent and intrusive ideas contribute to the affect-laden complexes and tension so characteristic of this personality.

Freud's brief essay "Character and Anal Eroticism" (1908) is notable not only for its clear description of the "anal character," the prime forerunner of contemporary conceptions of the compulsive personality, but for having stimulated all subsequent formulations of analytic character types. In this early paper Freud specified three distinct and pronounced anal character traits:

The persons whom I am about to describe are remarkable for a regular combination of the 3 following peculiarities: they are exceptionally orderly, parsimonious, and obstinate. Each of these words really cover a small group or series of traits which are related to one another. "Orderly" comprises both bodily cleanliness and reliability and conscientiousness in the performance of petty duties; the opposite of it would be "untidy" and "negligent." "Parsimony" may be exaggerated up to the point of avarice; and "obstinacy" may amount to defiance, with which irascibility and vindictiveness may easily be associated. The two latter qualities—parsimony and obstinacy—hang together more closely than the third, orderliness; they are, too, the more constant element in the whole complex. It seems to me, however, incontestable that all 3 in some way belong together. (1908, p. 83)

J. Sadger (1908, 1910) elaborated Freud's portrayal by noting that anal characters display a split or ambivalence in their behaviors; on the one hand, they exhibit responsibility and perserverence in assuming assigned tasks and, on the other, are strongly disposed to put off doing things until the very last moment.

Freud sought in 1913 to differentiate compulsive neurotic symptoms from the anal character type to which it corresponded. He concluded that the symptom reflects a breakdown in the individual's efforts to repress prohibited impulses and thoughts; in contrast, the character reflects successful repressions with supplementary reaction formations and sublimations. In a parallel essay, Jones (1918) extended the distinctions Freud had made between "obsessional" neuroses and "obsessional" (anal) character traits.

The most detailed of the early anal character formulations were those of Abraham (1921). Drawing upon Freud's and Jones's papers, Abraham presented a range of clinical features that characterized the "obsessional" type. The following excerpts from this seminal paper illustrate the diverse traits Abraham saw within this personality.

> [They] are inclined to be exaggerated in their criticism of others, and this easily degenerates into mere carping.... In some cases we meet with inaccessibility and stubbornness.... In others we find perserverence and thoroughness. ...
>
> There are [others] who avoid taking any kind of initiative...[and] we must not forget the tendency, often a very obstinate one, of postponing every action....
>
> Almost all relationships in life are brought into the category of having (holding fast) and giving.... We have now come very close to one of the classical traits...namely, his special attitude to money, which is usually one of parsimony and avarice.
>
> [This] over-emphasis of possession explains the difficulty... in separating... from objects of all kinds, when these have neither practical use nor monetary value.
>
> Pleasure in indexing and classifying... in drawing up programmes and regulating work by timesheets... is so marked... that the forepleasure they get in working out a plan is stronger than their gratification in its execution, so that they often leave it undone. (1921, pp. 378–388)

The next major analytic conception of the "compulsive" character was advanced by W. Reich in 1933. Reich's own words convey the "flavor" of his views:

> Even if the neurotic compulsive sense of order is not present, a *pedantic sense of order* is typical of the compulsive character. In both big and small things, he lives his life according to a preconceived, irrevocable pattern....
>
> This is related to another character trait, the ever-present penchant for *circumstantial, ruminative thinking*. There is a marked inability to focus

attention on what is rationally important about an object and to disregard its superficial aspects.

Frugality, often pushed to the point of *parsimony,* is a character trait in all compulsive characters and is intimately related to the others we have named. Pedantry, circumstantiality, tendency to compulsive rumination, and frugality are all derived from a single instinctual source: anal eroticism.

We have *indecision, doubt, and distrust.* In external appearance, the compulsive character exhibits strong *reserve* and *self-possession;* he is just as ill disposed towards affects as he is acutely inaccessible to them. He is usually even-tempered, lukewarm in his displays of both love and hate. In some cases, this can develop into a complete *affect-block.* (1949, pp. 209-211)

As Abraham was the prime explicator of the "anal" character in the 1920s and Reich the major contributor to the "compulsive" character in the 1930s, E. Fromm was the prime analytic theorist of the 1940s to provide additional insights into what he labeled the "hoarding orientation." Again, a quotation lets the theorist speak for himself:

[These] people have little faith in anything new they might get from the outside world; their security is based upon hoarding and saving, while spending is felt to be a threat. They have surrounded themselves, as it were, by a protective wall, and their main aim is to bring as much as possible into this fortified position and to let as little as possible out of it.

To him the outside world threatens to break into his fortified position; orderliness signifies mastering the world outside by putting it, and keeping it, in its proper place in order to avoid the danger of intrusion. His compulsive cleanliness is another expression of his need to undo contact with the outside world. Things beyond his own frontiers are felt to be dangerous and "unclean."...A constant "no" is the almost automatic defense against intrusion. (1947, pp. 65-67)

A more classical analytic rendition of "obsessive character traits" was formulated by the major 1950s theorist of the disorder, S. Rado. In his fine clinical portrayal of these personalities, Rado wrote:

The patient is overconscientious in his particular way. What he is mostly concerned about are the minutiae, the inconsequential details, the meticulous observance of minor rules and petty formalities.

A rough sketch...would depict him as highly opinionated and proud of his...avowed rationality, keen sense of reality, and "unswerving integrity." He may indeed be an honest man, but he may also turn out to be a sanctimonious hypocrite. He is the ultimate perfectionist. While very sensitive to his own hurt, he may, at the same time, be destructively critical, spiteful, vindictive, and given to...bearing grudges in trivial matters. Or, on the contrary, he may be overcautious, bent on avoiding...conflict. His "common sense" militates against what he views as fancies of the imagination: he is a "man of facts," not of fancies. (1959, pp. 325–326).

Rado's thesis concerning the origins of obsessive traits are well stated and also deserve selective quoting. Remaining true to Freud's assertion that the impact of the anal period is crucial to the development of the pattern, Rado continued:

> If the mother is overambitious, demanding and impatient . . . then the stage is set for the battle of the chamber pot.
>
> Irritated by the mother's interference with his bowel clock, the child responds to her entreaties with enraged defiance, to her punishments and threats of punishment with fearful obedience. The battle is a seesaw, and the mother . . . makes the disobedient child feel guilty, undergo deserved punishment and ask forgiveness. . . . It is characteristic of the type of child under consideration that his guilty fear is always somewhat stronger; sooner or later, it represses his defiant rage. Henceforth, his relationship to the mother, and soon to the father, will be determined by . . . guilty fear over defiant rage or *obedience* versus *defiance.*
>
> A few words should be added about the obsessive patient's "ambivalence." . . . we trace these manifestations uniformly to the underlying obedience-defiance conflict. . . . He ponders unendingly: must he give in, or could he gain the upper hand without giving offense. (1959, pp. 330, 336).

As was characteristic of the 1960s, the theoretical and clinical features ascribed to the compulsive were subjected to critical and quantitative scrutiny. For example, Sandler and Hazari (1960) evaluated the responses of 100 patients to an "obsessional" questionnaire using the centroid method of factor analysis. Their results indicated that obsessional character *traits* cluster in a different group than do obsessional *symptoms.* More significantly, they found that the character pattern cluster did indeed correspond to classical analytic features (e.g., systematic, methodical, thorough, well ordered, consistent, punctual, and meticulous). In another factor analytic study, a similar pattern of findings were obtained and cross-validated with both preselected and random patients (Lazare, Klerman, and Armor, 1966, 1970). As they phrased their results: "the obsessive factor both in the original and in the current study contains defining traits which were all predicted from psycho-analytic theory" (p. 283). Among these traits were emotional constriction, orderliness, parsimony, rigidity, superego, perseverence, and obstinacy. Also reflecting the empirical bent of the period, Walton and Presley (1973a, 1973b) rated 140 patients in an effort to extract distinctive components using a factor analytic matrix. Although blurred by certain intrusive "schizoid" elements, one of the components extracted was termed obsessional, having been composed of features such as stubbornness, meticulousness, and officiousness.

Formulations of a more theoretical nature were advanced by the end of the decade. Reinforced by both empirical data and conceptions concerning the role of ambivalence, such as posited by Rado, Millon (1969) put forth a theory-derived syndrome labeled "passive-ambivalence," a clinical pattern that paralleled in all major respects the character type variously called "anal," "compulsive," and "obsessional." To represent the deferential and self-constricting manner in which the obedience-defiance conflict is resolved, Millon proposed that the pattern be termed the "conforming" personality. The following descriptions and diagnostic criteria were developed in accord with this pattern. They served as the DSM-III initial working draft for the compulsive personality disorder.

> This pattern is typified by behavioral rigidity, emotional overcontrol and a conscientious compliance to rules and authority. Everyday relationships have a conventional, formal and serious quality to them and there is a conspicuous concern with matters of order, organization and efficiency. Perfectionism, smallmindedness and a lack of cognitive spontaneity are manifested in a cautious indecisiveness, procrastination and a tendency to be upset by deviations from routine. The characteristic air of austere and disciplined self-restraint precludes informality and easy relaxation.
>
> Since adolescence or early adulthood at least 3 of the following have been present to a notably greater degree than in most people and were not limited to discrete periods nor necessarily pompted by stressful life events.

1. Restrained affectivity (e.g., appears unrelaxed, tense, joyless and grim; emotional expression is kept under tight control).

2. Conscientious self-image (e.g., sees self as industrious, dependable and efficient; values self-discipline, prudence and loyalty).

3. Interpersonal respectfulness (e.g., exhibits unusual adherence to social conventions and properties; prefers polite, formal and correct personal relationships).

4. Cognitive constriction (e.g., constructs world in terms of rules, regulations, hierarchies; is unimaginative, indecisive and upset by unfamiliar or novel ideas and customs).

5. Behavioral rigidity (e.g., keeps to a well-structured, highly regulated and repetitive life pattern; reports preference for organized, methodical and meticulous work).

In response to preliminary personality committee discussions, the following modifications in criteria were proposed for a later draft.

A. Excessive emotional control (e.g., unable to relax, lack of spontaneous emotional response).

B. Excessive concern with matters of order, organization and efficiency (e.g., unduly meticulous, reliance on schedules).

C. Interpersonal reserve (e.g., relations with people are unduly conventional, serious and formal).

D. Excessive conformity to internalized standards (e.g., moralistic, or excessively judgmental of self or others).

    E.   Indecisiveness (e.g., procrastination, rumination).

The reader will be well prepared by now to proceed to a less formal and more discursive presentation of the major clinical features of this personality pattern.

CLINICAL PICTURE

The major characteristics of the compulsive personality are organized in terms of the usual fourfold grouping.

Behavioral Features

The grim and cheerless demeanor of compulsives is often quite striking. This is not to say that they are invariably glum or downcast but rather to convey their characteristic air of austerity and serious-mindedness. Posture and movement reflect their underlying tightness, a tense control of emotions that are kept well in check.

Compulsives are viewed by others as industrious and efficient, though lacking in flexibility and spontaneity. Many consider them to be stubborn, stingy, possessive, uncreative, and unimaginative. Quite typically, they tend to procrastinate, appear indecisive, and are easily upset by the unfamiliar or by deviations from routines to which they have become accustomed. Content with their "nose to the grindstone," many work diligently and patiently with activities that require being tidy and meticulous. Some judge these behaviors to be a sign of being orderly and methodical; others see it as reflecting a small-minded and picayune nature. Compulsive personalities are especially concerned with matters of organization and efficiency, and tend to be rigid and unbending about rules and procedures. These behaviors often lead others to see them as perfectionistic, officious, and legalistic.

The social behavior of compulsives may be characterized as polite and formal. They relate to others in terms of rank or status; that is, they tend to be authoritarian rather than equalitarian in their outlook. This is reflected in their contrasting behaviors with "superiors" as opposed to "inferiors." Compulsive personalities are deferential, ingratiating, and even obsequious with their superiors, going out of their way to impress them with their efficiency and serious-mindedness. Many seek the reassurance and approval of authority figures, experiencing considerable anxiety when they are unsure of their position. These behaviors contrast markedly with their attitudes toward subordinates. Here the compulsive is quite autocratic and condemnatory, often appearing pompous and self-righteous. This haughty and deprecatory manner is usually cloaked behind regulations and legalities. Not untypically, compulsives will justify their aggressive intentions by recourse to rules or authorities higher than themselves.

Self-Descriptions and Complaints

Compulsives take great pains to avoid recognizing the contradictions between their unconscious impulses and their overt behaviors. This they do by devaluing self-exploration. Thus, compulsives often exhibit little or no insight into their motives and feelings. To bolster this defensive maneuver, they demean the "personal equation," claiming that self-exploration is antithetical to efficient behavior and that introspection only intrudes upon rational thinking and self-control. Protectively, then, they avoid looking into themselves and build a rationale in which they assert that analyses such as these are signs of immature self-indulgence, traits that they view as anathema to civilized life.

Compulsives are good "organization men," typifying what has been termed the "bureaucratic personality." The compulsive's self-image is that of a conscientious, selfless, loyal, dependable, prudent, and responsible individual. Not only do these individuals willingly accept the beliefs of institutional authorities, but they believe that these authorities' demands and expectations are "correct." Compulsives identify with these strictures, internalizing them as a means of controlling their own repressed impulses and employing them as a standard to regulate the behavior of others. Their vigorous defense of institutional authorities often brings them commendation and support, rewards that serve to reinforce their inclination toward public obedience and moral self-righteousness.

It is characteristic of compulsives to be as harsh in their self-judgments as they are with others. In addition, they voice a strong sense of duty to others, feeling that they must not let the others down and, more significantly, not engage in behaviors that might provoke their displeasure. Although compulsives feel self-doubt or guilt for failing to live up to some ideal, they have no awareness that it is often their own ambivalence about achieving, their own unconscious desire to defy authority, that blocks them from attaining their public aspirations. They may rationalize their indecisiveness by the "wisdom" of "looking before one leaps," of delaying action until one is sure of its correctness, and of "aiming for high standards," which, of course demand the most careful and reflective appraisal. These philosophical cliches merely cloak an unconscious desire to undo the rigid mold into which compulsives have allowed their life to be cast.

Compulsives are contemptuous of those who behave "frivolously and impulsively"; emotional behavior is considered immature and irresponsible. To them, people must be judged by "objective" standards and by the time-proven rules of an organized society. Reactions to others must be based on "established" values and customs, not on "personal" judgments. What compulsives invariably fail to recognize is that they seek to judge others in accord with rules that they themselves unconsciously detest. They impose harsh regulations upon others largely to convince themselves that these rules can, in fact, be adhered to. If they succeed in restraining the rebellious impulses of others, perhaps they can be confident of successfully restraining their own.

Inferred Intrapsychic Dynamics

Appearing deliberate and well poised on the surface, the compulsive sits atop an internal powder keg. These personalities are beset by deep ambivalence and conflict, an inner turmoil that threatens to upset the balance they have so carefully wrought throughout life. They must preserve that balance and protect themselves against the intrusion into both conscious awareness and overt behavior of intensely contrary impulses and feelings. They must carefully avoid events that could dislodge and unleash these forces, causing them to lose favor with those in authority. Having opted for a strategy in which rewards and security are granted to those in power, they must, at all costs, prevent losing the powerful's respect and protection. To achieve this, they must take no risks and operate with complete certainty that no unanticipated event will upset their equilibrium. Avoiding external disruptions is difficult enough, but their greatest task is that of controlling their own emotions, that is, restraining the impulses that surge from within and from which they cannot escape. Their only recourse for dealing with these intrusive and frightening urges is either to transmute them or to seal them off. This they do by the extensive use of intrapsychic mechanisms. Because of the depth of their ambivalence and the imperative nature of its control, compulsive personalities employ more varied defensive mechanisms than any of the other pathological patterns.

Two of the most effective techniques for transforming negative impulses, yet finding outlets for them at the same time, are identification and sublimation. If compulsives can find a "punitive" model of authority to emulate, they can "justify" venting their hostile impulses toward others and perhaps receive commendation as well. For example, in one case the author observed that a child identified with his parents' strict attitudes by "tattling" and reproaching his brother; this enabled the child to find a sanctioned outlet for his otherwise unacceptable hostility. Much of the compulsive's self-righteous morality reflects the same process. Mechanisms of sublimation serve similar functions. Unconscious feelings of hostility that cannot be tolerated consciously are often expressed in socially acceptable ways through occupations such as judge, dean, soldier, or surgeon. Fiercely moralistic fathers and "loving," but overcontrolling, mothers are more common ways of restraint that often camouflage hidden hostility.

There are three intrapsychic mechanisms—reaction formation, isolation, and undoing—that do not provide an outlet for submerged hostile impulses but do serve to keep them in check. The ingratiating and obsequious manner of many compulsives, especially in circumstances that normally evoke frustration and anger in others, may be traced to a reaction formation of their hidden, rebellious urges. Not daring to expose their true feelings of defiance and anger, they must bind these feelings so tightly that their opposite comes forth. Compulsive individuals also compartmentalize or isolate their emotional response to a situation. They block or otherwise neutralize feelings that are normally aroused by a stressful event and thereby ensure against the possibility of reacting in ways that might cause embarrassment and disapproval. Should compulsives trespass the injunctions of authority figures or fail to live up to their expectations, they may engage in certain ritualistic acts to "undo" the evil or wrong they feel they have done. In this manner, they seek expiation for their sins, and they thereby regain the goodwill they fear may be lost.

Interpersonal Coping Style

The major force behind the behavior of compulsives is their fear of disapproval and their concern that their actions will be frowned upon and punished. This fear can be understood given their likely history of exposure to demanding, perfectionistic, and condemnatory parents. One would assume that by "toeing the line" and behaving properly and correctly, compulsives could put this concern aside and be relaxed and untroubled. But this does not prove to be possible because their conformity and propriety are merely a facade behind which lurks deeply repressed urges toward defiance and self-assertion. The ever-present threat that their rebellious and angry feelings will break into the open intensifies their fear of provoking disapproval. At some level, they sense the pretentiousness and insincerity of their public behavior. Thus, their fantasies may be a constant reminder of the disparity that exists between the front they present to others and the hostility they feel beneath. No matter how perfect their behavior may be in fact, no matter how hard they may attempt to prove themselves, this inner ambivalence remains. They must be alert to the possibility of detection at all times. Condemnation is a constant threat since their "true" feelings can be readily uncovered. To cope with both their fears and their impulses, compulsives engage in characteristic interpersonal behaviors that have been briefly addressed in previous sections. The following paragraphs summarize some of these features and touch upon other aspects not discussed earlier.

The compulsive person is extraordinarily careful to pay proper respect to those in authority. These individuals are not only correct and polite but ingratiating and obsequious. Their conduct is beyond reproach; they are ever punctual and meticulous in fulfilling the duties and obligations expected of them. These behaviors serve a variety of functions beyond gaining approval and the avoidance of displeasure. For example, by allying themselves with a "greater power" compulsives gain considerable strength and authority for themselves. Not only do they enjoy the protection and the prestige of another, but by associating their actions with the views of an external authority, they relieve themselves of blame should these actions meet with disfavor. Of course, by submerging their individuality and becoming chattels of some other power or person, compulsives alienate themselves, preclude experiencing a sense of true personal satisfaction, and lose those few remnants of personal identity they may still possess.

Compulsives are usually uncompromising and demanding in relationships with subordinates. This they do to bolster their deep feelings of inadequacy. Disrespect and disloyalty on the part of subordinates remind them all too painfully of their own inner urges and weaknesses. Moreover, this power over others provides them with a sanctioned outlet to vent hostile impulses. Should the others fail to live up to their standards, they feel just in reprimanding and condemning them.

Another aspect of the need for respect relates to property and possessions. The compulsive's behavior conveys the attitude "what is mine is mine and what is yours is yours; I will leave alone what you possess as long as you do likewise with mine." Just as these personalities learned in their struggle with parental restrictions to find a small sphere of behavior that was safe and above reproach, so too do they now gather and hold tight to their limited body of rights and possessions. As Fromm (1947) has put it, they will hoard and protect against all intrusions those few prized belongings they have struggled to acquire for themselves. Having been deprived of so many wishes and desires in childhood, they now nurture and protect what they have achieved. They fortify themselves and stave off those vultures who wish to deprive them of their resources. They are miserly and ungiving, and act as if their "fortune" could never be replenished.

There is a deeper and more devious basis for compulsives' demand that their possessions and privacy be secure. They dare not permit anyone to explore the emptiness of their inner self, the truly barren quality of their attainments and competencies. Of even greater import, they dread that others will uncover their rebellious urges, those angry and defiant feelings that lurk beneath their cloak of respectability and propriety. They must quickly stop others from exploring and possibly exposing the pretense of their very existence. Respect is a way of maintaining distance, then, a means of hiding what compulsives must keep from others and from themselves.

ASSOCIATED DISORDERS

As in earlier chapters, this section attempts to identify the most frequent Axis I and Axis II syndromes that covary with the personality under discussion. In addition, brief descriptions are given of the vulnerabilities that activate Axis I symptoms and the typical aims the Axis II personality seeks to achieve in coping with these vulnerabilities.

Concomitant Axis I Symptoms

Before proceeding, note should be made again of some of the factors that serve to differentiate and to interrelate Axis I and Axis II disorders.

Axis I clinical disorders usually take the form of dramatic signs that stand out in sharp relief against the more prosaic background of the patient's everyday style of functioning—what we have termed the *personality*. It has been our thesis that the patient's personality is the foundation for understanding his or her pathology. Axis I symptom disorders are extensions or disruptions in patients' characteristic personality styles; anchored to their past experience, they take on significance and meaning largely in that context. Because personality disorders possess pervasive vulnerabilities, a wide array of feelings and memories are quickly reactivated and unleashed in response to "duplicates" of the past. These inner forces rapidly override current realities and take over as the primary stimuli to which the person responds. As a consequence, the Axis I clinical symptom is less a function of present precipitants than it is of the past associations they evoke. It is this primacy of the reactivated past that gives clinical disorders much of their irrational and symbolic quality. However, the "hidden meaning" of the Axis I clinical symptom can be understood if seen in terms of the "inner stimulus" intrusions of Axis II personality vulnerabilities. In addition to reflecting the eruption of past memories and emotions, the Axis I disorder is shaped by the habitual coping style that characterizes the patient's Axis II personality. The behaviors exhibited, then, are "rational and appropriate" *if* seen in terms of the past that has been stirred up and the manner in which the patient has learned to cope with his/her vulnerabilities. With this as a precis, the discussion turns to the most prevalent Axis I disorders found among compulsive personalities.

Obsessive compulsive disorders. It is probable that compulsive personalities do in fact exhibit obsessive compulsive disorders with greater frequency than do other personality patterns. Some theorists contend that obsessive compulsive symptoms are not so much a matter of "disordered" coping as deeply ingrained strategies learned to contain socially forbidden impulses. Through widely generalized reaction formations, compulsives not only control their contrary inclinations but present a socially attractive front of conformity and propriety. The symptom of obsessive doubting leads these patients to reexamine the most trivial of decisions and acts. This excessive preoccupation with minor irrelevancies does enable them, however, to be distracted from the real source of their anxieties. Although self-doubting is a general characteristic of these personalities, it may become especially pronounced if a sudden eruption of feelings threatens to "expose them" or "give them away." Their pretense of equanimity may be readily disrupted by the intrusion of bizarre, hostile, or erotic thoughts. Stirring up intense fears of social condemnation, compulsives may "undo" these thoughts by a series of repetitive acts or rituals. For example, each morning, by washing his face and knotting his tie repeatedly, a compulsive man assured himself of his purity; the repetition of these easily mastered, if insignificant acts, strengthened his confidence in his ability to "clean up" and "tie down" his impulses.

Phobic disorders. Compulsives develop simple phobias primarily as a function of three anxiety precipitants: decision-making situations in which they anticipate being faulted or subjected to criticism; real failures that they wish to rationalize or avoid facing again; and surging impulses that they seek to counter, transform, or externalize lest these overwhelm controls and provoke social condemnation. In contrast to dependent and histrionic personalities, compulsives "hide" their phobias since their self-image would be weakened by such "foolish" and irrational symptoms. Thus, without public awareness, they displace their tensions into a variety of external phobic sources. This not only enables them to deny the internal roots of their discomforts, but, by making their anxiety into something tangible and identifiable, it becomes subject to control or avoidance.

Anxiety disorders. Compulsives are among the more frequent candidates for generalized anxiety disorders. Every act, thought, or impulse that may digress from the straight and narrow path is subject to the disapproval of an internal conscience or the punitive reactions of an external authority. Of equal importance, their anxiety is compounded by the presence within themselves of deeply repressed impulses that threaten to erupt and overwhelm their controls. Without rigid constraints, their tenuous social facade and psychic cohesion may be torn apart. Ever concerned that they will fail to live up to the demands of authority and constantly on edge lest their inner defiance break out of control, they often live in chronic states of anxiety. The constant presence of tension is so much a part of their everyday life that it is difficult to say where personality ends and where the anxiety symptom begins. On the positive side, many of these patients utilize the energy they derive from their tension to effective ends. Thus, the characteristic diligence and conscientiousness of compulsives reflect, in large measure, their control and exploitation of anxious energy. However, should these controls be shaken, there is a high probability that an acute attack or panic disorder will ensue.

Somatoform disorders. Compulsive personalities succumb to *conversion* disorders, albeit infrequently, as another means of containing the upsurge of forbidden impulses. Conversion disorders are not an easy "choice" for these patients, however, since to be ill runs counter to their image of self-sufficiency. Nevertheless—and in contrast to phobic symptoms, which are especially embarrassing in this regard—conversion symptoms enable these patients to advertise their illness as one of physical origin. It allows them not only to achieve the important secondary gains of attention and nurture but also to continue their belief that they are basically self-sufficient and merely unfortunate victims of "passing" sickness. Despite these gains, however, compulsives will feel most comfortable if they underplay their ailment, acting quite indifferent about it. Because they are likely to feel guilt over the surreptitious pleasure they gain in dependency, the conversion symptoms they acquire tend to be rather severe. Thus, they may exhibit the total immobilization of a bodily function (e.g., blindness, mutism, or complete paralysis of the legs). The severity of their symptoms not only reflects the sweeping character of their controls, as well as their need to "prove" the seriousness of their illness, but it frequently serves as punishment for intense guilt feelings. By becoming blind or by disabling their limbs, they sacrifice a part of themselves as penance for their "sinful" thoughts and urges.

Somatization and *hypochondriacal* disorders are also employed by compulsives as a way of rationalizing failures and inadequacies. Fearful that they will be condemned for their shortcomings, compulsives may seek to maintain self-respect and the esteem of others by ascribing deficiencies to some ill-defined ailment or "legitimate" physical illness. This maneuver may not only shield them from rebuke but may evoke praise from others for the few accomplishments they do manage to achieve. How commendable others must think they are for their conscientious efforts, despite their illness and exhaustion. Compulsives do frequently suffer real fatigue and physiologic symptoms as a consequence of their struggle to control undischarged inner angers and resentments. Bodily ailments may also represent a turning inward of repressed hostile impulses. Not infrequently, ailments such as these function as a displaced and symbolic self-punishment, a physical substitute for the guilt they feel after having expressed condemned emotions. Suffering not only discharges tension but serves as a form of expiation.

Psychosomatic disorders. As noted several times, compulsives keep under close wraps most of the tensions generated by their dependence-independence conflict. Through repression and other mechanisms, their resentments and anxieties are tightly controlled and infrequently discharged. As a consequence, physiological tensions are not dissipated, tend to cumulate, and result in frequent and persistent psychosomatic ailments, especially of the gastrointestinal variety. Also notable is the close correspondence between the compulsive life pattern and what is now termed "Type A" behavior, a style ostensibly correlated with cardiovascular difficulties.

Dissociative disorders. Compulsive personalities succumb to dissociative disorders on occasion and for a variety of reasons. Experiences of depersonalization and estrangement stem from the overcontrol of feeling. By desensitizing their emotions or by withdrawing feelings as part of everyday life, they begin to experience the world as flat and colorless, a place in which events seem mechanical, automatic, and unreal. Episodes of *amnesia* may occur if compulsives are otherwise unable to isolate and control their intense ambivalence. The coexistence of conflicting emotions may become too great a strain. Not only will the eruption of hostile or erotic impulses shatter the compulsive's self-image of propriety, but they may provoke the severe condemnation from others that is dreaded. Failing to restrain their urges, compulsives may be driven to disown their identity or to obliterate all past memories. *Fugue* states may be another way to discharge unbearable tensions in that they allow these patients to vent their contrary impulses without any conscious awareness and, hence, without having to assume responsibility for them. *Multiple personality* disorders, although rare, will enable the patient to retain his/her "true" identity most of the time yet gain periodic release through "other" selves.

Brief reactive psychoses and schizophreniform disorders.

Brief reactive psychoses and schizophreniform disorders occur on occasion in compulsive personalities. This usually follows a shattering of controls employed to restrain the repressed obedience-defiance conflict. Unable to keep these divisive forces in check, these patients may feel torn apart or engulfed in a sea of surging and contrary feelings that spill forth in a flood of incoherent verbalizations and bizarre emotions. Stereotyped grimacing, posturing, and mannerisms often reflect the patients' feeble efforts to contain their impulses or to damp down the confusion and disharmony that they feel.

Affective disorders.

More typical than these extreme psychotic episodes is the compulsive's proclivity to affective disorders, most frequently evident in periods of tense and anxious dejection. Faced with difficult decisions but unable to gain clear direction from others, these patients may experience intense anger toward themselves for their weakness and deep resentment toward others for what is seen as the latter's unyielding demands. Despite the intensity and direction of these feelings, compulsives dare not expose their own shortcomings nor their hostility toward others. Complicating matters further is the fact that they have been well trained to express self-reproval and guilt. Thus, rather than voice their defiance and vent their resentment, and thereby be subject to severe social rebuke, they turn their feelings inward and discharge anger toward themselves. This act of self-reproval serves as a form of expiation for their hidden oppositional thoughts and feelings. Moreover, by acting contrite they assume that no one will condemn and humiliate them. Unfortunately, compulsives have usually been subjected in the past to severe condemnation for any sign of weakness or incompetence. Thus, they find themselves trapped in a "bind." Whether they are contrite or whether they are defiant, they cannot be free of the fear that their actions will provoke further rejection. The agitated and apprehensive quality of their *major depressions* reflects both a struggle to contain their resentments and their fear that contrition will only prompt derision and condemnation.

On occasion, compulsives display a relatively benign but chronic "melancholy," currently termed *dysthymic disorder*. This may occur if they realize how empty their lives have been, how often they have denied themselves, and how much they have given up by conforming to external standards. Extended depressions of a melancholic nature are often interrupted, however, by brief periods of self-assertion and self-expression. Quite typically, feelings of anxiety will be activated during these brief "flings," turning them into rather short-lived episodes. More commonly, compulsives will exhibit classic forms of agitated depression, noted primarily by diffuse apprehension, marked feelings of guilt, and a tendency to complain about personal sin and unworthiness. As noted earlier, compulsives are likely to turn the angry and resentful components of their ambivalence inward and against themselves, claiming that they truly deserve punishment and the misery they now suffer.

Concurrent Axis II Personalities

With perhaps one or two exceptions, compulsives have been found to blend with almost every other personality type. Research employing the MCMI (Millon, 1977) narrows the most important combinations to two, one at a moderately serious level of pathology and the other at a more severe level. The former combination is characterized by strong dependent traits; the latter has significant paranoid features.

Compulsive-dependent mixed personality.
This amalgam has been recorded with considerable frequency in private practice settings and in clinics oriented toward the treatment of psychosomatic disorders; a two-to-one ratio of females to males shows up across diverse settings. The following MCMI report is based on the responses of a 42-year-old woman seen in a private group practice; she was referred for evaluation following an extended history of psychosomatic difficulties.

> This patient's behavior is typified by a submissive dependency, a compliance to rules and authority, and a willing submission to the wishes and values of others. There is a tendency to be self-effacing and noncompetitive, a fear of independent self-assertion, and a surface compliance to the expectations and demands of others. She voices a strong sense of duty to others, feeling that they must not have their expectations unmet. Her self-image, on the surface, is that of a considerate, thoughtful, and cooperative person, prone to be unambitious and modest. There are marked feelings of personal inadequacy as she tends to minimize attainments, underplay attributes, and downgrade abilities. The patient is overly respectful, even ingratiating with those in authority. The fear of provoking condemnation creates considerable tension for her, as well as occasional expressions of guilt. Her submissive behavior with those in authority may be traced in part to a reversal of hidden rebellious feelings.
>
> Lurking behind her front of propriety and restraint are intense contrary feelings that occasionally break through her controls. Rarely daring to expose these feelings, she binds them so tightly that life becomes overorganized in an anxiously tense and disciplined self-restraint. She lacks spontaneity and

flexibility, is often indecisive, tends to procrastinate, and is easily upset by deviations from routine. There is a marked denial of discordant emotions and a tendency to neutralize feelings normally aroused by distressful events.

The patient dreads making mistakes and fears taking risks lest these provoke disapproval and punishment. To avoid transgressions and obviate the unknown and potentially dangerous, she conveys a front of equanimity and social agreeableness. She is minimally introspective and displays a rigorous internal conscience, an inner gauge that serves to counter oppositional urges and thoughts. As a consequence of constraining feelings and denying emotional conflicts, she is inclined to develop numerous and persistent psychophysiological symptoms.

Compulsive-paranoid mixed personality. The second case has been selected to represent the personality mixture of compulsive and paranoid. The following MCMI computer report summarizes inferences about a 55-year-old field engineer who was referred following repeated difficulties with subordinates. Known as a tough but competent manager, he had recently begun to run into conflict with his division vice-president, claiming that he was not given adequate recognition for his efforts for the company. The MCMI narrative interpretation reads as follows:

> The patient's behavior is typified by a highly controlled but conflictful conformity to the conventions of propriety and authority. Also evident are periodic displays of suspiciousness, irritability, obsessional ideation, and moodiness. There is a tendency to compulsivity and denial, with a notable defensiveness about admitting psychological problems. However, there are occasional reports of feeling tense and high-strung. He anticipates derogation and humiliation from others, and there has been an inclination to self-blame and self-punishment that may have recently given way to outbursts of anger and persecutory accusations. There is a fear of expressing emotions, admitting shortcomings, and losing control.
>
> Efforts are made to maintain a disciplined self-restraint, and the patient rarely relaxes or lets down a guarded defensiveness. He typically appears grim and cheerless, exhibiting an anxiously tense serious-mindedness or perfectionism. Beneath a cooperative and controlled facade are marked feelings of personal insecurity, and he is vigilantly alert to avoid social transgressions that may provoke humiliation and embarassment. The patient's major defense has been to be excessively conforming, inhibiting behaviors that might evoke ridicule and contempt. There is a pattern of avoiding situations that may result either in personal censure or derision, and there is a dread of making mistakes or taking risks, lest these provoke disapproval. As a defensive maneuver, he restricts activities, operates within narrow boundaries, and confines himself to a rigid and, at times, self-righteous conformity to rules and regulations. By adhering vigorously to propriety and convention, by following the straight and narrow path, he seeks to minimize criticism and punitive reactions, particularly from persons in authority.
>
> The patient's defensive style has been undermined repeatedly, and there has been a growing tendency to be argumentative, resentful, and critical of others.

His marked self-doubts and deflated sense of self-esteem resulted in an earlier style of attachment to supportive institutional or bureaucratic organizations. In this way, the patient sought to associate his actions by identifying them with those in authority. Efforts are made to maintain a behavioral pattern that is consistent and unvarying, one in which independent actions are restrained and the strictures of authoritarian rules are rigidly complied with. Tendencies to perfectionism and concern with minor irrelevancies have distracted his attention from deeper sources of anxiety, inadequacy, and anticipated derogation.

To display weakness or abrogate the rules of social conventions was felt as a threat that might expose the patient to disapproval. Given his past experiences, the patient knows that others cannot be trusted to provide support. With each acquiescent submission to others, he has built an ever-larger residue of resentment. Thus, lurking behind his facade of propriety is a growing bitterness and disillusionment. These animosities churn within him. They will either break through to the surface in angry upsurges or be countered in ritualistic precautions or obsessive ruminations. Guilt and self-condemnation may be periodically exhibited, as when he turns his feelings inward and imposes severe punitive judgments and actions upon himself. Despite the tension it generates, such self-reproval is likely to serve as a release for his hostile and forbidden feelings. However, ambivalence is constantly present. On the one hand, there are strong desires to discharge hostility and, on the other, a constant fear that such expressions will prompt derision and rejection. As a residual of this ambivalence, he may have a history of persistent tensions, possibly evident in psychosomatic symptoms.

Differential Diagnostic Signs

Few problems of differential diagnosis are likely to arise with the compulsive personality. Difficulties are most probable, as is generally the case, with syndromes that frequently overlap or covary with the syndrome in the first place; these should be recorded, of course, as concurrent diagnoses. Separating the Axis I obsessive compulsive disorder from the Axis II compulsive personality is at times problematic; however, where the broad-ranging and varied features of personality have been present for an extended period, the Axis II diagnosis is fully justified, whether or not distinctive symptoms of obsessions or compulsions are evident.

PREDISPOSING BACKGROUND

This section explores factors that have been posited as contributing to the compulsive personality pattern. As before, the speculative nature of these determinants must be kept in mind.

Hypothetical Biogenic Factors

There are no distinguishing constitutional characteristics that can be considered typical of compulsive personalities. Some exhibit a marked diminution in activity and energy, attributable in all probability to their lifelong habit of constraint and inhibition. Few evidence a lively or ebullient manner; most are rigidly controlled and emotionally tight, and their failure to release pent-up energies is likely to dispose them to psychophysiologic disorders. Any speculation that the ambivalence of compulsives might reflect some intrinsic antagonism between opposing temperamental dispositions would seem presumptuous. Yet we do observe an opposition between intense fear and intense anger among these individuals. Both tendencies may be great and may account in part for their frequent indecisiveness and immobilization. Given their grim and joyless quality, we might also conjecture that many possess a constitutionally based anhedonic temperament. Translating these notions into tangible substrates, it might be hypothesized that regions of the limbic system associated with both "fear" and "anger" may be usually dense or well branched; conflicting signals from these areas might underlie the hesitancy, doubting, and indecisive behaviors seen in these patients. Similarly, the substrate for experiencing pleasure may be poorly developed, leading to the compulsive's typical stern countenance. Speculations such as these are highly conjectural.

Characteristic Experiential Histories

The determinants of the compulsive style are rooted primarily in interpersonal experience and reflect the behaviors the child learns as a means of coping with these experiences. This discussion formulates a developmental history with reference to a social learning model (Millon, 1969) that parallels many of the views of psychoanalytic theorists.

"Overcontrol" is a major concept in understanding how compulsives were trained to become what they are. It explains how compulsives acquired their style of behavior, as well as being descriptive of that style. The notion of overcontrol as a concept of child rearing may best be understood by contrasting it with other child-rearing practices. First, it differs from "overprotection" in that it reflects an attitude of parental firmness, if not repressiveness. Overprotection, most common in the history of the dependent personality, usually reflects a gentle and loving parental concern, a desire to cuddle and care for the child without harshness or hostility. Overcontrolling parents may also be "caring" but display this concern by "keeping the child in line"; they prevent children from causing trouble not only for themselves but for the parents as well. Overcontrolling parents are frequently punitive in response to transgression, whereas overprotective parents are likely to restrain the child more gently and lovingly, not with anger or threats.

Parental overcontrol is similar to parental hostility, a training process more typical of the history of the aggressive (antisocial) personality pattern. But there are important distinctions here as well. Hostile parents are punitive regardless of the child's behavior, whereas overcontrolling parents are punitive only if the child misbehaves. Thus, the parents of future compulsives are likely to expect their children to live up to their expectations and condemn them only if they fail to achieve the standards imposed. Overcontrol may be conceived, therefore, as a method of contingent punishment; that is, punishment is selective, occurring only under clearly defined conditions.

The contingency aspect of parental overcontrol makes it similar to the child-rearing experiences that characterize the history of the histrionic personality. Here, again, there are important differences. Future histrionics experience *irregular attention* and praise that is contingent on the performance of "good" behavior; they tend not to receive overt punishment or disapproval for "bad behavior." In contrast, future compulsives receive their praise, *not* irregularly but consistently, and they experience mostly negative or punitive reactions rather than positive comments and rewards. They become experts in learning what they must *not* do, so as to avoid punishment and condemnation, whereas histrionics learn what they can do, so as to achieve attention and praise. Future compulsives learn to heed parental restrictions and rules; for them, the lines of disapproved behaviors are set rigidly. However, as a consequence of experiencing mostly negative injunctions, they have little idea of what *is* approved. They know well what they must *not* do but do not know so well what they *can* do. The positive achievements of young compulsives often are "taken for granted" and only occasionally acknowledged by their parents; comments and judgments are almost exclusively limited to pointing out infractions of rules and boundaries the child must never transgress.

In sum, parental overcontrol is a restrictive method of child rearing in which punitive procedures are used to set strict limits upon the child's behavior. As long as these children operate within the approved boundaries they are likely to be secure from parental criticism and condemnation. Although overcontrol is a highly efficient training procedure, it is one fraught with pathological possibilities. These consequences during the second and third stages of neuropsychological development are examined next (the first stage is likely to have been "highly scheduled," but this is neither pathogenic nor distinctive to the development of the compulsive personality).

The second stage of development is notable for the fact that children begin their struggle to acquire autonomous skills and to achieve a sense of self-competence. At this time children become more assertive and resistant to parental directions and admonitions. Overcontrolling parents are likely to respond to these efforts with firm and harsh discipline. Some will physically curtail their children, berate them, withdraw love, and so on. Others will be relentless in their desire to squelch any bothersome transgression. Children who cannot find refuge from the parental onslaught either will submit entirely, withdraw into a shell, or be adamant and rebel. However, if these children can identify a sphere of behavior that is free of parental condemnation, they are likely to overvalue and indulge it. Not only will they restrict their activities to areas that meet parental approval, but they may become "experts" at them, perfectionists, if you will. Needless to say, they will stick within parentally circumscribed boundaries and not venture beyond.

Several consequences flow from this solution. Autonomy will be sharply curtailed, and the future compulsives will fail to develop the full range of competence feelings that other, less restricted children typically acquire. They are likely to develop marked doubts about their ability to deal with events beyond the confines to which they have been bound. They will hesitate to deviate from the "straight and narrow path," withdraw from new situations, and, hence, lack spontaneity, curiosity, and venturesomeness. Having little confidence in themselves and fearing parental wrath for even trivial misdeeds, they will learn to submerge their impulse toward independence and autonomy, and avoid exploring the unknown lest it lead them beyond approved boundaries. The future compulsive is like the dependent child in this regard; in contrast, however, the compulsive has accepted dependency, not for its comforts, love, and affection, but from guilt, shame, punishment, and the fear of rejection.

The third neuropsychological stage is characterized by the acquisition of self-initiative and a growing sense of one's personal identity. A prerequisite to their development is a well-established feeling of personal competence and autonomy, two features already impaired in the future compulsive. And to add insult to prior injury, overcontrolling parents continue to restrict and overdirect their children. They proffer advice and admonishments by which the children are expected to guide their behavior. Not only do they continue to be shaped excessively by parental directives, but the latter's counsel usually follows a narrow and well-defined course. As a consequence, young compulsives not only fail to learn to think for themselves but are guided in their thinking along highly conventional and adult lines. Rather than feeling free to engage in the imaginative play and creativity of childhood thinking, they are shaped to think in an overly mature fashion. They are led at an accelerated pace toward adulthood and are expected to "toe the line" in acquiring proper and upright attitudes. Parental overcontrol at this stage undermines children's opportunities to take the initiative and to acquire their own identity. They quickly become caricatures of adult propriety, "gentlemen" and "ladies," but automatons as well. Unable to face the novel and the unanticipated, they can act only if they are certain that their narrow band of approved behaviors is applicable and correct. They dare not venture on their own for fear that they are ill-equipped to meet challenges, or that they may overstep accepted boundaries. Their only recourse, then, is to simplify and organize their world, to be absolutely sure of what they can do, and to eliminate complexities that require decisions and initiative. Their environment must be a familiar one guided by explicit rules and standards, one in which they know beforehand what course of action is expected and approved.

To restate the foregoing in terms of the learning processes they reflect: The children learn *instrumentally* to avoid punishment by obediently acquiescing to parental demands and strictures. They are "shaped" by fear and intimidation to conform to the expectations and standards set down by their elders. Further, the children learn *vicariously* and by imitation. They model themselves after their parents' image by incorporating "whole hog" the rules and inhibitions that characterize their parents' standards and values. Moreover, they make a virtue of necessity. Thus, they feel proud and self-satisfied being "good" and "proper." This enables the children not only to master their dread of parental rejection but to gain the parents' commendation. Adoption of the parental model has its problematic side, however. Along with adult propriety, future compulsives incorporate the parents' strictness and punitive attitudes. They place themselves in a role that parallels theirs; as a result, they become stern, intolerant, and self-righteous tyrants who condemn the "immaturity and irresponsibility" of others. Another characteristic of the compulsive's learning history is its *insufficiency*, its narrow range of competencies and its inadequacies for dealing with novel and unforseen events . Thus, compulsives not only are fearful of violating rules but lack the wherewithal to change the unknown. Their behavioral narrowness is partly a matter of adaptive choice and partly a matter of having no alternatives.

There is another feature common to the developmental history of the compulsive: exposure to conditions that teach responsibility to others and a feeling of guilt when these responsibilities have not been met. As noted earlier, these youngsters are often "moralized" to inhibit their inclinations toward frivolous play and impulse gratification. Many are impressed by the shameful nature of such activities and are warned against the terrible consequences of mischief and "sin." Others may be told how pained and troubled their parents will be if they cause them embarrassment or deviate from the "path of righteousness." Long before children can understand the significance of these injunctions, they learn that they must adopt them as their own. In time, they will internalize these strictures and develop self-discipline and self-criticism, a "conscience" that will prevent them from transgressing the rights of others. They will be made to feel disloyal and disrespectful of their "well-meaning" parents if they balk at the latter's impositions and restraints. How inconsiderate a child must be "after all the things they have done." By promoting guilt, the child's anger is diverted from its original object and turned inward toward the self. It can be used to further curtail the child's inclinations toward disobedience or independence. Not only are these children now fearful of the consequences of their defiant impulses, but they have learned to feel guilty for merely thinking them. Now, by condemning themselves, they demonstrate their "good" intentions and thereby ward off reproach and criticism. And, as their own conscience and persecutor, they can always anticipate and avoid social condemnation.

PROGNOSTIC CONSIDERATIONS

As in previous chapters, this section addresses the features that perpetuate the personality style—that is, are themselves pathogenic of the pattern—followed by a brief exploration of some of the remedial steps that may prove useful in modifying the problem.

Perpetuation of the Compulsive Pattern

Given the conflicts and anxieties engendered by their strategy, why do compulsives resist exploring alternative coping methods? One answer, of course, is that they experience less pain by continuing, rather than changing, their style of behavior. Thus, discomforting as the strategy may be, it is less anguishing and more rewarding than any other they can envisage. Another answer is that much of what they do is merely the persistence of habit, the sheer continuation of what they have learned in the past. Thus, compulsives persevere, in part at least, not because their behavior is instrumentally so rewarding but because it is deeply ingrained, so much so that it persists automatically. None of this is unique to the compulsive personality. It is true of all personality patterns. Each style fosters a vicious circle such that the individual's adaptive strategy promotes conditions similar to those that gave rise initially to that strategy. Pathological personality traits are traps, self-made prisons that are perniciously self-defeating in that they promote their own continuation. The following paragraphs look at three of these self-perpetuating processes.

Pervasive rigidity. Compulsives dread making mistakes and fear taking risks lest they provoke disapproval. Defensively, they learn to restrict themselves to situations with which they are familiar and to actions they feel confident will be approved. They keep themselves within narrow boundaries and confine themselves to the repetition of the familiar. Rarely do they wander or view things from a different perspective than they have in the past. Moreover, compulsives are characteristically single-minded, have sharply defined interests, and can stick to "the facts" without deviation. To avoid the unknown—that is, the potentially dangerous—they maintain a tight and well-organized approach to life. They hold onto the "tried and true" and keep their nose to old and familiar grindstones. The price paid for this rigid and narrow outlook is high. Subtle emotions and creative imagination are simply incompatible with the deliberate and mechanical quality of the compulsive's style. Further, the repetitious going over the same dull routine prevents these persons from experiencing new perceptions and new ways of approaching their environment. By following the same narrow path, compulsives block their chances of breaking the bonds of the past. Their horizons are confined as they duplicate the same old grind.

Guilt and self-criticism. By the time compulsives attain adolescence, they are likely to have fully incorporated the strictures and regulations of their elders. Even if they could "get away with it" and be certain that no external power would judge them severely, they now carry within themselves a merciless internal "conscience," an inescapable inner gauge that ruthlessly evaluates and controls them, one that intrudes relentlessly to make them doubt and hesitate before they act. The proscriptions of "proper" behavior have been well learned and they dare not deviate irresponsibly. The onslaughts of guilt and self-recrimination are adamant and insidious. External sources of restraint have been supplanted with the inescapable controls of internal self-reproach. Compulsives are now their own persecutor and judge, ready to condemn themselves not only for overt acts but for thoughts of transgression as well. These inner controls stop them from exploring new avenues of behavior and thereby perpetuate the habits and constraints of the past.

Creation of rules and regulations. Most persons strive to minimize the constraints that society imposes. Laws are the price for a civilized existence, but we prefer as few as necessary. Compulsives are different. Not only do they live by rules and regulations, but they go out of their way to uncover legalities, moral prescriptions, and ethical standards to guide themselves and judge others. This attitude is understandable, deriving from their intense struggle to control raging impulses toward defiance that well up within them. The more restrictive the injunctions they find in legalities and external authority, the less effort they must expend on their own to control these contrary urges. Once more they trap themselves in a self-defeating circle. By creating or discovering new percepts to heed, they draw the noose even tighter around themselves and shrink their world into an ever-narrowing shell. Opportunities for learning new behaviors, or to view the world afresh and more flexibly, are further curtailed. Their own characteristic habits have increasingly narrowed their boundaries for change and growth.

Remedial Intervention

The behavioral style of the compulsive personality is not likely to change. These patients' mechanisms and interpersonal strategies do not foster so many new problems as they repeat old ones. As long as they are well prepared for the tasks they face it is likely that they will maintain an even keel through most of their life. Their "ships" are "tight," unventuresome and well-fortressed islands. Their world is well surveyed and stabilized. Responsibilities and relationships are kept clearly within the bounds of their capacities. They avoid exploring new directions and are reluctant, even obstinate, about making changes.

The inflexibility of the compulsive's approach may become an Achilles' heel for these personalities. Security and stability for them depend on a simple and well-ordered life. Should the unanticipated occur, or should stress supersede their defenses, their equanimity may falter. They may vacillate between diffuse anxiety, explosive outbursts, expressions of doubt and contrition, and any number of bizarre compulsions. If pressure mounts or continues over prolonged periods, they may decompensate into a florid disorder.

Compulsive personalities often seek therapy as a result of psychophysiologic discomforts. These persons often are beset with psychosomatic difficulties since they have difficulty in discharging internal tensions. Their repressed emotions churn within them, giving rise to numerous physical ailments. Among other reasons for seeking therapy are severe attacks of anxiety, spells of immobilization, sexual impotence, or excessive fatigue. Symptoms such as these threaten the compulsive style of efficiency and responsibility. Compulsives view these symptoms as products of an isolated physical "disease," failing to recognize, to the slightest degree, that they represent the outcroppings of internal ambivalence and repressed resentments.

Compulsive personalities are likely to regard therapy as an encroachment upon their defensive armor. They seek to relieve their symptoms but at the same time seek desperately to prevent self-exploration and self-awareness. The patient's defensiveness is deeply protective and must be honored by the therapist; probing should proceed no faster than the patient can tolerate. Only after building trust and self-confidence may one chance bringing to the open the patient's anger and resentment. For every piece of defensive armor removed, the therapist must be sure to bolster the patient's autonomy twofold. To remove more defenses than the patient can tolerate is to invite disaster. Fortunately, compulsives themselves are usually so well guarded that precipitous movement by the therapist is often ignored or intellectualized away. Nonetheless, caution is the byword with these personalities.

Supportive therapy is the major initial vehicle for treating these patients. Several psychopharmacologic agents may prove beneficial in alleviating periods of marked anxiety. Dosages should not be kept at a level where they cause the patient to feel significant decrements in efficiency and alertness. Also useful are behavior modification techniques designed to desensitize the patient to previously discomforting or anxiety-provoking situations. As noted earlier, cognitive reorientation methods, geared to developing insight, must be applied gradually and with discretion; these approaches often fail to accomplish their purposes since compulsives may grasp the problem they face, but only at an abstract or intellectual level. To rework the foundations of their life-style may require the long-term procedures of psychoanalytic therapy. However, personality reconstruction in these personalities is a slow, arduous, and often fruitless process. Compulsives are not especially amenable either to group or family therapy. They will often ally themselves with the therapist, refusing to participate wholeheartedly as patients, or experience extreme anxiety if forced to relinquish their defenses and expose their feelings in front of others.

Chapter 9

Passive-Aggressive Personality: The Negativistic Pattern

The passive-aggressive personality usually evolves when a child internalizes the inconsistencies and vacillations in parental attitudes and behaviors to which he/she was exposed, a feature of experience that is not uncommon in our complex and ever-changing society. What distinguishes so-called passive-aggressives is the fact that they were subjected to appreciably more than their share of contradictory parental messages. Their erraticism and capriciousness, their tendency to shift from agreeableness to negativism, simply mirror the inconsistent models and reinforcements to which they were exposed.

The overt picture of the DSM-III's passive-aggressive syndrome is strikingly dissimilar from that of the compulsive personality. According to Millon (1969), however, both share an intense and deeply rooted ambivalence about themselves and others. Compulsives deal with this ambivalence by vigorously suppressing the conflicts it engenders, and they appear as a consequence, to be well controlled and single-minded in purpose; their behavior is perfectionistic, scrupulous, orderly, and quite predictable. In contrast, the passive-aggressive, referred to in Millon's theory as the "active-ambivalent," fails either to submerge or to otherwise resolve these very same conflicts; as a consequence, the ambivalence of passive-aggressives intrudes constantly into their everyday life, resulting in indecisiveness, fluctuating attitudes, oppositional behaviors and emotions, and a general erraticism and unpredictability. They cannot decide whether to adhere to the desires of others as a means of gaining comfort and security *or* to turn to themselves for these gains, whether to be obediently dependent on others *or* defiantly resistant and independent of them, whether to take the initiative in mastering their world *or* to sit idly by, passively awaiting the leadership of others; they vacillate, then, like the proverbial donkey, moving first one way and then the other, never quite settling on which bale of hay is best.

The erratic pattern of behaviors observed among the passive-aggressive is similar to that employed by young children who explore, through trial and error, various actions and strategies in the hope of discovering which ones succeed for them. In this exploratory phase, children display considerable spontaneity, shifting in an almost random fashion from assertion to submission, to avoidance, to exploitation, to obstinacy, and so on. Most children meet with fairly stable parental responses to their varied behaviors, and, as a consequence, most learn to discern which actions and attitudes are acceptable and achieve their goals. This predictability in gauging the consequences of one's behaviors is not learned by future passive-aggressives for these children experience little in the way of parental consistency. Since they cannot discern a clear pattern of consequences for their behaviors, they continue on an erratic, "childish" course. The persistence of these childlike and capriciously unpredictable behaviors accounts in part for the frequency with which these personalities are referred to in adulthood as "emotionally immature."

The DSM-III characterization and diagnostic criteria of the passive-aggressive is unlike the other personality descriptions in the manual. In each of the other portrayals, several relatively distinct traits are identified as comprising the syndrome or personality pattern. In contrast, only one essential trait is specified in characterizing the passive-aggressive personality type, that of resistance to external demands. Several illustrations and consequences are spelled out in the manual, but they cannot substitute for the matrix of distinct, yet interrelated, traits that comprise a true *personality syndrome*. In line with this objection, the author, as a member of the DSM-III personality subcommittee, submitted the following critique in response to the sketchy and deficient penultimate draft. Unfortunately, in the author's opinion, the recommendations suggested had no impact on the final version.

I think the descriptive material for this personality is narrowly focused. As evident in the diagnostic criteria, we seem to be dealing with a tendency to resist authority as the prime and almost singular trait. Should we not be dealing with a much broader complex when we describe a disorder as a personality disorder? I would like to see additional factors added so as to characterize this as a personality rather than a symptom disorder. The following are my suggestions. First, I would like to see the name changed; "passive-aggressive" has a long history of mixed meanings; I think terms such as oppositional personality disorder or negativistic personality disorder capture the flavor of these patients more clearly. As far as essential features and diagnostic criteria, I would suggest some of the following: frequently irritable and erratically moody; a tendency to report being easily frustrated and angry; discontented self-image, as evidenced in feeling misunderstood and unappreciated by others; characteristically pessimistic, disgruntled and disillusioned with life; interpersonal ambivalence, as evidenced in a struggle between being dependently acquiescent and assertively independent; the use of unpredictable and sulking behaviors to provoke discomfort in others. I think each of the above will enrich the descriptive material we have. It will broaden the personality pattern and provide a complex of traits.

Relevant to the issue of the syndrome's narrow and limited focus are data obtained during the Task Force's field trials. Research seeking to gauge diagnostic agreement for each disorder resulted in a *Kappa* reliability figure of .21 for the passive-aggressive; the next poorest reliability among the personality disorders was .39, with the remainder of the group averaging close to .60. In effect, of all personality disorder descriptions, the passive-aggressive produces by far the poorest diagnostic agreement. Does the passive-aggressive portrayal suffer by comparison because it provides only one trait as a basis for identifying the clinical syndrome? The author thinks the answer is yes! Before proceeding to elaborate a more comprehensive conception for the passive-aggressive, the descriptive features noted in the DSM-III manual are recorded:

> The essential feature is a Personality Disorder in which there is resistance to demands for adequate performance in both occupational and social functioning; the resistance is expressed indirectly rather than directly. The consequence is pervasive and persistent social or occupational ineffectiveness, even when more self-assertive and effective behavior is possible. The name of this disorder is based on the assumption that such individuals are passively expressing covert aggression.
>
> Individuals with this disorder habitually resent and oppose demands to increase or maintain a given level of functioning. This occurs most clearly in work situations, but is also evident in social functioning. The resistance is expressed indirectly, through such maneuvers as procrastination, dawdling, stubbornness, intentional inefficiency, and "forgetfulness."
>
> The individual is ineffective both socially and occupationally because of the passive-resistant behavior....
>
> It is essential that this pattern of behavior occur in a variety of contexts in which more adaptive functioning is clearly possible.
>
> Often individuals with this disorder are dependent and lack self-confidence. Typically, they are pessimistic about the future but have no realization that their behavior is responsible for their difficulties. Although the individual may experience conscious resentment against authority figures, he or she never connects his or her passive-resistant behavior with his resentment. (p. 328)

Millon (1969) refers to this pattern as the "negativistic personality" to reflect this general contrariness and disinclination to doing things that others wish or expect of them. But beyond this passive-resistance there is a capricious impulsiveness, an irritable moodiness, a grumbling, discontented, sulky, unaccommodating, and fault-finding pessimism that characterizes their behaviors. They not only obstruct but dampen everyone's spirits as sullen malcontents and perennial complainers whose very presence demoralizes others. Although anguished and discontent with themselves, they never appear satisfied with others either. Even in the best of circumstances, they always seem to seek the "dark lining in the silver cloud." If they find themselves alone, they would prefer to be with others; if they are with others, they prefer to be alone. If someone gives them a gift, they dislike being obligated; if they fail to receive one, they feel slighted and rejected. If they are given a position of leadership, they complain bitterly about the lack of support they get from others; if they are not allowed to lead, they become critical and unsupporting of those who are.

HISTORICAL AND THEORETICAL ANTECEDENTS

The term "passive-aggressive personality" was first listed as part of the medical nomenclature in a War Department technical bulletin in 1945. Following a trial study of its utility in the Veterans Administration, it was formally introduced in the U.S. Joint Armed Services nosology in 1949. It was included next in the *Standard VA Classification* in 1951 as part of a new and broad category labeled "Character and Behavior Disorders," the first official recognition of the popular psychoanalytic designation *character disorder*. Character and behavior disorders subsumed two major syndromes: "Pathological Personalities" and "Immaturity Reactions." "Passive-aggressive" was listed among the latter group, along with "emotional instability," "passive-dependency," and "aggressive reaction." Guided by the VA nosology, the *Diagnostic and Statistical Manual of Mental Disorders* (DSM) developed by the American Psychiatric Association in 1952 included a passive-aggressive personality, differentiating it into three subtypes: a "pure" passive-aggressive, a passive-dependent, and an aggressive. Each of these types was considered a manifestation of the same underlying psychopathology and was ostensibly interchangeable in the same person. Although the 1968 edition (or second issue) of the DSM included a passive-aggressive type, it now took only one form; both passive-dependent and aggressive variants were dropped. The 1980 edition, or DSM-III, retains the earlier passive-aggressive personality, reactivates the passive-dependent type as a separate syndrome under the "dependent personality" label, and includes some aspects of the aggressive type as part of the antisocial personality description.

Although the passive-aggressive syndrome appears to be a prevalent disorder, its diagnostic reliability, as noted earlier, is extremely poor. Surprisingly, it has received rather scant theoretical and clinical attention despite having been listed in all three editions of the DSM. Tracing its ancestry and clinical forerunners proves to be a job of major proportions, requiring the uncovering of descriptively similar characterizations formulated under widely diverse syndrome labels. This worthy but comprehensive task is not attempted in this text. Rather a few clinical ancestors and a number of descriptively similar current conceptions are identified.

Clinicians inclined to biogenic explanations of psychopathology turn to the writings of Kraepelin, Bleuler, and Schneider most often for their hypotheses. What do these theorists offer us that is suggestive of the constellation of traits currently designated as the passive-aggressive personality? Kraepelin, for one, wrote about individuals with constitutions that incline them to behave in the characteristically ambivalent and contradictory manner that typifies the passive-aggressive. Employing the term "cyclothymia," first coined by Kahlbaum in the 1870s, Kraepelin (1913) referred to a depressively inclined variant as possessing "a special sensitiveness to the cares, troubles and disappointments of life. They take all things hard and feel the unpleasantness in every occurrence" (p. 219). Another variant of cyclothymia, those imbued with an irascible makeup, show "an extraordinary fluctuating emotional equilibrium and are strongly affected by all experiences, often in an unpleasant way" (p. 222).

Bleuler (1924) spoke of these personalities as being "irritable of mood" (*reizbare Verstimmung*), and Aschaffenburg (1922) described them as dissatisfied personalities who go through life as if they were perpetually wounded. Applying the lable "amphithymia," Hellpach (1920) depicted a similar pattern of fussy people who tend to be of a sour disposition, constantly fret over whatever they do, and make invidious and painful comparisons between themselves and those of a more cheerful inclination whose simpler and brighter outlook is both envied and decried. Of the constitutionalists, Schneider (1923) did best in capturing the essence of this personality type, whom he designated as "ill-tempered depressives." He summarized their prime features as follows:

> These tend to be cold, egotistical, morose and cantankerous. Sometimes also they are irritable and given to nagging and can be spiteful and malicious. They are doggedly pessimistic and rejoice when things go wrong. They are not given to wishing anyone well. (p. 81)

Theory-based "explanations" for these behaviors are to be found primarily in the writings of the early psychoanalysts. The clinical features of the passive-aggressive have been described in two different character types: the "oral sadistic melancholiac" and the "masochist." The first stems from ambivalences consequent to difficulties arising in the "oral biting" stage. That these consequences give rise to what has been called the "oral-sadistic" character, and that sadism and masochism are ostensibly two sides of the same coin, suggest the inevitable similarity between the two characterizations. The notion of the oral-sadistic, or melancholiac, character is discussed first.

It was Abraham (1924a) who first articulated a division of the oral stage into sucking and biting, with fixations arising at either substage and distinctive traits consequent to these fixations. In his initial descriptions, Abraham contrasted the clinical consequences of oral gratification with those who had been traumatized during the oral biting phase as follows: "The orally gratified person is identifying himself with the bounteous mother. Things are very different in the next, oral-sadistic stage, where envy, hostility, and jealousy make such behaviors impossible" (p. 398).

Since the theoretical framework that guides this chapter's clinical analysis is Millon's (1969) formulation of the "active-ambivalent" personality pattern, it is worthy of note that Abraham was the first to recognize that ambivalence was at the core of the oral-sadistic problem. Speaking of "melancholiacs," Abraham asserted that their moods and behaviors signified their effort to escape or otherwise deal with unresolved and deep rooted oral-sadistic ambivalence. He wrote as follows (1924b):

In the biting stage of the oral phase the individual incorporates the object in himself and in so doing destroys it.... It is in this stage that the ambivalent attitude of the ego to its object begins to grow up. We may say, therefore, that in the child's libidinal development the second stage, the oral sadistic phase, marks the beginning of its ambivalence conflict; whereas the first (sucking) stage should be regarded as pre-ambivalent.

The libidinal level, therefore, to which the melancholiac regresses after the loss of his object contains in itself a conflict of ambivalent feelings in its most primitive and therefore most unmodified form.... This ambivalent attitude remains inherent in the tendencies of the libido during subsequent phases of its development.... We meet this ambivalence everywhere in the patient's emotional life.

We are now in a position to understand why it is that the ambivalence of his instinctual life involves the melancholiac in quite especially grave conflicts which strike at the roots of his relation to his love-objects. The act of turning away from that original object round whom his whole emotional life revolved does not end there. It extends...finally to every human being. (pp. 451–453)

Menninger (1940) aptly portrayed the characteristic outlook and behavior of the oral-sadistic "melancholiac" in the following passage:

In the late oral stage the sadistic element of oral behavior develops. And this sadism in place of passive dependence makes the late oral-sadistic character in many ways the characterological opposite of the early oral character. The basic reaction is one of pessimistic distrust of the world. The world still owes the individual a living but instead of viewing it optimistically he is inclined to blame the world for everything unpleasant which happens to him. Instead of being easygoing, he is cantankerous, contemptuous, petulant. Instead of feeling that everything is right with the world, he is inclined to find everything wrong with it. Such individuals go through life making enemies instead of friends and constantly blame the other fellow for their shortcomings in accomplishment. Their social attitude is overdemanding and they are emotionally soured with the real world.... They become the perpetually discontented, moody people of unhappy temperament. (pp. 393–394)

The second line of psychoanalytic character depiction that can be viewed as a precursor to the passive-aggressive disorder is that known as the "masochistic" personality. Although the concepts of sadism and masochism were first formulated by Krafft-Ebing in his studies of psychopathologic sexual behavior in 1882, it was Freud and his disciples who developed a more contemporaneous explication of both phenomena. Prior to formulating his hypothesis that destructive behaviors are conceived best as derivatives of a death instinct, Freud referred to masochism as follows:

A child who behaves [with inexplicable naughtiness] is making a confession and trying to provoke punishment as a simultaneous means of setting his sense of guilt at rest and of satisfying his masochistic sexual trend. (1918, p. 28)

It was Reich (1933) who first conceptualized a comprehensive syndrome termed the "masochistic character," describing its essence as reflecting a passive form of aggression. The major traits he identified were:

a chronic, subjective feeling of *suffering* which is manifested objectively and especially stands out as a *tendency to complain.* Additional traits of the masochistic character are chronic tendencies to *inflict pain upon and to debase oneself* ("moral masochism") and an intense passion for tormenting others, from which the masochist suffers no less than his object. (1949, pp. 237-238)

A major feature of Reich's formulation of the masochist is the singular trait ascribed to the passive-aggressive in the DSM-III, that is, the disposition to obstruct others through passively provocative behaviors. Reflecting on the "infantile spite reaction" of one of his patients, Reich observed:

These provocations were attempts to make me strict and drive me into a frenzy.
It is not at all a question of punishment but of *putting* the analyst or his prototype, the parent, *in the wrong,* of causing him to act in a way which would give a rational foundation to the reproach "See how badly you are treating me."
There must be a meaning in the fact that the masochist provokes the analyst to put him in the wrong. The meaning is: "You are a bad person; you don't like me; on the contrary, you treat me horribly; I am right in hating you."
A deep *disappointment in love* lies behind the provocation. The masochist is especially fond of provoking those objects through whom he suffered a disappointment. Originally, these objects were intensely loved, and either an actual disappointment was experienced or the love demanded by the child was not sufficiently satisfied. (1949, pp. 242-243)

Reich's thesis of disappointment and disillusion is similar to formulations concerning other character types. What appears to distinguish the genesis of the masochistic pattern is the strategy the children acquired to spitefully "get back" at and torture their rejecting parents. Reich described this process by positing a series of hypothetical questions and patient responses. He illustrated the patient's complaint as follows:

"You see how miserable I am—love me!" "You don't love me enough—you are mean to me!" "You have to love me; I will force you to love me. If you don't love me, I'll make you angry!" The masochistic passion for torment, the complaints, the provocation, and the suffering can, in terms of their meaning— we shall discuss their dynamics later—be explained on the basis of the fantasized or actual non-fulfillment of a quantitatively inordinate demand for love.
The masochistic character seeks to bind the inner tension and threat of anxiety by an *inadequate* method, namely by *courting love through provocation and defiance.*

The defiance and the provocation are directed at the person who is loved and from whom love is demanded. In this way, the fear of losing love and attention is increased, just as the guilt feeling which one wants to be rid of is not diminished but intensified, for the beloved person is in fact tormented. This explains the extremely peculiar behavior of the masochist, who becomes more and more enmeshed in the situation of suffering, the more intensely he tries to extricate himself from it. (1949, pp. 245-246)

As will be evident in later detailed presentations of the passive-aggressive, Reich's conception of the masochistic character comes close to the mark.

Horney's formulation of "masochistic phenomena" bridges the theme of ambivalence first posited as central to these personalities by Abraham and the notion of spiteful suffering proposed by Reich. In her early writings on the subject, Horney noted (1939):

The masochist type despises himself for being dependent; because of his excessive expectations of his partner he is bound to become disappointed and resentful; he is bound to feel frequently unfairly treated. . . .

The conflict on the score of dependency is one between weakness and strength, between merging and self-assertion, between self-contempt and pride. . . .

The specific form of expressing wishes appears as a desperate cry . . . implying something like . . . "you have done me so much harm you are responsible for all my misery—you must do something for me."

The specifically masochistic way of expressing hostility is by suffering, helplessness, by the person representing himself as victimized and harmed.

The hostility . . . is not altogether merely defensive. It often has a sadistic character. . . . [It] springs from the vindictiveness of a weak and suppressed individual . . . who craves to feel that he too can subject others to his wishes and make them cringe. (pp. 261-263)

As noted earlier, the syndrome designated specifically as "the passive-aggressive personality" has stimulated few theoretical papers and research studies since its inclusion in the official nomenclature. However, two groups of recent investigators have surveyed its features and utility; their findings are briefly summarized next.

Whitman, Trosman, and Koenig (1954) studied a group of 62 patients diagnosed as passive-aggressive and compared their features to 338 other psychiatric outpatients. Despite differences, most patients showed "an intense ambivalent" relation to their parents and "came in complaining of anxiety." In deciphering the psychodymanics of their passive-aggressive behavior, Whitman et al. wrote:

When the aggression is inhibited by internal guilt or fear of external retaliation, regression to a dependent position occurs. This is revealed by passive behavior. Passive behavior may also be stimulated by inability to deal with the ambiguity of a role requirement. . . . The final step, dynamically, would be guilt over dependent needs . . . leading to pseudoaggression, the behavioral counter-

part being hostility. On the behavioral level, shame over a culturally unacceptable passive role leads to hostility. (p. 346)

In a more recent study (Small et al., 1970), 100 patients diagnosed as passive-
aggressive personalities were followed for periods of 7–15 years and compared
with matched controls. The investigators concluded their thoroughly detailed
study as follows:

> All of the investigators were impressed with...the subjects' ability to
> manipulate and misconstrue interpersonal situations. . . .
> Nevertheless, the majority of the subjects retained an active interest in
> interpersonal involvement. They were capable of giving and receiving affection,
> and most of their relatives and friends continued to hold them in esteem. In
> many instances this was despite frequent verbal battles and emotional outbursts,
> with the patients trying to influence and coerce others. The quality of the
> subjects' interactions with other people seemed to be intense, variable, and
> manipulative but with enduring relationships over long periods of time. . . .
> The illness was as likely to occur in males as in females and was characterized
> by interpersonal strife, verbal (not physical) aggressiveness, emotional storms,
> impulsivity, and manipulative behavior. Suicidal gestures and lack of attention
> to everyday responsibilities commonly accompanied this intensive style of
> relating. In both sexes there were prominent disturbances of affect, generally
> consisting of frequent, short-lived outbursts of anger or rage and often
> accompanied by tearfulness. (pp. 979–980)

Turning from the more psychodynamic approaches of the past several
decades, Klein and his associates (1969, 1973) have sought to identify
syndromal personality groups in terms of their pharmacologic response.
They consider the passive-aggressive type to be a dubious clinical entity,
providing an alternative in what they term the "emotionally unstable
character." The clinical features of the unstable character encompass characteristics that broaden the limited scope of the DSM passive-aggressive
portrayal. Their description stresses the likely biological instability and mood
lability of these patients, which consists of

> . . . short periods of tense, empty unhappiness, accompanied by inactivity,
> withdrawal, depression, irritability, and sulking, alternating suddenly with
> impulsiveness, giddiness, low frustration tolerance, rejection of rules, and
> shortsighted hedonism. . . .
> Patients with emotionally unstable personalities . . . are usually young, with a
> poorly developed conscience and generally immature attitudes, and are fre-
> quently irresponsible, hedonistic, extractive, and exploitive. Their marked
> affective lability is often not immediately noted as core pathology because of
> their complicated self-presentations. These range from a fragile, immature,
> dependent image, eliciting protectiveness from the observer, to a hard "wise
> guy" presentation expressing independence and lack of need for care. The
> patients are perplexed about their life goals, stating that they do not know who

they are, what they are, or what they want to be. They are also confused about issues of dependency, intimacy and self-assertion, often reacting in a disorganized, flighty, and despairing fashion. (1973, p. 186)

Descriptive material and diagnostic criteria for this personality syndrome were furnished by the author as the initial working draft for a "negativistic" syndrome; these were based on his theoretically derived "active-ambivalent pattern" (Millon, 1969). The features and criteria listed here encompass a broad range of characteristics reported in both the theoretical and research literature on the "emotionally unstable" and the "masochistic character," as well as recent reports on the "passive-aggressive;" hence the following includes features beyond those few noted in the final DSM-III draft. However, the breadth of this formulation is derived primarily by conceptualizing the features of this personality not only in terms of the "passiveness" of its aggression but as expressing the "activeness" of its ambivalence. The draft stated:

This pattern is typified by unpredictable moods, edgy irritability, social contrariness and a generally pessimistic outlook, notably the feeling of being cheated, misunderstood and unappreciated. An intense conflict between dependence and self-assertion contributes to an impulsive and quixotic emotionality. There is a pattern of sullen pouting, fault-finding, and stubbornness that is punctuated periodically by short-lived enthusiasms, angry outbursts and genuine expressions of guilt and contrition. Personal relationships are fraught with wrangles and disappointments, provoked often by the characteristic fretful, complaining and passive-aggressive behaviors.

Since adolescence or early adulthood at least 3 of the following have been present to a notably greater degree than in most people and were not limited to discrete periods nor necessarily prompted by stressful life events.

1. Irritable affectivity (e.g., is high-strung, quick-tempered and moody; reports being easily piqued and intolerant of frustration).

2. Behavioral contrariness (e.g., frequently exhibits passively-aggressive, obstinate, petulant, fault-finding and sulking behaviors; reveals a measure of gratification in demoralizing, obstructing and undermining the pleasures of others).

3. Discontented self-image (e.g., reports feeling misunderstood, unappreciated and demeaned by others; is characteristically pessimistic, disgruntled and disillusioned about life).

4. Deficient regulatory controls (e.g., fleeting thoughts and emotions are impulsively expressed in unmodulated form; external stimuli evoke rapid, capricious and fluctuating reactions).

5. Interpersonal ambivalence (e.g., conflicting and changing roles are assumed in social relationships, particularly dependent acquiescence and assertive independence; unpredictable and vacillating behaviors provoke edgy discomfort and exasperation in others).

CLINICAL PICTURE

This section discusses the central features of the so-called passive-aggressive pattern, detailing these characteristics in accord with the four levels of clinical analysis utilized in earlier chapters.

Behavioral Features

One of the problems that arise when focusing on the distinctive characteristics of a pathological personality type is that the reader is led to believe, incorrectly, that these individuals always display the features that have been described. This is not the case. Most personalities behave "normally" much of the time; that is, their behaviors are appropriate to the reality conditions of their environment. What a text such as this seeks to stress are those features that, by virtue of their frequency and intensity, *distinguish* certain personalities. Thus, "sullenness" may be used as a descriptor to characterize the passive-aggressive. But almost everyone behaves sullenly sometimes, and the passive-aggressive is not sullen much of the time. What distinguishes passive-aggressives is the ease with which they can be made to act in a sullen manner and the regularity with which this behavior is manifested. With this qualification in mind, the discussion turns to a description of the character-istic behaviors of this personality pattern. As noted earlier, the traits of the passive-aggressive are more broadly formulated here than in the DSM-III, and it is thereby conceptualized as a true personality syndrome. This extended formulation is guided primarily by the personality pattern described as the "active-ambivalent" or "negativistic" type by Millon (1969).

The personality pattern is best characterized by the rapid succession of changing behaviors and moods. Much of the time, these patients seem restless, unstable and erratic in their feelings. They are easily nettled, offended by trifles, and readily provoked into being sullen and contrary. There is often a low tolerance for frustration. Many are chronically impatient and irritable and fidgety unless things go their way. There are periods when they vacillate from being distraught and despondent at one moment, to being petty, spiteful, stubborn, and contentious, the next. At other times they may be enthusiastic and cheerful, but this mood is usually short lived. In no time, they are again disgruntled, critical, and envious. They often begrudge the good fortunes of others and are jealous, quarrelsome, and easily piqued by signs of indifference or minor slights. Emotions are "worn on their sleeves." Many are excitable and impulsive. Others suddenly burst into tears and guilt at the slightest upset. Still others often discharge anger or abuse at the least of provocations. The impulsive, unpredictable, and often explosive reactions of these personalities make it difficult for others to feel comfortable in their presence or to establish rewarding and enduring relationships with them. Although there will be periods of pleasant sociability and warm affection, most acquaintances of these personalities often feel "on edge," waiting for them to display a sullen and hurt look or become obstinate or nasty.

Self-Descriptions and Complaints

Passive-aggressives can be quite articulate in describing their subjective discomfort, but only rarely are they willing to explore or to admit any insights into its roots. In talking about their sensitivities and difficulties, they will not recognize that these reflect, in largest measure, their own inner conflicts and ambivalences. Self-reports alternate between preoccupations with personal inadequacies, bodily ailments, and guilt feelings, on the one hand, and social resentments, frustrations, and disillusionments, on the other. They will voice dismay about the sorry state of their life, their worries, their sadness, their disappointments, their "nervousness," and so on. Although most will express a desire to be rid of distress and difficulty, they seem unable, or perhaps unwilling, to find any solution.

Ambivalence characterizes the thinking of these persons. No sooner do they "see" the merits of approaching their problems one way than they find themselves saying, "but...." Fearful of committing themselves and unsure of their own desires or competencies, they find their thoughts shifting erratically from one solution to another. Because of their intense ambivalences, they often act precipitously, on the spur of the moment. Any other course for them would lead only to hesitation or vacillation, if not total immobility.

Passive-aggressives often assert that they have been trapped by fate, that nothing ever "works out" for them, and that whatever they desire runs aground. These negativistic persons express envy and resentment over the "easy life" of others. They are frequently critical and cynical with regard to what others have attained, yet covet these achievements themselves. Life, negativists claim, has been unkind to them. They feel cheated and unappreciated. Whatever they have done has been for naught. Their motives and behaviors have always been misunderstood and they are now bitterly disillusioned. The obstructiveness and pessimism that others have attributed to them are only a reflection, they feel, of their "sensitivity" or the pain they have suffered from physical disabilities or the inconsiderateness that others have shown toward them. But here again, the passive-aggressive's ambivalence intrudes. Perhaps, they say, it has all been a consequence of their own unworthiness, their own failures, and their own "bad temper." Maybe it is their own behavior that is the cause of their misery and the pain they have brought to others. Among these personalities, the ambivalent struggle between feeling guilt and feeling resentment permeates every facet of thought and behavior.

Inferred Intrapsychic Dynamics

A distinguishing clinical feature of passive-aggressives is their paucity of intrapsychic controls and mechanisms. Their moods, thoughts, and desires tend not to be worked out internally. Few unconscious processes are employed to handle the upsurge of feelings, and, as a consequence, these come readily to the surface, untransformed and unmoderated. These negativistic persons are like children in that they often react spontaneously and impulsively to passing emotions. As a result, there is little consistency and predictability to their reactions.

The behaviors of these overtly ambivalent personalities are even more erratic and vacillating than we might expect from their reinforcement history. They appear to have labored under a double handicap. Not only were they deprived of external consistency and control in childhood but, as a consequence of these experiences, never acquired the motivation and competencies of internal control. Unsure of what their environment expects of them and unable themselves to impose self-discipline and order, these persons seem adrift in their environment, bobbing up and down erratically from one mood to another.

As noted, these individuals failed to experience consistent parental discipline. What they did learn was through implicit modeling. In essence, they learned to copy the contradictory or capricious style of their parents. Deprived of conditions for acquiring self-control and modeling themselves after their opposing or erratic and ambivalent parents, these personalities never learn to conceal their moods for long and cannot bind or transform their emotions. Whatever inner feelings well up within them—be it guilt, anger, or inferiority—they spill quickly to the surface in pure and direct form.

This weakness of intrapsychic control would not prove troublesome if their feelings were calm and consistent, but they are not. Rooted in deep personal ambivalences, passive-aggressives experience an undercurrent of perpetual inner turmoil and anxiety. Their equilibrium is unstable. Their inability to anticipate the future as consistent or predictable gives rise to a constant state of insecurity. The frustration and confusion they feel turn readily to anger and resentment. Guilt often emerges and frequently serves to curtail this anger. In short, the actively ambivalent suffers a range of intense and conflicting emotions that, because of weak controls and lack of self-discipline, surge quickly and capriciously to the surface. The confusion of feelings that this creates is paralleled by a variety of erratic and contradictory mechanisms. Sometimes patients will turn their externally directed, hostile feelings back toward themselves, a mechanism termed by some as *introjection*, the converse of *projection*. For example, hatred felt toward others may be directed toward self, taking the form of guilt or self-condemnation. True to form, however, the passive-aggressive will alternate between introjection and projection. At one time, by projection, these persons will ascribe their destructive impulses to others, accusing the others, unjustly, of being malicious and unkind to them. At other times, by introjection, they will reverse the sequence, accusing themselves of faults that justifiably should be ascribed to others.

Thus, even in the use of unconscious mechanisms, the passive-aggressive behaves in an erratic and contradictory manner. Those at the receiving end of these seemingly bizarre intrapsychic processes cannot help but conclude that the person is behaving in an irrational manner and engaging in uncalled for outbursts and emotional inconsistencies.

Interpersonal Coping Style

Most persons acquire styles of relating to others that enable them to achieve an optimal level of satisfaction and security, as well as to maintain a reasonable degree of self-harmony. So-called normals may be differentiated from pathological personalities by the variety and character of the strategies they employ to achieve these goals. Healthy personalities draw upon their strategies flexibly as they face changing demands and pressures. Psychologically impaired individuals, however, tend to be inflexible. They approach different events as if they were the same and utilize the same strategies they acquired in childhood, even though these are presently inappropriate. Once having learned a particular style that has worked for them, it continues to be used as if it were a sacred rulebook for navigating the future.

The problem that faces passive-aggressives is quite different from that of most pathological personalities. Their difficulties stem *not* from the rigid character of their coping style but from its exaggerated fluidity. They are actively and overtly ambivalent, unable to find a satisfactory direction or course for their behavior. They vacillate and cannot decide whether to be dependent or independent of others and whether to respond to events actively or passively. Their dilemmas do not arise from an overcommitment to one strategy but from a lack of commitment. As a consequence, they vacillate indecisively in a tortuous and erratic manner from one mood and one course of action to another. They behave by fits and starts, shifting capriciously down a path that leads nowhere and precipitates them into endless wrangles with others and disappointments with themselves.

It would appear from the foregoing that the ambivalence and erratic course of the passive-aggressive would fail to provide the individual with any satisfactions or security. If this were the case, we would expect them to decompensate quickly. Few do. Hence, we are forced to inquire as to what gains and supports these individuals do achieve in the course of behaving in their vacillating and ambivalent manner.

Quite simply, being "difficult," quixotic, unpredictable, and discontent will produce certain rewards and avoid certain discomforts. The following are examples, drawn from the sphere of marital life, of the ingenious, though unconscious, mechanisms these personalites employ.

A passive-aggressive man, who is unwilling or unable to decide whether to "grow up" or remain a "child," explodes emotionally whenever his wife expects "too much" of him. Afterward, he expresses guilt, becomes contrite, and pleads forbearance on her part. By turning toward self-condemnation, he evokes her sympathy, restrains her from making undue demands, and maneuvers her into placating rather than criticizing him.

A woman, feeling the ambivalence of both love and hate for her husband, complains bitterly about his loss of interest in her as a woman. To prove his affections, he suggests that they go on a "second honeymoon," that is, take a vacation without the children. To this proposal, she replies that his plan only proves that he is a foolish spendthrift; in the same breath, however, she insists that the children come along. No matter what he does, he is wrong. She has not only trapped him but confused him as well. Her ambivalence maneuvers him, first one way and then the other. It forces him to be on edge, always alert to avoid situations that might provoke her ire, yet he can never quite be sure that he has succeeded.

The passive-aggressive's strategy of negativism, of being discontent and unpredictable, of being both seductive and rejecting, and of being demanding and then dissatisfied, is an effective weapon not only with an intimidated or pliant partner but with people in general. Switching among the roles of the martyr, the affronted, the aggrieved, the misunderstood, the contrite, the guilt-ridden, the sickly, and the overworked, is a tactic of interpersonal behavior that gains passive-aggressives the attention, reassurance, and dependency they crave while, at the same time, allowing them to subtly vent their angers and resentments. For all its seeming ineffectuality, vacillation recruits affection and support, on the one hand, and provides a means of discharging the tensions of frustration and hostility, on the other. Interspersed with self-deprecation and contrition, acts that relieve unconscious guilt and serve to solicit forgiveness and reassuring comments from others, this actively ambivalent strategy proves not to be a total failure at all.

ASSOCIATED DISORDERS

As in previous chapters this section outlines the major Axis I and Axis II disorders that frequently covary with the personality type under discussion. Similarly, matters of differential diagnosis are touched upon briefly.

Concomitant Axis I Symptoms

Anxiety disorders.   Passive-aggressive personalities experience prolonged and *generalized anxiety* disorders. In contrast to compulsive personalities, their passive-ambivalent counterparts, their discomfort and tension are exhibited openly and are utilized rather commonly as a means of either upsetting others or soliciting their attention and nurture. Which of these two instrumental aims takes precedence depends on whether the obedient-dependent or the defiant-independent facet of their ambivalence comes to the fore. Typically, passive-aggressives color their apprehensions with depressive complaints, usually to the effect that others misunderstand them and that life has been full of disappointments. These complaints not only crystallize and vent their tensions but are also subtle forms of expressing anger and resentment. Most commonly, passive-aggressives discharge their tensions in brief and frequent doses, thereby decreasing the likelihood of a significant, cumulative buildup and a consequent massive outburst. It is only when these negativistic persons are unable to discharge their inner anguish and hostile impulses that a full-blown *panic* attack may be precipitated. Having learned to utilize anxiety as a means of subtle aggression or as a way of gaining attention and nurture, some passive-aggressives claim to be experiencing anxiety when they are not genuinely feeling it.

Phobic disorders. As indicated, these personalities are more open about discharging their feelings than most other personality types. This ready and diffuse discharge of emotion has its self-defeating side. By connecting anxieties freely to any and all aspects of their life, they increase the likelihood that many, formerly innocuous, experiences and events will be fused with phobic qualities. These phobic symptoms may then be utilized for secondary gains, being employed to attract attention and to control or manipulate the lives of others.

Psychosomatic disorders. Among the principal origins of psychosomatic disorders (termed "psychological factors affecting physical conditions" in the DSM-III) are repetitive upsets of the body's homeostatic balance and chronic failures to dissipate physiological tension. These problems arise most frequently in patients who repeatedly find themselves in unresolvable conflict situations, such as when the discharge of tensions associated with one side of a conflict only increases the tensions engendered by the other side. This state of affairs describes the typical experience of ambivalent personalities. Both compulsives and passive-aggressives are trapped between acquiescent dependency, on the one hand, and hostile or assertive independence, on the other. When they submit or acquiesce to the wishes of others, they experience resentment and anger for having allowed themselves to be "weak" and having given up their independence. Conversely, if they are defiant and assert their independence, they experience anxiety for having endangered their tenuous dependency security. Although passive-aggressives do periodically discharge both sources of tension, their repetitive and chronically irritable behaviors reactivate these troublesome conflicts time and again. As a consequence, they often generate and accumulate tension faster than they can dissipate it. Moreover, because of their constantly fretful behaviors, their bodies are subjected repeatedly to vacillations in mood and emotion. As they swing from one intense feeling to another, their homeostatic equilibrium, so necessary for proper physiological functioning, is thrown off balance again and again. Not only do they experience an excess of chronic tension, then, but their systems rarely settle down into a smooth and regularized pattern. By keeping their bodies churning, they set themselves up for repeated bouts of psychosomatic discomfort.

Somatoform disorders. These negativistic personalities often display *hypochondriacal* and *somatization* symptoms in conjunction with their frequent psychosomatic disorders. Discontent, irritable, and fractious, they often use physical complaints as a weak disguise for hostile impulses, a veil to cloak their deeply felt anger and resentment. Feelings of retribution for past frustrations often underlie the excessive demands they make for special treatment. They seek not only to create guilt in others but to control the lives of family members and to cause them grief and financial cost. Although a significant proportion of these personalities were subjected in childhood to inconsistent parental treatment, most learned that they could evoke reliable parental attention and support when they were ill or when they complained of illness. As a consequence, when they need care and nurture, they may revert back to the ploy of physical complaints. Some may be sufficiently aware of the maneuvers they engage in so as to be justly diagnosed as exhibiting a *factitious disorder*. Others, less successful in evoking the care and sympathy they desire, have learned to nurture themselves, that is, to tend symbolically to their own bodily needs. Disillusioned by parental disinterest or inconsistency, these patients have learned to provide a hypochondriacal ministering to themselves, ensuring thereby a consistency in self-sympathy and self-gratification that can be obtained from no one else.

Because these personalities express their feelings rather openly and directly, tension builds up more slowly than in their passive ambivalent counterpart, the compulsive personality. Moreover, when emotional tension is discharged, it is less likely to be camouflaged. Thus, *conversion symptoms* among passive-aggressives are exhibited in fleeting or transitory forms such as intestinal spasms, facial tics, or laryngitis. Symptoms of this type often signify sporadic efforts to control anger and resentment. "Trained" to use physical ailments as instruments for manipulating others, their complaints of vague sensations and pains are designed in part to draw attention and nurturance, as well as to create concern and guilt in others.

Dissociative disorders. Accustomed to venting their contrary feelings quite directly, passive-aggressives exhibit dissociative symptoms only if they feel unduly restrained, shamed, or fearful of severe condemnation. Even under these circumstances, the frequency of dissociative disorders is low. Temper tantrums, which approach frenzied states in their overt appearance, are more common. However, in these episodes the patient rarely loses conscious awareness and is usually able to recall the events that transpired.

Affective disorders. These disorders are quite common among passive-aggressive personalities, ranging from occasional severe depressive episodes to more chronic forms of *dysthymic disorder*. Similarly, *cyclothymic disorders* with brief manic periods are not uncommon. Most frequently, passive-aggressive personalities display an agitated form of dysphoria. They characteristically vacillate between anxious futility, despair, and self-deprecation, on the one hand; and a bitter discontent and demanding irritability with friends and relatives, on the other. Accustomed to the direct ventilation of feelings, these personalities restrain their anger and turn it inward only when they fear its expression will result in severe humiliation or rejection. There is a great struggle between acting out defiantly and curtailing resentments. They exhibit as grumbling and sour a disaffection with themselves as they do with others. Moody complaints and generalized pessimism pervade the air. These attitudes serve as a vehicle of tension discharge, relieving them periodically of mounting inner- and outer-directed anger. Not to be overlooked also is the fact that sour moods and complaints often intimidate and make others feel guilty. These maneuvers enable the passive-aggressive to gain a measure of retribution for past disappointments by making life miserable for others.

Concurrent Axis II Personalities

In contrast to the DSM-III formulation, the passive-aggressive personality is conceived in this text as a comprehensive pattern of traits that will often overlap and combine as elements of other personality disorders. As such, we should anticipate finding amalgams and mixtures that display the features of two or more personalities. Research and multivariate cluster analyses with the MCMI (Millon, 1977) provide considerable data concerning the most prevalent of these personality combinations. These studies show that the passive-aggressive personality covaries most frequently with the DSM histrionic and borderline types.

Passive-aggressive-histrionic mixed personality.
This combination is seen most commonly among female patients in private practice settings and family agencies; among males it occurs with some frequency in drug rehabilitation programs. The following MCMI computer-generated interpretation was derived from the response of a 36-year-old married woman with two young children who recently began treatment in a psychoanalytically oriented private practice setting.

> The patient's behavior is typified by a high degree of emotional lability and short periods of impulsive acting out, alternating with depressive complaints, moodiness, and sulking. Notable also are hypersensitivity to criticism, a low frustration tolerance, immature behaviors, short-sighted hedonism, and a seeking of excitement and stimulation. Emotions surge readily to the surface, untransformed and unmoderated, evident in a distractible, flighty, and erratic style of behavior. Whatever inner feelings she may sense, be they guilt, anger, or desire spill quickly to the surface in pure and direct form.
>
> Moods tend to be brittle and variable with periods of high excitement and affability alternating with a leaden paralysis, fatigue, oversleeping, overeating, and an overuse of alcohol. She displays short-lived, dramatic, and superficial affects, reporting a tendency to be easily excited and then quickly bored. Mood levels are highly reactive to external stimulation. Feelings of desperation or euphoria are expressed histrionically and more intensely than justified by the situation. The patient behaves by fits and starts, shifting capriciously down a path that appears to lead nowhere, often precipitating wrangles with others and disappointments for self.

Cut off from needed external attentions, the patient may engage either in a frantic search for approval, become easily nettled and contentious, or become dejected and forlorn. There may be extreme cyclical swings, alternating periods of simulated euphoria and illusory excitements, intermingled with moments of hopelessness and self-condemnation. There are frequent depressive complaints, usually to the effect that others misunderstand her and that life has been full of disappointments. She may become disgruntled, critical, and envious of others, grudging their good fortunes with a jealous, quarrelsome, and irritable reaction to minor slights. There may be an unusual preoccupation with bodily functions and health, an overreaction to illness, and unreasonable complaints about minor ailments. Symptoms may be displayed exhibitionistically to gain attention and support.

Passive-aggressive-borderline mixed personality. The second most frequent profile was composed of the passive-aggressive–borderline combination. Here, the more severe features of the borderline tend to accentuate the moodiness and behavioral unpredictability that characterize the passive-aggressive. MCMI research suggests that this pattern may frequently be found among younger (Vietnam) veterans seen in VA mental hygiene clinics, chronic alcoholic patients "drying out" in jails and "stockades," and female psychiatric patients at half-way houses and day-care centers. The following narrative is taken from an MCMI computer report based on the responses of a 28-year-old divorced Vietnam veteran attending a weekly VA outpatient "medication" group treatment program.

The patient's behavior is typified by highly variable and unpredictable moods, an embittered and resentful irritability, and an untrusting and pessimistic outlook, notably the feelings of having been cheated, misunderstood, and unappreciated. An intense conflict between dependency and self-assertion contributes to an impulsive and quixotic emotionality. He exhibits deficient regulatory controls with fleeting thoughts and emotions impulsively expressed in unmodulated form and external stimuli evoking capricious and vacillating reactions. There is a pattern of negativism, sullen pouting, fault finding, and stubborneess that is punctuated periodically by short-lived enthusiasms, belligerent, and querulous outbursts and expressions of guilt and contrition.

The patient anticipates being disillusioned in relationships with others and often precipitates disappointments through obstructive behaviors. Though desperately seeking closeness and intimacy, he is deeply untrusting and fearful of domination, resists external influence, and is suspiciously alert to efforts that might undermine self-determination and autonomy. Personal relationships are fraught with wrangles and antagonisms, provoked often by his bitter complaining, passive-aggressive behaviors, touchiness, and characteristic irascible demeanor. The struggle between feelings of resentment and guilt, and the conflict over dependency and self-assertion permeate all aspects of his life.

The patient displays an unpredictable and rapid succession of moods, is invariably dysphoric in affect, seems restless, and is capricious and erratic in the expression of feelings. There is a tendency to be easily nettled, offended by trifles, and readily provoked into being fretful, contrary, and hostile. There is a low tolerance for frustration and he is impatient and fractious unless things go as desired. He will vacillate between being distraught and despondent, at one time; and being irrationally negativistic, petty, spiteful, and contentious, another. His disputatious and abrasive irritability precipitates exasperation in others, leading them to stereotype him as a person who dampens everyone's spirits, a perennial malcontent whose very presence demoralizes and obstructs the pleasures of others. There is a struggle between acting out and curtailing resentments. The sulking and unpredictable "blowing hot and cold" behaviors prompt others into reacting in a parallel capricious and inconsistent manner, causing them to weary quickly of him. As a result, he reports feeling misunderstood and unappreciated, at one time, and turning inward, expressing self-condemnation, the next.

The patient is overly sensitive to the attitudes of others, exhibiting an agitated defensiveness and brooding suspiciousness. Others are often seen as devious and hostile, and he repeatedly distorts their incidental remarks so as to appear deprecating and vilifying. He hesitates displaying weakness lest these be fatal concessions that will be misused by the malice anticipated from others. There is an alert vigilance against the possibility of attack or derogation, a defensive stance from which he can react at the slightest hint of threat. Feelings of retribution for past mistreatment underlie his hostility, envy and, suspiciousness. Unfortunately, these behaviors often set into motion a self-fulfilling prophesy, driving away potential well-wishers and creating unnecessary frictions, which are then seen by him as proof and justification for suspicion and hostility.

Differential Diagnostic Signs

Conceived in the broad sense in which the passive-aggressive is formulated here, the traits comprising this pattern share innumerable features with other symptom and personality disorders. Thus, the moodiness of this personality is a central feature of most affective disorders; the quick-tempered irritability and behavioral contrariness that characterize passive-aggressives are also found among antisocial types; the self-discontent and interpersonal ambivalence of this pattern are matched by the low self-esteem and conflicting attitudes toward others that typify avoidant personalities. In fact, it is the variegated, complex, inconstant, and erratic quality that is so unusual about the passive-aggressive. It is alone among the personality syndromes in that it possesses the entire mixture of traits seen more consistently and with less diversity among other types. This very heterogeneity and changeability are its distinguishing hallmarks.

It is in this last regard, the characteristic irregularity of mood and behavior, that the passive-aggressive, or what the author prefers to call the "active ambivalent" (Millon, 1969), may require differentiation from the DSM-III *cyclothymic disorder*. Both are "chronic," display either alternate or intermixed periods of intense affect that fail to approach psychotic proportions, and rarely, if ever, exhibit features such as delusions, hallucinations, or incoherence. There are two essential distinctions: first, the lifelong and consistent character of the personality pattern (passive-aggressive), which differs from the episodic and discontinuous nature of the disorder (cyclothymic); and second, the persistently negative tone of the passive-aggressive, as contrasted to the periodic manic or euphoric phases of the cyclothymic. A distinction may also be needed to differentiate the passive-aggressive's pessimistic and negative tone from that seen in the DSM-III *dysthymic disorder*, previously termed the "depressive neurosis." Both share a measure of chronicity, but the personality pattern is both more consistent and of greater duration. More significantly, the passive-aggressive exhibits a persistent resentful quality in interpersonal relations, a bitter, complaining, and quarrelsome irritability that is not evident in the down-in-the-dumps, more melancholic, and sad quality seen in the dysthymic syndrome. As encouraged in the multiaxial DSM-III format, concurrent diagnoses of Axis I and Axis II syndromes should be recorded if appropriate.

PREDISPOSING BACKGROUND

As noted in earlier chapters, under this topic a number of plausible etiologic hypotheses are proposed for the personality under study. The reader should be well conditioned by now to the highly conjectural nature of several of the speculations posited.

Hypothesized Biogenic Factors

Passive-aggressives do not exhibit a distinctive or characteristic level of biologic activation. There is reason, however, to believe that they may possess an intrinsic irritability or hyperreactivity to stimulation. They seem easily aroused, testy, high-strung, thin-skinned, and quick-tempered. Minor events provoke and chafe them. They become inflamed and aggrieved by the most incidental and insignificant acts of others. Of course, these hypersensitivities could stem from adverse experiences as well as constitutional proclivities. We may speculate further that these personalities possess some unusual mixture of temperaments. Their behavioral ambivalences may reflect the back-and-forth workings of conflicting dispositions and result in the erratic and contradictory emotional reactions they characteristically display. The reader must note that there is no substantive evidence to warrant placing confidence in these biogenic conjectures.

Passive-aggressive features are often observed among family members. Similarities such as these can arise, of course, entirely from the effects of shared experience and learning. But it is not unreasonable to propose that the biophysical substrate for affective irritability and for a sullen, pouting, and testy temperament may be transmitted by genetic mechanisms.

Along another line of speculation, a disproportionately high number of "difficult-to-schedule" infants may continue to exhibit their "biologically erratic" pattern throughout their lives and thereby be disposed to develop the features of ambivalence that characterize passive-aggressive personalities. Such fretful and "nervous" youngsters are good candidates for this pattern also because they are likely to provoke bewilderment, confusion, and vacillation in their parents. Thus, "irregular" children may set into motion erratic and contradictory reactions from parents that serve, in circular fashion, to reinforce their initial tendency to be spasmodic and variable.

Another biogenic source may be found in children who mature in an unbalanced progression or at an uneven rate. As with the difficult-to-schedule and erratic youngsters, they are likely to evoke inconsistent reactions from their parents more often than normally developing children. For example, "very bright" but "emotionally immature" youngsters may precipitate anger in response to the "childish" dimensions of their behavior but commendation in response to the "cleverness" they displayed while behaving childishly. Such children may very well become confused as to whether to continue or to inhibit their behavior since the reactions it prompted were contradictory. Similarly, precocious children may possess "immature" aptitudes and aspirations but lack the encouragement or opportunities to achieve these goals. This can lead to repetitive feelings of disappointment, a feature not dissimilar from the characteristic discontent of the passive-aggressive.

Turning to neurological and physiochemical hypotheses, it is conceivable that the affective excitability of this personality may arise from high reticular activity or sympathetic system dominance. Also speculative, but plausible, are proposals that implicate segments of the limbic system. Anatomically dense or well-branched neural pathways that subserve different and discordant emotions such as "anger," "sadness," and "fear" could underlie the ambivalent behaviors seen in this pattern. Of interest in this regard are recent suggestions that an "ambivalence" center may exist in the limbic region.

Data obtained in the development of the MCMI (Millon, 1977) suggest that the negativistic or passive-aggressive personality pattern is judged somewhat more prevalent among women than among men. Although speculative as a thesis, women may be subject to hormonal changes during their menstrual cycles that regularly activate marked, short-lived, and variable moods. Rapid changes in affect such as these may set into motion erratic behaviors and interpersonal reactions that lead to both the acquisition and perpetuation of an actively ambivalent personality pattern. No less plausible an explanation is that negative and obstreperous traits among men are judged as "tough-mindedness," where these very same characteristics among women are viewed as "bitchy" and "passive-aggressive." Note again that conjectures such as these are unconfirmed speculations.

Characteristic Experiential History

Although biogenic influences may dispose an individual to certain behaviors, the clinical pattern we observe is largely the result of the repetitive environmental influences to which the person was exposed.

The primary role of contradictory parental attitudes and inconsistent training methods in this personality pattern has been referred to often in this discussion. Every child experiences some degree of parental inconstancy, but future passive-aggressives have been exposed to appreciably more than their share. Their parents may have been in deep and continuing conflict regarding their attitude toward and handling of these children. The parents may have been quite different from each other in their own personality styles, thereby providing highly divergent and contradictory models for vicarious learning. They may have been inconsistent themselves, having swayed from hostility and rejection, at one time, to affection and love, at another. Each of these conflicting or erratic attitudes and models was experienced frequently, was pronounced in impact, and was present since early life.

As a result of these experiences, future passive-aggressives develop a variety of pervasive and deeply ingrained conflicts such as trust versus mistrust, competence versus doubt, and initiative versus guilt and fear. Their concept of self is composed of contradictory appraisals. Whatever judgment they make of themselves is likely to be matched by an opposing one. Is he/she a good person or bad; is he/she competent or incompetent? Every aspect of the behavior of these children is likely to have its positive and its negative side. No matter what they do or what they think, they will experience a contrary inclination or value by which to judge it.

The ambivalence that exists within passive-aggressives is compounded by their inability to gauge what to expect from the environment. How do they know when things are going well? Have they not experienced a capricious hostility in the past when things appeared to be fine? Such a child is terribly bewildered. Unlike the avoidant and the antisocial personalities, who "know" they will experience consistent humiliation or hostility, passive-aggressives are unable to predict what the future will bring. At any moment, and for no apparent reason, they may experience the kindness and support they crave. Even more probable, and for equally unfathomable reasons, they may be the recipients of hostility and rejection. They feel trapped in that they have no way of knowing which course of action on their part will bring them relief. Moreover, they have never learned to predict whether obedience or defiance will be instrumentally more effective. They vacillate; they are hostile, compliant, feel guilty, and so on, shifting erratically and impulsively from one futile action to another. Unable to anticipate what reactions their behaviors will elicit and having learned no way of reliably predicting whether the parents will be critical or affectionate, they can take nothing for granted. Thus, perverse as it may seem, they must be ready for hostility when most people would expect commendation and must assume humiliation when most would anticipate reward. They are eternally "on edge," in a state of continuous tension and alertness. Keyed up in this way, emotions build until such a child is "raw to the touch," overready to react explosively and erratically at the slightest of provocations.

The effects of contradictory and inconsistent parental behaviors may be summarized as follows. First, these children learn vicariously and unconsciously to imitate their parents' erratic, capricious, or conflicting actions and attitudes. Second, they fail to learn what behaviors will "pay off"; that is, they cannot develop a consistent and reliable strategy to achieve the rewards and security they seek. Third, they internalize conflicting attitudes toward themselves and others; for example, they do not know whether to think of themselves as competent or incompetent and are unsure as to whether they love or hate those upon whom they depend. Fourth, unable to anticipate the consequences of their actions, they get "tied up in emotional knots" and behave erratically and impulsively.

Second in importance only to parental behavioral inconsistency are styles of intrafamilial communication that transmit conflicting and incompatible messages. Such families may present a facade of mutuality that cloaks and serves to control hidden resentments and antagonisms. Thus, parents who smile and say "yes, dear" may convey through their facial expression and overly sweet tone of voice that they really mean "no, you miserable child." Expressions of concern and affection may be negated and undone in subtle and devious ways. Such parents may verbally assert their love for the child and thereby invite the child to demonstrate reciprocal affection, but they always seem to find some excuse to forestall or rebuff the affectionate response. Children in such settings are forced constantly into what are termed *approach-avoidance conflicts*. They are never sure what their parents really desire, and no matter what action they take, they find they cannot do right. Trapped in this double-bind, the children are unable not only to find a clear direction for their behavior but to extricate themselves from the irreconcilable demands that are made of them. This bind is often compounded by the fact that contradictions in parental messages are subtle or concealed. Thus, these children cannot chance accusing their parents of failing to mean what they say since there is no objective evidence to justify such an accusation. And not insignificantly, the consequences of accusing one's parents of dishonesty or deception are likely to be rather severe. Unable to discriminate a clear intent in these communications and fearful of misinterpreting them, the children may not only become confused and anxious, but they may learn through modeling to become equally equivocal and ambivalent in their own thinking and actions.

Paradoxical and contradictory parental behaviors are often found in "schismatic" families, that is, families where parents are manifestly in conflict with each other. In addition to their constant bickering, there is an undermining of one parent by the other through disqualifying and contradicting statements. Children brought up in this setting not only suffer the constant threat of family dissolution but, in addition, are often forced to serve as a mediator to moderate the tensions their parents generate. The children may be forced to switch sides and divide their loyalties from one moment to the next. They find that they are not free to be "themselves," for they must shift their attitudes and emotions to satisfy changing and antagonistic parental desires and expectations. Moreover, the different roles they must assume to placate their parents and to salvage a measure of family stability are markedly divergent. As long as the parents remain at odds, the children's behaviors and thoughts are likely to continue to be ambivalent and irreconcilable. A major consequence is that a child cannot identify consistently with one parent. These children end up modeling themselves after two intrinsically antagonistic figures and, hence, internalize opposing sets of attitudes, emotions, and behaviors. Rather sadly, schismatic families are ideal training grounds for the development of an actively ambivalent personality pattern.

Schismatic families also generate considerable anxiety and guilt in children. Not only are these youngsters in constant dread that the affections and supports of family life will dissolve, but they are often made to feel guilty for their contribution to its difficulties. To add insult to injury, they cannot help but feel dishonest and disloyal when forced to ally themselves first with one parent and then the other. Guilt and anxiety, internal influences that lead to behavior hesitation and to ambivalences in attitude and feeling, are produced also in nonschismatic families. Children can learn these emotional constraints through direct parental tuition. They may be taught to have an implacable inner "conscience" by which to gauge the "correctness" of their every behavior and thought. Methods of inculcating guilt and shame are outlined in the earlier discussion of the compulsive personality, the other ambivalent personality pattern. There is one significant difference. The future compulsive is likely to have been taught guilt in a consistent and unyielding manner, whereas the future passive-aggressive experiences such training more irregularly. Thus, the guilt of the "active" ambivalent, or passive-aggressive, personality is less firmly ingrained than in the "passive" ambivalent, or compulsive, personality. As a result, guilt often fails in its control function, and active-ambivalents "give in" frequently to their impulses. Their ambivalence is often seen in a vacillation between acting out, one moment, and feeling guilty, the next.

There is another feature that may be found with more than usual frequency in the background history of this personality. Many passive-aggressives report that they felt "replaced" by a younger sibling, and that parental affections were consequently withdrawn and redirected to a newborn child. Sibling competitions are, of course, experienced by many children, and what distinguishes the future passive-aggressive youngster, other than the frequency of such reporting, is not clear. A plausible thesis is that they experienced a marked change between earlier feelings of genuine parental security and its sudden termination upon the birth of the newborn child. Not uncommonly, mothers become overly preoccupied and attached to their "babies," often at the expense of older children. Children who previously experienced a deep bond with their mothers are likely to become severely upset with the advent of a new sib. This event may prove so distressing as to result in a deeply etched feeling that affections and security are not durable and that one must anticipate losing tomorrow what seemed so safe today.

It may be of interest to speculate as to how an event such as this would promote a passive-aggressive personality pattern. Surely, the shock of being "replaced" could create intense anxieties and strong feelings of jealousy and resentment. Children are likely, however, to hesitate in venting these feelings for fear of provoking more of the parental withdrawal they have already experienced. Moreover, these children may have been reprimanded and made to feel guilty for expressing envious feelings and occasional angry outbursts. As a result, "replaced" youngsters are likely to learn to "be sweet" and restrain their resentments when the parents are present but be "sneaky" and hostile when the parents are absent. This ambivalence and erraticism in dealing with feelings toward the sibling may become a prototype for later relationships. This is seen in certain repetitive sequences through which these personalities proceed in many of their social relationships. At first, there is a friendly, even overly enthusiastic, early association, followed by disappointment and hard feelings. They become attached to new and "marvelous" friends, only to find them "untrustworthy and disloyal" in short order. As they move from one social community or group to another, early enthusiasms quickly deteriorate into disillusionment and animosity.

Contributing further to ambivalence is the fact that these "replaced" children often are told how rewarding it is to "be a big brother or sister." It is all too clear, however, that "baby" gets almost all of mother's attention and affection. As a consequence, these children are forced into another bind. Should they grow up and get the dubious rewards of being an older child or should they remain "immature" and try to recapture the idyllic state of infancy? This conflict contributes further to the development of their ambivalence: to be assertively independent or to be clingingly dependent.

PROGNOSTIC IMPLICATIONS

Most pathological personalities feel some measure of stability and self-content with the life-style they have acquired. This is not typical among passive-aggressive personalities. Their feelings, attitudes, and behaviors allow for little internal equilibrium or consistent external gratification. They frequently live in a phenomenological state of discontent and self-dissatisfaction. Their irritability provokes them to behave unpredictably and to appear restless, sullen, and obstructive much of the time. Not only do they suffer an ever-present sense of inner turmoil, but they act out their discontent for all to see.

Perpetuation of the Passive-Aggressive Pattern

The following sections describe three aspects of the passive-aggressive style that perpetuate and intensify the troublesome behaviors and attitudes acquired in childhood.

Negativistic and unpredictable behaviors. Acting erratically, vacillating from one course to another, is a sheer waste of energy. By attempting to achieve incompatible goals, these persons scatter their efforts and dilute their effectiveness. Caught in their own crosscurrents, they cannot commit themselves to one clear direction, swinging indecisively back and forth, performing ineffectually, and experiencing a sense of paralyzing inertia or exhaustion.

In addition to the wasteful nature of ambivalence, passive-aggressives may actively impede their own progress toward conflict resolution and goal attainment. Thus, they frequently undo what good they previously had done. Driven by contrary feelings, they retract their "kind words" to others and replace them with harshness, or they undermine achievements they struggled so hard to attain. In short, their ambivalence often robs them of what few steps they secured toward progress. This inconstant "blowing hot and cold" behavior precipitates others into reacting in a parallel capricious and inconsistent manner. By prompting these reactions, passive-aggressives re-create the very conditions of their childhood that fostered the development of their unstable behaviors in the first place.

Most people weary of the sulking and stubborn unpredictability of these actively ambivalent personalities. Others are frequently goaded into exasperation and confusion when their persistent efforts to placate the passive-aggressive so frequently meet with failure. Eventually, everyone is likely to express both anger and disaffiliation, reactions that serve then only to intensify the passive-aggressive's dismay and anxiety.

Anticipating disappointment. Not only do passive-aggressives precipitate real difficulties through their negativistic behaviors, but they often perceive and anticipate difficulties where none in fact exist. They have learned from past experience that "good things don't last," that positive feelings and attitudes from those whom they seek love will end abruptly and capriciously and be followed by disappointment, anger, and rejection.

Rather than be disillusioned and embittered, rather than allowing themselves to be led down the "primrose path" to suffer the humiliation and pain of having their hopes dashed again, it would be better to put a halt to illusory gratifications and to the futility and heartache of short-lived pleasures. Protectively, then, passive-aggressives may refuse to wait for others to make the turnabout. Instead, they "jump the gun," pull back when things are going well, and thereby cut off experiences that may have proved gratifying had they been completed. The anticipation of being set back and left in the lurch prompts passive-aggressives into a self-fulfilling prophecy. By their own hand, they defeat their chance to experience events that could have promoted change and growth.

By cutting off the goodwill of others and by upsetting their pleasureable anticipations, passive-aggressives gain the perverse and negative gratification of venting hostility and anger. These acts, however, prove to be pyrrhic victories; not only do they sabotage their own chances for rewarding experiences, but they inevitably provoke counterhostility from others and increased guilt and anxiety for themselves. Their defensive action has instigated responses that perpetuate the original difficulty, setting into motion a vicious circle in which they feel further discontent and disappointment.

Re-creating disillusioning experiences. As noted earlier, interpersonal vacillation does gain partial gratifications for the passive-aggressive. And partial reinforcements, as we know from experimental research, strengthen habits and cause them to persist and recur. In the passive-aggressive this appears to take the form of unconscious repetition-compulsions in which the individual re-creates disillusioning experiences that parallel those of the past.

Despite their ambivalence and pessimistic outlook, passive-aggressives operate on the premise that they can overcome past disappointments and capture, in full measure, the love and attention they only partially gained in childhood. Unfortunately, their search for complete fulfillment can no longer be achieved since they now possess needs that are in fundamental opposition to one another; for example, they both want and do not want the love of those upon whom they depend. Despite this ambivalence, passive-aggressives enter new relationships as if a perfect and idyllic state could be achieved. They go through the act of seeking a consistent and true source of love, one that will not betray them as their parents and others have in the past. They venture into new relationships with enthusiasm and blind optimism; this time, all will go well. Despite this optimism, they remain unsure of the trust they really can place in others. Mindful of past betrayals and disappointments, they begin to test their new found "loves" to see if they are loyal and faithful. They may irritate others, frustrate them, and withdraw from them, all in an effort to check whether they will prove as fickle and insubstantial as those of the past. Soon these testing operations exhaust the partner's patience; annoyance, exasperation, and hostility follow. The passive-aggressive quickly becomes disenchanted; the "idol" has proved to be marred and imperfect; and the passive-aggressive is once more disillusioned and embittered. To vent their resentment at having been naive, these persons may turn against their "betrayers," disavow and recoil from the affections they had shown, and thereby complete the vicious circle. These experiences recur repeatedly, and with each recurrence, the passive-aggressives further reinforce their pessimistic anticipations. In their efforts to overcome past disillusionment, they have thrown themselves into new ventures that have led to further disillusion.

Remedial Interventions

These patients frequently decompensate into anxiety and depressive disorders. Therapists must be on guard to anticipate suicidal attempts since ambivalent personalities can act quite impulsively when they feel guilt, need attention, or seek a dramatic form of retribution. Major goals of therapy are to guide these patients into recognizing the sources and character of their ambivalence, and to reinforce a more consistent approach to life. Since these patients often enter treatment in an agitated state, an early treatment task is to calm their anxieties and guilt. Relieved of tension, many will lose their incentive to continue treatment. Motivating them to pursue a more substantial course of therapy may call for considerable effort on the part of the therapist since these personalities are deeply ambivalent about dependency relationships. They desire to be nurtured and loved by a powerful parental figure, but such submission poses the threat of loss and undermines the desire to maintain independence.

A seesaw struggle is often enacted between patient and therapist; the passive-aggressive is likely to exhibit an ingratiating submissiveness, one time, and a taunting and demanding attitude, the next. Similarly, these patients may solicit the therapist's affections, but when these are expressed, the patients reject them, voicing doubt about the genuineness of the therapist's feelings. When the therapist points out these contradictory attitudes, the patients may verbally appreciate the therapist's perceptiveness but not alter their attitudes at all.

Specific techniques should be noted. First, environmental pressures that aggravate the patient's anxieties should be removed. Intense anxieties tend to preoccupy the patient in the early phases of treatment; supportive therapy may be employed in their relief, as may pharmacological tranquilizing agents. If depressive features predominate, antidepressant drugs should be prescribed.

Formal behavior modification methods may be fruitfully explored to achieve greater consistency in social behaviors. More directive cognitive techniques may be used to confront patients with the obstructive and self-defeating character of their interpersonal relations. Cognitive approaches must be handled with caution, however, lest the patient become unduly guilt ridden, depressed, and suicidal. The greatest benefit derived through these approaches is to stabilize these patients, to "set them straight" and to help put reins on their uncontrollable vacillations of mood and behavior.

Because of the deeply rooted character of these problems and the high probability that unconscious resistances will impede the effectiveness of other therapeutic procedures, it may be necessary to explore the more extensive and prolonged techniques of psychoanalytic therapy. A thorough reconstruction of personality may be the only means of altering the pattern. Because family treatment methods focus on the complex network of relationships that often sustain this personality style, these may prove to be the most useful techniques available. Group methods may be fruitfully employed to assist patients to acquire more self-control and consistency in social situations.

Chapter 10

Schizoid Personality: The Asocial Pattern

There are pathological personalities who are distinguished by their aloof, introverted, and seclusive nature. They have difficulty in establishing friendships, prefer distant or limited involvements with others, and seem uninterested in (if not aversive to) social activities. In general, they appear to gain little satisfaction in personal relationships.

This chapter and Chapter 11 differentiate as *passive* and *active* variants two personality syndromes that share this "socially detached" pattern. Neither of these types is entirely homogeneous, but each does exhibit distinctive clinical features and experiential histories. One type, the passively detached variant, or what has been labeled the "schizoid personality" in the DSM-III, displays emotional and cognitive deficits that hinder the development of close or warm relationships. The other variant, the actively detached, or DSM-III "avoidant" personality, includes individuals whose experiences of interpersonal rejection and deprecation have led them to be mistrustful of and to keep distance from close relationships.

This chapter attends to schizoid personalities. These individuals are seen in every walk of life; they appear untroubled and indifferent, and function adequately in their occupations, but are judged by their associates as rather colorless and shy, seeming to prefer to be by themselves and to be lacking in the need to communicate with or relate affectionately to others. Typically, they remain in the background of social life, work quietly and unobtrusively at their jobs, and are rarely noticed even by those with whom they have routine contact. They would fade into the passing scene, to live their lives in a tangential and undisturbed inconspicuousness, were it not for the fact that there are persons who expect or wish them to be more vibrant, alive, and involved.

What appears most distinctive about these individuals is that they seem to lack the equipment for experiencing the finer shades and subtleties of emotional life. They appear especially unaware of, if not insensitive to, the feelings and thoughts of others. Some interpret their interpersonal passivity as a sign of hostility and rejection; it does not represent, however, an active disinterest but rather a fundamental *incapacity* to sense the moods and needs that are experienced by others, and that others normally expect will evoke thoughtful or empathic responses. Schizoid individuals are unfeeling, then, not by intention or for self-protective reasons, but because they possess an intrinsic emotional blandness and interpersonal imperceptiveness. They lack spontaneity, resonance, and color, are clumsy, unresponsive, and boring in relationships, and appear to lead dull, if not bleak, and stolid lives.

Because schizoids experience few rewards in social interaction, they often turn their talents and interests toward things, objects, or abstractions. As children, for example, they are likely to have been disinclined to competitive games and frolicsome activities, preferring to concentrate their energies on hobbies such as stamp or rock collecting, mechanical gadgets, electronic equipment, or academic pursuits such as mathematics or engineering. Many find considerable gratification in nonsocial and abstract activities, often developing rather intricate fantasy lives in conjunction with these. Unfortunately, the drab and withdrawn characteristics of developing schizoids often make them easy targets for teasing and condemnation by their peers, leading frequently to an intensification of their isolation and self-absorption activities.

In the past, the label "schizoid" was applied to individuals with a mix of features that the DSM-III now differentiates into three separate personality syndromes: the "schizoid," the "avoidant," and the "schizotypal." The designation "schizoid" is limited to personalities characterized by an intrinsic defect in the capacity to form social relationships. The label "avoidant" represents those who possess both the capacity and desire to relate socially, but who fear humiliation and disapproval, and, hence, distance themselves from such relationships. The term "schizotypal" is reserved for individuals who are noted by the eccentric character of their social communications and behaviors, and for an ostensive genetic linkage to schizophrenia. These distinctions are elaborated more fully and sharply as the discussion proceeds. For the present, portions of the DSM-III text for the personality labeled "schizoid" are reproduced:

> The essential feature is a Personality Disorder in which there is a defect in the capacity to form social relationships, evidenced by the absence of warm, tender feelings for others and indifference to praise, criticism, and the feelings of others. The diagnosis is not made if eccentricities of speech, behavior, or thought characteristic of Schizotypal Personality Disorder are present or if the disturbance is due to a psychotic disorder such as Schizophrenia.
>
> The individuals with this disorder show little or no desire for social involvement, usually prefer to be "loners," and have few, if any, close friends. They appear reserved, withdrawn, and seclusive and usually pursue solitary interests or hobbies. Individuals with this disorder are usually humorless or dull

and without affect in situations where an emotional response would be appropriate. They usually appear "cold," aloof, and distant.

Individuals with this disorder are often unable to express aggressiveness or hostility. They may seem vague about their goals, indecisive in their actions, self-absorbed, absentminded, and detached from their environment ("not with it" or "in a fog"). Excessive daydreaming is often seen. (p. 310)

HISTORICAL AND THEORETICAL ANTECEDENTS

The designation of "schizoid personality" could not have been made prior to Eugen Bleuler's formulation of the concept of schizophrenia, offered as an alternative to the diagnostic label of "dementia praecox" in 1911. Nevertheless, during the two decades prior to Bleuler's concept, Kahlbaum (1890), Binet (1890), and Hoch (1910) argued the view that the dramatic symptoms seen in clinical states such as dementia praecox were often accentuations of the individual's preexisting personality traits that had been thrust into sharp relief as a consequence of some unusual event or trauma. For example, Kahlbaum introduced the term "heboid" to represent the personality pattern that was structurally connected to clinical hebephrenia, referring to it as a "deviation of psychic individuality in social relationships."

Particularly relevant also to the syndrome of dementia praecox was August Hoch's study of the background histories and personal characteristics of these patients (1910). He was to conclude from this research that most had exhibited a "shut-in" personality that predated their manifest illness by several years. These "shut-in" types were described as

> persons who do not have a natural tendency ... to get into contact with the environment, who are reticent, seclusive, who cannot adapt themselves to situations, who are hard to influence ... and stubborn ... in a passive than an active way. They do not let others know what their conflicts are; they do not unburden their minds, are shy, and have a tendency to live in a world of fancies.
>
> What is, after all, the deterioration in dementia praecox if not the expression of the constitutional tendencies in their extreme form, a shutting out of the outside world, a deterioration of interests in the environment, a living in a world apart? (p. 219)

Farrar (1927) expanded Hoch's notion of "shut-in" personalities by distinguishing five subtypes: (1) the "backward" variant lacked ambition, appeared absent-minded, and was disinclined to attend to work or school responsibilities; (2) the "precocious" type was seen as bookish, serious-minded, and prudish, and was often considered as having been a model child; (3) the "neurotic" pattern was noted by frequent temper tantrums, self-centeredness, secretiveness, and persistent physical complaints; (4) the "a-social" style was best characterized by seclusiveness, an indifference to worldly affairs, and a preference for extended day-dreaming; and (5) the "juvenile" kind remained childlike and dependent, refusing to, or otherwise unable to, grow up.

Emil Kraepelin also wrote of a prodromal form of dementia praecox in the eighth edition of his text (1913). He described it as follows:

> Certain abnormal personalities with mild defect states...[are] a product of dementia praecox experienced in earliest childhood, and then brought to a standstill. (p. 237)

In addition to this prodromal variant of dementia praecox, which slows to a halt before reaching clinical proportions, Kraepelin also spoke of a healed and stable prepsychotic state. Notable in this formulation is the absence of the persistent deterioration that was so central to Kraepelin's original view that dementia praecox followed an inevitable downward course. Clearly, these "milder personality defects," though akin to dementia praecox, differed from the more serious and florid psychotic form. Using modern terminology, mild schizophrenic disorders that came to a standstill prior to decompensation would be likely to be labeled as "schizoid" personalities. Kraepelin, however, had his own terminology for these individuals, designating them as "autistic personalities" (1919). To him, the trait that disposed them to dementia praecox, and that characterized the prodromal and quiescent stages, was their tendency to "narrow or reduce their external interests and contacts and their preoccupation with inward ruminations" (p 213).

Eugen Bleuler coined the term *schizoidie* (1922, 1929) to represent a pattern of traits closely allied to Hoch's "shut-in" type and Kraepelin's "autistic" personality. The tendency to "schizoidness" was seen by Bleuler as present in everyone, differing among individuals only in the quantity of its potential biologic penetrance. In its clinical or schizophrenic form, this tendency achieved its full level of morbid intensity, whereas in moderate form it could assume the character of only a mild schizoid personality, described by Bleuler as "people who are shut in, suspicious, incapable of discussion, people who are comfortably dull" (1924, p. 441). The "fundamental symptoms" that Bleuler spelled out as pathognomonic for schizophrenia were to be found in reduced magnitude among schizoids. Referring to the prominent features found in these milder forms, Bleuler wrote:

> Even in the less severe forms of the illness, indifference seems to be the external sign of their state; an indifference to everything—to friends and relations, to vocation or enjoyment, to duties or rights, to good fortune or to bad. (1950, p. 40)

Applying the term *autism* to signify the characteristic detachment from reality and the predominance of the inner life among these individuals, Bleuler went on to note:

> Autism is not always detected at the very first glance. Initially the behavior of many patients betrays nothing remarkable. It is only on prolonged observation

that one sees how much they always seek their own way, and how little they permit their environment to influence them. (1950, p. 65)

Despite Bleuler's seminal contributions to the schizophrenic concept, it was Ernst Kretschmer (1925) who introduced the most subtle refinements of the schizoid character portrayal. Distinctions first posited by him closely parallel subsequent discriminations in theory (Millon, 1969) and are an important forerunner of the DSM-III differentiation between schizoid and avoidant types. Because of the originality of this demarcation, as well as the descriptive clarity and clinical astuteness of his text, more than the usual attention is devoted here to his contributions.

Although Kretschmer noted that schizoids might exhibit certain "peculiarities of character" in "different relative proportions," he identified two distinct subgroups, what he termed the "hyperaesthetic" and the "anaesthetic" schizoid types. The former group, the hyperaesthetics, are essentially equivalent to what the DSM-III has labeled the "avoidant personality." This syndrome is described more fully in the next chapter. For comparative purposes, however, a few phrases are quoted from Kretschmer to convey how this type contrasts with the anaesthetic, termed the "schizoid personality" in the DSM-III. Kretschmer portrayed the hyperaesthetic as follows:

> Timid, shy, with fine feelings, sensitive, nervous, excitable....
> Abnormally tender, constantly wounded... "all nerves."...
> [hyperaesthetics] feel all the harsh, strong colors and tones of everyday life... as shrill, ugly... even to the extent of being psychically painful. Their autism is a painful cramping of the self into itself. They seek as far as possible to avoid and deaden all stimulation from the outside. (1925, pp. 155–161)

Descriptively, and in contrast to the hyperaesthetic-avoidant, Kretschmer portrayed the anaesthetic-schizoid personality as follows:

> We feel that we are in contact with something flavorless, boring.... What is there in the deep under all these masks? Perhaps there is a nothing, a dark, hollow-eyed nothing—affective anemia. Behind an ever-silent facade, which twitches uncertainly with every expiring whim—nothing but broken pieces, black rubbish heaps, yawning emotional emptiness, or the cold breath of an arctic soullessness. (1925, p. 150)

Kretschmer's descriptive language is so colorful as to mislead us into feeling that we are reading about a lively and exciting personality rather than one devoid of affect and interpersonally numbing. Relating the characteristic social indifference and introversiveness of the anaesthetic schizoid, Kretschmer wrote:

> "Indifference" is a common schizoid variant of affective insensibility. It is an uninterestedness, which is ostentatiously manifested.. The indifferent knows

that he takes absolutely no interest in many things which are important to other people. (1925, p. 172)

The autism of the predominantly anaesthetic ... is unfeelingness, lack of affect response to the world about him, which has no interest for his emotional life, and for whose own rightful interests he has no feeling. He draws himself back into himself because he has no reason to do anything else, because all that is about him can offer him nothing. (1925, p. 162)

Characterizing the lack of vitality, spark, or liveliness among the schizoid, Kretschmer went on to say:

> The commonest type in our pre-psychotic material is that in which one finds affective lameness. ... The term "affective lameness" has a close connection with popular speech, which describes those people as "lame (contorted)," in whose behavior it is clearly manifest that the most outstanding symptom is a psychomotor one. ... "One could have wished that he were livelier." "He is a bit tepid." "He is absolutely lacking in life and temperament." Such are the commonest descriptions of young men suffering from affective lameness. This lack of liveliness, of immediately-reacting vivacity of psychomotor expression, is found also in the most gifted members of the group. ...
>
> "Lameness" implies ... the loss of immediate connection between the emotional stimulus and the motor response. It is for this reason that with the "comfortable" person we always have a feeling that we are in emotional rapport, even when he says nothing, while the "lame" appears to us strange, unsympathetic ... because we often cannot read in his face, or in his movements, the expression of what he is feeling, or, above all, the adequate reaction to what we are doing and saying to him. The essential quality ... is that he can stand there with a puzzled face and hanging arms ... in a situation that would electrify even one of the "comfortables." (1925, pp. 169–170)
>
> They are ... devoid of humor, and often serious, without exhibiting either sorrowfulness or cheerfulness.
>
> The expression "dullness" denotes [their] passive lack of feeling ... a phlegmatic state, which may distinguished ... by the lack of warm, emotional responsiveness toward mankind. (1925, pp. 172–173)

To Kretschmer, the root of the schizoid's "affective lameness" could be traced to constitutional temperament, a view shared by Bleuler. In contrast, psychoanalytic thinkers acquainted with this personality were, as expected, inclined to locate its origins in troublesome childhood events. However, and unlike most of their "character" types, early analytic theorists did not trace or derive the schizoid pattern from a particular stage of libidinal or psychosexual development. Nevertheless, several analytic theorists—notably W. R. D. Fairbairn, Helene Deutsch, and D. W. Winnicott—each described an analogous pattern in the early 1940s in terms of psychoanalytic metapsychology.

A major founder of the object-relations school of analysis, Fairbairn (1940) stressed the role of depersonalization, derealization, and disturbances of the reality-sense in a range of syndromes he variously termed schizoid "characters," "types," "states," and "personalities." These persons sense themselves as "artificial," as having the feeling that a "plate-glass" exists between them and others, as experiencing a strange unfamiliarity with familiar persons and, conversely, as experiencing familiarity or *déjà vu* with unfamiliar persons or situations. Among their prominent clinical characteristics are "an attitude of isolation and detachment, and a preoccupation with inner reality." Of special note to Fairbairn is their "difficulty over giving in the emotional sense" (p. 15), which they cope with by "playing roles" and by "exhibitionism." To Fairbairn:

> The significance of the exploitation of exhibitionism as defense lies in the fact that it represents a technique for giving without giving, by means of a substitute of "showing" for "giving." (1940, p. 16)

Especially significant to the schizoid pattern is their inability to perceive others as worthy of their empathy or love. This stems not only from their unwillingness to part with what little love they themselves possess, but because they feel that love "is too dangerous to release upon [their] objects" (p. 15). In line with his view that the root of the difficulty is traceable to oral libidinal strains, Fairbairn asserted that schizoids experience an

> unsatisfactory emotional relationship with their parents and particularly with their mothers.... the type of mother who is specially prone ... is the mother who fails to convince her child by spontaneous and genuine expressions of affection that she herself loves him as a person. (1940, p. 13)

As a consequence of such an upbringing, schizoids are incapable of either giving love or being loved. Using his analytic terminology, Fairbairn stated that they have learned to keep their libidinal objects at a distance, "depersonalizing the object and de-emotionalizing the object-relationships" (p. 15).

Deutsch (1942) described a group of highly similar schizoid types. Even more clearly than Fairbairn, she considered the central feature of experience to have been the impersonality and formality of the child's early relationships. Labeled the "as if" type, these personalities learn how to act with others but are devoid of the feeling and relatedness that usually are part of these actions. Deutsch wrote:

> The way of feeling and manner of life of this type forces on the observer the inescapable impression that the individual's whole relationship to life has something about it which is lacking in genuineness and yet outwardly runs along "as if" it were complete. (1942, p. 302)

In detailing her portrayal of this personality, Deutsch stated:

> The individual's emotional relationship to the outside world and to his own ego appears impoverished or absent ... there are individuals who are not aware of their lack of normal affective bonds and responses, but whose emotional disturbance is perceived ... only by those around them. (1942, p. 301)

As both Bleuler and Fairbairn had noted earlier, schizoids often appear quite "normal" upon first impression. Over time or upon closer inspection "the lack of real warmth brings such an emptiness and dullness to the emotional atmosphere" (p. 302) that relationships simply cannot last in any meaningful or rewarding sense. Deutsch described this quality as follows:

> All the expressions of emotion are formal.... all inner experience is completely excluded. It is like the performance of an actor who is technically well-trained but who lacks the necessary spark to make his impersonations true to life....
>
> Outwardly he conducts his life as if he possessed a complete and sensitive emotional capacity. To him there is no difference between his empty forms and what others actually experience.... The apparently normal relationship to the world...[is] a mimicry...despite the absence of object cathexis.
>
> Further consequences of such a relation to life are a completely passive attitude to the environment with a highly plastic readiness to pick up signals from the outer world and to mold oneself and ones's behavior accordingly.
>
> Another characteristic... is that aggressive tendencies are almost completely masked by passivity, lending an air of negative goodness. (1942, pp. 303–305)

Grinker, Werble, and Drye (1968), in research into so-called borderline syndromes, identified one subgroup whose characteristics clustered in accord with Deutsch's "as if" type. Among the notable features Grinker et al. uncovered were

> bland and adaptive behavior.... here was little evidence of negative behavior or affect... but what is also missing is manifestation of positive affect—in fact there is no evidence of love for anybody or anything. Furthermore, there is no indication of a well-developed sense of self-identity. (p. 87)

The final trait reported in this excerpt, that of a lack of a well-developed sense of identity, is central to D. W. Winnicott's (1945, 1956) formulation of what he termed "false self" personalities, a character type similar in its features to those described by Kretschmer, Fairbairn, and Deutsch. Winnicott portrayed this unfeeling and detached person as follows:

> In the cases on which my work is based there has been a true self, hidden and protected by a "false self."This false self is no doubt an aspect of the true self. It hides and protects it, and it reacts to the adaptation failures and develops a pattern corresponding to the pattern of environmental failure. In this way the true self is not involved in the reacting, and so preserves a continuity of being. This hidden true self suffers an impoverishment, however, that results from a lack of experience. The false self may achieve a deceptive false integrity, that is to say a false ego-strength.... The false self cannot, however, experience life, and feel real. (1956, p. 387)

H. Guntrip (1952) and R. Laing (1960), more recent followers of the object-relations and self-theory traditions of British psychoanalysis, have further elaborated Fairbairn's and Winnicott's notions of the "schizoid" personality. Both are exceptionally articulate. For example, Guntrip portrayed the schizoid as follows:

> Complaints of feeling cut off, shut off, out of touch, feeling apart or strange, of things being out of focus or unreal, of not feeling one with people, or of the point having gone out of life, interest flagging, things seem futile and meaningless, all describe in various ways this state of mind. Patients usually call it "depression," but it lacks the heavy black, inner sense of brooding, of anger and of guilt... in classic depression.
>
> External relationships seem to have been emptied by a massive withdrawal of the real libidinal self. Effective mental activity has disappeared into a hidden inner world; the patient's conscious ego is emptied of vital feeling and action, and seems to have become unreal... merely reporting [inner activities] as if it were a neutral observer, not personally in the inner drama of which [the patient] is a detached observer. The attitude to the outer world is the same: *non-involvement and observation at a distance without any feeling*, like that of a press reporter describing a social gathering of which he is not a part, in which he has no personal interest, and by which he is bored. (1952, p. 86)

Laing (1960) added to the false-self theme proposed by Winnicott and also portrayed the sense of schizoid detachment and impassivity:

> In the schizoid condition here described there is a persistent scission between the self and the body. What the individual regards as his true self is experienced as more or less disembodied, and bodily experience and actions are in turn felt to be part of the false-self system....
>
> This detachment of the self means that the self is never revealed directly in the individual's expressions and actions, nor does it experience anything spontaneously or immediately. The self's relationship to the other is always at one remove. The direct and immediate transactions between the individual, the other, and the world, even in such basic respects as perceiving and acting, all come to be meaningless, futile, and false....
>
> The final effect is an overall experience of everything having come to a stop. Nothing moves; nothing is alive; everything is dead, including the self. The self by its detachment is precluded from a full experience of realness and aliveness. (1960, pp. 82–87)

Picking up on Deutsch's concept of "as if," Arieti (1955) has proposed that the schizoids' insensitivity is a defense against their profound vulnerabilty to the pain of rejection. This vulnerability is so successfully repressed that no longer is there any pain or social longing. Arieti's formulation of the dynamics of the schizoid may be more applicable to the DSM-III conception of the avoidant personality.

Turning to an entirely different perspective, that of psychopharmacologic research, D. F. Klein (1970, 1977) suggested that the traditional schizoid syndrome confuses two distinct personality categories. Of note is the correspondence between Klein's specific suggestion in this regard and the differentiation Kretschmer made some 45 years earlier between hyperaesthetic and anaesthetic schizoids. Klein wrote:

> I believe the DSM-II schizoid personality...confuses two quite separate groups of people: the shy, socially backward, inept, obedient person who is fearful and therefore isolated but appreciates sociability and would like to be part of the crowd; and there is the asocial, eccentric, (imperceptive and undiplomatic) person who seeks to be alone and has difficulty in relationships with his peers, frequently resulting in social ostracism and scapegoating. (1970, p. 189)

The former group—the shy, fearful type, who appreciates sociability—parallels Kretschmer's hyperaesthetic and corresponds in several respects to the DSM-III avoidant personality. Similarly, the asocial and imperceptive type, who has difficulty in relating with peers, possesses qualities akin to Kretschmer's anaesthetic and to the DSM-III schizoid characterization.

A theoretically derived distinction that also results in two "schizoid" variants was formulated by Millon (1969) and proposed as a typological framework for the DSM-III personality subcommittee. Labeled the "passive-detached" and "active-detached" patterns, or alternatively the "asocial" and "avoidant" personalities, they are analogous to the differentiation proposed by Kretschmer between anaesthetics and hyperaesthetics. The text and criteria that follow served in 1975 as the initial working draft for the DSM-III schizoid (asocial) personality; Chapter 11 includes a comparable text and criteria for the avoidant personality.

> This pattern is typified by a rather quiet, colorless and impassive style of interpersonal behavior. Affectionate needs are markedly limited and desires for communication and close relationship with others are minimal. There is little capacity for experiencing pleasure and a pervasively bland emotional tone characterizes daily life. This introversive and apathetic pattern covaries with a general lack of vitality and motoric spontaneity, deficits in stimulus-seeking behavior, impoverished social sensibilities and a notable cognitive vagueness regarding interpersonal matters.
>
> Since adolescence or early adulthood at least 3 of the following have been present to a notably greater degree than in most people and were not limited to discrete periods nor necessarily prompted by stressful life events.
>
> 1. Affectivity deficit (e.g., exhibits intrinsic emotional blandness; reports weak affectionate needs and an inability to display enthusiasm or experience pleasure).
> 2. Mild cognitive slippage (e.g., evidences impoverished and obscure thought processes inappropriate to intellectual level; social communication often tangential and irrelevant).
> 3. Interpersonal indifference (e.g., possesses minimal "human" interests; is satisfied with and prefers a peripheral role in social and family relationships).

4. Behavioral apathy (e.g., ease of fatigability, low energy and lack of vitality; displays deficits in activation, motoric expressiveness and spontaneity).
5. Perceptual insensitivity (e.g., reveals minimal introspection and awareness of self; impervious to subtleties of everyday social and emotional life).

Following extended discussions, the originally proposed label for the DSM-III syndrome "asocial personality" was replaced with the designation "introverted personality." The term "asocial" had been preempted by the ICD-9 as an alternative label for the antisocial personality; confusion, especially in Europe, was thought inevitable. The substitute designation "introverted" was dropped in its turn because of objections from Jungian analysts. Finally, the label "schizoid" was reintroduced despite strong disagreements by members of the committee to the effect that this term conveyed different meanings in prior manuals, and that it would result in confusions with a new syndrome that had imprudently been labeled "schizotypal personality."

The following text and criteria were proposed at an intermediate phase of the committee's work:

> The essential features are a profound defect in the ability to form social relationships and to respond to the usual forms of social reinforcements. Such patients are characteristically "loners," who do not appear distressed by their social distance and are not interested in greater social involvement. Affectionate needs are markedly limited and there appears to be little capacity for experiencing pleasure.
>
> Deficits in stimulus-seeking are notable and these patients frequently maintain solitary interests and hobbies. The characteristic introversive pattern frequently covaries with a general lack of vitality and motor spontaneity. Habits of speech typically are slow and monotonous with few rhythmic or expressive gestures. A pervasively bland emotional tone characterizes daily life as does a lack of self-reflection and introspection.
>
> At least 3 of the following are characteristic of the patient's long term functioning and are not limited to discrete periods.

A. Social relationship deficits (e.g., has few friends or close bonds with others).
B. Interpersonal indifference (e.g., has minimal desire for social involvement and is unresponsive to praise or criticism).
C. Anhedonia (e.g., exhibits weak affectionate needs and is unable to readily experience pleasure or enthusiasm).
D. Behavioral apathy (e.g., displays low energy, motivation, or stimulus-seeking behavior).
E. Minimal self-reflection (e.g., rarely examines self-motives or personal relationships).

CLINICAL PICTURE

With the foregoing as a background, this section details the clinical characteristics of these individuals in a more systematic fashion.

Behavioral Features

The inability of schizoids to engage in the give-and-take of reciprocal relationships may readily be observed. They are rather vague and peripheral in group interactions, appearing to be involved in their own world of preoccupations. It is even difficult for them to mix with others in pleasant social activities, let alone those demanding leadership. When relating to others in a mandatory setting, as in school or work, their social communications are expressed not in a peculiar or irrational way but in a perfunctory, formal and impersonal manner.

Speech typically is slow and monotonous, characterized by an affectless vacancy and obscurities that signify either inattentiveness or a failure to grasp the emotional dimensions of human communication. Movements are lethargic and lacking in rhythmic or expressive gestures. They rarely "perk up" or respond alertly to the feelings of others; they are not intentionally unkind, however. They seem invariably preoccupied with tangential and picayune matters, rather passively detached from others and drifting along quietly and unobtrusively, as if in a world of their own.

Asocial individuals of this cast evidence underresponsiveness to all forms of stimulation. Events that normally provoke anger, elicit joy, or evoke sadness in others seem to fall on deaf ears. There is a pervasive imperviousness to emotions, not only to those of joy and pleasure. Feelings of anger, depression, or anxiety rarely are expressed. This apathy and emotional deficit are cardinal signs of the schizoid syndrome. Their generalized inability to be activated and aroused may be exhibited in a wide-ranging lack of initiative and the failure to respond to most reinforcements that prompt others into action. Thus, they are not only unmoved by emotional stimuli but seem to possess a general deficiency in energy and vitality. When they do become involved, it tends toward mental activities, such as reading or television watching, or toward physical activities that call for minimal energy expenditures, such as drawing, watch repairing, needlepoint, and so on.

Self-Reports and Complaints

Schizoid personalities rarely are introspective since the satisfactions to be found in self-evaluation are minimal for those who are incapable of experiencing deep emotions. This diminished introspectiveness, with its attendant lowering of insight, derives from another feature of the schizoid pattern. They display a vagueness and impoverishment of thought, a tendency to skim the surface of events, and an inability to convey articulate and relevant ideas regarding interpersonal phenomena.

This style of amorphous communication may be related to another trait, one referred to here as "defective perceptual scanning." It is characterized by a tendency to miss or blur differences and to overlook, diffuse, and homogenize the varied elements of experience. Instead of differentiating events and sensing their discriminable and distinctive attributes, schizoids tend to mix them up, intrude extraneous or irrelevant features, and perceive them in a somewhat disorganized fashion. This inability to attend, select, and regulate one's perceptions of the environment seems, once again, to be especially pronounced with social and emotional phenomena.

Schizoid personalities characterize themselves as bland persons who are reflective and introversive. Most seem complacent and satisfied with their lives and are content to remain aloof from the social aspirations and competitiveness they see in others. Self-descriptions, however, tend to be vague and superficial. This lack of clarity does not indicate elusiveness or protective denial on their part but rather their deficient powers to reflect on social and emotional processes. Interpersonal attitudes are no less vague and inarticulate. When adequately formulated, schizoids perceive themselves to be somewhat reserved and distant, lacking in much concern or care for others. Rather interestingly, they are able to recognize that others tend to be indifferent to them and their needs.

Inferred Intrapsychic Dynamics

Schizoids engage in few complicated unconscious processes. Relatively untroubled by intense emotions, insensitive to interpersonal relationships, and difficult to arouse and activate, they hardly feel the impact of events and have little reason to devise complicated intrapsychic defenses and strategies. They do harbor the residuals of past memories and emotions, but, in general, their inner world lacks the intensities and intricacies found in all other pathological personalities.

Interpersonal Coping Style

For the same reasons they fail to develop intrapsychic mechanisms, schizoids also tend not to learn complex interpersonal coping maneuvers. Their drives are meager and they lack the intense personal involvements sometimes conducive to painful emotional conflicts. This is not to say that they possess no drives or discords, but that those they do experience are of mild degree and of minor consequence. One of the distinctions of the schizoid personality, then, is the paucity (rather than the character or direction) of their interpersonal coping. If any factor in their generally feeble hierarchy of motives can be identified, it is their preference for remaining socially detached. This is not a "driving" need of theirs, as it is with the avoidant personality, but merely a comfortable and preferred state. When social circumstances press them beyond comfort, they may simply retreat and draw into themselves. Should social discord or demands become intense or persistent, they may revert to more severe coping reactions and display various pathological disorders such as "schizophrenic" syndromes.

ASSOCIATED DISORDERS

As in previous chapters, this section describes the Axis I and Axis II disorders that co-occur with the personality pattern under review. Considerations relevant to differential diagnoses are also noted.

Concomitant Axis I Symptoms

Complicated intrapsychic processes are not characteristic of the DSM-III schizoid personality. As described earlier, these individuals lack the affective intensity to activate those defensive mechanisms that comprise unconscious dynamics. Consequently, schizoids exhibit few of the intricate coping maneuvers and experience few of the symbolic symptom disorders usually recorded on Axis I.

Anxiety disorders. In common with all pathological personalities, schizoids do experience anxiety disorders. However, and in consonance with their flat and colorless style, intense emotionality is rarely exhibited, and states of chronic anxiety are almost never found. Nevertheless, two diametrically opposite sets of circumstances may prompt a flare-up of acute anxiety, or panic disorder: excessive stimulation or persistent understimulation. Schizoids may "explode" when they feel encroached upon or when faced with unusual social demands and responsibilities. Similar consequences may follow from marked understimulation. Here, the schizoid experiences feelings of depersonalization, a fearful sense of emptiness and nothingness, and a state of self-nonexistence, stagnation, barrenness, and unreality that becomes frightfully overwhelming and unbearable.

Affective disorders. Along similar lines, schizoids may exhibit brief and rather frenzied episodes of *manic* excitement in an attempt to counter the anxieties of depersonalization. Here, for but a fleeting period, they burst out of their characteristic retiring and unsociable pattern and into a frantic and bizarre conviviality. The wild, irrational, and chaotic character of their exuberance tends to run but a brief, if erratic, course before collapsing into their more typically subdued and inexpressive state.

Obsessive-compulsive disorders. Extended social isolation, with its consequent periods of "empty" rumination, often results in *obsessive* thinking, which the schizoid may be unable to block from conscious intrusion. Most of these thoughts are meaningless (e.g., "where did I see a chair with one leg?") and experienced without emotion but, nonetheless, may be so persistent and distracting as to upset the routine of daily activities. Some recurrent thoughts may become tension laden, pertain to forbidden impulses or prohibited desires, and, hence, evoke feelings of shame, disgust, or horror. The more desperately these patients try to rid themselves of these repugnant ideas, the more persistent and tormenting they may become. For example, a passing thought of poisoning a wayward wife may become fixed in a husband's mind; no matter how much he seeks to distract his attention from it, the thought returns time and again.

Dissociative disorders. As already noted, *depersonalization* disorders are rather common among schizoids. As an extension or elaboration of their more characteristic state, these patients often experience altered perceptions of themselves and a sense of self-estrangement, including feeling "mechanical," distant, and disembodied. Trancelike states akin to estrangement also occur, but here the patients' awareness is merely dimmed. They may report being in a "twilight" dream world, totally immersed in inner events, and entirely oblivious to their surroundings.

As a function of their habitual lack of interest in the events of everyday life, schizoids often fail to acquire a coherent and well-integrated core of attitudes necessary for organizing an "inner identity." Empty or devoid of a past, deficient in "psychic" cohesion, and insensitive to external promptings, they are subject to the kind of splitting or disintegration that inclines them to *dissociative* states.

Somatoform disorders. Although only modestly prevalent, *hypochondriacal disorders* will become prominent and salient features when they do occur in schizoids. Noted by the presence of prolonged periods of weariness and exhaustion, undiagnosable physical sensations, and persistent insomnia, these patients may fall into a state of diffuse irritability and report pains in different, unconnected, and changing regions of the body. Phenomenologically, these schizoids report experiencing a heaviness and a drab monotony to their lives. Despite this lethargy, they become fixated, exquisitely attuned to some facet of normal physiology, or uncharacteristically concerned with a minor change in their bodily functioning. These preoccupations seem to reflect a need on their part to "latch on" to something tangible about themselves, something that will assure them that they do, in fact, exist and are not insubstantial or disembodied.

Schizophrenic disorders. As noted earlier, schizoids may exhibit brief frenzied states of manic excitement; for similar reasons, they may succumb to other transient episodes, best diagnosed as *brief reactive psychoses* and *schizophreniform disorders*. The frenetic quality of their behavior is still prominent but, in contrast to the manic phase, exhibits significant elements of apprehension and agitation. Periods diagnosable as *disorganized (hebephrenic) schizophrenia* may also occur; here, the patient evidences a blend of irrational thinking and flat affect, punctuated every now and then by panicky outbursts and bizarre emotions. Phases of *catatonic schizophrenia* are also seen in these personalities. At these times, patients appear motivated by a desire to withdraw from external provocation rather than by a need to control untoward impulses, not that the latter should be overlooked as a factor. Faced with derogation and humiliation, schizoids may draw tightly into their shells, resistant to any form of stimulation that may demand that they think or feel. The grimacing and giggling often observed at these periods is a clue to their chaotic fantasy world.

The most characteristic feature of psychotic-level schizoid behavior is their profound lethargy and indifference to their surroundings. If they move, it is listlessly, languidly; they are perhaps best described as stuporous. Clothes droop as on a hanger, and their faces are lifeless and masklike. At best, speech is slow, labored, whispered or totally inaudible. Passively withdrawn and unresponsive, they do not participate or feel involved, perceiving events and things about them as unreal and strange. There is a characteristic emotional poverty, compounded by a dreamy detachment, a tendency to stand immobile or fixed in one place. Many sit habitually in a cramped, bent-over, and peculiar position, to which they return repeatedly if they are distracted or dislodged. Others not only show the typical lack of initiative but display an automatic obedience to the requests of others, even when these directives could result in severe physical discomfort or danger. Some become so profoundly detached that they fail to register or react to painful stimuli.

Concurrent Axis II Personalities

Research employing the MCMI (Millon, 1977) suggests that the schizoid or passively detached pattern covaries most frequently with the DSM-III dependent and schizotypal personality syndromes. Combination with the compulsive personality is also notable, though of lesser prevalence.

Schizoid-dependent mixed personality. This profile occurs most prominently among long-term institutionalized and half-way house psychiatric patients, ambulatory males at VA outpatient mental hygiene clinics, and, to a lesser degree, in prison settings and among chronic, physically ill patients who give evidence of emotional flattening and having "given up." The following MCMI computer-generated narrative was derived from the responses of a 54-year-old World War II veteran who attended brief monthly sessions at a nearby VA mental hygiene clinic for a 30-year period. He had experienced three extended psychotic episodes during this time; each was diagnosed as "chronic undifferentiated schizophrenia" and required hospitalization, the first for 3 years and the latter two for approximately 3-month periods each. Ambulatory for the past 8 years, he recently remarried and was experiencing difficulties in this relationship.

This patient's life-style is typified by a quiet, colorless, and dependent way of relating to others. His introversive pattern covaries with a general lack of vitality, deficits in social initiative and stimulus-seeking behaviors, impoverished affect, and a cognitive vagueness regarding interpersonal matters. Fatigability, low energy level, and weakness in motoric expressiveness and spontaneity are notable. He prefers a peripheral but dependent role in social and family relationships. There is a desire for social isolation that conflicts with strong dependency needs. Both stem from low self-esteem and inadequacies in autonomy and social competence.

The patient is inclined to be self-belittling and possesses a self-image of a weak and ineffectual person. Life is experienced as uneventful, with periods of passive solitude interspersed with feelings of emptiness and depersonalization. He evidences an indifference to social surroundings, is minimally introspective and generally insensitive to the subtleties of emotional life. Thought processes, though not deficient, are unfocused, particularly with regard to interpersonal matters. Social communication is often strained, self-conscious, and tangential.

There is a deficiency in the expression of affection, which may stem from an anhedonic inability to display enthusiasm or experience pleasure. He does exhibit a chronic but mild depressiveness. There is a marked tendency to keep to a simple, repetitive, and dependent life pattern. He avoids self-assertion, abdicates autonomous responsibilities, and is content to remain aloof from normal social aspirations. Disengaged from and disinterested in most of the rewards of active human relationships, he appears to others as apathetic and asocial. By restricting social and emotional involvements to a minimum, he perpetuates a life pattern of isolation and dependency.

Schizoid-schizotypal mixed personality. The second most frequent joint personality diagnosis found with the schizoid pattern is the DSM-III schizoid-schizotypal combination. A highly prevalent profile, it is seen most commonly in the chronically institutionalized, residents of half-way houses, and in such long-term outpatient settings as VA mental hygiene clinics. The following case report is based on response data given in answer to questions on the MCMI by a 44-year-old unmarried female who had been hospitalized for "schizophrenia" several times since late adolescence. She was currently residing in a half-way house located in a major metropolitan area, making what her supervisors referred to as a "quiet, if eccentric adjustment."

This patient's way of life is characterized by a quiet and inexpressive dependency. A marked deficit in social interest is notable, as are frequent behavioral eccentricities, occasional autistic thinking, and depersonalization anxieties. This intensely introversive pattern covaries with a lack of energy, deficits in social initiative and stimulus-seeking behaviors, impoverished affect, and confused thinking regarding interpersonal matters. She is likely to have acquired a peripheral but dependent role in social and family relationships. Her desire for social isolation conflicts with her strong dependency on others for support. Both stem from low self-esteem and inadequacies in autonomy and social competence.

The patient remains a detached observer of the passing scene, is character-istically self-belittling, and possesses a self-image of being a weak and ineffectual person. Rather than venturing outward, she has retreated defensively, increas-ingly remote from others and from sources of potential growth and gratification. Life is uneventful, with extended periods of solitude interspersed with feelings of being disembodied, empty, and depersonalized. She evidences a pervasive inadequacy in most areas, and there is a tendency to follow a meaningless, ineffectual, and idle pattern, drifting aimlessly and remaining on the periphery of social life.

Thought processes are unfocused, particularly with regard to emotional and interpersonal matters. Her estrangement from others has led to a loss of touch with reality. Social communication is often strained, self-conscious, and tangential, further alienating her from others. There is hesitation in expressing affection, which may stem from an anhedonic inability to display enthusiasm or experience pleasure.

She exhibits a distinct depressive tone, is occasionally morose, and is likely to display an erratic moodiness with multiple complaints. Beneath her more typical apathetic exterior, there are intense feelings of discontent and anger. This is evident in periodic displays of passive-aggressive, petulant, and fault-finding behaviors. More commonly, she is self-deprecating and self-punitive, and is disposed to constant but quiet worrying. There is a marked tendency to keep a simple, repetitive, and dependent life pattern with avoidance of self-assertion and indifference to normal social aspirations. Disengaged from and disinterested in most of the rewards of active human relationships, she appears to others as an unobtrusively strange, disconnected, and lifeless person. By restricting social and emotional involvements to a minimum, she perpetuates her life pattern of isolation and dependency.

Differential Diagnostic Signs

As has been often stated in this book, differential diagnosis is no longer the important issue it has been in the past since overlapping syndromes are not only recognized but encouraged in the multiaxial DSM-III format; this is especially true in Axis I and Axis II combinations.

The prime symptom that may require differentiation from the schizoid personality is likely to be *depersonalization disorder*. In general, the breadth and number of traits involved and the specific features of interpersonal "coolness" and social indifference should help distinguish the personality syndrome from the more narrow and transient nature of the symptom disorder.

Differentiations between schizoid personality and various *schizophrenic disorders* may not be necessary when overlapping symptoms are observed; both should be registered on their respective axes where appropriate. Where distinction rather than covariance is the issue, the centrality of delusions, hallucinations, and disordered thinking to the schizophrenic diagnosis clearly sets it apart from the more prosaic and nonpsychotic features of the schizoid.

Turning to Axis II personality syndromes, diagnostic difficulties are likely to be encountered most often by clinicians who are becoming acquainted for the first time with the new texts and criteria for the schizoid, schizotypal, and avoidant personalities. Differentiations among these syndromes will become less troublesome as the reader progresses through this text. A few words are in order in the interim.

First, schizotypal personalities are more "dramatically" eccentric than schizoids, who are characteristically flat, colorless, and dull. Schizotypals exhibit several classic schizophrenic signs, though not delusions or hallucinations. Notable among these features are ideas of reference, suspiciousness, magical thinking, and odd speech—as well as the social isolation and restricted or cold affect that they share with the schizoid. Of course, schizoid and schizotypal characteristics will covary, as illustrated in an earlier case. The qualities of both syndromes frequently intermesh when schizoids begin to decompensate and are treated in institutional settings where they may observe and then adopt a variety of "odd and peculiar" mannerisms via modeling and vicarious learning.

Second, diagnostic differentiations between schizoid and *avoidant* personalities are difficult to make upon initial observations since both tend to be socially hesitant and unresponsive. A nonempirical source of difficulty in this regard may arise among clinicians who consider all "bland exteriors" to signify an adaptive or defensive emotional blunting and withdrawal consequent to repressed childhood disappointments, conflicts, and anxieties. This theoretical assumption does not apply to the formulations of the schizoid as conceived in the DSM-III. Though presented atheoretically insofar as etiology is concerned, the DSM-III schizoid is seen as not conflicted, nor suffering either ambivalence or deep disillusion; this patients's affectless and detached qualities stem from inherent deficits. For those who hold to the conflict, disillusion, and defense models, the new avoidant personality designation represents the syndrome that derives from experiences of early rebuff or affectional deprivation. Avoidant types desire affect and social acceptance, whereas the similarly appearing schizoid is intrinsically unresponsive and indifferent to them. Avoidants may appear cooly detached, but they actually are restrained and fearful lest their intense desires be met with further rejection and humiliation. More is said about this distinction between the passively and actively detached types in the next chapter.

PREDISPOSING BACKGROUND

Despite the long history and diverse methods that have been employed in researching the variants of the "schizophrenic spectrum," few data show up with sufficient consistency to be useful in identifying definitive "causes." Taken in concert, however, these data provide a basis, at least, for speculating about some of the background characteristics that may be expected to be found in these individuals.

Hypothesized Biogenic Factors

Schizoids may display an autonomic-endocrine imbalance favoring the cholinergic or parasympathetic system. Similarly, measures of arousal and activation should suggest high thresholds and sluggish responsivity. An ectomorphic body build, signifying inadequate nutritional reserves and lowered physical and energy capacities, has also been reported with some regularity. Behavioral observations lead us to infer, further, that schizoids have not only an anhedonic temperament but a temperament that is characterized by a broadly generalized emotional unresponsiveness. We might suggest, therefore, that biological substrates for a number of drive states, such as sex and hunger, are also especially weak. Speculations concerning the particular brain regions involved in these deficits are noted in later paragraphs.

It must be reiterated again that the role of biophysical processes in psychopathology is almost entirely conjectural. Available research data often are contradictory or based on poorly designed studies. With this caveat in mind, a few of the more plausible hypotheses are detailed.

Since children inherit overt physical features from their parents, it is safe to assume that features of internal morphology and physiochemistry are similarly inherited. Specifically, it would seem that parents who are biologically limited in their capacity to experience intense emotions, or to be vigorous and active, possess associated structural and physiological deficiencies that they transmit genetically to their children. Translated in terms relevant to our topic, the schizoid pattern may arise because an individual is at the low end of a genetically based continuum of individual differences in neurological structures and physiochemical processes that subserve affectivity, interpersonal sensitivity, activation, and so on.

Another frankly speculative hypothesis is that a substantial number of adult schizoid personalities displayed low sensory responsivity, motor passivity, and a generally placid mood in infancy and early childhood. They may have been easy to handle and care for, but it is likely that they provided their parents with few of the blissful and exuberant responses experienced with more vibrant and expressive youngsters. As a consequence of their undemanding and unresponsive nature, they are likely to have evoked few reciprocal responses of overt affection and stimulation from their caretakers. This reciprocal deficit in sheer physical handling and warmth may have compounded the child's initial tendencies toward inactivity, emotional flatness, and general insipidity.

Given that the schizoid is not obviously organic, it is probable that biophysical defects, if any, would take the form, not of gross tissue damage, but of a numerical sparseness of neural cells or of thinly dispersed branching systems emanating from relevant functional regions. For example, a congenital aplasia in any of the centers of the limbic system may give rise to affectivity deficits. Since the subregions of this complex anatomical system may be differentially impaired, no two persons will possess identical deficits. Thus, some schizoid personalities may exhibit the consequences of deficiencies in the "pleasure" center, whereas others may display behaviors associated with an underdeveloped "aversive" center, and so on.

The apathetic character of the schizoid pattern may be traced to deficits in the reticular system. Our understanding of the diverse functions carried out by this widely ramified system is far from complete, but we do have reason to think that it subserves arousal and activation. Thus a feebly branched reticular formation may underlie the lethargy and lack of alertness that characterize this personality. The view that the reticular system is a major relay situation for intrabrain circuitry is also unverified, but it is plausible. Dysfunctions in the reticular system may give rise, therefore, to chaotic interneuronal transmissions, and these may lead, in turn, to deficient emotional learnings. In a disorganized system, the emotional dimension of an experience may be circuited peculiarly or fail to be anchored to the cognitive awareness of that experience. As a result of such "discoordinations" the person may possess an intellectual grasp of human relationships but obscure them with irrelevant or deficient emotional correlates. This breakdown in reticular coordination may account for the schizoid's deficiency in connecting cognitions with their normally associated emotions.

Hypotheses implicating neurohormonal disturbances have become increasingly popular, and specific attention has been drawn to the role of these chemicals in maintaining synaptic control. Excesses or deficiencies in various neurohormones may result in the proliferation and scattering of neural impulses or in the inhibition of efficient neural sequences. Any chemically induced source of synaptic dyscontrol could give rise to the cognitive or affective deficits that characterize the schizoid.

Characteristic Experiential Histories

The variety of influences that may shape personality are legion. Unfortunately, there is a paucity of well-designed research in the field. Despite the lack of consistent confirmatory data, there is sufficient reason to believe that the psychogenic hypotheses that follow have merit as plausible conjectures.

A lack of functional stimuli normally provided by the infant's caretakers will inevitably set the foundation for maturational and learning deficits. Insufficient stimulus nourishment during the first year of life is likely to result in the underdevelopment of neural substrates for affectivity and a deficient learning of interpersonal attachments. Constitutionally unresponsive infants who have a built-in stimulus barrier, or who elicit few reactions from their environment, may be subject to a compounding of their initial activation and sensory deficits. Such children receive little cuddling and affection from their parents and, as a consequence, are deprived of the social and emotional cues requisite to learning human attachment behaviors. Some may provide stimulation for themselves, but this is likely to take the form of inanimate objects (dolls, blankets, or blocks), which may result in attachments to things rather than to people. Given an inborn sensory or energy deficit, these "schizoid-prone" infants are likely to be deprived of stimuli necessary for the maturation of their "emotional" brain centers and for the learning of human attachment behaviors.

Similar consequences may occur among infants with entirely normal constitutional capacities and dispositions. An "average" child who is reared with minimal human warmth, either in an impersonal atmosphere or with cold and unaffectionate parents, will also be deprived of the early sensory and affective stimulation necessary for normal development. As a consequence, these youngsters are likely to acquire the interpersonally detached and affectless symptomatology of the schizoid pattern.

A brief excerpt from Deutsch's study of the "as if" personality may be useful at this point since it effectively captures the essence of the experiential history of many schizoids. The case described is that of an only child of "one of the oldest noble families in Europe" and portrays the character of the relationship between parent and child that was "quite in accordance with tradition." The child's care and training was delegated to "strangers." Deutsch wrote:

> On certain specified days of the week she was brought before her parents for "control." At these meetings there was a formal check of her educational achievements, and the new program and other directions were given her preceptors. Then after a cool, ceremonious dismissal, the child was returned to her quarters. She received no warmth and no tenderness from her parents, nor did punishment come directly from them. This virtual separation from her parents had come soon after her birth. Perhaps the most inauspicious component of her parents' conduct, which granted the child only a very niggardly bit of warmth, was the fact—and this was reinforced by the whole program of her education—that their sheer existence was strongly emphasized, and the patient was drilled in love, honor, and obedience towards them without ever feeling these emotions directly and realistically.
>
> In this atmosphere, so lacking in feeling on the part of the parents, the development of a satisfactory emotional life could scarcely be expected in the child. (1942, p. 306)

It is clear that children learn to imitate the pattern of interpersonal relationships to which they are repeatedly exposed. Thus, learning to be reticent and undemonstrative is often but an incidental product of observing everyday relationships within a family setting. Families that are characterized by interpersonal reserve and formality, or that possess a bleak and cold atmosphere in which members relate to each other in a remote or disaffiliated way, are likely breeding grounds for schizoid-prone children who will acquire deeply ingrained habits of social ineptness or insensitivity.

Fragmented or amorphous styles of family communications also set the stage for the schizoid style. Thus, to relate successfully with others requires the capacity to focus on what others are experiencing and communicating, and to convey appropriate and relevant reactions in response. Some children fail to learn how to attend and interpret the signals that others communicate, or fail to learn how to respond in meaningful and rational ways. Learning effective styles of interpersonal communication is a requisite to shared social behaviors. Without these skills, the individual cannot function comfortably with others and will appear detached, unresponsive, cold, and insensitive— traits we associate with the schizoid pattern. Family styles of communicating in which ideas are aborted or are transmitted in circumstantial or amorphous ways are likely to be mirrored in the growing child's own manner of communciation. Moreover, being exposed to unfocused and murky patterns of thought, these children will, both by imitation and by the need to follow the "logic" that surrounds them, attend to peripheral or tangential aspects of human communication, that is, to signs and cues that most people view as irrelevant and distracting. This way of attending to, thinking about, and reacting to events, when generalized beyond the family setting, will give rise to perplexity and confusion on the part of others. As a consequence, disjointed and meaningless transactions may come to characterize many of these children's interpersonal relations, leading them into isolation and social distance. These events can only foster cognitive obscurities and emotional deficiencies, traits that characterize this passive-detached, or schizoid pattern.

PROGNOSTIC CONSIDERATIONS

What does the future hold for the schizoid? This section explores personality features that are themselves pathogenic, that is, foster increments in the individual's difficulties. Also touched upon are some of the therapeutic steps that might help reverse these trends.

Self-Perpetuation of the Schizoid Pattern

The impassivity and lack of color of schizoids enable them to maintain a comfortable distance from others. But their preferred state of detachment is itself pathogenic, not only because it fails to elicit experiences that could promote a more vibrant and rewarding style of life but because it fosters conditions that are conducive to more serious forms of psychopathology. Among the more prominent factors that operate to this end are the following.

Impassive and insensitive behavior. The inarticulateness and affective unresponsiveness that characterize schizoids do little to make them attractive to others. Most persons are not inclined to relate to schizoids for any period, tending to overlook their presence in most settings and, when interacting socially, doing so in a perfunctory and unemotional way. Of course, the fact that others consider them as boring and colorless suits the asocial predilections of schizoids quite well. However, this preference for remaining apart and alone only perpetuates and intensifies their tendencies toward detachment.

Diminished perceptual awareness. The schizoid personality not only is socially imperceptive but tends to "flatten" emotional events, that is, to blur and homogenize experiences that are intrinsically distinct and varied. In effect, these personalities project their murky and undifferentiated cognitions upon discriminable and complex social events. As a consequence of this perceptual diffusiveness, they preclude the possibility of learning from experiences that could lead them to a more variegated and socially discriminating life.

Social Inactivity. Passively-detached schizoids perpetuate their own pattern by limiting severely their social contacts and emotional involvements. Only those activities required to perform their jobs or fulfill their family obligations are pursued with any diligence. By shrinking their interpersonal milieu, they preclude new experiences from coming to bear upon them. This is their preference, of course, but it only fosters their isolated and withdrawn existence since it excludes events that might alter their style.

Remedial Interventions

The prognosis for this moderately severe personality is not promising. Many appear limited by a constitutional incapacity for affective expression and physical vigor. These liabilities may be inborn or acquired as a consequence of early experience. Regardless of their origin, however, the affectivity and interpersonal deficits found in these individuals are chronic and pervasive features of their personality makeup. Coupling these ingrained traits with the chracteristic lack of insight and poor motivation for change, we can only conclude that the probability is small that they will either seek or succeed in a course of remedial therapy. If their deficits are mild and if the circumstances of their life are favorable, they will stand a good chance, however, of maintaining adequate vocational and social adjustments.

When schizoids do come to the attention of a therapist, the latter's efforts are best directed toward countering their withdrawal tendencies. A major therapeutic goal is to prevent the possibility that they will isolate themselves entirely from the support of a benign environment. Additionally, the therapist should seek to ensure that they continue some level of social activity to prevent them from becoming lost in fantasy preoccupations and separated from reality contacts. However, efforts to encourage much social activity are best avoided since their tolerance in this area is limited.

Psychopharmacological treatment methods may be indicated. Trial periods with a number of "stimulants" may be explored to see if they "perk up" energy and affectivity. These should be used with caution, however, since they may activate feelings the patient is ill-equipped to handle. Attempts to cognitively reorient the patient's attitudes may be made for the purpose of developing self-insight and for motivating greater interpersonal sensitivity and activity. Techniques of behavioral modification appear to be of little value other than to reinforce some social skills. For different reasons, little may be expected of psychoanalytic approaches since schizoids possess a relatively uncomplicated world of intrapsychic emotions and defenses. Group methods may prove useful in encouraging and facilitating the acquisition of constructive social attitudes. In these benign settings, schizoids may begin to alter their social image and develop both the motivation and skills for a more effective interpersonal style.

Chapter 11

Avoidant Personality: The Withdrawn Pattern

Being "socially detached" can arise from numerous etiological sources and unfold through divergent developmental lines. One group of detached individuals, the "schizoid personality" discussed in the previous chapter, is noted by its "passive" detachment. These persons lack the affective capacity necessary for successful social relationships. Because of their deficits they fail to respond to the usual incentives and punishments that both activate interpersonal behavior and stimulate socially relevant and mutually rewarding communcations.

In terms of surface behavior, a second group, referred to as the "avoidant personality," appears very much like the first. Closer inspection, however, reveals that these "actively" detached persons are quite dissimilar from the passive type. They are oversensitive to social stimuli and are hyperreactive to the moods and feelings of others, especially those that portend rejection and humiliation. Their extreme anxiety not only intrudes into their thoughts and interferes with their behaviors but also disposes them to distance themselves from others as a protection against the psychic pain they anticipate.

The distinction drawn here between passively detached (schizoid) and actively detached (avoidant) personality types corresponds closely to data generated in studies of schizophrenia that consistently uncover two contrasting sets of characteristics. Some researchers reviewing their data suggest that schizophrenic patients are distinguished best by a number of deficits, their *under*arousal, *under*motivation, and *in*sensitivities. Others assert with equal conviction and support that these patients are best characterized by their excessive reactivity, that is, *over*arousal, *over*motivation and *hyper*sensitivity.

The author's own theoretical work (Millon, 1969) leads to the conclusion that both sets of seemingly contradictory findings are correct, *if* viewed in terms of the distinction between active and passive detachment. Both detached patterns, passive (schizoid) and active (avoidant), are disposed toward the more severe schizophrenic disorders. Although the overt symptomatologies of the active and passive styles are highly similar, especially upon initial examination, their constitutional dispositions, experiential histories, and basic coping strategies are quite distinct. One group—the passive, or schizoid—will display chronic underreactivity, affectivity deficit, cognitive slippage, and interpersonal indifference; whereas the other—the active, or avoidant—will show up as chronically overreactive and hyperalert, with affective disharmony, cognitive interference, and interpersonal distrust among their major features. The author believes that the reason researchers have consistently turned up paradoxical and contradictory results in schizophrenia can be traced, in great measure, to their failure to recognize that a basic distinction exists between actively and passively detached personalities.

The features of the passively detached schizoid were elaborated in the preceding chapter. The actively detached, or avoidant, personality is the prime focus in this chapter. Before proceeding to trace the historical antecedents of this new official syndrome, its principal descriptive features are presented as given in the DSM-III.

> The essential feature is a Personality Disorder in which there are hypersensitivity to potential rejection, humiliation, or shame; an unwillingness to enter into relationships unless given unusually strong guarantees of uncritical acceptance; social withdrawal in spite of a desire for affection and acceptance; and low self-esteem.
>
> Individuals with this disorder are exquisitely sensitive to rejection, humiliation, or shame. Most people are somewhat concerned about how others assess them, but these individuals are devastated by the slightest hint of disapproval. Consequently, they withdraw from opportunities for developing close relationships because of a fearful expectation of being belittled or humiliated. They may have one or two close friends, but the relationships are contingent on unconditional approval. . . .
>
> They are distressed by their lack of ability to relate comfortably to others and suffer from low self-esteem.
>
> Depression, anxiety, and anger at oneself for failing to develop social relations are commonly present. (p. 323)

HISTORICAL AND THEORETICAL ANTECEDENTS

The label "avoidant personality" is new, having been coined by Millon (1969) as a descriptive designation for individuals distinguished best by their active, as opposed to passive, aversion to social relationships. Personality features of a cast similar to the avoidant have been scattered through the clinical literature, most frequently in conjunction with conceptions of the schizoid personality and in descriptions of phobic character traits. Although this literature is quite slim, an attempt is made here to identify a number of these historic parallels. Before doing so, it should be noted that the mistrustful interpersonal style of the avoidant and the characteristic developmental history of parental deprecation represent features that have been ascribed, notably by analytic theorists, to a broad range of other personality disorders— for example, to the schizoid character by Fairbairn (1940) and, more recently, to the narcissistic personality by Kohut (1971). This chapter, however, is concerned with those authors whose conceptions of both the phenomenology and etiology of the personality types they have studied appear to be clear forerunners of the DSM-III avoidant pattern.

The first portrayal that approximates the actively detached character of the avoidant was described in 1911 by Bleuler in his initial formulation of the schizophrenic concept. Discussing several of the contrasting routes that often lead to the psychotic syndrome, Bleuler recorded the early phase of certain patients as follows:

> There are also cases where the shutting off from the outside world is caused by contrary reasons. Particularly in the beginning of their illness, these patients quite consciously shun any contact with reality because their affects are so powerful that they must avoid everything which might arouse their emotions. The apathy toward the outer world is then a secondary one springing from a hypertrophied sensitivity. (1950, p. 65)

Another early description that coincides in certain respects with the avoidant trait constellation was presented by Schneider (1923) in his conception of the aesthenic personality. Although aesthenics are noted best by their extra-ordinary attention to and hypochondriacal concern with bodily functions, this basic preoccupation extends into the psychic realm as well. Schneider described this feature as follows:

> Just as the aesthenic patient no longer takes his bodily functions for granted so he loses the normal, carefree attitude to psychic functions. . . . All this is due in the first place to the chronic habit of self-investigation. . . . Psychic functioning as with bodily function becomes interfered with and starts to falter. . . .
> Feelings do not seem genuine, relationships appear lifeless and void. . . .
> All human activity needs a certain psychic half light or chiaroscuro if it is to be experienced as an integral part of the self. Actions tend to disintegrate if full attention is focussed on them in the same way as the body ceases to function smoothly if it is subjected to too much conscious interference. (1950, p. 141)

Reflecting on observations made by Kretschmer concerning aesthenics, Schneider noted that these patients also

> fail to relax after reacting to an experience though they may personally be no longer oppressed by it. A disturbed emotional undertow persists or the situation is deliberately prolonged. (1950, p. 143)

Turning more directly to the observations of Kretschmer leads to the first series of descriptions that presaged the avoidant personality in the majority of its elements. As discussed in the preceding chapter, Kretschmer identified two polarities of sensitivity among those with the schizoid temperament: the anaesthetic and the hyperaesthetic. Those whose constitutional dispositions cluster at the anaesthetic pole correspond closely to the DSM-III schizoid, described in detail in Chapter 10. It is the group that Kretschmer located at the hyperaesthetic end of the continuum, which exhibits sensibilities that foreshadow and exemplify the avoidant pattern. Kretschmer's own words illustrate his portrayal:

> In the hyperaesthetic type, there often develops a sharp antithesis: "I" and "The external world." There is a constant excited self-analysis and comparison: "How do I impress people? Who is doing me an injury? In what respect have I to forgive myself something? How shall I get through?" This is particularly true of gifted, artistic natures.... They are men who have a continual psychic conflict, whose life is composed of a chain of tragedies, a single thorny path of sorrow....
>
> [Here] we find the qualities of nervousness, excitability, capriciousness, anxiousness, tenderness, and, above all, sensitive susceptibility.... He behaves shyly, or timidly, or distrustfully, or as if he were pushed in to himself. He complains of nerve troubles. He keeps anxiously away from all coarse games and brawls....
>
> They are not restful in spirit, but, under the covering of a sulky silence, there always glimmers a spark of inner tension, which has the character of a complex, and springs from the accumulation of all the little everyday unpleasantness of office and family life; which get heaped up inside, which cannot be overcome, and which cannot be spoken out. (1925, pp. 167–174)

The key phrase depicting Kretschmer's hyperaesthetic, and one equally central to an understanding of the avoidant personality, was stated by him thus: "They seek as far as possible to avoid and deaden all stimulation from the outside" (p. 161). How sharply this differs from the anaesthetic, or DSM-III schizoid, who Kretschmer depicted as possessing "a certain psychic insensitivity, dullness...lack of spontaneity [and] affective imbecility" (p. 156).

Conceived as a formal entity, traditional psychoanalytic theorists have not proposed a diagnostic syndrome along the lines of the avoidant personality. The formulations of Fairbairn, Winnicott, Arieti, Guntrip, and Laing, however, using labels such as "schizoid" and "false-self," do correspond in several major respects to the developmental history and socially detached character of the avoidant type. Reference may be made to their views presented in the preceding chapter, and readers of their writings will no doubt find their descriptions as closely paralleling those of the DSM-III avoidant.

Along similar lines, the notion of a "phobic character" has been touched upon by a number of classically oriented analysts. Fenichel, for example, wrote:

> "Phobic characters" would be the correct designation for persons whose reactive behavior limits itself to the avoidance of the situations originally wished for. (1945, p. 527)

Rado, a major contributor to the classical analytic school, described a subgroup of his "overreactive disorders" as follows:

> I use the phrase *phobic avoidance* since phobia is the avoidance mechanism.
> The ... characteristic of the phobic avoidance mechanism is that it tends to spread, to reinforce one set of precautionary measures, to reinforce safeguards of the first order by new safeguards of the second order, the third order, and so forth. The more precautionary measures are introduced, the more the conditions of anxiety move along. (1969, p. 182)

Most recently, MacKinnon and Michels (1971), adhering to a relatively traditional analytic model, set forth a number of features of what they term "phobic character traits." They wrote:

> Far more common than the symptomatic phobia is the use of avoidance and inhibition as characterological defenses.... [It] is recognized as defensive avoidance only when the person's life situation exposes his inhibition as maladaptive....
> The individual is preoccupied with his security and fears any possible threat to it, constantly imagining himself in situations of danger while pursuing the course of greatest safety. (p. 149)

Breaking from the orthodox analytic mold, Horney (1945) proposed a personality characterization that she termed the "detached type" and described as exhibiting an interpersonal style of "moving away from people." The following excerpts illustrate her portrayal of this "interpersonally avoidant" and "actively detached" pattern:

> There is intolerable strain in associating with people and solitude becomes primarily a means of avoiding it....
> What is crucial is their inner need to put distance between themselves and others.... They draw around themselves a kind of magic circle which no one may penetrate....
> All the needs and qualities they acquire are diverted toward this major need for not getting involved....
> A ... precarious way to maintain self-sufficiency is by consciously or unconsciously restricting one's needs.... the underlying principle here is never to become so attached to anybody and anything so that he or it becomes indispensable.... Better to have nothing matter much.
> His goals are negative: he wants *not* to be involved, *not* to need anybody, *not* to allow others to intrude on or influence him.
> There is a general tendency to suppress all feeling, even to deny its existence. (pp. 73–82)

In subsequent writings, Horney elaborated a variety of "neurotic solutions" to conflict. Among the characteristics that typify the detached style are self-hate and self-contempt, which Horney aptly described as follows:

> On little or no provocation he feels that others look down on him, do not take him seriously, do not care for his company, and in fact, slight him. His self-

contempt adds considerably to the profound uncertainty he has about himself, and hence cannot but make him as profoundly uncertain about the attitudes of others toward him. Being unable to accept himself as he is, he cannot possibly believe that others, knowing him with all his shortcomings, can accept him in a friendly or appreciative spirit.

What he feels in deeper layers is much more drastic, and may amount to an unshakable conviction that others plainly despise him. (1950, p. 134)

Turning to entirely different quarters, several biologically oriented researchers have referred to syndromes that are also akin to the avoidant. On the basis of his early genetic family studies, Kallmann (1938), for example, came to speak of certain patients as suffering "schizoidia," describing them as exhibiting "autistic introversion, emotional inadequacy, sudden surges of temperament and inappropriate motor responses to emotional stimuli" (p. 162). Similarly, Kety and his associates (1968), in their discussions of the "schizophrenic spectrum," spoke of their fourth and final subgroup as possessing attributes similar to Kretschmer's "schizothymics," a familial disposition to schizophrenia characterized by clinical features such as "nervousness" "shyness," and "sensitivity." A more explicitly biological formulation is Klein's differentiation of two schizoid subtypes. The first he believes is aptly labeled as such in the DSM-III; it is noted by an intrinsic asocial inclination that is experienced as ego-syntonic. The second type, quite similar in its sensitivities to the DSM-III avoidant, Klein described as:

> The shy, socially backward, inept, obedient person who is fearful and therefore isolated but appreciates sociability and would like to be part of the crowd . . . seems to have an emotional state compounded of anticipatory anxiety [and] low self-esteem. (1970, p. 189)

A recent, and analytically oriented, theory that deals with the origins of schizophrenia describes the syndrome as possessing features that are prominent in the DSM-III avoidant personality. Set within an object-relations framework, Burnham, Gladstone, and Gibson attributed the primary clinical symptomatology of this group to what they termed the "need-fear dilemma"; they expressed the concern of this patient as follows:

> He has an inordinate need for external structure and control. He requires others to provide the organization and regulation which he is unable to provide for himself. . . . [His] very psychological existence depends on his maintaining contact with objects, whether as individuals or as part of a social structure. . . .
>
> The very excessiveness of his need for objects also makes them inordinately dangerous and fearsome since they can destroy him through abandonment. Hence he fears and distrusts them.
>
> [Among] efforts to avert or alleviate the pain of his need-fear dilemma [is] . . . object avoidance. . . .
>
> Avoidance takes various forms. In one form the person becomes quietly withdrawn and seemingly detached, unresponsive, and disinterested in others. . . .

> Withdrawal may be the patient's way of trying to maintain extremely tenuous
> internal equilibria by limiting potentially disruptive object contacts. . . .
> Attempts by others to engage him in interaction are regarded as intrusions which
> carry the threat of disorganization. His usual reaction is either a deepening of the
> gulf of unresponsiveness or an abrupt outburst of rage. (1969, pp. 27–31)

The diversity of syndromes posited in the past that parallel important clinical
segments of the avoidant personality should be a testament to its validity as a
clinical entity, despite its recency as a formal and official designation. Only
time will tell whether it is best conceived in purely descriptive terms or
through notions such as temperament (Kretschmer), developmental conflict
(Horney), or early object anxiety (Burnham). As conceived in the DSM-III, it
had its origins in a biosocial-learning theory (Millon, 1969) and was described
as the personality pattern representing an active-detached coping style. In
accord with this formulation, the following clinical features and diagnostic
criteria were presented by the author in 1975 as the initial working draft of the
avoidant syndrome for the personality subcommittee of the DSM-III Task
Force.

> This pattern is typified by an apprehensive and fearful mistrust of others.
> There is a depreciation of self-worth, a marked social awkwardness and a general
> distancing from interpersonal closeness. Desires for affection may be strong, but
> are self-protectively denied or restrained. Recurrent anxieties and a pervasive
> mood disharmony characterize the emotional life. Thought is periodically
> distracted and confused, and there is an overalertness to potential social
> derogation that is intensified by tendencies to distort events in line with
> anticipated rejection.
>
> Since adolescence or early adulthood at least 3 of the following have been
> present to a notably greater degree than in most people and were not limited to
> discrete periods nor necessarily prompted by stressful life events.
>
> 1. Affective dysphoria (e.g., notes a constant and confusing undercurrent of
>   tension, sadness and anger; exhibits vacillation between desire for affection,
>   fear and numbness of feeling).
> 2. Mild cognitive interference (e.g., relates being bothered and distracted by
>   disruptive inner thoughts; irrelevant and digressive ideation upsets effective
>   social communication).
> 3. Alienated self-image (e.g., describes life as one of social isolation and
>   rejection; devalues self and reports periodic feelings of emptiness and
>   depersonalization).
> 4. Aversive interpersonal behavior (e.g., tells of social pan-anxiety and distrust;
>   protectively seeks privacy to avoid anticipated social derogation).
> 5. Perceptual hypersensitivity (e.g., vigilant scanning for potential threats to
>   self; overinterprets innocuous behaviors as signs of ridicule and humilia-
>   tion).

Following several committee discussions, a number of modifications in the
diagnostic criteria were proposed and, with notable exceptions, served as the
principal components of the final DSM-III draft.

A. Excessive social withdrawal (e.g., distances self from close personal attachments; engages in peripheral social and vocational roles).

B. Hypersensitivity to rejection (e.g., apprehensively alert to signs of social derogation; interprets innocuous events as ridiculing).

C. Contingent personal relationships (e.g., is self-protectively unwilling to enter into relationships unless given unusually strong guarantees of being uncritically accepted).

D. Low self-esteem (e.g., devalues self-achievements and is overly dismayed by personal shortcomings).

E. Emotional dysphoria (e.g., experiences a confusing mixture of feeling tense, sad, angry, and lonely).

CLINICAL PICTURE

Avoidant personalities are acutely sensitive to social deprecation and humiliation. They feel their loneliness and isolated existence deeply, experience being "out of things" as painful, and have a strong, though often repressed, desire to be accepted. Despite their longing to relate and to be active participants in social life, they fear placing their welfare in the hands of others. Their social detachment does not stem, therefore, from deficit drives and sensibilities, as in the schizoid personality, but from an active and self-protective restraint. Although experiencing a pervasive estrangement and loneliness, they dare not expose themselves to the defeat and humiliation they anticipate. Since their affective feelings cannot be expressed overtly, they cumulate and are often directed toward an inner world of fantasy and imagination. Their need for affect and closeness may pour forth in poetry, be sublimated in intellectual pursuits, or be expressed in sensitively detailed artistic activities.

Unfortunately, isolation and protective withdrawal results in secondary consequences that further compound the avoidants' difficulties. Their obviously tense and fearful demeanor often elicits ridicule and deprecation from others. Expressions of self-doubt and anxious restraint leave them open to persons who gain satisfaction in taunting and belittling those who dare not retaliate. The additional humiliation they experience thereby not only confirms their mistrust of others but reactivates the wounds of the past.

With this precis in mind, the four levels of clinical data that help diagnose the avoidant pattern are detailed.

Behavioral Features

A shy and apprehensive quality characterizes avoidants. They are not only awkward and uncomfortable in social situations but seem to shrink actively from the reciprocal give-and-take of interpersonal relations. They often impose a strain upon others in face-to-face interactions. Their discomfort and mistrust often take the form of subtle testing operations, that is, guarded maneuvers by which they check whether others are sincere in their friendly overtures or are a deceptive threat to their security. Most observers who have only passing contact with avoidant personalities tend to see them as timid, withdrawn, or perhaps cold and strange—not unlike the image conveyed by the schizoid personality. Those who relate to them more closely, however, quickly learn of their sensitivities, their touchiness, evasiveness, and mistrustful qualities.

The speech of avoidants is generally slow and constrained. They exhibit frequent hesitations, aborted or fragmentary thought sequences, and occasional confused and irrelevant digressions. Physical behaviors tend to be highly controlled or underactive, although marked with periodic bursts of fidgety and rapid staccato movements. Overt expressions of emotion are typically kept in check, but this underresponsiveness overlays deep tension and disharmony. They exert great restraint, not only in the control of anxiety, but in controlling feelings of confusion and in subduing the upsurge of anger.

Self-Descriptions and Complaints

The active-detached, or avoidant, personality is hyperalert to the most subtle feelings and intentions of others. These individuals are "sensitizers," acutely perceptive observers who scan and appraise every movement and expression of those with whom they come into contact. Although their hypervigilance serves to protect them against potential dangers, it floods them with excessive stimuli and distracts them from attending to many of the ordinary yet relevant features of their environment.

Thought processes are not only interfered with by this flooding of irrelevant environmental details but are complicated further by inner emotional disharmonies that intrude and divert the avoidants' attentions. Combined with extraneous perceptions, these intrusive feelings upset their cognitive processes and diminish their capacity to cope effectively with many of the ordinary tasks of life. This cognitive interference is especially pronounced in social settings, where avoidants' perceptual vigilance and emotional turmoil are most acute.

Avoidants describe themselves typically as ill-at-ease, anxious, and sad. Feelings of loneliness and of being unwanted and isolated are often expressed, as are fear and distrust of others. People are seen as critical, betraying, and humiliating. With so trouble-laden an outlook, we can well understand why their social behavior is characterized by interpersonal aversiveness.

Disharmonious emotions and feelings of emptiness and depersonalization are especially noteworthy. Avoidant personalities tend to be excessively introspective and self-conscious, often perceiving themselves as different from others, and they are unsure of their identity and self-worth. The alienation they feel with others is paralleled, then, by a feeling of alienation from themselves. They voice futility with regard to the life they lead, have a deflated self-image, and frequently refer to themselves with an attitude of contempt and derision more severe than they hear from others.

Inferred Intrapsychic Dynamics

Protecting oneself from real and imagined psychic pain is a paramount goal in these personalities. Avoiding situations that may result in personal humiliation or social rejection is the guiding force behind their interpersonal relationships. Of equal threat is the avoidant's own aggressive and affectional impulses. These are especially distressing since these persons fear that their own behaviors may prompt others to reject and condemn them. Much intrapsychic energy is devoted to mechanisms that deny and bind these inner urges.

Avoidant personalities are beset by several notable conflicts. The struggle between affection and mistrust is central. They desire to be close, show affection, and be warm with others, but they cannot shake themselves of the belief that such actions will result in pain and disillusion. They have strong doubts concerning their competence and, hence, have grave concerns about venturing into the more competitive aspects of our society. This lack of confidence curtails their initiative and leads to the fear that their efforts at autonomy and independence will only fail and result in humiliation. Every route toward gratification seems blocked with conflicts. They are unable to act on their own because of marked self-doubt; on the other hand, they cannot depend on others because they mistrust them. Security and rewards can be obtained, then, neither from themselves nor from others; both provide only pain and discomfort. They are trapped in the worst of both worlds, seeking to avoid both the distress that surrounds them and the emptiness and wounds that inhere within them.

This latter feature is especially significant to an understanding of the avoidant for it signifies the fact that turning away from one's external environment brings little peace and comfort. Avoidants find no solace and freedom within themselves. Having internalized the pernicious attitude of self-derogation and deprecation to which they were exposed in earlier life, they not only experience little reward in their accomplishments and thoughts but find instead shame, devaluation, and humiliation. In fact, there may be more pain being alone with one's despised self than with the escapable torment of others. Immersing oneself in one's own thoughts and feelings is the more difficult experience since one cannot physically avoid oneself, cannot walk away, escape, or hide from one's own being. Deprived of feelings of worth and self-respect, these persons suffer constantly from painful thoughts about their pitiful state, their misery, and the futility of being themselves. Efforts that are even more vigilant than those applied to the external world must be expended to ward off the painful ideas and feelings that well up within them. These aversive signals are especially anguishing since they pervade every facet of the avoidants' makeup. It is their entire being that has become devalued, and nothing about them escapes the severe judgment of self-derision.

The avoidant's prime, if not sole, recourse is to break up, destroy, or repress these painful thoughts and the emotions they unleash. These personalities struggle to prevent self-preoccupations and seek to intrude irrelevancies by blocking and making their normal thoughts and communications take on different and less significant meanings. In effect, and through various intrapsychic ploys, they attempt to interfere actively with their own cognitions. Similarly, the anxieties, desires, and impulses that surge within them must be also restrained, denied, turned about, transformed, and distorted. Thus, they seek to muddle their emotions also, making their affective life even more discordant and disharmonious than it is typically. To avoidants it is better to experience diffuse disharmony than the sharp pain and anguish of being themselves. Despite their efforts at inner control, painful and threatening thoughts and feelings will periodically break through, disrupting more stable cognitive processes and upsetting whatever emotional equanimity they are able to muster. Fantasies occasionally serve as an outlet for venting frustrating impulses, but they too prove distressing in the long run since they point up the contrast between desire and objective reality. Repression of all feelings it often the only recourse, hence accounting for the avoidant's initial appearance of being flat, unemotional, and indifferent, an appearance that belies the inner turmoil and intense affect these persons truly experience.

Interpersonal Coping Style

As noted, avoidant personalities have a deep mistrust of others and a markedly deflated image of their own self-worth. They have learned to believe through painful experiences that the world is unfriendly, cold, and humiliating, and that they possess few of the social skills and personal attributes by which they can hope to experience the pleasures and comforts of life. They anticipate being slighted or demeaned wherever they turn. They have learned to be watchful and on guard against the ridicule and contempt they expect from others. They must be exquisitely alert and sensitive to signs that portend censure and derision. And, perhaps most painful of all, looking inward offers them no solace since they find none of the attributes they admire in others.

Their outlook is therefore a negative one: to avoid pain, to need nothing, to depend on no one, and to deny desire. Moreover, they must turn away from themselves also, away from an awareness of their unlovability and unattractiveness, and from their inner conflicts and disharmony. Life, for them, is a negative experience, both from without and from within.

Interpersonally, avoidants are best characterized as actively detached personalities, they are guided by the need to put distance between themselves and others, that is, to minimize involvements that can reactivate or duplicate past humiliations. Privacy is sought and they attempt to eschew as many social obligations as possible without incurring further condemnation. Any event that entails a personal relationship with others, unless it assures uncritical acceptance, constitutes a potential threat to their fragile security. They may deny themselves even simple possessions to protect against the pain of loss or disappointment. Efforts to comply with the wishes of others, no less to assert themselves, may have proved fruitless or disillusioning. Appeasement may have resulted in a loss of what little personal integrity they may have felt they still possessed, leading only to feelings of greater humiliation and disparagement. The only course they have learned that will succeed in reducing shame and humiliation is to back away, draw within themselves, and keep a watchful eye against incursions into their solitude.

In sum, these personalities avoid the anguish of social relationships by distancing themselves and remaining vigilant and alert to potential threat. This actively detached coping style contrasts markedly with the strategy of passively detached schizoids, who are perceptually insensitive to their surroundings. Avoidants are overly attentive and aware of variations and subtleties in their stimulus world. They have learned in the past that the most effective means of avoiding social rejection and deprecation is to be hyperalert to cues that forewarn their occurrence. By decreasing their relationships and diminishing their importance, they can minimize the hazards they fear surround them.

ASSOCIATED DISORDERS

As in prior chapters, this section discusses the several Axis I and Axis II disorders that frequently exist concurrently with the personality syndrome under review. Aspects of differential diagnosis are also discussed.

Concomitant Axis I Symptoms

Avoidant types are among the most vulnerable of the personality patterns to Axis I symptom disorders; they not only exhibit more of them but experience them more frequently and intensely than all other types—with the possible exception of the borderline personality, in whom these symptoms often achieve the characterological quality of chronicity. Because the avoidant designation is the newest of the official personality syndromes, its concomitant symptom disorders are elaborated more fully than usual.

Anxiety disorders.   The most common of the avoidant's symptoms is the *generalized anxiety disorder,* typically seen for prolonged periods and consisting of moderately intense and widely exhibited apprehensions. The interpersonal abilities of avoidants are barely adequate to the social strains and challenges they must handle. As such, they characteristically seem on edge, unable to relax, easily startled, tense, worrisome, irritable, preoccupied with calamities, and prone to nightmares; and they have poor appetites and suffer fatigue and intangible physical ailments. Some avoidants "adjust" to this pervasively uncomfortable state, but their lives are thereby limited and impoverished, restricted by the need to curtail their activities and relationships to just those few they can manage. Phenomenological apprehension is the most notable symptom voiced by these patients. They often report a vague and diffuse awareness that something dreadful is imminent, an experience compounded by the fact that they are unsure as to what it is that they dread and from where the danger may arise. This feeling of impending disaster periodically reaches intense proportions, as in an acute panic disorder. Frequently, avoidants will be precipitated into anxiety as a consequence of social encroachment. Their histories have made them hypersensitive to social derogation and humiliation. Not only have they acquired a marked distrust of others, but they lack the self-esteem to retaliate against insult and derision. When repeated deprecations occur, reactivating past humiliations and resentments, avoidants are unable to respond or fear responding as they would like. As a consequence, their frustration and tension may mount, finally erupting into an acute panic.

Phobic disorders.   Social phobias of course, are so deeply ingrained and pervasive a part of the avoidant that it is difficult to say where the personality trait ends and where the phobic symptom begins. Nevertheless, avoidant personalities may have particular phobic feelings about specific settings or persons that are of substantially greater magnitude than they possess toward most interpersonal situations. Avoidants tend to keep their phobias to themselves. For them, the phobic symptom does not serve as a means of soliciting social attention, as it does in dependents or histrionics, since they are convinced that such attentions will bring forth only ridicule and abuse. As with anxiety, phobias are an expression, albeit a symbolic one, of feeling encroached upon or of being pressured by excessive social demands. Crystallized in phobic form, these patients have an identifiable and circumscribed anxiety source that they can then actively avoid. In a similar manner, phobic symptoms may enable avoidants to redirect feelings of resentment that they dare not express toward the "true" object of these feelings. Dreading social rebuke, avoidants will seek some innocuous external source to keep their resentments in check. Through displacement and condensation, the selected phobic object may come to represent a symbolic, yet "real," basis for their anxieties and resentments.

Obsessive-compulsive disorders.   These may serve to distract these patients from reflecting on their "true" misery. Similarly, obsessive or compulsive preoccupations may serve to counteract feelings of estrangement or depersonalization by providing them with thoughts and behaviors that assure them that there is some tangible reality to life. Moreover, these ruminations and activities "fill up" time and distract their attention from anticipated social derision. For example, a 30-year-old severely avoidant man made a 360-degree turn each time he walked through a door. He believed that this act would change his personality, which, in turn, would disincline those he subsequently met from ridiculing him. Ritualistic behaviors such as these often signify a bizarre method of controlling socially condemned thoughts and impulses. Thus, this same patient put the index finger of his right hand to his lips, and then placed both hands in the back pockets of his trousers, whenever he felt the urge to speak obscenities or fondle the breasts of women passersby.

Somatoform disorders. Avoidant personalities exhibit *hypochondriacal disorders* to achieve a variety of different coping goals, such as countering feelings of depersonalization. They may become alert to bodily sounds and movements to assure themselves that they exist as "real" and alive. In more severe states, and because of their habitual social isolation and self-preoccupations, these bodily sensations may become elaborated into bizarre and delusional experiences. Discomforting bodily sensations may be used also as a symbolic form of self-punishment, representing the disgust, if not hatred, that some avoidants feel toward themselves. Fatigue in these personalities may be seen as an extension of the avoidant's basic detachment strategy. Thus, physical inertia can serve instrumentally as a rationalization to justify withdrawal from social contact.

A wide variety of *conversion disorders*—ranging from minor tics, generalized sensory anesthesias, and motor paralyses to the total loss of vision or hearing—may be exhibited by avoidant personalities. These symptoms do not occur frequently, however, since these patients wish to avoid situations that promote attention. Nevertheless, when they are unable to avoid social pressure or deprecation, and fear expressing their dismay directly or overtly, they may bind their anxieties into conversion symptoms. These symptoms are most likely to occur if strong impulses of counterhostility, which must be contained, have been stirred. Specifically, symptoms such as loss of vision and hearing may be understood if seen as an extension of their habitual avoidance strategy. By eliminating their sensory awareness, they no longer see or hear others deriding them. A severance of body functions, such as in sensory anesthesias or motor paralyses, may reflect the condensation and displacement of depersonalization anxieties. Thus, rather than experience a sense of "nothingness," avoidants may crystallize and contain this dreadful feeling by attaching it to one part of the body. Conversion symptoms may also reflect self-repudiation. Viewing themselves with derision and contempt, avoidants may utilize conversion as an expression of self-rejection. By disconnecting some part of themselves, they symbolize their desire to disown their body. Some conversion patients evidence *la belle indifference,* that is, a lack of concern about their bodily symptoms. Although this indifference to illness does occur, it is by no means typical of all conversion patients and would be expected among those who do not wish to draw attention to their ailment. For this reason, it is found in avoidant personalities who have serious concerns as to how others will react to their infirmity.

Dissociative disorders. As noted repeatedly, avoidant personalities experience frequent and varied forms of dissociative disorder. Feelings of estrangement may arise as a protective maneuver to diminish the impact of excessive stimulation or the pain of social humiliation. These symptoms may also reflect the patient's devalued sense of self. Thus, without an esteemed and integrated inner core to which experience can be anchored, events often seem disconnected, ephemeral, and unreal. Self-estrangement may also be traced to avoidants' characteristic coping maneuver of cognitive interference, which not only serves to disconnect normally associated events but deprives these persons of meaningful contact with their own feelings and thoughts. Experiences of amnesia may also arise occasionally as an expression of self-rejection. To be oneself is not a cheerful prospect for these persons, and life may be started anew by the act of disowning one's past identity. Brief frenzied states in which frustrated and repressed impulses are discharged may be commonly found in these patients, especially at advanced levels of severity.

Affective disorders.   Given their "detached" style, we might think that avoidants would not be among those who display affective disorders. This belief would be consistent with their characteristic effort to flatten emotions and suppress or otherwise interfere with feelings. Despite their efforts in this regard, these patients do sense a deep sadness, emptiness, and loneliness. Many express a yearning for the affection and approval they have been denied. Added to this melancholic tone is the contempt these patients feel for themselves and the self-deprecation they experience for their unlovability, weaknesses, and ineffectuality. Though hesitant to display this self-contempt before others, lest it invite a chorus of further derision, tactful probing will readily elicit both the self-deprecatory comments and the genuinely felt moods of futility and dejection. Repetitive affective disorders, particularly of a depressive nature, are therefore among their more notable Axis I symptoms.

Schizophrenic disorders.   Among the more severe or psychotic disorders, *disorganized schizophrenic* episodes signify a surrendering by the avoidant of all coping efforts. Although every pathological pattern may exhibit this disorder, it is an active coping maneuver in some personality types, thereby increasing the likelihood of its occurrence. Moreover, some personalities are more disposed than others to surrender their controls and thus to collapse into a fragmented state. Avoidant personalities are among those especially inclined to this disorder, not only because they are easily overwhelmed by external and internal pressures but because "disorganization" is an extension of their characteristic protective maneuver of interfering with their cognitive clarity. By blocking the flow of thoughts and memories, they effectively distract themselves and dilute the impact of painful feelings and recollections. Disorganized (hebephrenic) schizophrenia may arise, then, as a direct product of either intolerable pressures or self-made confusions, or both. The upshot is a clinical picture of "forced" absurdity and incoherence, and a concerted effort to disrupt cognitive logic and emotional stability.

Catatonic schizophrenic disorders signify a protective withdrawal, a retreat into indifference, and a purposeful uninvolvement and insensitivity to life so as to avoid the anguish it has produced. By disengaging themselves totally, avoidants need no longer feel the painful emotions they experienced before, no longer suffer the discouragement of struggling fruitlessly, and no longer desire and aspire, only to be frustrated and humiliated again. Faced with a sense of hopelessness and futility, severely troubled avoidants have given up, have become uncaring, neutral, flat, impassive, and "dead" to everything. This shutting off of emotions and the retreat into indifference are protective devices that can be employed easily by all individuals who have been overwhelmed by a sense of hopelessness and futility. Despite its ease as a coping maneuver, it appears with significantly greater frequency among avoidants whose lifelong strategies dispose them to emotional detachment and withdrawal. It is a "logical" extension then of their personality style. Unable to handle substantial overstimulation—be it from unexpected responsibilities, objective threat, or reactivated anxiety—they may overemploy their characteristic coping strategies and withdraw into a *catatonic stupor*, an impassive, unresponsive, and unfeeling state. Avoidant personalities can usually be identified at these times by their total muteness and their complete "tuning out" of the world, traits that result in an inner void and a picture of masklike stupor. At other times, a *catatonic rigidity* becomes the prominent feature, a purposeful recalcitrance and manifest uncooperativeness. Beneath the quiet and restrained exterior, however, lies a seething but controlled hostility. These avoidants are not only mute and immobile, then, but "bullheaded" and adamant about remaining in certain fixed and preferred positions, opposing all efforts to alter them. This rigidity is manifested in their body tension, with fists clenched, teeth gritted, and jaw locked tight and firm. Breaking periodically through this physical immobility may be stereotyped repetitive acts, bizarre gestures, grimaces, and peculiar tics, grins, and giggles. Every now and then inner impulses and fantasies may emerge briefly in a *catatonic excitement*, often discharged or enacted in strange, symbolic expressions. Obviously, there are active, though confused, thoughts and emotions churning beneath the passive catatonic exterior.

Severely disturbed avoidants may also show periods of *paranoid schizophrenia*, with their unsystematic and incoherent delusions. Distortions of reality are almost an inevitable consequence of prolonged periods of marked social isolation. In addition, brief delusional formations may develop if these patients are faced with severe depersonalization feelings or are thrust into situations of excessive responsibility and stimulation. These delusions are usually bizarre and nonsensical.

Concurrent Axis II Personalities

Avoidant features often develop in other personality patterns as they begin to withdraw socially and experience critical and unsupportive responses from others. Whether initially dependent, passive-aggressive, compulsive, or whatever, the troublesome moods and actions that these patients exhibit often provoke both the rejection and the humiliating experiences that characterize the background of the avoidant from the start. In addition to these insidiously developing similarities, there are personality syndromes that naturally combine with the avoidant pattern; these are discussed next.

Research utilizing the MCMI (Millon, 1977) shows that profiles including the avoidant pattern are shared most often with dependent, passive-aggressive, borderline, and schizotypal personalities. A brief case study of an avoidant-dependent combination is presented in Chapter 5. The following paragraphs illustrate the mixed features of an avoidant–passive-aggressive and an avoidant-borderline profile; an avoidant-schizotypal combination is presented in chapter 14.

Avoidant-passive-aggressive mixed personality.   This combination

has been found to be prevalent in ambulatory outpatient centers for chronic clients, such as half-way houses. Patients in medical-surgical clinics who are referred for psychological evaluations also show this profile frequently. The following "blind" MCMI computer report is based on the responses of a 46-year-old male veteran of the Korean War; he had been hospitalized several times on psychiatric grounds and was currently attending a "medication group" at a local community mental health center following several aborted suicide attempts.

> This patient's behavior is typified by a conflict between desiring detachment from others and fearing to be independent. He would like to be close and show affection but anticipates pain and disillusionment. Complicating the concern about venturing into close relationships is his markedly deflated self-esteem. Thus, any effort to make a go at independence is constrained by the fear that it will fail and result in humiliation. Although he has no alternative but to depend upon supporting persons and institutions, this behavior overlies deep resentments. Others have either turned against him or disapproved his efforts to achieve autonomy. He is often petulant and passively aggressive, and on occasion will attack others for failing to recognize his need for affection and nurturance. The dependency security he seeks is seriously jeopardized under these circumstances. To bind anger, and thereby protect against humiliation and loss, he has become anxious and withdrawn, feeling a pervasive dysphoric mood.
>
> The patient's discontent, outbursts, and moodiness frequently evoke humiliating reactions from others, and these rebuffs only serve to reinforce his self-protective withdrawal. Every avenue of gratification seems trapped in conflict. He cannot act alone because of marked self-doubts. On the other hand, he cannot depend on others because of a deep social mistrust. Disposed to anticipate disappointments, he often precipitates disillusionment through obstructive and negative behaviors. He reports feeling misunderstood, unappreciated, and demeaned by others; voices a sense of futility about life; has a deflated self-image; and frequently refers to self with contempt and deprecation. A depressive tone and anxious wariness are ever-present, evident in erratic displays of moodiness.

Unable to muster the wherewithal to overcome deficits, and unable to achieve the support desired from others, he is disposed to turn against himself, expressing feelings of unworthiness and uselessness. Expecting to be slighted or demeaned, he has learned to be watchful and on guard against the ridicule and contempt anticipated from others. He is therefore ever-alert and sensitive to minute signs of censure and derision. Looking inward offers him no solace since he sees none of the attributes admired in others in himself. This awareness intrudes upon his thoughts and interferes with effective behavior, upsetting his cognitive processes and diminishing his capacity to cope effectively with ordinary life tasks. During periods when stresses are minimal, he may deny past resentments and attempt to portray an image of general well-being and contentment. These efforts, however, give way readily under the slightest of pressures.

Avoidant-borderline mixed personality. The second profile combination, that composed of an avoidant-borderline amalgam, is found most often among chronic psychiatric patients who have experienced repeated psychotic episodes. It also shows up among those undergoing an acute or brief reactive psychosis. The automated printout of the MCMI computer analysis presented here is based on responses obtained from a 40-year-old divorced woman whose two preadolsecent children were placed in a foster home several years earlier. Her history shows more than 10 brief psychiatric hospitalizations.

This patient's behavior is characterized by a pervasive apprehensiveness and intense and variable moods that are noted by prolonged periods of dejection and self-deprecation, interspersed with normal spans, as well as episodes of withdrawn isolation or unpredictable and erratic anger. The expectancy that people will be rejecting and disparaging precipitates profound gloom, at one time, and irrational negativism or excitement, another. At times, despite a longing to relate and be accepted, she constrains these needs, protectively withdraws from threats to her fragile emotional balance, and maintains a safe distance from any psychological involvements. Retreating defensively, she may become remote from others and from needed sources of support. A surface apathy may be exhibited in these efforts to damp down or deaden excess sensitivities. Nevertheless, intense contrary feelings occasionally break through in manipulative and immature outbursts.

Deep resentments are difficult to bind toward those whom she has felt have been unsupportive, critical, and disapproving. The little security that she possesses, however, is threatened when these resentments are discharged. To protect against further loss, she makes repeated efforts to resist expressing anger, albeit unsuccessfully. When not withdrawn and drifting aimlessly in peripheral social roles, she is unpredictable, irritably edgy, and negativistic, engaging in innumerable wrangles and disappointments with others, vacillitating between moments of being agreeable, sullenly passive, and explosively angry. These difficulties are frequently complicated by genuine expressions of guilt and contrition that are mixed with feelings of being misunderstood, unappreciated, and demeaned by others.

Deprived of a sense of self-worth, she suffers constantly from painful thoughts about the pitiful and futile state of being oneself. This is compounded by her tendency to be extremely introspective. Thus, the alienation that she feels from others is paralleled by a feeling of alienation from self. There is a constant and confusing undercurrent of tension, sadness, and anger. Vacillation is exhibited between desires for affection, fear, and a general numbness of feeling. She has learned to be watchful, on guard against ridicule, and ever-alert to signs of censure and derision. She detects the most minute traces of annoyance expressed by others and makes the mole hill of a minor and passing slight into a mountain of personal ridicule and condemnation. She has learned that good things don't last, that affection will capriciously end, followed by disappointment and rejection. Anticipating rejection and deprecation, she frequently jumps the gun with impulsive hostility. What is seen is a cyclical variation of constraint followed by angry acting out, followed in turn by remorse and regret. These erratic emotions not only are intrinsically distressing, but they upset her capacity to cope effectively with everyday tasks. Unable to orient emotions and thoughts logically, she may at times become lost in personal irrelevancies and autistic asides. This inability to order ideas and feelings in a consistent and relevant manner only further alienates her from others.

Differential Diagnostic Signs

As with the new DSM-III schizoid personality, the avoidant syndrome may frequently be confused with similar disorders until clinicians have had adequate time and numerous cases to which to apply its criteria.

As far as Axis I distinctions are concerned, the only differentiation that may cause substantive difficulty is that between the avoidant personality and *social phobias*. They do overlap and may, of course, be simultaneously diagnosed. There are two prime distinctions. First, there is a pervasiveness and diffuseness to the personality's socially aversive behaviors, in contrast to the specificity of the phobic object and the intensity of the phobic response. Second, unless it covaries with the avoidant syndrome, the phobic symptom is not associated with the broad range of traits that characterize the personality, such as "low self-esteem," the "desire for acceptance," and so on.

In differentiating between avoidant and other Axis II personality syndromes, predicaments may occur in separating avoidants from schizoids, schizotypals, and borderlines.

As noted in Chapter 10, avoidant personalities desire social acceptance and feel their isolation deeply, whereas the *schizoid* is genuinely indifferent to social matters and is intrinsically blunted emotionally. *Schizotypal* personalities differ from avoidants in their obvious eccentricities, such as their odd speech, ideas of reference, and so on—essentially the features of schizophrenia without the presence of delusions or hallucinations; avoidants lack these dramatic peculiarities and bizarre behaviors, exhibiting instead the anticipation of humiliation, a fear of interpersonal rejection, low self-esteem, and the desire for social acceptance. *Borderline* personalities share many features in common with avoidant types. Here again, the avoidant's loneliness, stemming from intense social needs that are conflicted by equally intense social fears, is its paramount discriminating feature, whereas behavioral impulsivity, affective instability, and ambivalent relationships with others are the prime characteristics of the borderline.

PREDISPOSING BACKGROUND

As stated previously, personality represents the individual's pervasive style of functioning and arises as a consequence of the intricate and sequential interplay of both biological and psychological influences. As in earlier chapters, this section outlines several of the more plausible biogenic and psychogenic factors that underlie the development of the personality under review. Note again that the influences hypothesized here are neither necessary, sufficient, mutually exclusive, nor even contributory causes in all cases. They are posited as reasonable conjectures, and the author believes that any number of combinations of these determinants may shape the course of pathological personality development.

Hypothetical Biogenic Factors

The hypervigilance that characterizes the avoidant signifies a habitual high level of somatic arousal. The exterior behavioral sluggishness and inactivity is deceptive. It overlays an extremely low threshold for alertness and reactive readiness, which the avoidant goes to great pains to cover up. Chronic tension may be discerned in spasmodic and uncoordinated motor behaviors, and in a high degree of sensory distractibility. Many avoidants appear to the undiscerning eye to be quiet and shy, unperturbed by external events. The converse is actually true. They are preoccupied with and hyperalert to their surroundings, so much so that they often cannot concentrate on their work or responsibilities.

The hyperarousal of avoidants may reflect a biophysical sensory irritability or a more centrally involved somatic imbalance or dysfunction. Using a different conceptual language to refer to this biophysical speculation, it might be hypothesized that these individuals possess a constitutionally based fearful or anxious temperament, that is, a hypersensitivity to potential threat. The conjectures suggested here may be no more than different conceptual approaches to the same thesis; for example, a fearful temperamental disposition may simply be a "behavioral" term to represent a "biophysical" limbic system imbalance.

Genetic or hereditary predispositions to avoidant behavior cannot be overlooked. Diverse anatomic structures and processes provide the substrate for such complex psychological functions as those called "affective disharmony," "interpersonal aversiveness," and so on. These biophysical substrates vary substantially from person to person (Williams, 1973) and are clearly influenced in their structure by heredity. Studies that demonstrate a higher than chance correspondence among family members in such behaviors as social apprehensiveness and aversiveness are attributable in large measure to learning, but there is reason to believe, at least in some cases, that this correspondence can be ascribed in part to the common genotypic pool within families.

Infants who display temperamentally based hyperirritability, crankiness, tension, and withdrawal behaviors may not only possess a constitutional disposition toward an avoidant pattern but may prompt rejecting and hostile attitudes from their parents. Easily frightened and hypertense babies who are easily awakened, cry, and are colicky rarely afford their parents much comfort and joy. Such infants typically induce parental weariness, feelings of inadequacy, exasperation, and anger, attitudes and feelings that may give rise to a stereotype of a troublesome, whining, and difficult-to-manage child. In these cases, an initial temperamental tendency toward anxiety and tension may be aggravated further by parental rejection and deprecation.

Delayed or uneven maturation in any of the major spheres of sensory, sensorimotor, or cognitive functioning may signify an impaired biophysical substrate that can limit these children's capacity to cope adequately with the normal tasks they face at each developmental stage. Intrinsic deficiencies such as these may also be compounded by the children's self-conscious awareness of their inadequacies. Of no less potential as a factor intensifying these deficits are parental reactions to the child's atypical development. Parents who expect their children to progress successfully and rapidly through the usual developmental sequence may experience considerable dismay over the deviations and failures they observe. Perceived in this manner, delayed achievements often result in parental condemnation and ridicule, experiences that evoke feelings of social alienation and low self-regard on the part of the child.

A few speculations of an anatomical and biochemical nature may be in order. For example, avoidant personalities may experience aversive stimuli more intensely and more frequently than others because they possess an especially dense or overabundantly branched neural substrate in the "aversive" center of the limbic system. Another plausible speculation for their avoidant tendencies is a possible functional dominance of the sympathetic nervous system. Thus, excess adrenalin owing to any one of a number of autonomic or pituitary-adrenal axis dysfunctions may give rise to the hypervigilant and irritable characteristics of this personality. Imbalances of this kind may lead also to the affective disharmony and cognitive interference found among these patients. Deficiencies or excesses in certain brain neurohormones may facilitate rapid synaptic transmission and result in a flooding and scattering of neural impulses. Such individuals will not only appear overalert and overactive but may experience the avoidant's characteristic cognitive interference and generalized emotional dysphoria. Although individual differences in anatomy and physiology have been well demonstrated, we must recognize that speculations attributing complex forms of clinical behavior to biophysical variations such as proposed here are not only conjectural but rather simplistic. Even if differences in aversiveness ultimately were found to be connected to biological substrates, the psychological form and content of these tendencies would take on their specific character only as a function of the individual's particular life experiences and learnings, factors to which the discussion turns next.

Characteristic Experiential Histories

Any attempt to list the diverse life experiences that may give rise to an avoidant personality would be not only futile but misleading. It is not so much the particulars of the timing, setting, or source of these events that make them important, but rather the message these experiences convey to the individual. Diverse though they may be, these experiences possess one crucial theme in common: They depreciate the individual's self-esteem through either explicit or implicit rejection, humiliation, or denigration. Moreover, repeated exposure to such events not only fosters a deflated sense of self-worth but tends, ultimately, to produce the affective dysphoria, cognitive interference, alienated self-image, interpersonal distrust, and active social detachment so characteristic of this personality. Two of the primary sources of these derogating experiences are elaborated in the following paragraphs.

The first and major source is parental rejection and deprecation. Attractive and healthy infants may be subjected to parental devaluation, malignment, and rejection no less so than troublesome youngsters. Reared in a family setting in which they are belittled, abandoned, and censured, these children will have their natural robustness and optimism crushed, and will acquire instead attitudes of self-deprecation and feelings of social alienation. Before elaborating some of the features associated with parental derogation and hostility that lead to the avoidant personality, it may be instructive to note some points in common between the experiences of the aggressive (antisocial) personality and those of the avoidant. They are quite similar in certain respects; both are exposed to parental devaluation and condemnation, and both learn to be suspicious and to view the world as hostile and dangerous. There appear to be two main reasons why avoidants learn to actively detach from others, whereas the aggressive antisocials learn to rise up with counterhostility and assertive independence.

First, close inspection of the childhood of the avoidant personality indicates that parental rejection took the form primarily of belittlement, depreciation, and humiliation. Although these youngsters may have borne the brunt of occasional physical cruelty, the essential nature of the message conveyed by the persecutor was that the child was weak, worthless, and beneath contempt. As a consequence of being demeaned and belittled these children also learn to devalue themselves and, hence, develop little or no sense of self-esteem. Considered worthless, derided, and forlorn, they feel powerless to counterattack and overcome the humiliation and ridicule to which they were exposed. Aggressive antisocial children were objects of similar derogation from their parents, but they received or experienced a different message than did the future avoidants. Rather than being devalued in the attack, future aggressives learned to feel that they were a "power" that had to be contended with, that they could upset others, that they had the wherewithal to disrupt the moods, attitudes, and behaviors of others. Instead of feeling humiliated and belittled, each hostile onslaught to which they were exposed served to reinforce an image of their own influence and potency. Judging themselves as possessing the power to "cause trouble," they were spurred on to vigorous counter-hostility.

A second distinction between the avoidant and the aggressive antisocial may be traced to possible differences in temperament. It is not implausible that constitutionally apprehensive and timorous children and constitution-ally fearless and hardy youngsters would respond differentially to parental derogation and hostility. Parental attitudes such as these would be likely to produce an avoidant pattern in an anxious and fearful youngster, hence an avoidant personality, and an aggressive antisocial pattern in a dauntless and bold youngster.

The consequences of parental rejection and humiliation are undoubtedly many and diverse. Returning to the avoidant personality's development, some of these consequences are outlined as they might arise during each of the three stages of neuropsychological development.

Parents who manage their infants in a cold and indelicate manner during the *sensory-attachment* stage will promote feelings of tension and insecurity on the part of their offspring. Such infants are likely to acquire a diffuse sense that the world is harsh, unwelcoming, and discomforting. In their primitive and highly generalized way, they will be disinclined to attach themselves to others. Moreover, they may acquire a vague, yet deeply felt, mistrust of their human surroundings and, as a result, feel an ever-present sense of being isolated, helpless, and abandoned. Self-protectively, these youngsters may learn to "turn off" their growing sensory capacities and thereby diminish the discomfort they experience. By doing so, however, they may set the stage for an enduring and generalized habit of interpersonal withdrawal.

Parents who ridicule and belittle their offspring's first stumbling efforts during the *sensorimotor-autonomy* stage will markedly diminish these children's feelings of competence and confidence. Although these youngsters may develop fully normal language skills and motor aptitudes, they may begin to utilize these competencies in a hesitant and self-doubting manner. In effect, they have internalized as "valid" their parents' criticisms and deroga-tions. And, in time, they may come to disparage and revile themselves just as their parents had done. Harsh and self-critical attitudes such as these have far-reaching and devastating consequences. By belittling their own worth, these children have undone themselves as a source for soothing their wounds or gaining the esteem they cannot obtain elsewhere. As a consequence of this self-derogation, they have not only lost the approval and respect of others but can no longer obtain these from themselves. They are caught now in a web of both social and self-reproval. Moreover, they, themselves, have become prime agents of their own derogation and belittling. And this sets the roots of another cardinal feature of the avoidant, that of self-alienation.

The roots of self-depreciation begun in the sensorimotor-autonomy phase take firmer hold in the *intracortical-initiative* stage. The image of being a weak, unlovable, and unworthy person becomes implanted in a strong cognitive base. Avoidants judge themselves increasingly as unattractive, as pitiful persons who deserve to be scoffed at and ridiculed. Few efforts may be expended on their part to alter this image since nothing they attempt "can ever" succeed, given the deficits and inadequacies they see within themselves.

Avoidant youngsters often compound their plight by identifying with an ineffectual parent or parental surrogate. Seeking and finding a modicum of love and affection in this model, they learn to identify themselves with this "unwholesome" parental figure and thereby seal their fate. By abdicating their own identity for the dubious rewards provided by this ineffectual model, they undermine whatever possibilities they may have had for finding a more satisfying style of life. They now copy the insecurities and inadequacies of their sorrowful exemplar, learning to display the same social deficits and ineffectualities they observe.

Signs of the avoidant pattern are usually evident well before the child begins to participate in the give-and-take of peer relationships, school and athletic competitions, heterosexual dating (with its attendant anxieties), and so on. These early signs may stem from constitutional dispositions or the circumstances of family life. Whatever their origins, most school-age children already possess the hesitations and aversive tendencies that will characterize them more clearly in later life. But for other youngsters, the rudiments of social withdrawal and self-alienation have developed only minimally when they first encounter the challenges of peer group activities. Opportunities for enhancing competencies and for developing effective social skills remain good, unless they experience rejection, isolation, or the devastating ridicule that can so often be meted out by age-mates. As hesitant children venture to meet their peers at school, on the athletic field, at school dances, and so on, they are exposed to challenges that may tear down their sense of competence and self-esteem. Some will be shattered by daily reminders of their scholastic ineptitude; a few will be ridiculed for deficits in athletic prowess; others will experience cruel derogation because of a lack of attractiveness, vitality, and so on. Unable to prove themselves in any of the myriad intellectual, physical, or social spheres of peer competition, they are not only derided and isolated by others but become sharply critical toward themselves for their own lack of worthiness and esteem. Their feelings of loneliness and shame are now compounded by severe self-judgments of personal inferiority and unattractiveness. They can turn neither to others for solace and gratification nor to themselves.

PROGNOSTIC CONSIDERATIONS

The coping style employed by the avoidant personality is not a matter of choice. It is the principal, and perhaps only, means these individuals have found effective in warding off the painful humiliation experienced at the hands of others. Discomforting as social alienation may be, it is less distressing than the anguish of extending themselves to others, only to be rebuffed or ridiculed. Distance guarantees a measure of safety; trust only invites disillusion.

Perpetuation of the Avoidant Pattern

The coping maneuvers of avoidants prove self-defeating. There is a driven and frightened quality to their behaviors. Moreover, avoidants are adaptively inflexible because they cannot explore alternative actions without feeling trepidation and anxiety. In contrast to other personalities, the avoidant coping style is essentially negative. Rather than venturing outward or drawing upon what aptitudes they possess, they retreat defensively and become increasingly remote from others and removed from sources of potential growth. As a consequence of their protective withdrawal, avoidants are left to be alone with their inner turmoil, conflicts, and self-alienation. They have succeeded in minimizing their external dangers, but they have trapped themselves in a situation equally devastating.

Several behaviors that foster and intensity the avoidant's difficulties are noted here.

Active social detachment.

Avoidant personalities assume that the experiences to which they were exposed in early life will continue forever. Defensively they narrow the range of activities in which they allow themselves to participate. By sharply circumscribing their life, they preclude the possibility of corrective experiences that might lead them to see that "all is not lost" and that there are kindly persons who will neither disparage nor humiliate them.

A further consequence of detaching themselves from others is that they are left to be preoccupied with their own thoughts and impulses. Limited to the inner world of stimuli, they will reflect and ruminate about the past, with all the discomforts it brings forth. Since their experiences have become restricted largely to thinking about past events, life becomes a series of duplications. As a consequence, avoidants are left to relive the painful experiences of earlier times rather than be exposed to new and different events that might alter their outlook and feelings. Moreover, these self-preoccupations serve only to further widen the breach between themselves and others. A vicious circle may take hold. The more they turn inward, the more they lose contact with the typical interests and thoughts of those around them. They become progressively more estranged from their environment, increasingly out of touch with reality and the checks against irrational thought provided by social contact and communication. Away from the controls and stabilizing influences of ordinary human interactions, they begin to lose their sense of balance and perspective, often feeling puzzled, peculiar, unreal, and "crazy."

Suspicious and fearful behaviors.   Detached and mistrustful behaviors not only establish distance from others but evoke reciprocal reactions of disaffiliation and rejection. An attitude that communicates weakness, self-effacement, and fear invariably attracts those who enjoy deprecating and ridiculing others. Thus, the hesitant posture, suspicious demeanor, and self-deprecating attitudes of the avoidant will tend to evoke interpersonal responses that lead to further experiences of humiliation, contempt, and derogation—in short, a repetition of the past. Any apparent sensitivity to rebuff or obviously fearful and unassertive style will tend to evoke ridicule from peers, an experience that will only reinforce and intensity this personality's aversive inclinations.

Emotional and perceptual hypersensitivity.   Avoidant personalities are painfully alert to signs of deception, humiliation, and deprecation. As noted in an earlier case presentation, these patients detect the most minute traces of indifference or annoyance on the part of others and make the molehills of minor and passing slights into mountains of personal ridicule and condemnation. They are incredibly sensitive instruments for picking up and magnifying incidental actions and for interpreting them as indications of derision and rejection. This hypersensitivity functions well in the service of self-protection but fosters a deepening of the person's plight. As a result of their extensive scanning of the environment, avoidants actually increase the likelihood that they will encounter precisely those stimuli they wish most to avoid. Their exquisite antennae pick up and transform what most people overlook. In effect, their hypersensitivity backfires by becoming an instrument that brings to their awareness, time and again, the very pain they wish to escape. Their defensive vigilance thus intensifies rather than diminishes their anguish.

Intentional inferference.   Avoidants must counter the flood of threatening stimuli that they register as a consequence of their emotional and perceptual hypersensitivities. To assure a modicum of personal tranquility, they engage constantly in a series of cognitive reinterpretations and digressions. They may actively block, destroy, and fragment their own thoughts, seeking to disconnect relationships between what they see, what meanings they attribute to their perceptions, and what feelings they experience in response. Defensively, then, they intentionally destroy the clarity of their thoughts by intruding irrelevant distractions, tangential ideas, and discordant emotions. This coping maneuver exacts its price. By upsetting the smooth and logical pattern of their cognitive processes, avoidants further diminish their ability to deal with events efficiently and rationally. No longer can they attend to the most salient features of their environment, nor can they focus their thoughts or respond rationally to events. Moreover, they cannot learn new ways to handle and resolve their difficulties since their thinking is cluttered and scattered. Social communications also take on a tangential and irrelevant quality, and they may begin to talk and act in an erratic and halting manner. In sum, in their attempt to diminish intrusively disturbing thoughts, they fall prey to a coping mechanism that further aggravates their original difficulties and ultimately intensifies their alienation from both themselves and others.

Remedial Interventions

As evident from the foregoing, the prognosis for the avoidant personality is often poor. Not only are these persons' habits and attitudes pervasive and ingrained, as are all personality patterns, but they are usually trapped in an environment that provides them with few of the supports and encouragements they need to reverse their life-style. Moreover, because of their basic mistrust of others, they are unlikely to be motivated either to seek or to sustain a therapeutic relationship. Should they agree to treatment, it is probable that they will engage in maneuvers to test the sincerity and genuineness of the therapist's feelings and motives. Most often, they will terminate treatment long before remedial improvement has occurred. This tendency to withdraw from therapy stems not only from their doubts and suspicions regarding the therapist's integrity but also from their unwillingness to face the humiliation and anguish involved in confronting their painful memories and feelings. They sense intuitively that their defenses are weak and tenuous and that to face directly their feeling of unworthiness, no less their repressed frustrations and impulses, will simply overwhelm them, driving them into unbearable anxieties and even to (as they fear it) "insanity."

To add to these fears, the potential gains of therapy may not only fail to motivate the avoidant but may actually serve as a deterrent. It may reawaken what these personalities view as false hopes. That is, it may remind them of the dangers and humiliations they experienced when they tendered their affections to others but received rejection in return. Now that they may have found a modest level of comfort by detaching themselves from others, they would rather leave matters stand, keep to the level of adjustment to which they are accustomed, and not "rock the boat" they have so tenuously learned to sail.

When an avoidant enters a therapeutic relationship, the therapist must take great pains not to push matters too hard or too fast, since the patient may feel he/she has but a fragile hold on reality. The therapist should seek, gently and carefully, to build a sense of genuine trust. Gradually, attention may be turned to the patient's positive attributes, addressing these as a means of building confidence and enhancing feelings of self-worth. This is likely to be a slow and arduous process, requiring the reworking of long-standing anxieties and resentments, bringing to consciousness the deep roots of mistrust, and, in time, enabling the patient to reappraise these feelings more objectively.

Considering therapy from the viewpoint of formal technique, note that a first approach would be to assist the patient in arranging for a rewarding environment and facilitating the discovery of opportunities that would enhance self-worth. Supportive therapeutic approaches may be all such patients can tolerate until they are capable of dealing comfortably with their more painful feelings. Psychopharmacologic treatment may be used to diminish or control anxieties. Behavior modification may prove useful as a way to learn less fearful reactions to formerly threatening situations. As avoidants progress to trust and feel secure with their therapists, they may be amenable to methods of cognitive reorientation designed to alter erroneous self-attitudes and distorted social expectancies. The deeper and more searching procedures of psychoanalysis can be useful in reconstructing unconscious anxieties and mechanisms that pervade all aspects of these patients' behavior. Family techniques can be usefully employed to moderate destructive patterns of communication that contribute to or intensify avoidants' problems. Last, group therapy may assist these patients in learning new attitudes and skills in a more benign and accepting social setting than they normally encounter.

Part Three

Severe Personality Disorders

Chapter 12

Borderline Personality: The Unstable Pattern

All patterns of pathological personality—be they of mild, moderate, or marked severity—are deeply etched and pervasive characteristics of functioning that unfold as a product of the interplay of constitutional and experiential influences. The behaviors, self-descriptions, intrapsychic mechanisms, and interpersonal coping styles that evolve out of these transactions are embedded so firmly within the individual that they become the very fabric of his or her makeup, operating automatically and insidiously as the individual's way of life. Present realities are often mere catalysts that stir up these long-standing habits, memories, and feelings. Past learnings frequently persist inflexibly, irrespective of how maladaptive or irrational they now may be. Sooner or later they may prove to be the person's undoing. Self-defeating vicious circles are set up that precipitate new difficulties and often reactivate and aggravate earlier unfavorable conditions of life.

PRELIMINARY COMMENTS ON SEVERITY OF PERSONALITY PATHOLOGY

Chapters 12-14 describe the three most severe variants of personality pathology, the so-called borderline, paranoid, and schizotypal syndromes. As discussed previously, the author's prior theoretical and clinical work has led to a differentiation of the major personalities in terms of their level of structural coherence and interpersonal flexibility. As a précis of this final group of chapters, it may be useful to outline some of the criteria employed to assist in concluding that certain pathological patterns are more severe or grave than others. Although all of these personalities display an adaptive inflexibility, tend to promote self-perpetuating vicious circles, and hang on a tenuous emotional balance, there are substantive grounds for differentiating them in terms of levels of severity. Before doing so, it should be restated that personality structure is composed of complex traits that lie on a continuum of adaptiveness. Adaptiveness is a gradient, a matter of degree, and not a dichotomy. Notions such as health versus disease, abnormal versus normal, or psychotic versus nonpsychotic are polar extremes of a continuum that has intervening shades or gradations. An infinite number of discriminations may be made along these lines, but for certain purposes, refined distinctions may be neither feasible nor necessary. As long as we keep in mind that the pathological dimension of personality lies on a continuum, it will suffice to differentiate patients into a few broad classes such as mild, moderate, advanced, or severe.

In general, the patients discussed in the following chapters differ from those in preceding chapters by the frequency with which certain unusual symptoms arise, such as emotional outbursts, peculiar thinking, and bizarre behaviors. Inner (ego) controls have significantly weakened and these patients are driven to rather extreme measures as a means of maintaining their psychological balance and cohesion. Facing increased difficulty, they are ineffective in mobilizing their coping strategies, are less able to realistically appraise the stresses they face, and are unable to draw upon their prior competencies and resources. Some become overly rigid and constrictive in their thinking and behavior, such as the paranoid; or, conversely, they experience being cognitively confused and emotionally scattered, as borderlines and schizotypals often are. Should difficulties mount or their restitutive efforts continue to fail, these more severely disturbed personalities may abandon their attempts to mobilize their resources or to maintain their psychic cohesion, and thereby deteriorate into a florid psychotic disorder. In these more decompensated states, patients fail to discriminate between inner subjective experience and external reality; they are unable to carry out normal responsibilities or otherwise behave in accord with conventional social standards and expectations. As reality recedes further into the background, rational thinking disappears, previously controlled emotions erupt, and a disintegration and demoralization of self often takes hold. The upsurge of formerly repressed feelings and memories combines with new adverse experiences to undermine the individual's remaining coping capacities. Fearful of losing their tenuous hold on reality and threatened by surging emotions and uncontrollable and bizarre thoughts, these individuals succumb further. Deteriorating to more primitive levels of functioning and retreating into an inner and unreal world, they may ultimately fall into a persistent and more pernicious pattern of life. Despite the insidious and destructive sequence of decompensation, they will retain essentially the same basic perceptions, attitudes, and emotions they evidenced earlier in life. Advanced forms of personality pathology, no matter how bizarre and maladaptive they may become, remain consonant with the individual's lifelong history and style of functioning.

The levels to which this deterioration proceeds may be usefully separated into two broad categories.

1. At the first level, or what is here termed syndromes of *advanced personality dysfunction*, patients can no longer depend on their prior

mechanisms and strategies to work for them. No longer sure of the strategies' effectiveness, they are likely to become overly concerned about receiving the attention and support they previously assumed they could readily obtain. They may seek to mobilize their resources, shore up their strategies, and take a more active role than before. For example, a previously dependent personality may begin to feel severely threatened by separation anxieties. As former strategies waver and stumble, a less functional pattern of behaviors may evolve. The patient may engage in a series of frantic actions to regain security or display his/her frustration at having failed. Individuals who stabilize at these more extreme or advanced levels of personality dysfunction often remain ambulatory, despite transient psychotic episodes. The borderline, paranoid, and schizotypal syndromes are the major variants of these dysfunctional personality structures. Although deterioration may proceed to lower levels of decompensation, these syndromes do not signify diagnostic indecision, nor are they a way station between normality and total psychotic disintegration. Rather, they should be seen as crystallized, habitual, and enduring pathological patterns.

Two features distinguish these advanced dysfunctional personalities from those at less severe levels. The first has been termed *deficit social competence* (Millon, 1969) and refers to the erratic personal history of these patients and their failure to attain a level of social achievement commensurate with their natural aptitudes and talents. Faulty starts and repeated disruptions characterize their educational, vocational, and marital life. In contrast to the less severe types, who progress and achieve a modicum of social and vocational effectiveness, advanced dysfunctional personalities create endless complications for themselves and experience the same setbacks time and again. Despite these failures, many are fortunate in having strongly supportive or beneficent environments. Hence, they are able to "pull themselves together" periodically and "make a go of it again." This rapid recovery process contrasts to the fate of those at more severe levels of personality decompensation, who exhibit a more persistent downhill regression that eventuates in prolonged and often total social invalidism.

As evident from the foregoing, the second distinguishing feature of the advanced dysfunctional group is their *periodic, but reversible, psychotic episodes*. These severe transient disorders are characterized by the loss of reality contact and by both cognitive and emotional dyscontrol. Although psychotic eruptions occur with some frequency, their reversibility differentiates them from those at the decompensated level. Thus, in the dysfunctional patient, the reality break is brief and transitory, whereas in severely decompensated personalities it is prolonged and often permanent. Caught in their own adaptive inflexibilities and tendencies to foster new difficulties and self-defeating vicious circles, dysfunctional personalities experience constant upsets in their equilibrium and are subject to emotional eruptions and uncontrollable behaviors and thoughts. However, once these intense feelings are discharged, these patients regain a modicum of psychic balance—until such time as their tensions again mount beyond manageable portions.

As noted, three advanced dysfunctional personalities are distinguished. According to Millon (1969), they parallel, in somewhat less discriminable (but more severe) form, the eight personality patterns described in previous chapters. Thus, the *schizotypal* is an advanced and more dysfunctional variant of the detached patterns: the schizoid and avoidant types. The *borderline* is usually a moderately disintegrated, dependent, histrionic, compulsive, or passive-aggressive pattern; and the *paranoid* is a more severe personality type that is akin the narcissistic, antisocial, and, at times, compulsive and passive-aggressive patterns. A detailed review of the borderline is presented in this chapter ; the paranoid and schizotypal personalities are detailed in Chapters 13 and 14.

2. *Severely decompensated personality* is the term the author suggests for the most profoundly deteriorated of the personality types. As with their less severe counterparts, decompensated features are deeply rooted, pervasive, and relatively enduring. They usually require institutional care and treatment, and are distinguished from Axis I psychotic disorders by the breadth and persistence of their deterioration. Although psychotic disorders represent equal severity, they are of relatively briefer duration, are usually confined to a particular sphere of functioning (e.g., mood, thought, or behavior), and do not eventuate in a broad and enduring deterioration of the personality pattern.

Three clinical features may be noted in common among decompensated personality patterns (Millon, 1969).

First, there are significant signs of either *developmental immaturity* or *social invalidism*. Some patients appear to be "fixated," that is, developmentally arrested prior to full social maturity. For various reasons they have failed to acquire a repertoire of mature social skills. There are signs that they persistently fell behind their age-mates or deteriorated rapidly, but quite early in life. Other decompensated patients achieved a measure of social competence through childhood and adolescence but, under the weight of unrelieved stress, began to "regress" and revert to significantly more immature levels of function than previously displayed, a process here termed *invalidism*. A second feature distinguishing these severely decompensated personalities is their *cognitive disorganization*. This may be signified by illogical, disjointed, or fragmented thinking, often exhibited in obscure communications, seemingly random or irrelevant flights of fancy, and unsystematized delusions and hallucinations. Feelings of *estrangement* are the third cardinal feature of these personalities. Invalidism and cognitive disorganization often combine to produce feelings of self-worthlessness and a sense of inner disorder or "nothingness." The world is viewed as an alien, strange, and mechanical nightmare of shapes and movements. And looking inward, they perceive themselves to be disembodied, a foreign shell or a depersonalized object that is unconnected to their thoughts and "being."

Severely decompensated personalities evolve from the same biogenic and psychogenic roots as those found in less severe pathological types. These influences have simply been more injurious and persistent. Not infrequently, the more permanent decompensated state may insidiously develop following a series of transitory psychotic episodes. For various reasons—perhaps poor hospital management or unreceptive family conditions—these patients remain institutionalized, only to disintegrate progressively into a more pervasive and enduring pathological pattern. Isolated increasingly from normal social activities and having acquired the habits and rewards of hospital life, they give up efforts to regain a meaningful "outside" existence and allow themselves to slip into the emptiness of permanent decompensation.

Although several varieties of the severely decompensated personality have been discussed previously by the author (Millon, 1969), this text bypasses a detailed presentation, referring briefly to certain of their clinical features in describing the three dysfunctional types.

PRELIMINARY COMMENTS ON THE BORDERLINE CONCEPT

The label "borderline" has had a varied, if brief history. Despite its recent status as an official diagnostic entity in the DSM-III nomenclature, a status gained after considerable dispute, its use as a formal syndromal designation is most lamentable. In its pure linguistic sense, the term *borderline* conveys with clarity and utility a mid-level severity, or intermediary degree, of either personality functioning (Millon, 1969) or structural organization (Kernberg, 1967, 1970). However—and in contrast with other new DSM-III personality labels, such as narcissistic and avoidant—the *borderline* term neither connotes nor communicates a behavioral pattern that portrays distinctive stylistic features (Perry and Klerman, 1978). In concert with other colleagues on the DSM-III Task Force, the author strongly argued for the selection of alternative and more clearly descriptive designations. For example, the author's original working draft for this syndrome, prepared for the DSM-III personality subcommittee in 1975, termed it the "cycloid" personality. Since the descriptive features and diagnostic criteria for the final draft of the "borderline" personality disorder remained highly consistent with this early formulation, the author joined other outspoken committee members who vigorously dissented from the decision to choose so general and vague a label as *borderline* to represent what was a distinctive syndromal trait constellation. In his final memo on the issue, written in June 1978, the author commented as follows:

> I very much like the description of the borderline personality disorder; it portrays a very important population that has not been adequately described in previous DSM publications. However, I would like to register my strong agreement with the point raised... to the effect that *the label, borderline, is perhaps the most poorly chosen of all the terms selected for the DSM-III.* I know

a small segment of the profession feels that this is the most apt descriptive term for this population, but frankly, I find the word, borderline, to mean, at best, a level of severity and not a descriptive type. . . . Unless the word is used to signify a class that borders on something, then it has no clinical or descriptive meaning at all.

If we look at the clinical description that we have created for this disorder I am sure we can find a label that is more suitable and communicative than borderline. . . .

I would like the Personality Committee to reassess the term borderline. . . . [in addition to the original suggestions of cycloid and unstable] other alternative labels that might be considered are the following: *ambivalent* personality disorder, *erratic* personality disorder, *impulsive* personality disorder, *quixotic* personality disorder, etc. Any one of these (*labile* captures the flavor most clearly for me) would be far preferable than the meaningless borderline label. Please let's try not to fall prey to absurdities in the literature; let's not get hooked into a poor label which, when closely examined, has absolutely no relationship to the syndrome's clinical descriptions. One of the major advances of DSM-III is that it has sought to create labels and descriptions that are clearer, more explicit and more relevant than in the past. Let's not regress by introducing a bad and misleading label.

Although the term *borderline* was retained, its evolution in the deliberations of the DSM-III committee reinforces the notion that it is a specific diagnostic entity that has stabilized at an advanced level of dysfunction. More importantly, its clinical characteristics are not only those of a personality syndrome but one that falls within the broad spectrum of *affective disorders*. In this sense, it parallels the schizotypal syndrome, which was also conceived as an advanced level of personality dysfunction but within the schizophrenic disorder spectrum.

With the foregoing as an introduction, the major characteristics of the DSM-III borderline personality syndrome are briefly reviewed.

The most salient feature of this person is the depth and variability of moods. Borderlines tend to experience extended periods of dejection and disillusionment, interspersed occasionally with brief excursions of euphoria and significantly more frequent episodes of irritability, self-destructive acts, and impulsive anger. These moods are often unpredictable and appear prompted less by external events than by internal factors.

This text stresses the divergent background histories found among borderlines. In effect, they are conceived as advanced dysfunctional variants of the less severe dependent, histrionic, compulsive, and passive-aggressive personalities. The variety of borderline personalities reported in the literature are thereby more clearly differentiated and their frequently mixed symptom pictures are clarified. The model presented states that when these four less dysfunctional personalities prove deficient or falter under the strain of persistent environmental stress, they will frequently deteriorate into what we have labeled the "borderline personality pattern." For example, a *dependent* personality, faced with intense problems in areas of special vulnerability, will experience a sense of helplessness and hopelessness; these persons will exhibit brief, frantic, but futile efforts either to assert themselves and stand on their own, or to recapture by behaving in a forced, cheerful, and outgoing manner the attachment and support they desperately need. Similarly, the characteristic gregarious strategy of a *histrionic* personality may reach a feverish pitch of euphoric excitement, only to fall into the depths of futility, despondency, and self-destructiveness, should the person's restitutive efforts fail. Unsure of external approval and troubled by surging inner impulses, a *compulsive* personality may vacillate among marked self-condemnation, protestations of piety and good intentions, and impulsive outbursts of anger, followed by feelings of intense shame and guilt for "errors" and shortcomings. The preborderline pattern of behavior vacillation in a *passive-aggressive* personality will continue under increased stress but reach a more intense, unpredictable, and erratic pace, swinging into profound gloom at one time, and irrational negativism and chaotic excitement, the next. It is the instability of both behavior and affect, combined with their shared search for acceptance and approval, that justifies bringing these patients together into a single "borderline" syndrome despite their divergent histories and coping styles.

As a consequence of their "failed background," borderlines will have had rather checkered histories in their personal relationships and in school and work performance. Most will have exhibited an extreme unevenness in fulfilling normal social functions and responsibilities. Rarely do they persevere to attain mature goals. Their histories show repeated setbacks, a lack of judgment and foresight, tendencies to digress from earlier aspirations, and failures to utilize their natural aptitudes and talents. It is often easy to trace the consequences of their adaptive inflexibility and their involvement in self-defeating vicious circles. Many may have shown flashes of promise, stability, and achievement, but these periods usually are either short-lived or are dependent on the presence of a highly tolerant and supportive social system. Most fail to learn from their experiences and involve themselves in the same imbroglios, quandaries, and disappointments as they have before. Life is like a merry-go-round of getting into predicaments and discord, and then spending time extricating oneself from them. Few things are ever accomplished and much in life is undone. The borderline patient goes round in circles, covering the same ground as before, getting nowhere, and then starting all over again. This pattern contrasts to personalities at milder levels of pathological functioning whose strategies and behaviors, though self-perpetuating, are often instrumentally successful. The borderline's style of functioning falters frequently and leads these individuals to endless impasses and serious setbacks. Rather than finding and holding a secure niche for themselves in society, as many of the less severe personalities do, they upset their progress repeatedly, achieve a low level of social attainment, and find that they must start again from scratch. Despite these ups and downs, borderlines do manage to to recoup, to gain the wherewithal to pull themselves together, to find an "out," and to get enough of a foothold in normal life to prevent themselves from slipping into more pernicious and serious states. In contrast to the severely decompensated personality patterns, where realistic efforts to mobilize and defend onself have been abandoned, borderline patients gain enough reinforcement to motivate themselves to make a "go of it" again.

Despite this capacity to "regain one's wits" and take hold of life, borderline patients do experience transient periods in which bizarre behaviors, irrational impulses, and delusional thoughts are exhibited. These confusing episodes signify the tenuous character of their stability and controls. During these disturbed states, they may "drift out" of contact with their environment as if caught up in a momentary dream in which reality is blurred and fears and urges that derive from an obscure inner source take over and engulf them in an ocean of primitive anxieties and behaviors. Unable to grasp the illusory character of these inner stimuli, they may be driven to engage in erratic and hostile actions or embark on wild and chaotic sprees they may only vaguely recall. These episodes of emotional discharge serve a useful homeostatic function since they afford temporary relief from mounting internal pressures. When pressures cumulate beyond tolerable limits, they erupt through the patient's tenuous controls and are manifested in bizarre acts and thoughts. Upon release, these patients may sense a feeling of easement and quiescence. They may now regain a measure of psychic equilibrium until such time as these tensions again cumulate beyond manageable proportions. These transitory breaks from reality, traditionally termed "psychotic disorders," occur infrequently in the milder pathological personalities. Although less severely disturbed personalities do lose control occasionally, they usually retain a full awareness of reality. This contrasts not only with the borderline patient but with the paranoid and schizotypal as well. Each of these more advanced dysfunctional personalities exhibits marked breaks with reality at relatively frequent intervals. Every so often their intrapsychic world erupts and overwhelms them, blurring their awareness and releasing bizarre impulses, thoughts, and actions.

Patients who exhibit the borderline pattern can develop a healthier mode of adjustment or, conversely, decompensate into a more severe pattern of disorder. However, barring the presence of change-inducing events, they are likely to preserve their characteristic level and style of functioning. Through all their ups and downs, and despite the fluctuating mix of both mild and marked pathological features, borderlines remain sufficiently different from both the less and more severe personality syndromes to justify considering them a distinct clinical entity. Before detailing the historical and theoretical origins of the syndrome, the text of the disorder is reproduced, as presented in the DSM-III manual:

> The essential feature is a Personality Disorder in which there is instability in a variety of areas, including interpersonal behavior, mood and self-image. No single feature is invariably present. Interpersonal relations are often intense and unstable, with marked shifts of attitude over time. Frequently there is impulsive and unpredictable behavior that is potentially physically self-damaging. Mood is often unstable, with marked shifts from a normal mood to a dysphoric mood

or with inappropriate, intense anger or lack of control of anger. A profound identity disturbance may be manifested by uncertainty about several issues relating to identity, such as self-image, gender identity, or long-term goals or values. There may be problems tolerating being alone, and chronic feelings of emptiness or boredom.

Some conceptualize this condition as a level of personality organization, rather than as a specific Personality Disorder.

Quite often social contrariness and a generally pessimistic outlook are seen. Alternation between dependency and self-assertion is common. During periods of extreme stress transient psychotic symptoms of insufficient severity or duration to warrant an additional diagnosis may occur. (p. 321–322)

HISTORICAL AND THEORETICAL ANTECEDENTS

Prior to its current fashionable status, the label "borderline" was typically assigned when a clinician was uncertain about the diagnosis of a patient. Every clinician faces dilemmas as to whether certain observed ominous symptoms signify the presence of more severe pathology than first "meets the eye." Such patients appear to display both normal and psychotic features. At these times, clinicians handle this seeming incongruence by hedging, that is, "sitting on the fence." They wait until they can obtain a clearer picture of their patient's status or until some change occurs in behaviors before making the decision as to whether the patient is suffering a "neurosis" or a "psychosis." This common use of the borderline designation rests on the false premise that patients must fall in one of two categories of a dichotomy, that of "slightly sick" (neurosis) or "very sick" (psychosis). We now recognize that personality pathology lies on a continuum, that it is not an all-or-none phenomenon but one that may fall at any point along a continuous gradient. "Borderline" need not be used as a wastebasket for clinical indecision. It is currently conceived as a meaningful designation that reflects a real rather than a spurious or incongruous state of affairs: an advanced and potentially serious level of maladaptive personality functioning. Moreover, borderline syndromes need not represent transitory states between normality and frank pathology, that is, a way station that leads inevitably to more severe illness. The label signifies a habitual level of behavior, a durable pattern of disturbed functioning that stabilizes for substantial periods of time.

Although several clinical theorists have formulated the concept of "borderline" as representing a level of personality organization (Kernberg, 1967, 1970) or a degree of personality severity (Millon, 1969, Stone, 1980), rather than a specific character type possessing distinctive features, the DSM-III Task Force chose the latter course and applied the label to a discrete syndromal entity. Hence, this review of the literature is more narrowly focused than it would otherwise have been—that is, if it encompassed notions such as "borderline schizophrenia," "pseudoneurotic schizophrenia," and "latent psychoses," each of which is considered by some as part of a broad borderline spectrum. These latter clinical entities are bypassed in the present rendering of the historical forerunners of the DSM-III borderline since they more properly prefigure the "schizotypal personality" syndrome presented in Chapter 14.

Complicating this review further, the particular constellation of traits comprised in the DSM-III borderline syndrome has historical and theoretical precursors that antedate the latter, and the discussion therefore cannot be restricted to propositions that employ the recent designation of "borderline." There is a substantial body of literature on syndromes, *not* termed borderline, that possess clinical features clearly representing the pattern of affective and interpersonal instability that characterizes the DSM-III personality type. This review, therefore, does not begin with the borderline concept but with formulations that differ in designation but are clinically akin to it.

A further source of difficulty in furnishing a comprehensive yet relevant survey of borderline antecedents is the plethora of terms and the not inconsiderable disagreement that exists among theorists concerning the prime attributes of the syndrome (Perry and Klerman, 1978). Popular among psychoanalytic thinkers is the position that it is best conceived as a structural configuration or character organization that exists at a level of personality cohesion midway between neurotic and psychotic levels (Knight, 1953; Frosch, 1960; Kernberg, 1970). Certain biologically oriented researchers hold the view that it is best considered as a set of personality variants within an affective disorders spectrum (Klein, 1977; Akiskal et al., 1977). As noted earlier, those who consider it as essentially an incipient precursor or inchoate substrate for schizophrenia are discussed in Chapter 14, dealing with the schizotypal personality. Still others have formulated it as a stable and moderately severe level of functioning that encompasses a variety of different personality subtypes (Grinker et al., 1968, Millon, 1969).

The presentation must be formally divided to represent these diverse viewpoints. The ensuing paragraphs provide a prime example of how theoretically dissimilar perspectives can conceptualize the same diagnostic syndrome in divergent fashions.

Forerunners of the Borderline Syndrome

From the earliest literary and medical history, writers have recognized the coexistence within single persons of intense and divergent moods such as euphoria, irritability, and depression. Homer, Hippocrates, and Aretaeus, described with great vividness the related character of impulsive anger, mania, and melancholia, noting both the erratic vacillation among these "spells" and the personalities likely to be subject to them. However, as with most medical and scientific knowledge, these early writings were suppressed in medieval times. With the advent of the Renaissance, many of the observations of early Greek and Roman physicians were brought again to light, and studies of these patients were begun anew.

The first theorist to revive the notion of the covariation between impulsive and erratic moods in a single syndrome was Bonet, who applied the term *folie maniaco-melancolique* in 1684. Schacht and Herschel in the eighteenth century reinforced the view suggested in Bonet's terminology that these erratic and unstable moods followed a rhythmic or periodic regularity of highs and lows. Fixed in the minds of all subsequent clinicians was the belief in an inevitable periodicity of the manic-depressive covariation. In fact, the case histories described by Bonet, Schacht, and Herschel rarely followed so regular a pattern. Rather, they were episodic, erratic, and desultory in sequence, shifting almost randomly from depression, to anger, to guilt, to elation, to boredom, to normality, and so on in an unpredictable and inconsistent course. In 1854 Baillarger and Falret summarized the results of 30 years' work with depressed and suicidal persons. They reported that a large portion of these patients showed a course of extended depression, broken intermittently by periods of irritability, anger, elation, and normality. The terms *la folie circulaire* (Falret, 1854) and *folie à double forme* (Baillarger, 1854) were applied to signify the syndrome's contrasting and variable character. It was Kahlbaum who, in 1882, clearly imprinted the current belief in the fixed covariation of mania and melancholia. Although he saw them as facets of a single disease that manifested itself in different ways at different times— occasionally euphoric, occasionally melancholic, and occasionally excitable or angry—it was the primacy of the former two which rigidified future conceptions of the syndrome and redirected thinking away from its more typical and fundamental affective instability and unpredictability. He termed the milder variant of the illness, notable for its frequent periods of normality, *cyclothymia.* A more severe and chronic form of the same pattern was designated *vesania typica circularis.*

From a vantage quite different than Kahlbaum's, an American psychiatrist, C. Hughes, wrote in 1884 that "the borderland of insanity is occupied by many persons who pass their whole life near that line, sometimes on one side, sometimes on the other" (p. 297). Also writing of "borderline insanity," J. C. Rosse (1890) spoke of patients who drifted in a twilight between "reason and despair."

Kraepelin borrowed heavily from his German predecessor Kahlbaum's formulations but separated the "personality" and "temperament" variants of cyclothymia from the manifest or clinical state of the disease. Nevertheless, he proposed the name *maniacal-depressive insanity* for "the whole domain of periodic and circular insanity," including such diverse disturbances as "the morbid states termed melancholia . . . [and] certain slight colorings of mood, some of them periodic, some of them continuously morbid" (1896, p. 161). Convinced of the unitary character of this disease, Kraepelin wrote:

> I have become convinced all these states only represent manifestations of a single morbid process. It is certainly possible that later a series of subordinate groups may be . . . entirely separated off. But if this happens, then according to my view those symptoms will certainly not be authoritative which hitherto have usually been placed in the foreground. (1896, p. 164).

Kraepelin viewed "circular insanity" to be a unitary illness. Moreover, every disorder that gave evidence of mood disturbances—however regular or irregular; whatever the predominant affect, be it irritability, depression, or mania—was conceived to be a variant or "rudiment" of the same basic impairment. To him, the common denominator for these disturbances was an endogenous metabolic dysfunction that was "to an astonishing degree independent of external influences" (p. 173).

In his eighth edition of the monumental *Lehrbuch* (1909-1915), Kraepelin began to formulate a number of subaffective personality conditions that are quite comparable to current borderline criteria. Thus, he wrote:

> There are certain temperaments which may be regarded as *rudiments of manic-depressive* insanity. They may throughout the whole of life exist as peculiar forms of psychic personality, without further development; but they may also become the point of departure for a morbid process which develops under peculiar conditions and runs its course in isolated attacks. Not at all infrequently, moreover, the permanent divergencies are already in themselves so considerable that they also extend into the domain of the morbid without the appearance of more severe, delimited attacks. (1921, p. 118)

As noted in an earlier chapter, Kraepelin identified four temperament variants disposed to clinical manic-depressive disease. The irritable temperament, elsewhere described by Kraepelin as the "excitable personality," was conceived as a "mixture of the fundamental states." It parallels the borderline features closely, as illustrated in the following excerpts:

> The patients display from youth up extraordinarily great fluctuations in emotional equilibrium and are greatly moved by all experiences, frequently in an unpleasant way. . . .
> They flare up, and on the most trivial occasions fall into outbursts of boundless fury.
> The coloring of mood is subject to frequent change . . . periods are interpolated in which they are irritable and ill-humored, also perhaps sad, spiritless, anxious; they shed tears without cause, give expression to thoughts of suicide, bring forward hypochondriacal complaints, go to bed. . . .
> They are mostly very distractible and unsteady in their endeavors.
> In consequence of their irritability and their changing moods their conduct of life is subject to the most multifarious incidents, they make sudden resolves, and carry them out on the spot, run off abruptly, go traveling, enter a cloister. (1921, pp. 130-131)

Of special note is the extent to which Kraepelin's description encompasses the central diagnostic criteria of the DSM-III borderline, especially the impulsivity, unstable relationships, inappropriate and intense anger, affective instability, and physically self-damaging acts.

Kretschmer (1925) provided another precursor of the borderline in portraying patients who exhibited what he considers a mixed cycloid-schizoid temperament. Not quite as apt or congruent as is Kraepelin's text, it nevertheless captures a number of important elements of the borderline syndrome. Kretschmer depicted these patients as follows:

> Cases of agitated melancholia with violent motility symptoms, alien influences in the constitution...may be distinguished [by]...an admixture of humourless dryness, of a hypochondriacal, hostile attitude towards the world...of sharpness, nervousness, and jerky restless moodiness (not rhythmic cyclic modifications), of insufficient affective response, of a grumbling dissatisfaction, and of a display of sulky pessimism.... This kind...is not at all the prototype...of the cycloid character...Out of our material one could form a continuous series leading...from the typical cycloid over to the typical schizoid. (1925, p. 140)

Schneider, Kretschmer's prime European contemporary, came even closer to the mark of the borderline in his portait of the "labile" personality (1923). In his characterization of this type, Schneider wrote:

> The labile...has no chronic moodiness but is specifically characterized by the abrupt and rapid changes of mood which he undergoes.
> Sometimes the smallest stimulus is sufficient to arouse a violent reaction....It appears that there is some constitutional tendency toward sporadic reactions of a morose and irritable character....
> We are only interested here in behavior which clearly arises from periodic lability of mood. Such behavior has sometimes been called impulsive but the impulse...is only secondary and takes place against the periodic crisis of mood.
> Labile [persons] present a picture of shiftless, social instability. They develop sudden dislikes and distastes. They experience sudden restlessness.... Many... are socially shiftless and inconstant.
> As a social group...the more irritable ones are apt to get into trouble through impulsive violence, and the more inconstant ones have all sorts of chance lapses.
> We may wonder whether the mood shift of our labile personalities is a matter of cyclothymic...mood. Clinically everything speaks against cyclothymia. The transience of the mood and the general volatility are the chief contraindications. (1950, pp. 116–120)

Finally, a brief note should be made of the contribution of J. Kasanin (1933), who first coined the label "schizoaffective." Reviewing the atypical premorbid characteristics of several cases of young psychotics who were initially hospitalized with the diagnoses of acute schizophrenic episodes, Kasanin concluded that they appeared to possess the social dispositions and affective inclinations that are more typical of manic-depressives. The acute nature of the disorder and the blend of features portrayed in Kasanin's syndrome are somewhat tangential to the borderline formulation, yet the following quote suggests elements of comparability:

> A subjective review of their...personalities reveals that they are very sensitive, critical of themselves, introspective, very unhappy and preoccupied with their

own conflicts, problems, and sometimes with life in general. These conflicts and problems may go on for years before the patient breaks down. . . . The fact that there is comparatively little of the extremely bizarre, unusual and mysterious, is what perhaps gives these cases a fairly good chance of recovery. They do not exhibit any profound regression socially. . . . Their reaction is one of protest, or a fear, without the ready acceptance of the solution offered by the psychosis. (1933, p. 101)

Psychoanalytic Notions of Borderline Structures or Characters

The first formal publication to employ the designation of borderline was written by Adolf Stern in 1938. His paper was prompted by the increasing number of patients seen who could not be fit readily into standard neurotic or psychotic categories, and who were, in addition, refractory to psychotherapeutic interventions. Stern labeled these patients as comprising a "border line group of neuroses." Close examination led him to identify 10 symptoms, character traits, and "reaction formations" that, though not unique to the borderline group, were judged by him to be both more pronounced than in other neurotics and especially resistant to psychoanalytic efforts at resolution. Since a number of these 10 characteristics have remained as criteria for contemporary borderline conceptions it may be useful to record them briefly: "narcissism," a character trait consequent to deficient maternal affection; "psychic bleeding," a self-protective lethargy or immobility in respond to stress; "inordinate hypersensitivity," an undue caution or exquisite awareness of minor slights; "psychic rigidity," a persistent, protectively reflexive body stiffness in anticipation of danger; "negative therapeutic reactions," a quickness to display anger, depression, or anxiety in response to interpretive probes involving self-esteem; "feelings of inferiority," despite demonstrable evidence of self-competence, claiming a personal inadequacy so as to avoid adult responsibilities; "masochism," a depressively toned, self-pity, "wound-licking," and self-commiseration; "somatic anxiety," a presumption of one's constitutional inadequacy to function without external assistance; "projection mechanism," a tendency to attribute internal difficulties to ostensive hostile sources in the environment; and "difficulties in reality testing," nonpsychotic deficits in judgment and empathic accuracy.

Although close to a decade would pass before the borderline label reemerged in the formal literature, it was a popular, if colloquial, term that conveyed little more than the patient's intermediary or inchoate status, a loosely conceived designation bandied about informally at case conferences or in passing diagnostic dialogues. Two informal and occasionally overlapping trends emerged. Psychoanalysts such as Stern focused on the problem of identifying the "borderline" between neurotic characters or symptom disorders and similarly appearing, but more ominous and severe, forms of pathology. Although the roots and characteristic features of the syndrome are more broadly conceived by others, it was the analysts' concern and their related line of thinking that gradually evolved into the DSM-III formulation that has been labeled the 'borderline personality." The other, overlapping yet distinct, concern that arose was found among hospital-based clinicians, often biologically oriented, who sought to differentiate the manifest forms of schizophrenia from their "borderline" variants, characterized by designations such as "latent," "ambulatory," or "incipient." It was this latter desire and its related line of thought and research that ultimately shaped the syndrome and criteria for the DSM-III schizotypal personality. As indicated earlier, this chapter proceeds with antecedents more directly relevant to the contemporary borderline formulation.

Melitta Schmideberg (1947, 1959) was among a small group of clinicians to employ the "borderline" term in early post-World War II publications. In her first papers she characterized borderlines as unable to tolerate routine, incapable of developing insight, inclined to lead chaotic lives, and deficient in empathic capacity. To Schmideberg, the borderline concept represented a stable level of functioning that blends features of normality, neuroses, psychoses, and psychopathy. Also notable was her contention that there was no single and distinct entity that could be labeled "borderline"; rather, the term encompassed several trait mixtures and symptom constellations. She wrote of the syndrome as follows:

> It is not just quantitatively halfway between the neuroses and psychoses; the blending and combination of these modes of reaction produce something qualitatively different....
>
> One reason why the borderline should be regarded as a clinical entity is that the patient, as a rule, remains substantially the same throughout his life. He is stable in his instability, whatever ups and downs he has, and often keeps constant his pattern of peculiarity.
>
> Borderlines should be broken down into major subgroups, such as depressives, schizoids, paranoids....
>
> Borderlines suffer from disturbances affecting almost every area of their personality and life, in particular, personal relations and depth of feeling (1959, p. 399)

Another early theorist of the borderline syndrome, A. Wolberg (1952), posited a number of clinical features that also resemble those found in the DSM-III formulation. Of particular interest was her notion of the vicious circle within which the borderline-prone child becomes trapped. Notable in this sequence are: ambivalence between wishing to be seen as "good" by one's parents, accompanied by a resistance to obeying them; a mixed feeling of anxiety and depression leading to the need for constant reassurance of love that fails to be forthcoming; a consequent hypersensitivity to anticipated rejection from others; a growing feeling of personal failure, loneliness, and emptiness; a projected hostile acting out against others, followed by contrition and guilt; self-punitive and self-damaging behaviors such as drug or alcohol addiction; and increased anxiety and depression—and the vicious circle begins anew.

Although Knight (1953) focused his attention on young adults undergoing schizophrenic-like states or transient psychotic episodes, his paper was a seminal contribution in that he brought to the foreground the importance of "ego weakness" as a crucial element in characterizing the borderline personality structure. In essence, he concluded that psychotic episodes were likely to occur in borderline character structures. Superficial neurotic symptoms provide a "holding position," but, ultimately, the weak ego defenses display themselves in both microscopic (interview behavior) and macroscopic (life history and behavior) forms. Conceptualizing his incisive and fruitful studies from an ego-analytic perspective, Knight wrote:

> The superficial clinical picture—hysteria, phobia, obsessions, compulsive rituals—may represent a holding operation in a forward position, while the major portion of the ego has regressed far behind this in varying degrees of disorder.
> We conceptualize the borderline case as one in which normal ego functions of secondary process thinking, integration, realistic planning, adaptation to the environment, maintenance of object relationships, and defenses against primitive unconscious impulses are severely weakened.
> Other ego functions, such as conventional (but superficial) adaptation to the environment and superficial maintenance of object relationships may exhibit varying degrees of intactness. And still others, such as memory, calculation, and certain habitual performances, may seem unimpaired.
> In addition to these . . . evidences of ego weakness [there is a] . . . lack of concern about the realities of his life predicament; . . . the illness developed in the absence of observable precipitating stress, or under . . . relatively minor stress; . . . the presence of multiple symptoms and disabilities, especially if these are regarded with an acceptance that seems ego-syntonic; . . . lack of achievement over a relatively long period, indicating a chronic and severe failure of the ego to channelize energies constructively; . . . vagueness or unrealism in planning for the future with respect to education, vocation, marriage, parenthood, and the like. (1953, pp. 5-8)

J. Frosch initiated a series of explorations in the 1950s into what he termed the "disorders of impulse control," many of which typify the DSM-III borderline (e.g., quick-tempered irritability). It was not until his papers on the "psychotic character" (1960, 1964, 1970), however, that Frosch made his contributions more directly relevant to contemporary borderline conceptions. Adhering to a more orthodox psychoanalytic perspective than Knight's ego-orientation, Frosch summarized his position as follows:

> We are not dealing with a transitional phase on the way to or back from psychosis, or a latent, or larval psychosis which may become overt. We are dealing with characterological phenomena peculiar to persons who may never show psychosis and who establish a reality-syntonic adaptation. . . .
> The psychotic character is dominated by psychotic processes and modes of adaptation. . . . There is a propensity for regressive dedifferentiation and an underlying fear of disintegration and dissolution of the self. The psychotic

reactions of fragmentation, projective identification, ego splitting, etc., can also be observed in the psychotic character, especially during periods of decompensation. . . .

He retains a relative capacity to test reality, albeit with techniques frequently consistent with earlier ego states. Object relations, although at times prone to primitivization, as in psychosis, are nonetheless at a higher infantile level. There appears to be a push toward establishing contact with objects, though the simultaneously existing fear of engulfment by the object frequently leads to complications.

The ego is constantly threatened by breakthroughs of id-derived impulses. (1970, pp. 47–48)

Influenced by the articulate and cogent theses of Stern and Knight, and of the British object-relations theorists Klein, Fairbairn, and Winnicott in particular, Kernberg's recent writings (1967, 1970, 1975, 1977, 1979, 1980) on the "borderline personality organization" have become a prime force in establishing the status and attention given the syndrome in contemporary literature. Combining the central role assigned by Knight to impaired ego functions and the diverse symptom criteria spelled out by Stern, Kernberg has constructed a complex, multilevel, and multidimensional nosology based on psychoanalytic metapsychology. This schema encompasses not only the borderline ego structure, or organization, but a wide range of syndromes that are hierarchically ordered in terms of both specific type and pathological severity. Paralleling a similar nosological matrix by Millon (1969), which is based on a social-learning rather than a psychoanalytic metapsychology, it conceives the borderline concept as a particular form of significantly weakened personality organization. Neither Kernberg nor Millon, nor for that matter Knight or Schmideberg, suggest that the "borderline" label be employed as a specific or distinct diagnostic type: Rather, they contend that it is best treated as a supplementary diagnosis that conveys the dimension of severity in "ego" functioning and "object" relations.

Despite the diversity of forms this personality may take, borderlines do possess certain stable and enduring psychostructural features in common, according to Cary (1972) and Kernberg (1979). In reviewing the clinical manifestations of the borderline personality, which Kernberg considers intermediary between neurotic and psychotic organizations, he wrote:

Clinically, when we speak of patients with borderline personality organizations, we refer to patients who present serious difficulties in their interpersonal relationships and some alteration in their experience of reality but with essential preservation of reality testing. Such patients also present contradictory characteristics, chaotic co-existence of defenses against and direct expression of primitive "id contents" in consciousness, a kind of pseudo-insight into their personality without real concern for nor awareness of the conflictual nature of the material, and a lack of clear identity and lack of understanding in depth of other people. These patients present primitive defensive operations rather than repression and related defenses, and above all, mutual dissociation of contradictory ego states reflecting what might be called a "nonmetabolized" persistence of early, pathological internalized object relationships. They also show "nonspecific" manifestations of ego weakness. The term "nonspecific" refers to a lack of impulse control, lack of anxiety tolerance, lack of sublimatory capacity, and presence of primary process thinking, and indicates that these manifestations of ego weakness represent a general inadequacy of normal ego functioning. In contrast, the primitive defensive constellation of these patients and their contradictory, pathological character traits are "specific" manifestations of ego weakness. (1975, pp. 161–162)

Borderline Conceptions Within the Affective Disorder Spectrum

It was mentioned earlier that a drift has occurred in the theoretical and research literature, as well as in the formulations of the DSM-III, toward conceiving the borderline syndrome as a personality variant that falls within the spectrum of affective disorders; in this respect, it parallels the schizotypal personality syndrome, which has been increasingly conceived as fitting the schizophrenic spectrum. The major exponents of this view are found most prominently among researchers of a biological persuasion, but a number of psychoanalytically oriented theorists have also offered suggestions of a similar cast.

Although referring only tangentially to Kraepelin's views, which address the same thesis directly and cogently, E. Jacobson (1953), an important analytic theorist, recorded her experiences with a group of "cyclothymic depressives" who gave evidence of "simple depression . . . without psychotic symptoms, yet belong to the manic-depressive group" (p. 52). As would be anticipated, Jacobson sought to interpret the behavior of these "borderline" cyclothymics in psychoanalytic terms. To her, their behaviors reflected an effort to find solutions to psychosexual conflicts through regressive maneuvers. An "inherited constitution" might be operative, but, according to Jacobson, these affective borderlines more than likely experienced emotional deprivation, had poor self versus object differentiations, and displayed a "remarkable vulnerability, and intolerance of frustration, hurt and disappointment" (p. 55).

More relevant to current conceptions of the borderline are the affective symptoms that B. R. Easser and S. R. Lesser (1965) described in their psychoanalytic formulation of the "hysteroid" borderline type. This group of patients exhibits the outward behaviors of the classical hysterical (histrionic) personality but are unquestionably a more deeply disturbed variant. Worthy of mention is that the features of Easser and Lesser's hysteroid are akin to the symptoms outlined in Kernberg's portrayal of the infantile personality (1967, 1970), a character type he judged structurally at the "lower level" (borderline) of organization. The affinity of the hysteroid to both an affective style and a borderline severity is well portrayed in the following (Easser and Lesser, 1965):

In many instances the hysteroid would appear to be a caricature of the hysteric, much as the hysteric has been said to be a caricature of femininity. Each characteristic is demonstrated in even sharper dramatic relief. The bounds of social custom and propriety are breached. The latent aggressivity of the exhibitionism, the competitiveness and the self-absorption becomes blatant, insistent, and bizarre. The chic becomes the mannequin; the casual, sloppy; the bohemian, beat.

The adaptational functioning of the hysteroid is erratic. Inconstancy and irresponsibility cause the patient to suffer realistic rebuffs, injuries, and failure.

The hysteroid starts friendships with great hopes and enthusiasm. The friendship commences with idolatry and ends in bitterness when the expectation of rescue, nurture and care is not fulfilled. These relational ruptures are often succeeded by detachment, isolation, depression, and paranoid-like trends.

The hysteroid's family life is often...disturbed, disorganized, and inconsistent.

Grosser fluctuations of the hysteroid personality are to be anticipated from the more infantile fixation and the consequent weaker integration and synthesis of the ego. Thus we encounter less emotional control, a lessened ability to hold and tolerate tension, and more proneness to action and depression. (pp. 399-400)

Entering from the perspective of differential responsiveness to pharmacologic agents, D. Klein has raised serious questions concerning the validity of the borderline syndrome as a unified diagnostic entity (1975, 1977). This challenge notwithstanding, he has proposed a series of ostensibly distinct personality disorders that exhibit clinical features frequently associated with recent descriptions of the borderline syndrome. In addition to asserting that the borderline designation subsumes, in effect, several heterogeneous subtypes, he contends further that their characterological and severity dimensions are secondary to their shared affective symptomatology. In essence—and in accord with Kraepelin's contention some 70 years earlier to the effect that an endogenous metabolic defect was at the core of the disturbance—Klein argued that an affective dysfunction lies at the heart of the vulnerability of these syndromes. Three personality types—the phobic-anxious, the emotionally unstable, and the hysteroid dysphorics—are identified as subject to this vulnerability; each displays a long-term and somewhat atypical affective disorder. Several brief excerpts characterizing these patterns are provided in Chapters 5 and 9 and these are not repeated here. Worthy of note, however, is the symptomatologic affinity between Klein's pharmacologically deduced hysteroid dysphoric type and Easser and Lesser's analytically derived hysteroid portrayal. Also notable are the close parallels between Klein's three "atypical affective" syndromes and three of the four borderline syndromal clusters obtained empirically by Grinker, Werbel, and Drye (1968), whose work is discussed shortly.

Passing mention must be made, however, of another group of contemporary biological researchers, H. S. Akiskal et al. (1977), who have studied and marshalled data from a variety of pharmacologic and family sources that support the position that what they term "cyclothymia" is, in essence, a subclinical or borderline personality condition found in biological relatives of manic-depressives, which predisposes those afflicted to the clinical form of the illness, a view quite reminiscent once more of Kraepelin's early thesis.

The work of Grinker et al. (1968) is especially noteworthy in being the first systematic empirical investigation employing explicit criteria both for including a borderline population sample and excluding potentially confounding schizophrenic-like patients. Selection criteria resulted in young adults with short-term hospitalizations, good interim functioning, and florid, attention-gaining behaviors; these criteria were employed to minimize the schizophrenic confound and oriented the study population along affective lines. Data from 51 patients were subjected to a cluster analysis and resulted in both common features and differentiation into four major subtypes. Among the elements that appear to be shared by all variants are

> *anger* as the main or only affect, defect in *affectional* relationships, absence of indications of *self-identity* and *depressive* loneliness (p. 176)

The four subgroups were described as follows. The first, which Grinker et al. termed the "psychotic border," was

> characterized clinically by inappropriate and negative behaviors.... These patients were careless in their personal grooming and slept and ate erratically.... [Their] perception of self and others ... revealed deficiencies.... These patients manifested essentially negative effects ... with occasional angry eruptions in an impulsive manner. In addition, depression of recognizable duration was present. (p. 83).

The second cluster, or "core" borderline group, was characterized by the following:

1. Vacillating involvement with others
2. Overt or acting-out expressions of anger
3. Depression
4. Absence of indications of consistent self identity (p. 87).

The third group, the affectless, defended "as if" persons, represents a syndrome similar to the DSM-III schizoid personality. As discussed in Chapter 10, Deutsch's "as if" type appears to be the forerunner, not of the borderline disorder as we currently conceive it to be, but of the affectless, unempathic, interpersonally detached schizoid.

The fourth borderline category, labeled "the border with the neurosis," revealed defects in self-esteem and confidence, and a depressive quality not associated with anger or guilt feelings. The prime qualities were summarized by Grinker et al. as follows:

1. Childlike clinging depression (anaclitic)
2. Anxiety
3. Generally close resemblance to neurotic narcissistic characters (p. 90)

A review of the findings reported by Grinker et al. suggests that their fourth group, rather than exhibiting parallels with the newly conceptualized DSM-III narcissistic pattern, is appreciably more similar to the manual's newly formulated dependent personality. The first of their subtypes, referred to as the "psychotic border" is akin to Klein's hysteroid dysphorics, to Millon's cycloid personalities, and to the DSM-III borderline characterization. Their so-called core borderline group overlaps also with the DSM-III borderline description and has affinities with Klein's emotionally unstable character and Millon's negativistic personality.

The recent work of Gunderson and his colleagues (Gunderson and Singer, 1975; Gunderson, Carpenter, and Strauss, 1975; Gunderson, 1977, 1979) has led them to strongly advocate the borderline as a discrete personality disorder that can be clearly described and differentially diagnosed from both schizophrenic syndromes and neurotic states. Benefiting from a thorough review of prior work and opportunities to carry out a series of empirical studies, Gunderson et al. characterized the borderline as showing intense affect, either hostile or depressed; an absence of flatness or pleasure, but frequent depersonalization; a background of episodic and impulsive behavior that may include self-damaging acts such as drug overdoses, alcoholism, or promiscuity; identity disturbances that are often cloaked by superficial identifications; brief psychotic episodes; and interpersonal relationships that vacillate between superficiality, dependency, and manipulativeness.

Finally, the theoretical propositions of Millon (1969) provide a schema for conceptualizing the borderline as a level of personality disorganization with several subvariants. To Millon, the so-called borderline, schizotypal, and paranoid personalities of the DSM-III exhibit a series of characteristics in common, notably a chronic and periodically severe pathology in their overall structure and a checkered history of disruptions, predicaments, and disappointments in personal relationships and in school and work performance. Deficits in social attainments may also be prominent, as evidenced in an apparent inability to learn from prior difficulties, a tendency to precipitate self-defeating vicious circles, digressions and setbacks from earlier aspirations, and a failure to achieve a consistent niche in life that is consonant with natural aptitudes and potentials. Although all these personalities are able to function on an ambulatory basis, there is likely to have been repetitive but transient episodes in which extreme or bizarre behaviors were exhibited. More specifically, the descriptions and criteria that follow were written by Millon in 1975 as the initial working draft of the "borderline cycloid" for the DSM-III Task Force personality subcommittee.

This pattern is typified by intense, variable moods and by irregular energy levels, both of which appear frequently to be unrelated to external events. Those with predominant euphoric moods often experience brief spells of dejection, anxiety or impulsive anger; where the characteristic mood is depressed, transient periods of anxiety, elation and anger may be interspersed. There is a notable fear of separation and loss with considerable dependency reassurance required to maintain psychic equilibrium. Strong ambivalent feelings, such as love, anger and guilt, are often felt toward those upon whom there is dependence.

An appraisal of personal background and history reveals both of the following:

1. Social attainment deficits (e.g., experienced serious, self-precipitated setbacks in scholastic, marital or vocational pursuits; repeated failure to maintain durable, satisfactory and secure roles consonant with age and aptitudes).
2. Periodic mini-psychotic episodes (e.g., experienced several brief and reversible periods in which either bizarre behaviors, extreme moods, irrational impulses or delusional thoughts were exhibited; short lived breaks from "reality," however, are often recognized subsequently as peculiar or deviant).

Since adolescence or early adulthood at least 3 of the following have been present to a notably greater degree than in most people and were not limited to discrete periods nor necessarily prompted by stressful life events.

1. Intense endogenous moods (e.g., repetitive failure to be in normal mood not readily attributable to external sources; affective state either characteristically depressed or excited, or noted by recurring periods of dejection and apathy interspersed with spells of anger, anxiety or euphoria).
2. Dysregulated activation (e.g., experiences desultory energy level and irregular sleep-wake cycle; describes time periods suggesting that affective-activation equilibrium was constantly in jeopardy).
3. Self-condemnatory conscience (e.g., reveals recurring self-mutilating and suicidal thoughts; periodically redeems moody behavior through contrition and self-derogation).
4. Dependency anxiety (e.g., preoccupied with securing affection and maintaining emotional support; reacts intensely to separation and reports haunting fear of isolation and loss).
5. Cognitive-affective ambivalence (e.g., portrays repeated struggle to express attitudes contrary to inner feelings; conflicting emotions and thoughts simultaneously experienced toward others, notably love, rage and guilt).

The preceding text was subsequently revised in line with Klein's characterizations of the "emotionally unstable character disorder" and was labeled the "unstable personality disorder." Still later work reported by Spitzer, Endicott, and Gibbon (1979) was undertaken with the view of including the major criteria proposed by Kernberg. Following extended discussions and compromises of a political rather than substantive nature, the syndrome was designated the "borderline personality."

CLINICAL PICTURE

Patients categorized as borderline personalities display a wide variety of clinical features. Certain elements do stand out as relatively distinct and these are the prime focus here. As in prior chapters, these characteristics are separated into four broad categories.

Behavioral Features

The most striking characteristic of borderlines is the intensity of their affect and the changeability of their actions. Rapid shifts from one mood and attitude to another are not inevitable aspects of the everyday behavior of the borderline, but they do characterize extended periods when there has been a break in control. Most borderlines exhibit a single, dominant outlook or frame of mind, such as a self-ingratiating depressive tone, which gives way periodically, however, to anxious agitation or impulsive outbursts of inappropriate temper or anger. Self-destructive and self-damaging behaviors, although relatively infrequent, are usually recognized subsequently as having been foolish and irrational. It is the unpredictability and the impetuous, erratic, and unreflected impulsivity that characterizes the borderline's tempers and actions, rather than the presence of a pattern of smoothly and repetitively swinging emotions that go from one end of the affective continuum to the other. This brittle, labile, and unsustainable quality contrasts to the cyclical regularity of contrasting moods that is often believed to typify these patients.

Self-Descriptions and Complaints

There is either a confusion or a diffusion in borderlines' conception of themselves. They have considerable difficulty in maintaining a stable sense of "who they are," conveying rapidly shifting presentations of self, or in formulating any clear sense of personal identity. A major consequence of this uncertainty is the lack of a consistent purpose or direction for shaping one's attitudes, behaviors, or emotions. Unable to give coherence to their existence, they have few anchors or guideposts to either coordinate their actions, control their impulses, or construct a goal-oriented means for achieving their desires. Feeling scattered and unintegrated, they vacillate, responding as a child would to every passing interest or whim and shifting from one momentary course to another. They remain aimless, unable to channel their energies or abilities, incapable of settling down on some path or role that might provide a basis for fashioning a unified and enduring sense of self.

As a secondary consequence of their unsure or unstable self-identities, borderlines tend to become exceedingly dependent on others, if they were not so already. Not only do they need protection and reassurance to maintain their equanimity, but they become inordinately vulnerable to separation from these external sources of support. Isolation or aloneness may be terrifying not only because borderlines lack an inherent sense of self but because they lack the wherewithal, the know-how, and equipment for taking mature, self-determined, and independent action. Unable to fend adequately for themselves, they not only dread potential loss but often anticipate it, "seeing it" happening when, in fact, it is not. Moreover, since most borderlines devalue their self-worth, it is difficult for them to believe that those upon whom they depend could think well of them. Consequently, they are exceedingly fearful that others will depreciate them and cast them off. With so unstable a foundation of self-esteem, and lacking the means for an autonomous existence, borderlines remain constantly on edge, prone to the anxiety of separation and ripe for anticipating inevitable desertion. Events that stir up these fears may precipitate extreme efforts at restitution such as idealization, self-abnegation, and attention-gaining acts of self-destruction or, conversely, self-assertion and impulsive anger.

Matters are bad enough for borderlines, given their identity diffusion and separation anxieties, but they are also in intense conflict regarding dependency needs and often feel guilt for past attempts at self-assertion and independence. In these quests for self-determination and self-identity, many have been subjected to ridicule and isolation, resulting in feelings of distrust and anger toward others. Borderlines cannot help but be ambivalently anxious. To assert themselves endangers the security and protection they desperately seek from others by provoking the latter to reject and abandon them. Yet, given their past, they know they can never entirely trust others nor fully hope to gain the security and affection they need. Should their anxiety about separation lead them to submit as a way of warding off or forestalling desertion, they expose themselves to even further dependency and, thereby, an even greater threat of loss. Moreover, they know they experience intense anger toward those upon whom they depend, not only because it shames them and exposes their weakness but also because of the others' power in having "forced" them to yield and acquiesce. This very resentment becomes then a threat in itself. If they are going to appease others to prevent abandonment, they must take pains to assure that their anger remains under control. Should this resentment be discharged, even in innocuous forms of self-assertion, their security will be severely threatened. They are in a terrible bind. Should they "strike out" alone, no longer dependent on others who have expected too much or have demeaned them, or should they submit for fear of losing what little security they can gain thereby?

To secure their anger and to constrain their resentment, borderlines often turn against themselves in a self-critical and self-condemnatory manner. Despising themselves, they voice the same harsh judgments they have learned to anticipate from others. They display not only anxiety and conflict but overt expressions of guilt, remorse, and self-belittlement. It is these feelings that occasionally take hold, overwhelm them, and lead to the characteristic self-damaging and periodic self-destructive acts.

Inferred Intrapsychic Processes

As just noted, the hostility of borderlines poses a serious threat to their security. To experience resentment toward others, let alone to vent it, endangers them since it may provoke the counterhostility, rejection, and abandonment they fear. Angry feelings and outbursts must not only be curtailed or redirected toward impotent scapegoats but intrapsychically reversed and condemned. To appease their conscience and to assure expiation, they may reproach themselves for their faults, and purify themselves to prove their virtue. To accomplish this goal, their hostile impulses are intrapsychically inverted. Thus, aggressive urges toward others may be turned upon themselves. Rather than vent their anger they will openly castigate and derogate themselves, and voice exaggerated feelings of guilt and worthlessness. Some borderlines become notably self-recriminating. They belittle themselves, demean their abilities, and derogate their virtues, not only as a means of diluting their aggressive urges but to assure others that they themselves are neither worthy nor able adversaries. The self-effacement of these borderlines is an attempt, then, both to control their own hostility and to stave off hostility from others. Among other borderlines, where hostile impulses are more deeply ingrained as a form of self-expression, these feelings must be counteracted more forcefully. Since these patients are likely to have displayed their anger more frequently and destructively, they must work all the harder to redeem themselves. Instead of being merely self-effacing and contrite, they will often turn upon themselves viciously, claiming that they are despicable and hateful persons. These condemnatory self-accusations may at times reach delusional proportions, and such patients may reject every rational effort to dissuade them of their culpability. In these cases, it is the struggle to redeem oneself that often leads to self-mutilation and physical destruction.

Interpersonal Coping Style

The borderline is more ambivalent about relationships with others than are most personality syndromes. Moreover, these individuals have been less successful in fulfilling their dependency needs, suffering thereby considerably greater separation anxieties. Their concerns are not simply those of gaining approval and affection but of not submitting to others, yet preventing further loss. Since they already are on shaky grounds, borderlines' actions are directed less toward accumulating additional reserves of support and esteem than toward preserving the little security they still possess.

At first, borderlines will employ their characteristic coping styles with increased fervor in the hope that they will regain their footing. Some may become martyrs, dedicated and self-effacing persons who are "so good" that they are willing to devote or sacrifice their lives for some greater purpose. The usual goal of these borderlines is to insinuate themselves into the lives of others who will not merely "use" them but need them and, therefore, not desert them. Self-sacrificing though they may appear to be, these borderlines effectively manipulate others to protect against the separation they dread. Moreover, by "sacrificing" themselves, they not only assure continued contact with others but serve as implicit models for others to be gentle and considerate in return. Virtuous martyrdom, rather than a sacrifice, is a ploy of submissive devotion that strengthens the attachments borderlines need.

The intolerance of being abandoned and the feeling of emptiness and aloneness consequent to the borderline's failure to maintain a secure and rewarding dependency relationship, cumulate into a reservoir of anxiety, conflict, and anger. Like a safety valve, these tensions must be released either slowly or through periodic and often impulsive outbursts against others. Since borderlines seek the goodwill of those upon whom they depend, they will try to express their inner tensions subtly and indirectly at first. Depression is among the most common of these covert expressions. Thus, the pleading anguish, despair, and resignation voiced by borderlines serve to release tensions and to externalize the torment they feel within themselves. For some, however, depressive lethargy and sulking behavior are a means primarily of expressing anger. Depression serves as an instrument for them to frustrate and retaliate against those who have "failed" them or "demanded too much." Angered by the "inconsiderateness" of others, these borderlines employ their somber and melancholy sadness as a vehicle to "get back" at them or "teach them a lesson." Moreover, by exaggerating their plight and by moping about helplessly, they effectively avoid responsibilities, place added burdens upon others, and thereby cause their families not only to take care of them but to suffer and feel guilt while doing so. In addition, the dour moods and excessive complaints of these borderlines infect the atmosphere with tension and irritability, thereby upsetting what equanimity remains among those who have "disappointed" them. Similarly, suicidal threats, gambling, and other impulsively self-damaging acts may function as instruments of punitive blackmail, a way of threatening others that further trouble is in the offing, and that they had best "make up" for their prior neglect and thoughtlessness.

ASSOCIATED DISORDERS

As in prior chapters, this section outlines several of the major Axis I symptom disorders that are associated with the personality under review. Special attention is given to concurrent or covariant Axis II personality disorders since the borderline pattern is in great measure a more advanced or dysfunctional variant of the less problematic or milder personality types. Points useful in the differential diagnosis of the borderline pattern are briefly discussed as well.

Concomitant Axis I Symptoms

One of the distinguishing features of borderline personalities is the wide variety of covariant symptoms they exhibit over time. The affective instability and diminished controls that characterize the pattern result in the periodic emergence of a number of different Axis I disorders. Only the more common of these are noted here.

Anxiety disorders.   Brief eruptions of uncontrollable emotion occur in borderline patients, who often experience states of *generalized anxiety*. For varied reasons, traceable to particular vulnerabilities or coping inadequacies, these patients fear the imminence of an impending disaster or feel that they are being overwhelmed or will disintegrate from the press of forces that surge within them. These anxieties may follow a period of mounting stress in which a series of objectively trivial events cumulate to the point of being experienced as devastating and crushing. At other times, it is when the patients' unconscious impulses have been activated and break through their controls that we see this dramatic upsurge and emotional discharge. As the more acute phases of these attacks approach their culmination, the patient's breathing quickens, the heart races, and the patient perspires profusely and feels faint, numb, nauseous, chilly, and weak. After a few minutes (or at most one or two hours), the diffuse sense of fear, with its concomitant physical symptoms, begins to subside, and the patient returns to a more typical level of composure. There are others, more intense periods when a sweeping disorganization and overwhelming *panic disorder* take hold. This borderline's controls have completely disintegrated and the patient is carried by a rush of irrational impulses and bizarre thoughts that often culminate in a wild spree of chaotic behavior, violent outbursts, terrifying hallucinations, suicidal acts, and so on. These extreme behaviors may be justly diagnosed as *brief reactive psychoses*. In either case, we see transitory states of both intense anxiety and ego decompensation that terminate after a few hours, or at most no more than one or two days, following which the patient regains his/her "normal" equilibrium. Should these eruptions linger for weeks or recur frequently, with bizarre behaviors and terrifying anxieties persisting, it would be more correct to categorize the impairment as a specific psychotic disorder.

Obsessive-compulsive disorders.   Borderline patients will occasionally exhibit *compulsive disorders*, as seen in an irresistible preoccupation with some absurd but "safe" activity that serves to distract them from confronting more painful sources of discomfort. Also, through reaction formation, they may pursue these activities as a subterfuge for socially unacceptable impulses. Thus, symbolic acts of compulsive "undoing" serve not only to void past sins but to ward off anticipated future punishment and social rebuke. Moreover, the self-punitive and redemptive aspects of the undoing ritual often diminish the oppressive buildup of guilt. For example, insistence on order and cleanliness, so untypical of the borderline's characteristic behavior, and the self-righteous air with which they perform these acts distract others from their previous irrationalities, and this often also evokes the secondary gains of attention and approval.

Somatoform disorders. These have as their primary goal the blocking from awareness of the true source of the borderline's anxiety. Despite the price these patients must pay in diminished bodily functioning, they remain relatively free of tension by accepting their disability. The "choice" of the symptom and the symbolic meaning it expresses reflect the particular character of an individual's underlying difficulties and the secondary gains he or she wishes to achieve. Both the problems and the gains that borderlines seek stem from their basic vulnerabilities and habitual coping style. This interplay can be illustrated with three brief examples: One borderline patient, whose pattern of life has been guided by the fear of social rebuke, may develop an arm paralysis to control the impulse to strike someone whom he/she hates; another borderline may suddenly become mute for fear of voicing intense anger and resentment; a third patient may lose his/her hearing as a way of tuning out ridiculing voices, both real and imagined. Somatoform symptoms rarely are the end product of a single cause or coping function. Over-determined, they reflect a compromise solution that blends several emotions and coping aims. Thus, a paralyzed arm may not only control an angry impulse but also may attract social sympathy, as well as discharge the patient's self-punitive and guilt feelings.

Dissociative disorders. Borderline personalities are likely to vent brief, but highly charged, angry outbursts during *psychogenic fugue* states. Repressed resentments occasionally take this form and erupt into the open when these patients have felt trapped and confused or betrayed. Moreover, it is not unusual for borderlines to brutalize themselves, as well as others, during these fugues. They may tear their clothes, smash their fists, and lacerate their bodies, thereby suffering more themselves than do their presumed assailants. Most frequently, these violent discharges are followed by a return to their former state. In some cases, however, borderlines may disintegrate into one or another of the more prolonged psychotic disorders. Though strange and fearsome, fugues do not come as totally unexpected to friends and family members of borderlines since the symptoms of this disorder are but extremes of their long-term pattern of impulsiveness, behavioral unpredictability, and self-damaging acts.

Affective disorders. Overt and direct expressions of hostility tend to be exhibited only impulsively by borderlines since they fear these actions will lead others to reject them. A major form of anger control is to turn feelings of resentment inward into hypochondriacal disorders and mild depressive episodes. Not only may they overplay their helplessness and futile state, but the borderline's "sorrowful plight" may create guilt in others and cause them no end of discomfort as they try to meet the borderline's "justified" need for attention and care. Of course, devious coping maneuvers such as these often prove fruitless and may evoke exasperation and rebuke from others. Should such a course prevail, borderlines may turn their anger upon themselves even more intensely. Protestations of guilt and self-reproval come to the fore as they voice a flood of self-deprecatory comments about their own personal shortcomings, the inordinate and despicable demands they have made of others, their history of irresponsibility, unworthiness, evil actions, and so on. Self-derision and thinly veiled suicidal threats not only discharge borderlines' anger but manage to get others to forgive them and offer assurances of their devotion and compassion.

As evident from the preceding, borderlines succumb frequently to *major depressions.* In the more retarded form of depression, borderlines gain some measure of control over their inner conflicts and hostile impulses. Referred to earlier, they do this by turning their angry feelings inward, that is, by taking out their hatred upon themselves. Guilt and self-disparagement are voiced for their failures, impulsive acts, contemptuous feelings, and evil thoughts. Feelings of emptiness, boredom, and "deadness" also are frequently reported. In the more self-punitive depressions, borderlines manage to cloak their contrary impulses by seeking redemption and asking absolution for their past behaviors and forbidden inclinations. Not infrequently, this sadness and melancholy solicit support and nurture from others. As in other symptom disorders, this is a subtle and indirect means of venting hidden resentment and anger. Helplessness and self-destructive acts make others feel guilty and burden them with extra responsibilities and woes.

The affective disorder features of the borderline are rather mixed and erratic, varying in quality and focus according to the patient's special vulnerabilities. It is essentially a composite of depression and hostility, although not as extreme as either when one of these is the predominant affect. Quite often we see an incessant despair and suffering, an agitated pacing, a wringing of hands, and an apprehensiveness and tension that are unrelieved by comforting reassurances. The primary components at these times are hostile depressive complaints and a demanding and querulous irritability. These patients may bemoan their sorry state and their desperate need for others to attend to their manifold physical ailments, pains, and incapacities. In other borderlines, the depressive picture is colored less by critical and demanding attitudes, and more by self-blame and guilt. In others still, we see anxious self-doubting, expressions of self-hate, a preoccupation with impending disasters, suicidal thoughts, feelings of unworthiness, and delusions of shame and sin. Borderlines are especially prone, however, to agitated depressions. These disorders are an extension of their personality style—unstable relationships and feelings, self-destructiveness, identity confusion, complaints, irritability, and grumbling discontent, usually interwoven with expressions of guilt and self-condemnation. Their habitual style of acting out their conflicts and ambivalent feelings becomes more pronounced at these times and results in vacillations between bitterness and resentment, on the one hand, and intropunitive self-deprecation, on the other.

Some borderlines display periods of *bipolar disorder* similar to schizo-affective states, displaying a scattering of ideas and emotions, and a jumble of disconnected thoughts and aimless behaviors. In some cases, there may be an exuberance, a zestful energy and jovial mood, that is lacking among true schizophrenic types. Although the ideas and hyperactivity of these borderlines tend to be connected only loosely to reality, they have an intelligible logic to them and appear consonant with the predominant mood. In other cases, behaviors and ideas are fragmented, vague, disjointed, and bizarre. Here, the borderlines' moods are varied and changeable, inconsistent with their thoughts and actions, and difficult to grasp and relate to, let alone empathize with. Albeit briefly, some borderlines successfully infect others for short periods with their conviviality and buoyant optimism. They may become extremely clever and witty, rattling off puns and rhymes, and playing cute and devilish tricks. This humor and mischievousness rapidly drains others, who quickly tire of the incessant and increasingly irrational quality of the borderlines' forced sociability. In addition to their frenetic excitement and reckless race from one topic to another, they may display an annoying pomposity and self-expansiveness as well. Boastfulness becomes extremely trying and exasperating, often destroying what patience and goodwill these patients previously evoked from others.

Schizoaffective disorders.   Without external support and lacking a core of inner competence, borderlines may disintegrate into a schizoaffective disorder. However, and in line with most patients exhibiting this disorder, we often see beneath their confusion and bizarre acts a need for affection and emotional support. Their regressive eating and soiling, for example, may reflect a search for nurturant care and attention. Even their stereotyped grimacing may signify their pathetic effort to attract the goodwill and approval of those upon whom they now wish to depend.

Concurrent Axis II Personalities

Both theory (Millon, 1969) and research (Millon, 1977) show that the borderline pattern overlaps almost invariably with every other personality disorder; the schizoid and antisocial types are about the only likely exceptions. More often than not, it develops insidiously as an advanced or more dysfunctional variant of its concurrent personality types.

Before proceeding to describe in detail the major subvariants of the borderline syndrome, it should be noted that its features occasionally are displayed in combination with *narcissistic* personalities and with *avoidant* personalities; borderline characteristics show up rarely among schizoids and antisocials. In both narcissists and avoidants what we observe are brief episodes of impulsivity and affective instability that mimic the more intrinsic traits of the borderline. A key notion in the previous sentence is brevity, that is, the evanascent nature with which these covariant symptoms exhibit themselves. Impulsive anger, affective instability,and self-destructive acts are not, nor do they appear to become, integral character traits of either of these two personalities. Narcissists succumb to them fleetingly following severe psychic deflation, that is, a loss of a significant source of status or fantasied self-esteem; during these transitory episodes they will appear "borderline" but only until they can regain their benignly arrogant composure. The avoidant may also succumb to the borderline's more overtly exhibitionistic symptoms following a painful psychic blow. However, avoidants are much more apt to decompensate, if at all, along schizotypal lines. They intensify at these times their established pattern of social anxiety and isolation, their self-created cognitive interference, and their flat and constricted affect. The discussion returns now to those subtypes of the borderline that share its prime features in a more enduring and integrated fashion.

Borderline-dependent mixed personality. These patients wish to be self-effacing, sweet, Pollyanna like, pliant, and submissive individuals who shun competition and avoid initiative. Easily discouraged, they seek to attach themselves to one or two persons upon whom they can depend, with whom they can experience reciprocal affection, and to whom they can be loyal and humble. Unfortunately, these borderlines' strategy of cooperation and compliance has not been notably successful. They have put all their eggs in one basket; someone specific has been chosen upon whom the patient is excessively dependent. This attachment has not proved to be secure. As a result, the borderline's lifeline has connected him/her to an unreliable anchor and his/her psychic equilibrim has been in constant jeopardy. These borderlines exhibit an anxious and persistent preoccupation with security. Their pathetic lack of inner resources and their marked self-doubts lead them to cling to whomever they can and to submerge every remnant of autonomy and individuality they possess. This insecurity has precipitated conflict and further distress. Borderline-dependents easily become dejected and depressed, feeling hopeless, helpless, and powerless to overcome their fate. Every task or decision has become weighty and unnerving. Even the simplest of responsibilities feel as if they demand more energy than the borderline can muster. Life seems to be empty and vacant, yet it feels heavy and burdensome. They "know" they cannot go on alone and begin to turn against themselves, feeling unworthy, useless, and despised. Should their futility grow, they may regress to a state of marked apathy and infantile dependency, requiring others to tend to them as if they were infants. However, borderline-dependents sometimes reverse their habitual passive and dependent style, seeking actively, for example, to solicit attention and security. During these brief periods they may become exceedingly cheerful and buoyant, trying to cover up and counter their underlying despondency. Others may disown their submissive and acquiescent past and display outbursts of explosive and angry resentment, wildly attacking others for having exploited and abused them and for having failed to see how needful they have been of encouragement and nurturance. Not infrequently, a frightening sense of isolation and aloneness may overwhelm these patients, driving them into a panic in which they cry out for someone to comfort and hold them, lest they sink into an oblivion of nothingness.

The following MCMI computer printout was generated on the basis of the responses of a 29-year-old male who had been seen periodically in outpatient centers ever since the age of 16. He had been hospitalized for three brief psychotic episodes during that time span.

The patient's behavior is typified by marked dependency needs, the depth and variability of recurring moods, and prolonged periods of dejection and self-depreciation that are interspersed with normal spans, as well as episodes of high energy and impulsive, angry outbursts. There is an anxious seeking for reassurance from others to maintain equanimity, and he is especially vulnerable to fears of separation from those who provide this support. The fear of being abandoned leads him to be overly compliant at one time, profoundly gloomy the next, and irrationally argumentive and negativistic another. He is viewed by some as submissive and cooperative, and by others as unpredictable, irritable, and pessimistic. He repeatedly struggles to express attitudes contrary to inner feelings, often portraying conflicting emotions simultaneously toward others, notably love, rage, and guilt.

Notable also are the patient's desultory energy levels, easy fatiguability, and irregular sleep-wake cycle, suggesting that affective-activity equilibrim is in constant jeopardy. As a consequence, he vacillates between being tense and high-strung, manipulative, and moody, and is particularly sensitive to the pressures and demands of others. The frequent vacillation between moments of social agreeableness and being sullen or passively aggressive is typically followed by expressions of contrition.

The patient often complains bitterly about the lack of care expressed by others and of being treated unfairly, behaviors that keep others constantly on edge, never knowing if they will be reacted to in a cooperative or a sulky manner. Although still making efforts to be obliging and submissive to others, he has learned to anticipate disappointments, makes the mole hill of a passing indifference into a mountain of personal ridicule, and frequently precipitates interpersonal difficulties by constantly doubting the genuineness of interest others may express. These irritable testing maneuvers have begun to exasperate and alienate those upon whom he depends. Guilt, remorse, and self-condemnation are expressed at times when he has been threatened by separation and disapproval, all in the hope of regaining lost support and reassurance. Not uncommonly, he will exhibit helplessness and clinging behaviors, in addition to displaying suspiciousness, anxiety, and depression. However, others have grown increasingly weary of these behaviors, leading him to react by vacillating erratically between expressions of gloomy self-deprecation and being petulant and bitter. The struggle between dependent acquiescence and assertive independence has constantly intruded into his life. The inability to regulate emotional controls, the feeling of being misunderstood, and the unpredictable moods expressed, all contribute to innumerable wrangles and conflicts with others and to a persistent tense, resentful, and depressed tone.

Borderline-histrionic mixed personality. These patients are similar to their less severe counterparts in that both often exhibit flighty, capricious, labile, evasive, and superficial behaviors. In the borderline variant, however, we observe more extreme efforts to cope with events, many of which serve only to perpetuate and deepen the patient's plight. For example, most borderline-histrionics have not mastered the techinques of soliciting approval and ensuring a constant stream of support and encouragement. Because of their excessively flighty and capricious personal relationships, they may have experienced long periods without a secure and consistent source of affection. As noted in Chapter 5, when these patients are deprived of the attentions they crave, they may intensify their strategy of gregariousness and seductiveness, becoming dramatically exhibitionistic and infantile. Extreme hyperactivity and distractibility are often evident, as are frenetic gaiety, exaggerated boastfulness, and an insatiable need for social excitement. Fearful of missing any source of attention, they may display a frantic conviviality, an irrational and superficial euphoria in which they lose their sense of propriety and judgment. Having experienced repeated rebuffs or having had their efforts to solicit attention fail and lead to rejection, they now fear a permanent loss of attention and esteem, and may succumb to hopeless and bitter self-re-criminations. No longer confident in their seductive powers and dreading the decline of their former vigor, charm, and youth, they fret and doubt their worth and attractiveness. Anticipating desertion and disillusioned with themselves, they ponder a future of emptiness, boredom, and aloneness. Such worries beget further worries, and doubts raise only more doubts. Ultimately, their gloom may turn to agitation, to increased self-derogation, irritability, and self-destructive impulses. In time, reality begins to be distorted so that everything, no matter how valued or exciting it formerly was, now seems worthless, bleak, and barren.

Borderline-compulsive mixed personality. Despite their affective instability and impulsiveness, these individuals still possess the remnants of a few pure compulsive traits, such as attempting to be methodical, industrious, conscientious, and orderly. They also seek to comply to the strictures of society and remain small-minded, perfectionistic, grim, and humorless. They recognize that support and reward are contingent largely on compliance and submission. They had learned in the past that one had to be good "or else." Borderline-compulsives are less certain, however, than their less severe variant that rewards will, in fact, follow compliance. They are no longer sure that diligence and acquiescence gain approval or forestall desertion. Their compliant and conscientious behaviors do not "pay off" anymore, and they are justly distressed and resentful. The pact made with parents and other authority figures has been abrogated too often; others have failed to fulfill their share of the bargain. The resentment and anger these borderlines feel for having been coerced into submission, and then betrayed, churns within them and presses hard against their formerly strong controls. Persistently breaking through the surface, these feelings erupt in angry and sudden outbursts of fury and vituperation. The unbridled intensity of their anger draws its strength not only from immediate precipitants but from a deep reservoir of animosity that has been filled over years of felt oppression and coercion.

Resentments that are discharged overtly or remain seething near the surface are experienced as a threat to equanimity. Angry impulses create anxiety because they jeopardize security. Such hostility is doubly dangerous. Not only is it directed at the very persons upon whom the borderlines depend, thereby undermining the strength of those to whom they look for support, but, in addition, it will likely provoke their wrath, leading to outright condemnation and desertion. To counter their angry impulses, borderline-compulsives may become excessively rigid and constrained, muzzling and binding all traces of resentment. Severe self-condemnation frequently becomes a dominant symptom. Struggling feverishly to control their surging anger, they turn their feelings inward and impose upon themselves harsh judgments and punitive actions. Accusations of their own unworthiness are but mild rebukes for the self-derogation and guilt they feel. Self-mutilation and suicide, symbolic acts of self-desertion, may become the only punishment that "fits the crime."

Borderline-passive-aggressive mixed personality.   These patients may be difficult to distinguish from their less severe counterparts. The overt symptoms of the advanced dysfunctional borderline are, of course, more intense, and psychotic episodes occur with greater frequency than in the milder variant. Both, however, are well characterized by their unpredictability and by their restless, irritable, impatient, and complaining behaviors. They are judged by associates as disgruntled, discontent, stubborn, sullen, pessimistic, and resentful. Easily disillusioned and slighted, they tend to be envious of others and feel unappreciated and cheated in life. Despite their resentment of others, these borderlines fear separation from them. These patients are ambivalent, trapped by conflicting inclinations to "move toward, away, or against others." They vacillate perpetually, first finding one course of action unappealing, then another, then a third, and back again. To give in to others is to lose hope of independence, but to withdraw is to be isolated. Borderline–passive-aggressives have always resented their dependence on others and hate those to whom they have turned to seek security, love, and esteem. In contrast to their milder counterpart, the borderlines feel they never had their needs satisfied and never felt secure in their relationships.

The borderline–passive-aggressive openly registers disappointments, is stubborn and recalcitrant, and vents angers directly, only to recant and feel guilt and contrition. These patients are indecisive and oscillate between apologetic submission, on the one hand, and stubborn resistance and contrariness on the other. Unable to get hold of themselves and unable to find a comfortable niche with others, these borderlines become increasingly testy, bitter, and discontent. Resigned to their fate and despairing of hope, they vary unpredictably between two pathological behavior extremes. At one time, they voice feelings of worthlessness and futility, are highly agitated or deeply depressed, express guilt and are severely self-condemnatory and self-destructive. At other periods, their negativism may cross the line of reason, break out of control, and drive them into maniacal rages in which they make excessive demands of others and viciously attack those who have "trapped" them and forced them into intolerable conflicts. Following these wild outbursts, however, they may turn their hostility inward, be remorseful, plead forgiveness, and promise "to behave" and "make up" for their unpleasant and miserable past. These resolutions are usually short-lived.

Decompensated borderline personality. The previously described borderline personality variants exhibit "mixed" clinical signs and fluctuate between relatively "normal" and distinctly pathological behaviors. This contrasts with the decompensated borderline, who displays a consistent and pervasive impairment that rarely is broken by lucid thoughts and conventional behaviors. Decompensated borderlines often require institutionalization since they are unable to manage alone, appear to make few efforts to "get hold" of themselves, and are incapable of filling any acceptable societal role. They possess two features in common with all severely decompensated states: diminished reality awareness and cognitive and emotional dyscontrol. These patients fail to discriminate between subjective fantasy and objective reality. External events take on a dreamlike quality and become a hazy and phantasmagoric world of fleeting and distorted impressions colored by internal moods and images. They no longer grasp the threats they face or the rewards they may gain. Pain and pleasure become blurred, causing them to behave in a purposeless, irrational, or bizarre manner. Controls in thought and emotion are deficient, and there is a sense of internal disunity and disorganization in their social communications. Ideas are jumbled and take the form of peculiar beliefs or delusions. Stereotyped behaviors may be exhibited. Subjective imaginings become reality and are projected upon the outer world as hallucinatory perceptions.

Notable at this stage is the emergence of a persistent social invalidism, most clearly evident in the patient's inability to assume responsibility for his or her own care, welfare and health. Acceptance of social invalidism as a way of life is not difficult for borderline patients, given their lifelong orientation to dependency. As their efforts to maintain a normal social life are abandoned, they succumb readily into a helpless and autistic state. This withdrawal into self, without external purpose or the controls of social reality, only increases the likelihood of cognitive disorganization. Whatever coherent thoughts these borderlines do possess are colored by an oppressive and melancholy tone. To avoid painful preoccupations such as these, they may try to focus on "offbeat" or cheerful thoughts, a process that accounts in part for their erratic ramblings. These cognitive digressions rarely are sustained. Sensing the futility of their efforts to alter their mood and preoccupation, decompensated borderlines block or retard their thought processes, resulting thereby in the slow and laborious responses that often characterize them. Should these efforts fail also, they may disassemble or disorganize their ruminations to protect themselves against the anguish their thoughts evoke. As a consequence, their cognitive processes are disjunctive and autistic, manifesting themselves either in sudden changes of focus or as incoherent ramblings.

Behaviors and emotions also tend toward the bizarre, with capricious bursts of energy and irrational exuberance scattered unpredictably in an otherwise more sluggish and lugubrious style. Some may exhibit no motor activity, a physical inertia, a weighty and stooped posture, and downcast and forlorn expression. Fragmented delusions and hallucinations are not uncommon. These symptoms usually express themselves as obsessive fears of impending disaster or in strange and undiagnosable bodily ailments. Self-deprecation, remorse, and guilt are prominent aspects of their disorganized delusions. Feelings of estrangement in these borderlines are rooted in their growing sense of aloneness and apartness from the attachments they previously had established. Socially rebuffed and often institutionalized, they not only experience separation from "loved" ones but are immersed in new and strange environments. Geared to turn to others for guidance and support, these borderlines are now keenly aware of their aloneness and the frightening unfamiliarity of their surroundings. Most feel desperately removed and lost, perplexed and bewildered in a strange and unreal world.

Differential Diagnostic Signs

Borderlines typically manifest so many and so wide-ranging a group of associated disorders that differential diagnosis becomes an academic matter of minor clinical significance. This is true of both covariant Axis I symptoms and Axis II personality disorders. The major issue that deserves a modicum of attention relates to the distinction between the psychotic Axis I *affective disorders* and various borderline personality patterns, a distinction often difficult to make on the basis of overt clinical features alone. The principal difference between them lies in the developmental history of the impairment; psychotic affective disorders usually have a rapid onset. Although those disposed to severe affective disorders have evidenced prior social difficulties and competency deficits, most have managed to maintain their psychic equilibrium for extended periods. In contrast, borderline personalities show a consistently lower level of functioning. Another distinction between the Axis I affective disorders and the borderline patterns is the role of external precipitants. The borderline patient's disturbance appears to reflect the operation of internal and ingrained defects in personality, whereas in the psychotic symptom disorders there is evidence that the current maladaptive behavior is, in part at least, a product of external or environmental stress. Further, as these stresses are reduced, disordered patients quickly regain their coping power and former level of functioning. This rapid return to equilibrium is not evident among borderline personalities. Disorders, therefore, are transitory, of relative short duration, in contrast to the more permanent and disturbed life-style of the borderline personality. This brings us to another distinction between these severe psychic states. Disordered patients feel their symptoms to be discordant and therefore exert some, albeit futile, efforts "to fight" them off. The emotions they experience may be spoken of as "ego-dystonic," that is, alien, strange, and unwanted. In contrast, borderlines tend to become indifferent or accepting of their pathological behaviors. Their actions and moods are taken for granted, are "ego-syntonic," that is, seem to be an inevitable or natural part of their lives.

The relative comfort with which bizarre traits are experienced in borderline patients reflects in large measure the insidious manner in which these traits developed. They are integrated bit by bit into the very fabric of the patient's personality makeup. In contrast, Axis I psychotic disorders often appear relatively abruptly, disrupting the patient's accustomed mode of functioning. In this respect, Axis I symptoms often stand out as isolated and dramatic deviations from a more typical style of behavior: They erupt, so to speak, as bizarre accentuations or caricatures of the person's more prosaic style.

Despite the points of distinction noted, the line between Axis I affective disorders and the Axis II borderline personality is often a blurred one. Diagnostic complications are compounded further in these cases by the fact that episodes of symptom disorder may gradually blend into a more permanent borderline pattern. For a variety of reasons—persistent stress, the "comforts" of hospitalization, and so on—patients often "get caught" in the web surrounding their disorder and fail to "pull out" of what may otherwise have been a transitory episode.

Difficulties in separating borderline from *schizotypal* personalities will occur because these patterns occasionally blend, especially when the borderline begins to decompensate. Nevertheless, the key distinction lies in the features that differentiate schizophrenic-like symptoms versus affective-type symptoms. The diagnostic criteria spelled out in the DSM-III represent the key differentiations well. Thought and perceptual pathologies characterize the socially isolated schizotypal, whereas mood instability and ambivalence typify the interpersonally dependent borderline.

PREDISPOSING BACKGROUND

It is the author's contention that we will find the same complex of determinants in the borderline syndrome as we do in its less severe variants: the dependent, histrionic, compulsive, and passive-aggressive personalities.

The primary differences between them are the intensity, frequency, timing, and persistence of a host of potentially pathogenic factors. Those who function at the borderline level may begin with less adequate constitutional equipment or be subjected to a series of more adverse early experiences. As a consequence of their more troublesome histories, they either fail to develop an adequate coping style in the first place or decompensate slowly under the weight of repeated and unrelieved difficulties. It is the author's view that most borderline cases progress sequentially through a more adaptive or higher level of functioning before deteriorating to the advanced dysfunctional state. Some patients, however, notably childhood variants, never appear to "get off the ground" and give evidence of a borderline pattern from their earliest years.

The developmental history of the borderline personality is reviewed here by subdividing the presentation into the four personality types the author believes are disposed to deteriorate into the syndrome. This review should help clarify the varied pictures that are seen among patients diagnosed as borderline. With exceptions relevant to the more advanced, or borderline, stage of dysfunction, these hypotheses frequently summarize material presented in earlier chapters. Toward the end of minimizing repetitions, views concerning biogenic and experiential influences are presented together.

Borderline-dependent personality etiology. The biogenic background of these borderlines is likely to include a disproportionately high number of bland and unenergetic relatives. A melancholic and fearful infantile pattern is not infrequent and often gives rise to parental overprotection. Speculations may be proposed regarding various limbic, reticular, or adrenal imbalances to account for their typical low activation levels and their vulnerability to fear, both of which may elicit protective and nurtural responses in beneficent environments.

The characteristic experiential history appears to have been parental overprotection, leading to an unusually strong attachment to, and dependency on, a single caretaking figure. Perpetuation of overprotection into late childhood may have fostered a lack of autonomous capabilities and a self-image of incompetence and inadequacy. These children accentuate these weaknesses by abdicating self-responsibility and by clinging to others, thereby restricting their opportunities to learn skills for social independence.

In contrast to their personality counterparts who stabilized at milder levels of pathology, borderlines were increasingly rebuffed as time progressed by those upon whom they depended. The intense anxieties engendered by these later separations precipitated mood vacillations, marked self-disparagements, and guilt, as well as an occasional psychotic episode. In addition, these patients perpetuated their plight by abdicating self-responsibility and clinging tenaciously to others. Borderlines placed themselves in vulnerable positions. Increasingly devoid of capacities for autonomy, they found themselves viewed with exasperation by those upon whom they depended. Failures to gain support from others may have led either to marked self-disparagement or to frenetic efforts to solicit attention. These erratic behaviors and mood swings are likely to have fostered increased inner disharmony and maladaptation, resulting in intrapsychic dyscontrol and psychotic episodes.

Borderline-histrionic personality etiology.   Biogenically, these patients may have close relatives who exhibit high autonomic reactivity. Other evidence suggesting a constitutional predisposition is hyperresponsitivity in early childhood. A temperamental inclination such as this not only exposed them to a high degree of sensory stimulation but may have elicited frequent and intense reactions from others. Another speculation might suggest neurally dense or low-threshold limbic, reticular, or adrenal systems as underlying their sensory reactivity.

Among the more plausible experiential influences in this syndrome is an unusually varied and enriched sequence of early sensory experiences that built in a "need" for stimulus diversity and excitement. Parental control by contingent and irregular reward may have established the habit of feeling personally competent and accepted only if behaviors were explicitly approved by others. These youngsters may have been exposed to exhibitionistic and histrionic parental models. Another background contributor may have been exposure to rapidly changing societal values, resulting in extreme exteroceptivity, that is, an excessive dependence on external cues for guiding behavior. In time, the pattern of capriciousness and seductiveness in interpersonal relations may have fostered rather than resolved difficulties. Emotional shallowness and excessive demands for attention and approval often undermine enduring relationships. Thus, the originally skilled seductiveness of the histrionic style may not only foster new difficulties but may have faltered as an instrumental strategy. Shallow and capricious, they give little in return for their subtle, though excessive, demands upon others. Further, because of their exteroceptive orientation and their intrapsychic repressions, they have failed to acquire the inner resources to draw sustenance from themselves. As a result, they are on unsure footing, constantly on edge and never quite sure that they will secure the attention and esteem they require from others. Anxious that they will be cut adrift and left on their own, they proceed through affective mood swings of simulated euphoria in which they seek to solicit the attention they need, periods of brooding dejection and self-deprecation, followed by impulsive outbursts of resentment and hostility. These persistent and unpredictable mood changes result only in further interpersonal complications. When their dread of desertion reaches monumental proportions, they may lose control and feel swept up either in a chaotic cry for help or a deep and intransigent gloom.

Borderline-compulsive personality etiology.As children, these patients learned to conceive their worth in proportion to the degree of their success in meeting parental demands, feeling that they would be punished and abandoned if they failed to heed their parent's strictures. The future borderlines felt especially vulnerable to error, knowing that they had to keep within approved boundaries, yet being unsure of exactly what these boundaries were. Fearing transgression, they modeled themselves closely after authority figures, repressing all inclinations toward autonomy and independence lest these behaviors provoke their wrath and desertion. They learned to follow rules, failed to develop initiative, and lacked spontaneity and imagination. Overtrained to be conventional and to feel guilt and self-reproach for failing to subscribe to the rigid prescriptions of their elders, they sacrificed their own identity to gain favor and esteem from others. This lifestyle perpetuated their difficulties. Their rigidity and conformity precluded growth and change, kept them from genuinely warm human relationships, and alienated them from their own inner feelings. Constantly tense for fear that they would overstep approved lines, they found themselves unable to make decisions or act assertively. Their indecisiveness may have turned to guilt for having let others down. Thinking of themselves as frauds and failures led to increased self-derogation. In time, their controls weakened and their repressed angers and resentments erupted, thereby reinforcing their fear and guilt, and setting the cycle in motion again.

Borderline-passive-aggressive personality etiology. The negativistic, discontented, and erratic quality of these patients is largely attributable to early parental inconsistency. Most failed to be treated in even a moderately predictable fashion, being doted upon one moment and castigated the next—ignored, abused, nurtured, exploited, promised, denied, and so on, with little rhyme or reason as they saw it. These borderlines learned to anticipate irrationality, to expect contradictions, and to know, however painfully, that their actions would bring them rewards one time but condemnation the next. Parental behaviors may have served as models for vacillation, capriciousness, and unpredictability. In others, schisms may have existed between parents, tearing the child's loyalties first one way and then the other. These borderline types learned that nothing is free of conflict and that they are trapped in a bind. Despite feeling mishandled and cheated, they received enough attention and affection to keep them hoping for some harmony and a secure dependency. Unfortunately for these borderlines, these hopes rarely were fulfilled. Not only did external circumstances continue to be inconsistent, but the patients themselves perpetuated further inconsistencies by their own vacillations, unpredictability, unreasonableless, sullenness, and revengful nature. Having learned to anticipate disappointment, they often "jumped the gun," thereby alienating others before the latter rejected them. In addition, inner tensions kept churning close to the surface, leading them to act impulsively and precipitously. This lack of controls resulted in endless wrangles with others and precluded achieving the affections these patients so desperately sought. Angry and pessimistic, they may have become violent at times, exploding with bitter complaints and recriminations against the world, or, conversely, they may have turned against themselves, becoming self-sacrificing, pleading forgiveness, and derogating themselves through impulsively self-damaging acts. Unable to "get hold" of themselves, control their churning resentments and conflicts, or elicit even the slightest degree of approval and support from others, and guilt-ridden and self-condemnatory, this borderline will often slide from impulsive actions into more serious psychotic disorders. Unless aided therapeutically, these borderlines may become disorganized cognitively, become estranged from themselves, and sink into the sheltered obscurity of institutional life.

Decompensated borderline personality etiology. Tendencies toward decompensation are usually aggravated by the cumulation of repetititve pathogenic experiences. Not only are early behaviors and attitudes difficult to distinguish, but, in addition, the individual may be exposed to a continuous stream of destructive events that accelerate the pathological decline. Not the least of these accelerating factors are the borderline's own coping behaviors, which foster new problems and perpetuate vicious circles. As with other more advanced personality dysfunctions, borderlines experience serious incursions upon their psychic equilibrium, giving rise to short-lived and usually reversible psychotic episodes. These bizarre periods normally subside following the reduction of stress. In some cases, however, psychotic episodes persist until they become an ingrained and enduring pattern. Perhaps the circumstances of stress failed to diminish or the patient became trapped, so to speak, in the web of his/her own coping maneuvers. Not infrequently, the rewards and comforts acquired during the episode were greater than those the patient obtained preceding it. Whatever the cause or combination of causes, some borderline patients fail to "pull themselves together" and override what is usually a transient psychotic period. It is in these cases that we often see the progressive deterioration into a decompensated borderline pattern. At these times, patients begin to feel that their "normal" relations with others are bogged down and hopeless. They also experience an intolerable decline in their self-worth. As they defensively isolate themselves from social pain and humiliation, their feelings of helplessness and self-derogation increase. They may soon experience a measure of relief as they accept the inevitability of invalidism. There are gains to be eked out through collapse and withdrawal. Not only will others care for them, but they need meet no responsibilities nor struggle to achieve goals in a world with which they cannot cope. They give up their struggle for a meaningful social existence and allow themselves to sink increasingly into a pervasive listlessness, a disorganization of control and thought, an invalidism in which they care little and do little to care for themselves.

PROGNOSTIC CONSIDERATIONS

As in prior chapters, this section describes how aspects of the behavioral style of the personality pattern under discussion perpetuate and intensify the difficulties that characterize that personality. A few words are said also concerning steps that might be taken toward the end of remedying these difficulties.

Perpetuation of the Borderline Pattern

It is difficult to see the utility of any of the borderline's characteristic behaviors, let alone to grasp what gains the patient may derive by vacillating among them. Clinging helplessness, resentful stubbornness, hostile outbursts, pitiable depression, and self-denigrating guilt seem notably wasteful and self-destructive. Although these genuinely felt emotions are instrumentally useful in eliciting attention and approval, releasing tensions, wreaking revenge, and avoiding permanent rejection by redeeming onself through contrition and self-derogation, they ultimately intensify and subvert the borderline's efforts for a better life.

Despite short-term gains, these behaviors are self-defeating in the end. By their affective instability and self-deprecation, these patients avoid confronting and resolving their real interpersonal difficulties. Their coping maneuvers are a double-edged sword, relieving passing discomforts and strains but in the long run fostering the perpetuation of faulty attitudes and strategies.

A major tactic taken by borderlines is a reversal of their traditional roles, a strategy that only alienates them from their more accustomed states. Thus, when these patients exaggerate or intensify their habitual style of soliciting their needs, and fail to gain what they sought, they may "renunciate" their characteristic coping style, even if for a brief period. For example, the borderline-dependents, rather than acting weak and submissive, will reverse their more typical behaviors and assert themselves, becoming either gay and frivolous or demanding and aggressive. In this manner they take on a new and rather unusual mode of coping as a substitute method for mastering their anxieties. Unable to quiet fears that refuse to be solved by their habitual behaviors and discouraged and annoyed at the futility of using these strategies, they disown them, divest themselves of these deficient coping mechanisms and supplant them with dramatically new instrumentalities. The goal of these borderline-dependents remains the same, that of denying or controlling their anxiety, but they have uncovered a new strategy by which to achieve it, one diametrically opposed to that used before. This erratic, if not radical, shifting from one strategy to another accounts in part for the unstable, impulsive, and unpredictable pattern observed in these patients.

These radical changes in behavior style are not only seen by others as bizarre but are usually even less effective in the long run than the patients' more established strategies. They have adopted attributes that are foreign to their "natural" self. Unaccustomed to the feelings they seek to simulate and the behaviors they strive to portray, their actions have an "unreal," awkward, and strained manner. The upshot of this reversal in coping style is a further failure to achieve their goals, leading to increased anxiety, dismay, and hostility. Not only have these simulations alienated the borderlines from their real feelings, but the pretensions they display before others have made them even more vulnerable to exposure and humiliation. Whatever temporary gains achieved by these new forms of coping and tension discharge, they are self-defeating in the long run. The forced cheerful or hostile behavior of the borderline wears people down and provokes them to exasperation and anger, which, in turn, will only intensify the anxieties and conflicts the patient feels.

As these "last ditch" means of coping prove self-defeating, the patients' tensions and depressions mount beyond tolerable limits and they may begin to lose control. Psychotic behaviors may burst forth and discharge a torrential stream of irrational emotions. Borderline-dependents, for example, may shriek that others despise them, are seeking to depreciate their worth, and are plotting to abandon them. They may make inordinate demands for attention and reassurance or threaten to commit suicide and thereby save others the energy of destroying them slowly. Under similar circumstances, borderline-compulsive personalities may burst into vitriolic attacks upon their "loved ones" as their deep and previously hidden bitterness and resentment surge into the open. They may accuse others of having aggressed against them, unjustly viewing them as frauds and failures. Utilizing intrapsychic projection, they may ascribe to others the weakness and ineptness they now feel within themselves. It is "they" who have "always" been deficient and who should now be punished and humiliated. "Righteously indignant," these patients flail outward, castigating, condemning, and denouncing others for their frailty and imperfections. Needless to say, the counterreactions this provokes only further intensifies these borderlines' plight. Once more, their own behavior is the pathogenic source, the spur to further condemnation and denigration.

Remedial Interventions

Despite the many commonalities among borderlines, it is well to remind ourselves that there are many personality variants in which borderline characteristics are intermeshed. However, by grouping these individuals into a single syndrome we will be alerted to the important features these patients share. As clinicians, we know that each individual possesses a distinctive history; moreover, our patients are seen therapeutically at different stages in their disturbance. Some are well compensated, whereas others are not. Some are bolstered by supporting families, while others face destructive environmental conditions. All of these factors must be assessed before we can gauge the patient's prognostic picture and recommend a remedial course of therapy.

The borderline classification refers to a deeply ingrained personality pattern; nothing but the most prolonged and intensive therapy will produce substantial changes. Despite this pessimism, the prognosis of borderlines, though serious, is not as problematic as, for example, the schizotypal personality. Most borderlines seek and have maintained occasional satisfactory social relationships. Their need for attention and approval, their history of at least partial encouragement in childhood, their interest in soliciting some support and nurturance, and their desire to restrain contrary and troublesome impulses, all decrease the probability of inevitable decompensation. Even following psychotic episodes, these patients often recover quickly and return to their former functional level. If these patients can find an emotionally nurturant environment and are reinforced in their need for acceptance and attachment, they can live periodically in comfort and relative tranquility, maintaining a reasonably secure hold on reality. However, should the attentions and supports that borderlines require be withdrawn and should their strategies prove wearisome and exasperating to others, precipitating their anger and unforgiveness, then their tenuous hold on reality will disintegrate and their capacity to function will wither. At these times, they will succumb either to a somber depression or to an erratic and explosive surge of assertion and hostility. Care should be taken to anticipate and head off the danger of suicide during these episodes.

Another major concern is the forestalling of a more permanent decompensation process. Among the early signs of such a growing breakdown are marked discouragement and a persistent dejection. At this phase, it is especially useful to employ supportive therapy and cognitive reorientation. Efforts should be made to boost these patients' sagging morale, to encourage them to continue in their usual sphere of activities, to build their self-confidence, and to deter them from ruminating and being preoccupied with their melancholy feelings. Of course, they should not be pressed beyond their capabilities, nor told to "snap out of it," since their failure to achieve these goals will only strengthen the patients' growing conviction of their own incompetence and unworthiness.

Should depression be the major symptom picture, it is advisable to prescribe any of the suitable antidepressant agents as a means of buoying the patient's flagging spirits. These should be supplemented, where indicated, by a course of electroconvulsive treatments. Should suicide become a threat, or should the patient lose control or engage in hostile outbursts, it may be advisable to arrange for brief institutionalization.

During more quiescent periods serious efforts to alter the borderline's basic psychopathology may be attempted. A primary goal in this regard is the facilitation of autonomy, the building of confidence, and the overcoming of fears of self-determination. In all likelihood, this will be resisted. Borderline patients often feel that the therapist's efforts to encourage them to assume self-responsibility and self-control are a sign of rejection, efforts to "be rid" of them. This may engender disappointment, dejection, and even rage, reactions that must be anticipated, given the borderline's characteristic style, and must be dealt with if fundamental personality changes are to be explored. If a sound and secure therapeutic alliance has been established, these patients may learn to tolerate their contrary feelings and dependency anxieties. Learning to face and handle their unstable emotions must be coordinated with the strengthening of healthier self-attitudes and interpersonal relationships. The therapist may serve as a model to demonstrate how feelings, conflicts, and uncertainties can be approached and resolved with reasonable equanimity and foresight. Group and family methods may be utilized to test these newly learned attitudes and strategies in a more natural social setting than found in individual treatment.

Chapter 13

Paranoid Personality: The Suspicious Pattern

Among the more prominent features of paranoid personalities are their mistrust of others and their desire to stay free of relationships in which they might lose the power of self-determination. They are characteristically suspicious, guarded, and hostile; tend to misread the actions of others; and respond with anger to what they frequently interpret as deception, deprecation, and betrayal. Their readiness to perceive hidden motives and deceit precipitates innumerable social difficulties, which then confirm and reinforce their expectations. Their need to distance from others, combined with their tendency to magnify minor slights, results in distortions that occasionally cross the bounds of reality.

A feature that justifies considering paranoids among the more severe personalities is the inelasticity and constriction of their coping skills. The unyielding and obdurate structure of their personality contrasts markedly with the lack of cohesion and instability of the borderline's personality. Whereas borderlines are subject to a dissolution of controls and to a fluidity in their responsiveness, paranoids display such inflexible controls that they are subject to having their rigid facade shattered.

Entirely insignificant and irrelevant events are often transformed by paranoids so as to have personal reference to themselves. They may begin to impose their inner world of meanings upon the outer world of reality. As Cameron once put it (1963), they create a "pseudo-community" composed of distorted people and processes. Situations and events lose their objective attributes and are interpreted in terms of subjective expectations and feelings. Unable and unwilling to follow the lead of others and accustomed to drawing power within themselves, paranoids reconstruct reality so that it suits their dictates. Faced by a world in which others shape what occurs, they construct a world in which they determine events and have power to do as they desire. In contrast to their less severe counterparts, the paranoid's need for autonomy and independence has been undermined often and seriously. These personalities counter the anxiety their experiences create by distorting objective reality and constructing in its stead a new reality in which they can affirm their personal stature and significance.

Historically among the first and more uniformly portrayed of the personality disorders, the paranoid is described as follows in the DSM-III manual:

> The essential feature is a Personality Disorder in which there is a pervasive and unwarranted suspiciousness and mistrust of people, hypersensitivity, and restricted affectivity....
>
> Individuals with this disorder are typically hypervigilant and take precautions against any perceived threat. They tend to avoid blame even when it is warranted. They are often viewed by others as guarded, secretive, devious and scheming. They may question the loyalty of others, always expecting trickery. For this reason, there may be pathological jealousy.
>
> When individuals with this disorder find themselves in a new situation, they intensely and narrowly search for confirmation of their expectations.... They are concerned with hidden motives and special meanings. Often, transient ideas of reference occur, e.g., that others are taking special notice of them or may be saying vulgar things about them.
>
> Individuals with this disorder are usually argumentative and exaggerate difficulties by "making mountains out of molehills." They often find it difficult to relax, usually appear tense, and show a tendency to counter-attack when they perceive any threat. Though they are critical of others, and often litigious, they have great difficulty accepting criticism themselves.
>
> These individuals' affectivity is restricted, and they may appear "cold" to others. They have no true sense of humor and are usually serious. They may pride themselves on always being objective, rational, and unemotional. They usually lack passive, soft, sentimental and tender feelings.
>
> Individuals with this disorder are...viewed as hostile, stubborn and defensive. They tend to be rigid and unwilling to compromise. They often generate uneasiness and fear in others. Often there is an inordinate fear of losing independence or the power to shape events in accord with their own wishes.
>
> They usually avoid intimacy except with those in whom they have absolute trust. They show an excessive need to be self-sufficient, to the point of egocentricity and exaggerated self-importance. They avoid participation in group activities unless they are in a dominant position....
>
> They are often envious and jealous of those in positions of power. They have disdain for persons seen as weak, soft, sickly or defective. (p. 307–308)

HISTORICAL AND THEORETICAL ANTECEDENTS

The term *paranoia* can be traced back over 2000 years in the medical literature, preceding the writings of even Hippocrates. Translated from the Greek it means "to think beside oneself," and it was used rather freely in ancient times as a general designation for all forms of serious mental disturbance. The word disappeared from the medical lexicon in the second century and was not revived again until the eighteenth century. Heinroth, following the structure of Kantian psychology, utilized the term in 1818 to represent a variety of disorders. Those of the intellect were termed "paranoia"; disturbances of feeling were called "paranoia ecstasia." Also proposed were the parallel concepts of *Wahnsinn* and *Verrücktheit* (the latter term is still in use as a label for paranoia in modern-day Germany). Griesinger picked up the term *Wahnsinn* in 1845 to signify pathological thought processes and applied it to cases that exhibited expansive and grandiose delusions. In 1863 Kahlbaum suggested that paranoia be the exclusive label for delusional states.

The French psychiatrist V. Magnan (1886) described a subgroup of patients, which he termed *bouffées délirantes des dégénérés*, who gave evidence of preexisting traits that disposed them to psychotic disorders. Among the paranoic group displaying these preconditions, he isolated a subset that he labeled *délire chronique*. This syndrome followed a course similar to dementia praecox, but it usually began later in life and was characterized by delusions that showed a "striking degree of systematization." Magnan considered the development of *délire chronique* to progress slowly through four stages. At first, patients exhibited a general irritability, pessimism, and hypochondriacal preoccupation; subsequently, they deteriorate to the point of making delusional interpretations of events, visualizing florid hallucinations, and, finally, succumbing to the inevitable dementia. Magnan's developmental thesis appears to have been the first formulation of the paranoid concept to have explicitly conceived of its premorbid "personality" history.

Following the German usage, particularly the proposals of Kahlbaum, in 1895 Kraepelin narrowed the meaning of the term *paranoia*, restricting it to highly systematized and well-contained delusions in patients who otherwise lacked signs of personality deterioration. Recognizing that paranoia, as he described it, applied to a small portion of cases, Kraepelin adopted a label first used by Guslain in the early nineteenth century, "paraphrenia," to signify impairments displaying a mixture of the delusional elements of paranoia and the deterioration features of dementia praecox. Kraepelin believed that as many as 40 percent of patients who exhibited paranoid delusions ultimately deteriorated to dementia praecox, that the bulk of the remainder decompensated to the paraphrenic level, and that a very small proportion retained the characteristic nondeterioration of pure paranoia. In his early writings on the subject, Kraepelin appears to have conceived the systematized delusions of paranoia to be a first stage of what could turn out to be a general deterioration process. In the second stage, if it occurs at all, the patient decompensates to paraphrenia, identified by bizarre thoughts and perceptual hallucinations; in this form, Kraepelin specified that many functions of personality that are not directly associated with thought and intellect remain moderately well preserved. For example, the patient's mood is not unstable or fragmented but is consistent with his or her disordered ideas. For many patients, however, paraphrenia is a transitional second stage that eventuated in dementia praecox. At this final level, all personality functions have disintegrated. Thus, the patient's moods are both incongruous and random, and no longer consonant with the delusional content. In his early publications, Kraepelin referred to the totally deteriorated cases of paranoia by the term "dementia paranoides." Subsequently, he claimed that "when the delusions and... emotions... may be observed with complete indifference to the natural relations of life...[these disorders] are more correctly to be brought under the head of dementia praecox" (1896, p. 512).

It was not until the monumental eighth edition of his *Lehrbuch* (1909–1915) that Kraepelin formally addressed the premorbid character of individuals disposed to paranoid conditions. Writing about those he explicitly termed paranoid personalities, Kraepelin portrayed their characteristics as follows:

> The most conspiciously common feature was the feeling of uncertainty and of distrust towards the surroundings.... The patient feels himself on every occasion unjustly treated, the object of hostility, interfered with, oppressed. His own people treat him badly.... In indefinite hints he speaks of secret connections, of the agitation of certain people. Things are not as they ought to be; everywhere he scents interested motives, embezzlement, intrigues....
>
> Such delusional ideas, which emerge sometimes on one occasion, sometimes on another, are closely accompanied by a great *emotional irritability* and a *discontented, dejected* mood. The patient is difficult to get on with, is fault-finding, makes difficulties everywhere, perpetually lives at variance with his fellow-workers, on trivial occasions falls into measureless excitement, scolds blusters and swears.
>
> As a rule, heightened self-consciousness can be easily demonstrated. The patients boast of their performances, consider themselves superior to their surroundings, make special claims, lay the blame for their failure solely on external hindrances.
>
> [The paranoid] seems to me to be essentially a *combination of uncertainty with excessive valuation of self*, which leads to the patient being forced into hostile opposition to the influences of the struggle for life and his seeking to withdraw himself from them by inward exaltation. Further a strong personal coloring of thought by vivid feeling-tones, activity of the power of imagination and self-confidence might be of significance. (1921, pp. 268–271)

As in his depiction of so many of the disorders for which he is better known, Kraepelin beautifully portrayed the essential features of the paranoid personality, a description as apt today as it was when written.

Other theorists of repute in the first decade of the century also wrote of traits they associated with the paranoid condition. Albeit briefly and tangentially, each formulated concepts similar to contemporary notions of the paranoid character. For example, K. Birnbaum (1909), best known for his progressive views of the "sociopath," preceded Kraepelin in speaking of paranoids as possessing overvalued ideas that were heavily charged with emotion and dominated the individual's psychic life. Even earlier E. Bleuler (1906) ascribed the development of paranoia to the patient's premorbid "excessive stability" of affect. He asserted that paranoids made no more errors or misinterpretations of life events than did normal persons. The essential pathological feature is the "fixity" of their errors. They possess a resistance to change that leads to the rigidification of beliefs and ultimately, by being compounded over time, the implacable delusional system we term paranoia. A. Meyer (1908, 1913) conceived of the paranoid developmental process in a fashion similar to Bleuler. In addition to the inability of paranoids to adjust their beliefs to the facts, he noted their inclination to isolate themselves and to counter the efforts of others to correct or otherwise influence their misinterpretation of events.

Another early nonanalytic theorist of note was Schneider (1923). He characterized these traits as a specific personality type, speaking of such individuals as "fanatic psychopaths." Although disavowing the appropriateness of the label "paranoid personality," his portrayal of the fanatic is very much in line with our contemporary conception of the paranoid. The following excerpts taken from the final edition of his personality text illustrate these parallels quite well:

> Ideas of fanatic personalities differ from those of depressive or insecure personalities in that the ideas are held much more assertively and combatively. Where sthenic [drive energies] are less in evidence there is a tendency for the fanatic ideas to issue in schemes and programmes. If the over-valued idea relates to a personal difference or a civil dispute, every effort is concentrated on laying low the offender utterly....
>
> There are fanatics who are expansive . . . tenacious personalities who elaborate their experience in a most vigorous way and are uninhibitedly aggressive. (1950, pp. 97–98)

A tangential note is Schneider's strong stance on the separation he believed should be made between personality and pathology, nowhere stated more directly than in his discussion of how delusions are independent of the personality structure of the "fanatic" patient. His position on this controversial issue was stated as follows:

> In our view delusion-formation has nothing to do with traits of personality and there are serious objections to attempts which endeavor to associate the two. Delusion cannot be explained away in terms of a particular personality, its development and inner conflicts. (1950, p. 99)

Schneider's assertions on this issue were set in clear opposition to the well-known psychoanalytic contention that clinical symptoms have distinct ontogenetic origins and character substrates. It is appropriate, therefore, that the discussion turns next to the analyst's prime exponent.

Freud first conceived of paranoia in 1896 as a "neuropsychosis of defense," a formulation that laid the foundation for considering all mental disorders to result from a psychodynamic process with specific developmental roots. Not only did this early paper establish the important concept of projection, but his success in elucidating the delusional symptom as a faulty attempt at self-remediation contributed significantly toward establishing the utility of an intrapsychic approach to psychopathology. Specifically, Freud considered the paranoid symptom to signify a series of intrapsychic transformations. First, there is a breakdown in the effectiveness of repression as a defense against unacceptable impulses. This results in the alternative use of denial, reaction formation, and projection mechanisms. The product of these more circuitous intrapsychic maneuvers gains conscious form in a delusion. Freud utilized this particular intrapsychic sequence to elucidate how paranoia derives from unsuccessfully repressed homosexual urges. It was in the famous case of Schreber that Freud (1911) was provided with an excellent opportunity to illustrate this previously formulated model. Simplifying Freud's logic, he asserted that Schreber's homosexual impulse for another man, in the form "I love him," was *denied*; because the urge was viewed consciously as repugnant, it was altered through *reaction formation* to its opposite, "I do not love him, I hate him." The next step, that of *projection*, altered the attitude further: "It is not that I hate him, but that he hates me." Finally, since his newly emergent hatred required an acceptable justification, he reverted to the more conventional mechanism of *rationalization* and concluded, "I hate him because of his hatred for me." Freud conceived a wide range of persecutory, erotic and jealousy delusions as essentially progressing through similar psychodynamic sequences and transformations.

Despite the seminal role he played in formulating his model of paranoia, Freud did not construct an explicit basis for either the origins or the structure of a paranoid character type. It was S. Ferenczi and K. Abraham who suggested that the foundation for this personality might be first established during the anal period. Abraham wrote:

> If we bear in mind the great significance of anal eroticism in the psychogenesis of paranoia ... we can understand this ... behavior as an anal-character formation, and therefore as a precursor of paranoia. (1921, p. 391)

Explicating this connection more fully, Menninger wrote:

> The character traits of the anal expulsive period are chiefly those of megalomania and suspiciousness.... The individual who constantly is extremely conceited, very ambitious, and makes unwarranted claims upon his own abilities but is inclined to attribute his failures to the jealousy of rivals is a personality determined chiefly by fixations in the anal expulsive period. Such individuals are closely related to the paranoid character, on the one hand, and to

homosexual characters, on the other. . . . These character traits [derive] from the
megalomania connected with early consciousness of sphincter control and from
the reaction formation against the homosexuality of this period. (1940, p. 394)

A few words concerning the contributions of E. Kretschmer and W. Sheldon
should be recorded to identify yet another explanatory schema for the
paranoid character. In 1918 Kretschmer wrote of a syndrome that he labeled
"paranoia sensitiva"; these personalities were noted as being extraordinarily
sensitive to the negative judgments of others, hence leading them to restrict
their social contacts. Although formulated in this early book as a subset of
paranoid disorders, the primary traits that Kretschmer ascribed to them depict
the characteristics of the recently formulated "avoidant personality." For
example, Kretschmer noted that they were anxiety-prone, liable to feelings of
inferiority and melancholy, socially shy or hesitant, and morbidly disposed to
introspection. In his later writings (1925), these same features were ascribed
also to patients considered close to the hyperaesthetic pole of the schizoid
temperament, as discussed in Chapter 11. More consistent with present-day
conceptions of the paranoid personality was Kretschmer's "expansive reaction type." This temperament inclined those who were so endowed to become
sensitive, suspicious, irritable, tenacious, uninhibitedly aggressive, and,
ultimately, combatively paranoid.

Sheldon (Sheldon, 1940; Sheldon and Stevens, 1942), Kretschmer's prime
disciple, proposed a temperament variant that he labeled "somatatonia." It
served as the substrate for what he termed the "paranoid component," an
inclination to "fight against something" and to be antagonistic and resentful
of others. Those possessing this component will be openly aggressive if they
can successfully present themselves in this manner. Those who fail in these
overt actions will use indirect methods of attack or, if need be, limit themselves
to internal ruminations of hostility or persecution.

Brief mention should be made of the perceptive analyses of paranoid
phenomena by N. Cameron (1943, 1963). A short excerpt will illustrate the
aptness and clarity of his formulation of the paranoid personality:

> The paranoid personality is one that has its origin in a lack of basic trust.
> There is evidence that in many cases the paranoid person has received sadistic
> treatment during early infancy and that he has, in consequence, internalized
> sadistic attitudes toward himself and others. Because of his basic lack of trust in
> others the paranoid personality must be vigilant in order to safeguard himself
> against sudden deception and attack. He is exquisitely sensitive to traces of
> hostility, contempt, criticism or accusation. (1963, p. 645)

Finally, the following text and criteria were written for the DSM-III Task
Force personality subcommittee by the author as the initial draft for the
paranoid syndrome. Derived from his theoretical model (Millon, 1969) as an
extreme variant of the "independent" coping style, it places the paranoid
personality at an advanced level of dysfunction, equal in that respect to the
DSM-III borderline and schizotypal syndromes.

This pattern is typified by a suspicious and vigilant mistrust of others, resistance to external sources of influence and a fear of losing the power of self-determination. There is an undercurrent of veiled hostility, tendencies toward self-importance, the presence of fixed, but essentially irrational, belief systems, and an inclination to misinterpret the incidental actions of others as signs of deception and malevolence. The hypersensitive readiness to perceive threat, to experience envy or jealously and to assign malice to others precipitates frequent social difficulties.

An appraisal of personal background and history reveals both of the following:

1. Social attainment deficits (e.g., experienced serious, self-precipitated set-backs in scholastic, marital or vocational pursuits; repeated failure to maintain durable, satisfactory and secure roles consonant with age and aptitudes).

2. Periodic mini-psychotic episodes (e.g., experienced several brief and reversible periods in which either bizarre behaviors, extreme moods, irrational impulses or delusional thoughts were exhibited; short-lived breaks from "reality," however, are often recognized subsequently as peculiar or deviant).

Since adolescence or early adulthood at least 3 of the following have been present to a notably greater degree than in most people and were not limited to discrete periods nor necessarily prompted by stressful life events.

1. Vigilant mistrust (e.g., exhibits edgy defensiveness against anticipated criticism and deception; conveys extreme suspiciousness, envy and jealousy of others).

2. Provocative interpersonal behavior (e.g., displays a disputatious, fractious and abrasive irritability; precipitates exasperation and anger by hostile, deprecatory demeanor).

3. Tenacious autonomy (e.g., expresses fear of losing independence and power of self-determination; is grimly resistant to sources of external influence and control).

4. Mini-delusional cognitions (e.g., grossly distorts events into personally logical, but essentially irrational, belief systems; embellishes trivial achievements in line with semi-grandiose self-image).

5. Persecutory self-references (e.g., entirely incidental events are construed as critical of self; reveals tendency to magnify minor and personally unrelated tensions into proofs of purposeful deception and malice).

CLINICAL PICTURE

As in prior chapters, the presentation of the characteristics of the personality under review is divided into the four sections that are this text's standard format.

Behavioral Features

Paranoids are constantly on guard, mobilized, and ready for any real or imagined threat. Whether faced with danger or not, they maintain a fixed level of preparedness, an alert vigilance against the possibility of attack and derogation. They exhibit an edgy tension, an abrasive irritability, and an ever-present defensive stance from which they can spring into action at the slightest offense. Their state of rigid control never seems to abate, and they rarely relax, ease up, or let down their guard.

The experiential history of paranoids often gives them reason to be mistrustful and to fear betrayal or sadistic treatment. To counter these sources of threat, they have learned to distance themselves from others and to remain strong and vigilant, not only as a protective stance but as a means of vindication and triumph over potential attackers. To assure their security, they go to great pains to avoid any weakening of their resolve and to develop new and superior powers to control others. One of their major steps in this quest is the desensitization of tender and affectionate feelings. They become hard, obdurate, immune, and insensitive to the suffering of others. By so doing they protect themselves against entrapment and against being drawn into a web of anticipated deceit and subjugation. To assume a callous and unsympathetic stance is not difficult for paranoids. Not only is it a successful defensive maneuver against entrapment, but it also allows them to discharge their resentments and angers.

As a further means of assuring self-determination, paranoids assume an attitude of invincibility and pride. Convincing themselves that they have extraordinary capacities, they can now master their fate alone, as well as overcome every obstacle, resistance, and conflict. All traces of self-doubt are dismissed and they repudiate all nurturant overtures from others. Thus assured, they will never dread having to need or to depend on anyone.

To be coerced by a power stronger than themselves provokes extreme anxiety. Paranoids are acutely sensitive to any threat to their autonomy, resist all obligations, and are cautious lest any form of cooperation be but a ploy to seduce them and force their submission to the will of others. This attachment anxiety, with its consequent dread of losing personal control and independence, underlies much of the paranoid's characteristic resistance to influence. Fearful of domination, these personalities watch carefully to ensure that no one robs them of their will. Circumstances that prompt feelings of helplessness and incompetence, or decrease their freedom of movement, or place them in a vulnerable position subject to the powers of others, may precipitate a sudden and ferocious "counterattack." Feeling trapped by the dangers of dependency, struggling to regain their status, and dreading deceit and betrayal, they may strike out aggressively and accuse others of seeking to persecute them. Should others accuse them accurately of thinking, feeling, or behaving in ways that are alien to their self-image, they are likely to claim that powerful and malevolent sources have coerced them with malicious intent. These accusations may become grossly pathological and signify the presence of an incipient psychotic disorder, as when they locate these powers among an unidentifiable "they" or as a "voice," "communist," or "devil."

Self-Descriptions and Complaints

The paranoid's lack of trust seriously distorts perceptions, thoughts, and memories. All of us are selective in what we perceive and infer, based on our pattern of needs and past experiences. Unfortunately, the learned feelings and attitudes of paranoids produce a deep mistrust and pervasive suspiciousness of others. They are notoriously oversensitive and disposed to detect signs everywhere of trickery and deception; they are preoccupied with these thoughts, actively picking up minute cues, then magnifying and distorting them so as to confirm their worst expectations. To complicate matters further, events that fail to confirm their preformed suspicions "only prove how deceitful and clever others can be." In an effort to uncover the assumed pretense, they will "test" others and explore every nook and cranny they can to find some justification for their beliefs. These preconceptions rarely are upset by facts. Paranoids dismiss contradictions and confirm their expectations by seizing upon real, although trivial or irrelevant, data. Even more problematic is that they create an atmosphere that provokes others to act as they anticipated. After testing the "honesty" of their "friends" and constantly cajoling and intimidating others, the paranoid will provoke almost everyone into exasperation and anger.

The unwillingness of paranoids to trust sharing their doubts and insecurities leaves them isolated and bereft of the reality checks that might restrain their suspicions. Driven to maintain secrecy, they become increasingly unable to see things as others do. Lacking closeness and sharing, and with no one to counter the proliferations of their imagination, they concoct events in support of their fears or their wishes, pondering incessantly over deviant ideas, putting together the flimsiest of evidence, reshaping the past to conform to preconceptions, and building an intricate logic to justify their distortions. Left to their own devices, paranoids are unable to validate their speculations and ruminations. Little difference exists in their mind between what they have seen and what they have thought. Momentary impressions and hazy memories become fact. Chains of unconnected facts are fitted together. An inexorable course from imagination to supposition to suspicion takes place, and soon a system of invalid and unshakable beliefs has been created.

Inferred Intrapsychic Dynamics

Unable to accept faults and weaknesses within themselves, paranoids maintain their self-esteem by attributing their shortcomings to others. Repudiating their own failures, they project or ascribe them to someone else. They possess a remarkable talent for spotting the most trifling deficiencies in others. Both indirectly and directly they point to and exaggerate the minor defects they uncover among those they learn to despise. Rarely does their envy and hostility subside. They are touchy and irritable, ready to humiliate and deprecate anyone whose merits they question, and whose attitudes and demeanor evoke their ire or contempt.

Paranoids transform events to suit their self-image and aspirations. Even patients who are noted for their rigidity and hyperalertness to the environment begin to exhibit a lowering of controls and a loosening of the boundaries between reality and fantasy. These transformations create innumerable and troublesome end products. The three found most commonly among paranoids are described here: denial of any personal weakness and malevolence, the projection of these traits upon others, and the aggrandizement of self through grandiose and persecutory fantasies.

Troubled by mounting and inescapable evidence of inadequacy and hostility, paranoids are driven to go beyond mere denial. They not only disown these personally humiliating traits but throw them back at their real or imagined accusers. They claim that it is "they" who are stupid, malicious, and vindictive. In contrast, they are innocent and unfortunate victims of the incompetence and malevolence of others. By a simple reversal, paranoids not only absolve themselves of fault but find a "justified" outlet for their resentment and anger. If paranoids are found to have been in error, others should be blamed for their ineptness. If they have been driven to become aggressive, it is only because the evil of others has provoked them. They are innocent, and justifiably indignant, unfortunate and maligned scapegoats for the blundering and the slanderous.

Faced with persistent derogation and threat, paranoids will seek vigorously to redeem themselves and reestablish their sense of autonomy and power. However, they may have no recourse to achieve these ends except through fantasy. Unable to face their feelings of inadequacy and insignificance, they may begin to fabricate an image of superior self-worth. Left to ruminate alone, they may construct proofs of their eminence through intricate self-deceptions. Renouncing objective reality, they supplant it with a glorified self-image. They endow themselves with limitless powers and talents, and hence need no longer be ashamed of themselves or fear others. They can now "rise above" petty jealousies, "understanding all too clearly" why others seek to undermine their stature and virtue. The meaning of the malicious and persecutory attacks of others is obvious; it is the paranoid's eminence and superiority that they envy and seek to destroy.

Interpersonal Coping Style

Beneath the obvious mistrust and defensive vigilance of the paranoid stirs a current of deep resentment toward others who "have made it." To paranoids, most people have attained their wealth and esteem unjustly. To make matters worse, they have been overlooked and are bitter for having been treated unfairly and slighted by those "high and mighty cheats and crooks" who dupe the world. Only a thin veil hides these bristling animosities.

Paranoids detest being dependent, not only because it signifies weakness and inferiority but because they dare not trust anyone. To lean on another is to be exposed to ultimate betrayal and to rest on ground that will give way when support is needed most. Rather than chance deceit, paranoids strive to be the makers of their own fate, free of all personal entanglements and obligations. Bad enough to trust others; even worse is to be subject to their control.

As must be evident from the foregoing, the confidence and pride of paranoids cloak but a hollow shell. Their arrogant pose of autonomy rests on insecure footings. Extremely vulnerable to challenge, their defensive facade is constantly weakened by real and fantasied threats. In their efforts to reassert their power and invincibility, they resort to any course of action that will shore up their defenses or thwart their detractors. Hostility for the paranoid serves both defensive and restitutive measures. Not only is it a means of countering threats to their equilibrium, but it helps restore their image of self-determination and autonomy. Once released, this hostility draws upon a reserve of earlier resentments. Present angers are fueled by animosities from the past. Desire for reprisal and vindication spurred by prior humiliations are brought to the surface and discharged into the stream of current hostility. Every trivial rebuff is a painful reminder of the past, part of the plot whose history is traced back to early mistreatments. Trapped in what they see as a timeless web of deceit and malice, the fears and angers of paranoids may mount to monumental proportions. With their defenses in shambles, their controls dissolved, and their fantasies of doom running rampant, their dread and fury increase. A flood of hostile energies may erupt, letting loose a violent and uncontrollable torrent of vituperation and aggression. These psychotic outbursts are usually brief. As the surge of fear and hostility is discharged, these patients typically regain their composure and seek to rationalize their actions, reconstruct their defenses, and bind their aggression. This subsiding of bizarre emotions does not lead to a "normal" state but a return to their former personality pattern.

ASSOCIATED DISORDERS

The paranoid personality is a well-established and clinically familiar syndrome. This section touches only briefly on the concomitant Axis I symptom disorders associated with the syndrome; most are of a psychotic nature. Paranoids are usually overly sensitive about appearing "strange or bizarre" and, hence, display few of the milder and more controllable Axis I symptoms. When their defenses disintegrate or shatter, however, we see only the more extreme or psychotic level symptoms. The multidiagnosis format of the DSM-III encourages concurrent personality diagnosis. For this reason, and in contrast to discussions of the syndrome by other authors, most of the attention in this section is allotted to concurrent personality disorders that covary with the paranoid. Issues of differential diagnosis are also briefly presented.

Concomitant Axis I Symptoms

Paranoid disorders. Paranoid personalities develop delusional paranoid disorders and paranoia insidiously, usually as a consequence of anticipating or experiencing repeated mistreatment or humiliation. Acute paranoid episodes may be precipitated by the shock of an unanticipated betrayal. In these acute phases, previously repressed resentments may surge to the surface and overwhelm the patient's former controls, quickly taking the form of a delusional belief, usually persecutory in nature. During these episodes, typically brief and rather chaotic, patients both discharge their anger and project it upon others. Note that the resentments and suspicions of the paranoid usually do not cumulate and burst out of control. Rather, these patients continue to be persistently touchy, secretive, and irritable, thereby allowing them to vent their spleen in regular, small doses. Only if their suspicions are aggravated suddenly do they take explosive or irrational form.

Anxiety disorders. Severe *generalized* anxiety disorders may take the form of diffuse apprehensions or fears of the unknown, often distracting the patient from dealing effectively with matters of daily routine. Paranoids may complain of their inability to concentrate and of being unable to enjoy previously pleasurable activities and pursuits. No matter what they do, they feel unable to avoid pervasive and interminable apprehension. They sense themselves incapable of distinguishing the safe from the unsafe. Some become notably irritable and view minor responsibilities as momentous and insurmountable tasks. Distress mounts when they become aware and self-conscious of their growing incompetence and tension. Soon this self-awareness becomes a preoccupation. Observing themselves, paranoids sense tremors, palpitations, muscular tightness, "butterflies in the stomach," cold sweats, a feeling of foreboding, and, ultimately, the dread of imminent collapse. Their awareness of their own frailty has not only perpetuated their fright but feeds on itself until it builds to monumental proportions. Unless they can distract or divert their attention elsewhere, the paranoids' controls may give way. The upsurge of unconscious fears and images that flood to the surface may inundate and overwhelm them, resulting in an acute anxiety attack or *panic disorder*.

Affective disorders. Paranoids, especially those with a strong blend of narcissistic features, may evidence a self-exalted and pompous variant of *manic disorder*. Faced with realities that shatter their illusion of significance and omnipotence, they may lose perspective and frantically seek to regain their status. No longer secure in their image of superiority, they attempt through cheerful and buoyant behaviors to instill or revive the blissful state of former times when they believed their mere existence was of value in itself. They are driven to their excited state in the hope of reestablishing their lost exalted status.

Schizophrenic disorders. In contrast to the buoyant and manic hyperactivity that may be seen in the paranoid-narcissist, paranoid-antisocial personalities are subject more to the *schizophrenic: catatonic excited* disorders. These paranoids move about in a surly and truculent manner and explode into uncontrollable rages during which they threaten and occasionally physically assault others with little or no provocation. At these times, they unleash a torrent of abuse and storm about defiantly, cursing and voicing bitterness and contempt for all. They may lunge at and assail passersby quite unpredictably, shouting obscenities at unseen but hallucinated attackers and persecutors. It is the quality of irrational belligerence and fury, the frenzied lashing out, that distinguishes these paranoids from others.

Paranoid-compulsive personality mixtures are also subject to *schizophrenic disorders*, but of the *catatonic stupor* and *negativism* varieties. Their physical uncooperativeness is but a passive expression of deeply felt resentments and angers. The body tightness we observe reflects an intense struggle to control seething hostility, and their physical withdrawal and obduracy helps avoid contacts with events that could provoke and unleash their hostile impulses. Their catatonic postures both communicate and control their anger. They may be seen as bizarre extensions of their habitual coping style, a means of controlling contrary urges by protective restraint and rigid behavior. The gestures and grimaces of these patients convey symbolically an abbreviated and immediately restrained expression of their aggressive urges.

Concurrent Axis II Personalities

As noted in the prior chapter, there are both theoretical rationales (Millon, 1969) and supportive empirical data (Millon, 1977) to indicate that the paranoid covaries in profile combination with specific other personality types. In these mixed cases, the paranoid dimension is often an insidious and secondary development, fusing slowly into the fabric of an earlier and less dysfunctional coping style. Although paranoid-like features may be exhibited in almost every other personality disorder, they tend to become integral components of only four of the patterns previously described: the narcissistic, the antisocial (aggressive), the compulsive, and the passive-aggressive.

Before proceeding to discuss these personality combinations, it should be noted that no single attribute may be found universally in all paranoid personalities. The great majority of patients do evidence the constellation of behaviors described in the "clinical picture" section, but the focus on these common symptoms should not obscure the many variations of the impairment. What follows expresses but a small fraction of the diversity seen among paranoids. As a further caveat, note that the distinctions drawn here are not so sharply defined in reality. There are numerous overlappings in which traces of features associated with each subvariety may be found in the others. "Pure" textbook cases are rarely met.

Paranoid-narcissistic mixed personality.   These individuals are similar to their less severe counterparts. They seek to retain their admirable self-image, tend to act in a haughty and pretentious manner, and are naïvely self-confident, ungenerous, exploitive, expansive, and presumptuous, displaying a supercilious contempt and arrogance toward others. In contrast to the more mildly dysfunctional narcissists, who are likely to have achieved a modicum of success with their optimistic veneer and exploitive behaviors, paranoid-narcissists have run hard against reality. Their illusions of omnipotence may periodically have been shattered, toppling them from their vaulted self-image of eminence. Accustomed to seeing themselves as the center of things, they cannot bear the lessened significance now assigned them. Their narcissism has been severely wounded. Not only must they counter the indifference and humiliation found in reality, but they must reestablish their pride through extravagant claims and fantasies. Upset by assaults against their self-esteem, paranoid-narcissists reconstruct their image of themselves even further and ascend beyond the status from which they fell. By self-reinforcement they endow themselves with exalted competencies and powers. They dismiss any evidence that conflicts with their newly acquired and self-designated importance. Whatever flimsy talents and accomplishments they possess are embellished, creating thereby a new self-image that brushes aside objective reality.

Lacking internal discipline and cognitive control, paranoid-narcissists allow their reparative fantasies free rein to embroider a fabric of high sheen and appeal, caring little for the fact that their claims are unwarranted. Their grand assertions become fixed and adamant, for they are necessary elements in regaining an identity of significance and esteem. These paranoids go to great lengths to convince themselves and others of the validity of their claims, insisting against obvious contradictions and the ridicule of others that they deserve to be catered to, and that they are entitled to special acknowledgment and privileges. But the evidence in support of their assertions is as flimsy as a house of cards, easily collapsed by the slightest incursion. Unable to sustain this image before others and rebuffed and powerless to gain the recognition they crave, these paranoid-narcissists turn more and more inward for salvation. Taking liberties with objective facts and wandering further from social reality and shared meanings, they concoct an ever more elaborate world of fantasy. They may don the role and attributes of some idolized person, someone whose repute cannot be questioned by others. As this identification takes root, these paranoids begin to assert a new identity: a noble and inspired leader, a saint or powerful political figure, or an awesome and talented genius. Crossing the line into psychotic delusions, they may propose grandiose schemes for "saving the world," for solving insurmountable scientific problems, for creating new societies, and so on. These schemes may be worked out in minute detail and are formulated often with sufficient logic to draw at least momentary attention and recognition from others.

Paranoid-antisocial (aggressive) mixed personality. These paranoids are characterized best by their power orientation, their mistrust and resentment of others, and by their belligerent and intimidating manner. There is a ruthless desire to triumph over others, to vindicate themselves for past wrongs by cunning revenge or callous force, if necessary. In contrast to their nonparanoid counterpart, these personalities have found that their efforts to outwit and frustrate others have only prompted the others to inflict more of the harsh punishment and rejection to which they were previously subjected. Their strategy of arrogance and brutalization has backfired and they seek retribution, no longer as much through direct action as through fantasy.

Persistent and humiliating setbacks have confirmed these paranoids' expectancy of aggression from others. Of course, they have by their own hand stirred up much hostility and disfavor. Their argumentative and "chip-on-the-shoulder" attitude has provoked ample antagonism from others. Isolated and resentful, they now turn increasingly to themselves to cogitate and to mull over their fate. Left to their own ruminations, they begin to concoct plots in which every facet of their environment plays a threatening and treacherous role. Moreover, through projection, they attribute their own venom to others, ascribing to them the malice and ill will these patients feel within themselves. The line draws thin between objective antagonism and imagined hostility. Slowly, the belief takes hold that others are intentionally persecuting them. Alone, feeling all the more threatened, and with decreasing self-esteem, their suspicions now cross the line into psychotic delusions.

Essential to these paranoids is their need to retain their independence from the malice and power of others. Despite all adversity they cling tenaciously to the belief in their self-image of autonomy and strength. This may be seen in the content of the persecutory delusions. The malevolence of others is viewed neither as casual nor random. Rather, it is seen as designed to intimidate, offend, and undermine the patients' self-esteem. "They" are out to weaken the patients' "will," destroy their power, spread lies, thwart their talents, conspire to control their thoughts, and to subjugate them. Paranoid persecutory themes are filled with the dread of being forced to submit to authority, of being made soft and pliant, and of being tricked to surrender self-determination.

Paranoid-compulsive mixed personality. These individuals are similar to the moderately severe compulsive personality. However, in contrast to their milder and borderline-compulsive counterparts, who retain the hope of achieving protection through the good offices of others, paranoid-compulsives renounce their dependency aspirations and assume a stance of independence. Despite their growing hostility and the repudiation of conformity and submissive respect as a way of life, they retain their basic rigidity and perfectionism. They are now all the more grim and humorless, tense, controlled and inflexible, small-minded, legalistic, and self-righteous. These features of their makeup are even more deeply embedded and internalized as a fixed habit system. They may have found it necessary to discard their dependence on others as their primary source of reward, but the remnants of their lifelong habit of overcontrol and faultlessness are not as readily abandoned. Thus, they continue to seek the clarity of rules and regulations, cannot tolerate suspense, and impose order and system on their life. Deprived now of the guidelines of those others they have spurned, these paranoids lean increasingly upon themeselves and become their own ruthless slave drivers in search for order and power. Often there is an obsessive concern with trivial details and an excessive intellectualization of minor events, all to the end of obtaining internal perfection and faultlessness.

In this newly created independence, paranoid-compulsives have freed themselves from their prior constraints of submission and propriety. They may discharge the hostility they previously repressed. With little hesitation, they will impose their self-created standards upon others, demand that others submit to their way of doing things, and attack them with the same punitive attitudes to which they themselves were earlier subjected. The impossible regulations they set for others allow them to vent hostilities and to condemn others for their failures. Now they can give others what they themselves received. They despise and hate others openly for their weaknesses, their deceits, and their hypocrisy—feelings that they previously experienced within themselves, had once successfully repressed, and still try to conceal by condemning them in others.

Despite their public repudiation of being conforming and submissive persons, paranoid-compulsives cannot free themselves entirely of feeling conflict and guilt. Although they try to justify their aggressive manner they cannot fully square these actions with their past beliefs. Moreover, their present overt arrogance reactivates past anxieties, for they cannot escape remembering the retaliation their own hostile actions provoked in the past. Deep within paranoid-compulsives, then, are the remnants of guilt and the fear of retribution. Both elements give rise to persecutory beliefs. They have learned from past experience to anticipate disfavor and criticism in response to contrary and nonconforming behaviors. Consequently, as they scan their environment they "see" in the movements and remarks of others the hostility they anticipate. Further, to deny or justify their behaviors, they project their anger upon others. This mechanism proves self-defeating since it leads them to "find" hostile intent where none, in fact, exists. Last, inner feelings of guilt reactivate self-condemnatory attitudes. Part of their self feels that they should be punished for their resentments and behaviors. Thus, in combination, their anticipations, projections, and guilt lead them inexorably to believe that others are "after them," seeking to condemn, punish, belittle, and undo them.

Paranoid-passive-aggressive mixed personality. These patients may be differentiated from their less severe counterparts and the equally ill borderline–passive-aggressives by the presence of periodic delusions. In common with their affiliated syndromal patterns, these paranoids are noted by their discontent, pessimism, stubbornness, and vacillation. However, this paranoid is more aggressively negativistic and faultfinding, and is almost invariably sullen, resentful, obstructive, and peevish, openly registering feelings of jealousy, of being misunderstood, and of being cheated. Rarely can these patients sustain good relationships, and they re-create endless wrangles wherever they go. Demoralized by these failures, they forego all hopes of gaining affection and approval from others and decide to renounce these aspirations in preference for self-determination.

Although they assert their new found independence with prideful self-assurance, paranoid–passive-aggressives remain irritable, dissatisfied, and troubled by discontent and ambivalence. They cannot forget their resentments and their feeling of having been mistreated and exploited. They will often perceive the achievements of others as unfair advantages, preferential treatments that are undeserved and have been denied to them. Disgruntlement and complaints mount. Fantasies expand and weave into irrational envy. Their grumbling comments turn to overt anger and hostility. Each of these may feed into a theme of unjust misfortune. If unchecked, they are whipped, bit by bit, into a psychotic delusion of resentful jealousy. In similar fashion, erotic delusions may evolve among these patients. Although they consciously repudiate their need for others, passive-aggressive–paranoids still seek affection from them. Rather than admit these desires, however, they will defensively project them, interpreting the casual remarks and actions of others as subtle signs of amorous intent. However, they are unable to tolerate these "attentions" since they dread further betrayal and exploitation. As a consequence, these paranoids will insist that they must be "protected" against erotic seduction by others. Innocent victims may be accused of committing indignities, of making lewd suggestions, or of molesting them.

Decompensated paranoid personality. These individuals are extremely vulnerable to the strains of life and are easily precipitated into psychotic disorders. Events that promote mistrust, expectations of sadistic treatment, or the loss of self-determination result in defensive vigilance, secretive withdrawal, and, ultimately, the delusions that are so characteristic of paranoids when they succumb to frank psychoses. Not infrequently, the persistent isolation and delusional ruminations of moderately dysfunctional paranoids may become more deeply entrenched and result in a more permanent decompensated pattern.

The contrast in the clinical picture between the advanced dysfunctional paranoid and the decompensated paranoid is more striking than that found between other dysfunctional patterns and their decompensated counterparts. Although the transition is likely to have been a gradual one, spotted along the way with several "disordered" episodes, the final decompensated state reflects a major and sharp transformation. Certain fundamental changes take place; superficial appearances tend to accentuate them, however. The dramatic change in the clinical picture between these two functional levels may account in part for Kraepelin's decision to subsume the decompensated cases, which he originally termed "dementia paranoides," under the dementia praecox label.

Most obvious is that the air of arrogant independence and self-assertion that characterizes many dysfunctional paranoid personalities sharply deflates when they succumb to the decompensated level. In contrast to borderlines and schizotypals—their dysfunctional level counterparts, who have always appeared more or less ineffectual, weak, or vacillating—dysfunctional paranoids have fostered the image of being cocky, self-assured, willful, and dominant. Thus, they fall a great distance when they finally topple, and the contrast is quite marked.

Despite these overtly dramatic changes, the decompensated paranoid remains defensively guarded against influence, coercion, or attachments of any kind. These patients are still mistrustful and suspicious, fearful that those upon whom they now must depend for survival will be deceitful or injurious. Through the haze of their disorganized thought processes, they will still distort objective reality to fit their delusional "pseudocommunity." Not only are they estranged from others and unable to share common perspectives, but they will continue their attempt to ward off the influence of others. Despite their psychic collapse, they will persist, however feebly, in their struggle to retain self-determination and keep intact at least some remnants of their shattered self-image. The traces of their past arrogance and self-assurance are now submerged, however, in ineffectualities and confusions. Where self-determination and independence characterized earlier behavior, we observe a pervasive invalidism and dependence on others for care and survival. Although cognitive processes were always distorted and narrow in focus, they once possessed an intrinsic order and logic to them. Now they are fragmented, disjunctive, and delusional. Previously, ideas were communicated in a self-confident and often articulate manner. Now they tend to be stated with hesitation and doubt. Ideas frequently are tangential, expressed in incoherent phrases, or scattered in disjointed flights of fancy. Emotions still retain their veiled hostility, but the "fight" is lacking. Anger seems devoid of feeling and the spark of intense resentment has burned out. Behavior that was once dominant, intimidating, or contemptuous has become aversive, secretive, and bizarre. The whole complex of self-assurance and social belligerence has disintegrated, leaving an inner void, a hesitation, and a fragmented shadow of the former being.

The role of being an invalid has been hard for these patients to accept. Their mistrust of others and their lifelong orientation toward self-determination make it difficult to accept the weakness and dependence that their new ineffectual role imposes on them. They have no choice, however. Their behaviors are grossly disturbing and impossible to tolerate in normal social environments. Institutional life may be a sanctuary for some, and "illness" may be a convenient rationalization for their repeated failures. Others may assert that "forced" hospitalization only proves the validity of their persecutory beliefs in that it verifies the deceit of others and the resentment "the world" has always felt toward them. Distorted thus, many decompensated paranoids accept their fate of hospital invalidism and become less contentious and resistive. Though still secretive and easily affronted, they may no longer be difficult to manage. Unfortunately, their formerly organized world collapses across a number of fronts. As they become increasingly detached from social contact, lost in their own reveries, they have little need to maintain the logic of consensual thinking. They slip easily, then, into an inchoate world of dreamlike fantasy, with all its disjointed and phantasmagoric elements. As their formerly prideful self-image sinks into shame and humiliation, they may begin to engage in the destruction of their own cognitive processes. These paranoids would rather not think, if all they can think about is their humiliation and the "shameful" state in which they now find themselves. When painful thoughts such as these intrude into consciousness, they disassemble and twist them into digressive and irrelevant paths, ultimately creating disorganization where cognitive order and clarity previously existed. They become estranged from themselves for similar reasons. Previously apart from others by choice, they now separate and jettison their own being. Unable to tolerate their present state, they become a disembodied emptiness, a nonentity that is no longer capable of feeling the anguish of being who they are.

Differential Diagnostic Signs

There are several listings in the DSM-III that resemble the paranoid personality. Most relevant are "paranoid disorder," "paranoia," and "schizophrenic disorder, paranoid type." All three syndromes are distinguished by the presence of persistent psychotic symptoms such as delusions and hallucinations, which are not intrinsic to the paranoid personality syndrome unless a psychotic episode is superimposed. Specifically, the description of the "paranoia" category states that it develops insidiously and possesses "a permanent and unshakable delusional system accompanied by preservation of clear and orderly thinking." "Paranoid disorder" is the broader syndrome within which paranoia is subsumed; it does not require that the delusional system be "permanent and unshakable." Finally, the syndrome noted as "schizophrenia disorder, paranoid type" is described as evidencing incoherence, loose associations, hallucinations, and fragmented delusions. In surveying these descriptions, it appears that the progression from "paranoia" to "paranoid disorder" to "schizophrenia, paranoid type" reflects, primarily, differences in degree of personality deterioration. Thus, in "paranoia" the delusions are highly systematized and the personality largely intact; in the "paranoid disorder" the delusions lack the systematization seen in paranoia but fall short of the fragmentation and deterioration of the "schizophrenic paranoid."

The paranoid's dread of attachment and fear of insignificance are similar to the concerns of the *schizotypal*. Both distance from close personal relationships and are vulnerable to the threat of external control. These commonalities may lead to some difficulties in differentiating between these syndromes. There are, however, several clear distinctions between them. For example, schizotypals experience little satisfaction in being themselves; thus, their fantasies generate feelings of low, rather than high, self-worth. They turn from others *and* from themselves, being neither socially attached nor possessing a valued sense of self. Paranoids turn from others, but their active fantasy life creates an enhanced self-image. Faced with the loss of external recognition or power, paranoids draw upon their internal sources of supply to compensate for rebuff and anguish. On other dimensions—and in contrast with schizotypals, who tend toward the apathetic and indifferent—paranoids are often energetic, driven, argumentative, and hostile. As noted earlier, in the more decompensated states, the pictures of schizotypals, paranoids, and borderlines begin to merge, making discrimination extremely difficult at the symptomatological level. Differentiation in these cases may be more accurately made with reference to developmental histories.

PREDISPOSING BACKGROUND

There is no unique set nor sequence of determinants in the dispositional background of paranoid personalities. Different combinations and orders of events may give rise to the syndrome. The preceding discussion has formally recognized some of these divergent lines by differentiating the paranoid syndrome into several variants; the discussion of backgrounds is arranged according to these differences. Note again that the propositions presented are provisional hypotheses, not facts. There is little in the way of dependable evidence from systematic and well-designed research to justify making definitive statements.

Paranoid-narcissistic personality etiology.   These individuals typically were overvalued and indulged by their parents, given the impression that their mere existence was of sufficient worth in itself. Few developed a sense of interpersonal responsibility, failing to learn how to cooperate, to share, or to think of the interests of others. Unrestrained by their parents and unjustly confident in their self-worth, their fantasies had few boundaries, allowing them to create fanciful images of their power and achievements. The social insensitivity and exploitiveness of these future paranoids led inevitably to interpersonal difficulties. Once beyond the protective home setting, they ran hard against objective reality. Their illusion of omnipotence was challenged and their self-centeredness and ungiving attitudes were attacked. In time, their image of eminence and perfection was shattered. Rather than face or adapt to reality, or build up their competencies to match their high self-esteem, they turned increasingly to the refuge of fantasy. Rationalizing their defects and lost in their imaginary gratifications, they retreated and became further alienated from others. As new rejections and humiliations cumulated, the narcissistic-paranoids moved more into themselves, soon beginning to confuse their fantasy compensations for objective reality. In their imaginative world they redeemed themselves and reasserted their pride and status. Their lifelong habit of self-reinforcement enabled them to weave alibis and proofs of their own perfection and grandiosity with supreme facility. Protected by these fantasies, they remained indifferent to others, successfully compensating for the others' "jealous criticism" and their malevolent lies and "distortions."

Paranoid-antisocial (aggressive) personality etiology. Biogenically, many of these patients appear to come from families with a disproportionately high number of members who display vigorous energy and an irascible temperament. As children, these patients are likely to have been active and intrusive; they exhibited frequent temper outbursts and were considered to be difficult to manage and found to precipitate difficulties. Aspects of their thick-skinned and aggressive temperament may be traced to constitutionally low thresholds of ·reactivity in the limbic and reticular systems.

The characteristic experiential history of these paranoids suggests that they were subjected to parental antagonism and harrassment. Many served as scapegoats for displaced parental aggression. Instead of responding with anxiety as a consequence of this mistreatment, they acquired the feeling that they had "to be contended with" and that they could cause trouble and "get a rise" out of others through their obdurate and provocative behaviors. In addition, many learned vicariously to model themselves after their aggressive parents. The paranoid-antisocial learned to perceive the world as harsh and unkind, a place calling for protective vigilance and mistrust. Many also acquired the self-confidence to fend for themselves.

Through their own aggressive actions these future paranoids found they could disturb others and manipulate events to their suiting. Mistrustful of others and confident of their powers, they rejected parental controls and values, and supplanted them with their own. Rebellious of parental authority, they developed few inner controls, often failing to learn to restrain impulses or to avoid temptations.

Similar learnings are acquired by children reared in broken families and disorganized subcultures. Impulse controls are not learned and children gain their outlook on life wandering "on the street" in concert with equally destitute and disillusioned peers. There are few congenial and socially successful models for them to emulate, and the traditional values and standards of society are viewed as alien, if not downright hypocritical and hostile. Aggressive toughness seems mandatory for survival, and these youngsters learn quickly to adopt a "dog-eat-dog" attitude and to counter hostility with the same. Anticipating resentment and betrayal from others, future antisocial-paranoids moved through life with a chip-on-the-shoulder attitude, bristling with anger and reacting before hostility and duplicity actually occurred. Resentment and antagonism were projected. Dreading being attacked, humiliated, or powerless, they learned to attack first.

In contrast to their less severe prototype, paranoid-antisocials experienced repeated rebuffs. Their confidence weakened, they could not successfully sustain their assertive and vindictive strategy. Faced with repeated setbacks, they redoubled their isolation from others, preferring fantasy as a means of nursing their wounds. Their growing apartness from social life, their gnawing mistrust of relationships, and the devastating feeling that they may have lost their powers of self-determination, lead these paranoids into increasingly irrational suspicions and, ultimately, their delusions of persecution.

Paranoid-compulsive personality etiology. These persons have a background of parental overcontrol through contingent punishment. Most have striven to meet parental demands and to avoid errors and transgressions, thereby minimizing punitive treatment and the threat of abandonment. In early life they sought to model themselves after authority figures, foregoing their independence and following the rules with utmost precision. As a consequence of their rigid conformity, they lack spontaneity and initiative, are unable to form deep and geniune relationships, and are indecisive and fearful of the unknown. For various reasons, differing from case to case, the security these paranoids sought to achieve through submission and propriety was not attained. Lacking guidance and support from others, intolerant of suspense, and dreading punishment lest repressed anger erupt, they drew into themselves, turned away from their dependent conformity, and sought solace, if they could, within their own thoughts. Although renouncing their dependency, compulsive-paranoids cannot relinquish their lifelong habits. Thus, feelings of guilt and fear become acute as they begin to assert themselves. Anticipating punishment for their nonconforming behaviors and feeling that such actions deserve condemnation, they project these self-judgments upon others and now view them to be hostile and persecutory.

Paranoid-passive-aggressive personality etiology. These paranoids often evidence irregular infantile patterns and an uneven course of maturation, traits that often promote inconsistent and contradictory styles of parental management. Their characteristic irritable affectivity may be attributed to low neurophysiological thresholds or responsivity.

Most of these patients are likely to have acquired their negativistic irritability and discontent in response to inconsistent parental treatment. Many were subjected to capricious vacillations in parental emotion and interest. Thus, their parents may have been affectionate one moment and irrationally hostile the next. These erratic behaviors often serve as a model for vicarious learning and imitation. Similar learnings are often acquired in schismatic families where parents vie for their children's loyalties, creating not only confusion and contradictory behaviors but feelings of guilt and anxiety. Early learnings are perpetuated by the future paranoids' own actions. Intransigence, disgruntlement, and behavioral inconsistency result in difficult personal relationships and the persistence of chaotic and erratic experiences. Should these events lead to painful setbacks and severe disappointments, these paranoids will have learned to forego their dependency needs, gradually relinquishing all hope of affection and approval from others. They begin to see others as having been given preferential and undeserved treatment. Their complaints and discontent begin to take on an irrational quality. Jealousy delusions may come to the fore, and accusations of infidelity, deceit, and betrayal are made against innocent relatives and friends.

Decompensated paranoid personality etiology. As patients discard the coping style of the basic paranoid level, they harshly reject all forms of dependence, refuse to ally themselves with anyone they consider "inferior," and begin to suspect that others will undo them the first moment they can. Their resentments are now overt. Moreover, humiliated time and again, they reconstruct reality totally to suit their needs and illusions. As fantasy supplants reality and as delusions lead them further astray, the decompensation process speeds up. The more they drift into the boundless and undisciplined character of their inner world, the more their thoughts become fluid and disorganized. Repeated belittlement and censure take their toll. Their reveries are interrupted more and more with thoughts of persecution, dismay, and anguish. Inchoate suspicions of malignment and deceit gradually are transformed into irrational delusions. Unable to cope directly with these threats, their tensions erupt into overt hostile attacks or delusional fantasies. This stage, with its periodic psychotic episodes, may disintegrate further. There is a marked withdrawal from social contact. The shock and humiliation of hospitalization, their loss of self-determination, and their frightening dependence on others may shatter their fragile underpinnings and its remnants of a delusional self-image. Protectively withdrawing, they sink into a primitive and diffuse world unchecked by reality and social controls. The logic of delusional systems loses its coherence and order. Disorganized fantasies blur into reality, hallucinations are projected, and cognitive associations are dismembered. Bizarre emotions and a sense of disorientation and estrangement come to the fore. The final shameful collapse to the role of hospital invalid crushes their once exalted self-image. Cognitively disorganized, they try to deny and destroy the intrusions of their own painful thoughts and memories, thereby becoming increasingly estranged from themselves. All that remains is a thin thread connecting the present to the past. These few mementos they either hold fast, turning them over and over again in their thoughts, or dismiss and deny, thereby rejecting the very fact of their prior existence.

PROGNOSTIC CONSIDERATIONS

This final section of the discussion again addresses aspects that contribute new difficulties for the patient or exacerbate established ones. The processes of self-perpetuation are what makes pathology itself pathogenic. In line with the established format, there is a brief presentation of steps that may help remedy these difficulties.

Perpetuation of the Paranoid Pattern

Despite its utility as a defensive maneuver, the gains of the projection mechanism are short-lived in that they ultimately intensify the paranoid's plight. By ascribing slanderous and malevolent attitudes to others, these persons now face threat where none, in fact, may have existed. Thus, by their own subjective distortion, they have created a hostile environment from which there can be no physical escape. Moreover, their unjust accusations are bound to provoke feelings of exasperation and anger in others. Projection may thereby transform neutral overtures into the very hostility they feared.

Delusions are a natural outgrowth of the paranoid pattern. Two factors, dependence on self for both stimulation and reinforcement, are conducive to their development. Insistent on retaining their autonomy, paranoids isolate themselves and are unwilling to share the perspective and attitudes of others. Withdrawn from social communion, they have ample time to cogitate and form idiosyncratic suppositions and hypotheses. These speculative ruminations are "confirmed" as valid since it is the patient alone who is qualified to judge them. The delusions that paranoids construct differ from those seen in other pathological patterns. Accustomed to independent thought and convinced of their superiority, they are skillful in formulating beliefs and confident in their correctness. As such, their delusions tend to be systematic, rational, and convincing. By contrast, the occasional delusions of the borderline and schizotypal appear illogical and unpersuasive, arise under conditions of emotional duress, and consequently appear bizarre, scattered, and unsystematic.

The paranoid's characteristic attitude of independence and self-confidence is largely spurious. These personalities maintain their illusion of superiority by rigid self-conviction and exaggerated bluff. Time and again, their competencies are shown to be defective and they are made to look foolish. As a consequence, their precarious equilibrium and their self-anointed status and pride are upset easily and too often. To regain belief in their invincibility, they may be driven to extreme and pathological measures. Rather than accepting the reality of their weaknesses, they assert that some alien influence undermines them and causes them to fail and be humbled before others. Ineffectuality and shame must be attributed to some irresistible and destructive power. As their suspicions of a "foreign force" grows and as their vigilance against humiliation crumbles, paranoids increasingly distort reality. Not only do they deny the possibility that their failures are self-caused, but they are unwilling to ascribe these failures to mere "pedestrian" powers. Rather, they see their loss as reflecting the malicious workings of devils, x-rays, magnetism, poisons, and so on. Delusions of influence and persecution signify both their dread of submission and their need to bolster their pride by attributing shortcomings to the action of formidable forces. In time, their self-glorification and persecutory delusions form a systematic pattern. Soon the "whole picture" comes into sharp relief. One delusion feeds another, unchecked by the controls of social reality. Minor fabrications, employed initially to cope with the humiliations of reality, eventually become complex schemes that are more "real" than reality itself.

Remedial Interventions

As with other personality patterns, the prospects for the paranoid are poor. Habits and attitudes are deeply ingrained and pervade the entire fabric of functioning. Modest inroads are possible, of course, but these are likely to merely diminish the frequency of troublesome episodes rather than revamp the basic personality style.

Most paranoid personalities do not succumb to serious and persistent delusions. Nevertheless, they are regarded by most associates as suspicious, testy, or supercilious people. A small number attain considerable success, especially if they are genuinely talented or happen by good fortune to attract a coterie of disciples seeking a supremely confident, if somewhat deranged, leader.

Despite difficult social relationships, the long-range prognosis for the paranoid is not as poor as that of the schizotypal, one of its advanced dysfunctional counterparts. Paranoids can obtain satisfactions from themselves; schizotypals do not. Faced with external derogation, paranoids can nurture themselves until their wounds are sufficiently healed. Schizotypals, lacking faith both in themselves and others, remain empty-handed. Compared to borderlines, their other dysfunctional counterpart, paranoids have both an advantage and a disadvantage insofar as prognosis is concerned. Borderlines characteristically maintain reasonably good interpersonal relations. As a consequence, they gain some of the support and encouragement they need. Furthermore, borderlines turn to others during difficult periods, often soliciting enough affection and security to forestall a further decline. In contrast, paranoids tend to remain socially obnoxious and keep to themselves when relationships turn sour. Behaviors such as these increase their isolation, not only resulting in an intensification of their suspicions and secretiveness but giving rise to further social estrangement. To the borderlines' disadvantage is their lack of internal reserve, which leads them to slip into a state of helplessness should they fail to evoke external support. This is not the case with paranoids. Not only will they refuse to submit to weakness and indolence, but they will struggle to "pull themselves up by their own bootstraps."

Therapeutic work with paranoids is a touchy proposition at best. Few come willingly for treatment. Therapy signifies weakness and dependency, both of which are anathema. Many therapists fall into the trap of disliking these patients since their suspicions and hostility readily provoke discomfort and resentment. Therapists must resist being intimidated by the arrogance and demeaning comments of these patients. Weakness is not a trait paranoids could accept in someone in whom they have placed their trust. Other problems can complicate the therapeutic effort. Excessive friendliness and overt sympathies often connote deceit to these patients, a seductive prelude to humiliation and deprecation. As paranoids tend to view it, they have suffered pain at the hands of deceptively "kind" people. Nor can therapists question these patients about their distorted attitudes and beliefs. This may drive them to concoct new rationalizations. It may intensify their distrust and destroy whatever rapport has been built. Conceivably, it may unleash a barrage of defensive hostility or precipitate an open psychotic break. The beliefs, self-confidence, and image of autonomy and strength of paranoids should not be directly challenged. These illusions are too vital a part of their style; to question them is to attack the patient's fragile equilibrium.

What then is a good approach to take with these patients?

Essentially, the therapist must build trust through a series of slow and progressive steps. A quiet, formal, and genuine respect for the patient as a person must be shown. The therapist must accept, but not confirm, the patients' unusual beliefs and allow them to explore their thoughts and feelings at a pace they can tolerate. The major initial goal of therapy is to free patients of mistrust by showing them that they can share their anxieties with another person without the humiliation and maltreatment to which they are accustomed. If this can be accomplished, paranoids may learn to look at the world not only from their own perspective but through the eyes of others. If they can trust the therapist, they can begin to relax, relinquish their defenses, and open themselves to new attitudes. Once they have accepted the therapist as someone they can trust, they may be able to lean on the therapist and accept his/her thoughts and suggestions. This may become a basis for a more generalized lessening of suspicions and for a wider scope of trusting and sharing.

Regarding specific modes of therapy, it is simplest to say that technique is secondary to building trust. Nevertheless, psychopharmacologic agents may be of value during anxious or acting-out periods. Institutionalization may be required if reality controls break down. During outpatient treatment, it is advisable that environmental irritants be reduced. Behavioral and psychoanalytic therapies cannot be employed without the prior development of trust; their applicability and effectiveness are questionable in any case. Nondirective cognitive approaches may be indicated as a first approach, to be followed (where appropriate) by other measures. The choice of second-stage therapeutic methods depends on both practical and ultimate goals. At best, therapy is likely to control or moderate rather than reverse the basic personality pattern.

Chapter 14

Schizotypal Personality: The Eccentric Pattern

Clearly manifest in the schizotypal personality are a variety of persistent and prominent eccentricities of behavior, thought, and perception. These characteristics mirror—but fall short of, in either severity or peculiarity—features that would justify the diagnosis of clinical schizophrenia. It is the author's contention (Millon, 1969) that these "odd" schizotypal symptoms contribute to and are derivatives of a more fundamental and profound social isolation and self-alienation. Although the schizotypal syndrome should be seen as an advanced dysfunctional personality, akin in severity to both the borderline and paranoid types, it may be best understood as a more grave form of the pathologically less severe schizoid and avoidant patterns.

In general, these three syndromes—schizoid, avoidant, and schizotypal—are characterized by an impoverished social life, a distancing from close interpersonal relationships, and an autistic, but nondelusional, pattern of thinking. Because of their more advanced state of pathology, schizotypals frequently lead a meaningless, idle, and ineffectual existence, drifting from one aimless activity to another, remaining on the periphery of societal life, and rarely developing intimate attachments or accepting enduring responsibilities. Their characteristic oddities in behavior and thought—such as magical thinking, illusions, circumstantial speech, suspiciousness, and ideas of reference—stem in part from their withdrawn and isolated existence. This separateness from conventional relationships and modes of communication precludes their being exposed to "corrective" perspectives that might mitigate their autistic preoccupations. To paraphrase what was stated in an earlier chapter, the more individuals turn inward, the more they lose contact with the styles of behavior and thought of those around them. As they become progressively estranged from their social environment, they lose touch with the "conventions of reality" and with the checks against irrational thought and behavior that are provided by reciprocal relationships. Increasingly detached from the controls and stabilizing influences of repetitive, though ordinary, human affairs, they may lose their sense of behavioral propriety and suitability, and gradually begin the process of acting, thinking, and perceiving in peculiar, unreal, and somewhat "crazy" ways—hence, their manifest and prominent eccentricities.

In consequence, and because they lack either the means or the desire to experience the joy and vibrancy of a "personal" life, schizotypals become devitalized and numb, wander in a dim and hazy fog, and engage in bizarre activities and curious thoughts that have minimal social purpose or meaning. As the reader proceeds through this chapter, it will become more clear as to why schizotypals avoid participating in social reality. Briefly, there is no reason to aspire to be part of normal social life when they believe that nothing can spark their flat existence or provide them with feelings of joy. As a consequence, they move through life, not only like automatons possessing impenetrable barriers to shared meanings and affections, but also estranged from the aspirations, spontaneity, delight, and triumph of selfhood.

Before proceeding to the more detailed presentation of the schizotypal, a few words should be said about controversies concerning its selection as a diagnostic label. Perhaps second only to the disputation that surrounded the choice of the borderline term, the introduction of this new designation raised serious objections on the part of several members of the Task Force. The issue of the substantive validity of the syndrome as a distinct personality entity remained active in the deliberations of the committee to the very end, resolved in part only by a study undertaken by Spitzer, Endicott, and Gibbon (1979). The reader's appraisal of the internal coherence and differential diagnostic properties of the schizotypal constellation may be aided by a review of its historical and theoretical antecedents, furnished in the next section. For the present, attention is focused on problems associated with the use of "schizoid" and "schizotypal" as two, ostensibly distinct, personality designations. Numerous objections concerning potential confusions these terms might engender were raised by Task Force members. Thus, in a memo to his Task Force colleagues in December 1978, the author wrote:

> I took upon myself the opportunity to explore empirically views...concerning possible confusions that might exist with the terms schizoid and schizotypal as separate personality disorders....my own data, limited though they are in terms of the size and diversity of the sample, show that many would be inclined to think that schizoid and schizotypal are synonymous, particularly in suggesting dispositions to schizophrenia....[I] think the introduction of the term schizotypal and the reapplication of the label schizoid to mean something different than it meant in DSM-II, is only going to lead to confusion and to a diminishment in utility of the Personality Disorders axis.

Two, among several, concurring views expressed at this late date by Task Force members are excerpted here:

Using both schizoid and schizotypal is asking for trouble. I have a nagging feeling that if we cut out schizoid and leave schizotypal then what will happen is that people will equate schizotypal with schizoid and not understand the other term.

Introducing the term Schizotypal, which will be new to most clinicians, met with dismay and annoyance when I described it to a sophisticated clinical group here. Both Schizoid and Schizotypal Personality Disorders are described with a central criterion of severe social isolation.

As noted earlier, the reader should be able to assess distinctions between these two syndromes following opportunities to review their associated histories and data, and opportunities to test DSM-III differential criteria with "real," rather than theoretically abstract, patients. It is the author's view that substantive clinical grounds exist for separating them, if for no other reason than their levels of severity and their consequences. Nonetheless, the selection of such similar diagnostic labels seems to have been most unwise when appropriate alternative designations were available. Despite the lamentable nature of this decision, there is no ambiguity in the DSM-III descriptive characterization of the schizotypal syndrome, which states in part:

The essential feature is a Personality Disorder in which there are various oddities of thought, perception, speech and behavior that are not severe enough to meet the criteria for Schizophrenia. No single feature is invariably present. The disturbance in the content of thought may include magical thinking (or in children, bizarre fantasies or preoccupations), ideas of reference, or paranoid ideation. Perceptual disturbances may include recurrent illusions, depersonalization, or derealization (not associated with panic attacks). Often, speech shows marked peculiarities: concepts may be expressed unclearly or oddly or words used deviantly, but never to the point of loosening of associations or incoherence. Frequently, but not invariably, the behavioral manifestations include social isolation and constricted or inappropriate affect that interferes with rapport in face-to-face interaction.

Varying admixtures of anxiety, depression, and other dysphoric moods are common. . . . During periods of extreme stress transient psychotic symptoms may be present. (p. 310)

HISTORICAL AND THEORETICAL ANTECEDENTS

In contrast with the comparatively extensive early literature on the paranoid syndrome, and more similar to the "borderline" label in their shared recency, the diagnostic term "schizotypal" provides few leads to the diligent investigator who seeks to trace its historical roots. Coined as a syndromal designation as late as the 1950s, the constellation of traits it encompasses may be found under descriptive labels that are quite far afield. This review is not limited, therefore, to a literature bound by adherence to the "schizotypal" designation. On the other hand, the purview is not enlarged so broadly as to include historical entities more properly conceived as forerunners of the new borderline syndrome, a diagnostic class identified by its characteristic affective and interpersonal instability. Rather, attention is focused on earlier syndromes that closely approximate the principal characteristics of the schizotypal pattern—social isolation and eccentricities in behavior, thought, and perception. First, a few paragraphs are devoted to reviewing the historical evolution of schizophrenia, the syndromal prototype of which schizotypal is ostensibly a dilute and nonpsychotic personality variant.

An English neurologist, Willis, reported in 1674 having observed a pathological sequence in which "young persons who, lively and spirited, and at times even brilliant in their childhood, passed into obtuseness and hebetude during adolescence." Better known historically are the texts written in 1852 and 1853 by the Belgian psychiatrist Morel, who described the case of a 14 year-old boy who had been a cheerful and good student, but who progressively lost his intellectual capacities and increasingly became melancholy and withdrawn. Morel considered cases such as these to be irremediable and ascribed the deterioriation to an arrest in brain development that stemmed from hereditary causes. He named the illness "dementia praecox" (*demence precoce*) to signify his observation that the degenerative processes began at an early age and progressed rapidly.

K. L. Kahlbaum (1863) and E. Hecker (1871) described two other forms of mental deterioration. They applied the term "hebephrenia" to conditions that began in adolescence, usually started with a quick succession of erratic moods followed by a rapid enfeeblement of all functions, and finally progressed to an unalterable psychic decline. The label "catatonic" was introduced to represent "tension insanity" in cases where the patient displayed no reactivity to sensory impressions, lacked "self-will," and sat mute and physically immobile. These symptoms ostensibly reflected brain structure deterioration.

Emil Kraepelin considered hebephrenia and dementia praecox to be synonymous prior to the fifth edition of his psychiatric text (1896). In that highly original treatise, he concluded that the diverse symptom complexes of catatonia and hebephrenia, as well as certain paranoid disturbances, displayed a common theme of early deterioration and ultimate incurability. As he conceived them, each of these illnesses was a variation of Morel's original concept of dementia praecox. By subsuming the disparate symptoms of these formerly separate syndromes under the common theme of their ostensive early and inexorable mental decline, Kraepelin appeared to bring order and simplicity to what had previously been diagnostic confusion. In line with the traditions of German psychiatry, Kraepelin assumed that a biophysical defect lay at the heart of this new coordinating syndrome. In contrast to his forebears, however, he speculated that sexual and metabolic dysfunctions were the probable causal agents, rather than the usual hypothesis of an anatomic lesion. Among the major signs that Kraepelin considered central, in addition to the progressive and inevitable decline, were discrepancies between thought and emotion, negativism and stereotyped behaviors, wandering or unconnected ideas, hallucinations, delusions, and a general mental deterioration.

Kraepelin's observations and syntheses were challenged and modified in significant proposals offered by Eugen Bleuler in Switzerland and Adolf Meyer in the United States.

Observing hundreds of dementia praecox patients in the early 1900s led Bleuler (1911) to conclude that it was misleading to compare the type of deterioration they evidenced with that found among patients suffering from metabolic deficiencies or brain degeneration. Moreover, the reactions and thoughts of his patients were qualitatively complex and often highly creative, contrasting markedly with the simple or meandering thinking that Kraepelin observed. Furthermore, not only did many of his patients display their illness for the first time in adulthood, rather than in adolescence, but a significant proportion evidenced no progressive deterioration, which Kraepelin considered the sine qua non of the syndrome. Thus, to Bleuler, the label "dementia praecox" was a misleading designation in that it characterized an age of onset and a course of development that were not supported by the evidence.

The "primary symptoms," as Bleuler saw them, were disturbances in the associative link among thoughts, a breach between affect and intellect, ambivalence toward the same objects, and an autistic detachment from reality. The variety of cases that displayed these fragmented thoughts, feelings, and actions led Bleuler, in 1911, to term them "the group of schizophrenias," a label selected to signify what he saw to be a split (*schism*) within the mind (*phrenos*) of these patients. Although he considered schizophrenia to be a diverse set of disorders, he retained the Kraepelinian view that the impairment stemmed from a unitary disease process that was attributable to physiologic pathology. Schizophrenics shared a neurological ailment that produced their common primary symptoms. Schizophrenics also exhibited several "secondary symptoms," such as hallucinations and delusions, the content of which Bleuler ascribed to the patients' distinctive life experiences and to their efforts to adapt to their basic disease. Psychogenic factors shaped the particular character of the schizophrenic impairment, but Bleuler was convinced that experience could not in itself "cause" the ailment.

Along similar lines, Adolf Meyer suggested in 1906 that dementia praecox was not an organic disease but a maladaptive way of "reacting" to stress, fully understandable in terms of the patient's constitutional potentials and life experiences. To him, these maladaptive reactions led to what he termed "progressive habit deteriorations," which reflected "inefficient and faulty attempts to avoid difficulties" (1912, p. 98). Symptoms of psychopathology were seen as the end product of abortive and self-defeating efforts to establish psychic equilibrium. His well-reasoned "psychobiological" approach to schizophrenia, which he preferred to call "paregasia" to signify its distorted or twisted character, was the most systematic recognition to date of the interactive and progressive nature of pathogenesis. Of special note also was

Meyer's view that paregasia could be present in dilute and nonpsychotic form, that is, without delusions, hallucinations, or deterioration. He considered the classic psychotic symptoms to be advanced signs of a potentially, but not inevitably, evolving habit system that might stabilize at a prepsychotic level. In its nonclinical state, paregasia could be detected by a variety of attenuated and "soft" signs that merely suggested the manifest psychotic disorder. Meyer's proposal of a self-defeating and maladaptive reaction system (personality) that parallels schizophrenia in inchoate form was a highly innovative, but unheeded, notion. In many respects, Bleuler and Meyer's ideas on this matter were the primary forerunners of the schizotypal syndrome; that is, they shared the view that a constitutional defect or disposition can evolve into a moderately dysfunctional and enduring personality system under a regimen of life experiences that prevent these potentials from being exacerbated into a manifest clinical state.

Both Bleuler and Meyer expanded Kraepelin's more limited conception of the inevitable and fixed course of dementia praecox by recognizing both nondeteriorating and intermediary cases, a position that Kraepelin accepted in his later years when writing of "autistic personalities" (1919) and those whose dementia is "brought to a standstill short of its full clinical course" (p. 237) Nevertheless, there were those who retained Kraepelin's earlier insistence on the inevitable deterioration in dementia praecox. For example, Langfeldt (1937) stressed the notion that some "schizophrenic" patients do follow an inevitable course of decompensation, whereas others do not. This distinction led him to reserve the schizophrenic label for those he termed "process" types, who eventually did deteriorate; he coined the word "schizophreniform" for those he referred to as "reactive" types, patients whose symptoms were more affectively tinged and followed intense and acute precipitants. Process schizophrenics presumably possessed premorbid "schizoid" personalities that would progress insidiously to the clinical state with minimal external promptings. As this deterioration progresses, previously inchoate signs of "ego-boundary disturbances," associative thought defects, and feelings of depersonalization gain increasing prominence.

The theme of a nonpsychotic form of schizophrenia was brought into sharp focus in a seminal paper by G. Zilboorg (1941). Referring to these patients as "ambulatory schizophrenics," Zilboorg took strong exception to the practice of creating "euphemistic labels" (such as "borderline cases," "incipient schizophrenia," and the like) when what was observed were merely less advanced forms of the basic schizophrenic disease process. Devising new terms was seen as both misleading and unjustified. To quote Zilboorg, it is as if we would

> refuse to make a diagnosis of appendicitis merely because the appendix has not ruptured and no peritonitis has as yet set in.... Schizophrenia is not *dementia praecox*.... [it] is a generic name covering a certain type of psychopathological processes. That these... should present themselves in various

degrees of intensity, various stages of development—from the earliest to most advanced forms—and in various degrees of overtness of clinical manifestations, should be self-understood. (1941, p. 151)

Considering the flagrant symptoms of delusions, hallucinations, and flatness of affect to be "terminal phenomena" that belong to advanced cases only, Zilboorg wrote of the ambulatory schizophrenic as follows:

> These patients seldom reach the point at which hospitalization appears necessary either to the relatives or to the psychiatrist, and...they appear "to walk about life" like any other "normal" person—although they remain inefficient, peregrinatory, casual in their ties to things and to people...Such individuals remain more or less on the loose in the actual or figurative sense, outwardly and inwardly....
>
> Suffice it here to say that the shallowness of affect so conspicuous in the external aspects of the clinical picture should not be mistaken either for the absence of affect or for some special mysterious disturbance of what is called the "emotional sphere"....The emotion appears lacking in the schizophrenic only because that part of his personality which deals with external realities of life...play a minor role in his life. (1941, pp. 154–155)

Another early, yet formal, recognition of a stable, prepsychotic form of schizophrenia evolved in psychodiagnostic studies undertaken by Rapaport et al. (1945–1946, 1968). Searching for subgroups within the broad spectrum of clearly diagnosed schizophrenics, they identified an important patient population that they termed "preschizophrenics," described as follows:

> These were cases...whose adjustment was so precarious that schizophrenia-like withdrawal tendencies in the guise of anxiety and inhibition, or schizophrenialike ideational productions in the guise of obsessive-phobic thought, had already penetrated into their everyday life; thus any strain or stress could precipitate a schizophrenic psychosis, but under favorable conditions they might continue with such preschizophrenic behavior or ideation without an acute break. (1968, p. 57)

Of particular note was the subdivision of the preschizophrenic group into two categories, the "inhibited" (coarctated) type and the "overideational" type. They described these types as follows:

> [The preschizophrenic] group was subdivided into two categories. One of these, [the inhibited] was characterized by blocking, withdrawal, marked anxiety, feelings of strangeness, incompetence, extreme inhibition of affect and some kind of sexual preoccupation....The other group, [the overideational], was characterized by an enormous wealth of fantasy, obsessive ideation, obsessions and a preoccupation with themselves and their bodies; these subjects were intensely introspective and preoccupied with their own ideas. (1968, p. 58)

Although following similar lines of diagnostic assessment, Schafer concluded (1948) that clearer distinctions should be made among the preschizophrenic group; thus, he replaced the labels "coarctated" (inhibited) and "overideational," substituting in their stead the terms "schizoid character," "incipient schizophrenia," and "schizophrenic character." The schizoid was described briefly and possessed essentially the same features that are included under that designation in this text. The incipient form reflected what the term implies—behaviors, thoughts, and perceptions that suggest a psychotic break is imminent. Last, Schafer's notion of a schizophrenic character approached in certain details many of the symptoms incorporated in the DSM-III schizotypal personality syndrome. Taking as his guide Zilboorg's formulation of ambulatory schizophrenia, Schafer wrote:

> This diagnostic term is applied to those patients in whom a lifelong, insidious, and extensive development of schizophrenic disorganization has taken place, and in whom this development appears to have reached an essentially stable state, the schizophrenic mechanisms seeming to be integrated into the character make-up. There has been no acute break and there is no reason to anticipate a rapid process of deterioration. The classical secondary symptoms (hallucinations, delusions) are absent, but the primary disorders of thinking and affect are evident upon clinical examination. Usually the major diagnostic features are bizarre, impulsive acts which are fantastically and blandly rationalized, and wild flights of fancy, the products of which often remain indistinguishable from fact in the patient's mind. Phobic, obsessive-compulsive, psychopathic, and histrionic features may all merge in these cases. As a rule, the orderly front they put up is adequate for most routine or simple social situations. (1948, p. 86)

The concept of "latent schizophrenia," signifying the presence of "concealed" catatonic and paranoid symptoms, was first posited by Bleuler, but it was not brought to the fore as a potential diagnostic entity until so formulated in a paper by P. Federn (1947) and, later, in the concept of "latent psychosis" described by G. Bychowski (1953). Referred to as persons who cloak their deeper pathology under the guise of neurotic manifestations, latent schizophrenia "reveals itself by the patient's behavior and mannerisms, earlier than by his verbal productions" (Federn, 1947, p. 141). To Bychowski, the cardinal feature was the ease with which "primary processes" spilled into their thoughts and speech. Social communication was thereby often scattered, evidencing excesses in condensation and personal allusions. The "depressive" inclinations that Bychowski observed in these patients suggest that many may have been more typical of what we currently label "borderline personalities."

The superimposition of neurotic symptoms as a cloak for deeper schizophrenic processes was brought to its clearest and most articulate form by P. Hoch and P. Polatin (1949) in their formulation of "pseudoneurotic schizophrenia." Elaborating the concept in detail in later papers (Hoch and Cattell, 1959; Hoch et al., 1962), these investigators took pains to stress that the entity they described was a stable variant of schizophrenia, which, though occasionally precipitated into a clinical psychosis, more characteristically retained its distinctive features and "ambulatory" status over extended periods of time. Displaying a conglomeration of traits and clinical features that formed a unique constellation, the pseudoneurotic schizophrenic exhibited a variety of signs that both mimicked and dramatized classical neurotic symptomatology, as well as suggesting in a more subtle or less striking form the thought disorders and dysregulated emotions that typify clinical schizophrenia. In the first paper on the syndrome, Hoch and Polatin offered the following descriptive features as a basis for the diagnosis:

> Some inappropriate emotional connections ... are not rarely present, and a lack of modulation, of flexibility in emotional display is demonstrated. ... Many of these patients show the cold, controlled, and at the same time, hypersensitive reactions to emotional situations, usually over-emphasizing trivial frustrations and not responding to, or by-passing, major ones. At times lack of inhibition in displaying certain emotions is especially striking in otherwise markedly inhibited persons. ...
>
> From the diagnostic point of view the most important presenting symptom is what the writers call pan-anxiety and pan-neurosis. Many of these patients show, in contrast to the usual neurotic, an all-pervading anxiety structure which does not leave any life-approach of the person free from tension. ... In connection with this diffuse anxiety, a pan-neurosis is also present. The patients usually do not have one or two different neurotic manifestations, but all symptoms known in neurotic illness are often present at the same time. ...
>
> In all the writers' cases they observed that the patient usually told of a great many sexual preoccupations showing autoerotic, oral, anal homosexual and heterosexual tendencies. ...
>
> Quite a number of the patients with this pseudoneurotic symptomatology develop psychotic episodes which are, however, often of short duration. ... In these short-lived psychotic attacks (micro-psychosis) usually three elements appear simultaneously which are very significant. The patient expresses hypochondriacal ideas, ideas of reference, and feelings of depersonalization. They are often interlocked. (1949, pp. 250–253)

The specific term "schizotypal" was coined by S. Rado in a paper delivered in 1950 to the New York Academy of Medicine; this concept was briefly expanded in an address in 1953 to the American Psychiatric Association and further developed in several publications in 1956 and later. Conceiving the label as an abbreviation of "schizophrenic phenotype" (indicating its ostensive representation in overt form of an underlying hereditary predisposition or genotype), Rado specified the existence of two inherited defects, that of an "integrative pleasure deficiency" and a "proprioceptive diathesis." The following excerpt from an early paper details these defects and articulates their consequences with clinical clarity and astuteness:

> In general, *absence of sufficient pleasure* slows down and hinders psychodynamic integration. ... In particular, (1) it weakens the motivating power of the welfare emotions, such as pleasurable desire, joy, affection, love and pride; (2) it weakens the counter balancing effect ordinarily exerted by the welfare

emotions on the emergency emotions, thus allowing fears and rages to rise to excessive strength; (3) it reduces the coherence of the action-self, which is viewed as the highest integrative system of the organism, and the very basis of its self-awareness; (4) it undermines the schizotype's self-confidence and sense of security in relation to both himself and his social environment; (5) it makes the development of a well-integrated sexual function impossible; (6) it limits the schizotype's capacity for the appropriate enjoyment of his life activities, as well as for love and affectionate give and take in human relationships.

The *proprioceptive diathesis* further damages the composition of the action-self.... This two-fold impairment of the action-self appears to be the deepest root of the patient's tormenting lack of self-confidence and also, of his feeling that he is hopelessly different from other people. Furthermore, brittleness of the impaired action-self predisposes the patient to disintegrative breakdown marked by thought disorder. (1956, p. 226)

Referring to the efforts individuals make to compensate for their innate defects as "schizoadaptation," Rado stated that its success depends on the interplay of three reparative processes: the careful husbanding of the scarce pleasure capacity; the ability to shift the burden of adaptive tasks to others, despite ambivalent overdependency; and the adequacy with which non-emotional thoughts can replace limited pleasurable feelings. Rado did not see the schizotypal pattern as inevitably fixed but as an adaptive developmental process that can move forward and back between four stages: compensated, decompensated, disintegrated, and deteriorated. He described the stages and sequence as follows:

Compensated schizotypal behavior means that in favorable circumstances the schizotype may go through life without a breakdown.... In decompensated schizotypal behavior, "emergency dyscontrol" is marked by the production of inappropriate or excessive fears and rages. An attack of emergency dyscontrol is bound to break the compensatory system of adaptation and thus precipitate decompensation, characterized by what appears to be a scramble of phobic, obsessive, depressive, and still other overreactive mechanisms....

The stage of disintegrated schizotypal behavior is known as overt schizophrenic psychosis. Disorganization of his action-self has reduced the patient to adaptive incompetence, the disintegrative process resulting in thought disorder, activity disorder, and the like.... The process of schizotypal disintegration may go on for an indefinite period of time. There is, however, a chance of spontaneous remission, as well as a threat of progressive deterioration. Deteriorated schizotypal behavior is marked by a progressive cessation of function, a nearly complete withdrawal from the adaptive task. (1969, pp. 254-255)

Attracted by Rado's schizotypal formulation, P. Meehl (1962) constructed a brilliant, speculative theoretical model. Essentially, Meehl sought to articulate how an inherited "neural integrative defect," which he labeled "schizotaxia," evolved through "all known forms of social history" into the phenotypic personality organization that Rado termed the "schizotype." The reader is referred to Meehl's paper for his masterly neurologic–social-learning thesis. A brief quote summarizing his general theme will suffice here:

> I hypothesize that the statistical relation between schizotaxia, schizotypy, and schizophrenia is class inclusion: All schizotaxics become, *on all actually existing social learning regimens*, schizotypic in personality organization; but most of these remain compensated. A minority, disadvantaged by other (largely polygenically determined) constitutional weaknesses, and put on a bad regimen by schizophrenogenic mothers (most of whom are themselves schizotypes) are thereby potentiated into clinical schizophrenia. What makes schizotaxia etiologically specific is its role as a *necessary* condition. I postulate that a nonschizotaxic individual, whatever his other genetic makeup and whatever his learning history, would at most develop a character disorder or a psychoneurosis; but he would not become a schizotype and therefore could never manifest its decompensated form, schizophrenia. (1962, p. 832)

In line with the growing conviction that schizophrenia is genetically based yet possesses a variety of phenotypic forms depending on polygenic mixtures and environmental potentiators, S. Kety, D. Rosenthal, P. Wender, and F. Schulsinger (1968) set out to develop a strategy to "disentangle" genetic and environmental variables. Unsure of what clinical conditions the concept of schizophrenia actually subsumed, they reviewed its history and concluded that there were basically four variants that had been designated as either schizophrenia itself or as closely related to schizophrenia. They grouped these variants into what they spoke of as the "schizophrenic spectrum" since it was possible to align and differentiate them reasonably well on grounds such as clinical severity and chronicity. The first subcategory, termed "chronic schizophrenia," was seen to correspond to Kraepelin's initial formulation of dementia praecox, with its poor prepsychotic adjustment, progressive deterioration, and prominence of Bleuler's "primary" symptoms; this group is variously referred to as "true" and "process" schizophrenia in contemporary literature. The second group, labeled the "acute schizophrenic reaction," exhibited a good premorbid history, appeared to have been precipitated by external events into a rapid decompensation, was noted by Bleuler's more dramatic "secondary" symptoms, and had a good long-term prognosis. The third, or "borderline" schizophrenic, group is summarized in greater detail shortly since it best parallels the DSM-III schizotypal syndrome. The fourth, final, and most distal variant, whose location on the schizophrenic spectrum is questioned by some, received the label "inadequate personality"; more akin to the DSM-III schizoid than schizotypal personality, its historical ancestry and diagnostic features can be reviewed best by reference to Chapter 10. Returning to the borderline schizophrenic subgroup, Wender has summarized its essential characteristics as follows:

> [There is] a chronic history of psychological maladaptation with abnormalities in the following areas: (1) *Thinking*—strange, vague, illogical mentation

which tends to ignore reality, logic and experience, and results in poor adaptation to life experiences; (2) *Affective life*—characterized by "anhedonia," the inability to experience intense pleasure, so that the individuals report a history of never having been happy (although they may never have been seriously depressed); (3) *Interpersonal relations*—characterized by a tendency to polar opposites which may include either the absence of deep, intense involvement with other people or excessively "deep" and dependent involvement with others. There also exist possible difficulties in sexual adjustment which may be characterized by either a very low sexual drive or a promiscuous and chaotic pattern of sexual interaction; (4) *Psychopathology*—characterized not only by its intensity but by its lack of constancy with multiple neurotic manifestations that may shift frequently (obsessive concerns, phobias, conversion symptoms, psychosomatic symptoms, etc.); severe, widespread anxiety and occasionally short-lived episodes, designated as "micropsychotic," during which the individual experiences transient delusions, hallucinations, feelings of depersonalization or de-realization. The course of these disturbances tends to be lifelong, generally without deterioration, and the illnesses seem refractory to neuroleptic drugs. (1977, p. 112)

Drawing upon his theoretically based model of psychopathology (Millon, 1969), the author constructed a syndrome at the mid-level of personality severity based on the "detached" coping style. Labeled in the model as the "schizoid personality," it corresponds in the DSM-III to the new schizotypal syndrome. It was conceived in the theory as a more severe variant of the passively detached DSM-III schizoid and the actively detached DSM-III avoidant personalities. Although these two subtypes share many clinical features in common, important characteristics differentiate them, especially those associated with the experience and expression of affect and anxiety. As in the case of the DSM-III borderlines and paranoids, several subtypes of the schizotypal are expected since advanced dysfunctional personality patterns are seen as superimposed on less severe character types. The following descriptive text and criteria were conceived with these considerations in mind. They were written by the author in 1975 for the DSM-III personality subcommittee as the first working draft of what ultimately was labeled the "schizotypal" syndrome.

This pattern is typified by a marked deficit in social interest, a shunning of close interpersonal relationships, frequent behavioral eccentricities, non-delusional autistic thinking and depersonalization anxieties. There is a tendency to follow meaningless, idle and ineffectual lives, drifting aimlessly and remaining on the periphery of societal living. Some possess significant activation, affective and cognitive deficiencies, appearing listless, bland, unmotivated and obscure, only minimally connected to the external world. Others are anxiously tense and withdrawn, fearful and intentionally seclusive, inclined to damp down hypersensitivities and to disconnect from anticipated external threats.

An appraisal of personal background and history reveals both of the following:

1. Social attainment deficits (e.g., experienced serious, self-precipitated setbacks in scholastic, marital or vocational pursuits; repeated failure to maintain durable, satisfactory and secure roles consonant with age and aptitudes).

2. Periodic mini-psychotic episodes (e.g., experienced several brief and reversible periods in which either bizarre behaviors, extreme moods, irrational impulses or delusional thoughts were exhibited; short-lived breaks from "reality," however, are often recognized as peculiar or deviant).

Since adolescence or early adulthood at least 3 of the following have been present to a notably greater degree than in most people and were not limited to discrete periods nor necessarily prompted by stressful life events.

1. Social detachment (e.g., prefers life of isolation with minimal personal attachments and obligations; has drifted over time into increasingly peripheral social and vocational roles).

2. Behavioral eccentricity (e.g., exhibits frequent odd or peculiar habits; is perceived by others as unobtrusively strange or different).

3. Non-delusional autistic thinking (e.g., social communication interspersed with personal irrelevancies, obscurities and tangential asides; appears self-absorbed and lost in daydreams with occasional blurring of fantasy and reality).

4. Either (a) Anxious wariness (e.g., reports being hypersensitive, apprehensively ill-at-ease, particularly in social encounters; is guarded, suspicious of others and secretive in behavior) or (b) Emotional flatness (e.g., manifests a drab, sluggish, joyless, and spiritless appearance; reveals marked deficiencies in activation and affect).

5. Disquieting estrangement (e.g., reports periods of depersonalization, derealization and dissociation; experiences anxious feelings of emptiness and meaninglessness.

The final text and criteria for the syndrome were based on a study carried out and reported by Spitzer, Endicott, and Gibbon (1979) to clarify distinctions that might be drawn between what were then tentatively termed in the deliberations of the DSM-III Task Force as the "Unstable (Borderline)" and "Schizotypal" personalities. Following guidelines established earlier by relevant Task Force members, Spitzer et al. consulted other theorists and researchers at work in the field for further advice toward the goal of constructing two subsets of potentially discriminating criterion item lists. Although procedures for data gathering, analyzing, and cross-validating these criterion sets were carried out with exceptional diligence, the final item lists were found to highly correlate when utilized with a heterogeneous patient population. However, within a select group of more disturbed or dysfunctional patients, borderline and schizotypal item subsets did show a high degree of independence. The data of these studies—though far from fully convincing either clinically, methodologically, or statistically—provided sufficient "hard" evidence to justify separating the two syndromes and to utilize their respective item lists as inclusion criteria for the DSM-III.

CLINICAL PICTURE

Although important distinctions exist among subvariants of the schizotypal syndrome, they do share a number of features, and it is these to which attention is directed in the following four sections. Some points characterizing these subtypes are noted; a more detailed discussion of these differentiations is postponed until the "associated disorders" section.

Behavioral Features

Some schizotypals are aloof and isolated and behave in a bland and apathetic manner since they experience few pleasures and have need to avoid few discomforts. It would appear, then, that they should have little reason to acquire instrumental behaviors. Why then would they develop superstitions, referential ideas, and illusions, and engage at times in frenetic activity and vigorous coping? In essence, these "passive" schizotypals have enough awareness of the fruits of life to realize that other people do experience joy, sorrow, and excitement, whereas they, by contrast, are empty and barren. They desire *some* relatedness, *some* sensation, and *some* feeling that they are part of the world about them. Although avoiding more than they can handle comfortably, they also feel considerable discomfort with less than they need, especially since less brings them close to nothing. Their recurrent illusions, their magical and telepathic thinking, and their ideas of reference may be viewed as a coping effort to "fill the spaces of their "emptiness," the feeling that they are "going under" and are bereft of all life and meaning.

Other schizotypals more actively control expressions of intense affect since they fear being humiliated and rejected. They are inexpressive and socially isolated for protective reasons. Their constricted affect and interpersonal reserve do not arise because of intrinsic emotional or social deficits but because they have bound their feelings and relationships to protect against the possibility of rebuff. Alienated from others and themselves, they too may sense the terror of impending nothingness and of a barren, depersonalized, and nonexistent self. Such feelings prompt them also to engage in bizarre behaviors, beliefs, and perceptions that enable them to "reaffirm reality." It is for this reason among others that we observe the ideas of reference, the clairvoyance, the illusions, and the "strange" ideation that typify the schizotypal.

Self-Descriptions and Complaints

The deficient or disharmonious affect of schizotypals deprives them of the capacity to experience events as something other than flat and lifeless phenomena. They suffer a sense of vapidness in a world of cold and washed-out objects. Moreover, schizotypals feel themselves to be more dead than alive, insubstantial, foreign, and disembodied. As existential phenomenologists might put it, they are threatened by "nonbeing." Detached observers of the passing scene, these patients remain uninvolved, looking from the outside not only with regard to others but with regard to themselves as well. Many pathological personalities experience periods of inner void and social detachment, but the feeling of estrangement and depersonalization is an ever-present and insistent feature of the schizotypal's everyday existence. This persistent detachment and disavowal of self distinguishes the unreal and meaningless quality of their lives and gives rise to a frightening sense of emptiness and nothingness. As already noted, the schizotypal may be overwhelmed by the dread of total disintegration, implosion, and non-existence—feelings that are countered by imposing or constructing new worlds of self-made reality, an idiosyncratic reality composed of superstitions, suspicions, illusions, and so on. The more severe attacks of depersonalization may precipitate wild psychotic episodes, irrational outbursts in which these patients frantically search to build a sense of reality to fill their vacant existence.

Inferred Intrapsychic Dynamics

Schizotypals are often faced with excess, rather than deficit, stimulation. This is likely to occur when social demands and expectations press hard against their preferred uninvolved or withdrawn state. Unable to avoid such external impositions, some schizotypals may react either by "blanking out," drifting off into another world, or by paranoid or aggressive outbursts. Undue encroachments upon their complacent world may lead them to disconnect socially for prolonged periods, during which they may be confused and aimless, display inappropriate affect and paranoid thinking, and communicate in odd, circumstantial, and metaphorical ways. At other times, when external pressures may be especially acute, they may react with a massive and psychotic outpouring of primitive impulses, delusional thoughts, hallucinations, and bizarre behaviors. Many schizotypals have stored up intense repressed anxieties and hostilities throughout their lives. Once released, these feelings burst out in a rampaging flood. The backlog of suspicions, fears, and animosities has been ignited and now explodes in a frenzied cathartic discharge.

Interpersonal Coping Style

When motivated or prompted to relate to others, schizotypals are frequently unable to orient their thoughts logically, and they become lost in personal irrelevancies and in tangential asides that seem vague, digressive, and with no pertinence to the topic at hand. They are "out of touch" with others and are unable to order their ideas in terms relevant to reciprocal, social communication. This pervasive disjunctiveness, this scattered, circumstantial, and autistic feature of their thinking, only further alienates them from others.

The social achievements of the typical schizotypal usually indicate an erratic course in which the person has failed to make normal progress. School and work histories show marked deficits and irregularities, given their intellectual capacities as a base. Not only are they frequent "drop outs," but they tend to drift from one job to another and are often separated or divorced, if they ever married. Their deficits in achievement competence derive from and, in part, contribute to their social anxieties and feelings of unworthiness. Moreover, there is a listlessness and a lack of spontaneity, ambition, and interest in life. Schizotypals are able to talk about only a few relatively tangible matters, usually those things that demand their immediate attention. If they do sustain a conversation, they may press it beyond the appropriate or suitable, digressing into highly personal, odd, or metaphorical topics. More commonly, they lack the spark to initiate action or to participate socially, seemingly enclosed and trapped by some force that blocks them from responding to and empathizing with others. This inability to take hold of life, to become a member of a "real" society, and to invest one's energies and interests in a world of others, lies at the heart of their pathology.

ASSOCIATED DISORDERS

As in the prior two chapters, the focus here is concentrated on personalities that most frequently covary with the syndrome under review. Brief attention is given both to the schizotypal's concomitant Axis I symptom disorders and to points of differential diagnosis.

Concomitant Axis I Symptoms

Although schizotypals occasionally exhibit a wide range of DSM-III anxiety, somatoform, and dissociative disorders, these are touched upon only in passing as the chapter progresses. Primary interest is directed to the more severe, psychotic-level schizophrenic disturbances to which the schizotypal is especially prone.

Disorganized schizophrenic disorders. Particularly subject to disorganized (hebephrenic) schizophrenic disorders, schizotypals are identifiable by their incongruous and fragmented behaviors. At these times they seem totally disoriented and confused, unclear as to time, place, and identity. Many will exhibit posturing, grimacing, inappropriate giggling, and peculiar mannerisms. Speech tends to ramble into "word salads" composed of incoherent neologisms and a chaotic mishmash of irrelevancies. Ideas are colored with fantasy, illusion, and hallucination, and scattered with bizarre and fragmentary delusions that have no apparent logic or function. Regressive acts such as soiling and wetting are not uncommon, and these patients often consume food in an infantile or ravenous manner.

Catatonic schizophrenia and schizophreniform episodes. These latter episodes will occur when the tide of unconscious anxieties and impulses surges forward and these patients sink rapidly into a hazy world of fleeting and dreamlike impressions. Subjective moods and images become fused with, and ultimately dominate, objective realities. Overt behaviors are distorted and guided by primary process thinking and thereby appear purposeless, disjointed, irrational, stereotyped, and bizarre. There is a disunity and disorganization to speech and communication. Ideas are conveyed in an inchoate or jumbled fashion, reflecting delusions that are projected onto the world in hallucinatory perceptions. Controls are abandoned and random emotions break loose. No seeming purpose exists to their behaviors, other than the ventilation of momentary impulses. Unable to grasp reality or coordinate feelings and thoughts, these schizotypals may regress into a totally helpless catatonic invalidism.

Residual schizophrenia. In the residual schizophrenic state, bizarre thoughts and emotions churn close to the surface but are managed and held in check by the schizotypal. However, should these feelings overpower the patient's tenuous controls, particular disorders are likely to occur, such as hebephrenic states or brief schizophreniform episodes. These latter episodes tend to be characterized by a mixture of terror and fury. In less severe reactions, we observe more terror than fury; violence usually is controlled or neutralized. In more extreme cases, a full-fledged catatonic excitement may emerge, with unconscious impulses rising to the foreground and producing the turbulent picture that typifies these disorders. These eruptions often are useful safety valves. By discharging hidden and pent-up feelings, the schizotypal's cumulative tensions subside temporarily. For a brief period, these patients can vent emotions that they would not dare express in the course of their everyday life. Chaotic and aberrant as they appear, and as they are, these outbursts serve an adaptive function.

Concurrent Axis II Personalities

Research (Millon, 1977) and theory (Millon, 1969) suggest that the schizotypal syndrome covaries most frequently with the *schizoid* and *avoidant* personalities. It would appear from this work that the schizotypal pattern develops insidiously until it becomes an integral but more dysfunctional coping style that supersedes one of the two less severe personality types. Hence, what we observe clinically in the schizotypal is a mixture of its own constellation of traits superimposed upon either the passively detached schizoid style or the actively detached avoidant style. The following sections detail some of the more distinctive clinical features of these two sets of personality combinations; the concluding section addresses the characteristics of those schizotypals who continue to regress to a decompensated form.

Schizotypal-schizoid mixed personality. Notably insensitive to feelings, these individuals often experience a separation between their thoughts and their physical body. There is a strange sense of nonbeing or nonexistence, as if their floating conscious awareness carried with it a depersonalized or identityless human form. Behaviorally, these personalities tend to be drab, sluggish, and inexpressive. They possess a marked deficit in affectivity and appear bland, indifferent, unmotivated, and insensitive to the external world. Cognitive processes seem obscure, vague, and tangential. They are either impervious to, or miss the shades of, interpersonal and emotional experience. Social communications are responded to minimally or with inappropriate affect or peculiar ideas, or in a circumstantial and confused manner. Speech is often monotonous, listless, or inaudible. Most people consider them to be unobtrusive and strange persons who drift on the periphery of life or who fade into the background, self-absorbed, wool gathering, and lost to the outside world.

The schizotypal-schizoid will occasionally experience the awesome terror of feeling "dead," nonexistent, petrified. Detached from the world and insensitive to their own feelings, these patients may become terrified by a frightening sense of "nothingness," of passing through a barren, cold, lifeless existence. The disaster of losing "self," of becoming a walking automaton, a petrified object without meaning or purpose, may overwhelm these patients, driving them into a bizarre psychotic state in which they create "tangible" illusions to which they can relate, self-referential ideas that give them a significance they otherwise lack, bizarre telepathic powers that enable them to communicate with mythical or distant others—all in a desperate effort to reaffirm their existence in reality. Sinking into a lifeless void, they catch themselves, struck by a sense of becoming a thing and not a being. This dread, this catastrophic sense of nothingness, causes them to grasp at anything, real or fantasied, by which they can convince themselves that they do, in fact, exist. On the brink of feeling totally annihilated, they struggle desperately to confirm their being, clinging tenaciously to whatever meaning and feeling they can find in or impute to their surroundings. As in their "pure" schizotypal counterpart, these eccentricities are attempts to forestall the void of oblivion and nothingness.

These schizotypals occasionally succumb to psychotic disorders when faced with too much, rather than too little, stimulation. Painfully uncomfortable with social obligations or personal closeness, they will feel encroached upon if pressed into responsibilities beyond their limited tolerance. During these periods, schizotypal-schizoids may either explode, bursting into frenetic activity to block the intrusions forced upon them, or simply "fade out," become blank, lose conscious awareness and "turn off" the pressures of the outer world.

Schizotypal-avoidant mixed personality. As with their pure "avoidant" counterparts, these personalities are restrained, isolated, apprehensive, guarded, and shrinking. Protectively, they seek to "kill" their feelings and desires, bind their impulses, and withdraw from social encounters, thereby defending themselves from the pain and anguish of interpersonal relationships. The surface apathy and seeming indifference of these patients is not, as it is in the schizotypal-schizoid, owing to an intrinsic lack of sensitivity but to their attempt to restrain, damp down, or deaden excessive sensitivity. In addition to their social isolation, schizotypal-avoidants depreciate their self-worth. There is an abandonment of self and a disowning and remoteness from feeling and desire. The "real" selves of these personalties have been devalued and demeaned, split off, cast asunder, and rejected as humiliating or valueless. Not only are these schizotypals alienated from others, then, but they find no refuge and comfort in turning to themselves. Their isolation is twofold. So little is gained from others, and only a despairing sense of shame is found within themselves. Without the rewards of self or others to spur them, they drift into personal apathy and social isolation. Having little hope of gaining affection and security, schizotypal-avoidants learn that it is best to deny real feelings and aspirations. Cognitive processes are intentionally confused in an effort to disqualify and discredit rational thinking. In their stead are substituted fantasy worlds that might provide some respite from the anguish of realistic thought. But these, too, hold brief interest since the outer world keeps intruding and "shames" these patients back to reality.

Disharmonious affects, irrelevant and tangential thoughts, and an increasingly severe social bankruptcy develop as schizotypal-avoidants are forced to build an ever-tighter armor around themselves. Their characteristic eccentricities derive from this wall of isolation and insularity that they have constructed. Like the schizotypal-schizoid, they are subject to the devastating terror of "nothingness," the feeling of imminent nonexistence. By insulating themselves, shrinking their world, and deadening their sensitivities, they have laid the groundwork for feeling emptiness and unreality. To counter the anxieties of depersonalization and derealization, they may be driven into excited and bizarre behaviors, contrive peculiar and hallucinating images, and shout utterly unintelligible but beseeching sounds, all in an effort to draw attention and affirm their existence as living beings. They may manuever irrationally just to evoke a response from others, simply create a stir to prove that they are real and not a mirage of empty, floating automatons such as they sense themselves to be. Failing in this effort to quiet their anxieties, as is likely, they may turn to a "make-believe" world of superstitions, magic, and telepathy—anything that they can fashion from their imagination that will provide them with a "pseudocommunity" of fantasied persons and objects to which they can safely relate.

Schizotypal-avoidant personalities are most likely to be precipitated into a frank psychotic disorder when confronted with painful humiliation and derogation from others. Although they have sought by active withdrawal and isolation to minimize their social contacts, this coping defense is not impenetrable. Should their armor be pierced and their protective detachment assaulted and encroached upon, they will not only experience the anguish of the present but will have reactivated within them the painful memories of past assaults. Under these pressures, the schizotypal-avoidant may burst into a flood of erratic, hostile, and bizarre reactions. Fearful lest they be further humiliated and injured, and unable to govern the onrush of previously repressed anxieties and angers, these patients may lose all controls and be drowned in a wave of chaotic and primitive impulses. Thus, at the moment their external world inundates them, their inner world erupts. What we see is a frantic struggle to escape beings smothered and submerged.

The following MCMI (Millon, 1977) computer-generated printout reflects the responses of a 58-year-old veteran who had been hospitalized numerous times for psychiatric disabilities. Classified a "chronic undifferentiated schizophrenic" for many years, his personality pattern and level of severity appear closest to the schizotypal-avoidant combination. This personality amalgam is common among chronic schizophrenics and is found with considerable frequency in settings that care for such individuals.

This patient's behavior is typified by an intensely apprehensive mistrust of others and a tendency to withdraw from social encounters. Behavioral eccentricities, magical thinking, illusions, and depersonalization anxieties are evident occasionally. He has become a detached observer of the passing scene, increasingly isolated from others and from sources of potential growth and gratification. Desires for closeness and affection are present but are self-protectively denied or restrained. The patient avoids as many social and personal obligations as possible without incurring further condemnation. Any commitment to others constitutes a potential threat to his fragile hold on reality. A suspiciousness, recurrent social anxieties, and a pervasive mood disharmony characterize his emotional life. Extended periods of solitude are interspersed with feelings of emptiness and depersonalization.

The tendency to be overly concerned with social rebuff is intensified by ideas of reference and an inclination to perceive events in line with anticipated rejection. The patient often feels persecuted, humiliated, and disparaged by others. There is notable lack of initiative, a self-effacement of aptitudes, and a general avoidance of autonomous behaviors. Despite strong desires to relate and be accepted, he denies these needs and maintains a safe measure of interpersonal distance. In order to forestall further rejection he is noncompetitive, behaves submissively, and depreciates personal self-worth. The patient may assume a passive interpersonal role, accepting whatever support can be found and willingly submitting to the demands of others to fulfill a modicum of dependency needs. Almost totally dependent on nurturant persons or institutions, he has assumed increasingly ineffectual social and vocational roles. There may be a tendency to follow a meaningless and idle life, drifting aimlessly and remaining on the periphery of life.

This patient's self-image is that of weakness, fragility, and ineffectuality. Ordinary stresses and responsibilities are experienced as excessively demanding. The passive life-style and behavioral sluggishness may be deceptive, however, overlying anger, anxiety, and depression that he goes to great pains to restrain and control. Similarly, surface appearances of affective blandness may cover an emotional dysphoria, a constant undercurrent of tension, sadness, and rage. He frequently appears self-absorbed, lost in daydreams, with occasional blurrings of fantasy and reality. Personal irrelevancies, odd speech, and tangential asides are common since he appears unable to order his ideas in ways relevant to reciprocal, social communication. Intentional cognitive interference may be attempted in his effort to disqualify and discredit rational thoughts and the distressful elements they contain. To counteract the effects of self-reflection, he may flatten emotionally tinged experiences, that is, suppress and dilute events that stir disturbing memories and feelings. These defensive efforts preclude behaviors that could lead to a more socially rewarding life-style. Also self-defeating is the persistent self-depreciation of aptitudes and competencies. His scattered, suspicious, and occasional autistic thinking only further alienates others. The affective unresponsiveness, bizarreness, and withdrawal behaviors lead others to view him as a peculiar and disconnected person. All of these factors contribute to the maintenance of his detached, socially anxious, and ineffectual pattern.

Decompensated schizotypal personality.   Though the clinical appearance of decompensated schizotypals is clearly more deteriorated than their less severe counterparts, they still retain many of the same features. The lack of social relatedness remains among the most striking characteristics. Cognitive processes are even more markedly disorganized, evidencing both bizarre and fragmented qualities. Speech is almost invariably tangential and incoherent, tending to be scattered with neologisms mixed into rambling "word salads." Behavior is extremely eccentric and spotted with peculiar mannerisms and automatisms. Affect either is totally lacking, creating a drab and flat appearance, or is characterized by inappropriateness and incongruity. Hallucinations and delusions have become quite common, though often fleeting and scattered. Connections among passing events and thoughts become either vague or overinvolved. Social communication loses its focus and wanders into generalities and abstractions, the significance of which is difficult to grasp. Sequences of ideas become disjointed and fragmented. Metaphorical or stereotyped phrases may be endlessly repeated. Seemingly random thoughts become fused, creating neologisms that may be thrown together in disconnected sentences. Delusions and hallucinations tend to be loosely structured and transitory, in contrast to the more logical, ingrained, and systematized delusional belief of paranoid personalities. These unsystematized delusions and perceptions are typically dissolved and forgotten almost as readily as they were formed. Some seem to "stick," however, although they never attain the logic and coherence of paranoid beliefs.

The chaotic thought processes of decompensated schizotypals are not wholly meaningless. Their irrational quality stems from the fact that internal images become mixed in a rather chancelike manner with unrelated environmental events. Lacking cognitive control, schizotypals allow stimuli from divergent origins to flow together into a common stream, resulting in odd perceptions, disjointed behaviors, and incoherent verbalizations. By abandoning their cognitive controls, they have lost choice and selectivity. The hierarchy of relevance and suitability that differentiated among stimuli and responses has been leveled. Everything seems to have equal impact, and all responses have an equal probability of expression. Unable to scan the environment selectively and unable to distinguish the salient from the irrelevant, their thoughts become scattered and disorganized, a potpourri of fragmented delusions, transitory hallucinations, and obscure and circumstantial talk. As decompensated schizotypals succumb further, they jettison all traces of pride and control, abandoning whatever social amenities and facades they may have previously acquired. Most strikingly, they lose touch with the meaning and structure of social behavior and with the form and syntax of language and communication. Their actions and verbalizations are invariably peculiar and idiosyncratic. The styles and rules of interpersonal relations mystify them, and they seem puzzled by the sequence and purpose of social discourse and the reciprocal pattern of person-to-person interaction. Unable to make sense out of their environment, they perceive reality as unreal, a game whose moves are made by unseen hands in accord with strange and unfathomable regulations. The person has become a "nonbeing in the world." Perplexed and bewildered, such patients are unable to grasp the significance of what surrounds them and feel doomed to wander in an alien and frightening environment. They feel homeless, estranged nonparticipants at the mercy of enigmatic, capricious, and hazardous powers. Standing alone, they are not only confused but devoid of the means to mitigate their despair and their dread of the strange and ominous forces that surround them.

The social estrangement of decompensated schizotypals is paralleled by an equally terrifying estrangement from themselves. As noted earlier, these patients often seek to destroy, disarrange, or clutter their thoughts and memories. They may have purposely made their behavior incongruous, jumbled their ideas, and swung from one mood to another without rhyme or reason. By successfully interfering with "real" thinking and feeling, they may have protected themselves from the anguish it produced. Unfortunately, several equally disturbing consequences result from this purposeful self-disjunction. Observing his/her own behavior, the patient now sees something foreign: a strange, unknown, and peculiar being, a frightening and unpredictable creature that the person cannot recognize. Both participant and spectator, the patient observes his/her own self with terror. These personalities cannot match what now emanates from themselves with what they know to have been themselves. They look on aghast, unable to control the impulses, bizarre grimaces, and strange outbursts that emerge from within them. Some alien force must reside within, some power that causes them to act as they do. This body and these behaviors surely cannot be theirs. Try as they may, however, these patients cannot escape the fright of self-awareness. Separation from self must be total. They must disown themselves, not only their feelings and thoughts but their total being. It is at this point of self-abandonment that the schizotypal patient disintegrates into a final and profoundly severe personality pattern.

Differential Diagnostic Signs

Only a few points are noted in this last of the differential diagnostic sections. The major considerations relevant to distinguishing among similar syndromes have been recorded several times in earlier chapters. Thus, given the multiaxial system of the DSM-III, the schizotypal designation may be diagnosed concurrently with any number of Axis I and Axis II disorders.

Differential concerns should be few. The schizotypal syndrome is a chronic and pervasive life-style that exhibits and subsumes a wide constellation of Axis I features that may be diagnosed as separate symptoms when they are found singly or for brief time periods. Thus, *depersonalization disorder,* so intrinsic a part of the schizotypal syndrome, would be independently diagnosed if there were no covariant patient symptoms such as social isolation, suspiciousness, or a host of eccentricities of thought, perception, and behavior.

Various *schizophrenic disorders* may be seen concomitantly with the schizotypal syndrome, an expected covariance given the theoretical and empirical basis for constructing the personality syndrome in the first place. A major issue, one more of nosologic consistency than substantive discrimination, is the separation of *schizophrenia: residual type* from schizotypal personality. The diagnostic criteria are highly similar. However, "residual" is to be employed only if a prior psychotic episode has occurred. Since schizotypals ostensibly experience transient psychotic episodes, usually those of a schizophrenic nature, then it would appear that they always must coexist multiaxially—except before the schizotypal's first schizophrenic episode. So be it.

PREDISPOSING BACKGROUND

As noted in earlier chapters, it is the author's contention that personality patterns evolve from a complex interaction of biogenic and psychogenic factors. Prior descriptions of personality syndromes have sought, albeit too briefly, to identify the most probable combinations of influence that contribute to these psychopathologies. Among the more significant factors were heredity, constitutional dispositions; stimulation at sensitive periods of neurological maturation; parental feelings, communications, and methods of behavioral control; and the individual's own self-defeating attitudes, behaviors, and coping strategies. In the following sections these influences are grouped as done in Chapters 12 and 13, focusing on background features that characterize the two major variants of the schizotypal syndrome, the schizotypal-schizoid (passively detached style) and the schizotypal-avoidant (actively detached style). In addition, special attention is given to the deterioration process that takes form in a decompensated schizotypal pattern.

Schizotypal-schizoid personality etiology. These passively oriented schizotypals may be unfortunate carriers of a defective family inheritance. There are some data supporting the contention that genetic factors conducive to affective and cognitive deficits underlie the eccentricities of many of these personalities. Although families do "breed" the characteristics of the schizo-typal-schizoid, it is difficult to conceptualize the nature of the genetic mechanisms involved or even to state unequivocally that such mechanisms do in fact operate. Families may very well "breed" this pattern through interpersonal experience and not through biological inheritance at all. Among other biogenic factors that may be conducive to the development of this schizotypal is a passive infantile pattern, which may initiate a sequence of impoverished stimulation and parental indifference. Also possible, though speculative, are anatomic deficits or neurochemical dysfunctions in either reticular, limbic, sympathetic, or synaptic control systems, resulting in diminished activation, minimal pleasure-pain sensibilities, and cognitive dysfunctions.

Those hindered in early life with constitutional insensitivities often experience marked stimulus impoverishment during their "oral," or sensory-attachment stage. This may set in motion an underdeveloped biophysical substrate for affectivity and deficient learning of social attachment behaviors. Other experiential factors of note are family atmospheres of indifference, impassivity, or formality, which may provide models for imitative learning and thereby establish the roots for lifelong patterns of social reticence, interpersonal insensitivity, and discomfort with personal affection and closeness. Family styles of fragmented and amorphous communication may also contribute. Thus, exposure to disjointed, vague, and pointless interactions may give rise to the development, not only of inner cognitive confusions, but to unfocused, irrelevant, and tangential interpersonal relations. Experiences paralleling those of early childhood are often repeated and cumulative. In addition, stereotypes of the child's early "character" often take firm root, shape subsequent social attitudes, and preclude any changes in interpersonal style. Problematic relationships of this nature often get caught in a web of reciprocally destructive reactions, which then only aggravate earlier maladaptive tendencies.

Often overlooked among processes that perpetuate the individual's initial experiences are his or her own behaviors and coping styles. In the developmental background of schizotypal-schizoids, the following appear to be especially self-defeating: affective deficits that "flatten" emotional experiences and perceptual insensitivities and cognitive obscurities that blur distinctions among events that might otherwise enhance and enrich their lives. As a consequence, opportunities for realizing stimulating and varied experiences, so necessary to alter the characteristically apathetic state, are precluded or diluted. To add further insult to these injuries, the early passive and cognitively insensitive behaviors of schizotypal-schizoids make them unattractive and unrewarding social companions. Unable to communicate with either affect or clarity, they likely were shunned, overlooked, and invited to share few of the more interesting experiences to which others were drawn. Failing to interchange ideas and feelings with others, they remained fixed and undeveloped, continuing therefore in their disjointed, amorphous, and affectless state. Restricted in their social experiences, they acquired few social skills, found it increasingly difficult to relate socially, and perpetuated a vicious circle that not only fostered their isolated life but accentuated their social inadequacies and cognitive deficiencies.

Alienated from others and marginal members of society, schizotypal-schizoids turned increasingly to solitary thoughts. Over time, shared social behaviors became fully subordinate to private fantasy. In solitude their thoughts were left to wander unchecked by the logic and control of reciprocal social communication and activity. What they found within themselves was hardly rewarding, a barren, colorless void that offered no basis for joyful fantasy. Their inner personal world proved to be as "dead" and ungratifying as objective reality. They had no choice, so it seemed, but to turn to "unreal" fantasies. These, at least, might fill in the void and give their existence some substance. Interest moved toward the mystical and magical, to "needed" illusions and ideation that enabled the person to become a central, rather than a peripheral and insignificant figure.

Schizotypal-avoidant personality etiology.

There is evidence that these individuals have a family history of apprehensive or cognitively "muddled" relatives, suggesting the possibility that genetic dispositions may be operative. A fearful infantile pattern was not uncommon in this personality, often precipitating parental exasperation and rejection. Some have evidenced an irregular sequence of maturation, resulting in the development of an imbalance among competencies, an inability to handle excess emotionality, and the emergence of social peculiarities. The possibility of an underlying excess in limbic and sympathetic system reactivity, or a neurochemical acceleration of synaptic transmission, likewise may be posited. Dysfunctions such as these could give rise to the hypersensitivity and cognitive "flooding" that characterize these patients.

Many schizotypal-avoidants were exposed to an early history of deprecation, rejection, and humiliation, resulting in feelings of low self-esteem and a marked distrust of interpersonal relations. Others may have been subjected to belittlement, censure, and ridicule, not only from parents but also from sibs and peers. During the sensory-attachment phase of development they may have been treated in a harsh and unwelcoming fashion, thereby learning protectively to keep distance from their environment and to insulate their feelings. Ridicule from others in response to their efforts during the sensorimotor-autonomy stage may have led to feelings of personal incompetence and low self-worth. A further consequence of these experiences is that the children learn not only to avoid the appraisals of others but to demean themselves as persons as well. Continuation into the intracortical-initiative stage only intensifies feelings of low self-esteem and increases self-critical attitudes. Future schizotypal-avoidants now devalue, censure, and belittle themselves as others had in the past. Some are subjected to deprecation and humiliation at the hands of their adolescent peers. Social alienation, heterosexual failure, and minimal vocational and competitive success during this period add further insults to the earlier injuries.

Unfortunately, the coping strategies acquired by schizotypal-avoidants to fend off the pain of life fostered rather than resolved their difficulties. In an effort to minimize their awareness of external discomfort, they turned inward to fantasy and rumination, but this also proved to be self-defeating. Not only were their inner conflicts intense, but they spent much of their reflective time reliving and duplicating the painful events of the past. Their protective efforts only reinforced their distress. Moreover, given their low self-esteem, their inner reflections often took the form of self-reproval. Not only did they fail to gain solace from themselves, but they found that they could not readily escape from their own thoughts of self-derogation, from feelings of personal worthlessness and the futility of being themselves. In an effort to counter these oppressive inner thoughts, they may have sought to block and destroy their cognitive clarity, that is, to interfere with the anguish of their discordant inner emotions and ideas. This maneuver not only proved self-defeating, in that it diminished their ability to deal with events rationally, but it further estranged them from communicating effectively with others. Even more destructive, self-reproval and cognitive interference alienated them from their own existence. Having no place to go, they began to create a new, inner world, one populated by "magical" fantasies, illusions, telepathic relationships, and other odd thoughts that would provide them not only with an existence but one that was more significant and potentially rewarding than that found in reality.

Decompensated schizotypal personality etiology. Why does the schizoypal deteriorate further? Certainly these patients have had little reason to face reality, a life full of anguish and humiliation. Having failed repeatedly to cope with their adversity, they had no option but to withdraw, "tune out" reality and reduce contact with events that evoked nothing but shame and agony. At first, they sought this respite from painful reality. Unchecked by social judgment, their fantasies had free rein to salve their wounds. These reveries often blurred into a dreamlike state, lost any organization, and became fragmented, discontinuous, and ephemeral. Despite its usefulness in blocking reality, the patients found that their dream world was not a haven but a nightmare. Whatever meaning they drew from these reveries reminded them of their misery, of past misfortunes, and of having become nothing but failures, humiliated nonentities bereft of status and hope. Their inner personal world proved no less painful than that of reality. Faced with the pain of being themselves, they turned away, not only from others but also from their own being. But this was no simple task. This effort, like so many that preceded it, proved a further undoing. Trapped in the web of self-made confusions, they could not gain a clear focus and could not organize themselves to find some meaningful purposes to their existence. Ultimately, they began to sink into an abyss of nothingness, an estrangement from both the outer world and subjective self.

It is evident from the preceding that the emergence of the decompensated schizotypal pattern is a progressive and insidious process. The kernel was set in place in childhood and developed into manifest clinical form through imperceptible steps. It is not necessary to elaborate each step in the developmental sequence preceding the final pattern.

At this final stage, external events are seen as a distant screen upon which phantoms move in a strange and purposeless automaticity. Voices appear to emanate from alien sources, creating a muted cacophony of obscure and bewildering sounds. A visual fog descends, enshrouding the patient's eyes and ears, dampening the senses and giving events a shadowy, pantomimic quality. Inner thoughts are no more articulate or meaningful. Within the self is a boundless region of fantasy, delusion, inchoate images, and sensations. An unanchored and rudderless ship in a whirling sea, the patient drifts without a compass, hither any yon, buffeted by waves of past memories and future illusions. Dreams, reality, past, and present, a potpourri of random pieces merge and are then dismembered. To these patients, their own physical presence is foreign, a detached corpse. They sense themselves floating, a disembodied mind filled with fleeting, disconnected, jumbled, and affectless impressions. There is a frightening collapse of meaning and existence as the very sense of life is lost.

PROGNOSTIC CONSIDERATIONS

The future of the schizotypal syndrome is perhaps the least promising of all personality types. This section briefly summarizes factors that contribute toward the downward progression. A few words concerning remedial approaches are also included.

Perpetuation of the Schizotypal Pattern

The final spiral to deterioration usually occurs only after repeated or prolonged periods of hospitalization. Among the experiences that foster this deterioration are those of *social isolation* and *dependency training*. Both can be consequences of troublesome family environments or understaffed hospital systems.

Schizotypals who are segregated from social contact, "kept at home," or (if institutionalized) allowed to drift into "back" wards without encouragement to relate to friends, relatives, fellow patients, or staff, will inevitably deteriorate with the passage of time. Social confinement not only perpetuates but intensifies deficits in cognitive organization and social skills. Under continued stimulus and social deprivation, these patients will lose what competencies they may have had formerly.

Perhaps no less damaging is an excess in "protective" care, a tendency to patronize and coddle the patient. Though schizotypal patients often become social invalids, they will not regain normal skills and responsibilities if they are exposed to a regimen of inadvertent dependency training. Extreme devotion to their welfare may be of great value, but it may do them an ultimate disservice. Schizotypals who relinquish their former activities and restrict themselves to the directives of family members or hospital personnel may learn to lean too much on others and not enough on themselves. Prolonged guidance and shielding of this kind may lead to a progressive impoverishment of competencies and self-motivation, and result in a total helplessness. Under such ostensibly "good" regimens, schizotypals will be reinforced to learn dependency and apathy.

Other factors, which stem from the patient's own behavior, will foster further personality deterioration. Thus, it is not only through neglect or mismanagement that schizotypals experience decreased social contact. As noted earlier, to protect themselves from painful humiliation and rejection, they have learned to withdraw from reality and disengage themselves from social life. Even though exposed to active and inviting social opportunities, many schizotypals will participate only reluctantly, preferring to keep to themselves. The consequences of self-insulation for them are no different than for those who have been isolated by protective or neglectful management. Without active and relatively normal interpersonal relationships, these patients will recede further into social stagnancy and become increasingly impoverished and deteriorated.

Progressively decompensating schizotypals not only terminate relationships with others but with themselves as well. Fantasy may have been an early refuge, but there are few consistent gratifications to be gained from this source either. The content of fantasy turns too often to preoccupations with past misfortunes and injustice. In the end, schizotypals are unable to escape the futility and anguish of being who they are. To protect against this self-inflicted misery, they often destroy their own thoughts, cluttering, blocking, and disarranging their memories and feelings, and thus contributing to the cognitive disorganization that is so characteristic of the decompensated level. Disoriented as they may be, however, schizotypal patients will still sense the irrational and bizarre in their behavior. Nothing less than a total abandonment of self will do. Finally, they are driven to jettison themselves and disavow their very existence. In contrast to the less severe personality patterns, decompensated schizotypals may ultimately accept the calm and deathlike emptiness that takes hold, this permanent escape from being themselves. They have, in effect, "chosen" nothingness.

Remedial Intervention

Significant differences between them necessitate separating the discussion of the schizotypal into schizoid and avoidant variants.

Briefly, *schizotypal-schizoids* have a poor prognosis. Most are limited in their constitutional capacity for affectivity and activation. Few are motivated to sustain therapeutic relationships and, left to their own devices, will isolate themselves increasingly from social activities. The therapist's primary goal should be the prevention of the deleterious consequences of social isolation. Through environmental management, efforts should be made to increase the patient's involvement in interpersonal activities. Several psychopharmacological agents may be explored to determine whether they stimulate activation and affectivity. Efforts to enhance social interest must proceed in a slow, step-by-step manner, however, so as not to push the patient beyond tolerable limits. Clearer and more focused styles of thinking may be fostered by employing careful and well-reasoned therapeutic communications. Since schizotypal-schizoids are not totally devoid of feeling, the therapist should be alert to those spheres of life in which the patient possesses positive emotional inclinations, seeking to encourage activities consonant with these tendencies. Group therapy may facilitate the development of social skills. It would be wise, however, to precede or combine group programs with individual treatment sessions so as to forestall untoward social discomforts on the part of this patient.

Schizotypal-avoidant personalities also have poor prognostic prospects. The pattern is deeply ingrained. These patients rarely live in an encouraging or supportive environment. Probing into personal matters is experienced as painful, even terrifying. They distrust close personal relationships such as occur in most forms of psychotherapy. Therapy sets up what they see as false hopes and necessitates painful self-exposure. Most would rather leave matters be, keep to themselves, and remain insulated from the potential of further humiliation and anguish. Should they enter treatment, schizotypal-avoidants tend to be guarded, constantly testing the therapist's sincerity. A "false move" is likely to be interpreted as verification of the disinterest and deprecation the patient has learned to anticipate from others.

Trust is essential. Without a feeling of confidence in the genuineness of the therapist's motives, these patients will block the therapist's efforts and, ultimately, terminate treatment. Equally important is that the patient find a supportive social environment. Treatment will be difficult enough, a long and an uphill battle, unless external conditions are favorable. The primary focus should be to enhance these patients' self-worth and to encourage them to recognize their positive attributes. Pride in self and valuing one's constructive capacities are necessary first in rebuilding the patients' motivation. No longer alienated from themselves, they have a basis for overcoming their alienation from others. With a sense of self-worth, the therapist may guide these patients to explore positively rewarding social activities. Initiating such experiences may be a crucial point in what otherwise might have been a downward progression.

Pharmacologic agents should be employed to help curb the expression of irrational impulses. As far as other techniques are concerned, supportive methods are primary in the early stages. Cognitive and group techniques are best employed in the mid-phases of treatment, that is, after adequate rapport and trust have been established. Psychoanalytic methods should not be considered until the patient's tendency toward detachment is well under control. Analytic procedures such as free association, the neutral attitude of the therapist, or the focus on dreams may only foster autistic reveries and social withdrawal. Institutionalization, when necessary, should be brief. Hospital settings too often breed isolation, reward "quiet" behaviors, and provide models of eccentric belief and perception, each of which can lead to increased detachment and bizarre preoccupations.

References

Abraham, K. (1921). Contributions to the theory of the anal character. In *Selected Papers on Psychoanalysis* (English translation, 1927). London: Hogarth.

Abraham, K. (1924a). The influence of oral eroticism on character formation. In *Selected Papers on Psychoanalysis* (English translation, 1927). London: Hogarth.

Abraham, K. (1924b). A short study of the development of the libido, viewed in the light of mental disorders. In *Selected Papers on Psychoanalysis* (English translation, 1927). London: Hogarth.

Abraham, K. (1925). Character-formation on the genital level of the libido. In *Selected Papers on Psychoanalysis* (English translation, 1927). London: Hogarth.

Adler, A. (1964). *Problems of Neurosis.* New York: Harper.

Aichorn, A. (1935). *Wayward Youth.* New York: Viking.

Akiskal, H. S.; Djenderedjian, A. H.; Rosenthal, T. L.; and Khani, M. K. (1977). Cyclothymic disorder: Validating criteria for inclusion in the bipolar affective group. *American Journal of Psychiatry*, 134, 1227–1233.

Alexander, F. (1923). *Psychoanalysis of the Total Personality* (English translation, 1930). New York: Nervous and Mental Disease Publications.

Alexander, F. (1930). The neurotic character. *International Journal of Psychoanalysis*, 11, 292–313.

Alexander, F. (1935). *Roots of Crime.* New York: Knopf.

Alker, H. A. (1972). Is personality situationally specific or intrapsychically consistent? *Journal of Personality*, 40, 1–16.

Allen, F. (1950). The psychopathic delinquent child. *American Journal of Orthopsychiatry*, 20, 223–265.

Allport, G. W. (1937). *Personality: A Psychological Interpretation.* New York: Holt.

American Psychiatric Association (1952). *Diagnostic and Statistical Manual of Mental Disorders* (DSM-I). Washington, D. C.: Mental Hospitals Service.

American Psychiatric Association (1968). *Diagnostic and Statistical Manual of Mental Disorders* (DSM-II). Washington, D.C.: American Psychiatric Association.

American Psychiatric Association (1980). *Diagnostic and Statistical Manual of Mental Disorders* (DSM-III). Washington, D.C.: American Psychiatric Association.

Ansbacher, H. L.; and Ansbacher, R. (1956). *The Individual Psychology of Alfred Adler.* New York: Basic Books.

Arieti, S. (1955). *Interpretation of Schizophrenia.* New York: Brunner.

Armstrong, J. S.; and Solberg, P. (1968). On the interpretation of factor analysis. *Psychological Bulletin, 70,* 361–364.

Aschaffenburg, G. (1922). Constitutional psychopathies. In *Handbook of Medical Practice,* Vol. 4. Leipzig: Barth.

Baillarger, M. (1854). De la folie à double forme. *Année medicales psychologie, 27,* 369–384.

Bandura, A.; and Walters, R. H. (1959). *Adolescent Aggression.* New York: Ronald.

Bartemeier, L. H. (1930). The neurotic character as a new psychoanalytic concept. *American Journal of Orthopsychiatry, 1,* 512–519.

Bartko, J. J.; Strauss, J. S.; and Carpenter, W. T. (1971). An evaluation of taxometric techniques for psychiatric data. *Classification Society Bulletin, 2,* 1–28.

Beck, A. T. (1963). Thinking and depression. *Archives of General Psychiatry, 9,* 324–333.

Beck, A. T. (1967). *Depression: Clinical, Experimental, and Theoretical Aspects.* New York: Harper and Row.

Bem, D. J. (1972). Constructing cross-situational consistencies in behavior: Some thoughts on Alker's critique of Mischel. *Journal of Personality, 40,* 17–26.

Binet, A. (1890). Double consciousness in health. *Mind, 15,* 46–57.

Birnbaum, K. (1909). *Die psychopathischen Verbrecher.* Leipzig: Thieme.

Birnbaum, K. (1914). *Die psychopathischen Verbrecher* (2nd ed.). Leipzig: Thieme.

Bleuler, E. (1906). *Affectivität, Suggestibilität, Paranoia.* Halle: Marhold.

Bleuler, E. (1911). *Dementia Praecox oder Gruppe der Schizophrenien.* Leipzig: Deuticke, And *Dementia Praecox* (English translation, 1950). New York: International Universities Press.

Bleuler, E. (1922). Die probleme der Schizoidie und der Syntonie. *Zeitschrift fuer die gesamte Neurologie und Psychiatrie, 78,* 373–388.

Bleuler, E. (1924). *Textbook of Psychiatry* (English translation). New York: Macmillan.

Bleuler, E. (1929). Syntonie-schizoidie-schizophrenie. *Neurologie und Psychopathologie, 38,* 47–64.

Block, J. (1971). *Lives Through Time.* Berkeley: Bancroft.

Block, J. (1977). Advancing the psychology of personality: Paradigmatic shift or improving the quality of research. In D. Magnusson and N. S. Endler (Eds.), *Personality at the Crossroads: Current Issues in Interactional Psychology.* Hillsdale: Erlbaum.

Bonet, T. (1684). *Sepulchretum.* Paris.

Burnham, D. L.; Gladstone, A. I.; and Gibson, R. W. (1969). *Schizophrenia and the Need-Fear Dilemma.* New York: International Universities Press.

Bursten, B. (1972). The manipulative personality. *Archives of General Psychiatry, 26,* 318–321.

Bursten, B. (1973). Some narcissistic personality types. *International Journal of Psychoanalysis, 54,* 287–300.

Buss, A. H. (1966). *Psychopathology.* New York: Wiley.

Buss, A. H.; and Plomin, R. (1975). *A Temperament Theory of Personality Development.* New York: Wiley.

Bychowski, G. (1953). The problem of latent psychosis. *Journal of the American Psychoanalytic Association, 4,* 484–503.

Cameron, N. (1943). The paranoid pseudo-community. *American Journal of Sociology, 49,* 32–38.

Cameron, N. (1963). *Personality Development and Psychopathology.* Boston: Houghton Mifflin.

Cameron, N.; and Margaret, A. (1951). *Behavior Pathology.* Boston: Houghton Mifflin.

Cary, G. L. (1972). The borderline condition: A structural-dynamic viewpoint. *Psychoanalytic Review, 59,* 33–54.

Cattell, R. B. (1957). *Personality and Motivation Structure and Measurement.* New York: World.

Cattell, R. B. (1965). *The Scientific Analysis of Personality.* Chicago: Aldine.

Cattell, R. B. (1970). The integration of functional and psychometric requirements in a quantitative and computerized diagnostic system. In A. R. Mahrer (Ed.), *New Approaches to Personality Classification,* pp. 9-52. New York: Columbia University Press.

Chodoff, P. (1974). The diagnosis of hysteria: An overview. *American Journal of Psychiatry,* **131,** 1073-1078.

Chodoff, P.; and Lyons, H. (1958). Hysteria, the hysterical personality, and "hysterical" conversion. *American Journal of Psychiatry,* **114,** 734-740.

Cleckley, H. (1941). *The Mask of Sanity.* St. Louis: Mosby.

Coriat, R. C. (1927). Discussion of "The Constitutional Psychopathic Inferior." *American Journal of Psychiatry,* **6,** 686-689.

Deutsch, H. (1942). Some forms of emotional disturbance and their relationship to schizophrenia. *Psychoanalytic Quarterly,* **11,** 301-321.

Donath, J. (1897). The anankast (psychic compulsive states). *Archiv fuer Psychiatrie und Neurologie,* **29,** 211-230.

Easser, R.; and Lesser, S. (1965). Hysterical personality: A reevaluation. *Psychoanalytic Quarterly,* **34,** 390-402.

Ekehammer, E. (1974). Interactionism in personality from a historical perspective. *Psychological Bulletin,* **81,** 1026-1048.

Ellis, H. (1898). Auto-erotism: A psychological study. *Alienist and Neurologist,* **19,** 260-299.

Endler, N. S.; and Magnusson, D. (1976). Toward an interactional psychology of personality. *Psychological Bulletin,* **83,** 956-974.

Epstein, S. (1977). Traits are alive and well. In D. Magnusson and N. S. Endler (Eds.), *Personality at the Crossroads: Current Issues in Interactional Psychology.* Hillsdale: Erlbuam.

Epstein, S. (1979). The stability of behavior: I. On predicting most of the people much of the time. *Journal of Personality and Social Psychology,* **37,** 1097-1126.

Erikson, E. (1950). *Childhood and Society.* New York: Norton.

Escalona, S. (1968). *Roots of Individuality.* Chicago: Aldine.

Escalona, S.; and Heider, G. (1959). *Prediction and Outcome.* New York: Basic Books.

Escalona, S.; and Leitch, M. (1953). *Early Phases of Personality Development.* Evanston: Child Development Publications.

Esquirol, E. (1838). *Maladies Mentales* (2 vols.). Paris: Bailliere.

Eysenck, H. J. (1952). *The Scientific Study of Personality.* London: Routledge and Kegan Paul.

Eysenck, H. J. (1957). *The Dynamics of Anxiety and Hysteria.* New York: Praeger.

Eysenck, H. J. (1960). *The Structure of Human Personality.* London: Routledge and Kegan Paul.

Eysenck, H. J. (1967). *The Biological Basis of Personality.* Springfield, Ill.: C. C. Thomas.

Eysenck, H. J.; and Eysenck, S. B. G. (1969). *Personality Structure and Measurement.* London: Routledge and Kegan Paul.

Fairbairn, W. R. D. (1940). Schizoid factors in the personality. In *Psychoanalytic Studies of the Personality* (1952). London: Tavistock.

Falret, J. (1854). De la folie circulaire. *Bulletin del l'Academie Médicale,* **19,** 382-394.

Farrar, C. F. (1927). Quoted in D. Henderson and R. D. Gillespie, *A Textbook of Psychiatry.* London: Oxford.

Federn, P. (1947). Principles of psychotherapy in latent schizophrenia. *American Journal of Psychotherapy,* **1,** 129-139.

Fenichel, O. (1945). *The Psychoanalytic Theory of the Neurosis.* New York: Norton.

Ferenczi, S. (1952). *Further Contributions to Theory and Technique of Psychoanalysis.* New York: Basic Books.

Feuchtersleben, E. (1847). *Lehrbuch der arztlichen Seelenkunde.* Vienna: Gerold.

Fiske, D. W.; and Maddi, S. R. (Eds.) (1961). *Functions of Varied Experience.* Homewood: Dorsey.

Fleiss, J. L.; and Zubin, J. (1969). On the methods and theory of clustering. *Multivariate Behavior Research,* **4,** 235-250.

Forman, M. (1975). Narcissistic personality disorders and the oedipal fixations. *Annual of Psychoanalysis,* Vol. 3, pp. 65-92. New York: International Universities Press.

Freud, S. (1896). Further remarks on the defence-neuropsychoses. In *Collected Papers* (English translation, Vol. 2, 1925). London: Hogarth.

Freud, S. (1908). Character and anal eroticism. In *Collected Papers* (English translation, Vol. 2, 1925). London: Hogarth.

Freud, S. (1910). Leonardo da Vinci and a memory of his childhood. In *Standard Edition of the Works of Sigmund Freud* (Vol. 2, 1957). London: Hogarth.

Freud, S. (1911). Psychoanalytic notes upon an autobiographical account of a case of paranoia (Dementia paranoides). In *Collected Papers* (English translation, Vol. 3, 1925). London: Hogarth.

Freud, S. (1914). On narcissism: An introduction. In *Collected Papers* (English translation, Vol. 4, 1925). London: Hogarth.

Freud, S. (1915a). The instincts and their vicissitudes. In *Collected Papers* (English translation, Vol. 4, 1925). London: Hogarth.

Freud, S. (1915b). Some character types met with in psycho-analytic work. In *Collected Papers* (English translation, Vol. 4, 1925). London: Hogarth.

Freud, S. (1918). From the history of an infantile neurosis. In *Collected Papers* (English translation, Vol. 3, 1925). London: Hogarth.

Freud, S. (1932). Libidinal types. In *Collected Papers* (English translation, Vol. 5, 1950). London: Hogarth.

Friedlander, K. (1945). Formation of the antisocial character. *Psychoanalytic Study of the Child,* **1,** 189-203.

Fromm, E. (1947). *Man for Himself.* New York: Rinehart.

Frosch, J. (1960). Psychotic character. *Journal of the American Psychoanalytic Association,* **8,** 544-555.

Frosch, J. (1964). The psychotic character. *Psychiatric Quarterly,* **38,** 81-96.

Frosch, J. (1970). Psychoanalytic considerations of the psychotic character. *Journal of the American Psychoanalytic Association,* **18,** 24-50.

Gedo, J. D.; and Goldberg, A. (1973). *Models of the Mind.* Chicago: University of Chicago Press.

Gouster, M. (1878). Moral insanity. *Review of Scientific Medicine,* **38,** 115-131.

Greenacre, P. (1945). Conscience in the psychopath. *American Journal of Orthopsychiatry,* **15,** 495-509.

Greenacre, P. (Ed.) (1953). *Affective Disorders.* New York: International Universities Press.

Griesinger, W. (1845). *Mental Pathology and Therapeutics* (English translation, 1867). London: New Syndenham Society.

Griesinger, W. (1868). A little recognized psychopathic state. *Archiv fuer Psychiatrie und Neurologie,* **1,** 626-631.

Grinker, R. R.; Werble, B.; and Drye, R. C. (1968). *The Borderline Syndrome.* New York: Basic Books.

Gunderson, J. G. (1977). Characteristics of borderlines. In P. Hartcollis (Ed.), *Borderline Personality Disorders,* pp. 173-192. New York: International Universities Press.

Gunderson, J. G. (1979). The relatedness of borderline to schizophrenic disorders. *Schizophrenia Bulletin,* **5,** 17-23.

Gunderson, J. G.; Carpenter, W. T.; and Strauss, J. S. (1975). Borderline and schizophrenic patients: A comparative study. *American Journal of Psychiatry,* **132,** 1257-1264.

Gunderson, J. G.; and Singer, M. T. (1975). Defining borderline patients: An overview. *American Journal of Psychiatry,* **132,** 1-10.

Guntrip, H. (1952). A study of Fairbairn's theory of schizoid reactions. *British Journal of Medical Psychology,* **25,** 86-104.

Guslain, J. (1826). *Traité sur l'alienation mentale.* Amsterdam.

Hartmann, H. (1958). *Ego Psychology and the Problem of Adaptation.* New York: International Universities Press.

Healy, W.; and Bronner, A. (1926). *Delinquents and Criminals: Their Making and Unmaking.* New York: Macmillan.

Hecker, E. (1871). Die Hebephrenie. *Archive fuer Pathologie, Anatomie und Physiologie,* **52,** 394-429.

Heinroth, J. C. (1818). *Lehrbuch der Störungen des Seelenlebens.* Leipzig: Thieme.

Hellpach, W. (1920). Amphithymia. *Zeitschrift fuer die gesamte Neurologie und Psychiatrie,* **19,** 136-152.

Hempel, C. G. (1961). Introduction to problems of taxonomy. In J. Zubin (Ed.), *Field Studies in the Mental Disorders,* pp. 3-22. New York: Grune and Stratton.

Henderson, D. K. (1939). *Psychopathic States.* London: Chapman and Hall.

Henderson, D.; and Gillespie, R. D. (1927). *A Text-Book of Psychiatry.* London: Oxford.

Henderson, D.; and Gillespie, R. D. (1940). *A Text-Book of Psychiatry* (5th ed.). London: Oxford.

Heymans, G.; and Wiersma, E. (1906-1909). Beitrage zur speziellen Psychologie auf Grund einer Massenuntersuchung. *Zeitsehrift fuer Psychologie,* **42, 46, 49, 51.**

Hirt, E. (1902). *Die Temperamente.* Leipzig: Barth.

Hoch, A. (1910). Constitutional factors in the dementia praecox group. *Review of Neurology and Psychiatry,* **8,** 463-475.

Hoch, P. H.; and Cattell, J. P. (1959). The diagnosis of pseudoneurotic schizophrenia. *Psychiatric Quarterly,* **33,** 17-43.

Hoch, P. H.; Cattell, J. P.; Stahl, M. O.; and Pennes, H. H. (1962). The course and outcome of pseudoneurotic schizophrenia. *American Journal of Psychiatry,* 118, 106-115.

Hoch, P. H.; and Polatin, P. (1949). Pseudoneurotic form of schizophrenia. *Psychiatric Quarterly,* **23,** 248-276.

Horney, K. (1937). *The Neurotic Personality of Our Time.* New York: Norton.

Horney, K. (1939). *New Ways in Psychoanalysis.* New York: Norton.

Horney, K. (1942). *Self Analysis.* New York: Norton.

Horney, K. (1945). *Our Inner Conflicts.* New York: Norton.

Horney, K. (1950). *Neurosis and Human Growth.* New York: Norton.

Hughes, C. H. (1884). Moral (affective) insanity: Psycho-sensory insanity. *Alienist and Neurologist,* **5,** 296-315.

Jacobson, E. (1953). Contribution to the metapsychology of cyclothymic depression. In P. Greenacre (Ed.), *Affective Disorders,* pp. 49-83. New York: International Universities Press.

Jacobson, E. (1964). *The Self and the Object World.* New York: International Universities Press.

Jahoda, M. (Ed.) (1958). *Current Concepts of Positive Mental Health.* New York: Basic Books.

Janet, P. (1901). *The Mental State of Hystericals: A Study of Mental Stigmata and Mental Accidents* (English translation). New York: Putnam.

Jaspers, K. (1913). *Allegemaine Psychopathologie.* Berlin: Springer.

Jaspers, K. (1925). *Allegemaine Psychopathologie* (2nd ed.). Berlin: Springer.

Jaspers, K. (1948). *General Psychopathology* (English translation). London: Oxford.

Jones, E. (1918). Anal character traits. In *Papers on Psychoanalysis* (1938). London: Ballière, Tindall and Cox.

Jung, C. G. (1921). *Psychologische Typen.* Zurich: Rascher.

Kahlbaum, K. L. (1863). *Die Gruppierung der psychischen Krankenheiten.* Danzig: A. W. Kafemann.

Kahlbaum, K. L. (1882). *Uber zyklisches Irresein, Irrenfreund.* Berlin.

Kahlbaum, K. L. (1890). Heboidophrenia. *Allgemaine Zeitschrift fuer Psychiatrie,* **46,** 461–482.

Kahn, E. (1928). *Psychopathischen Personlichkeiten.* Berlin: Springer.

Kahn, E. (1931). *Psychopathic Personalities* (English translation). New Haven: Yale University Press.

Kallmann, F. J. (1938). *The Genetics of Schizophrenia.* New York: Augustin.

Karpman, B. (1941). On the need for separating psychopathy into two distinct clinical types: Symptomatic and idiopathic. *Journal of Criminal Psychopathology,* **3,** 112–137.

Kasanin, J. (1933). Acute schizoaffective psychoses. *American Journal of Psychiatry,* **97,** 97–120.

Kendell, R. E. (1968). The classification of depressive illnesses. *Maudsley Monograph Number 18.* London: Oxford.

Kendell, R. E. (1975). *The Role of Diagnosis in Psychiatry.* Oxford: Blackwell.

Kernberg, O. F. (1967). Borderline personality organization. *Journal of the American Psychoanalytic Association,* **15,** 641–685.

Kernberg, O. F. (1970). A psychoanalytic classification of character pathology. *Journal of the American Psychoanalytic Association,* **18,** 800–822.

Kernberg, O. F. (1975). *Borderline Conditions and Pathological Narcissism.* New York: Jason Aronson.

Kernberg, O. F. (1977). The structural diagnosis of borderline personality organization. In P. Hartcollis (Ed.), *Borderline Personality Disorders.* New York: International Universities Press.

Kernberg, O. F. (1979). Two reviews of the literature on borderlines: An assessment. *Schizophrenia Bulletin,* **5,** 53–58.

Kernberg, O. F. (1980). *Internal World and External Reality.* New York: Jason Aronson.

Kety, S. S.; Rosenthal, D.; Wender, P. H.; and Schulsinger, F. (1968). Mental illness in the biological and adoptive families of adopted schizophrenics. In D. Rosenthal and S. S. Kety (Eds.), *Transmission of Schizophrenia,* pp. 345–362. Oxford: Pergamon Press.

Klein, D. F. (1967). The importance of psychiatric diagnosis in prediction of clinical drug effects. *Archives of General Psychiatry,* **16,** 118–126.

Klein, D. F. (1970). Psychotropic drugs and the regulation of behavioral activation in psychiatric illness. In W. L. Smith (Ed.), *Drugs and Cerebral Function.* Springfield, Ill.: C. C. Thomas.

Klein, D. F. (1971). Approaches to measuring the efficacy of drug treatment of personality disorders: An analysis and program. In *Principles and Problems in Establishing the Efficacy of Psychotropic Agents.* U. S. Department of Health, Education and Welfare, Public Health Service, Publication Number 2138, pp. 187–204.

Klein, D. F. (1972). *Psychiatric Case Studies: Treatment, Drugs and Outcome.* Baltimore: Williams and Wilkins.

Klein, D. F. (1975). Psychopharmacology and the borderline patient. In J. E. Mack (Ed.), *Borderline States in Psychiatry*, pp. 75–92. New York: Grune and Stratton.

Klein, D. F. (1977). Psychopharmacological treatment and delineation of borderline disorders. In P. Hartcollis (Ed.), *Borderline Personality Disorders*, pp. 365–383. New York: International Universities Press.

Klein, D. F.; and Davis, J. (1969). *Diagnosis and Drug Treatment of Psychiatric Disorders.* Baltimore: Williams and Wilkins.

Klein, D. F.; Honigfeld, G.; and Feldman, S. (1973). Prediction of drug effect in personality disorders. *Journal of Nervous and Mental Diseases*, **156**, 183–198.

Knight, R. P. (1953). Borderline states. *Bulletin of the Menninger Clinic*, **17**, 1–12.

Koch, J. L. (1891). *Die psychopathischen Minderwertigkeiten.* Ravensburg: Maier.

Kohut, H. (1966). Forms and transformations of narcissism. *Journal of the American Psychoanalytic Association*, **14**, 243–272.

Kohut, H. (1968). The psychoanalytic treatment of narcissistic personality disorders. *Psychoanalytic Study of the Child*, **23**, 86–113.

Kohut, H. (1971). *The Analysis of Self.* New York: International Universities Press.

Kollarits, J. (1912). *Charakter und Nervositat.* Budapest: Knoedler.

Kraepelin, E. (1887). *Psychiatrie: Ein Lehrbuch* (2nd ed.). Leipzig: Abel.

Kraepelin, E. (1889). *Psychiatrie: Ein Lehrbuch* (3rd ed.). Leipzig: Barth.

Kraepelin, E. (1896). *Psychiatrie: Ein Lehrbuch* (5th ed.). Leipzig: Barth.

Kraepelin, E. (1903–1904). *Psychiatrie: Ein Lehrbuch* (7th ed.). Leipzig: Barth.

Kraepelin, E. (1904). *Lectures on Clinical Psychiatry* (English translation). New York: Wood.

Kraepelin, E. (1909–1915). *Psychiatrie: Ein Lehrbuch* (8th ed.). Leipzig: Barth.

Kraepelin, E. (1913). *Psychiatrie: Ein Lehrbuch* (8th ed.), Vol. 3. Leipzig: Barth.

Kraepelin, E. (1919). *Dementia Praecox and Paraphrenia.* Edinburgh: Livingstone.

Kraepelin, E. (1921). *Manic-Depressive Insanity and Paranoia.* Edinburgh: Livingstone.

Krafft-Ebing, R. (1867). *Moral Insanity—Its Recognition and Forensic Assessment.* Berlin: Erlangen.

Krafft-Ebing, R. (1882). *Psychopathia Sexualis* (English translation, 1937). New York: Physicians and Surgeons Books.

Kretschmer, E. (1918). *Der sensitive Beziehungswahn.* Berlin: Springer.

Kretschmer, E. (1925). *Korperbau und Charakter.* Berlin: Springer Verlag. And *Physique and Character* (English translation). London: Kegan Paul.

Kretschmer, E. (1926). *Hysteria* (English translation). New York: Nervous and Mental Disease Publishers.

Laing, R. D. (1960). *The Divided Self.* Chicago: Quadrangle.

Langfeldt, G. (1937). The prognosis in schizophrenia and the factors influencing the course of the disease. *Acta Psychiatrica Scandinavica*, Supplementum 13.

Lasch, C. (1978). *The Culture of Narcissism.* New York: Norton.

Lazare, A.; Klerman, G. L.; and Armor, D. (1966). Oral, obsessive, and hysterical personality patterns. *Archives of General Psychiatry*, **14**, 624–630.

Lazare, A.; Klerman, G. L.; and Armor, D. (1970). Oral, obsessive and hysterical personality patterns: Replication of factor analysis in an independent sample. *Journal of Psychiatric Research*, **7**, 275–290.

Lazursky, A. (1906). *An Outline of a Science of Characters.* St. Petersburg: Lossky.

Leary, T. (1957). *Interpersonal Diagnosis of Personality.* New York: Ronald.

Lewis, A. (1974). Psychopathic personality: A most elusive category. *Psychological Medicine*, **4**, 133–140.

Levy, D. M. (1951). Psychopathic behavior in infants and children. *American Journal of Orthopsychiatry*, **21**, 223-272.

Lombroso, C. (1872-1885). *L'Uomo delinquente*. Bocca: Torina.

Lorr, M. (1975). Convergences in personality constructs measured by four inventories. *Journal of Clinical Psychology*, **31**, 182-188.

Lorr, M.; and Manning, T. T. (1978). Higher-order personality factors of the ISI. *Multivariate Behavioral Research*, **13**, 3-7.

MacKinnon, R. A.; and Michels, R. (1971). *The Psychiatric Interview in Clinical Practice*. Philadelphia: W. B. Saunders.

Maddi, S. R. (1968). *Personality Theories: A Comparative Analysis*. Homewood: Dorsey.

Maddi, S. R.; and Propst, B. (1971). Activation theory and personality. In S. R. Maddi (Ed.), *Perspectives on Personality*. Boston: Little, Brown.

Magnan, V. (1886). *Lecons cliniques sur les madadies mentales*. Paris: Battaille.

Magnusson, D.; and Endler, N. S. (Eds.) (1977). *Personality at the Crossroads: Current Issues in Interactional Psychology*. Hillsdale: Erlbaum.

Marmor, J. (1953). Orality in the hysterical personality. *Journal of the American Psychoanalytic Association*, **1**, 656-671.

Maudsley, H. (1874). *Responsibility in Mental Disease*. London: King.

Maxwell, A. E. (1971). Multivariate statistical methods and classification problems. *British Journal of Psychiatry*, **119**, 121-127.

McDougall, W. (1908). *Introduction to Social Psychology*. New York: Scribners.

Meehl, P. (1962). Schizotaxia, schizotypy, schizophrenia. *American Psychologist*, 17, 827-838. Reprinted in T. Millon (Ed.), *Theories of Psychopathology and Personality* (2nd ed., 1973). Philadelphia: W. B. Saunders.

Meissner, W. W.. (1979). *The Paranoid Process*. New York: Jason Aronson.

Menninger, K. (1940). Character disorders. In J. F. Brown (Ed.), *The Psychodynamics of Abnormal Behavior*, pp. 384-403. New York: McGraw-Hill.

Menninger, K. (1963). *The Vital Balance*. New York: Viking.

Meumann, E. (1910). *Intelligenz und Wille*. Leipzig: Barth.

Meyer, A. (1906). Fundamental conceptions of dementia praecox. *British Medical Journal*, **2**, 757-760.

Meyer, A. (1908). The problem of mental reaction-types, mental causes and diseases. *Psychological Bulletin*, **5**, 245-261.

Meyer, A. (1912). Remarks on habit disorganizations in the essential deteriorations. *Nervous and Mental Disease Monographs*, **9**, 95-109.

Meyer, A. (1913). The treatment of paranoic and paranoid states. In W. White and S. Jelliffe (Eds.), *Modern Treatment of Nervous and Mental Diseases*, pp. 274-285. Philadelphia: Lea and Febiger.

Millon, T. (Ed.) (1967). *Theories of Psychopathology*. Philadelphia: W. B. Saunders.

Millon, T. (1969). *Modern Psychopathology: A Biosocial Approach to Maladaptive Learning and Functioning*. Philadelphia: W. B. Saunders.

Millon, T. (Ed.) (1973). *Theories of Psychopathology and Personality* (2nd ed.). Philadelphia: W. B. Saunders.

Millon, T. (1977). *Millon Clinical Multiaxial Inventory Manual*. Minneapolis: National Computer Systems.

Millon, T.; and Millon, R. (1974). *Abnormal Behavior and Personality*. Philadelphia: W. B. Saunders.

Mischel, W. (1968). *Personality Assessment*. New York: Wiley.

Mischel, W. (1969). Continuity and change in personality. *American Psychologist*, **24**, 1012-1018.

Mischel, W. (1973a). Toward a cognitive social learning reconceptualization of personality. *Psychological Review*, **80**, 252-283.

Mischel, W. (1973b). On the empirical dilemmas of psychodynamic approaches: Issues and alternative. *Journal of Abnormal Psychology*, **82**, 335-344.

Mischel, W. (1979). On the interface of cognition and personality: Beyond the person-situation debate. *American Psychologist*, **34**, 740-754.

Morel, B. A. (1852-1853). *Traité theorique et pratique des maladies mentales*, Vols. 1 and 2. Paris and Nancy: Bailliere.

Murphy, L. B., et al. (1962). *The Widening World of Childhood*. New York: Basic Books.

Murphy, L. B.; and Moriarty, A. E. (1976). *Vulnerability, Coping and Growth*. New Haven: Yale University Press.

Näcke, P. (1899). Die sexuellen perversitaten in der irrenansalt. *Psychiatrie en Neurologie Bladen*, **3**, 14-21.

Nagera, H. (1964). Autoeroticism, autoerotic activities, and ego development. *Psychoanalytic Study of the Child*, **19**, 240-255.

Offer, D.; and Sabshin, M. (1974). *Normality: Theoretical and Clinical Concepts of Mental Health* (rev. ed.). New York: Basic Books.

Olweus, D. (1977). A critical analysis of the "modern" interactionist position. In D. Magnusson and N. S. Endler (Eds.), *Personality at the Crossroads: Current Issues in Interactional Psychology*. Hillsdale: Erlbuam.

Palombo, J. (1976). Theories of narcissism and the practice of clinical social work. *Clinical Social Work Journal*, **4**, 147-161.

Partridge, G. E. (1927). A study of 50 cases of psychopathic personality. *American Journal of Psychiatry*, **7**, 953-974.

Patridge, G. E. (1928). Psychopathic personality and personality investigation. *American Journal of Psychiatry*, **8**, 1053-1064.

Partridge, G. E. (1930). Current conceptions of psychopathic personality. *American Journal of Psychiatry*, **10**, 53-99.

Perry, J. C.; and Klerman, G. L. (1978). The borderline patient. *Archives of General Psychiatry*, **35**, 141-150.

Phillips, L. (1968). *Human Adaptation and Its Failures*. New York: Academic Press.

Piaget, J. (1952). *The Origins of Intelligence in Children*. New York: International Universities Press.

Piaget, J. (1956). The general problems of the psychobiological development of the child. In J. M. Tanner and B. Inhelder (Eds.), *Discussions on Child Development*, Vol. 4. New York: International Universities Press.

Pinel, P. (1801). *Traite medico-philosophique sur l'alienation mentale*. Paris: Richard, Caille et Ravier.

Pinel, P. (1806). *A Treatise on Insanity* (Translated by D. Davis). New York: Hafner.

Prichard, J. C. (1835). *A Treatise on Insanity*. London: Sherwood, Gilbert and Piper.

Quay, H. C. (1964). Personality dimensions in delinquent males as inferred from the factor analysis of behavior ratings. *Journal of Research in Crime and Delinquency*, **1**, 33-37.

Quay, H. C.; and Werry, J. S. (Eds.) (1979). *Psychopathological Disorders of Childhood* (2nd ed.). New York: Wiley.

Queyrat, F. (1896). *Les caractéres et l'education morale*. Paris: Alcan.

Rado, S. (1956). Schizotypal organization: Preliminary report on a clinical study of schizophrenia. In S. Rado and G. E. Daniels (Eds.), *Changing Concepts of Psychoanalytic Medicine*, pp. 225-236. New York: Grune and Stratton.

Rado, S. (1959). Obsessive behavior. In S. Arieti (Ed.), *American Handbook of Psychiatry*, Vol. 1. New York: Basic Books.

Rado, S. (1969). *Adaptational Psychodynamics.* New York: Science House.

Rapaport, D. (1958). The theory of ego autonomy: A generalization. *Bulletin of the Menninger Clinic,* **22,** 13-35.

Rapaport, D.; Gill, M. M.; and Schafer, R. (1945-1946). *Diagnostic Psychological Testing* (2 vols.). Chicago: Year Book Publishers.

Rapaport, D.; Gill, M. M.; Schafer, R.; and Holt, R. R. (1968). *Diagnostic Psychological Testing* (rev. ed.). New York: International Universities Press.

Reich, A. (1960). Pathologic forms of self-esteem regulation. *Psychoanalytic Study of the Child,* **15,** 215-232.

Reich, W. (1933). *Charakteranalyse.* Leipzig: Sexpol Verlag.

Reich, W. (1949). *Character Analysis* (3rd ed.). New York: Farrar, Straus and Giroux.

Ribot, T. (1890). *Psychologie des sentiments.* Paris: Delahaye and Lecrosnier.

Roback, A. A. (1927). *The Psychology of Character.* New York: Harcourt, Brace.

Robins, L. (1966). *Deviant Children Grown Up.* Baltimore: Williams and Wilkins.

Rosenfeld, H. (1964). On the psychopathology of narcissism. *International Journal of Psychoanalysis,* **45,** 332-337.

Rosenthal, D.; and Kety, S. S. (Eds.) (1968). *The Transmission of Schizophrenia.* Oxford: Pergamon.

Rosse, J. C. (1890). Clinical cases of insanity and imbecility. *American Journal of Insanity,* **47,** 263-267.

Rush, B. (1812). *Medical Inquiries and Observations upon the Diseases of the Mind.* Philadelphia: Kimber and Richardson.

Sadger, J. (1908). Psychiatrish-neurologisches in psychoanalytischer Beleuchtung. *Zeitschrift fuer gesamte Medizin,* **7,** 92-104.

Sadger, J. (1910). Analerotik und analcharakter. *Die Heilkunde,* **4,** 11-20.

Sandler, J.; and Hazari, A. (1960). The obsessional: On the psychological classification of obsessional character traits and symptoms. *British Journal of Medical Psychology,* **33,** 113-122.

Schafer, R. (1948). *The Clinical Application of Psychological Tests.* New York: International Universities Press.

Schmideberg, M. (1947). The treatment of psychopaths and borderline patients. *American Journal of Psychotherapy,* **1,** 45-55.

Schmideberg, M. (1959). The borderline patient. In S. Arieti (Ed.), *American Handbook of Psychiatry,* Vol. 1, pp. 398-416. New York: Basic Books.

Schneider, K. (1923). *Die psychopathischen Persönlichkeiten.* Vienna: Deuticke.

Schneider, K. (1950). *Psychopathic Personalities* (9th ed., English translation). London: Cassell.

Schwartz, R. A.; and Schwartz, I. K. (1976). Are personality disorders diseases? *Diseases of the Nervous System,* **86,** 613-617.

Scott, W. A. (1958). Social psychological correlates of mental illness and mental health. *Psychological Bulletin,* **55,** 65-87.

Sheldon, W. H. (1940). *The Varieties of Human Physique: An Introduction to Constitutional Psychology.* New York: Harper.

Sheldon, W. H. (1954). *Atlas of Men: A Guide for Somatotyping the Male of All Ages.* New York: Harper.

Sheldon, W. H.; and Stevens, S. S. (1942). *The Varieties of Temperament: A Psychology of Constitutional Differences.* New York: Harper.

Shoben, E. J. (1957). Toward a concept of the normal personality. *American Psychologist,* **12,** 183-189.

Sjöbring, H. (1914). *Den Individualpsykologiska Frageställningen Inom Psykiatrien.* Dissertation, Upsala University.

Sjöbring, H. (1973). Personality structure and development: A model and its applications (English translation). *Acta Psychiatrica Scandinavica,* Supplement 244.

Skinner, B. F. (1953). *Science and Behavior.* New York: Macmillan.

Small, I. F.; Small, J. G.; Alig, V. B.; and Moore, D. F. (1970). Passive-aggressive personality disorder: A search for a syndrome. *American Journal of Psychiatry,* **126,** 973-983.

Spitzer, R. L.; Endicott, J.; and Gibbon, M. (1979). Crossing the border into borderline personality and borderline schizophrenia. *Archives of General psychiatry,* **36,** 17-24.

Stern, A. (1938). Psychoanalytic investigation of and therapy in the border line group of neuroses. *Psychoanalytic Quarterly,* **7,** 467-489.

Stone, M. H. (1980). *The Borderline Syndromes.* New York: McGraw-Hill.

Strauss, J. S. (1973). Diagnostic models and the nature of psychiatric disorder. *Archives of General Psychiatry,* **29,** 445-449.

Strauss, J. S. (1975). A comprehensive approach to psychiatric diagnoses. *American Journal of Psychiatry,* **132,** 1193-1197.

Sullivan, H. S. (1947). *Conceptions of Modern Psychiatry.* New York: Norton.

Task Force on Nomenclature and Statistics, American Psychiatric Association (1976). *DSM-III in Midstream.* Conference Publication, Missouri Institute of Psychiatry.

Thomas, A.; and Chess, S. (1977). *Temperament and Development.* New York: Brunner/Mazel.

Thomas, A.; Chess, S.; and Birch, H. G. (1963). *Behavioral Individuality in Early Childhood.* New York: New York University Press.

Thomas, A.; Chess, S.; and Birch, H. G. (1968). *Temperament and Behavior Disorders in Children.* New York: New York University Press.

Tramer, M. (1931). Psychopathic personalities. *Schweizer medizinische Wochenschrift,* **217,** 271-322.

Tuke, D. H. (1892). *Dictionary of Psychological Medicine.* Philadelphia: Blakiston.

U.S. Joint Armed Services (1949). *Nomenclature and Method of Recording Psychiatric Conditions.* Washington, D.C.: Department of Defense.

Veterans Administration (1951). *Standard Classification of Diseases.* Washington, D.C.: Veterans Administration.

Wachtel, P. L. (1973). Psychodynamics, behavior therapy and the implacable experimenter: An inquiry into the consistency of personality. *Journal of Abnormal Psychology,* **82,** 324-334.

Walton, H. J.; Foulds, G. A.; Littman, S. K.; and Presley, A. S. (1970). Abnormal personality. *British Journal of Psychiatry,* **116,** 497-510.

Walton, H. J.; and Presley, A. S. (1973a). Use of a category system in the diagnosis of abnormal personality. *British Journal of Psychiatry,* **122,** 259-263.

Walton, H. J.; and Presley, A. S. (1973b). Dimensions of abnormal personality. *British Journal of Psychiatry,* **122,** 269-276.

War Department Technical Bulletin (1945). Nomenclature and Recording Diagnoses. Number 203. Washington, D.C.: War Department

Wender, P. H. (1977). The scope and the validity of the schizophrenic spectrum concept. In V. M. Rakoff, H. C. Stancer, and H. B. Kedward (Eds.), *Psychiatric Diagnosis.* New York: Brunner/Mazel.

Werner, H. (1940). *Comparative Psychology of Mental Development.* New York: Follett.

Westphal, C. (1877). Über Zwangsvorstellungen. *Berliner klinische Wochenschrift,* **2,** 239-262.

Whitman, R. M.; Trosman, H.; and Koenig, R. (1954). Clinical assessment of passive-aggressive personality. *Archives of Neurology and Psychiatry,* **72,** 540-549.

Williams, R. J. (1973). The biological approach to the study of personality. In T. Millon (Ed.), *Theories of Psychopathology and Personality* (2nd ed., 1973). Philadelphia: W. B. Saunders.

Willis, T. (1684). Quoted in R. Semelaigne. *Alienistes et philanthropes* (1912). Paris: Battaille.

Winnicott, D. W. (1945). Primitive emotional development. In *Collected Papers* (1958). London: Tavistock.

Winnicott, D. W. (1956). On transference. *International Journal of Psychoanalysis*, **37**, 382-395.

Wittels, F. (1930). The hysterical character. *Medical Review of Reviews*, **36**, 186-190.

Wittels, F. (1937). The criminal psychopath in the psychoanalytic system. *Psychoanalytic Review*, **24**, 276-283.

Wolberg, A. (1952). The "borderline patient." *American Journal of Psychotherapy*, **6**, 694-701.

Wolf, E. (1976). Recent advances in the psychology of the self: An outline of basic concepts. *Comprehensive Psychiatry*, **17**, 37-46.

Zetzel, E. R. (1968). The so-called good hysteric. *International Journal of Psychoanalysis*, **49**, 256-260.

Zilboorg, G. (1941). Ambulatory schizophrenia. *Psychiatry*, **4**, 149-155.

Author Index

Subject Index

Active-ambivalent personality pattern, 61, 92, 244-272
Active-dependent personality pattern, 60, 91, 131-156
Active-detached personality, 61, 92, 297-324
Active-independent personality pattern, 61, 91, 181-215
Active-passive dimension, 52, 58-62
 Adler's conception, 52
 Millon's conception, 58-62
Active trait, 38-39
Adaptive inflexibility, 9
Adaptive learning, 71-72
Advanced personality disorder, 328-330
Affectionless personality, 43
Affective component, 35
Affective disorders:
 among avoidant personalities, 311
 among borderline personalities, 354-356
 among compulsive personalities, 233-234
 among dependent personalities, 119
 among histrionic personalities, 145-146
 among narcissistic personalities, 170-171
 among paranoid personalities, 384-385
 among passive-aggressive personalities, 260-261
 among schizoid personalities, 286
Aggressive personality pattern, 53, 157, 181-215
Aggressive-sadistic personality, 56
Aggressive sociopath, 45
Agoraphobia, 123-124
Alaxia, 40

Alternative data levels, 12-14
Ambition-ridden personality, 43
Ambivalent personality types, 59, 216-243, 244-272
Amorphous personality, 28
 Heymans and Wiersma's conception, 28
 Queyrat's conception, 28
Anal-expulsive personality, 49
Anal-retentive personality, 49
"Anankast," 219-220
Antisocial personality, 181-215
 associated disorders, 203-206
  antisocial-paranoid mixed personality, 205
  anxiety, 204
  axis I symptoms, 203-204
  axis II personalities, 204-205
  differential diagnostic signs, 205-206
  paranoid, 204
 clinical picture, 198-203
  behavioral features, 198-199
  inferred intrapsychic dynamics, 200-201
  interpersonal coping style, 201-203
  self-descriptions and complaints, 199-200
 historical and theoretical antecedents, 183-198
  Alexander, 193-195
  Bartemeier, 193
  Bursten, 195-196
  Cameron and Margaret, 197
  Cleckley, 192
  Freud, 192-193

447